ANCIENT EGYPT

ANCIENT EGYPT
Reconstructing the Past

Pamela Bradley

CAMBRIDGE
UNIVERSITY PRESS

PUBLISHED BY THE PRESS SYNDICATE OF THE UNIVERSITY OF CAMBRIDGE
The Pitt Building, Trumpington Street, Cambridge, United Kingdom

CAMBRIDGE UNIVERSITY PRESS
The Edinburgh Building, Cambridge CB2 2RU, UK   www.cup.cam.ac.uk
40 West 20th Street, New York, NY 10011–4211, USA   www.cup.org
10 Stamford Road, Oakleigh, Melbourne 3166, Australia
Ruiz de Alarcón 13, 28014 Madrid, Spain

First published 1999

Edited by Fiona Sim
Cover and text design by Juno Creative Services
Typesetting by Arc Typography
Illustrations by David Evans and Adam Bradley
Printed in Australia by Star Printery

Typeset in 10/12 Garamond Light. System QuarkXPress®

National Library of Australia Cataloguing in Publication data
Bradley, Pamela
Ancient Egypt: reconstructing the past

Bibliography.
Includes index.
ISBN 0 521 77656 2

1. History, Ancient – Methodology. 2. Egypt – History – To 332 B.C.
   3. Egypt – Civilization – To 332 B.C. I. Title.

932.01

ISBN 0 521 776562 paperback

CONTENTS

List of illustrations

List of maps

ABOUT THIS TEXT

This text is divided into four parts which cover:

- the historical periods of Egyptian history referred to as the Old, Middle and New Kingdoms (these are terms used by scholars to focus on certain changes that occurred in Egyptian history)
- Egyptian society as it developed and changed in each of these periods
- the impact of significant individuals and groups on the society and historical period in which they lived.

Because it has been difficult to establish an accurate chronology for Egyptian history, scholars, museums and writers of texts are often at variance with one another over dates. The dates ascribed to historical periods, important events and significant individuals in this text tend to follow the chronology used by J Baines and J Málek in the *Atlas of Ancient Egypt.*

There is extensive use in the text of both written (primary and secondary) and archaeological sources as well as diagrams, tables, maps and line drawings. At the end of each chapter there is a diagrammatic summary of the preceding information, a number of activities based on the sources and essay topics.

It is hoped that the written and pictorial material presented in this book will help students and those interested in Egyptian history to:

- appreciate the difficulties of writing a connected history of Egypt due to the nature of the sources
- understand the need to use a variety of sources in trying to piece together the mosaic of ancient life and society
- assess the different interpretations of the sources by archaeologists and historians as well as scholars in scientific fields
- ask historical questions, particularly with regard to controversial issues
- understand the impact of particular individuals, groups and institutions on their own and later times
- identify some of the beliefs on which ancient Egyptian society was based
- recognise factors contributing to change in particular periods of Egyptian history
- feel a sense of responsibility to conserve the monuments of Egypt's past and develop an interest in reading more about ancient Egypt and in studying history for leisure.

The summaries and activities at the end of each chapter have been designed to help students analyse and make deductions from a wide range of written and archaeological sources and evaluate the reliability of those sources; organise information in a variety of ways; present, in written form, an argument supported by evidence and empathise with individuals and groups from the past.

The following icon, which is the hieroglyphic symbol for the equipment of an Egyptian scribe, indicates that there is a series of tasks to be completed.

PART
ONE

Introduction

OVERVIEW

Part 1 includes information and concepts which form the basis for understanding pharaonic history.

The nature of ancient Egyptian civilisation was determined to a large extent by the physical environment in which the people lived. The predominant forces of nature which influenced their lives were the Nile and its annual inundation, the deserts which encroached on the fertile ribbon of land adjacent to the river and the ever-present sun.

Chapter 1:
- stresses the duality of Egypt by distinguishing between the *Two Lands* of Upper and Lower Egypt and by defining the terms *Red Land* and *Black Land*
- explains the link between the physical environment and the distinctive lifestyle and beliefs of the ancient Egyptians.

Because of the lack of historical records and the nature of the written sources, it has been very difficult to write a connected history of ancient Egypt. Gardiner emphasised this fact when he said that the history of Egypt is 'merely a collection of rags and tatters'.[1]

Chapter 2:
- deals with the main sources of written information available to historians and the key to their decipherment — the Rosetta Stone
- discusses the advantages and disadvantages of particular written sources in building up a picture of the past

1

- notes the difficulties of developing an accurate chronology for Egyptian history
- looks at Egyptian myths and legends as sources of information
- outlines the types of archaeological sources which are used to confirm or refute the written records
- points out the amount of conjecture used in filling in the gaps in the sources.

The Archaic Period (the first two dynasties of kings after the unification of the *Two Lands* in c. 3100 BC) was the formative time of Egyptian history. The pattern of kingship and the institutions of a centralised state were established. These developments laid the basis for the great accomplishments of the Old Kingdom or Pyramid Age.

Chapter 3:
- outlines the developments that appear to have occurred during the Predynastic Period
- looks at the evidence for the unification of Upper and Lower Egypt into one kingdom
- notes the apparent development of the concept of divine kingship and its various aspects.

The physical environment of ancient Egypt

Most civilisations have been influenced by their environment. Ancient Egypt owed much of its character to the nature of the Nile River, the length and shape of the river valley, the enclosing deserts and the climate. The Greek historian Herodotus (c. 490–420 BC) summed it up when he said:

> Not only is the Egyptian climate peculiar and the Nile different in its behaviour from other rivers elsewhere, but the Egyptians themselves in their manners and customs seem to have reversed the ordinary practices of mankind.[1]

The Nile River and the sun were the two great forces which dominated the lives of the ancient Egyptians. Their gifts of water, fertile soil and warmth created life. On the other hand they had the potential to bring destruction and death.

The Nile River

The Nile, referred to by the ancient Egyptians as simply *Iteru* or *The River* transformed an almost waterless waste of desert into one of the most fertile areas on earth.

The Nile's source is in tropical Africa. The White Nile begins in Lake Victoria in east Africa, while the Blue Nile starts in Lake Tana in the snow-covered Ethiopian mountains. Further downstream the Blue Nile is joined by the Atbara River. At the present-day city of Khartoum, in the Sudan, these two large river systems merge to form the Nile.

The river's source

Until the construction of the Aswan Dam this century, the Nile cut its way for over 1300 kilometres through the deserts of Nubia. Its flow was interrupted six times by rocky cataracts (rapids) before it entered Egypt.

The traditional southern boundary of ancient Egypt was just south of Aswan at the First Cataract. Massive boulders and outcrops of pink and black granite formed a series of rapids extending over six kilometres.

The First Cataract

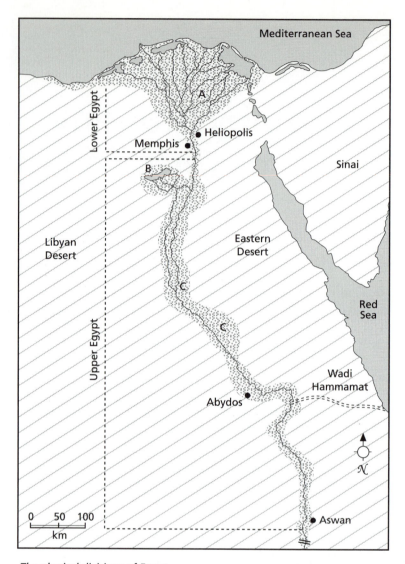

The physical divisions of Egypt

The Black Land

A The Delta

B The Faiyum

C The Nile Valley

The Red Land

The First Cataract
at Elephantine

An island known as *Abu* or *Elephant Land* (later called Elephantine Island) commanded this frontier area where the river plunged and swirled over the huge granite obstructions. Classical writers reported that during flood time the roaring of the waters was so great as to cause deafness.

For the next 800 kilometres the river wound its way northwards through a narrow valley hemmed in first by sandstone and then limestone cliffs. In places the fertile strip of land bordering the Nile was so narrow that the desert hills almost rose up out of the river. At other places the muddy river flats extended many kilometres on either side of the Nile.

The Faiyum

Further north, a branch of the Nile flowed westward into a depression 50 metres below sea level. This depression caught the surplus floodwaters and acted as a reservoir when the water level of the Nile was low. The

Some of the boulders that interrupt the Nile's flow at the First Cataract

land which was periodically reclaimed from this huge lake was fertile and rich in wildlife. Today it is referred to as the Faiyum.

Just north of the ancient capital of Memphis (near modern Cairo), the river divided into a number of large branches (seven reported by Herodotus) and many smaller ones as it slowly wound its way to the Mediterranean Sea. Silt was deposited in a large triangular or fan-shaped formation which the Greeks called the *delta* because of its resemblance to the shape of the fourth letter of their alphabet.

It has been observed that the valley, Faiyum and delta areas looked and still look like the long stem, bud and flower of the lotus that played an important part in Egyptian symbolism for 3000 years. According to that symbolism it was the opening lotus flower from which the sun god was born.

A lotus flower

The annual inundation or flood of the Nile

Every year at the same time the Nile flooded. This annual flood, referred to as the inundation, was without doubt the most important event in the lives of the Egyptian people. It sustained life along the valley.

During June, the Nile began to rise and green water (containing vegetable matter) appeared everywhere along the valley between Aswan and Memphis. The waters continued to rise and by August they were a dark, muddy colour (because of the eroded material they contained). The floodwaters reached their peak during September and after several weeks the level began to drop. By May of the following year, the river level was at its lowest.

The timing of the flood and the height of the waters were critical for the inhabitants of the valley. Ancient records indicate that when the river rose to seven and a half metres at Elephantine Island there was enough water to supply the needs of the country. A flood level over eight metres was dangerously high while a height of six metres was perilously low.

Height and timing of the flood

What caused this annual inundation?

A view of the fertile Nile Valley

During late spring and early summer (in the northern hemisphere), the normal equatorial rains of central Africa were supplemented by water from the melting snows and the summer monsoons in the mountains of Ethiopia. As the water poured down the valleys of the Ethiopian highlands, it eroded the adjacent land. The free stone dust was carried along by the Blue Nile and Atbara River and eventually deposited as a dark, rich silt over the valley flats of Egypt when the river broke its banks.

Accumulations of this alluvium or alluvial soil (silt carried and deposited by rivers and streams) made the Nile Valley into one of the most fertile areas on earth.

Effects of the flood

The Nile's life-giving waters and annual deposits of rich, black soil enabled the Egyptians to develop a prosperous agricultural society instead of remaining as desert-dwelling nomads. From this agricultural society grew one of the world's greatest civilisations.

As Herodotus remarked, 'Egypt is the gift of the river'.[2]

The Black Land

Fertile black mud

The land known as Egypt in antiquity was called the *Black Land* or *Kemet* because of the fertile black silt or mud which the Nile, in flood, deposited over the valley every year.

The Black Land comprised:

- the long, narrow river valley enclosed by desert cliffs (Upper Egypt)
- the huge, lush, fan-shaped lowland area known as the delta (Lower Egypt).

The Two Lands of Upper and Lower Egypt

In ancient times these two distinct physical regions were known as *The Two Lands* — *The Land of Upper Egypt* and *The Land of Lower Egypt*. Although the Nile river united these two lands into one country, each one had a distinctive character. (Refer to the map on page 4.)

Upper Egypt or *Shemau*

Upper Egypt extended from the First Cataract to just north of the ancient capital of Memphis, a distance of approximately 800 kilometres. It comprised a long, narrow trough, between three and eighteen kilometres wide, cut into the desert cliffs. It was somewhat isolated from outside contact by the forbidding deserts on either side. It was a five- to eight-day journey from the Nile across the eastern desert to the Red Sea.

The amount of land available for growing food was limited and it was a constant battle for the inhabitants to keep the desert sands from covering their valuable farmland. These farmers depended totally on the yearly flood for their survival.

The excessively dry heat of Upper Egypt was occasionally tempered by the cooling effects of the north wind, and the perpetual sunshine produced a brilliant light.

Lower Egypt or *To-mehu*

Lower Egypt was a broad triangular or fan-shaped area of land with its apex just north of Memphis and its base extending along the Mediterranean coastline. It covered an area twice the size of the valley and was more naturally fertile than Upper Egypt. Its marshes were thick with

Sandstone cliffs that enclose the Nile Valley

papyrus and other reeds and teemed with bird and animal life. The desert was further away from the settlements of Lower Egypt and the climate was milder and moister than Upper Egypt.

Because of its Mediterranean coastline Lower Egypt had closer contact with other cultures although it was more vulnerable to infiltration and invasion.

The *Two Lands* differed in more than just physical features. The people spoke different dialects and some would have probably felt like foreigners in the other's land. Also, each land had its own distinguishing emblems and protective deities:

- Upper Egypt — the sedge (a type of reed) and the vulture goddess, Nekhbet
- Lower Egypt — the bee and the cobra goddess, Wadjet (Edjo).

Before these Two Lands were united into one kingdom (c. 3100 BC), each one had its own ruler who wore a distinctive crown — the tall conical White Crown of Upper Egypt and the Red Crown of Lower Egypt.

The Red Land

In contrast to the fertile Black Land of the valley and delta, the deserts were referred to as the *Red Land* or *Deshret* because of their dominant colour.

Land of the Dead

The desert plateaux and cliffs bordering the valley, where the Egyptians buried their dead, built some of their temples and hunted wild animals, were the only parts of the desert regarded as part of Egypt proper.

Oases

The Egyptians referred to the entire desert area west of the Nile as Libya. It was a desolate region of rocks and sand dunes broken only by a line of oases. This desert held little interest for the Egyptians although the oases provided trade links with the more remote areas. During later periods of Egyptian history the oases were used as places of political banishment. This inhospitable desert isolated Egypt from the west, except for the narrow coastal strip approaching the delta.

To the east of the Nile Valley, high forbidding desert mountains stretched away to the Red Sea. There were several routes through the mountains, which followed dry river beds called wadis.

Minerals and stones

This desert was exploited extensively by the Egyptians for its minerals as well as for its abundant supply of building and semi-precious stones. To the north, a route led from the delta area to the Sinai Peninsula where the Egyptians mined copper and turquoise.

Nubia

The land south of the First Cataract was referred to as Nubia, parts of which were incorporated into Egypt at various times. Lower Nubia, the area between the First and Second Cataract, seems to have been regarded almost as Egyptian by right. Not only was Nubia exceptionally rich in gold but it was the main route through which passed the more exotic products of tropical Africa, so prized by the Egyptians.

The effect of the physical environment on Egyptian lifestyle and beliefs

The ancient Egyptians developed a distinctive lifestyle and belief system because:

- they lived in a long, narrow valley and marshy delta enclosed by barren, inhospitable deserts
- they were totally dependent on the life-giving waters of the Nile
- they enjoyed a climate where the sun shone constantly and where there was virtually no rain.

Lifestyle

Almost all activities in Egypt, from the more mundane tasks of the farmer to the coronation of the king, were determined by the Nile and its annual flood.

The yearly calendar

There were three seasons in the yearly calendar.

1 Akhet

2 Perit

3 Shemu.

The shadouf, an ancient device for raising water, still in use along the Nile

Akhet was the season of the flood which began sometime in July. The first day of the inundation, when the life-giving waters began to rise, was one of only two days when a king could hold his coronation.

The king's coronation

At this time most of the large-scale building activities were carried out since the extensive floodwaters allowed barges, transporting the massive blocks of stone, to get closer to the building sites. While their land was under water, farmers were often conscripted to work in gangs on the construction of temples and other major works. Normally they had little to do at this time except hand feed their animals and repair equipment.

Perit, which began in November was called the *Season of Coming Forth*. It was the time of sowing the seeds. The first day of this season was the only other time that the king could be officially crowned. On the first five days of Perit the kings also held their important 30-year jubilee or Sed (also called Heb-sed) festival. Since the purpose of this festival was to rejuvenate the king's powers it was natural that it should be celebrated when the land had been rejuvenated by the silt-carrying floodwaters.

Heb-sed festival

This was the period of most intensive activity along the Nile. Farmers raced against time to conserve the floodwaters by repairing dykes and cleaning out ditches and canals; to spread the rich silt; to plough the fields and sow the seed before the land began to dry out too much.

Shemu was the season of harvest and began sometime in early March. A celebration held at the beginning of the harvest season, the Festival of Min, god of fertility, was possibly the highlight of the year for the Egyptian peasant farmer.

Harvest and tax collection

It was a hectic time of the year. Farmers harvested, threshed, winnowed, stored and transported the grain and flax while scribes recorded the harvest, carried out the census, assessed and collected the taxes.

Administration

A nilometre, used to calculate the height of the flood

All Egyptians, from the lowliest peasant farmers to the highest officials, depended on the Nile for their survival. For this reason it was necessary to have a central authority to control water supplies. Due to the great length of the Nile valley, a huge bureaucracy of government officials, skilled in calculation, measurement and writing was needed:

- to make predictions about the timing and nature of the flood
- to plan irrigation works
- to organise local community effort to get the land back in order after the flood
- to re-survey the land and mark out farm boundaries which had disappeared under the floodwaters.

A *normal* flood could be easily controlled. However, sometimes emergencies occurred. A flood level about 1.5 metres lower than normal at Elephantine Island meant food shortages and a series of low-level floods could cause a life-threatening famine. However, a water level 30 to 60 centimetres higher than normal was destructive, causing serious damage to houses, dykes and canals. Such emergency situations could only be handled by a large-scale community effort.

Conscripted gangs

Local nobles, responsible to the central government, conscripted, organised and supervised large work gangs to build and maintain irrigation schemes. This unpaid work was onerous but necessary.

Land was valued and taxes, in the form of produce, were assessed by government officials on the basis of the height of the flood. For example, some land always received the benefit of the flood and so had the potential for a good harvest. On the other hand, some parcels of land were covered with water some years and not others. Plots further away from the river very rarely received the life-giving floodwater and silt.

Nilometers were built along the Nile to measure the maximum, minimum and average flow of the flood. Usually these were built in the form of a staircase leading from the river. As the floodwaters rose up through the staircase, the amount of water was determined by grooves cut in the walls. The Greek geographer, Strabo, reported:

Measurement of floodwaters

> There are marks which measure the height of the water for irrigation. They are used by the farmers to measure the flow of the water, by the bureaucrats (officials) to establish the amount of taxes. In fact the higher the water the higher the taxes.[3]

Communication and transportation

The river was the chief highway of the ancient Egyptians. It linked and united the scattered villages and towns along its 900 kilometre length from the delta to the First Cataract. The inhospitable desert on both sides of the river made travel overland difficult and the Egyptians did not have wheeled vehicles or horses until approximately 1600 BC.

Water highways

Travel up and down the river was made easier by the prevailing wind and the Nile current. Since the prevailing wind blew from north to south, boats travelling south or upstream (towards the source) could use their sails. The river current ran from south to north so boats heading north or downstream (towards the mouth) were helped by the current. The Egyptian hieroglyph for *travelling south* or *going upstream* was a boat with a sail while the hieroglyph for *travelling north* or *going downstream* was a boat with oars.

The heiroglyph for upstream (or travelling south)

The number of boats, either depicted in tomb paintings or as models among the funerary goods in tombs, indicate the importance of this form of travel to the ancient Egyptians.

The heiroglyph for downstream (or travelling north)

A Nile boat (from the tomb of Sennefer)

Building, crafts and decorative arts

The rich alluvial soil and the swamps and marshes of the *Black Land* provided building materials for domestic architecture, resources for many Egyptian crafts and decorative themes for Egyptian art.

The barren expanses of desert which comprised the *Red Land* provided the Egyptians with many of the resources for their sacred buildings and for funerary and temple equipment.

Brick making

Nile mud was used for brick making. Sun-dried mud-brick was the basic material for all domestic buildings, including the palaces of the kings. It was the ideal building material in a land which was virtually rainless. The mud was always at hand, the bricks were quick to make and repairs to buildings could be carried out easily. Unfortunately very few of these buildings have survived.

Ancient mud-bricks

Building stone

Limestone and sandstone from the desert cliffs bordering the Nile were the chief building materials used in temples and tombs. The limestone quarry at Tura across the river from Giza, was the source of the finest limestone blocks used as casing stones for the pyramids. The harder pink and black granite from Aswan was used for gateways, columns, obelisks and as the facing stones in the burial chambers of kings. Granite was also used for the sarcophagi (huge stone outer coffins) of royalty.

The papyrus reed which grew profusely along the marshy banks of the river and in the swamps of the delta provided the raw materials for many items used in everyday life.

Papyrus products

Every part of the papyrus plant was used by the Egyptians. From it they made flat-bottomed fishing and fowling skiffs, sandals, ropes, baskets, mats and a fine white paper also called papyrus. This valuable product was used by priests, officials and wealthy people only. See Chapter 6 for details on the manufacture of papyrus.

A papyrus collector

Fowling in the papyrus marshes using a papyrus skiff

The deserts were exploited for a variety of building and semi-precious stones and valuable metals such as gold and copper. Fine statues were sculpted from basalt and reddish quartzite, beautiful translucent jars and vessels were crafted from alabaster, funerary items and jewellery were made from gold and semi-precious stones like turquoise, and tools were manufactured from copper.

Valuable stones and minerals

Many of the motifs used in decorating private and public buildings were taken from the river landscape. Sculpted friezes and painted scenes on the walls and floors of royal palaces and the houses of wealthy officials depicted darting birds, fish, ducks and flowering reeds. The papyrus plant and the blue and white lotus flowers were common motifs used by crafts-men and architects. The halls of the great temples featured massed columns, designed to look like reeds, lotus flowers and buds, and palms. These halls were meant to create an impression of the lush vegetation of the primeval marshes.

Ducks in the papyrus marsh, from Akhetaten

An alabaster lamp in the shape of three lotus flowers, from the tomb of Tutankhamun

Above: Flower column from the Temple of Karnak

Right: Bud columns from the Temple of Karnak

Religious beliefs and morality

Egyptian religious beliefs were partly inspired by the nature of the land and its climate. The physical environment was reflected in:

- their view of creation
- the nature of their gods
- their belief in life after death and the nature of the afterlife.

The Egyptian concept of creation

The Egyptian concept of creation was expressed in a number of myths or stories. Although they varied from one another in some of the details, the myths contained a number of common elements. It does not take too much imagination to see that these beliefs were based on the Egyptians' observation of the environment around them.

Elements of the myths	Features of the environment
At first the whole earth was covered with water (*the waters of chaos* or the *primeval ocean called Nun*).	During the annual inundation the Nile valley was covered with water.
A mound of earth or an island (*the primeval mound*) emerged from the waters.	As the floodwaters receded small hills or mounds of earth emerged.
The first god appeared on this mound and created life (*the first time*).	From the rich silt which covered the land, new life sprang up.

The nature of the gods

Many of the Egyptian gods symbolised some aspect of the natural environment such as the sun, the Nile River and the rejuvenating flood and silt which supported new life. Some gods represented the qualities found in the creatures that lived along the Nile valley, such as the falcon and cobra.

Re (Ra), the sun god, was the most important deity throughout Egyptian history. He was depicted in many forms — as a falcon-headed man with a sun disk on his head, as a scarab beetle pushing a sun disk ahead of him, as a bennu bird which rose at dawn to herald the new day, and sometimes as a child arising from an opening lotus flower.

Re

Hapi, was the spirit of the Nile. The Egyptians depicted him as a man with:

Hapi

- a pendulous belly (the sign of a prosperous, well-fed man in Egypt)
- the breasts of a woman (fertility and nourishment)
- a cluster of lotus and papyrus plants on his head (plant symbols of Upper and Lower Egypt)
- a girdle or belt (similar to those worn by fishermen along the river)
- a table of offerings (abundance).

Prayers were offered to him for a *good* flood. He was praised in hymns as the one who comes to nourish Egypt and as the creator of every good thing. Refer to the *Hymn to Hapi* at the end of this chapter (Question 2).

Osiris symbolised the energy behind the life-giving flood (the silt) and the resultant new growth.

Osiris

Seth was always associated with the desert. To the Egyptians, the desert was a dangerous and inhospitable place full of wild animals. It was also where the dead were buried. The Egyptians associated Seth, as god of the desert, with every other frightening thing in nature — wind, rain, storms and thunder.

Seth

A representation of Hapi, the spirit of the Nile

Belief in life after death

To the Egyptians, the cycle of life, death and rebirth was apparent in the patterns of nature.

- The sun appeared to *die* each evening in the west and be *reborn* each morning in the east.
- The germinating seed sprouted from the parched earth after the annual flood of the Nile.

The contrast between the fertile area of cultivation (the *Black Land*) and the aridity of the desert (the *Red Land*) was a constant reminder to the Egyptians of the contrast between life and death. The western desert became the *Land of the Dead*, where the necropolises or *cities of the dead* (cemeteries) were located. The jackal that roamed the desert became the symbol of Anubis, god of the dead and guardian of the necropolis.

During the New Kingdom, most people believed that they would spend eternity in the *Fields of Reeds*, a place which closely resembled the delta with its lush meadows, watercourses and canals. Kings were thought to spend eternity riding across the sky in the boat of the sun god, Re.

Attitudes and morality

Conservatism

Because of the constant sunshine and the regularity of the flood the ancient Egyptians developed a conservative attitude to life. Nothing much changed from one year to the next — their civilisation continued with little change for over 3000 years. Rather than adopt a totally new belief or idea, they were more likely to graft the new concept onto the old.

Security

The long, narrow, fertile valley of the Nile enclosed by deserts on both sides, provided a secure environment for its inhabitants. Although the deserts were not total barriers to invasion and foreign influences, the Egyptians, for a substantial part of their history, were confident in their relative isolation and prosperity.

Parochialism

However, due to the narrowness of their land the people tended to have a parochial (narrow and inward-looking) outlook and were distrustful of foreigners. The Egyptians described non-Egyptians in a derogatory way, using words such as *vile* and *wretched* when referring to the Bedouin tribesmen of the deserts, the Nubians from the south and the various groups from Syria and Palestine to the north-east. It was not until a group of Asiatic infiltrators, known as the Hyksos, established themselves in the delta about 1600 BC and spread their rule over much of the Nile Valley, that the attitudes of the Egyptians changed. Their sense of security was seriously threatened at this time. When they eventually expelled the Hyksos from Egypt they were forced to move further afield to protect their land. As a result they adopted a wider view of the world.

Egyptian morality reflected the society's total dependence on the water provided by the Nile. It was regarded as just as serious to divert or withhold a neighbour's water supply as it was to commit theft or murder. Many officials in their tomb inscriptions made particular reference to the fact that they had not dammed water, preventing others from obtaining their share. When facing judgment before the gods, Egyptians listed the sins they had not committed. One of these was: *I have not fouled running water.*[4]

Conclusion

The Egyptians always saw life as a duality — the *Two Lands* of *Upper* and *Lower Egypt*; the fertile area of cultivation (Black Land) and the inhospitable barren deserts (Red Land) and the two sides of the river, the east where people generally lived and the west where they were buried.

Chapter review

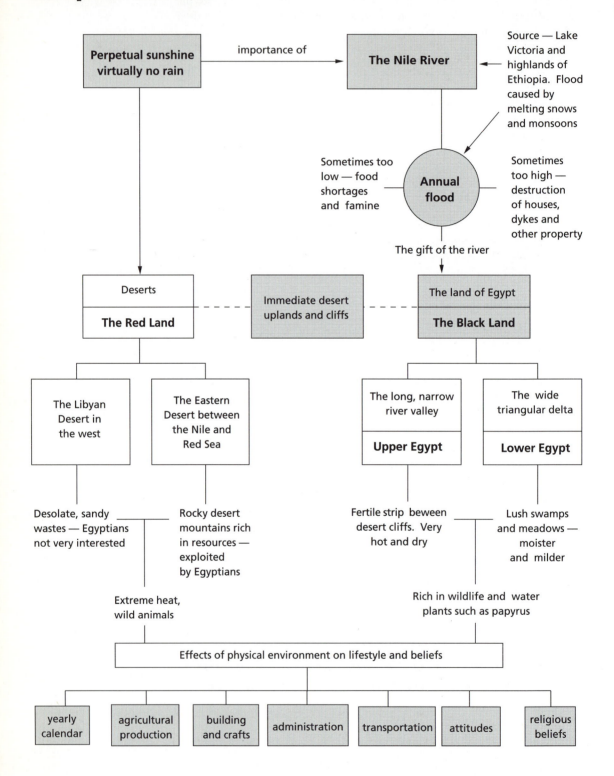

The physical environment of ancient Egypt

REVISION QUESTIONS AND ESSAY TOPICS

1 **The following extracts are from Book 2: 8–29 of** *The Histories* **by Herodotus, a Greek historian, who lived during the fifth century BC and who spent some time in Egypt.**

> *From the coast inland as far as Heliopolis* ... the country is broad and flat, with much swamp and mud ... Southwards of Heliopolis the country narrows. It is confined on the one side by the range of the Arabian mountains which run north and south and then continue without a break in the direction of the Arabian Gulf. In these mountains are the quarries where the stone was cut for the pyramids at Memphis ... On the Libyan side of Egypt there is another range of hills where the pyramids stand; these hills are rocky and covered with sand, and run in a southerly direction ... Above Heliopolis, then, for a distance of four days' voyage up the river Egypt is narrow, and the extent of the territory, for so important a country, is meagre enough. Between the two mountain ranges — the Libyan and the Arabian — it is a level plain, in its narrowest part, so far as I could judge, not more than about two hundred furlongs (about 40 kilometres) across. South of this the country broadens again ... My own observation bears out the statement made to me by the priests that the greater part of the country I have described has been built up by silt from the Nile ...*
>
> *As things are at present those people (those who live in the delta region) get their harvests with less labour than any one else in the world, the rest of the Egyptians included ... Concerning the sources of the Nile, nobody I have spoken with, Egyptian, Libyan or Greek, professed to have any knowledge ... As far as Elephantine I speak as an eye-witness, but further south from hearsay. The most I could learn was that beyond Elephantine the country rises steeply; and in that part of the river boats have to be hauled along by ropes. If the rope parts, the boat is gone in a moment, carried away by the force of the stream.*[5]

* Heliopolis was the centre of the sun cult and was located north of the capital of Memphis.

a How did Herodotus obtain his information? Find at least two pieces of supporting evidence from the extracts.

b What did the Egyptians call the two areas described below:

> 'From the coast inland ... the country is broad and flat, with much swamp and mud ...'
> 'Southwards of Heliopolis the country narrows'?

c To what was Herodotus referring when he spoke of the Arabian mountains?

d What physical feature was Herodotus describing when he said, 'In that part of the river the boats have to be hauled along by ropes'?

e How accurate are the observations made by Herodotus that:

> 'the greater part of the country was built up by Nile silt'
> 'the farming in the delta was easier than elsewhere in Egypt'?

f   Find a quote from Herodotus which describes the features shown in the photo below.

2 The following hymn is an adaptation of translations by Erman, *Literature* p. 149 and Wilson in *Ancient Near-Eastern Texts*, pp. 372–373.

> *Praise to you, Hapi, sprung from the earth, come to nourish Egypt!*
> *Hapi, of secret ways and darkness by day, your followers sing to you!*
> *You flood the fields that Re has made, to satisfy all who thirst,*
> *Your dew descends from the sky to let the waterless desert drink.*
> *Friend of Geb,* lord of Nepri, you promote the arts of Ptah.*#*
> *Lord of the fishes,*
> *You make the wild fowl stream south and none falls down from heat.*
> *Maker of barley and wheat, it is through you that the temples celebrate.*
> *When your flow is sluggish, noses are blocked and everyone is poor;*
> *As the number of sacred loaves goes down, a million men perish.*
> *When your waters plunder the whole land rages,*
> *Great and small call out;*
> *People's lives are changed by your coming,*
> *When Khnum^ fashions you.*
> *When you flood, the earth is glad and every belly rejoices,*
> *Laughter is on every face and every mouth is smiling.*
>
> *Hapi, the light-maker who comes from the dark,*
> *You fatten the herds, your might fashions everything,*
> *None can live without you.*
> *People are clothed with the flax from your fields,*
> *For you have made Hedj-hotep+ serve you;*
> *You anoint with your unguents,*
> *You are the like of Ptah.*
> *All types of crafts exist because of you,*

All books of godly words are products from the sedges.
Coming out above from the cavern, you want your coming secret.
If your rise is insufficient, the people dwindle,
A year's food supply is lost.
The rich man looks concerned, everyone is seen with weapons,
Friends do not attend to each other.
Cloth is wanting for one's clothes, noble children lack their finery.
There is no eye-paint, no one is anointed.
Songs to the harp are made for you, one sings with clapping hands;
Your children hail you, crowds adorn themselves for you,
Who comes with riches, adorning the land.
You make every body thrive;
You sustain the heart of pregnant women,
And love a multitude of herds.
When you rise ... men feast on the meadow's gift,
Decked with the lotus for the nose,
And all the things that sprout from the earth ...
Good things are strewn about the houses,
The whole land leaps for joy.
O Hapi, when you overflow, sacrifice is made for you ...
Fowl is fattened for you, desert game is snared for you,
As one repays your bounty.
Offerings are made to all the gods of that which you have provided,
Choice incense, oxen, goats and birds in a great sacrifice.

Oh joy when you come!
Oh joy when you come, O Hapi!
You feed men and herds with your meadow gifts.
Oh joy when you come![6]

* Geb was the god of the earth
\# Ptah was a creator god and the patron god of craftsmen
^ Khnum was a creator god of Elephantine, the divine potter
\+ Hedj-hotep was the weaver god.

a Who was Hapi?

b Where did the Egyptians believe Hapi lived? Find supporting evidence from the hymn.

c Why is Hapi described in the hymn as the 'Friend of Geb'?

d What benefits did the annual flood bring to the Egyptian farmer? Find three pieces of supporting evidence from the hymn.

e List some of the words in the hymn which reveal the feelings of the Egyptians when a *good* flood arrived.

f Hapi is described as a 'promoter of the crafts'.

To what craft does the line 'All books of godly words are products from the sedges', refer?

Find evidence from the hymn of another craft which depended on the annual flood.

g   Find a line from the hymn which best describes the following illustration.

Bas-relief from the pyramid of Unas

h   Explain why, according to the hymn, the rich were so concerned during a bad year (when the flood level was too low) that some even carried weapons.

i   To what do each of the following lines refer?

'When your flow is sluggish, noses are blocked and everyone is poor.'

'When your waters plunder the whole land rages.'

'When you rise, men feast in the meadow's gifts.'

3   Essay topics

a   Comment on Herodotus' statement that 'Egypt is the gift of the river'.[7]

b   Describe the concerns that a family of Egyptian peasant farmers might have had as they waited anxiously for the Nile's water level to rise in July. How would they and their neighbours have reacted when the long-awaited flood finally broke the river's banks and flowed across their land.

Use the information in the Hymn to Hapi as a guide.

Sources for Egyptian history

In the fifth century BC the Greek historian Herodotus, on a visit to Egypt, marvelled at the number and size of the monuments, some of which were already over 2000 years old.

Numerous material remains

> About Egypt I shall have a great deal more to relate because of the number of remarkable things which the country contains, and because of the fact that more monuments which beggar description are to be found there than anywhere else in the world.[1]

Visitors to Egypt today still gaze in amazement at these monuments — the pyramids, the massive stone statues, the painted rock-cut and masta-ba tombs, and the mortuary and cult temples. With their incised and painted hieroglyphic texts they provide a wealth of information on the art and culture of the ancient Egyptians.

Despite the number of inscriptions that have survived, there are few reliable records of those events which affected Egyptian development and which influenced the lives of individuals. James maintains that 'the raw material for the writing of a satisfactory Egyptian history is insufficient and sketchy'[2] and Gardiner says that 'what is proudly advertised as Egyptian history is merely a collection of rags and tatters'.[3]

Historical information limited

Written sources

The written records left by the ancient Egyptians are to be found:

- carved into the walls of temples
- inscribed on stelae found in tombs, temples, and wherever else the ancient Egyptians felt the need to leave a monument to commemorate a victorious battle, a successful mining or quarrying expedition, the founding of a new city or the construction of a building

Where the sources are found

- painted or inscribed on coffins, sarcophagi, canopic chests and other funerary items
- written with reed pens on papyrus fragments or rolls
- written or scratched on broken pieces of pottery or limestone flakes (ostraca).

None of these written sources of information could be read before the nineteenth century.

The Rosetta Stone — deciphering the ancient scripts

A black basalt stone, discovered in 1798 at Rosetta (Rashid) in the Egyptian delta, provided the key to understanding the mysterious Egyptian picture-writing (hieroglyphics).

The Rosetta Stone

The Rosetta Stone, as it became known, was an inscription in honour of an Egyptian pharaoh called Ptolemy Epiphanes (196 BC). It was written in Greek and in two Egyptian scripts — hieroglyphic and a popular shorthand version called demotic. Since the Greek text could be read, it was possible to translate that section of the inscription. However, it took years of dedicated work before Jean Francois Champollion cracked the code in 1824. Many more years passed before there was enough material in the form of original documents or copies of inscriptions for historians to fully make use of the key provided by Champollion and others who followed him.

Hieroglyphic script

Since the Egyptians had one word which stood for both *writing* and *drawing*, the miniature images used to record their language were pleasing to the eye as well as the mind.

These images, usually carved deeply into the stone walls and columns of temples, were called hieroglyphics which meant *sacred carvings* in Greek. In some of the later Old Kingdom pyramids hieroglyphics were used to record prayers and magical spells.

However, the word is now applied to all Egyptian writing which is pic-torial, including the signs painted on the walls of tombs and inside coffins as well as those written/drawn with reed pens on religious papyri.

Hieroglyphic writing was a combination of ideograms (pictures which stand for exactly what they represent), phonograms (pictures which stand for sounds) and alphabetic consonants. No vowels were written. For example:

Nature of hieroglyphs

- a billowing sail means *wind*
- a picture of a loaf stands for the letter *t*, a mouth stands for the letter *r*
- a swallow stands for the sound *wr* as well as the word *great*
- a beetle which stands for the sound *hpr* also means to *become*.

Because these miniature signs could be ambiguous it was often neces-sary to add another sign, called a determinative, to clarify what was meant. The deciphering of hieroglyphic writing was further complicated by the fact that sometimes it read from top to bottom, sometimes from right to left and sometimes from left to right.

Ambiguity of hieroglyphs

Hieratic script

Hieratic script was a simplified form of hieroglyphic script, developed to make writing quicker and easier. It was particularly suited to writing on papyrus. It first appeared in the Old Kingdom as an abbreviated form of hieroglyphics but gradually became more cursive with some of the original signs replaced with strokes. The demotic script on the Rosetta Stone was not in use until c. 700 BC.

*Deeply incised hieroglyphs from
the Temple of Karnak*

*Painted hieroglyphs
from the tomb of a
noble at Aswan*

Cartouches

A feature of the Rosetta inscription was the oval *rope-loop* or *royal ring*, called a cartouche. Cartouches surrounded the names of kings and queens and this helped Champollion decipher the hieroglyphs.

In the written records cartouches were always placed around two of the five names of the king — the one he was given at birth and the one he assumed when he came to the throne. These rope rings were believed to magically protect the king. They were also a symbol for *that which the sun-disk encircles* and alluded to the king's authority over the world.

*A cartouche from the
wall of a temple*

The nature of the written sources

Monumental inscriptions associated with the kings and the gods

The hieroglyphic records carved on the walls of temples and on free-standing stelae are called monumental inscriptions. The purpose of these inscriptions was to glorify the king by commemorating his deeds and virtues and to honour the gods. The king's achievements were always displayed in very public places.

These royal inscriptions reflected the Egyptian belief in the king as:

- a god
- the protector of his people
- a leader of the nation during war
- the intermediary between the gods and the people.

They included records of military campaigns, either described as a single event or in an annalistic form (a year by year account); treaties and decrees; building activities and dedication ceremonies; mining, quarrying and trading expeditions and endowments and offerings made to the gods. They also depicted the king in his role of high priest and highlighted the monarch's physical prowess.

These inscriptions were a form of propaganda.

A free-standing official stela erected by Amenhotep III on the site of his mortuary temple in western Thebes

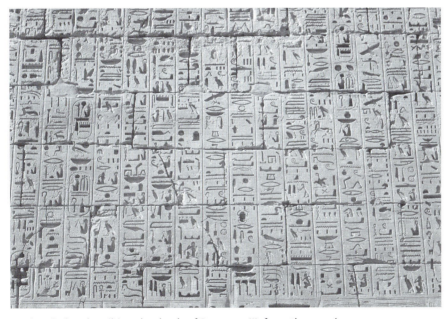

An inscription describing the deeds of Ramesses III, from the remains of the Temple of Medinet Habu, western Thebes

Above: A monumental inscription of Ramesses III fighting a battle, from the remains of the Temple of Medinet Habu, western Thebes

Right: A rock stela on Sehel Island near the First Cataract which describes a famine during the reign of King Djoser

Funerary texts

The Egyptians believed in life after death. In order to pass safely to the next life they relied on a whole collection of magical spells and prayers. These are now referred to as funerary texts.

Pyramid Texts

During the latter part of the Old Kingdom a large number of these incantations and prayers were inscribed on the walls of the royal burial chambers. They first appeared in the pyramid of King Unas, the last ruler of the Fifth Dynasty and then in the pyramids of Sixth Dynasty kings and queens. These texts are known as the *Pyramid Texts* and their purpose was to ensure the well-being of the king in his next life in the sky with the gods.

Coffin Texts

By the Middle Kingdom, well-to-do Egyptians also wanted to join the gods in the afterlife. They began to inscribe the inside of their coffins with spells to protect them and guide them safely to the next life. These spells and prayers, although based on the older Pyramid Texts, included new material and are referred to as the *Coffin Texts*.

The Book of the Dead

During the New Kingdom, the funerary texts were written on papyrus rolls and placed near the body of those people who could afford a copy. This papyrus book was referred to by the Egyptians as *The Book of Coming Forth By Day* but is more commonly known today as *The Book of the Dead*. It was divided into a number of chapters or spells for particular purposes, such as protecting the parts of the body and successfully passing the tests in the Hall of Judgment. However, not every copy was the same. Those who could afford it had individual copies made with their own choice of chapters. The less wealthy bought off the shelf versions. The *Book of the Dead* grew out of the Pyramid and Coffin Texts.

Records associated with civil administration

The autobiographies of officials

The administration of Egypt was run by a vast bureaucracy of officials at the head of which was the vizier, *first under the king*. Like the king, these high officials left a record of their achievements but whereas kings recorded their deeds in very public places, private individuals could only properly record their achievements in their tombs. The personal record found in the tombs of non-royal individuals is sometimes referred to as the tomb autobiography.

Some of these inscriptions simply include a list of titles granted to the tomb owner by the king and a brief description of the duties carried out on behalf of the king. These records, which are always expressed in stereotyped phrases, reveal little of the official's life and character and always give credit to the king for whatever the official achieved.

Glorification of the king

There are some which give more specific and precise career details and provide some insight into the character of the tomb owner. Many of these, however, belong to provincial officials who carried out activities beyond the borders of Egypt. Sometimes these officials carved more informative records of their achievements in remote mining and quarrying regions.

Some career details

The autobiography of a vizier, the highest official in the land, was sometimes accompanied by a detailed account of his official duties and responsibilities.

Official dispatches and records of judicial proceedings

Egyptian scribes kept careful records. Most of the official documents in museums around the world are dated from the late New Kingdom.

Many were found in the remains of the administrative buildings associated with the mortuary temple of Ramesses III (Medinet Habu). Others were found in the village of Deir el-Medina in western Thebes which was home to the craftsmen who built and decorated the royal tombs in the Valley of the Kings. A collection of letters from the late Eighteenth Dynasty were found in the ruins of the ancient city of Akhetaten (modern Amarna).

Letters, dispatches and reports sent to and from officials throughout Egypt were written on papyrus and dealt with such business as water resources, grain supplies, the collection of taxes and the census, the progress of building projects, problems with royal workmen and so on.

Nature of official dispatches

Reports and letters sent to and received from the local native princes of Syria and Palestine and the great kings of the eastern empires, such as Babylon were inscribed in cuneiform (wedge-shaped signs) on clay tablets. These were written in Akkadian, the diplomatic language of the day. Egyptian scribes later translated and transcribed the messages onto papyrus for storage in the official Egyptian archives. The collection of

The Amarna Letters

clay tablets found at Amarna are referred to as the Amarna Letters. These give some insights into the relationship between the Egyptian pharaoh and foreign princes, as well as the problems faced by Egyptian administrators and local rulers.

Some of the surviving official records concern judicial matters. One of these, known as the Amherst Papyrus, is a particularly illuminating document. It deals with the interrogation of tomb robbers from the village of Deir el-Medina who were arrested and brought before the court of the vizier. The account of their trial included accusations of corruption among district officials.

There are also records of legal disputes over ownership, inheritances and non-payment of debts that were handled in the local courts.

Workers' registers

The scribes who supervised the workmen from Deir el-Medina kept careful registers in which they recorded details about the amount of work completed, equipment issued to the workmen, the number of tools broken and replaced, and absenteeism among the workers.

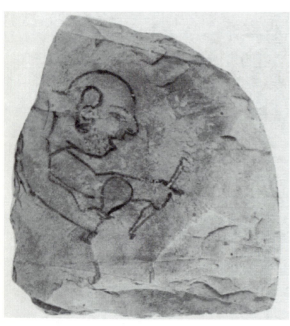

Ostracon of a workman breaking stone with a spike and mallet

Instructions

This type of text is found in all Egyptian periods and reflects the ethical standards of society. These *instructions* were brief teachings aimed at guiding the members of the noble/official class in correct behaviour.

Domestic records

Written records about the everyday life of the ordinary Egyptians are sadly lacking. Those found in the village of Deir el-Medina throw some light on domestic life, although they are not necessarily typical of other settlements.

Thousands of ostraca (broken pieces of pottery and limestone flakes covered with hieratic writing and sketches) reveal something of the concerns of the ordinary people and their sense of humour. These fragmentary records include personal letters, complaints about neighbours, stories, laundry lists, accounts of festivals, the brewing of beer, getting drunk, presents sent to each other, medical complaints, and offerings made to their personal gods.

No records by peasants

Unfortunately, what is known about the lives of the peasant farmers was recorded by members of other classes — nobles depicted the ideal agricultural life in their tombs while scribes often emphasised the miserable aspects of the peasants' lifestyle.

Problems associated with the written sources

Despite the amount of written material found in Egypt, there is a real lack of historical data. Scholars attempting to write a history of Egypt have to take into account some of the following factors:

- the inequality in the preservation of records from one historical period to another and from one geographical area to another
- the disproportionate number of records associated with funerary beliefs, burial practices and temple worship
- the idealised and distorted versions of events (propaganda) presented in the monumental inscriptions
- the conservatism which led ancient Egyptians to record what was traditional rather than what really happened
- the focus in the texts on the activities of men of the upper classes. Where women are mentioned it is from a male perspective
- the lack of a sense of chronology (sequence of events) on the part of Egyptian scribes.

Lack of historical data

Inequality in the preservation of the records

The number of records which have survived from one period to another varies considerably. For example, the few surviving inscriptions from the Old Kingdom (the Pyramid Age) are mostly fragmentary lists of kings, funerary prayers, magical spells, lists of offerings to the gods, some moral instructions and graffiti. There are some, but not many, informative details from tomb biographies.

Few historical records from Old Kingdom

The Egyptians who lived during politically unstable and economically depressed periods tended to leave fewer records. In contrast, the records from the New Kingdom are much more numerous and informative.

Most historical records have been found in the desert uplands rather than the area of cultivation along the river where the Egyptians lived and worked. Objects and records buried in the hot, dry desert sands were preserved, while those buried in the alluvial soil of the valley and the delta deteriorated quickly. This was due to the excessive moisture, the rising level of the water table and the activities of the dense rural populations. Most buildings in the river valley, including the palaces of the kings, were built of mud-bricks which deteriorated rapidly. The towns of present day Egypt now cover the debris of successive ancient settlements. Since the desert fringes, where most of the records have been found, are in Upper Egypt, there is a marked disparity in our knowledge of Upper and of Lower Egypt.

Records preserved in desert sands

A disproportionate number of sources of a funerary and religious nature

There is far more information available concerning the Egyptians' religious and funerary beliefs and practices than about anything else. This is because most Egyptians buried their dead in the preserving sands of the deserts adjoining the river valley. Also their tombs and mortuary temples were built of highly durable stone.

Unlike palaces and houses, cult temples (*mansions of the gods*) built on the alluvial flats were able to survive in the moister conditions because they were constructed of stone.

Egyptologists have tended in the past to concentrate their attentions on the cemeteries and temples of the two greatest ancient cities — Thebes and Memphis/Sakkara.

Distortion and propaganda in the monumental inscriptions

Many of the records left behind by the pharaohs are 'slanted away from reality'.[4] The monumental inscriptions (hieroglyphic texts and larger-than-life reliefs of kings and gods carved on the walls of temples) were intended as official propaganda. Since Egyptian kings were regarded as gods, the main purpose of these records was to maintain the god-like status of the king by describing the events of his reign in the most favourable light. 'In general it may be said that anything sinister or unsuccessful in the careers of the pharaohs was carefully suppressed.'[5] For example, military set-backs and disastrous defeats were generally ignored or transformed into a situation where the divine and superhuman power of the king saved the day. Internal conspiracies and attempted assassinations are often only discovered by chance references in other sources.

Pharaohs did not hesitate to *borrow* the great deeds of those who had ruled before them. They sometimes even went so far as to obliterate the scenes and texts of their predecessors from the walls of the temples and claim the achievements as their own.

The inscriptions on the walls of tombs belonging to the great nobles contain some of the boastful quality of the royal texts because Egyptians thought it was important to advertise their achievements. These records have to be treated cautiously.

Tradition rather than truth

Similar themes from one period to another

The Egyptians believed that what was done *on the first occasion* or *in the time of the ancestors* was what should always be done. In their written records as well as their pictorial representations, the Egyptians depicted what was traditional rather than what really happened. For example, all pharaohs were shown as conquerors smashing the skulls of their enemies or trampling them underfoot, no matter whether an individual ruler ever faced an enemy or not. As Gardiner comments, 'Often this love of the time-honoured and the typical led to downright falsification'.[6]

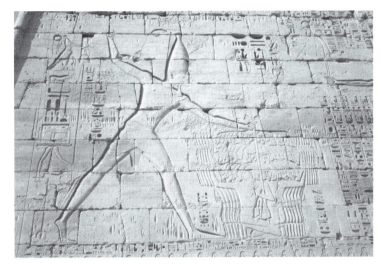

A New Kingdom pharaoh (Ramesses III) smashing the heads of his enemies, from the Temple of Ramesses at Medinet Habu

Male bias in the texts

Only a small percentage of the population of ancient Egypt could read and write. Almost all of these were men of the scribal and noble classes. Therefore most written records were written by males, from a male point of view and for male readers. It is difficult to build up a picture of the life of Egyptian women.

What we do get from the records is 'an idea of the ideals concerning women and their place in society, and of the types of female behaviour that might have fallen outside the prescribed limits'.[7]

Difficulties with chronology

Modern historians see events as part of a chain with causes and effects. Ancient Egyptians did not look for causes or feel the need to record events chronologically and systematically. In fact, they did not have a consistent way of reckoning time and only felt obliged to record the deeds of those kings whom they believed were deserving of honour.

Egyptians dated events according to:

No consistent way of reckoning time

- a specific year in a king's reign such as 'the year of fighting and smiting the northerners'[8]
- a census of cattle held every two years — 'in the year of the second enumeration of all the large and small cattle of the north and south'. If an event happened in an odd year it might be referred to 'as the year after the second numbering of all oxen'[9]
- the regnal year of a pharaoh (the reign of a pharaoh) — in the fifteenth year of Senwosret (Sesostris) III or in year 22 of Thutmose III and so on.

**Omissions in
King Lists**

Not only are the surviving lists of Egyptian kings fragmentary, but certain noteworthy rulers have been omitted while less significant ones have been included.

Also it has been difficult for historians to identify some of the kings from the names in the lists. Each Egyptian king had a number of names, such as the one he was given at birth and the one adopted on becoming pharaoh. (In the first two dynasties, kings had only two names and it was not until the Fourth Dynasty that they adopted the full titulary of five names which they retained throughout pharaonic history.) Identification of a particular pharaoh becomes difficult if his birth name was used in one record and his throne name was used in another.

Dynasties

Establishing an accurate chronology for Egyptian history has presented many problems. Egyptian history is conventionally divided into a number of dynasties or lines of kings from the same family. These 31 dynasties from c. 3100–332 BC are grouped into larger time-spans according to political, social and cultural patterns and changes. For example dynasties three to six are grouped into the period referred to as the *Old Kingdom*.

**Manetho and discovery
of the King Lists**

This division of Egyptian history into dynasties was based on the work of a priest called Manetho who lived in Heliopolis in the third century BC. Historians later modified his chronology when more reliable ancient texts were found. These included:

- the Palermo Stone, a fragment of diorite inscribed with selected events from the reigns of the earliest kings — from Menes (believed to be the first king of the *Two Lands*) to those of the Fifth Dynasty

- the King List inscribed on a wall in the temple of Seti I at Abydos. This list is part of a scene showing King Seti I and his son, Ramesses II, making offerings to about 76 of their ancestors who are represented by cartouches enclosing their names

- the Turin Canon of Kings, a papyrus document written in hieratic about the time of King Ramesses II.

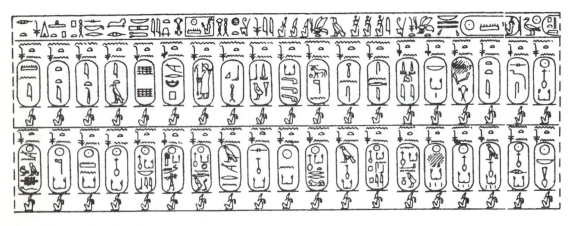

Part of the Abydos King List

Other records that have helped historians develop a more accurate chronological framework include:

- dated labels on pottery food-jars found in the ruins of royal palaces
- entries made in the registers kept by scribes in charge of craftsmen working on the royal tombs at Thebes
- astronomical texts.

Even when all available sources have been used, many of the dates ascribed to the periods, dynasties and individual kings are doubtful.

The chronology used by scholars and featured in modern texts varies considerably.

Dynastic periods	Egyptian Antiquities Organisation	Department of Antiquities, British Museum	Cyril Aldred	J Baines and J Málek
Early Dynastic Period — Archaic Dynasties 1–2	c. 3000–2705 BC	c. 3100–2686 BC	c. 3168–2705 BC	c. 2920–2649 BC
Old Kingdom — Dynasties 3–6	c. 2705–2230 BC	c. 2686–2181 BC	c. 2705–2230 BC	c. 2649–2150 BC
First Intermediate Period — Dynasties 7–10	c.2155–2134 BC	c. 2181–2133 BC	c. 2230–2035 BC	c. 2150–2040 BC
Middle Kingdom — Dynasties 11–12	c. 2134–1781 BC	c. 2133–1674 BC	c. 2035–1720 BC	c. 2040–1640 BC
Second Intermediate Period — Dynasties 14–17	c.1781–1550 BC	c.1674–1567 BC	c. 1720–1550 BC	c. 1640–1532 BC
New Kingdom — Dynasties 18–20	c. 1550–1070 BC	c.1567–1085 BC	c. 1550–1070 BC	c. 1550–1070 BC
Third Intermediate Period — Dynasties 21–24	c. 1070–712 BC	c. 1085–709 BC	c. 1070–712 BC	c. 1070–712 BC
Late Period — Dynasties 25–30	712–332 BC	709–332 BC	712–332 BC	712–332 BC

A comparison of chronologies used by various scholars and organisations

The examples in the table on page 35, used in publications between 1978–1988, reveal these variations. They are the approximate dates used by:

- the Egyptian Antiquities Organisation
- the Department of Egyptian Antiquities in the British Museum
- the noted Egyptologist Cyril Aldred and
- the authors of *Atlas of Ancient Egypt*, J Baines and J Málek.

According to the noted Egyptologists, John Baines and Jaromír Málek, the margin of error in these dates varies from about 150 years for the beginning of the First Dynasty to about ten years for the New Kingdom and Third Intermediate Period. The dates for the Twelfth Dynasty of the Middle Kingdom are fairly precise, while those for the Eighteenth and Nineteenth Dynasties of the New Kingdom vary according to which astronomical calculations a particular scholar used.

In this text, the author has tended to follow the dates suggested by Baines and Málek.

Myths and legends as sources

The ancient Egyptians told numerous stories to explain their beliefs about the creation of the earth, the important deities, their origins and places of worship and some of their funerary practices.

Transmitted orally

Because there were a number of versions of these myths it is very difficult to work out the nature of Egyptian beliefs and practices from them. Some of these can be deduced from references to the myths and legends in the religious and magical texts (*Pyramid* and *Coffin Texts* and *The Book of the Dead*), temple inscriptions (festivals and rituals) and occasional papyrus documents.

Prehistoric origins

Most of the myths and legends had prehistoric origins and were altered and added to through each historic period, depending on which city and deity were pre-eminent at the time.

Recorded at a later date

The fullest versions of these stories were usually written down at a late period. Some were recorded by the Greeks, who tried to associate their own gods with the Egyptian deities, and some by priests and others during the Ptolemaic Period (332–30 BC) when a Macedonian Greek/Egyptian dynasty ruled over Egypt.

Each of the important cult centres throughout Egypt had its own version of the creation of the world in which its cult god played a major role. There were common features in all of these stories and these have already been mentioned in Chapter 1. Two of these are referred to as the Heliopolitan and Memphite doctrines. More detail is given on these creation myths in later chapters.

Osirian myth

Two of the best known stories in Egyptian mythology concerned:

- the life, death and resurrection of Osiris
- the battle between Horus, the son of Osiris, and his uncle Seth for control of the Egyptian throne.

No full account of the Osiris myth as told by the Egyptians themselves has survived — perhaps because it was so well known they felt no need to write it down. However, parts of the story can be put together from references to Osiris in the religious texts, rites depicted on temple walls, funerary objects found in tombs and so on. These tend to substantiate the complete version of the Osiris legend (*De Iside et Osiride*) told by Plutarch, the Greek writer of the first century AD.

Osiris had once been a good king of Egypt who taught the arts of civilisation to his people. He was murdered by his jealous brother Seth who cut up his body and scattered the parts all over Egypt. Osiris' wife, Isis, and her sister wandered the length and breadth of Egypt collecting the pieces of Osiris' body. With the help of the gods (Re, Anubis and Thoth) Osiris was restored to life. Although the dead king was resurrected he was not able to take his place on the throne again and instead ruled the Underworld as king. Osiris' son, Horus, took revenge on Seth for his father's death and was given the throne of Egypt by the gods.

This story of Osiris reflects many of the beliefs and practices followed throughout pharaonic history.

A secondary historical source — Herodotus

During the fifth century BC, the Greek historian Herodotus visited Egypt, which at that time was part of the Persian Empire. The information he collected was included in the history he wrote about the conflicts between the Greeks and the Persians.

A traveller in Egypt in the fifth century BC

As a tourist in Egypt he travelled as far as the First Cataract and was excited by everything he saw and heard — the weird religious beliefs, the magnificent buildings, the strange customs and the Egyptians' ancient wisdom. Apart from his own observations, he relied on information gathered from priests and native interpreters.

He states at the beginning of his work that he did not necessarily believe everything that he was told, but felt obliged to write it down since it was what people living at the time believed had happened.

Herodotus' interpretation of what he saw and heard was obviously influenced by his own background, experiences and beliefs. In his account of what he saw and heard, recorded in Book 2 of his *Histories*, Herodotus:

- does not mention the great monuments at Thebes or the Sphinx at Giza
- gives a detailed description of the process of mummification which in many aspects is reliable
- provides some valuable geographical information particularly about the delta region
- gives many details on Egyptian religion, although he is not generally reliable in this area

- indicates that he knew of the existence of Menes, the first king of the *Two Lands*, although his account of early Egyptian monarchy is generally poor.

Studying a written document

The following chart suggests some of the things to look for when studying a written document.

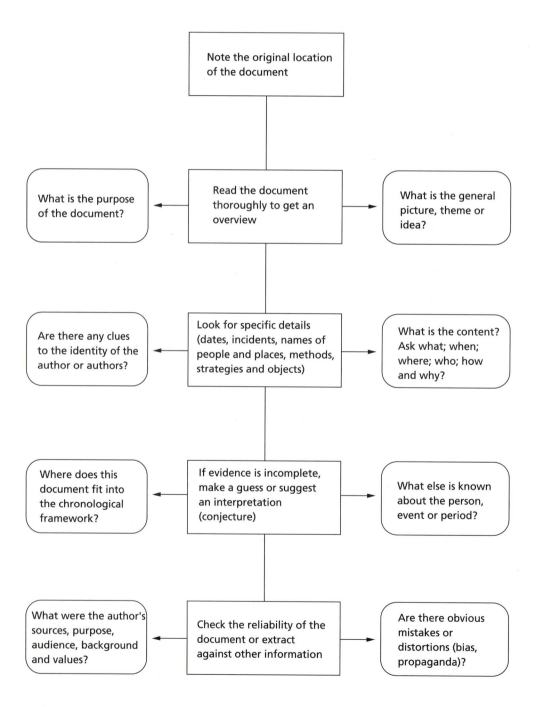

Archaeological sources

Archaeological remains can be grouped under three headings. Those associated with:

- temples
- tombs
- towns.

The following diagram and photographs illustrate some of the major archaeological sources for Egyptian civilisation.

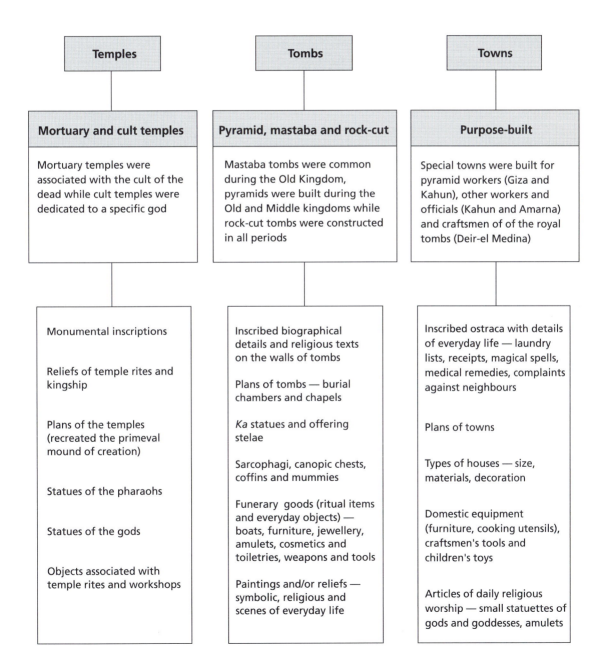

Above: An alabaster sphinx at Memphis

Right: A colossal statue of Amenhotep III in western Thebes

Below: The pylons of a New Kingdom temple from western Thebes

A mastaba tomb at Giza

The remains of a workers' town at Deir el-Medina

Conclusion

To reiterate what James says in his work *Pharaoh's People*, despite the wealth of source material in the area of art and culture, 'the raw material for the writing of a satisfactory Egyptian history is insufficient and sketchy'. [10]

However, historians study every scrap of relevant written information and supplement this with evidence from archaeological material. They then attempt to fit what they discover into a complicated mosaic, filling in the gaps by guesswork or speculation. The way historians interpret the source material is often affected by their own beliefs and values. This leads to a wide variety of opinions about specific events in Egyptian history and the lives of particular individuals.

Chapter review

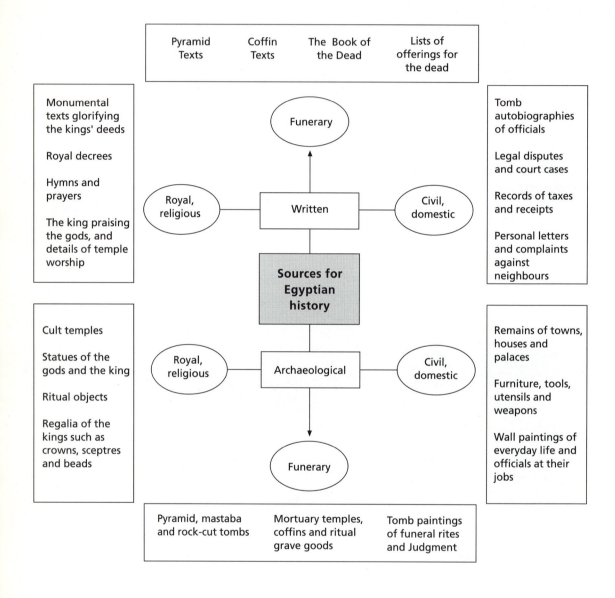

REVIEW QUESTIONS AND ESSAY TOPICS

1 **Identifying written sources.**
Read through the six extracts below and then answer the following questions.

  i   *The Count, Governor of Upper Egypt, Chamberlain, Warden of Nekhen, Mayor of Nekheb, Sole
Companion, honoured by Osiris Foremost-of-the-Westerners, Weni [says]: I was a fillet-wearing
youth under the majesty of King Teti, my office being that of custodian of the storehouse, when
I became inspector of [tenants] of the palace ... When I became overseer of the robing-room under
the majesty of King Pepi, his majesty gave me the rank of companion and inspector of priests of
his pyramid town.*[11]

  ii   *Chapter 43 — To retain one's head*

   Formula for not letting the head of N be cut off in the necropolis (city of the dead)

   *I am the Great one, son of the Great one,
The Fiery one, son of the Fiery one,
To whom his head was given after having been cut off.
The head of Osiris shall not be taken from him,
My head shall not be taken from me!
I am risen, renewed, refreshed,
I am Osiris!*[12]

  iii   *If you are mighty, gain respect through knowledge
And through gentleness of speech.
Don't command except as is fitting
He who provokes gets into trouble* [13]

  iv   *The gang made merry before him for four full days, drinking with their wives and children —
60 people from inside [the village] and 60 people from outside.*[14]

  v   *The Royal Scribe and Chief of the Treasury, Suty, salutes Pharaoh:
Greetings! This letter is to inform my good lord of his flourishing affairs within the Place of Truth,
namely of his workforce, and about their annual expenditure, by account [thus]:*[15]

  vi   *Thereupon the forces of the Foe of Khatti (the Hittites) surrounded the followers of his majesty who
were by his side. When his majesty caught sight of them he rose quickly, enraged at them like his
father Mont*. ... His majesty was mighty, his heart stout, one could not stand before him. All his
ground was ablaze with fire; he burned all the countries with his blast. His eyes were savage as he
beheld them; his power flared like fire against them. He heeded not the foreign multitude; he
regarded them as chaff. ... His majesty slew the entire force of the Foe of Khatti, together with his
great chiefs and all his brothers, as well as all the chiefs of all the countries that had come with him,
their infantry and their chariotry falling on their faces one upon the other. His majesty slaughtered
them in their places; they sprawled before his horses and his majesty was alone, none other with him.*[16]

   * Mont (or Montu) was a Theban god of war

  a   To what category of written record do each of these extracts belong?
Explain each of your answers.

  b   Where would extracts i, ii and vi have been originally located?

  c   Which extracts would have been written in hieroglyphics and which ones would have been
written in hieratic?

d   On what materials were extracts ii, iv and v written?

e   Explain why the information in extract vi can not be accepted by historians as it is.

2   Analysing a document.

The Mayor of Western Thebes, Ramose, greets the Chief Workmen Nebnufer and Qaha with the entire gang as follows:

See now, the Governor and Vizier, Paser, has sent to me, saying: 'Let the dues be brought for the workmen of the Royal Tomb, namely vegetables, fish, firewood, jars of beer, victuals and milk. Do not let a scrap of it remain outstanding... [Do not] let me find anything of their dues [held back as] balance. [And even] you take care [over this].'[17]

a   What type of document is this?

b   What is its purpose?

c   Who is its author?

d   By whose authority has this document been written?

e   Who are the people referred to as *the entire gang*?

f   Who provides them with their basic needs?

j   What appears to have been the problem?

h   Put the people mentioned in this document in order according to their official positions.

i   What does this document indicate about Paser?

3   Essay topic.

Researching into Ancient Egypt is like trying to repair a tapestry with gaping holes where much of the design is lost. From what is left some idea of the pattern may be gained, but where too much has gone to be recovered it is no good just pulling together the remaining threads to cover the hole as if nothing were missing. One can fill the hole with a new design from one's imagination, but only at the risk of going far beyond the original.[18]

Explain what Robins means in the quote above.

CHAPTER
3

The formative years of Egyptian greatness

The years from c. 5000–3100 BC are referred to as the Predynastic Period of Egyptian civilisation — that long period of time before the *Two Lands of Egypt* were united under the rule of one king.

The Predynastic Period was marked by a revolution in food production, advances in technology, growth in population, increased war-like activity among the local communities, and a political amalgamation of towns and villages into two clearly defined parts of the country — the Kingdoms of Upper and Lower Egypt.

About 3100 BC, the lands of Upper and Lower Egypt were united under one king. Menes is the traditional name given to the leader who established the First Dynasty of Egyptian rulers, although the inscriptional evidence points to a ruler called Narmer.

The period covering the first two dynasties of rulers is often referred to as the Archaic Period (c. 3000–2705). These were the formative years of Egyptian history — a 'time of trial and discovery' [1] when many of the Egyptian institutions and traditions were established. This statement is based on the view held by the majority of Egyptologists. However, there are others who admit that science, technology, architecture and the hieroglyphic system of the Archaic Period show virtually no signs of development and appear to have been complete at the beginning.

The information in this and following chapters follows the conventional viewpoint. However, you should realise there is still a great deal of mystery surrounding this period.

During these early years a centralised state was organised with the king as its nucleus. It is generally believed that the concept of divine kingship (the king as a god) was worked out in detail and a pattern set for the next 3000 years. Memphis was established as the capital of the Two Lands and a bureaucracy of high officials, to govern the united lands on the king's behalf, began to evolve. As the institutions of a centralised state were slowly established, developments in writing, mathematics and astronomy occurred.

*Places of significance
during the Predynastic
and Archaic periods*

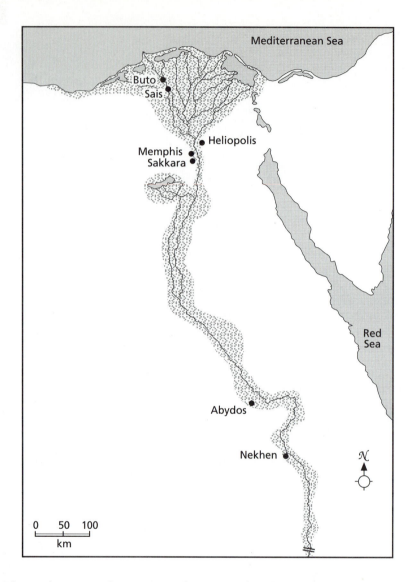

The Archaic Period was not without its political tensions and struggles. These occurred in the long process of consolidation after the unification of Upper and Lower Egypt.

Sources of evidence for the Predynastic and Archaic periods

Most of the evidence for the Predynastic Period comes from the almost indestructible pottery of the earliest settlers along the Nile. Other material remains found in shallow pit-graves include baskets, bone and ivory combs and figurines, beads, decorated palettes for mixing cosmetics, mace-heads (a mace is a club-like weapon), arrow heads, and a few bodies which had been preserved in the dry sands. The bodies in these pit-graves were wrapped in skins or matting and placed in a foetal position on their left sides.

**Evidence from
pit graves**

Evidence of the events which marked the transition from Predynastic times to the Archaic Period is found on the so-called *Scorpion Mace-head* and the famous *Narmer Palette* which is the earliest known Egyptian historical record in existence.

The tombs in the royal cemeteries at Abydos in Upper Egypt and Sakkara, near Memphis, are the chief sources of evidence for developments in the Archaic Period.

Royal cemeteries

The Predynastic Period

The map on page 46 shows the places of significance during the Predynastic and Archaic periods. The diagram that follows outlines the developments that pre-historians believe occurred along the Nile Valley over a period of approximately 2000 years (from c. 5000–3100 BC).

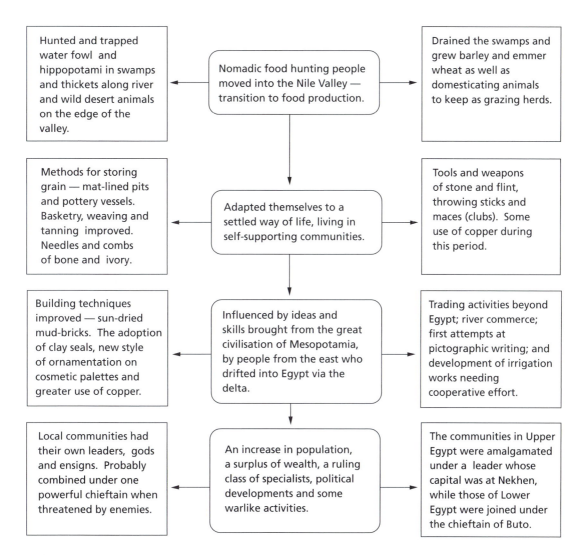

Hunted and trapped water fowl and hippopotami in swamps and thickets along river and wild desert animals on the edge of the valley.

Nomadic food hunting people moved into the Nile Valley — transition to food production.

Drained the swamps and grew barley and emmer wheat as well as domesticating animals to keep as grazing herds.

Methods for storing grain — mat-lined pits and pottery vessels. Basketry, weaving and tanning improved. Needles and combs of bone and ivory.

Adapted themselves to a settled way of life, living in self-supporting communities.

Tools and weapons of stone and flint, throwing sticks and maces (clubs). Some use of copper during this period.

Building techniques improved — sun-dried mud-bricks. The adoption of clay seals, new style of ornamentation on cosmetic palettes and greater use of copper.

Influenced by ideas and skills brought from the great civilisation of Mesopotamia, by people from the east who drifted into Egypt via the delta.

Trading activities beyond Egypt; river commerce; first attempts at pictographic writing; and development of irrigation works needing cooperative effort.

Local communities had their own leaders, gods and ensigns. Probably combined under one powerful chieftain when threatened by enemies.

An increase in population, a surplus of wealth, a ruling class of specialists, political developments and some warlike activities.

The communities in Upper Egypt were amalgamated under a leader whose capital was at Nekhen, while those of Lower Egypt were joined under the chieftain of Buto.

Developments that occurred along the Nile Valley from c. 5000–3100 BC

**Amalgamation of
river communities**

During the Predynastic Period two clearly defined groups of local communities evolved. Those along the river valley of Upper Egypt amalgamated under a powerful leader who established his capital at Nekhen/Hierakonopolis. The communities of the delta region were grouped together under a chieftain whose capital was at Buto.

These rulers of Upper and Lower Egypt wore distinctive crowns and their kingdoms were associated with particular emblems and protective deities. These crowns, emblems and goddesses formed an important part of royal symbolism throughout Egyptian history.

The table below shows the symbols associated with the Two Lands and their kings.

Upper Egypt	Lower Egypt
The White Crown	The Red Crown
The vulture goddess, Nekhbet of Nekhen	The cobra goddess Wadjet of Buto
The sedge	The bee

Symbols of the Two Lands of Upper and Lower Egypt

War-like activities at the end of the Predynastic Period

From the decoration on slate palettes and mace-heads found at the site of Nekhen in Upper Egypt, this period seems to have been a time of continuous struggle. There is evidence of fighting between the people of Upper and Lower Egypt as well as between the people of the valley and the desert nomads. It appears from a painted tomb at Nekhen that some of these battles were fought on water.

A number of palettes depict a king represented as a bull or lion, driving captives before him or holding them by a rope. These captives usually symbolise a particular district or group of people. Sometimes the standards of districts and the symbols of townships are depicted.

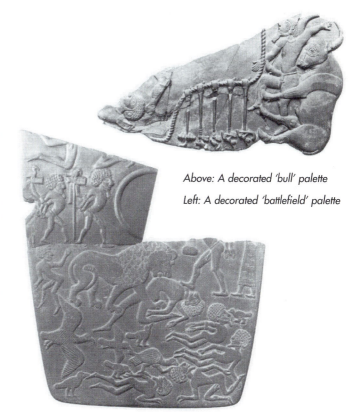

Above: A decorated 'bull' palette

Left: A decorated 'battlefield' palette

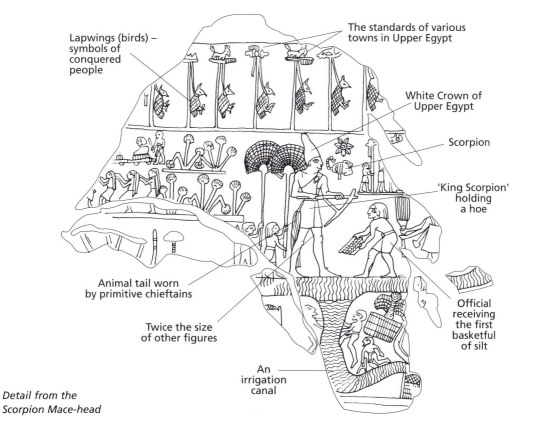

Lapwings (birds) – symbols of conquered people

The standards of various towns in Upper Egypt

White Crown of Upper Egypt

Scorpion

'King Scorpion' holding a hoe

Official receiving the first basketful of silt

Animal tail worn by primitive chieftains

Twice the size of other figures

An irrigation canal

Detail from the Scorpion Mace-head

King *Scorpion*

The first king or powerful chieftain of Upper Egypt about whom there is any evidence, is referred to as the *Scorpion King*. A decorated limestone mace-head from this period depicts a larger-than-life figure, wearing the White Crown of Upper Egypt with a hieroglyph of a scorpion near his head — hence the name.

Historians believe *Scorpion* carried out campaigns against Lower Egypt and probably prepared the way for his successor, Narmer, to unite the Two Lands. The scenes on this mace-head and on the fragments of another, reveal something of Scorpion's conquests as well as the status of a Predynastic king.

The Scorpion Mace-head

The decoration on the mace-head, illustrated more clearly in the line drawing on page 49, depicts the following:

- The king, twice as tall as all other figures (an indication of his divine status) wearing the conical White Crown of Upper Egypt, a tunic over one shoulder and the animal tail of a primitive chieftain, attended by fan-bearers.

- Men, below the king who is holding a hoe, digging an irrigation canal. An official appears to be presenting the king with the first basketful of silt. The king seems to be involved in an agricultural rite.

- A frieze of the standards of various nomes or provinces in Upper Egypt from which hang small birds (plovers or lapwings) by rope. These birds were symbolic of the conquered people of Lower Egypt.

A scene on a fragment of another mace-head shows *Scorpion* wearing the Red Crown of Lower Egypt and holding the flail or whip (symbols of royal authority), with the god Horus dragging a captive before him.

It is generally believed that King *Scorpion* did not unite the two lands but that he carried out the conquests which permitted his successor to do so.

The unification of the Two Lands

Narmer Palette evidence for unification

About 3100 BC, a king of Upper Egypt, believed to be Narmer, conquered Lower Egypt and united the Two Lands. The evidence for this achievement comes from a large commemorative palette, the Narmer Palette, found in near-perfect condition at Hierakonopolis. Both the front (obverse) and the back (reverse) of this half metre–high slate palette are covered with very clear reliefs (carvings).

Details of the Narmer Palette

Details on front

On the front or obverse of the palette are the following details:

- Two heads of the goddess Hathor (depicted as a cow) surround a very early form of a cartouche, called a *serekh*, enclosing Narmer's name.

- Narmer, proportionately larger than the other figures on the palette, and wearing the Red Crown, is accompanied by his sandal-bearer and foot-washer, who is shown as half the size of the king. Preceding the king is a priest and four standard-bearers. There is a ship which probably transported him to where his enemies were.

- Rows of bound and decapitated bodies with their heads between their legs indicate Narmer's victory.

- Serpent-like creatures with intertwined necks and held by leashes may have represented the union of the Two Lands.

- The king, represented as a mighty bull, appears to be trampling a rebel and battering down the walls of an enemy town.

The back or reverse of the palette features the following details:

Details on back

- Hathor heads and the Narmer serekh.

- A huge figure of the king wearing the White Crown of Upper Egypt and the kilt, animal tail and protective bead apron of a primitive chieftain. In his right hand he holds a mace ready to smash the head of a captive whom he holds in his left hand. Again the king is accompanied by his sandal-bearer.

- The falcon, which represented the king as the incarnation of the falcon god, Horus, is holding another captive by a rope. The captives are from the delta region which is indicated by the papyrus plant, symbol of Lower Egypt.

- Two of the king's enemies are shown either fleeing or drowning. Their city is symbolised by an image that could represent a rectangular fortress or the facade of a palace.

Slate palette of Narmer — front (on left) and back (on right)

Narmer's conquest of Lower Egypt and unification of the country was probably carried out over a period of time rather than achieved in one campaign only. The political unification of the Two Lands took two dynasties to be consolidated.

The union of the Two Lands was regarded by later Egyptians as the most important event in their history — a *First Time* event similar to the creation of the universe.

The Archaic Period — First and Second dynasties

Narmer or Menes?

The Turin Canon of Kings, Herodotus and Manetho all record that a king called Menes was the founder of the First Dynasty. Herodotus said that he was told by the priests that 'it was Min (Menes), the first king of Egypt'[2], who founded Memphis as the capital of a united land.

What about the evidence of the Narmer Palette? Were Menes and Narmer the same person, were there two kings or was Menes a legendary figure?

Although it cannot be proven, most historians believe that they were the same person. Gardiner outlines the controversy over this in *Egypt of the Pharaohs.*

Memphis, the capital of a united Egypt

Menes (Narmer) established the new royal residence and capital city at a place on neutral ground near the apex of the delta. According to Herodotus, the land on which the new capital was built was reclaimed from the river by diverting its course.

> The river used to flow along the base of the sandy hills on the Libyan border, and this monarch, by damming it up at the bend one hundred furlongs (20 kilometres) south of Memphis, drained the original channel and diverted it to a new one half-way between the two lines of hills... On the land which had been drained by the diversion of the river, King Min (Menes) built the city which is now called Memphis — it lies in the narrower part of Egypt — and afterwards on the north and west sides of the town excavated a lake, communicating with the river, which protects it on the east.[3]

Administrative centre of the Two Lands

This new residence-city, known as Memphis, was referred to as *White Walls* because of the fortified walls which surrounded it. The city was protected from the annual flood by a huge embankment. Memphis' importance as a royal and administrative centre is supported by the large number of huge mastaba tombs in the necropolis (cemetery) at nearby Sakkara.

For as long as the monarchy lasted in Egypt, Memphis was a pre-eminent city, although there is virtually nothing left of it today. It was significant as the site where the Egyptian kings were crowned and where they usually held their important jubilee and rejuvenation ceremony —the Sed festival. This was generally held after the king had been on the throne for many years (usually 30). A mace-head shows King Narmer, clothed in what appears to be the cloak usually associated with the Sed festival. If this fragment does depict part of the Sed ritual, then Narmer probably reigned for a long time.

First and Second dynasty rulers

Historians have identified the names of seventeen First and Second dynasty rulers, two of whom were women — queens Neith-hotep and Meryt-Neith. The evidence for these queens being ruling monarchs is based on the serekhs or rectangular frames surrounding their names and the size of their tombs.

Seventeen rulers identified

These queens seem to have been linked with Neith, a patron goddess of Lower Egypt, associated with war. Since other women buried in the royal cemeteries at Abydos and Sakkara also had 'Neith' as part of their name, Emery[4] has suggested that the early kings may have taken women from Lower Egypt as wives in order to strengthen the union of the Two Lands. There is also evidence that King Aha (second of the First Dynasty kings) founded a temple to Neith and that several kings made journeys to worship at a temple dedicated to Neith. Apart from references to religious festivals, not much is known about the individual rulers.

Early dynastic queens

There is scanty evidence that King Aha may have carried out a campaign against Nubia, that King Djer fought in Sinai and that King Den fought with the tribes of the eastern desert and defeated some unknown place or group referred to as 'Wer-ka'. That these early kings mined in Sinai is suggested by the four turquoise and amethyst bracelets and the copper tools found in the tomb of King Djer. The contents of the tomb of King Djet indicate that there was a degree of trade possibly via the Red Sea.

Fragmentary evidence of achievements

There was some innovation in tomb building during this time, particularly in the reigns of Den and Semerkhet of the First Dynasty and of the Second Dynasty kings, Hetepsekhemy and Netjeren.

Despite the lack of details about the individual rulers of the Archaic Period, the traditions that they established were followed for as long as a pharaoh sat on the throne of Egypt. Wilson, in *The Culture of Ancient Egypt*, maintains:

> that the first two dynasties were too busy setting up the state and the traditions of the state to undertake any modification of the form of their culture[5]

Establishment of the pattern of kingship

As the concept of the divine kingship evolved during the time of Menes/Narmer and his successors, traditions and institutions that supported this concept developed as well; some of these are shown in the diagram on the next page.

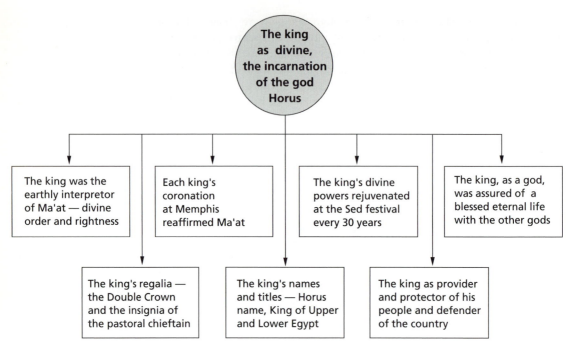

The king as divine, the incarnation of the god Horus

- The king was the earthly interpretor of Ma'at — divine order and rightness
- Each king's coronation at Memphis reaffirmed Ma'at
- The king's divine powers rejuvenated at the Sed festival every 30 years
- The king, as a god, was assured of a blessed eternal life with the other gods

- The king's regalia — the Double Crown and the insignia of the pastoral chieftain
- The king's names and titles — Horus name, King of Upper and Lower Egypt
- The king as provider and protector of his people and defender of the country

Setting the pattern of kingship for 3000 years

The king as the incarnation of Horus

From the time of Menes/Narmer, every king of Egypt was given the title of *Horus*. The generally held belief is that the king was regarded as the incarnation or earthly form of the falcon god Horus and, as such, was divine. However, some scholars believe that, at this time, the king was considered as the *representative* of Horus on earth rather than the *incarnation* of the god.

Whatever the case, Horus, the falcon god, was chosen as the one who was embodied in or who was represented by the king. Why?

It has been suggested that because Narmer came from a region which was a centre of Horus worship, the god became the symbol of the victorious king. However, Frankfort, in his book *Kingship and the Gods*, says that this was not the main reason for associating the king with Horus. Falcons were a common sight in Egyptian skies and these majestic birds must have created an impressive sight as they soared upwards into the sky until they disappeared from sight or hovered motionless high above the earth. They represented everything that was mysterious in nature. Falcon gods were worshipped in many parts of the country in Predynastic times and it is easy to see why the early Egyptians made Horus their supreme god.

Falcon worship widespread

Horus, whose wide-spread wings represented the sky and whose fierce eyes were the sun and moon, was referred to as the *Lord of Heaven*, *Lord of the Horizon* and the *Distant One*. This was the obvious god to be regarded as the 'animating spirit of the ruler of Egypt'.[6]

Horus and Re

From earliest times, the Egyptians worshipped a form of the sun god. In the Archaic period, Horus was that sun god. The sun god was later associated with Re, the sun god of the city of On or Heliopolis as Re-Horakhte or *Horus in the Horizon*. During the Fourth and Fifth dynasties, Re replaced Horus as the supreme god and there was a corresponding change in the divine status of the king.

Royal names

The king, as the embodiment of Horus, was given what is called a Horus name which was a statement of the king's god-like (divine) qualities.

Horus name

The Horus name was written vertically in a rectangular frame called a *serekh*. Later, royal names were contained within a cartouche. These rectangular serekhs represented the facade of a brick palace with the king as the falcon perched on top.

Royal serekhs

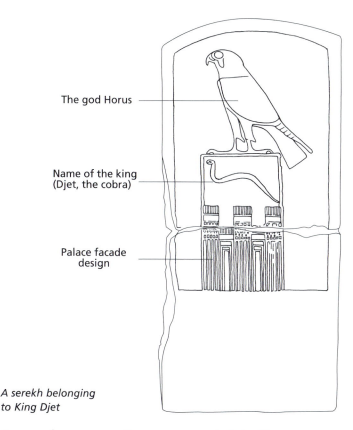

The god Horus

Name of the king
(Djet, the cobra)

Palace facade
design

*A serekh belonging
to King Djet*

A second name sometimes accompanied the Horus name or was used separately. This second name was introduced by the symbol of the sedge and the bee which stood for the title *King of Upper and Lower Egypt*. It might also be introduced by the symbol of the vulture and cobra or the *Two Ladies* title.

Additional names

For most of Egyptian history the kings of Egypt had five names and titles of which the Horus name was the oldest. This list of names and titles was referred to as the royal titulary but it did not reach its full form until the Fifth Dynasty. For the first few dynasties the kings were generally known by their Horus name.

The regalia of the king

Although the Two Lands were united into one kingdom, each part of the country retained its identity and emblems. This is reflected in the Double Crown worn by all Egyptian kings after unification. This crown combined the tall conical White Crown of Upper Egypt with the Red Crown of Lower Egypt.

The trappings of the primitive pastoral chieftains seen on the Scorpion Mace-head and the Narmer Palette were incorporated into the ceremonial regalia of Egyptian kings. They included:

- an artificial beard, reminiscent of a goat beard, which was attached to the king's chin
- the tail of a bull or lion, which hung from a girdle or belt, symbolically protected the king's back
- a *shemset* girdle with an apron made of pendant beads or narrow strips of leather which covered the king's loins
- the flail and crook, symbols of the primitive shepherd, which the king carried.

The Double Crown of Egypt

The king's coronation and Sed festival

During the Archaic Period the ceremonies associated with the two most important events of the king's life — the coronation and the Sed festival — were set in place. Refer to Chapter 6 for details of these ceremonies.

Significant events in the king's life

The Sed festival (heb-sed) was usually held after the king had been on the throne for 30 years and was repeated every three years after that. Its main purpose was to symbolically rejuvenate the king's powers so that he could continue to rule effectively.

Both the coronation and the Sed festival were held at Memphis and lasted for five days. Every part of the coronation and Sed ritual was carried out twice since the king was the ruler of both Upper Egypt and Lower Egypt.

The coronation ceremonies ended with the king's *circuit of the White Walls* or procession around the walls of Memphis. The main ritual of the Sed festival was a symbolic race over a field which represented the land of Egypt.

The divine role of the king

Ma'at versus chaos

The Egyptians believed in the concept of *ma'at* or divine order established at the time of creation. They believed that without ma'at there would be chaos in both the physical and spiritual world.

The king was regarded as the representative of divine order on earth. When he died the people feared an outbreak of chaos and disorder. It was imperative to get the next king crowned as soon as possible in order to re-establish harmony, stability and security in the kingdom.

Since the king, as the embodiment of ma'at, interpreted and articulated the law, there was no need to draw up a code of laws.

As the incarnation or representative of a god on earth, the king was expected to have power over the Nile and to win new agricultural lands. As well as bringing fertility and prosperity to the land the god-king was believed to protect his people from evil and dangers in both human and animal form.

The king as the source of Egypt's prosperity

Representations of early kings such as Menes, Aha, Djer and Den show them smiting the Bedouin of the eastern desert, the Libyans to the west and the Nubians to the south. The kings are also depicted hunting wild animals, symbols of evil, in the deserts and spearing the hippopotamus, symbol of Seth, in the marshlands.

The king as protector of his people

The responsibilities of the king to uphold the divine order of the world by fighting evil, defending his land and sustaining life, continued throughout Egyptian dynastic history.

Fifteen hundred years after Menes, kings of Egypt were still being depicted:

- wielding a mace or some other weapon over their heads ready to smite the *wretched* enemies of Egypt who cowered before them
- single-handedly defeating huge foreign armies
- symbolically fighting evil as they engaged in hunting forays in the deserts
- providing life-giving waters.

The afterlife of a king

Even from the earliest times it is apparent that Egyptians believed in some form of continued existence after death. Their beliefs about what form this afterlife took are not known. However, in these early dynasties, as in all periods of Egyptian history, the king was believed to have a different afterlife to that of everyone else.

Although Wilson says that 'in the earliest dynasties only those who carried within them the germ of divinity were sure of eternal life after death',[7] it is probably more accurate to say that only the kings were assured of an afterlife with the gods.

An afterlife spent with the gods

It is likely that the kings expected to join the company of gods in the sky when they died, although as Spencer points out, 'the Egyptians did not necessarily hold a single view of the next world at any one time'.[8]

Judging by the subsidiary burials of sacrificed retainers around the tombs of First Dynasty rulers, it appears that 'there was an expectation that the lifestyles of master and servant would continue unchanged after death'.[9]

Royal tombs

The kings and queens of the First and Second dynasties were buried in elaborate brick and wood-lined pit graves at Abydos and in large rectangular mud-brick tombs called mastabas (from the Arabic word for *bench*) at Sakkara.

Cemeteries at Abydos and Sakkara

The names of some rulers have been found associated with burials at both places. Some scholars believe that these kings were buried at Sakkara and that the Abydos tombs were merely cenotaphs to symbolise the king's hold over Upper Egypt. More recent evidence suggests that many of the First Dynasty rulers were actually buried at Abydos, although it appears that the majority of Second Dynasty kings were interred at Sakkara. Scholars are still divided on this question.

When the royal tombs at Abydos in Upper Egypt were excavated by Sir Flinders Petrie, nothing of their superstructure remained. It is generally believed that the tombs had vaulted roofs. The burial chambers were cut into the rock and lined with mud-bricks. Several other underground chambers contained food offerings as well as small objects such as stone vessels, mud jar seals impressed with the names of First and Second dynasty kings, ivory and ebony tablets, and the earliest royal jewellery.

Subsidiary burials

Each tomb was marked with a stone stela inscribed with the ruler's name. Some of these early royal tombs were surrounded by smaller burial chambers adjoining one another. The evidence from these seems to indicate that at least during the First Dynasty, royal servants and women of the harem were buried at the same time as their king or queen. These people may have willingly gone to their death with their ruler in the hope they might have a share in the afterlife. At Abydos more than 1300 of these subsidiary burials have been discovered.

One of the best preserved tombs at Abydos belonged to Queen Meryt-Neith and, judging by the size of her tomb and the number of subsidiary burials around it, she appears to have been a reigning monarch and not just a queen consort.

Mastaba of King Djer

At Sakkara, the mastaba tombs were much larger than the tombs at Abydos. They comprised a superstructure (above the ground) of many storage chambers and a substructure (below the ground) of from five to seven compartments, of which the central one was the burial chamber. The largest mastaba in the area may have belonged to King Djer, the third king of the First Dynasty. The facade of the superstructure was decorated with niches and panelling similar to that on the front of a palace. Its burial chamber appears to have been lined with wood and decorated with strips of gold. On the outside of the superstructure a number of carved bull's heads were mounted on a low bench. Sixty-two subsidiary burials were associated with Djer's tomb.

Mastaba of Queen Meryt-Neith

Another mastaba recorded the name of Meryt-Neith, the same queen whose tomb was found at Abydos. On the outside of this mastaba was a rock-cut pit, almost 18 metres long, which probably held a large boat. Once again, associated with Meryt-Neith's tomb (if in fact it was her actual burial site) were 20 subsidiary graves, still containing the bodies and burial goods of craftsmen. This practice of sacrificial burials was discontinued by the Second Dynasty.

Importance of early dynastic queens

The number of huge tombs belonging to royal women indicate the importance of chief queens and queen mothers during this period. Throughout Egyptian history, royal women, particularly heiress queens, were held in the greatest esteem.

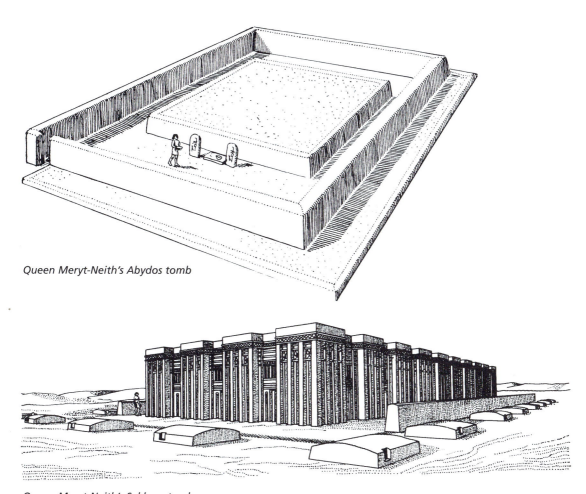

Queen Meryt-Neith's Abydos tomb

Queen Meryt-Neith's Sakkara tomb

It has been difficult to identify the tombs of the nobles during this period since many have no name associated with them. However, it appears that there was not such a vast difference in the size of royal and noble tombs in the first two dynasties as there was in the Third, Fourth and Fifth dynasties.

Establishment of a centralised administration

The most important achievement during the Archaic Period was the organisation of the kingdom so that it would run smoothly. Since everyone's survival depended on the annual flood and the subsequent agricultural production, it was essential to have an efficient centralised administration to control the irrigation policy; coordinate the large-scale agricultural projects; carry out tax assessments and the census of cattle; record the yields of grain and the distribution of seed to farmers; re-survey boundaries washed away during the flood; and to keep records of the maximum, minimum and average height of the Nile during flood.

Agricultural and irrigation policies

**Officials of first
two dynasties**

Not much is known about the officials who supervised these and other activities on behalf of the king, during the first two dynasties. They were probably recruited from the king's immediate family.

By the time of Djoser, second king of the Third Dynasty, the chief administrative official of the state was the vizier. The only evidence of such an official in the Archaic Period is an obscure reference on the Narmer Palette. However, it is likely that a member of the royal family, who held a high priesthood in the Temple of the Sun at Heliopolis, acted in this capacity. There were also chancellors appointed during the First Dynasty — one to control the storehouse of Upper Egypt (the White Treasury) and another in charge of the storehouse of Lower Egypt (the Red Treasury).

The creation and organisation of a centralised state would not have been possible without:

- the development of writing. This was aided by the availability of papyrus. A blank roll of papyrus found in the tomb of King Den is evidence that papyrus as a writing material was already being manufactured in the First Dynasty

**Skills needed
for a centralised
administration**

- the mastery of mathematical calculation (decimals and fractions), measurement of time by observation of the heavens and an accurate calendar to predict the annual rise of the Nile and to decide auspicious times for important state festivals

- the existence of a body of men, such as priests and scribes, who were skilled in these areas.

The Temple of the Sun at Heliopolis, just north of Memphis, was a centre of learning as well as religion. The priests attached to this temple studied writing (hieroglyphic and hieratic scripts), mathematics and astronomy. Their knowledge of the movements of the planets and stars helped them draw up a more precise calendar than that used by the farmers. The official calendar was based on the rising of the star Sirius and consisted of 12 months of 30 days each with an extra five days added at the end of the year.

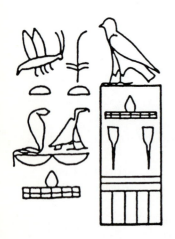  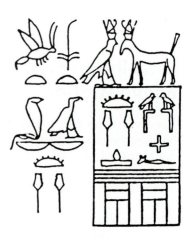

Serekhs of three Second Dynasty kings, Hetepeskhemy, Peribsen and Khasekhemwy

Evidence of political struggles

The Archaic Period was not without its political struggles. The main sources of evidence for this political rivalry are the serekhs of the kings.

The name of the first Second Dynasty king, Hetepeskhemy, means *The Two Powers are at Peace*, which may indicate that there was some upheaval at the end of the First Dynasty.

King Hetepeskhemy

The serekh of a Second Dynasty king called Peribsen was not surmounted by the falcon god Horus but by the Seth animal. Did Peribsen no longer see himself as the incarnation of Horus? There may have been a struggle between two rival groups prior to his reign.

King Peribsen

The last king of the Second Dynasty, Khasekhemwy, obviously provided a compromise between the two groups since his serekh combined the falcon of Horus and the Seth animal.

King Khasekhemwy

Conclusion

The kings and nobles of the Archaic Period established the pattern of kingship which lasted for approximately 3000 years, set up the institutions of an efficient centralised state and prepared the way for the incredible accomplishments of the Old Kingdom.

Chapter review

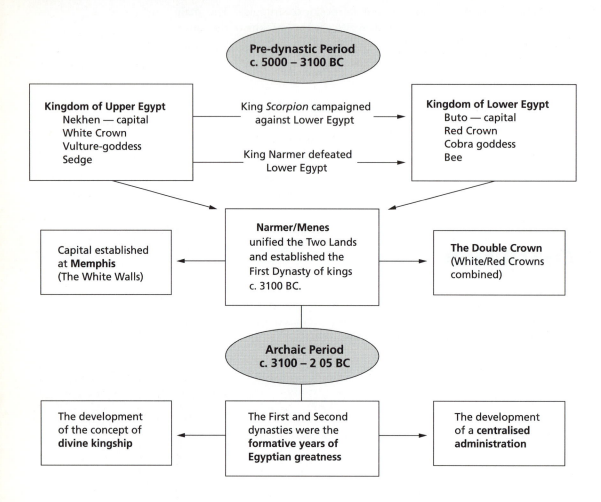

Pre-dynastic Period
c. 5000 – 3100 BC

Kingdom of Upper Egypt
 Nekhen — capital
 White Crown
 Vulture-goddess
 Sedge

King *Scorpion* campaigned
against Lower Egypt

King Narmer defeated
Lower Egypt

Kingdom of Lower Egypt
 Buto — capital
 Red Crown
 Cobra goddess
 Bee

Capital established
at **Memphis**
(The White Walls)

Narmer/Menes
unified the Two Lands
and established the
First Dynasty of kings
c. 3100 BC.

The Double Crown
(White/Red Crowns
combined)

Archaic Period
c. 3100 – 2 05 BC

The development
of the concept of
divine kingship

The First and Second
dynasties were the
**formative years of
Egyptian greatness**

The development
of a **centralised
administration**

REVISION QUESTIONS AND ESSAY TOPICS

1 **Look carefully again at the back and front of the Narmer Palette (page 51) and answer the following questions:**

a How do historians know the name of the king on this palette?

b The king is shown on the palette in three forms. What are they?

c Explain the way the king is depicted on the back of the palette.

d Describe the two pieces of evidence on the front of the palette which indicate the king's conquests.

e What is the evidence shown on the back of the palette which illustrates the king's conquest of Lower Egypt?

f What evidence is there on the front of the palette that Narmer unified the Two Lands?

g What is the importance of the Narmer Palette to historians?

2 **Identify the symbols shown below and explain the significance of each one.**

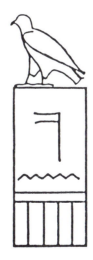

3 **Essay topic**

Explain why most Egyptologists believe that the Archaic Period was the formative age of Egyptian history.

The Old Kingdom:
the Pyramid Age

OVERVIEW

The information in Chapters 4 and 5 generally follows the line of orthodox Egyptology. However, because of the limited amount of written and archaeological evidence and the refusal of many modern Egyptologists to accept new scientific evidence, there are likely to be many inaccuracies in the traditional accounts of the period.

It is highly likely that the commonly-held view will be challenged in the near future as experts from fields such as astronomy, geology, metallurgy, seismology, chemistry and engineering, combine their findings with techniques based on modern computer technology.

The Old Kingdom is often referred to as the Pyramid Age. It comprised four dynasties or lines of rulers — the Third to the Sixth dynasties. Because of the difficulties involved in establishing an accurate chronology for Egyptian history, it is not possible to put firm dates on this period. For example, the Third Dynasty is believed to have been founded anywhere from c. 2705 BC to c. 2649 BC while the Sixth Dynasty ended somewhere between 2230 BC and 2150 BC. The dates used in Part 2 are those suggested by Baines and Málek in *Atlas of Ancient Egypt*. Refer back to Chapter 2 for information on chronology.

During the Third Dynasty, King Netjerykhet Djoser (Zoser) and his vizier/architect, Imhotep, built the first pyramid tomb — the Step Pyramid at Sakkara. It is believed that during this time religious beliefs may have been undergoing a transition. Imhotep and others after him experimented with new building materials and techniques. The god-like status and power of the king developed throughout the Third Dynasty.

Third Dynasty

Fourth Dynasty

Sneferu, the first king of the Fourth Dynasty, completed at least three pyramids, one of which was the first true pyramid. He was succeeded by his son Khufu (Cheops), for whom it is generally believed the massive Great Pyramid at Giza was constructed. Khafre (Cephren) and Menkaure (Mycerinus) are believed to have been responsible for the other two pyramid complexes on the plateau at Giza. These Fourth Dynasty pyramids appear to reflect the power and status of the god-kings. This was the peak of the Old Kingdom.

Fifth Dynasty

The Fifth Dynasty was marked by the growing importance of the cult of the sun god whose priests became very powerful. Their influence over royalty at this time is reflected in three changes that occurred. The kings built smaller pyramids for themselves but constructed elaborate sun temples to the sun god, Re; many Fifth Dynasty kings incorporated *re* as part of their name, and from this time the king was referred to as the *Son of Re*.

Sixth Dynasty

The Sixth and last dynasty of the Old Kingdom saw an increase in the independence and power of the great nobles at the expense of royalty. This change was reflected in the location of their tombs. Many nobles felt independent enough to be buried in their own districts rather than near Memphis. In their huge and beautifully decorated tombs, these Sixth Dynasty nobles proudly recorded all their achievements. At the end of the Sixth Dynasty centralised authority broke down and a period of chaos resulted (the First Intermediate Period).

Almost all evidence for *life* during the Old Kingdom comes from those architectural and artistic features associated with *death*. The reliefs carved into the walls of the mastaba and rock-cut tombs of officials of the Old Kingdom and the surviving grave goods, provide a glimpse into the everyday life of the Egyptian people.

Limited evidence for the life of Old Kingdom royalty

Although the well-being of the god-kings was the chief concern of all social groups, from the peasants to the nobles, very little is known about the way of life of the kings of the Old Kingdom. The limited information available concerns significant events during their reigns such as the jubilee or Sed festival. However, some insight into the personal life of the kings can be gained from the tomb inscriptions of their high officials.

More evidence for the life of officials, craftsmen and peasants

Unlike the lives of the kings, those of the nobles and officials are better documented. The vivid scenes found on the walls of such Fifth and Sixth dynasty officials as Ptahhotep, Ti, Mereruka, Kagemeni and Ankhmahor (at Sakkara); Kaemankh, Idu and Nefer (at Giza) and Kahep and Pepiankh (at Akhmin and Meir), provide details about:

- the activities they carried out on behalf of their king

- the behaviour expected of them in public life
- their family life and relationships
- the activities carried out on their estates
- the work supervised by them in the temple workshops.

The various techniques and tools used by Old Kingdom craftsmen such as carpenters, metalworkers, jewellers and sculptors are also depicted in the tomb reliefs. The evidence for the skills of these ancient craftsmen are the ritual and funerary grave goods which have survived the depredations of the tomb robbers, the surviving *ka* statues of royalty, as well as the tomb reliefs themselves.

Themes associated with food production, particularly the yearly agricultural cycle, tend to dominate the walls of the tombs of the nobles. This is the main source of information for the activities of the peasant farmers, herders and rural labourers in Old Kingdom Egypt. Unfortunately, these tomb scenes provide only glimpses of the lives of this important social group.

The Egyptians of the Old Kingdom believed in life after death but only royalty was thought to spend eternity in the company of the gods. While the kings seem to have enjoyed both an astral and solar afterlife, the rest of the population believed that their eternal life would be similar to their earthly existence.

Belief in a life force or *ka*, which continued to exist in the tomb after death, explains the funerary practices carried out by Old Kingdom Egyptians such as mummification and the tomb features such as *serdabs*, ka statues, offering stelae and false doors.

Evidence for funerary beliefs and practices

The main development in embalming during the Old Kingdom was the practice of removing the internal organs. However, this process was probably used only on the bodies of royalty. Mummification was still at a primitive stage by the end of the Old Kingdom.

The changes that occurred in the construction and *decoration* of mastaba and rock-cut tombs during the Old Kingdom reflected the need to adequately protect the body and provide for the deceased in the afterlife.

Sources of evidence for this period

There are few written records from the Old Kingdom. Those that have survived are fragmentary and generally associated with religion and the afterlife. However, some give biographical details of the leading officials of the day.

The major sources of evidence for the period are archaeological. These include the mastaba tombs and pyramid complexes at

Sakkara, Giza, Dahshur, Abusir and Meidum, the rock-cut tombs
in the cliffs at Aswan and the surviving grave goods and ka statues. These provide evidence for:

- political, social and religious changes
- the power and status of the god-king
- the status of the noble/official class
- technological advances
- religion and funerary beliefs and practices
- some personal details of individuals
- aspects of the life of the nobles, craftsmen and peasants.

The map below shows the location of the Old Kingdom necropolises (cemeteries).

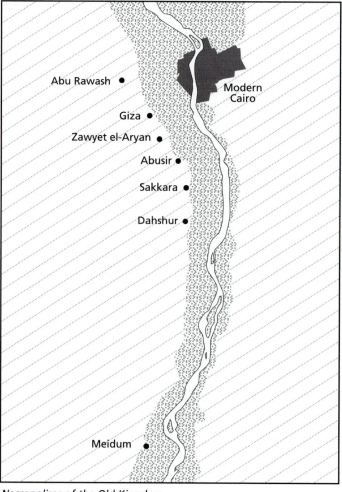

Necropolises of the Old Kingdom

The experimental phase of pyramid building

From mastaba to step pyramid — the Third Dynasty

The Third Dynasty (c. 2649–2575 BC) marked the beginning of a new era. With the reign of its second king, Djoser (Netjerykhet), the age of the pyramids began. Djoser's vizier and architect, the famed Imhotep, began the experimentation in pyramid-building which culminated in the magnificent Giza pyramids of the Fourth Dynasty.

The developments in royal tomb construction, from mastabas to Djoser's Step Pyramid during the Third Dynasty, provide evidence of the growing power and status of the kings.

Djoser

Among the kings listed in the Turin Canon, the name of Djoser was written in red ink which indicated that his reign was considered exceptional for some reason. The construction of a unique funerary complex, centred on the Step Pyramid was probably the achievement referred to in the ancient record.

Unfortunately, very little is known about King Djoser except that he must have had absolute power in order to demand the resources and manpower needed to construct the Step Pyramid complex. The size and uniqueness of his eternal home, and the more than 40 000 polished stone and alabaster bowls, cups, dishes and goblets found in one shaft of his pyramid, point to the increasing status of the kings at this time in comparison to the nobles.

The only other sources for his reign are:

- a *ka* statue of him found in the serdab, an enclosed cellar-like room at the entrance to the king's mortuary temple
- fragments of reliefs showing some aspects of his Sed festival

Sources for his reign

- two rock inscriptions — one on the island of Seheil at Aswan which describes a famine during his reign and another in Sinai which points to mining activities there.

Imhotep

Vizier and architect

Imhotep was the king's vizier or the chief official in the state, and master architect of the Step Pyramid complex. An inscription on the base of a statue of Djoser described Imhotep as:

> Chancellor of the King of Lower Egypt, the First One under the King, the Administrator of the Great Mansion, the Hereditary Noble, the High Priest of Heliopolis, the Chief Sculptor and the Chief Carpenter.[1]

This inscription, in which his name and titles were given equal pride of place with those of the king, shows the great respect which Djoser must have had for Imhotep.

During much of the Old Kingdom, the person appointed by the king as vizier was usually one of his close relatives, such as a son or a cousin. However, the evidence seems to suggest that Imhotep did not belong to the royal family although he had great authority in the royal house.

As vizier, he was in complete control of all aspects of the administration, particularly the building works of the king. The person who held this position needed to be highly educated. Those Egyptians with the greatest knowledge at this time were the high priests from the cult centre of the sun god at On or Heliopolis (from the Greek helios — sun and polis — city) as it was called later.

High priest of Heliopolis

As a high priest of Heliopolis, Imhotep:

- had exceptional knowledge in mathematics and astronomy — he was an expert in measuring time and space. These abilities would have aided him in designing and supervising the construction of the Step Pyramid complex
- developed expertise in medicine. Over 2000 years later he was worshipped by the Greeks as a god of healing. The Greeks identified Imhotep with their own god of medicine, Asclepios.

Patron of scribes

He was also respected as one of the great sages or wise men of his time and scribes throughout Egyptian history made him their patron. However, it was for his brilliance as an architect that he was most remembered.

The Step Pyramid complex at Sakkara

Owing to the work of dedicated archaeologists (C. M. Firth, J. E. Quibell and J. P. Lauer) this century, it is relatively easy today to picture what the magnificent burial complex of Djoser at Sakkara (Saqqara) looked like over 4600 years ago.

The design of the complex was unique. Imhotep may have intended to make Djoser's *house of eternity* (tomb) a recreation of the king's earthly home — the palace and its surroundings at Memphis or *White Walls*.

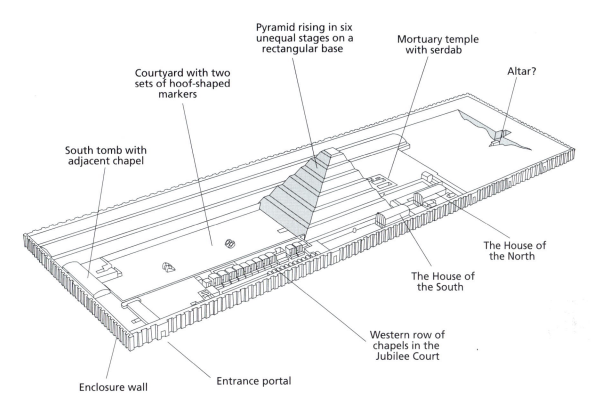

Pyramid rising in six unequal stages on a rectangular base

Mortuary temple with serdab

Altar?

Courtyard with two sets of hoof-shaped markers

South tomb with adjacent chapel

The House of the North

The House of the South

Western row of chapels in the Jubilee Court

Enclosure wall

Entrance portal

Plan of the Step Pyramid complex

The design also emphasised the Two Lands of Upper and Lower Egypt over which the king ruled.

A unique complex

The 15 hectare site selected by Imhotep for Djoser's funerary complex, was a rocky plateau on the edge of the western desert overlooking the capital of Memphis. The site was not far from the mastaba cemetery of the First and Second dynasty kings and queens.

The plan above shows the layout of the complex within its enclosure wall.

The complex comprised the following features:

Features

- the Step Pyramid, the mortuary temple and serdab

- a large mastaba-type tomb and chapel on the southern boundary, referred to as the Southern Tomb

- the Great Court

- the Jubilee or Sed Court with two rows of dummy shrines, a podium and vestibule

- the so-called Houses of the South and the North

- the palace-facade enclosure wall with 13 false doors

- decorative features which translated the building techniques of the past into stone.

The Step Pyramid

The Step Pyramid

Building material

In constructing Djoser's tomb, Imhotep experimented with stone as a building material. All previous royal tombs had been made of mud-bricks but Imhotep decided to use small, brick-size blocks of local limestone for the interior and pure white Tura limestone for the outer surfaces. The Step Pyramid appears to have been the first building in Egypt ever made completely from stone.

Small limestone blocks used in the Step Pyramid

From mastaba to Step Pyramid

Superimposed mastabas

The 60-metre-high pyramid was built as a series of mastabas, gradually decreasing in size. The six-stepped pyramid was the result of successive changes of plan by Imhotep. Some of these modifications can be clearly seen in the construction while others are based on conjecture.

What motivated Imhotep to experiment with superimposed mastabas will never be known, but the Pyramid Texts (found in later pyramids) may provide a clue. These texts were concerned with the afterlife of royalty. When Djoser died he was expected to ascend into the sky to spend eternity with the gods. One early view maintained that he would spend eternity among the imperishable stars while another held that he would accompany the sun god, Re, as he rowed across the heavens. Whichever view was held at this time (and there is a suggestion that religious beliefs may have been undergoing a transition), the king needed to gain access to the heavens.

A corner of the Step Pyramid, showing the original mastaba

The following spell from the Pyramid Texts may explain why Imhotep eventually decided on a step pyramid design.

A 'staircase to heaven'

> **A staircase to heaven is laid for him (the king) so that he may mount up to heaven thereby.**[2]

To the peasants working in the fields around Memphis, the gleaming white limestone pyramid on the desert plateau would certainly have seemed like a brilliant stairway to heaven for their god-king.

The chart on page 74 shows the changes in construction as Imhotep experimented and transformed the original mastaba into the first pyramid.

Underground chambers

The subterranean structures were the most complex of any pyramid. The burial chamber of the king was at the bottom of a 28-metre shaft and was designed as a huge sarcophagus. It was surrounded by a series of chambers, some of which were lined with blue faience tiles that imitated the reed matting on the walls of houses. A labyrinth of corridors, chambers and galleries, with a few reliefs of the king, led away from the burial chamber in all directions.

A labyrinth of corridors and chambers

A   Mastaba

Phase 1

The original square mastaba was close to 8 metres in height with sides 26.5 metres in length. It was made of solid stone and faced with Tura limestone.

Phase 2

The mastaba was extended by 4.3 metres on all sides but the addition was slightly lower than the original height. Again it was faced with fine white limestone.

Phase 3

The eastern end of the mastaba was lengthened by approximately 9 metres to give it a rectangular appearance.

B Step Pyramid

Phase 4

Adoption of a new revolutionary design. The base was extended on all sides and three mastaba-type steps were added, producing a four-stepped pyramid.

Phase 5

Finally the base was extended a further 61 metres on the north and west to support a total of six steps which were dressed with fine white Tura limestone.

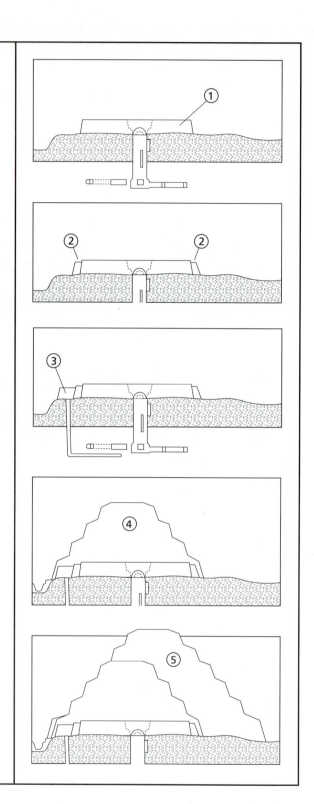

Changes in construction, from mastaba to Step Pyramid

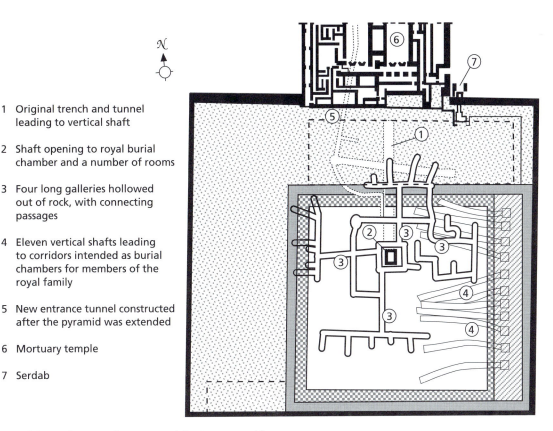

1 Original trench and tunnel
   leading to vertical shaft

2 Shaft opening to royal burial
   chamber and a number of rooms

3 Four long galleries hollowed
   out of rock, with connecting
   passages

4 Eleven vertical shafts leading
   to corridors intended as burial
   chambers for members of the
   royal family

5 New entrance tunnel constructed
   after the pyramid was extended

6 Mortuary temple

7 Serdab

Plan of the underground structure of the Step Pyramid

During the third alteration to the superstructure, Imhotep had eleven
vertical shafts sunk into the rock to a depth of approximately 33 metres.
Each one of these led to a horizontal corridor probably intended for the
members of Djoser's family.

It has been estimated that there were 400 rooms and approximately 5.7
kilometres of passageways.

The royal burial chamber was robbed in ancient times but two alabaster
sarcophagi, one containing the mummy of an eight-year-old boy, were
found in the fifth of the 11 corridors. In another gallery, 40 000 cups,   **Surviving objects**
bowls, dishes and goblets were stacked on top of one another. These
were made of the finest polished stone and many were crafted to resem-
ble metal vessels and basketware.

Mortuary temple and serdab

Attached to the north side of the pyramid was a mortuary temple which   **Funerary rites**
was connected to the burial chamber by a tunnel. This was where the
mortuary priests prayed for the deceased and made daily offerings of
food and drink.

At the entrance to the temple was a small stone room without a door.
This cellar-like chamber is referred to as a *serdab* and contained a life-

The original ka statue of Djoser found in the serdab, now in the Egyptian museum, Cairo

like statue of Djoser. It was believed that the king's life force or ka would inhabit the statue in order to receive the daily offerings. Two holes at eye level allowed the ka statue to see what offerings were made and to smell the burning incense.

The rest of the complex

According to Edwards, the 'other buildings around the Step pyramid were without precedent or parallel'[3] and so Egyptologists can only guess at their purpose. Imhotep may have designed the complex so that the king, in his next life, could continue to live as he had in his palace at Memphis, ruling over the Two Lands of Upper and Lower Egypt and symbolically rejuvenating his powers during the Sed festival.

The southern tomb

In the south-western corner of the enclosure Imhotep ordered the construction of another tomb. The two upper rooms are similar to the mortuary temple attached to the Step Pyramid while the tiny burial chamber, at the bottom of a deep shaft, duplicated the funerary chambers below the pyramid. The walls were decorated with the same blue tiles, representing the reed matting of houses, and there are also a number of reliefs depicting the king celebrating the Sed festival.

There are three possible explanations for the construction of this tomb.

Possible explanations

1 Since the burial chamber was far too small for an average person, it may have been a dummy tomb intended for a symbolic sacrifice of the king during the Sed festival.

2 It is likely that the First and Second dynasty tradition of building two tombs for the king, in his capacity as ruler of Upper and of Lower Egypt, was continued. Whereas the kings of the Archaic Period had one tomb at Sakkara and one (perhaps a cenotaph) at Abydos, Djoser incorporated both of them within the same complex. The southern tomb may have represented the Abydos cenotaph. Considering the number of duplicated features in the complex, the latter explanation seems the most likely.

3 It is possible that the southern tomb was intended for the king's ka. Egyptians often interred a statue of the king in a special burial. This tomb could be the forerunner of the subsidiary pyramids of the Fourth Dynasty.

The Great Court and the Jubilee or Sed Court

The Great Court and the so-called Sed Court are believed to have been designed by Imhotep for the re-enactment in the next life of the king's Sed festival during which his right to rule was reaffirmed. (See Chapter 6 for details of the Sed festival.)

On either side of the Sed Court were 13 dummy stone buildings representing the shrines of the districts of Upper and Lower Egypt. They were made of solid stone with imitation open doors. The facades of these buildings featured slender columns, at the head of which were large round holes probably meant to hold the flag poles bearing the emblems of the provinces. At the south end of the court are the remains of a stone dais for the king's throne.

Dummy buildings

In the Great Court are two B-shaped or hoof-shaped constructions which are believed to have been markers between which the king ran the symbolic race during the Sed festival. They were probably meant to represent the extent of the Two Lands of Egypt over which the king ruled.

The dais for the king's thrones (which were placed back to back, one representing Upper Egypt and the other Lower Egypt) in the Sed or Jubilee Court

Dummy shrines in the Sed or Jubilee Court

The Houses of the North and the South

These dummy buildings lying to the north of the Sed Court have no clear purpose but may have been part of the Sed festival ritual. It is thought that the southern building may have represented the Predynastic sanctuary of Nekhen in Upper Egypt while the northern building represented the corresponding sanctuary at Buto in Lower Egypt.

The enclosure wall and main entrance

The House (or Pavilion) of the North

The enclosure wall

The huge, pure white limestone wall enclosing the complex was approximately 1500 metres in circumference and about ten metres high. It was probably a copy of the famous *White Walls* built around Memphis by Menes/Narmer. At intervals along the panelled exterior were 14 towered gateways. Thirteen of these were false entrances, the stone carved to imitate wooden planks and hinges. The actual doorway was in the south-east corner and the complex was entered along a colonnaded passageway.

Design features of the complex

Some of the features incorporated by Imhotep into the complex:

- served a structural purpose
- symbolised the Two Lands
- imitated the natural features of the primeval marsh of creation and buildings of the remote past
- reproduced some of the domestic architecture that surrounded the king during his life.

Imhotep used small blocks of limestone, not much larger than mud-bricks, as the techniques needed for quarrying and handling large blocks of stone had not yet been mastered. The full potential of stone was not known at this stage so Imhotep used no free-standing columns in the complex. All piers and columns were attached to the wall at one point.

The lotus and papyrus, plant symbols of Upper and Lower Egypt, were used extensively for decoration, particularly in the capitals of columns. Most features such as the dummy chambers on either side of the Sed Court, were duplicated to represent Upper and Lower Egypt.

Looking through into the Great Court

Imhotep attempted to recreate in stone the plant life of the primeval marshes that the Egyptians believed existed at the time of creation. These included bundles of rushes, the stalks of the papyrus reeds and even the pendant leaves of a plant that was extinct by the time of the Third Dynasty. The fluted columns are believed to represent the bundles of reeds or palm-ribs which were used as supports in primitive buildings. Stake fences which surrounded and protected primitive sanctuaries were also imitated in stone.

Recreation of the primeval marshes

Palaces and houses of the time featured panelled walls, timber logs across the roofs, battened and hinged wooden doors, bundles of reeds tied together and coated in mud, papyrus and palm fences, and matting on the walls. Imhotep had all of these features built out of stone as decoration on the buildings at Sakkara.

Domestic features

The godlike status of Djoser was reflected in Imhotep's masterpiece, which Edwards describes in the following words:

> To review the Step Pyramid as a whole: it is certainly not an exaggeration to describe it as one of the most remarkable architectural works produced by the ancient Egyptians. That later generations regarded it

with exceptional esteem is clear, not only from the veneration which they accorded to Imhotep, but also from hieratic graffiti on the passage walls of the northern and southern buildings, which record the admiration felt by some Egyptians who visited the monument more than a thousand years after it was built. No other pyramid was surrounded with such an array of imposing buildings to supply the needs of the king in his after-life.[4]

Djoser's successors

The evidence suggests that Djoser's successors followed his example and also built step pyramids. However, from the remains of these later tombs it appears that they were never completed.

Sekhemkhet

Close to the south-west corner of the enclosure wall of the Step Pyramid, Sekhemkhet, Djoser's successor, began a similar tomb complex. Although this was never finished, excavators believe that it was probably planned from the beginning as a seven-step pyramid. The blocks of stone used in it were larger than those in Djoser's pyramid. The total enclosure for Sekhemkhet's complex was as long as that of Djoser but only two-thirds the width. The sections of the wall which remain show that they were identical to Djoser's, with a panelled facade, bastions and imitation double doors. Sekhemkhet's complex also included a southern mastaba.

North of Sakkara, at Zawyiet el-Aryan, is a building referred to as the Layer Pyramid. This is believed to have been built for another Third Dynasty king called Khaban. Although this tomb was never completed, it looks as if the architects were following the same design as the pyramid of Sekhemkhet.

Huni

The mystery of Huni and the Meidum Pyramid

The last king of the Third Dynasty was the little known Huni who supposedly reigned for 24 years. The pyramid at Meidum, about 50 kilometres south of Memphis is often ascribed to him. However, many scholars doubt that this pyramid really was built for him for the following reasons:

• No mention of his name has been found at or near Meidum.

• No member of his family and none of his officials were buried there.

• Later Egyptians attributed the Meidum pyramid to Huni's successor, Sneferu. The name given to it by the ancients was *Djed Sneferu* (*Sneferu Endures*).

• Several sons of Sneferu and their wives were buried in mastabas at Meidum.

It is possible that Huni started the pyramid at Meidum and that Sneferu completed it (see page 83). However, a large unexcavated enclosure to the west of the complex of Djoser and Sekhemkhet at Sakkara, could hold the key to Huni's burial place.

Seven small step pyramids, which Edwards believes 'belong to the same stage in technical achievement as the step pyramids of Djoser and Sekhemkhet'[5] were built along the Nile Valley as far as Elephantine. There is no evidence that these were ever built as tombs.

Small pyramids along the Nile

Who built them and for what purpose? A German archaeologist, Werner Kaiser, believes that they were all the work of Huni. His name was inscribed on a granite cone close to the step pyramid at Elephantine. However, an inscribed stela in front of the small pyramid at Seila bore the name and titles of Huni's successor, Sneferu.

The most likely explanation for these small step pyramids scattered along the Nile, is that they were symbols of the king's power placed in the provinces to remind the people of his authority. A less likely theory is that they represented the primeval mound that emerged from the waters of chaos during creation.

During the Third Dynasty the state was becoming more focused on the person of the god-king. Diverse elements within the state were drawn together by a well organised bureaucracy to provide for his well-being in this and the next life. From the Third Dynasty onwards, there was a marked differentiation in the size of the tombs of the kings in relation to those of their nobles and officials. This trend reached its peak during the next dynasty.

The peak of achievement — the Fourth Dynasty

During the Fourth Dynasty (c. 2575–2465 BC) the Old Kingdom reached its peak. The massive pyramid complexes soaring above the mastaba tombs of the nobles and officials at Dahshur and Giza are evidence of:

Architecture as main source of evidence for this dynasty

- the divine status of the kings and the vast gulf that separated the god-king from the rest of the population at this time
- the centralised nature of the state, focused on the person of the king
- the importance of the sun (solar) cult and the Egyptian view of the afterlife
- the dependence of the nobles and officials on the king for an afterlife
- the incredible technical achievements of the Egyptians.

A number of architectural developments during this dynasty indicated that there had been a religious shift. These included the 'true' pyramid form, a different type of pyramid complex and the positioning of the mortuary temple on the east, facing the rising sun, rather than on the north, as in the Third Dynasty.

Since the true pyramid was a symbol of the sun god it appears that there was a change from an astral (star) cult to a solar cult at this stage. Perhaps there was an acceptance of a new or altered view of the after-life. However, as was the case throughout Egyptian history, earlier beliefs and practices were not discarded but incorporated into the new belief system. See Chapter 7 for details.

King Sneferu and Queen Hetepheres

Sneferu was the first king of the Fourth Dynasty. His marriage to Hetepheres, the daughter of King Huni, last king of the Third Dynasty, ensured his accession to the throne.

Evidence for the reign of Sneferu and his *Great Royal Wife* Hetepheres, is drawn chiefly from the pyramid complexes at Dahshur and Meidum as well as from the Palermo Stone and the grave goods from the tomb of Hetepheres.

Sneferu's achievements

Sneferu is believed to have reigned for 24 years, although the fragments of the Palermo Stone record the events of only six years of his reign. During this six-year period he sent an expedition to restore order in Nubia, when his forces are supposed to have taken 7000 captives and 20 000 sheep and oxen. He also sent a fleet of 40 ships to the Phoenician coast to bring back cedar wood, some of which was used in the con-struction of his pyramids. From an inscription in Sinai, it appears that he promoted copper mining in the peninsula as well.

However, of all his achievements, none equals the construction of three pyramid complexes, each designed at some point to be his eternal home. That he was a truly great king is attested by the fact that his mor-tuary cult flourished for centuries after his death and that he was remem-bered by the Egyptians of later ages as an 'ideally beneficent and good-humoured monarch'.[6]

Sneferu's pyramids

Sneferu was responsible for the construction of the first true pyramid. It appears that he built at least two pyramid complexes on the desert plateau at Dahshur, about seven kilometres south of Sakkara. He was probably also the builder of the pyramid at Meidum, further south. If he did not start the construction of the Meidum Pyramid (often referred to as Huni's Pyramid), then he certainly completed it.

The Meidum Pyramid was built originally as a step pyramid but com-pleted as a true pyramid. The southern pyramid at Dahshur, referred to as the *Bent* or *Rhomboidal Pyramid*, was planned as a true pyramid but not completed as such. The northern pyramid at Dahshur (sometimes called the *Red Pyramid*) was planned and completed as a true pyramid.

Massive physical resources (approximately nine million tonnes of stone on the three pyramids alone according to Edwards) and advanced tech-

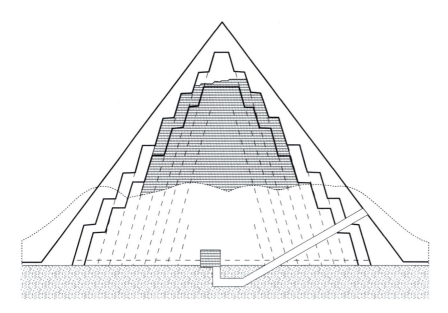

Stages in the construction of Meidum Pyramid

nical skills would have been required to build three tomb complexes in a reign of 24 years. This fact has given rise to the theory that Sneferu did not build the original step pyramid at Meidum but simply transformed his predecessor's tomb into a true pyramid.

According to Fakhry:

> We know from ancient sources that King Sneferu had two pyramids, which have been identified at Dahshur. It would be unusual for a king to have three such monuments. Sneferu's predecessor, King Hu (Huni) reigned for at least twenty-four years. In my opinion Huni built his monument at Meidum, but it was either left unfinished at the time of his death or considered too simple. During Sneferu's reign, this unfinished (or too modest) building was enlarged and completed. Consequently we can consider the completion of the pyramid at Meidum and its complex to date from the reign of Sneferu.[7]

Views about Sneferu's ownership of three pyramids

The remains of the pyramid at Meidum

The Bent Pyramid

The Northern Pyramid

However, Edwards maintains that Sneferu was the original owner of the Meidum Pyramid. He says that:

> If all the available information — technical, archaeological and epi-graphical (inscriptional) — be marshalled, the picture which emerges is clear. Sneferu, early in his reign, began to build his step pyramid at Meidum.[8]

Possible sequence of pyramid construction

Edwards then proceeds to outline the order in which he believes Sneferu built his three pyramids.

1 At the beginning of his reign Sneferu ordered the construction of the step pyramid at Meidum, intending to be buried there when he died.

2 It appears that at some stage he changed his mind and began the construction of the first (southern) pyramid at Dahshur. Although he planned this as a small true pyramid with an angle of incline of 60 degrees, the builders ran into trouble. Cracks began to appear when the pyramid had reached about 37 metres in height. Although the base was enlarged and the angle reduced to 54 degrees 31 minutes, cracks continued to appear. At about 54 metres in height the builders changed the design once again. The angle was reduced to 43 degrees 21 minutes, giving the pyramid a strange bent appearance, hence the name the *Bent* Pyramid.

Bent Pyramid

3 Sneferu then began the construction of the first true pyramid — the northern Dahshur pyramid — with an angle of incline maintained at 43 degrees 31 minutes, giving it a flattish appearance. Edwards believes that it was still being built towards the end of Sneferu's life because the dates on some of the casing stones corresponded to the sixteenth census of his reign. Censuses were generally held biennially (every two years) during the Old Kingdom and were used to date the events of a king's reign. It seems that Sneferu introduced an annual census after the seventh biennial one, so that during his reign seven biennial and ten annual censuses were held. By doing this, Sneferu may

First true pyramid

have hoped to increase revenue to pay for the building of
a second pyramid.

4   While the northern pyramid at Dahshur was still being built,
Edwards believes that Sneferu began to transform the Meidum
Pyramid and build a new mortuary temple. Dates on some of
the casing stones suggest that this construction work was being
carried out during the fifteenth, sixteenth and seventeenth
censuses of the king's reign. It is likely that the work was
unfinished when he died.

Gardiner tends to agree with Edwards. He says, 'The balance of evidence ... seems to point to the unpalatable conclusion that Sneferu did
possess three pyramids'.[9] The following diagram points to the evidence
for Sneferu's ownership of three pyramid complexes.

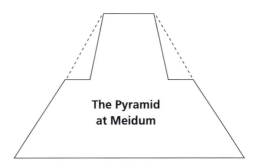

Graffiti from the Sixth Dynasty mention Sneferu's name.

Other graffiti by visitors of the Eighteenth Dynasty indicate that they came to Meidum to *see the beautiful temple of King Sneferu.*

The Pyramid at Meidum

Two of Sneferu's sons, his eldest Nefermaet and Rehotep, the high priest of Heliopolis, their wives, Itet and Nofret, plus other members of the royal family were buried near the pyramid.

Stelae in the mortuary chapel bear the king's names and titles.

Reliefs in the valley temple show the king wearing the Double Crown and the Sed garment, performing ritual ceremonies.

The Bent Pyramid at Dahshur

The name of Sneferu was written in red ochre on a block lying beneath the floor of the upper chamber.

The king's name was also on a stone on an outer casing block.

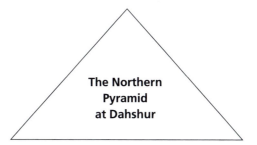

Reliefs found in the mortuary temple show Sneferu wearing Sed festival dress.

Other members of Sneferu's family including his son, Kanofer, and other sons and daughters were buried in mastabas to the SE of the pyramid.

The Northern Pyramid at Dahshur

Inscriptions from the reign of Pepi I found near the pyramid indicate that there were mortuary priests attached to the two Dahshur pyramids.

Sneferu's Horus name, *Nebmaet, w*as written in red ochre on a casing stone.

Evidence pointing to Sneferu's ownership of three pyramid complexes

A relief of Sneferu in his Sed regalia, from Dahshur

Why Sneferu ordered the construction of three tombs is not known and, according to Edwards, 'it is not possible to deduce in which of the three pyramids Sneferu was buried'.[10] Fakhry, however, is convinced that 'this king was buried in the Bent Pyramid of Dahshur, in the upper burial chamber at the end of the western gallery'.[11]

Evolution of the pyramid complex

Along with the evolution of the true pyramid form, a pyramid complex, quite different to that of the Third Dynasty, evolved. This type of complex, which continued to be built until the end of the Old Kingdom, comprised:

- the pyramid
- a mortuary temple on the eastern side of the pyramid
- one or more subsidiary pyramids
- a *temenos* or enclosure wall
- a valley temple on the edge of the area of cultivation
- a causeway leading from the valley temple to the mortuary temple.

It is believed that Sneferu was the first king to build a valley temple and causeway, although it cannot be said with certainty.

The valley temple of the Bent Pyramid revealed that the walls of temples were decorated with reliefs much earlier than had previously been thought. The plan of this temple and the 1400 or so fragments of reliefs discovered indicate that this building was magnificent. 'It would have borne comparison with anything now known of its kind from the Old Kingdom.'[12]

The causeway of the Bent Pyramid, like that of the Meidum Pyramid, was unroofed. Later causeways were roofed over.

Satellite pyramids

South of the Bent Pyramid was a small pyramid, the precise purpose of which is unknown. It was probably intended to fulfil the same function as the south tomb in Djoser's Step Pyramid complex. One or more of these small satellite pyramids were added to pyramid complexes from the time of Sneferu.

The basic elements comprising the pyramid complex evolved further under Sneferu's son and successor, Khufu, and reached their fully developed form at the time of Khufu's son, Khafre.

The discovery of the tomb of Hetepheres

Status of the queen

Hetepheres was possibly the most influential Old Kingdom woman. Not only was she the daughter of a god-king (Huni) and the wife of a god-king (Sneferu) but her eldest son was King Khufu, believed to be the builder of the Great Pyramid at Giza. An inscription in her tomb described her as:

> The mother of the King of Upper and Lower Egypt, follower of Horus, she who is in charge of the affairs of the harem, whose every word is done for her, daughter of the god (begotten) of his body, Hetepheres.[(13)]

The discovery of her funerary equipment in a tomb near that of her son on the Giza plateau proved to be one of the most important finds of the Old Kingdom.

How and where was it found?

In 1925 a team of American archaeologists led by George Reisner was working near the causeway of the Great Pyramid of Khufu. The team photographer was having trouble getting his tripod to stand up straight because the ground was too hard and uneven. When he moved his tripod to a new position, one of the legs broke through the ground into a hole. After examination it was found that the ground around the hole was covered with plaster which appeared to be a seal covering the entrance to a shaft. Since this plaster seal was not damaged in any way, it was likely that what lay beneath it was untouched. When the first layer of stones was removed a rubble-filled shaft was revealed.

What was discovered?

It took the excavators 13 days to clear the 30-metre-deep shaft, at the bottom of which they found a wall of stone blocks. When the first block was removed, the glow of a candle revealed an alabaster sarcophagus (large outer coffin).

The following day, by means of mirrors, the excavators reflected sunlight into the burial chamber. They discovered that the floor was covered with gilded rods, the remains of furniture from which the gold had flaked, and vessels of gold, copper and stone. Close to the floor the excavators found some gold hieroglyphs which spelled out the name of Hetepheres. As well as the funerary items, there were also workmen's tools lying about.

The state of the chamber walls — with holes which appeared to have been carelessly plugged with stones — suggested that the tomb may have been robbed. However, the precious objects were still on the floor and the outer plaster seal had not been damaged.

The state of the tomb

There was great excitement among the officials when it was time to open the alabaster sarcophagus. However, their excitement turned to intense disappointment when the heavy lid was raised and the sarcophagus was found to be empty.

Despite the absence of the queen's mummy, the tomb was filled with wonderful funerary objects which included:

- an alabaster canopic chest containing the Queen's embalmed viscera (internal organs) suspended in brine
- a bed with a partial covering of gold and a gold panelled footboard with a black and blue floral design

Elaborate funerary objects

- a canopy-frame made of wood encased with gold and with poles ending in lotus buds
- two armchairs encased in gold
- a carrying chair with poles terminating in gold-covered palm capitals and hieroglyphic inscriptions inlaid in ivory panels
- alabaster and gold vessels
- eight alabaster vases filled with unguents (sweet-smelling substances for rubbing on the body) and kohl (a black powder used for outlining the eyes)
- a box containing 20 silver bracelets or anklets inlaid with lapis lazuli, carnelian and malachite in the shape of butterflies
- gold razors and knives and a gold manicure set.

Reassembled bedroom furniture from the tomb of Hetepheres

What happened to Hetepheres' mummy?

Theory of a reburial

George Reisner advanced a theory that the tomb at Giza was not the original burial site of Hetepheres. He suggested that she was originally buried near her husband, Sneferu, at Dahshur but that tomb robbers had broken into her burial chamber and removed her body with its jewellery of gold and precious stones. It is possible that some of the necropolis guards were the actual tomb robbers and that they were disturbed before they could remove any of the larger items. Her son, Khufu, may have ordered a new tomb to be built in secret close to his own eternal home (the Great Pyramid), which was being constructed at the time. It is possible that the terrible news of the disappearance of his mother's body was kept from Khufu and that he thought the alabaster sarcophagus that was eventually lowered into the hurriedly prepared tomb still contained his mother's embalmed body.

Evidence of a reburial

The evidence to support Reisner's theory of a reburial includes:

- the absence of a body and the untouched plaster seal
- the crude nature of the tomb for a woman of such status

- the placement of the objects which indicates that they had been pushed in quickly
- the proximity of the sarcophagus to the entrance of the burial chamber which suggests that it had been lowered into the tomb after the funerary objects. This was very unusual
- the abandoned tools of workmen and holes plugged with stones instead of being plastered over, indicating a rushed job
- the lack of a superstructure which indicates the need to maintain complete secrecy. In normal circumstances a queen of Hetepheres' status would have had an elaborate tomb.

What was the significance of this discovery?

Hetepheres' tomb is the only one from the Old Kingdom found with many of its contents still intact. Its contents provide evidence of:
- the skills of the Fourth Dynasty craftsmen
- the kind of funerary equipment that must have been placed in other tombs of the period
- the status of royal women during the Old Kingdom
- the types of furnishings used in the apartments of royal women
- the developments in the embalming process used for royalty. The removal and preservation of internal organs may have occurred earlier in the case of kings.

Khufu (Cheops)

Khufu, the son of Sneferu and Hetepheres, is believed by Egyptologists to have been the builder of the Great Pyramid of Giza. However, the only evidence for this is a scrawled graffiti inside the relieving chambers above the so-called 'King's' chamber. There are serious doubts now about the authenticity of this inscription. See Appendix A.

Little known about Khufu

Despite the enormous technical advancements that were made during Khufu's reign, very little else is known about him. According to the ancient records, he reigned for 23 years, had several wives and many children. He is believed to have carried out building projects apart from the construction of his pyramid and exploited the Sinai, Nubia and the eastern desert for their mineral wealth.

Apart from these scanty facts, our knowledge of Khufu comes from secondary sources such as the Westcar Papyrus (a Middle Kingdom document), and the writings of Herodotus (fifth century BC) and Manetho (third century BC). These sources are critical of Khufu, particularly with regard to his religious policy. However, it is important to remember when these views were recorded.

Herodotus' view of Khufu

Herodotus reported that Khufu closed down temples and prevented his subjects, whom he treated as slaves, from practising their religion.

Manetho recorded that Khufu showed disrespect for the gods, and the Westcar Papyrus suggests that he closed at least one temple and did not make offerings to the gods on a regular basis.

Khufu as a tyrant

The extract below is from Book 2 of Herodotus' *Histories*.

> Up to the time of Rhampsinitus (Sneferu), Egypt was excellently governed; but his successor Cheops (to continue the story which the priests gave me) brought the country into all sorts of misery. He closed all the temples, then, not content with excluding his subjects from the practice of their religion, compelled them without exception to labour as slaves for his own advantage. One hundred thousand men laboured constantly, and were relieved every three months, by a fresh lot. It took ten years' oppression of the people to make the causeway for the conveyance of the stones ... The pyramid itself was twenty years in the building ... But no crime was too great for Cheops: when he was short of money, he sent his daughter to a bawdy-house with instructions to charge a certain sum — they did not tell me how much. This she actually did, adding to it a further transaction of her own ... [14]

How accurate is Herodotus' view? Herodotus' belief, that Khufu was a tyrant who enslaved his people, was based on his own standards and those of his age — the fifth century BC, over 2000 years after Khufu's lifetime. It is a mistake made by many writers throughout history. The same must be said about the priests who gave Herodotus much of his information. It is unlikely that they would have known a great deal about events so far in the past.

Herodotus could not envisage such a massive monument being built by anything other than slave labour. He failed to understand the Egyptians' attitude to their king. To them the king was a god on earth, who was responsible for maintaining the order, fertility and prosperity of the land, and they were willing to work on his eternal resting place. The peasants and craftsmen probably believed that if they were of service to their king in this life, then they might continue to be needed by him in the next life as well. Also most of the unskilled work (such as dragging the huge blocks) was probably carried out during the flood when farmers had fewer tasks to do.

Evidence refutes the idea of a tyranny

Other pieces of evidence which tend to refute Herodotus' view of the wicked tyrant oppressing his people are:

- the stable economic situation which he left. This allowed his son, Khafre, to build a pyramid almost as massive as that of his father
- the continuation of the cult of Khufu for many centuries after his death
- the fact that the name of Khufu, inscribed on protective scarabs in later ages, was thought to be a very powerful charm.

It would seem that Khufu 'was an able and energetic ruler during whose reign the land flourished and art reached perfection'.[16]

However, there may have been some truth in Herodotus' statement that Khufu closed down temples as there seem to have been religious changes during his reign. Some scholars believe that Khufu may have banned the use of statues for anyone other than the gods or the god king. The reason for this belief is that there appear to have been no ka statues placed in the tombs at this time.

Possible religious changes

The Great Pyramid — *The Horizon of Khufu*

The Great Pyramid was supposedly built as the eternal resting place for the body of King Khufu.

> Not only is it the largest monument of its kind ever constructed, but for excellence of workmanship, accuracy of planning, and beauty of proportion, it remains the chief of the Seven Wonders of the (Ancient) World.[15]

The Egyptian people believed that the king was appointed by the gods to rule on earth. As he was the only link they had with the gods, his welfare was the most important consideration in their lives. Only through the king would the gods provide for them. When he died he went to join the gods and the care of his soul was even more important than his welfare in life.

Khufu as the link between the gods and his subjects

The cult of the sun god and the Great Pyramid

Sun worship had been practised throughout Egypt in one form or another since Predynastic times. As early as the First Dynasty, when the worship of Re became fused with the cult of the god-king Horus, the rule of the king in this and the next life was associated with the sun god. The temples to the sun god at Heliopolis were among the most important and influential institutions in Egypt.

Worship of the sun from early times

However, during the Fourth Dynasty the solar cult became even more closely associated with the concept of supreme rule by the king. This was reflected in the construction of true pyramids which were symbols of the sun god. It was the vast knowledge of the priests of Re which was

The Great Pyramid of Khufu

the basis of the great technological developments of this period. Sneferu's vizier, Prince Kanufer, and Khufu's vizier and architect, Hemon, were high priests of Re at Heliopolis.

Although the priests of Re played a prominent role in shaping religious and political history, their power did not peak until the Fifth Dynasty.

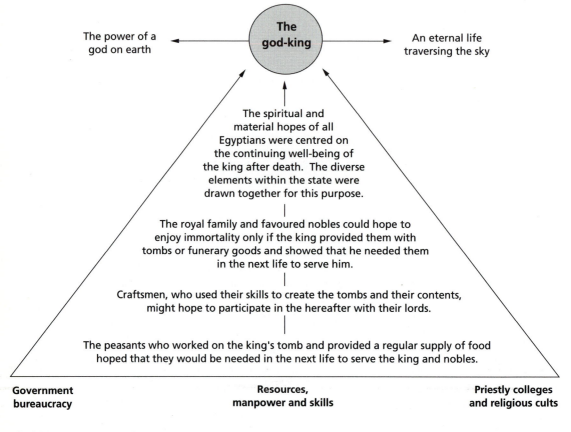

The king's status as a god

The significance of the pyramid shape

The ben-ben stone

The Great Pyramid was a symbol of the sun god. It is believed to have been a huge representation of a sacred stone, in the shape of a pyramidion, known as the *ben-ben*. This stone was worshipped in the temple of the sun god at Heliopolis.

There are several views as to the symbolic meaning of this stone. The most commonly held view is that the ben-ben represented the original mound that emerged from the waters of chaos during creation. It was this stone on which the sun god, Re-Atum, first manifest himself and created the world.

Primeval mound

The true pyramid may have represented a monumental mound. From earliest times, graves were covered with a tumulus or mound, and these were later incorporated into the mastaba and step pyramid tombs. A massive natural mound was left in the middle of the site on which the Great Pyramid was erected. It was incorporated into the pyramid's lower levels. The mound was regarded as a symbol of existence. It is possible that the king, buried under the mound (pyramid), was thought to receive a renewal of existence.

The other view is that the ben-ben stone represented the rays of the sun shining down on earth. As a representation of the rays of the sun, the pyramid provided a ramp by which the dead king could mount to heaven. The Pyramid Texts, found in later pyramids, suggest that the step pyramid tombs of the Third Dynasty represented stairways by which the kings could climb to heaven among the *imperishable stars*. By the Fourth Dynasty it seems that the king was believed to join Re by mounting a ramp formed by the sun's rays — 'Heaven hath strengthened for thee the rays of the sun that thou mayest lift thyself to heaven as the eye of Re'.[17]

Ben-ben as the rays of the sun

A ramp to heaven

Whether the ben-ben of Heliopolis represented the primeval mound or the rays of the sun, the kings of the Fourth and subsequent dynasties were buried under the symbol of the sun god.

There appears to have been a change from an astral (star) cult to a solar (sun) cult from the Third to the Fourth dynasty. However, the true pyramids still contained architectural features associated with the earlier beliefs. For example, the entrances to the Old Kingdom pyramids were always on the northern face, aligned with the circumpolar stars.

The site of the Great Pyramid

Khufu chose the plateau of Giza, to the north of Dahshur, as the site for his pyramid complex. His successors, Khafre and Menkaure, followed his example. Around these three complexes (pyramids, associated temples, causeways, satellite pyramids, queens' pyramids and boat pits) were the ordered rows of rectangular mastaba tombs belonging to the members of their families and to the officials who served them.

Giza, like all the sites chosen by kings of the Old Kingdom (Sakkara, Meidum, Dahshur, Abu Roash and Abusir), was:

Advantages of Giza Plateau

- on the western side of the Nile
- on the edge of the desert above the valley but not too far from the river
- within reasonable proximity to the capital city of Memphis and the residence of the king.

Why were these considerations of importance to the pyramid builders? The Egyptians believed that the west, where the sun *died* every day, was the land of the dead. Therefore most royal cemeteries throughout Egyptian pharaonic history were located on the west bank.

To avoid having their eternal homes flooded each year when the Nile broke its banks, the kings chose sites high enough to escape the inundation. However, the flood played an important part in the construction of the pyramids. Most of the huge blocks of stone used in the pyramids and their temples had to be transported by boat. Limestone came from Tura on the eastern side of the river and granite and basalt were quarried near Aswan over 800 kilometres to the south. It is believed that most of these stone blocks were transported during the flood season when they could be brought closer to the building site.

Because the king needed to inspect the pyramid in its various stages of construction, the site had to be fairly close to his residence.

Two other factors influenced Khufu's choice of Giza. The rock base on the plateau was free from any defects which might cause subsidence or cracking and there was an abundant supply of local limestone for the core of the pyramid.

Challenges facing the pyramid builders

Khufu's pyramid was an incredible leap forward in terms of size, technical expertise and organisation of both physical and human resources.

The architect(s) of the Great Pyramid had to find ways to:

- quarry the limestone and the harder granite and basalt
- transport the huge blocks from the quarries by boat and move them onto the Giza plateau
- level the surface of the base and ensure a perfect square
- achieve an exact orientation on the four cardinal points
- raise the blocks to the required height and lay them in position so that they held together internally and were arranged in a regular fashion externally.

> There was no standard manual for pyramid building in the early, experimental era of the giant pyramids.[18]

No iron tools

It has been estimated that the Great Pyramid complex contains about 2 700 000 cubic metres of stone. Since the ancient Egyptians used only tools of wood, stone and copper, how they cut through stones as hard as granite and basalt is 'one of the truly perplexing questions of pyramid age masonry'.[19] Refer to Appendix B for comments on the use of iron in ritual objects.

Massive quantity of stone

Approximately 2 300 000 blocks of limestone, weighing on an average 2.5 tonnes, made up the core and casing of the pyramid alone. This was obtained from the plateau itself and from the quarries of Tura across the river. Hard pink granite from Aswan was used in the internal passageways and chambers as well as for the temples and funerary equipment. The nine great granite beams in the roof of the 'burial' chamber were over 5.5 metres in length and weighed between 25 and 40 tonnes.

On the basis of the length of Khufu's reign and the number of blocks in his pyramid, it has been estimated that the ancient quarry workers would have had to cut 322 cubic metres of stone daily. Since an average stone block in the pyramid core was approximately one cubic metre in size, this means that the workmen had to cut around 322 stones per day. An interesting experiment (the 'Nova experiment'), carried out by Mark Lehner and a team of masons and workers, to test current theories about the Great Pyramid, found that 12 quarrymen could cut 8.5 stones per day. However, these modern workmen cut only limestone (softer than granite and basalt), used iron tools and a winch and only worked for 22 days. From this information Lehner and his team calculated that in Khufu's day about 1212 men could possibly cut the required amount of stone daily. He concluded that the skill of the ancient Egyptians was not the result 'of some mysterious technology or secret sophistication but of generations of practice and experience'.[20]

Some idea of how the ancient Egyptians transported these huge blocks from the quarries to the pyramid site can be gained from:

Evidence of
transportation

- the discovery of the oldest paved road in history at Lisht in the Faiyum area
- tomb and temple scenes showing the transportation of huge blocks on specially-built barges and the movement of a colossal statue belonging to Djehuthotep (shown in Chapter 8). This latter scene showed that the Egyptians used manpower for hauling building blocks, statues and obelisks.

In 1993, geologists investigating ancient Egyptian stone quarries made a discovery which throws more light on the technological advancement of Fourth Dynasty builders. In the Faiyum area, about 70 kilometres south of Giza, geologists identified what they believe is the oldest paved road in existence, estimated to have been built between 2600 and 2200 BC. It linked a basalt quarry and the remains of a stoneworkers' camp with an ancient lake.

Oldest known
paved road

This length of road, approximately 12 kilometres long and up to 11 metres wide, was made from wooden beams inserted into a base of limestone chips and mortar. This solid base was covered with another layer of limestone and gypsum chips. Alluvial mud was placed over this to provide a smooth surface. As the human-drawn sleds (there were no wheeled wagons at this time) were dragged over the road, water was poured under the sled runners to act as a lubricant. It is generally believed that wooden rollers were placed under the sleds and moved from back to front as the sled was pulled along. Lehner's Nova experiment proved that 20 men could easily pull a two tonne block along a lubricated track.

Edwards, in Chapter 8 of *The Pyramids of Egypt*, outlines what he considers the most likely methods used by the ancient builders to achieve a level base and orientate the pyramid to the four cardinal points. However, his views are now being questioned.

Edwards believes that the bases of pyramids were levelled by means of cutting channels in the surface, filling them with water and marking its level before draining it away. Lehner doubts that any method using water would have worked because of the difficulty of filling channels over a base area of 5.3 hectares with water carried in pots slung over a pole. He suggests also, that in the heat of Egypt much of the water would have evaporated before the levelling was completed.

Levelling, orientation
and alignment

Internal structure and elements in the complex of Khufu's pyramid

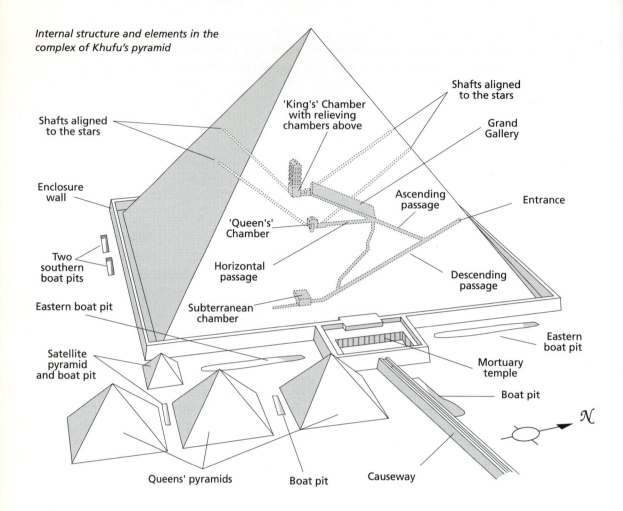

Whereas Edwards believes that the builders oriented the pyramid by the stars, Lehner suggests that they might have used the 'sun and shadow' method which he and his assistants used in the Nova experiment.

How the ancient builders aligned the axes and diagonals of the pyramid is not known. Somers, Clark and Engelbach, in *Ancient Egyptian Masonry*, believe that they achieved this by sighting objects on the ground some distance away.

Theories about ramps

The most controversial issue surrounding the construction of the pyramids concerns the lifting and placing of the stones in their courses and the laying of the casing stones. It is generally thought that a system of ramps was used but what type and how many is still a matter of conjecture. The use of ramps was the only possible way of doing this in the absence of the pulley. Various theories include the use of long supply ramps with foothold embankments, helicoidal ramps which spiralled around the pyramid and internal ramps with external stairs. Each one presents a problem.

From the construction of the small experimental pyramid built by the Nova team, it was found that there were problems in placing the stones towards the apex. Perhaps levers were used.

Herodotus recorded that it took 100 000 men to build the Great Pyramid. However, Lehner says that it is more likely that a conscripted labour force of only 20 000–30 000 worked at any one time. It is possible that they worked for a period of three months before being replaced. There is evidence that these pyramid workers were divided into crews of 2000 and these were further divided into gangs of 1000 which in turn were subdivided into smaller working teams.

Main features of the Great Pyramid

The table below summarises the main features of the Great Pyramid.

Size	Height Length of sides Area	Originally 146 metres high Average 230 metres long Covers an area of 5.3 hectares.
Materials	Type	The core is made of local limestone blocks and the outer casing is of fine Tura limestone. What is believed by Egyptologists to be Khufu's burial chamber and the ceiling of the grand gallery are constructed of pink Aswan granite.
Amount		Approximately 2 300 000 blocks
Weight		Blocks average about 2.5 tonnes. Some weigh much more.
Structural features	Base and faces	The base is almost a perfect square and the greatest difference in the length of the sides is 4.4 centimetres. The level varies only one centimetre from the SE to the NE corner. The faces are oriented exactly to the north, south, east and west and incline at an angle of 51 degrees 52 minutes.
	Joints in the	These average half a millimetre wide, so that the blocks casing blocks fit perfectly together.
	Entrance	The entrance is in the centre of the north face, about 20 metres from the base
	Internal chambers and galleries	The 47-metre-long grand gallery which leads up to the 'king's chamber', has an 8.5 metre-high corbelled roof (a roof supported by projections of stone on the faces of the walls) and is the most majestic passageway in any pyramid.
		There are three internal chambers — the so-called king's chamber (although it is called the 'king's chamber' there is no evidence that Khufu was buried here), the middle chamber, often incorrectly called the 'queen's chamber' (no queen was buried in it) and a subterranean chamber, 30 metres below the base of the pyramid.
		The 'king's chamber' is high in the body of the pyramid and possibly reflects the increasing identification of the king with the sun god, whose rays the pyramid symbolises. Its roof is made of nine monolithic slabs of granite 5.5 metres long and each estimated to weigh somewhere between 25 and 40 tonnes.
		Because of the larger-than-life niche in the 'queen's' chamber, it has been suggested that this may originally have been sealed off to form a type of *serdab* (cellar-like chamber).
		The roughly hewn subterranean chamber possibly represented the Underworld.
		Although some scholars believe that the three chambers indicate changes to the plan during construction, they are more likely to have been built as part of a symbolic plan, each catering for different aspects of the king's spiritual welfare.
		Shafts, leading from the two major chambers, probably served a ritual purpose associated with the stars. (Refer to Appendix C.)

The grand gallery in Khufu's pyramid

Other buildings associated with the Great Pyramid complex

The Great Pyramid, like all pyramids from the time of Sneferu, was the focal point of a complex of buildings. Unfortunately, much of Khufu's pyramid complex has disappeared or, like his valley temple, is still buried under the modern village of Kafr-es-Samman. There is enough left of his mortuary temple to see that the plan differed from Sneferu's simple mortuary temple and Khafre's large and more elaborate one. Fakhry believes that 'some unknown development in the royal mortuary cult must have led to radical changes in the plan of the pyramid temples'.[21]

Only recently has a satellite pyramid, for the king's ka, been located in front of the right-hand queen's pyramid. This was excavated when a modern road, running close to the pyramid, was removed.

On the eastern side of the pyramid are three subsidiary pyramids, possibly built for a number of queens, one of whom was Khufu's wife, Henutsen.

Boat pits

Five empty boat-shaped pits were found near Khufu's pyramid. The practice of placing boats beside the tombs of kings had been carried out from early dynastic times. However, until 1954, when two further boat pits were located, hidden under the rocks and sand close to Khufu's pyramid, no large Old Kingdom vessel had been found.

An empty boat pit

Only one pit was excavated* and found to contain a dismantled, flat-bottomed, cedar funerary boat. It consisted of 12 224 separate pieces, varying in size from ten centimetres to 23 metres in length. These pieces were arranged methodically in 13 layers. For 14 years each piece of the boat was recorded, chemically treated to preserve it and then carefully put together like a jigsaw puzzle. The restored 43 metre boat, complete with deck-house and six pairs of oars, averaging seven metres in length, is in near-perfect condition.

The first five boat-shaped pits are believed to have been part of the symbolic layout of the pyramid complex and represented the boats used by the king in his afterlife to sail across the heavens with the sun god by day and beneath the earth by night. These are often referred to as *solar* boats. The other two pits, containing the disassembled boats, probably served another purpose. These are believed to have been connected with the royal funeral. Anything connected with the funeral 'was considered highly charged'.[22] To neutralise the energy of the funerary boats, they were dismantled and buried just outside the mortuary complex.

From the graffiti scribbled on the sides of the opened pit, it is obvious that Khufu's son and immediate successor, Djedefre, who buried his father, was responsible for finishing the work and sealing the pit.

*   The other pit was examined by camera and its contents were found to be similar to those in the excavated pit. It was decided to leave it untouched.

A restored funerary boat

One of the subsidiary pyramids believed to belong to a queen

Khufu's successors

Possible dynastic problems

The various king lists and an inscription in the Wadi Hammamat give Khufu's successors as Djedefre, Khafre, Baufre, Djedefhor, Menkaure, Shepseskaf and Dedeptah.

There seems to have been some dynastic problem towards the end of Khufu's reign or soon after his death. Khufu had several wives — among them Queen Henutsen and another who is believed to have been a Libyan woman. A conflict between two branches of Khufu's family may have broken out, with each line of offspring gaining support from among the priests and nobles.

Djedefre

Pyramid at Abu Roash

Djedefre, Khufu's immediate successor, may have been the son of Khufu's Libyan queen. The fact that he built his own pyramid some eight kilometres north of Giza at Abu Roash, rather than near his father's tomb may indicate a split in the family. This seems to be the most likely explanation. The break does not appear to have been caused by religious differences since his pyramid complex followed the traditional form, although it was incomplete at Djedefre's death. Djedefre reigned for a short time, possibly eight years and was succeeded by Khafre, another of Khufu's sons.

Khafre (Cephren)

Khafre, who was described by Herodotus in much the same way as Khufu, built his tomb complex next to his father's at Giza. His pyramid was only slightly smaller than the Great Pyramid. Its impressive appearance today is due to the fact that it was built on slightly higher ground than the Great Pyramid and still retains some of its outer casing stones at the apex.

The Pyramid of Khafre

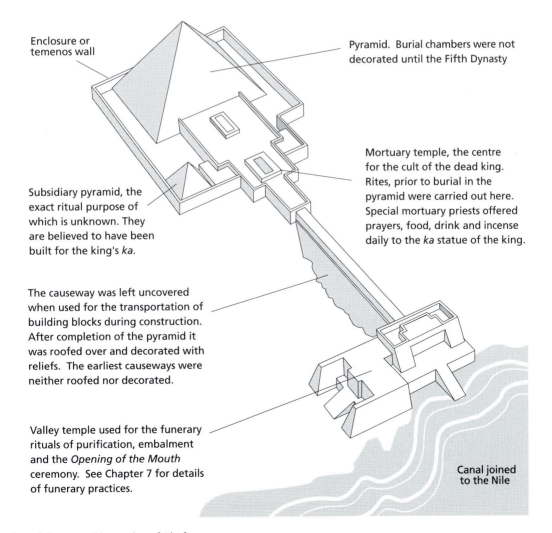

Enclosure or temenos wall

Pyramid. Burial chambers were not decorated until the Fifth Dynasty

Mortuary temple, the centre for the cult of the dead king. Rites, prior to burial in the pyramid were carried out here. Special mortuary priests offered prayers, food, drink and incense daily to the *ka* statue of the king.

Subsidiary pyramid, the exact ritual purpose of which is unknown. They are believed to have been built for the king's *ka.*

The causeway was left uncovered when used for the transportation of building blocks during construction. After completion of the pyramid it was roofed over and decorated with reliefs. The earliest causeways were neither roofed nor decorated.

Valley temple used for the funerary rituals of purification, embalment and the *Opening of the Mouth* ceremony. See Chapter 7 for details of funerary practices.

Canal joined to the Nile

Plan of the pyramid complex of Khafre

The traditional pyramid complex

Final form of pyramid complex

During Khafre's reign the pyramid complex developed into the form it was to retain for the rest of the Old Kingdom, and Khafre's complex is the best preserved of all pyramid complexes. Even today, his valley temple is superb and the remains of his mortuary temple indicate its original magnificence.

From this time there are five identifiable elements in the mortuary temple — an entrance hall, a broad columned hall, five statue niches, five storage chambers and an inner sanctuary with a stela and false door.

The following labelled drawing illustrates the elements of a mortuary temple.

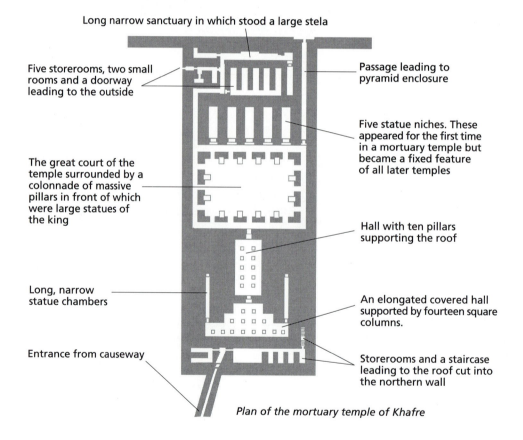

Long narrow sanctuary in which stood a large stela

Five storerooms, two small rooms and a doorway leading to the outside

Passage leading to pyramid enclosure

Five statue niches. These appeared for the first time in a mortuary temple but became a fixed feature of all later temples

The great court of the temple surrounded by a colonnade of massive pillars in front of which were large statues of the king

Hall with ten pillars supporting the roof

Long, narrow statue chambers

An elongated covered hall supported by fourteen square columns.

Entrance from causeway

Storerooms and a staircase leading to the roof cut into the northern wall

Plan of the mortuary temple of Khafre

The Sphinx

Close to Khafre's valley temple and at the lower end of his causeway is the 73-metre-long Great Sphinx — the outstretched body of a lion with a human head. The word *sphinx* is of Greek origin and means *to bind together*.

Symbolism of the lion

The lion was a solar animal and the embodiment of royal power. It was often depicted as the guardian of sacred places. The priests of Heliopolis seem to have incorporated the symbolism of the lion into their doctrine,

Right: A diorite statue of Khafre from his valley temple

Left: Part of the remains of the valley temple of Khafre

considering it as the protector of the gates which led to the Underworld. This may explain the recumbent body of the lion protecting the necropolis of Giza. Refer to Appendix D.

The human head of the Sphinx, which faces the rising sun, is believed to represent the sun god Atum, with the emblems of royalty (*nemes* headdress, ureaus, false beard and crown). Although there is no firm evidence, many Egyptologists believe that the features of the Sphinx are those of Khafre. Edwards suggests that this may have been because the Heliopolitan priesthood believed that the dead king actually became the sun god when he died.

Face of the Sphinx

The human-headed lion is sitting in a ditch below the level of the Giza plateau. Remains of the Sphinx temple are to be found in front of the lion's paws. This temple was oriented east to west with chapels at either end and an altar in the centre. This suggests that it could have been a solar temple, perhaps the forerunner of the sun temples built during the Fifth Dynasty. An interesting recent discovery indicates that there are tunnels under the Sphinx.

Most Egyptologists attribute the carving of the Great Sphinx to King Khafre. It is believed to have been fashioned out of a mound of poor quality limestone left over after the stone for the core of Khafre's pyramid had been quarried.* However, no contemporary inscription has been found pointing to the exact age of the Sphinx or its association with Khafre, except for the extremely weathered features of the face. Recent scientific evidence points to a far greater age for the Sphinx than the reign of Khafre. In 1992, an American geologist, Professor Robert M. Schoch of Boston University, redated the Great Sphinx.

Link with Khafre

Questions about the chronology of the Sphinx

He reported:

> I remain convinced, thus far, that the standard story told by Egyptologists as to when the Great Sphinx was created — namely, by the Old Kingdom Egyptians during the reign of Khafre — does not hold up under close examination.[23]

---

* Despite the poor quality of the limestone, the Sphinx has survived due to long periods when it was covered with sand. It must have been completely buried during the fifth century BC because none of the classical writers (eg, Herodotus) mentioned it.

The Sphinx and the pyramids of Khufu and Khafre

This view is strongly refuted by traditional Egyptologists such as Mark Lehner.

In his investigations of the Sphinx, Schoch looked at:

• weathering patterns on the Sphinx and its enclosure walls
• the underlying limestone of the Sphinx and valley temples in relation to the granite facing blocks
• ancient repairs to the body of the Sphinx
• the sub-surface weathering of the Sphinx enclosure by means of a seismic geophysical survey.

Of all forms of weathering found on the Giza plateau, weathering caused by heavy rainfall is the oldest. Schoch found evidence of this form of weathering only on the body of the Sphinx and the walls of the Sphinx enclosure. Well-documented Old Kingdom tombs on the Giza plateau and fragile mud-brick mastabas from the First and Second dynasties on the Sakkara plateau, reveal only wind weathering. On the body of the Sphinx, wind weathering is noticeable on top of the weathering caused by heavy rainfall. Schoch tentatively suggests that the Sphinx 'may have been carved prior to the last major period of precipitation in this part of the Nile Valley'[24] somewhere between 5000 and 10 000 years ago.

Evidence for Old Kingdom restoration of Sphinx

Schoch believes that the body of the Sphinx underwent repairs during the Old Kingdom, and this has been substantiated by Dr Zahi Hawass of the Egyptian Antiquities Organisation. His report at the international symposium on the Great Sphinx, held in Cairo in 1992 stated:

> It seems that the Sphinx underwent restoration during the Old Kingdom because the analysis of samples found on the right rear leg proved to be of Old Kingdom date.[25]

Seismic surveys have shown that the limestone below the surface of the Sphinx enclosure on the eastern, northern and southern sides has been weathered 50–100 per cent deeper than on the western side (the back part of the sphinx). A possible explanation for this is that when the

Sphinx was first carved, only the front and sides were exposed as it was meant to be viewed from the front only. The rump of the lion, which originally was still part of the bedrock, was *freed* later, perhaps at the time of Khafre. It may have been at this time that the carving was also given its kingly head.

Schoch realises that more seismic surveys have to be carried out in the area of the Sphinx and on the Giza plateau and sums up his findings so far as follows:

> Taking into account ... the evidence for a two stage construction of the Sphinx-associated temples, the research that has been carried out concerning different modes of weathering on the Giza plateau and the seismic surveys in the area of the Sphinx complex which give data on the sub-surface depth and distribution of weathering around the monument, and considering the fact that attribution of the carving of the Sphinx is based on circumstantial evidence to begin with, I find one conclusion inescapable: the initial carving of the core body of the colossal sculpture predated the time of Khafre. [26]

The remains of the granite casing stones of Menkaure's pyramid

Menkaure (Mycerinus)

Following the death of Khafre there appears to have been further family problems. Two kings, Baufre and Djedefhor (other sons of Khufu), followed in quick succession. Their reigns must have been very short since there was only five years between the reigns of Khafre and Menkaure.

A number of short reigns after Khafre

According to Herodotus, Menkaure was a mild, just and generous king who reversed the policies of Khufu, freed the people from slavery and allowed them to return to their everyday work. The Egyptians honoured him more than any other king. Despite Herodotus' praise for Menkaure, there is no contemporary record of his life or character.

Menkaure is believed to have built the third great pyramid tomb on the Giza plateau, although it was never completed. It was substantially smaller than those of Khufu and Khafre, with a base about a quarter of the area and with one-tenth of the building mass of the Great Pyramid. It appears that there was now a trend, which continued throughout the remainder of the Old Kingdom, to give more attention and resources to the construction and decoration of the mortuary temples than to the pyramids. However, despite its size, its lower section was cased in granite and had his pyramid been completed it would have looked magnificent.

Menkaure died unexpectedly and was succeeded by Shepseskaf whose exact relationship to Menkaure is unknown.

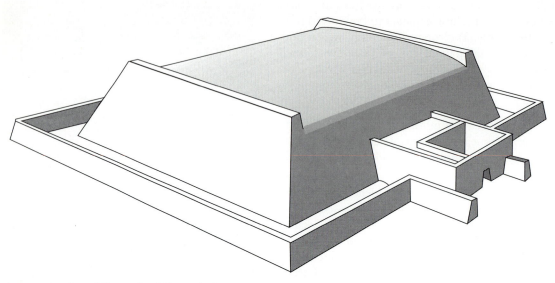

A reconstruction of the tomb of Shepseskaf

Shepseskaf

It appears that Shepseskaf, who reigned for only four years, broke with the Heliopolitan tradition in several ways:

- He did not build a pyramid tomb (the symbol of the sun god), but rather a mastaba similar to a large, rectangular sarcophagus (see the illustration above).
- He chose the Memphite necropolis of Sakkara as the location for his tomb rather than the Giza plateau.
- He did not include *re* as part of his name like his four predecessors
- His eldest daughter was married to a palace official who was loyal to the priests of Ptah and after the marriage, the king's son-in-law was declared High Priest of Ptah.

These changes in Fourth Dynasty tradition may have been a move to limit the influence of the priests of the sun god at Heliopolis over royalty.

Dedeptah

The name of the last king of the dynasty, Dedeptah, seems to indicate an increase in the influence of the priests of Ptah of Memphis at this time.

Drawing of the relief showing Khent-kawes with the false beard and ureaus of kingship, from the gateway of her tomb

Queen Khent-kawes

Queen Khent-kawes may have been a daughter of Menkaure. She was certainly a woman of very high status. Although her name is never enclosed in a cartouche, she is depicted on the granite gateway of her tomb wearing the false beard and ureaus of kingship.

She is believed to have been the mother of two of the Fifth Dynasty kings, possibly Weserkaf and Neferirkare. An inscription at the entrance to her tomb described her as 'the Mother of Two Kings of Upper and Lower Egypt'. The identity of her husband is not known but he may have been a high priest of Heliopolis.

Although some scholars attribute two tombs to her, one at Giza, near her father and another at Abusir, it is now thought that there were two queens with this name who lived a generation apart. One is believed to have been the mother of Neferirkare and the other his wife. Lehner says they both appear to have ruled as kings in their own right.

Khent-kawes' tomb at Giza was in the form of a huge sarcophagus of limestone blocks set on a panelled podium. 'The tomb is more conspicuous than that of any other queen of the Fourth Dynasty.'[27]

The other tomb at Abusir took the form of a small pyramid.

Conclusion

During the Fourth Dynasty, the resources of the kingdom and the energies of the people were devoted to providing for the welfare of the god-king in this life and the next. In such a centralised system, the king's power was absolute and he was the focus of the cult of the sun god. There were signs towards the end of the dynasty of the waning influence of the priesthood of Heliopolis over royalty. However, by the Fifth Dynasty the priests of Re not only regained their former influence but acquired unprecedented authority.

Absolute power of god-king

Despite some minor dynastic problems, the Fourth Dynasty was a time of considerable economic and political stability. The evidence for this is the massive building projects that were carried out, particularly by Sneferu, Khufu, Khafre and Menkaure. All the greatest pyramids were built at this time and this would have been impossible under chaotic conditions. Never again would Egyptian kings build on such a monumental scale and with such technical precision.

Relative economic and political stability

The expertise of the architects and builders carried over to the artists and craftsmen who produced such objects as the elegantly simple furniture of Queen Hetepheres and the powerful diorite statue of Khafre.

Since art may be said to mirror the spirit of the age, the architecture and art of this period are the main sources of information for the lifestyle and beliefs of the Egyptian people.

Chapter review

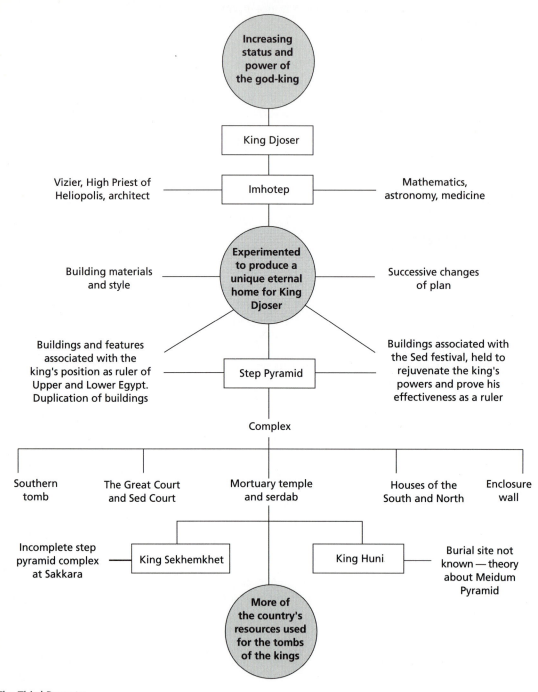

The Third Dynasty

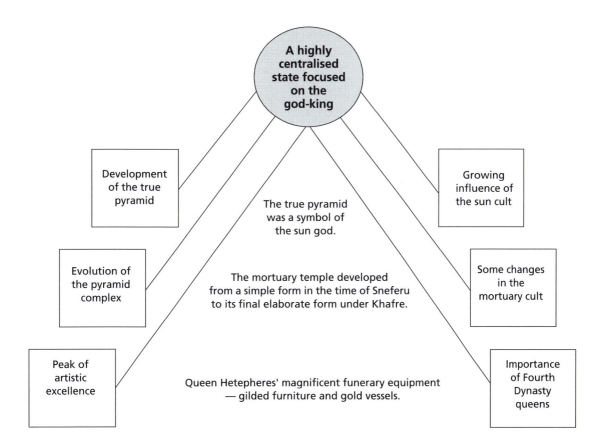

The Fourth Dynasty

REVISION QUESTIONS AND ESSAY TOPICS

1 Identify the architectural features of the Step Pyramid complex at Sakkara which are shown in the figures below.

(C)

(A)

(B)

a What do each of these photos reveal about building techniques during the Third Dynasty?

b What does each feature represent or what was its purpose?

2 Write a short answer (about one paragraph) to each of the following:

a For what accomplishments was Imhotep respected in later ages?

b What major changes in building techniques occurred during the Third Dynasty?

c What does the Step Pyramid complex indicate about the position of the king during the Third Dynasty?

d How did the Step Pyramid reflect Egyptian beliefs about the afterlife of a king at that time?

e Describe the successive changes of plan carried out by Imhotep in his construction of Djoser's tomb.

3 The photo below shows two gold vessels which were part of the funerary equipment found in the tomb of Queen Hetepheres.

a   Who was Queen Hetepheres?

b   Where was her funerary equipment discovered? Describe the tomb.

c   Explain why the sarcophagus and grave goods of such an important queen were buried in a makeshift tomb?

d   What other objects were found in the tomb?

e   What was the importance of this discovery?

4   **There is very little historical evidence for the personalities of the kings of the Fourth Dynasty and the events of their reigns.**

a   What is meant by historical evidence?

b   What are the main sources of information for the reigns of Sneferu, Khufu, Khafre and Menkaure?

c   What is known about the events of their reigns?

d   What was the view of the classical writer, Herodotus, of these kings?

e   Comment on the accuracy of Herodotus' view. Take into account:
  • when he lived
  • his sources
  • the values of his day.

5   **Study the plan below of the Giza necropolis and answer the following questions.**

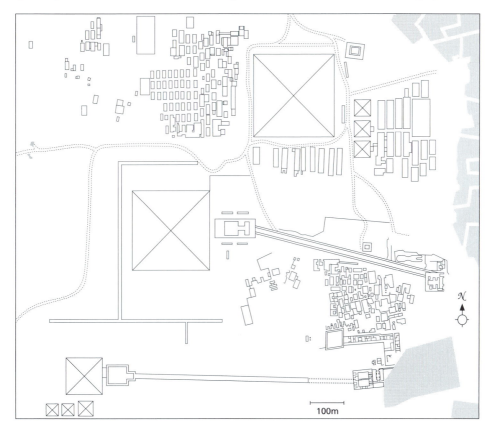

100m

Plan of the Giza necropolis

a Apart from the three main pyramids, what other features are shown on this plan of the Giza necropolis? For each feature identified:

- name the person or group for whom it was built
- describe its appearance and any unusual details
- explain its function.

b List the main features of the Great Pyramid — size, materials, architectural details inside and out.

c What was the significance of the pyramid shape?

d Why is the pyramid complex of Khafre of such interest to Egyptologists?

e What does this plan reveal about the position and status of Fourth Dynasty kings?

6 Essay topics

a Comment on Edwards' remark that 'it is certainly not an exaggeration to describe it (the Step Pyramid complex) as one of the most remarkable architectural works produced by the ancient Egyptians'.[28]

b What evidence do the massive pyramid complexes provide for archaeologists and historians about developments in the Fourth Dynasty?

CHAPTER
5

Religious and political changes

Sun temples and Pyramid Texts — the Fifth Dynasty

During the Fifth Dynasty (c. 2465–2323 BC), the priests at the cult centre of Heliopolis exerted an unprecedented influence over royalty. This was due to the enthusiasm exhibited by the kings of this dynasty for the cult of the sun god, Re. The kings adopted the title *Son of Re* as a more permanent part of their titulary and more rulers than previously included *re* as part of their official name.

There is evidence from the Palermo Stone that the Fifth Dynasty kings gave many gifts of land as well as abundant offerings to the sun god and its Heliopolitan priesthood. The kings built elaborate sun temples, while their own pyramid tombs were constructed of inferior materials. The contrast between the sun temples and the kings' pyramid complexes illustrates the decline in the absolutism of the king.

The Heliopolitan priesthood and the solar cult

In a land like Egypt where the sun was one of the two dominating forces of nature (the other being the Nile), it was natural for the people to worship the sun as a god. Solar (sun) worship had been practised throughout Egypt in one form or another since Predynastic times. Popular beliefs about the sun god varied from place to place as did the names by which the god was known and the way it was represented — Re, Atum, Kheper and Re-Horakhte.

Solar worship since Predynastic times

The Heliopolitan doctrine

The priests of the sun god at On or Heliopolis (the *city of the sun*) formulated the first state religion. They took the various popular beliefs

**First state religion
centred on Heliopolis**

about the sun and superimposed them one upon the other. They also amalgamated the various names for the sun god. By doing this they indicated to people throughout Egypt that the sun god they worshipped was the same as the one worshipped in the cult centre at Heliopolis.

The priests also very cleverly incorporated into their doctrine beliefs associated with the nature cult of Osiris which had originated in Busiris (the delta area) and then spread to Abydos (Upper Egypt). It was a very shrewd religious and political move to assimilate the gods of the Osiris cult into the Heliopolitan family of gods.

It was the usual practice throughout Egyptian history never to discard older ideas but rather to incorporate them with the new. In modifying the various interpretations of the sun worship into one doctrine and amalgamating the beliefs associated with Osiris with those of the sun, the priests were acting in the spirit of Egyptian tradition.

Each of the important cult centres throughout Egypt had its own version of the creation of the world in which its cult god played a major role. There were common features in all of these stories. One variant of the Heliopolitan version is described below:

> In the beginning there was nothing but a vast ocean or watery waste called Nun. Out of these waters of chaos emerged the primeval (first) hill or mound in the shape of the pyramidal stone or ben-ben which stood in the sanctuary of Heliopolis. It was on this mound that the god Atum-Re, by an act of will, created himself either in human form or in the shape of a bennu bird and brought light to the darkness. Atum-Re then created from himself other gods. He gave birth to his son, Shu, the god of air, by spitting him out and to his daughter, Tefnet, the goddess of moisture, by vomiting her up. This couple, Shu and Tefnet, created Nut, the sky-goddess and Geb, the earth-god. By placing himself between Nut and Geb, Shu separated the sky from the earth. The sky-goddess lowered herself onto Geb at night and together they created four children — Osiris, Seth, Isis and Nephthys. The gods ruled upon the earth and this was called the First Time. The temple of Atum-Re at Heliopolis was built at the place where the creator god first manifest himself. [1]

*A bennu bird alighting
on the ben-ben*

This group of nine gods is referred to as the Great Ennead of Heliopolis. Osiris and Isis had a son called Horus who founded another family of gods called the Small Ennead.

The political influence of the Heliopolitan priesthood

The temples at Heliopolis were among the most important and influential institutions in Egypt and the priests played a prominent role in shaping the country's religious and political history.

An educated elite

These priests were an educated elite. By studying the heavens as part of their worship, they developed a great understanding of astronomy and measurement. This knowledge, which was jealously guarded as part of the mysteries of their religion, was the basis of the great technological developments that took place during the previous two dynasties. However, their influence appears to have been threatened towards the end of the Fourth Dynasty by the priesthood of Ptah at Memphis. King Shepseskaf broke with the Heliopolitan tradition and the last king of the Fourth Dynasty included *ptah* as part of his name — Dedeptah.

It has been suggested that the priests of Heliopolis carried out an 'inspired, imaginative and successful campaign to boost their dwindling reputation'.⁽²⁾ According to a later text called the Westcar Papyrus, it was prophesied that the wife (Reddedet) of a priest of Heliopolis, impregnated by the sun god, would give birth to three sons who would rule Egypt as the first kings of a new dynasty. The first born of these *sons of the sun god* would also be the high priest of Heliopolis. Reddedet may be identified with Queen Khent-kawes, the mother of two kings of the Fifth Dynasty, Weserkaf (Userkaf) and Neferirkare.

Political campaign to increase power

The priests of Re also seem to have come to a compromise with the priests of Ptah. Prior to the Fifth Dynasty, kings usually appointed their viziers from among members of their own family. Those chosen were often already priests of Heliopolis. During the Fifth Dynasty, this practice ceased and viziers were selected from the leading noble families of Memphis, the cult centre of Ptah. It is interesting to note that five viziers of the Fifth Dynasty were named Ptahhotep and were buried at Sakkara while many of the kings they served were buried at Abusir, just south of Giza.

The following evidence points to the influence of the cult of the sun during the Fifth Dynasty.

- The practice, started in the Fourth Dynasty, of compounding *re* with the king's name, became the custom in the Fifth Dynasty. Some of the names of Fifth Dynasty kings were Sahu*re*, Neferirka*re*, Shepseska*re*, Nefere*fre*, Nuiser*re* and Djedka*re*-Isesi.

- The title *Son of Re* was permanently added to the king's titulary, being placed between the cartouches containing his throne name (praenomen) and birth name (nomen).

Hieroglyphic symbol meaning Son of Re

- Six of the Fifth Dynasty kings ordered the construction of elaborate sun temples at a site approximately eight kilometres south of Giza. These are believed to have been based on the plan of the temple of Atum-Re at Heliopolis. The contrast between these elaborate buildings and the pyramids of the king, indicates some weakening of the status of the king.

- From the remains of Weserkaf's pyramid complex it appears

that mortuary temples were now built to the south of the pyramid where they would receive sun all day.

- The *Pyramid Texts*, a collection of spells and prayers found in the chambers of the pyramid of Unas (Wenis), last of the Fifth Dynasty kings, mention only Re-Atum and the family of gods associated with the Heliopolis view of creation. There is no mention of Ptah of Memphis.

Pyramids and sun temples

During the Fifth Dynasty, the kings not only built their own pyramid complexes but constructed a new type of monument called a sun temple dedicated to their *father* the sun god. Gardiner suggests that because these kings could not hope to equal the magnificence of their predecessors' building activities, they chose a site some miles south of Giza for their pyramids (Abusir) and another site a short distance away for their sun temples (Abu Gurab). However, not all Fifth Dynasty kings built their pyramids at Abusir.

Sites

The first king and the last two kings of the dynasty — Weserkaf (Userkaf), Djedkare-Isesi and Unas (Wenis) — built their pyramid complexes at Sakkara, close to the Step Pyramid. Sahure, Neferirkare, Neferefre and Niuserre (Nyweserre) built theirs at Abusir between Giza and Sakkara.

Decline in workmanship

Although the pyramid complexes of the Fifth Dynasty kings followed the same pattern as their predecessors, their construction and materials were inferior. From the time of King Niuserre there was a further decline in the standard of workmanship. The pyramids were composed of a core of small stones with an outer casing of limestone and as a result most of them are today barely recognisable as pyramids.

Remains of the pyramid of Neferirkare at Abusir

All complexes had a satellite pyramid and a number of subsidiary pyramids for the queens. For the first time, during the reign of Djedkare-Isesi, a queen's pyramid included all the elements of a king's complex though on a reduced scale.

Despite their inferior construction, the pyramid complexes of the Fifth Dynasty included reliefs which 'surpassed in artistic magnificence anything which had previously been attempted'.[3]

Features of two Fifth Dynasty pyramid complexes

The complexes of Sahure and Unas have provided valuable evidence of events, aspects of royal life and religious changes. The complex of Sahure featured magnificent wall reliefs and an elaborate drainage system. The walls of Sahure's valley and mortuary temples and his causeway corridor were covered with thousands of square metres of reliefs cut into fine Tura limestone. The German archaeologists who originally excavated the pyramids of Abusir believed that there were over 10 000 metres of wall reliefs in Sahure's complex.

Sahure's fine wall reliefs

One of the subjects depicted time and again was the king triumphing in some form over his enemies, the Libyans and Asiatics. In one of these reliefs the king is shown killing a Libyan chief whose family appears to be pleading for mercy. It seems that during Sahure's reign many Libyan captives, including women and children, plus hundreds of thousands of cattle, sheep and asses were taken as booty.

These reliefs also provide evidence of trading connections with Syria or Palestine. The king and his officials are shown watching the departure of 12 sea-going vessels. In another relief the same expedition is welcomed back by the king. On board the ships are Asiatics who appear to be traders.

The architects of Sahure's pyramid complex devised a system of drainage for removing the occasional rain water and also for getting rid of the fluids used in temple rituals. The run-off from rain flowed into channels cut into the paving. Ritual liquids were collected in copper-lined basins. Beneath these basins were copper pipes which ran under the mortuary temple, the open enclosure and the causeway.

Advanced drainage system

Despite the fact that Unas' pyramid was the smallest of all the Old Kingdom pyramids, it included features of great importance to historians. These were:

Importance of the pyramid of Unas

- the decorated causeway connecting the pyramid with the valley temple
- the *Pyramid Texts* on the walls of the burial chamber.

Unas' 750-metre-long causeway is the best preserved of any from the Old Kingdom. It was originally designed as a covered way for the funeral procession of the king. The ceiling was painted blue with gold stars to represent the sky and the walls were brightly painted with a variety of detailed scenes which provide valuable information about this period.

The surviving fragments of wall decoration depict:

- boats transporting granite palm-tree columns along the Nile from the quarries at Aswan

- craftsmen making objects of gold and silver

**Evidence of
Unas' reign**

- labourers carrying out gathering and harvesting activities on the king's estates

- wild animals being hunted in the desert

- servants bringing goods to the king's tomb

- emaciated victims of famine. This is a very interesting fragment because kings usually depicted only those events or activities which they wanted remembered forever. It is probable that King Unas provided relief for these starving people.

Remains of the covered roof of Unas' causeway

The Pyramid Texts

Unas' burial chamber was the first to be decorated since the tomb of Djoser. Immediately around the king's black basalt sarcophagus, the walls were covered with alabaster and this was carved and painted to represent an archaic divine reed shrine open to the sky. Like his causeway, the roof of the burial chamber was covered with gold stars on a blue background.

However, the most significant feature of this chamber and adjacent corridors is the collection of 283 spells, prayers and utterances called the *Pyramid Texts* which were carved into the white alabaster and limestone walls. The hieroglyphic images were filled with blue paint to make them stand out more clearly.

Such texts were not found in any previous pyramid but were a feature of all pyramids of the Sixth Dynasty. For this reason it has been suggested that perhaps Unas was the first king of the Sixth Dynasty rather than the last king of the Fifth.

From the pyramids of the kings and queens of these two dynasties, a total of 759 spells have been identified, although no one pyramid contains all texts. These texts form the oldest surviving Egyptian religious and funerary literature.

Oldest religious literature

The Egyptians believed in the power and magic of the written word — that thoughts expressed in the written form could become real. It was believed that these texts, by their power and magic, would assist the kings and queens to pass safely into the next life and ensure their continued enjoyment of eternal life. For example, if the written spell said:

Magical power of the written word

> Rise up, O [King's name]!
> Take your head
> Collect your bones,
> gather your limbs,
> Shake the earth from your flesh![4]

then the Egyptians believed that the king would be resurrected with his body intact.

If the text said:

> Nut, your mother, spreads herself above you,
> She conceals you from all evil
> Nut protects you from all evil
> You, the greatest of her children![5]

then the king would be protected on his journey to the afterlife.

The Egyptians believed that the written word could also harm as well as protect. For this reason, the priests and sculptors who carved these spells on the walls took certain precautions. Because some of the hieroglyphic signs were symbols of potentially dangerous entities (snakes, scorpions, lions and humans), the images were drawn as though unfinished to render them harmless. For example:

- The image of a snake might be drawn as if cut in two, a scorpion might be depicted without its tail and a man or wild animal might be represented without limbs.
- Some animals were depicted with a line drawn through their body or had their hindquarters covered with plaster.

Pyramid Texts and ceiling decoration of Unas' burial chamber

Such signs are referred to as mutilated hieroglyphs.

It has been suggested that the *Pyramid Texts* may have formed part of the incantations spoken by the priests during the various stages of the funeral procession. Perhaps the kings of the late Old Kingdom wanted to make doubly sure of a happy afterlife by having the same spells and prayers written on the walls of their burial chambers.

Origin in distant past

Although these spells and prayers first appeared in the written form during the late Fifth Dynasty, their origin appears to have been in the distant past. Some of the utterances describe ancient funerary beliefs and practices which no longer applied in the Fifth and Sixth dynasties. Some examples are shown in the table below.

The Pyramid Texts	
An amalgamation of Pre-dynastic and Dynastic religious funerary spells	
Very ancient spells (nos 273–4)	References to the king as a hunter who catches and eats the gods in order to acquire their attributes.
A Predynastic spell (no. 662)	Reference to a time when royalty were buried in graves dug in the sand.
An early Dynastic spell (no. 355)	References to royalty buried in brick mastabas.
Third Dynasty spells (nos 267 and 619)	Reference to the Step Pyramid as a stairway to heaven.
Later Old Kingdom spells (nos 508 and 599)	References to the pyramid ramp on which to mount to heaven and to the enduring nature of the pyramid shape.

Edwards suggests that because of the constant references to the solar cult in the *Pyramid Texts*, they were very likely the work of the priests of Heliopolis. It is believed that at some stage in the Fifth Dynasty, the priests made a collection of old religious and funerary spells and prayers to which they added new incantations. The later spells referred to practices which had been adopted during the Pyramid Age.

Sun temples

Niuserre's sun temple

Six of the nine Fifth Dynasty kings built sun temples, although only two have been found. That of King Niuserre is the only one preserved well enough to give some idea of the layout of these temples to Re.

The evidence suggests that the sun temples served both a religious and economic purpose. Reliefs found in a long narrow chamber of Niuserre's temple, called the Room of the Seasons, portrayed all the activities during the Egyptian year. Aldred suggests this was like 'a visual hymn of praise to the sun god for all his bounty'.[6] This might support the view that:

> The power derived from the communion of god and king in the sun temple enabled the king to guarantee the welfare of the whole land and the proper functioning of everything connected with it.[7]

Religious purpose

An alabaster basin in the court of Niuserre's sun temple, used either for the collection of blood or for purification

Fragments of papyri from the reign of Neferirkare, called the Abusir Papyri indicate that the sun temples served a practical purpose as well as a religious one. It appears that the staff of the sun temples were responsible for delivering provisions (the joints of an ox, three kinds of bread and beer) twice daily to the king's mortuary temple. These offerings were later divided up between temple personnel.

Practical purpose

Every day at least one ox was killed in the temple slaughterhouse as an offering to the deceased king. Large alabaster basins sunk into the ground in the temple precinct were once believed to be for the collection of the blood of the slaughtered animals. However, Verner doubts that this was the site of the temple abattoir because there were no remains of animal bones nor of knives and other implements needed for the slaughtering of animals. He suggest that the animals were slaughtered elsewhere.

It is highly likely that granaries, bakehouses and breweries were part of the sun temple complex also.

Features of the sun temple

It appears that each sun temple had a name such as *Horizon of Re, Field of Re* and *Pleasure of Re* had elements in common with pyramid complexes. The labelled reconstruction below shows the main architectural features of the complex.

About the time of King Nuiserre, there was a decline in the dominance of Re. Niuserre's successor, Menkauhor, was the last Fifth Dynasty king to build a sun temple.

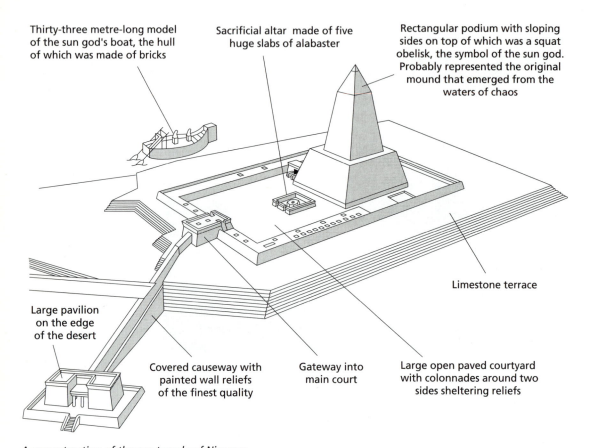

Thirty-three metre-long model of the sun god's boat, the hull of which was made of bricks

Sacrificial altar made of five huge slabs of alabaster

Rectangular podium with sloping sides on top of which was a squat obelisk, the symbol of the sun god. Probably represented the original mound that emerged from the waters of chaos

Limestone terrace

Large pavilion on the edge of the desert

Covered causeway with painted wall reliefs of the finest quality

Gateway into main court

Large open paved courtyard with colonnades around two sides sheltering reliefs

A reconstruction of the sun temple of Niuserre

Remains of the alabaster altar in the court of Niuserre's sun temple

The growing independence of the nobles — the Sixth Dynasty

There are discrepancies in the king lists for this period. Manetho, the Turin Canon and the Abydos King List vary considerably with regard to the names of the kings and the lengths of their reigns. Some details are known about events during the rule of Teti I, Pepi I, Merenre and Pepi II from the tomb biographies of their officials, but the period at the end of Pepi II's reign is very hazy.

The following table summarises some of the events that occurred during the reigns of these kings (c. 2323–2150 BC).

King	Reign	Events
Teti I	30 years?	Not much is known about his reign. His queen was Iput, whose pyramid was close to his at Sakkara
		Issued a charter of immunity to the dependents of a temple in Abydos, exempting them from taxation and other onerous tasks.
		Believed to have been assassinated by a bodyguard.
Weserkare	?	?
Pepi I	53 years?	Developed trading links with Lebanon and east Africa.
		Ordered a number of military campaigns against rebellious Sand-dwellers to the north-east, perhaps as far as Palestine.
		Celebrated a *Sed* festival.
		Married the two daughters of a local hereditary noble named Khui from Abydos.
		Dealt with a number of palace conspiracies against his rule.
Merenre	7–10 years?	Sent many expeditions to East Africa for ivory, ebony, animal skins and incense.
Pepi II	Over 90 years?	Came to the throne as a child of six. His mother ruled as regent until he came of age.
		Celebrated at least two *Sed* festivals.
		Issued a charter of immunity to the dependants of a temple in Coptos. The generosity of the king contributed to the depletion of his revenue.
		Had some problems with tribes in Nubia.
		Built the largest pyramid complex of the Sixth Dynasty.
Merenre II	c.1 year	As the son of Pepi I he was an old man when he came to the throne.

There is evidence that this dynasty was marked by:

* some political instability
* shortfalls in revenue
* the growing independence of the provincial nobles.

Political instability and shortfalls in royal revenues

Power struggles

There are some indications of a number of power struggles during this period. For example:

* Manetho mentioned that Teti I was assassinated by his own bodyguard.
* The fragmentary records of Weserkare indicate that they were deliberately damaged.
* During the reign of Pepi I there was at least one palace conspiracy involving a queen and possibly a vizier (refer to the tomb biography of Weni later in this chapter).
* A possible co-regency between Pepi I and his son, Merenre, to secure succession to the throne, suggests that there may have been threats to his position.
* The extremely short reigns of Pepi II's successors indicate a possible struggle for power at the end of the dynasty.

Decrease in royal revenues

Predecessors' extravagances

The physical resources needed to construct the pyramid complexes of the Fourth Dynasty and the elaborate sun temples of the Fifth Dynasty contributed to the depletion of the state's revenue in the Sixth. Also, from the Fourth to the Sixth dynasties, kings rewarded their loyal courtiers with gifts of tombs, funerary items and valuable areas of land from the royal estates. Because much of this land was exempt from taxation, the total area from which the king could raise revenue was gradually reduced.

Exemptions from taxation

The records show that a number of Sixth Dynasty pharaohs issued decrees which exempted certain temples and their priesthoods from contributing to the royal revenue. Other groups were exempt from working on the king's behalf. For example, Pepi I issued a decree which stated:

> My majesty has commanded the exemption of this chapel (of Queen-mother Iput) and [what belongs to it] in serfs and large and small cattle. [There is no] claim [whatever against it]. As to any commissioner who shall travel south on any mission, my majesty does not permit him to charge any travel expenses to the chapel. Nor does my majesty permit to supply the royal retinue. For my majesty has commanded the exemption of this chapel.[8]

The population of two agricultural villages that had contributed income and labour during the building of the two pyramids of Sneferu in the Fourth Dynasty were exempted forever from any further demands from royalty. The decree stated:

> My majesty has commanded that these two pyramid-towns be exempt for him in the course of eternity from doing any work of the Palace, from doing any forced labour for any part of the royal Residence, or from doing any corvee (forced public service, such as clearing canals, building and so on) at the word of anybody in the course of eternity.[9]

Wilson, in *The Culture of Ancient Egypt*, maintains that the kings inadvertently damaged the economy of Egypt by issuing these charters of immunity in order to win the support of powerful groups (refer to Chapter 6).

As the amount of revenue available was reduced, no longer did the pyramid tombs of the kings soar above the mastabas of their nobles and officials. Previous rulers had exploited the resources of Egypt to such an extent that Sixth Dynasty kings were forced to use inferior building materials and cheaper techniques.

Poorly constructed pyramids

The remains of a Sixth Dynasty pyramid at Sakkara with the Third Dynasty Step Pyramid in the background

The pyramids at Sakkara are in a dilapidated condition today because of their poor construction. Their core was made from small blocks of coarse local limestone and rubble, with a facing of finer limestone. However, the walls of the burial chambers of kings and queens were inscribed with Pyramid Texts. Perhaps as the absolute power of the kings declined they felt the need for written spells and prayers to help them safely reach the afterlife.

The growing independence of the nobility

Changes in administration

By the Sixth Dynasty, the king's nobles 'had discovered their powers through the business of setting up and extending the Egyptian state'. [10]

Importance of provincial centres

A number of developments within the bureaucracy took place in the late Fifth and Sixth dynasties. Administration of the provinces was not carried out solely from the capital of Memphis but increasingly from provincial centres such as Abydos, Akhmin, Dendera, Edfu and Elephantine.

Before the Fifth and Sixth dynasties, local governors or nomarchs* and other provincial officials, had been appointed by the king. However, gradually their positions became hereditary and as members of their families inherited the title and position, they became more powerful. Even though they were still subordinate to the king and stressed their loyalty to him, their tomb inscriptions reveal 'an unaccustomed absence of servility in their relationship with the king'. [11]

In response to this development the king had men appointed who acted as overseers of these provincial nobles. They were given titles such as *governor* or *overseer of the south* or *overseer of Upper Egypt*. The kings also appointed two viziers, one stationed in Upper Egypt and responsible for the administration in the southern regions. The other worked from Memphis.

Gradual decentralisation

Although the kings rewarded the achievements of particular nobles with lands and titles, it is possible that some of their generosity was aimed at retaining the loyalty of the powerful men in the nomes. There was a gradual shift of power from the capital to the provinces (decentralisation). This is seen in the number of official tombs built in provincial cemeteries.

By the end of the dynasty the provincial nobles took the opportunity to set themselves up as independent rulers and tried to shake off the control of the weakened central government.

Location and size of tombs

It had always been the ambition of high officials to be buried alongside their king or at least buried in the same necropolis, but as many of them became more self-confident, they no longer believed this was necessary.

Sakkara tombs of Mereruka and Kagemeni

Some Sixth Dynasty nobles, such as Mereruka, the son-in-law of Teti I and Kagemeni, the vizier, still chose to be buried at Sakkara close to their ruler. Their tombs were large and elaborate and indicated their great wealth. For example, Mereruka's tomb (see Chapter 7) had 33 chambers and corridors while Kagemeni's may have been two-storey. There is evidence that Kagemeni's mastaba included two rooms, each over ten metres long, specifically to house funerary barges.

* A nome was an administrative area like a province.

However, during this period many provincial nobles chose to be buried in their own districts (Zawyet el Amwat, Mer, Akhmin, Dendera, Edfu and Aswan) rather than near the tombs of the kings at Sakkara. This was the beginning of a trend towards political, social and economic decentralisation.

Provincial cemeteries

The powerful officials who worked on the king's behalf in the frontier area around Aswan, cut elaborate tombs into the faces of the cliffs overlooking the river. These provincial officials, working so far from the capital of Memphis, had great responsibility over their districts and were encouraged to use their initiative. They proudly recorded their achievements in the service of the king.

**Rock-cut tombs
at Aswan**

The autobiographical texts in their tombs show that many of them were more than just administrators — some were warriors and explorers. The most famous of these officials were Weni, Harkhuf and Mekhu, all of whom had the title *overseer* or *governor of the south*. Weni's career, which was inscribed on a limestone slab in the wall of a small chapel at Abydos, spanned the reigns of Teti I, Pepi I and Merenre. Harkhuf's record of service was carved into the facade of his tomb at Aswan. He served under Merenre and Pepi II.

The size, location, reliefs and texts of these tombs provide evidence for:

- the wealth of the king's high officials in comparison to lesser officials
- the growing power and independence of the provincial governors
- events at court
- the trading and quarrying expeditions, building activities and military campaigns carried out on behalf of the kings and the honours that the rulers bestowed on their officials.

The officials who brought back exotic and rare products as well as captives were richly rewarded for their efforts, although some of them lost their lives in the service of their king.

*The facade of the rock-cut tomb
of Harkhuf in the cliffs at Aswan*

Tomb biographies of Sixth Dynasty officials

Weni

Weni's career began during the reign of Teti I when he became 'a custodian of the storehouse'.[12] Under the rule of Pepi I, Weni was made 'senior warden of Nekhen'[13] and was given responsibility for hearing cases in secret, particularly those things which concerned the royal harem. 'When there was a secret charge in the royal harem against Queen Weret-yamtes',[14] Weni was sent alone to investigate because the king trusted him.

A military commander

In a campaign which the king ordered against the Asiatic 'Sand-dwellers' (nomadic desert tribesmen or Bedouin), Weni was appointed as commander of a huge army composed of 'many tens of thousands from all of Upper Egypt ... from Lower Egypt'[15] and from Nubia. Although the army included officials with a higher status than Weni, such as 'counts, seal-bearers, sole companions of the palace, chieftains and mayors of towns, chief priests',[16] the king chose Weni as overall commander. He was apparently appointed because of his ability to negotiate and discipline the troops.

The tomb of Merenre with his black granite sarcophagus, quarried under the supervision of Weni

It is apparent that Pepi I was faced with a number of rebellions among the Sand-dwellers because Weni led an army against them five times. On one occasion he carried out a strategy which involved ferrying half his troops by boat and attacking the enemy from behind, while the other half of his troops made a frontal attack by land. He 'caught them all and slew every marauder among them'.[17]

Under the leadership of King Merenre, Weni was made 'Count and Governor of Upper Egypt from Yebu in the south to Medenyt in the north'.[18] He maintained peaceful conditions on the frontier, keeping the neighbouring Nubian tribesmen in check and was diligent in looking after the king's revenue. It is recorded in his tomb that in one year he collected twice as much as normal.

Governor of Upper Egypt

Weni was dispatched to a number of quarrying regions in Upper and Middle Egypt to supervise the cutting of Merenre's black granite sarcophagus, a false door and libation stone for the king's chapel, granite lintels for the doorways and a huge alabaster altar. These tasks were far from easy. For example, the granite sarcophagus and parts of the king's mortuary chapel had to be transported to the pyramid 'in six barges and three tow-boats of eight ribs in a single expedition'.[19] To ferry the alabaster altar from Hatnub in Middle Egypt Weni built a barge 'of acacia wood of sixty cubits in length and thirty cubits in width' (about 30 metres long and 15 metres wide).[20] This was achieved in 17 days in the middle of summer when the river level was very low.

Supervisor of mining expeditions

Harkhuf

Harkhuf, who was Governor of the South during the reigns of Merenre and Pepi II, led four major exploratory and trading expeditions into Nubia. In his tomb high in the cliffs west of Aswan he described himself as 'Chief of scouts'[21] and caravan conductor.

Explorer in Nubia

The lands to the south of the First Cataract were rich in products such as gold, ebony, ivory, animal skins and incense. These were in great demand by the pharaohs. Harkhuf and his father, Iri, were sent by Merenre to Yam (believed to be the area south of the Second Cataract) to 'open the way to that country'.[22] He did this in seven months, bringing back 'all kinds of beautiful and rare gifts'.[23] His second expedition, to Irtjet, took eight months and again he returned with huge quantities of exotic goods.

During his third expedition, Harkhuf travelled westward to unexplored areas along the *Oasis Road*. This was also known as the *Elephant* or *Ivory Road* and may be the same route used today for transporting camels from the Sudan to the markets in Egypt.

When Harkhuf found that the ruler of Yam had gone off to fight the Tjemeh to the west, he went after him and became involved in the fighting. The ruler of Yam was so appreciative of his help that he provided Harkhuf with an escort of troops for his return journey through the lands of Irtjet, Setju and Wawat. When the chief of this confederacy saw the size of the army with Harkhuf he gave him cattle and sheep and showed him the way over the mountains. From this expedition Harkhuf

Exotic products brought back by Harkhuf

returned with 'three hundred donkeys laden with incense, ebony, oil, panther skins, elephants' tusks throw sticks and all sorts of good things'. (24) When he reached Egypt, the king sent his 'master of the cool rooms' (25) by boat to greet Harkhuf and provide him and his men with date wine, cakes, bread and beer.

Harkhuf's fourth expedition was carried out during the reign of Pepi II. The king was still a child at this time and when he heard that Harkhuf was bringing back a dancing pygmy, he was so excited that he wrote him a letter. Pepi promised Harkhuf 'many worthy honours for the benefit of your son's son for all time'(26) if he delivered the dancing pygmy to him sound and well. The king instructed Harkhuf to protect his prize by ordering 'worthy men to be around him on deck, lest he fall into the water', to guard his tent at all times and 'inspect him ten times at night'.(27) Receiving this letter from the child-king was the highlight of Harkhuf's life. He was so delighted with it that he had it inscribed on the facade of his tomb.

Mekhu and Sabni

Held in high regard by Pepi II

These two noblemen were father and son and were buried side by side at Aswan. Mekhu was governor of the south under Pepi II but was attacked and killed by desert tribesmen while on an expedition for the king in lower Nubia. Sabni, his son, travelled to Nubia to recover his father's body and punish his murderers. Pepi II held Mekhu in such high regard that he sent royal embalmers and mortuary priests to Elephantine with special linen and oils for the mummification. After his father was buried, Sabni travelled to the capital of Memphis to hand over the products collected by Mekhu during his ill-fated expedition.

Pepinakht

Military expeditions to Nubia and Red Sea coast

Pepinakht was another nobleman from Elephantine who led several military campaigns into Nubia to suppress rebellions. He brought back captives, including the children of chieftains who were to be used as hostages. On one occasion he returned with two Nubian rulers in order to negotiate a peaceful settlement.

The inscription in the tomb of Pepinakht also records how he was sent to the Red Sea coast to punish local tribesmen for killing a group of Egyptians. The murdered men had been building a boat on the Red Sea coast in preparation for a trading expedition to the Land of Punt. Pepinakht retaliated by killing large numbers of Sand-dwellers.

Conclusion

During the Fifth Dynasty there was 'a weakening of the kingship through priestly collaboration with the throne'.(28) The *Pyramid Texts*, which are one example of the influence of the priests of Heliopolis at this time, are a major source for understanding Egyptian funerary beliefs and burial practices during the Old Kingdom.

The Sixth Dynasty saw 'the provinces [come] into ever greater prominence'.[29] Although the kings of this period do not appear to have been weak men, the absolute power of the kingship declined in comparison with that of the hereditary provincial nobles. Problems at court increased after the death of the incredibly long-lived Pepi II and economic conditions continued to worsen.

The collapse of the Old Kingdom

At the end of the reign of Pepi II, Egypt experienced a long period of decline. The following factors have been suggested as possible reasons why the Old Kingdom collapsed.

A decline in economic conditions

The massive pyramid complexes of the Fourth Dynasty kings, Sneferu, Khufu, Khafre and Menkaure and the elaborate sun temples of the Fifth Dynasty used up vast amounts of resources. The size and workmanship of the pyramids of the Fifth and Sixth dynasty kings are evidence of the tremendous strain placed on the nation's resources by the building activities of the previous dynasty. Kings of the Sixth Dynasty granted perpetual endowments of land from the royal estates and charters of immunity from taxation.

Excessive use of resources

Foreign trade was disrupted by rebellions in Nubia and a threat to the Egyptian merchant colony at Byblos (Lebanon). The decline in foreign goods coming into the country also affected the kings' revenue.

Decline in foreign trade

It has been suggested that about 2350 BC Egypt began to experience drier conditions. This may have been the result of a change in the pattern of climate in Ethiopia — the monsoons may not have brought the usual heavy rains. A reduction in the rainfall in east Africa over a period of time would have caused a series of disastrously low Niles. Associated with the lack of adequate water supplies would have been dust storms and the encroachment of the desert into the areas of cultivation. There had obviously been some low Niles at the time of Unas because his causeway was decorated with reliefs showing starving people. The changing climatic conditions may have grown progressively worse.

Lack of rain and a series of low Niles

A gradual decline in the prestige and status of the kings from the Fourth Dynasty

The unprecedented patronage of the cult of Re by the rulers of the Fifth Dynasty allowed the solar priests to increase their influence at the expense of the kings.

During the Fifth Dynasty, the chief posts in the administration and provincial governorships became hereditary positions. The bureaucracy became increasingly independent and filled with men who no longer owed their positions to the king and no longer felt the need to be buried alongside the king.

Independence of bureaucracy

Foreign trade was a royal monopoly and when this declined the king's prestige suffered.

The king's prestige suffered as he failed to fulfil his duties to the people

As the climate became drier throughout Egypt, the kings were unable to fulfil their responsibilities to their subjects. One of the roles of the god-king was to maintain the prosperity of Egypt. This involved 'controlling' the flow of the Nile and ensuring the fertility of the soil.

If the god-king could no longer carry out his divine responsibilities on behalf of the nation, the whole economic and political system would collapse. In the period immediately after the death of Pepi II, the kings, unable to restore prosperity to the land, reigned for only short periods before being replaced.

Chapter review

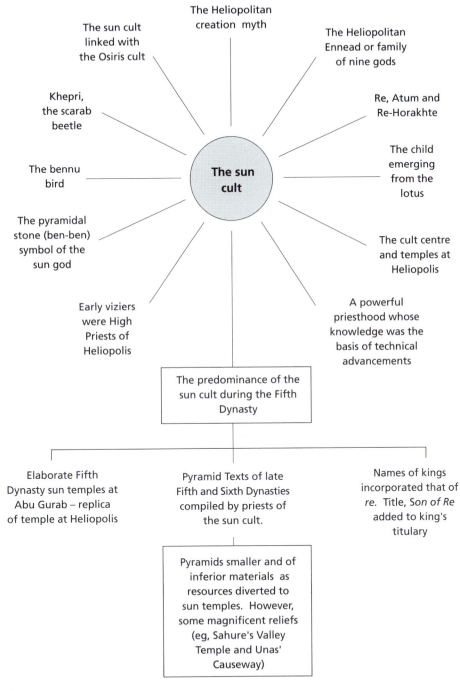

The Fifth Dynasty

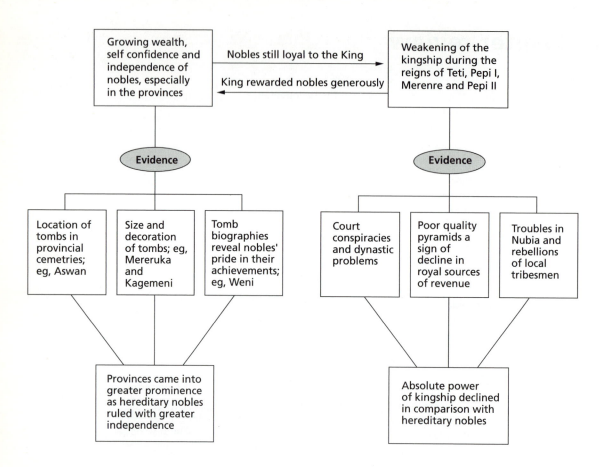

The Sixth Dynasty

REVISION QUESTIONS AND ESSAY TOPICS

1 Look carefully at the archaeological remains shown in the photos below and answer the questions associated with each one.

a What part of Unas' pyramid complex is shown in the next photo?

b What would it have originally looked like?

c What purpose did this feature serve?

d Why are the remains of this part of Unas' complex so valuable to historians?

e Identify the features shown in the two photographs below.

f Where would these have been found?

g Why was the discovery of these of great importance to historians?

h Explain why Fifth Dynasty pyramids are not much more than mounds of rubble today when the pyramids of their predecessors of the Fourth Dynasty are still in such magnificent condition.

A Fifth Dynasty pyramid

2 Identify the object shown in the figure below.

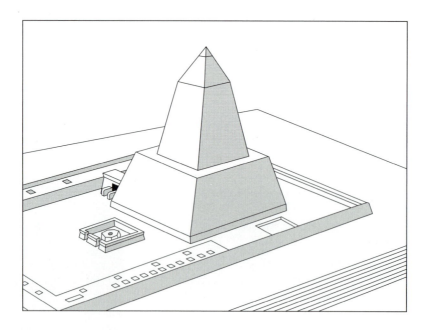

a   What was the significance of this feature in the sun temple?

b   What did the ben-ben symbolically represent?

c   What is thought to have been the main purpose of the Fifth Dynasty sun temples?

d   What other functions were carried out there? What evidence is there for these functions?

3 The following extracts from the *Pyramid Texts* provide evidence of the importance of the sun cult during the Fifth Dynasty. Read these extracts carefully and then answer the questions underneath.

Utterance 217

Re-Atum, this Unas comes to you,
A spirit indestructible
Who lays claim to the place of the four pillars
Your son comes to you,
May you cross the sky united in the dark,
May you rise in lightland, the place in which you shine!
...Seth, Nephthys, go proclaim to Upper Egypt's gods
And their spirits:
'This Unas comes, a spirit indestructible, ...'
Osiris, Isis, go proclaim to Lower Egypt's gods
And their spirits:
'This Unas comes, a spirit indestructible, ...'
Re-Atum, your son comes to you,
Unas comes to you,
Raise him to you, hold him in your arms,
He is your son of your body, forever. [30]

Utterance 253

Hand of Unas in hand of Re!
O Nut, take his hand!
O Shu, lift him up! [31]

Utterance 263

The sky's reed-floats (rafts) are launched for Unas
That he may cross on them to Lightland, to Re;
The sky's reed-floats are launched for Unas
That he may cross on them to Horakhte, to Re. [32]

Utterance 273

Unas has risen as Great One, as master of servants,
He will sit with his back to Geb, ... [33]

a What is an ennead? Which members of the ennead of gods, in the Heliopolis version of the creation myth, are mentioned in these extracts?

b Which of the various names referring to the sun god are used in these extracts?

c Explain how the quote 'Re-Atum your son comes to you ... he is your son, of your body forever', relates to a prophecy supposedly made by the priests of Heliopolis in an attempt to increase their influence with the kings of the Fifth Dynasty.

d What additional title was added to a king's list of names and titles in the Fifth Dynasty?

e Explain in one sentence what these extracts indicate about the afterlife of the king.

f What is the importance of the Pyramid Texts to historians?

4 **The photo below shows the site of the Sixth Dynasty cliff tombs at Aswan.**

a   Who was buried in these Aswan cliff tombs?

b   How did these tombs at Aswan differ from those of the nobles Mereruka and Kagemeni at Sakkara?

c   What were some of the activities carried out on behalf of their king by the men buried in these Aswan tombs? Give some specific examples.

d   Why did they choose to be buried so far from their king?

5 **The following two extracts come from the tombs of Weni at Abydos and the nomarch of the Twelfth Nome of Hierakonopolis.**

Weni was senior warden of Nekhen at this stage in his career.

> When I begged of the majesty of my lord (Pepi I) that there be brought for me a sarcophagus of white stone from Tura, his majesty had a royal seal-bearer cross over with a company of sailors under his command to bring me this sarcophagus from Tura. It came with him in a great barge of the court, together with its lid, a doorway lintel, two doorjambs and a libation-table. Never before had the like been done for any servant — but I was excellent in his majesty's heart. [34]

The autobiography of the nomarch of Hierakonopolis:

> I claimed from King Pepi II the honour of obtaining a sarcophagus, funerary wrappings and oils for my father. I asked the king to make my father a prince and, and the king made him a prince and awarded him the Gift-which-the-King-gives. [35]

a   Which king was Weni serving at this time?

b   In what ways did the king show his gratitude to Weni?

c   Who or what was a nomarch?

d   What changes had occurred in the status of nomarchs from the Fifth Dynasty?

e   During whose reign did the nomarch of Hierakonopolis live?

f   What does the second extract reveal about the relationship between some provincial nobles and the king towards the end of the Sixth Dynasty?

g   How does his attitude differ from that expressed by Weni? Provide evidence from the extracts.

h   What were the most common royal gifts given to nobles?

i   Apart from rewards for good service what other reason may have prompted the kings to give so generously to the provincial nobles?

j   How might these rewards and gifts have contributed to the weakening of the king's position.

k   In what other ways did the Sixth Dynasty kings inadvertently weaken their own economic position?

6   Essay topics

a   Explain why the priesthood of Re-Atum at Heliopolis had a unique influence over the kings of the Old Kingdom. What evidence is there to suggest that their power increased substantially during the Fifth Dynasty?

b   Comment on Wilson's statement that 'there was a gradual weakening of the king's power through the advance of the independent authority of the nobles' and 'a progressive decentralisation away from the king'.[36]

c   Use the following diagram to explain why the Old Kingdom collapsed at the close of the Sixth Dynasty.

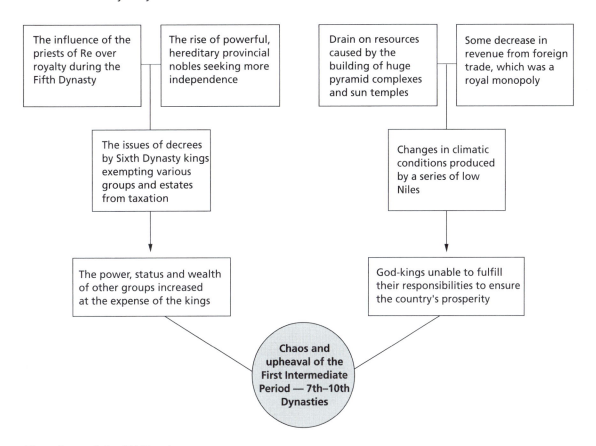

The collapse of the Old Kingdom

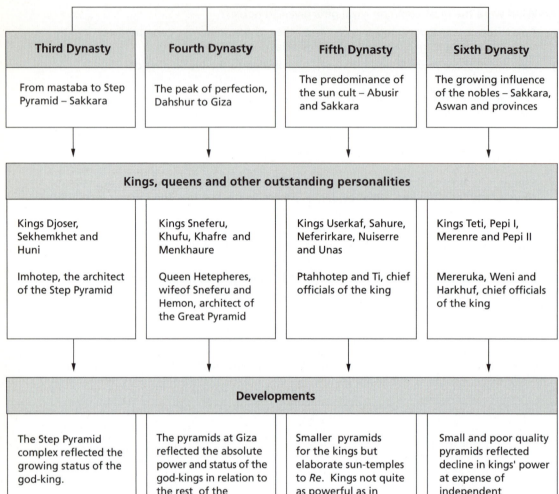

Third Dynasty	Fourth Dynasty	Fifth Dynasty	Sixth Dynasty
From mastaba to Step Pyramid – Sakkara	The peak of perfection, Dahshur to Giza	The predominance of the sun cult – Abusir and Sakkara	The growing influence of the nobles – Sakkara, Aswan and provinces

Kings, queens and other outstanding personalities

Kings Djoser, Sekhemkhet and Huni Imhotep, the architect of the Step Pyramid	Kings Sneferu, Khufu, Khafre and Menkhaure Queen Hetepheres, wifeof Sneferu and Hemon, architect of the Great Pyramid	Kings Userkaf, Sahure, Neferirkare, Nuiserre and Unas Ptahhotep and Ti, chief officials of the king	Kings Teti, Pepi I, Merenre and Pepi II Mereruka, Weni and Harkhuf, chief officials of the king

Developments

The Step Pyramid complex reflected the growing status of the god-king. Innovations in building techniques – first large construction in stone. The beginning of the growth of the sun cult – Imhotep, who designed the Step Pyramid was a high priest of the sun god at Heliopolis	The pyramids at Giza reflected the absolute power and status of the god-kings in relation to the rest of the population Great technological advancements in building Inceasing influence of the priests of the sun god, Re, over royalty The shape of the pyramid reflected the influence of Heliopolis .	Smaller pyramids for the kings but elaborate sun-temples to *Re*. Kings not quite as powerful as in previous dynasty Decline in standard of pyramid building The cult of Re was predominant and its priests very powerful. The kings were called the *Sons of Re* and the Pyramid Texts reflected the influence of the priests of Heliopolis	Small and poor quality pyramids reflected decline in kings' power at expense of independent and powerful nobles who built elaborate tombs Strain on resources during previous dynasties and decline in royal wealth due to exemptions from taxes for priests and nobles Pyramid Texts continued to be inscribed in the tombs of kings and queens

The Pyramid Age

The life of the king and his people

The structure of Old Kingdom society

The pyramids, with their brilliant capstones, soaring above the capital of Memphis and the necropolises at Sakkara and Giza, reflected the god-like status and absolute power of the king. The pyramid shape can also be used to represent the way Egyptian society was organised.

The god-king was the capstone, remote and isolated from his subjects. The bulk of the Egyptian people (the peasants) formed the broad base of the pyramid. Above the peasants ranged a variety of craftsmen, lesser officials, high-ranking officials to whom the king delegated his secular and religious powers and members of the royal family.

Egyptian society was hierarchical but not necessarily rigid. It was possible for a man of reasonably humble background to rise to a position of power, especially as the state grew and the king needed the services of more men of ability. Weni, who served under three kings, was one such official. However, it was the normal pattern for the son of a peasant to continue to carry out the tasks of a peasant and the son of an official, by the end of the Old Kingdom, to inherit his father's position.

The hierarchical nature of Egyptian society

The god-king

It is extremely difficult to appreciate the power and authority of the king during the Old Kingdom because he was regarded as divine. He was believed to be the earthly incarnation of the falcon god, Horus, the Son of Re, the sun god and to become Osiris when he died.

Since he was divine, even his relatives and closest officials had to follow strict rules of behaviour when they were in his presence. It is believed that they had to kiss the ground when approaching him. An Old Kingdom story tells how a prince, who was the king's son-in-law and the high priest of Ptah, was granted the great honour of kissing the king's sandal rather than the ground.

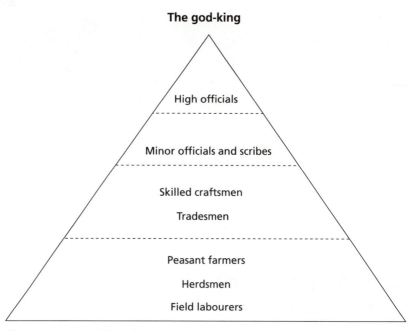

The organisation of Egyptian society

At no time was the king's personal name permitted to be used. The Egyptians believed in the power of the spoken word for good or evil. As it was possible to harm someone by speaking his name in a derogatory way, the people avoided using the king's name. During the Old Kingdom, when speaking of or referring to the king, his subjects used such terms as *Horus, the lord of the palace; His Majesty, my lord; The Great Double Hall* and *The Great House (Per' aa)*. Per' aa was the origin of the title *pharaoh* which was used to refer to the king during the New Kingdom.

The divine kingship was emphasised by:

- the many names and titles each king bore and the cartouche which always surrounded his name when carved or written
- the special regalia and insignia worn or carried by the king on official occasions
- the size and shape of his tomb which was a symbol of the sun god and the original mound of creation
- the representation of him in reliefs — towering above all others, symbolising the whole community in all activities, conducting rituals to the gods in all temples and smiting the enemies of Egypt.

The crowning of a king

It was important to all Egyptians that a new king should be crowned as soon as possible after the death of the previous ruler. The people believed that the king represented *ma'at* or right order in the universe and they feared that without a king on the throne chaos might prevail.

However, a king could not be crowned at just any time during the year. Each coronation was believed to represent the recreation of the world. It was timed to correspond to one of two important events in the agricultural cycle — the first day of the *Season of Inundation* when the Nile began to rise, or the first day of the *Season of Coming Forth* when the first seeds were sown.

Timing of the coronation

To protect the state until the previous ruler was embalmed and buried, the heir to the throne took control of the government immediately. In the meantime the priests of the *house of life* (a special place in the temple where books were written and interpretations made) began to prepare the titulary (names and titles) of the new king.

Before the previous king was buried, the heir to the throne, accompanied by royal princes, high officials and priests, travelled by royal barge to major cities throughout Egypt, presenting what has been called *The Mystery Play of Succession*. This was a mimed preview of the coronation in which all those accompanying the heir took part. Only when the heir had conducted the burial rites for his father, who had become Osiris, could he be crowned and take the throne as the living Horus.

Mystery play of succession

The coronation, which took five days, was held in the capital of Memphis and is believed to have followed the pattern set by Menes when he became the first king of a united Egypt. Since the king was the ruler of Upper and Lower Egypt, the rituals were repeated twice in two pavilions representing the primitive chapels of Predynastic times.

Before the coronation ceremonies proper, the king had to be purified by the priests who wore masks in the form of the various gods. This purification was carried out in a sacred pool in the temple enclosure. A high priest, in his leopard skin garment, invested the king with his royal powers and duties, by presenting him with the crowns and other sacred insignia.

Purification

The king wore the animal tail of an archaic chieftain, hanging from his belt. On the soles of his sandals were portrayed the enemies of Egypt. After leaving the sacred chapel he received his *great names*. The ceremonies ended with the *circuit of the White Walls* or a procession around the walls of Memphis.

Ceremonial regalia

The king's coronation was commemorated again during the Sed festival.

The Sed festival (heb-sed)

The most important ceremony in the king's life, apart from the coronation was the Sed festival or the king's jubilee. The reliefs and texts dealing with the Sed festival are the best sources for understanding the nature of Egyptian kingship since they illustrate the king's connections with the gods, the land of Egypt and the Egyptian people. The Sed festival, based on an ancient ritual, was celebrated as long as pharaohs ruled Egypt. Although there may have been some variations from one period to another, the basic format was always the same.

The Sed as evidence of Egyptian kingship

The Step Pyramid complex of King Djoser of the Third Dynasty is an important source of evidence for this festival — it incorporates a full-scale dummy of the festival court and buildings as well as reliefs of various Sed rituals. Refer to Chapter 4 for details about King Djoser and the Step Pyramid.

Purpose of the festival

There were two purposes for the celebration of this festival. They were:

1   to ritually rejuvenate the king's powers so that he could continue to rule effectively

2   to commemorate the king's accession to the throne by recreating the coronation ceremony.

It was celebrated after the king had been on the throne for a long time, usually 30 years. However, some kings during the New Kingdom held it earlier.

The origin of the festival

The festival was a very ancient one even in the days of King Djoser. It is believed that in primitive times when a ruler's powers appeared to be fading, he was expected to run a race over a fixed course in front of his subjects. This was a test of his prowess and was intended to show that he was still competent to rule. If he failed this test he was ceremonially put to death and replaced with a more vigorous leader. The Sed festival probably developed from this practice. Although the name *Sed* has not been satisfactorily explained, some scholars suggest that it meant *to slay* or *to slaughter*.

First Dynasty seals depicting this race have been found at Sakkara and are the earliest evidence of the Sed festival. By the Third Dynasty the *test* had developed from the running of a race to an elaborate five-day celebration.

Preparations

When the decision to hold a Sed festival was made, massive preparations were put into effect and officials and priests throughout the kingdom were notified well in advance.

Timing of the Sed festival

The jubilee could only begin on the first day of the *Season of Coming Forth* when the land, renewed by the flood, was prepared for planting. The festival symbolised the renewal of all the benefits given by the gods through the person of the king.

The celebrations took place in a huge complex of buildings specially prepared for the occasion.

Festival buildings

- A special area or hall (the festival hall), where the great throne stood, was constructed. Sometimes it was built within the enclosure of an existing temple but often a new temple was dedicated at this time.

- A building called the *palace* was erected to serve the king during the festival. It was where he changed his costume

and insignia and where he rested between
ceremonies. In later times this palace was
sometimes an elaborate structure but during
the Old Kingdom it was generally built in
simple Predynastic style.

- To accommodate the statues or standards of
  the gods who were brought from each part
  of the country, temporary shrines of reeds
  and matting had to be built. These were
  called *houses of the Sed festival* and were
  built on opposite sides of the *festival court*
  or the *court of the great ones* (the gods
  of the land).

  The shrines which housed the gods from
  Upper Egyptwere built on the eastern side
  of the court and resembled the primitive
  shrine of Nekhbet, patron goddess of that
  region. The shrines of the gods of Lower
  Egypt, on the western side, resembled
  the chapel of the goddess of Lower Egypt,
  Wadjet. In the court was a canopied dais
  on which two thrones stood back to back.

- An open area or *racecourse*, symbol of the land
  over which the king ruled, was set aside as well
  as an area to hold ceremonial banquets.

The buildings were then dedicated and purified.
During the *lighting of the flame* ceremony, the shrines,
the court and *great throne* were illuminated for five
days before the festival started.

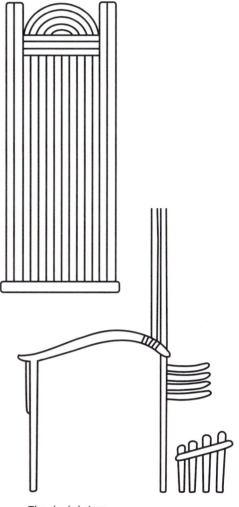

The dual shrines

Personnel involved

Although the ordinary people were not allowed to attend the festival
ceremonies in the temple precincts, they probably joined in the celebrations by lining the route from the harbour to the temple. In this way
they would at least see the arrival of the country's highest officials and
the statues of the gods which were brought from all over Egypt. They
might have been fortunate enough to catch a glimpse of the king and
his court as they met the more important of the kingdom's officials. It is
possible that the people participated in other ways but nothing is
known of this. Since the reliefs show figures called *subjects*, it is
believed that the people of Egypt were represented in some way.

It is difficult to know just what part the members of the administration,
such as the vizier, treasurer and so on, played in the celebrations since
the records refer to participants by primitive titles. These titles such as *the*   **Primitive titles**
herdsmen of Nekhen, the great ones of Upper and Lower Egypt and *chief*
of Pe probably disguise important members of the government. Royal
princes and kinsmen as well as priests also played an important role.

Foot-washing of King Nuiserre

Festival ceremonies

The festival opened with a great procession in which the king, the statues of the gods, priests and all officials took part.

Gifts from the king

Gifts from the king, in the form of cattle and sheep, were then dispensed to the priests of the various gods. These gifts emphasised the prosperity of the land for which the king was responsible, and the effectiveness of his rule. Two officials, with the titles *hereditary prince* and *master of the king's largess*, presided over this ceremony. The major gods also received individual gifts.

Visits to shrines

For the next two or three days the priests of the chief deities paid homage to the king and he in turn visited the shrines of the gods in the *court of the great ones*. Each of these solemn visits followed traditional forms with the king retiring to the *palace* to change his attire and insignia according to the purpose of the ritual.

> Thus, in a series of moves and countermoves, visits to shrines and demonstrations of loyalty before the throne are woven all the varied bonds which unite the realm and the ruler, the ruler and the gods. [1]

Re-enactment of coronation

A key part of the celebration was the re-enactment of the coronation. The king mounted the dais and as he sat on one throne he was crowned with the White Crown of Upper Egypt. He moved to the other throne and the ritual was repeated as he was crowned with the Red Crown of Lower Egypt. A parade of officials and deputations including ten chiefs from Upper Egypt and ten from Lower Egypt approached the throne to offer allegiance.

The most important ceremony was the *dedication of the field* which was the ritual race of primitive times. During this ritual the king *ran* a course (it may have been a brisk walk) over a rectangular piece of land which represented Egypt. He *ran* to the east, west, north and south of the field twice — once as the king of Upper Egypt, wearing the White Crown and once as the king of Lower Egypt, wearing the Red Crown.

A king being enthroned during the Sed festival

Ritual 'race'

For the race he wore the short royal kilt with the bull's tail attached, a special necklace and the appropriate crown. He carried a whip in one hand and a document, called *the Secret of the Two Partners* (Horus and Seth) or *the Will of My Father*, in the other. As he ran he chanted:

> I have run holding the Secret of the Two Partners, the will which my father has given me before Geb. I have passed through the land and touched its four sides: I run through it as I desire.[2]

The document was similar to a will and indicated that the god-king had inherited the land of Egypt. By running through the entire land (to each side of the rectangular field) with the document in his hand, the king took possession of his inheritance and reaffirmed his right to rule over Egypt. Reliefs of the king striding across the field with the document in his hand became the symbol of the entire Sed festival.

Nuiserre dedicating the field (the Sed race)

Concluding ceremony

The concluding ceremony was also carried out twice. The king was carried in a box-like litter to the chapel of a god of Lower Egypt where he was handed a crook, flail and welfare sceptre called the *was sceptre*. Two officials beside him proclaimed the king's power four times, thus ensuring the welfare of Egypt. Then he was taken in a basket-shaped litter to the shrine of a god of Upper Egypt where he was handed a bow and arrows. By shooting the arrows to the four points of the compass the king signified that the land of Egypt was protected.

Finally the king returned to the *court of the great ones* and gave an offering of ointment, linen, food and drink to the *royal ancestors*. This last act of the festival renewed the link between the king and the royal line.

Redford says of the Sed festival:

> no better means could be imagined to bring the nation together and to remind its citizens of the political system to which they owed their all.[3]

The king's official names

At the time of the First Dynasty the king had only one official name — the Horus name (see Chapter 3). As his power increased and political and religious changes occurred during the Old Kingdom, his list of titles and names grew until he had five *great names*.

Two of the king's names were enclosed in cartouches. These were:

- the name he was given when he was born
- the name he was given when he became king.

The Egyptians didn't think it fitting that a king should be known by the same common name he had when he was a prince, so he was given a special name when he came to the throne. His throne name and his individualised titulary were chosen by the priests in the *house of life*.

The five-part titulary expressed the Egyptians' concept of kingship.

The king's five great names

1   The king's first *great name* identified his aspect as the earthly incarnation of the god Horus.

2   The second name emphasised his double nature and was preceded by the *Two Ladies* or the goddesses representing Upper and Lower Egypt — the vulture goddess, Nekhbet and the cobra goddess, Wadjet.

3   The significance of the third name, the *Golden Horus* name is somewhat obscure but it probably expresses the divinity of the king. Gold which never decays may have represented the flesh of gods and kings as divine beings.

4   The fourth name was his throne or coronation name and was preceded by the title, *King of the South* (Upper Egypt) *and the North* (Lower Egypt), shown by the symbols of the sedge and the bee.

5   The final name was his solar name or that of his birth and was preceded by the term *Son of Re*. The figure below illustrates the

full titulary of an Egyptian king. Although the names and titles belong to a New Kingdom pharaoh, they show how these names were written.

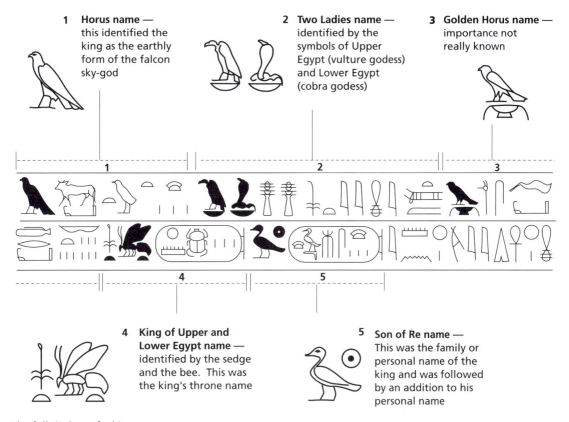

The full titulary of a king

The divine powers and responsibilities of the king

As the living incarnation of Horus and the son of Re, the king was the intermediary between the gods and the people of Egypt.

The few surviving documents (from the New Kingdom) describe the king as being the *ka* or life force of the nation, as maintaining *ma'at* or the right order of things and as having all the powers of the gods. He was believed to bring light to the land like Re, to make the land fertile with the life-giving aspects of Osiris, to defend Egypt against her enemies just as Bastet defended Re and to punish those who disobeyed him with the ferocity of the lion-headed goddess Sekhmet.

Egyptians believed the king embodied god-like qualities

The state (the land and its people) was his property and responsibility. He ruled it by *divine utterance*. What the king said was law, what he liked was justice and what he hated was what was wrong. All property, personal freedom, religious and secular powers, status and rank were transferred by him to others. The following diagram illustrates the divine powers and responsibilities of the king.

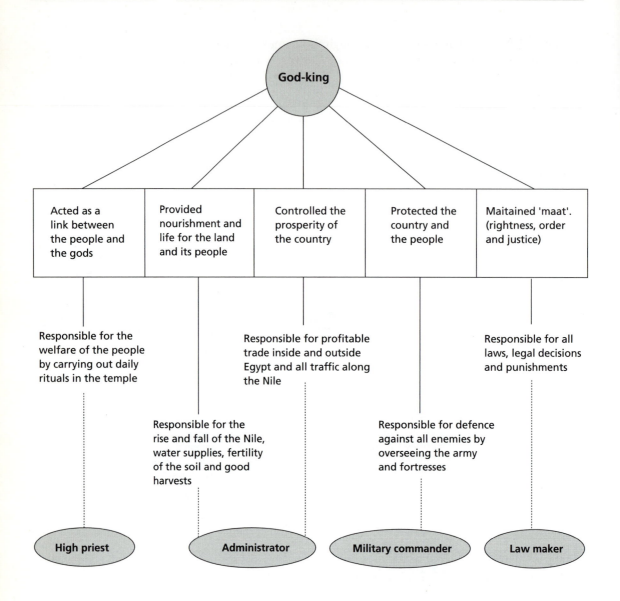

The divine powers of the king

The king as intermediary between the gods and the people

High priest

The most important role of the king was as high priest of every god in the land. In theory he was the only one entitled to enter the holy of holies and officiate at temple rituals in the chief cult centres throughout Egypt.

The king's chief function, to perform the daily ritual to every god, was delegated to others. The high priest of every cult temple became the king's representative and carried out the sacred rituals which were necessary if the right order of things, established at the time of creation, was to be maintained.

The king as chief judge, administrator and military commander

Although the king was the source of all justice and was responsible for the fertility, prosperity and defence of the land, he delegated these responsibilities to a number of very capable officials. These officials were at first recruited from the king's immediate family but as the tasks of administration increased, many non-royals held the positions of vizier, seal-bearers, treasurers, governors of the south and military leaders. These men were supported by an educated elite and numerous lesser officials.

Royal women

Very little is known about specific Old Kingdom queens but the size, location and contents of their tombs indicate that they had a high status and were regarded with great respect. Some of them were priestesses.

Those who were the mothers of kings were given special titles and during the Fourth and Fifth dynasties they were buried in small replicas of their husbands' pyramid tombs.

From the Pyramid Texts inscribed in their tombs it appears that they expected to spend eternity, like their husbands, with the gods.

A king in the costume of a god

Everyday life of royalty

Life at court during the Old Kingdom can only be deduced from the inscriptions found in the tombs of the king's officials whose titles indicate their responsibility to him. They recorded the duties they performed for their ruler and the honours he bestowed on them.

Since the king was regarded as a god, his day started with the same ritual that was carried out for every god throughout the land. He was:

- given a ritual bathing to restore his life force
- anointed with precious oils and clothed
- invested with the royal insignia by the priests
- accompanied to the temple to officiate at further ceremonies.

It is obvious from the titles of some of his courtiers that much time was spent attending to the person of the king. Some of the many personal attendants at court were *chief manicurist, chief pedicurist of the court, keeper of the royal robes, overseer of the cosmetic box, sandal-bearer of the king, director of music, wig-maker of the king, guardian of the royal jewels, chief court physician, physician of the belly, palace eye expert, chief of dental physicians* and *physician of the internal fluids*.

The king's personal attendants

Although the king was surrounded by officials and experts who attended to his every need and ran the state on his behalf, his own daily responsibilities were probably great. He would have spent part of the day in discussions with his vizier (second only to the king and often one of his own family). Other activities carried out on a more irregular basis might have included:

The king's duties

- receiving delegations
- consulting with his architects and inspecting major building works, particularly the stage of construction of his own pyramid
- attending festivals and temple dedications in major cities along the Nile
- making tours of inspection.

Like the members of the noble class, the king would have spent some time with his family. The king's chief wife was usually a member of the royal family. Since the king was a god it was important to keep the royal line pure so he was usually married, quite young, to someone very close to him such as a sister or half-sister. However, the king was not restricted to one wife. He had many lesser wives and large numbers of concubines, many of whom had children to him.

The women of the king's household lived in special apartments, usually in a restricted part of the palace. This was referred to as the harem. From time to time the harem was the source of palace intrigues and conspiracies as some royal women attempted to promote their own sons. This apparently occurred during the reign of Pepi I.

Harems – sources of possible conspiracies

However, generally the harem would have been a source of pleasure for the king. A story, referring to the reign of Sneferu, described how the king ordered 20 of the most beautiful young women in the palace to row, naked, up and down the lake in the palace grounds. Each maiden was given an oar of ebony, gold and silver and a fishing net. The old king's heart was gladdened by the site of these fresh young girls and their beautiful surroundings.

Apart from the time spent with his family and visits made to the harem, the king probably relaxed by listening to music, and watching dancers. The tomb of Harkhuf records how excited the young Pepi II was when he received word that the explorer, Harkhuf, was returning from one of his expeditions with a pygmy dancer. To Pepi, this present was worth more than all the other exotic gifts from the lands to the south.

Like the nobles, the kings enjoyed the exhilaration of hunting and trapping wild animals in the desert. Reliefs in the temple of the Fifth Dynasty king, Sahure, show him hunting wild animals such as gazelles and antelope.

There is almost nothing known about the life of royal women in the Old Kingdom. A wall painting in the tomb of a Fourth Dynasty queen, Meresankh II, shows the queen enjoying a boating expedition with her mother, Queen Hetepheres.

Royal dress

On normal occasions, the king probably dressed little differently from his high officials, wearing a variation of the pleated linen kilt. His jewellery, particularly his encrusted collars, was obviously more elaborate. On state occasions he would wear one of several crowns, an artificial beard, a wig, a leopard skin (insignia of a priest) or archaic animal tail, and carried the crook and flail, symbols of authority which involved persuasion and compulsion.

Royal women dressed in long, narrow linen sheaths and wore an abundance of bracelets and anklets. In the tomb of Queen Hetepheres, for example, was a box containing 20 silver inlaid bracelets.

Royal women boating, from the mastaba of Queen Merysankh

From the Pyramid Texts it seems that the king ate five meals a day. One of his officials, called *he who is head of the reversion* was responsible for distributing the remains of these meals to those at court.

Royal meals

The only surviving royal furniture from the Old Kingdom comes from the tomb of Hetepheres, wife of Sneferu and mother of Khufu. Its beauty and simplicity provide some evidence for the domestic elegance enjoyed by Old Kingdom royalty.

The official class and the administration of the state

The king's palace at Memphis (the *Great House*) was not only the home of the royal family and the king's many personal servants but also the centre of government.

Just as Egyptian society was organised in a hierarchical form, so too was the government. Every official had a precise title.

The vizier

At all times during the Old Kingdom, the man who was *first under the king* was the vizier. In various texts, the vizier was described as the *eyes and ears of the king, as leader of the great men of the south and the north* and as *second only to the king in the court and the palace.*

Second only to the king

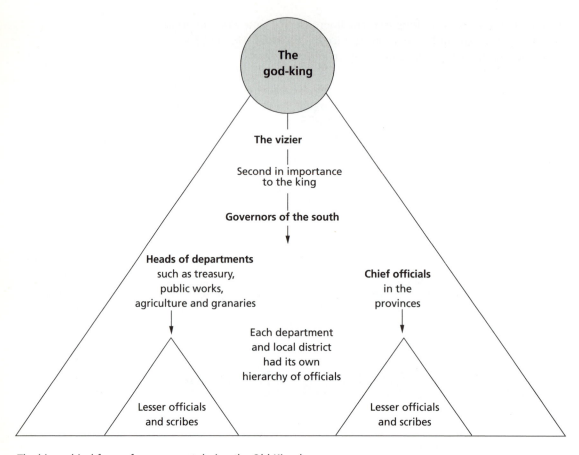

The hierarchical form of government during the Old Kingdom

During the earlier part of the Old Kingdom, the vizier was usually a very close relative of the king, perhaps a son. He was probably a high priest of the Temple of the Sun at Heliopolis as well. However, from the time of the Fifth Dynasty, the vizier was more frequently chosen from one of the noble families attached to the cult of Ptah of Memphis.

Female vizier

There is evidence that a woman, named Nebet, held the position of vizier in the reign of Pepi I.

The person chosen for this position had to have an ability to organise, since he was *sealbearer of the king of Lower Egypt, master of all the king's works, chief justice, chief treasurer* and *controller of all provincial governors.*

Some of his responsibilities included:

• supervising the treasury and all the precious belongings of the king

• collecting and valuing all the precious things *that are given by heaven or brought forth by the earth, or brought down by the Nile*

• judging cases and dispensing justice

- receiving and sending dispatches to officials in the provinces
- supervising the census (the counting of all cattle and fields) and assessing and collecting the taxes
- organising all mining, quarrying and building projects
- controlling the Nile traffic.

The practical work of each department under the vizier was carried out by a chief superintendent and a hierarchy of lesser officials, including vast numbers of scribes of all ranks.

What the correct titles and specific duties of these officials were is rather difficult to say. The Egyptians loved titles, and during the Fifth and Sixth dynasties the number of people with the same title increased. Many of these titles were probably honorific (a reward from the king) and involved no specific areas of responsibility. Because of this, some of the holders of these titles added the word *real* to them. For example, a Fifth Dynasty noble called Tepem'ankh (in his tomb biography) called himself:

An official of high standing

> The *real* nearest friend of the king
>
> The *real* judge and chief of the district
>
> The *real* judge and chief scribe.

The titles mentioned in Old Kingdom tombs of the Fifth and Sixth dynasties numbered about 2000. The reason for the vast number was that high officials often created a specific title for each function of their administrative and judicial work. For example, if a provincial governor had to pass on royal orders he might refer to himself as *privy councillor of the royal orders*. If he was in charge of public works he probably called himself *superintendent of the works of the king*. As a tax collector he might be referred to as *superintendent of the sacrificial and provision houses* and so on. Such a proliferation of titles has made it difficult for historians to work out who carried out what tasks.

Nomarchs

In the provinces or *nomes* the administration was in the hands of the leading noble landowner. He was referred to as the nomarch or provincial governor. These officials were directly responsible to the vizier but due to their distance from the capital of Memphis, many of them wielded great power.

Provincial governors

Nomarchs presided over a local court of justice, had at their disposal a body of troops and were responsible for the annual census, collection of taxes and irrigation works in their local area.

Towards the end of the Old Kingdom they became more independent of the central administration and the kings were forced to appoint an official called *overseer* or *governor of the south* to keep these nomarchs in check.

Governors of the south

Scribes

Because the Egyptians kept records of everything, scribes (those who could read, write and calculate) were found in every government department, in every temple and on every estate. They were responsible for measuring, inspecting, checking, rationing and recording.

Scribal training necessary for an official

Scribes were found at all levels in the administrative hierarchy because the Egyptians valued learning. A man who became a scribe was on the first rung of the official ladder.

Some remained simply clerks and secretaries writing dispatches to provincial officials on behalf of the king and vizier and recording legal decisions. Others became legal specialists, who drew up contracts in the vizier's court. Still others, because of their abilities to manage resources, both physical and human, reached positions of great power. Higher officials often included 'scribe' among their accumulated titles.

The administration of resources

The prosperity of the Egyptian state depended on the administration of resources, and scribes were concerned with system and detail.

Rationing of resources

One area in which scribes played a vital role was in the rationing of commodities. Because Egypt had a non-money economy and people were paid in goods, the scribes intervened in all areas of agricultural life. For example, they:

- measured yields of grain on the threshing floor
- supervised the storage of grain in the granaries as well as the production of bread and beer
- re-surveyed the fields after the flood
- distributed seed
- calculated the taxes and often punished tax evaders
- counted the animals during the census
- recorded the level of the Nile
- administered the water supplies.

On both royal and private estates, scribes were responsible for making the payments of commodities to all personnel. These included a basic ration of beer, bread and grain and possibly other items such as linen and meat.

A papyrus found in the pyramid temple of King Neferirkare of the Fifth Dynasty concerned the records of a number of estates associated with the king's mortuary cult. This showed the meticulous way in which the scribes had kept records of the daily income, daily offerings and rations to staff. They had drawn up a table to cover a 30-day month and each column had a heading naming the source of the foodstuffs, the kind of foodstuffs and the state they were in when delivered.

The skills of the scribes were used extensively on building, quarrying and irrigation projects. They were responsible for the management of labour, materials and rations. They:

- calculated the volume of materials to be moved, the labour units required and rations needed
- carefully scrutinised the work carried out by the army of people involved on a building project, from the architects to the skilled craftsmen and labourers. They then calculated the rewards each deserved
- checked on the tools issued and kept a record of those broken.

There are no records of the materials, labour and rations used during the building of the pyramids of Giza but some details are known about a quarrying expedition to Wadi Hammamat. The personnel involved in this expedition were 80 officials and 186 660 skilled and unskilled workers. The whole enterprise was managed by only eight scribes. The organisation of physical and human resources for the building of the pyramids would have been massive.

A seated scribe from the Fifth Dynasty

Scribes were also involved in:

- the activities of temples. They kept inventories of all temple property and supervised the activities in the temple workshops, particularly the weighing of gold and precious metals
- controlling traffic along the Nile and the movement of goods along the caravan routes of Nubia as well as supervising the valuable trade in cedar from Lebanon.

Priests

High priests of the cult temples were not spiritual leaders although their main purpose was to carry out the daily ritual to the god (refer to Chapter 16 for details on the daily temple rites). They were chiefly administrators of temple income and property. There was very little division in ancient Egypt between the secular and sacred world.

The Abusir Papyri, from the temples of Neferirkare, Raneferef and Khent-kawes, throw some light on the secular duties of priests. They organised the temple workforce, made regular inspections of temple buildings checking for damage, kept accounts, supervised the distribution of goods that flowed into the temple and maintained exhaustive inventories of temple property.

Priests as administrators

Although certain priests were permanently attached to the temple, the majority were part-time members of the temple hierarchy. Before taking up their period of service several times a year, these lay priests fumigated themselves with incense, cut their nails and removed all hair from their bodies. During their times of service in the temple they remained celibate but once they returned to their homes to resume their normal life they were free to live as ordinary men. While on temple duty they received a share of the daily offerings and the produce from the temple estates.

Part-time priests

Specialist priests

Some members of the temple community were specialists. For example, there was the lector priest who read the ritual and others who had knowledge in law, architecture and medicine.

The number of medical specialists attending the king indicates that during the Old Kingdom there was a vast knowledge of medical treatments. These men were probably trained as specialist priests in the cult centres of Heliopolis and Memphis.

Evidence for medical knowledge in this period comes from:

- the famous medical texts of later periods which are believed to have been copies of Old Kingdom texts
- tomb reliefs showing joints being manipulated, an operation on a foot and a circumcision
- mummies which show signs of dental work and treatment to various parts of their anatomy.

Medical knowledge

There is a well-known story about King Neferirkare of the Fifth Dynasty who, when he witnessed his vizier suffer a stroke, ordered his experts to find a remedy from the medical records.

Official positions held by women

Apart from Nebet, mentioned previously, women did not hold high official positions. Although there were some among the lower ranking officials, they were usually in the service of other women. For example, during the Fifth Dynasty there were:

- female overseers of the musical performers for the king and the cult gods
- female overseers of the women's quarters
- female overseers of the king's dining hall
- female inspectors of dancing and entertainment
- female overseers of wig-makers and weavers.

Some women had priestly duties associated with their father's mortuary rites.

Behaviour expected of the official class

Ptahhotep, a Fifth Dynasty vizier, left a record of instructions to his son in which he outlined some of the rules an official was expected to follow. These included the correct way to behave when dealing with those above and below him in the administrative hierarchy.

Ptahhotep's advice

He advised those who were leaders to always 'seek out every beneficent deed that your conduct may be blameless'.[4] Administrators should not be overconfident or arrogant because of their knowledge, but should pay careful attention to the speeches of petitioners and be free from greed. Ptahhotep also stressed that those officials who were sent with messages 'from one great man to another' should be totally reliable and 'give his message as he said it'.[5]

In everyday life Ptahhotep emphasised the need to be trustworthy, to think carefully before speaking and to never utter words in anger. He believed it was more appealing to be gentle than to be too strong. Refer to the activities at the end of this chapter for further extracts from the *Instructions of Ptahhotep*.

Lifestyle of the official class

Family relationships

The *Instructions of Ptahhotep*, the reliefs in the tombs of nobles such as Mereruka, and Old Kingdom statuary groups provide some idea of family relationships among the upper classes.

In the tomb reliefs, the nobleman was always depicted as much larger than everyone else. Sometimes the wife was shown as the same size as her husband and sometimes much smaller. Her size did not indicate an inferior social status. Wives were usually buried in the same tomb as their husbands, although some women who held religious positions or were divorced or unmarried may have had their own tombs.

Social status of women of the official class

Meresankh and his wife

Meresankh and his two daughters

There is no evidence as to the form of marriage that was practised during the Old Kingdom but it was a legal arrangement. Ptahhotep emphasised that it was important for a successful man to establish his own household and to treat his wife with love and respect.

**Obligations of a
husband to his wife**

> Love your wife with ardour. Fill her belly, clothe her back; ointment
> soothes her body. Gladden her heart as long as you live... Keep her
> from power, restrain her... Thus you will make her stay in your house.[6]

In her book, *Black Land, Red Land*, Mertz comments as follows on
Ptahhotep's advice.

> If there is no romance in Ptahhotep, there is another element which
> is very pleasant. Although the husband should be the master, his
> supremacy should be established by fairness and consideration, not by
> brute force.[7]

A man was also expected to treat his concubines kindly.

A nobleman had only one legal wife with whom he shared his social
life and whose children were his heirs. In some of the tomb scenes
there appears to be genuine affection between some husbands and
wives. For example, Mereruka and his wife are shown in two scenes
sharing several intimate moments — Mereruka watching his wife
preparing their bed and attentively appreciating her as she plays the
harp. There are also some Old Kingdom statuettes showing husbands
and wives embracing each other.

Obligations of a wife

One of the chief obligations of a wife was to 'be a fertile field for her
lord'[8] and present her husband with many children. A woman gained
added prestige with motherhood. Although a man counted himself
lucky to have both male and female children, he hoped that his wife
might give him a son whom he could see grow to manhood. Only a
boy could play the part of Horus at his father's funeral and make the
necessary offerings. There are many examples from the Old Kingdom
of devotion of a son to his father. For example, the tomb of Sebni at
Aswan records how Sebni's father was killed while on an expedition for
the king in the land of Nubia far to the south. When Sebni heard of his
father's death he set out on the same dangerous journey to find and
bring back his father's body for proper burial.

Ptahhotep emphasised to his son the importance of developing a good
character:

- He warned him about the dangers of approaching the women's
  quarters in the houses he might visit — 'A thousand men are
  turned away from their good' for the enjoyment of 'a short
  moment like a dream'.[9]

- He urged him not to boast about his ability and to learn
  from all people, including the uneducated — 'Don't be proud
  of your knowledge, consult the ignorant and the wise'.[10]

- He advised him to guard against speaking badly of others —
  'Guard against reviling speech which embroils one great with
  another'[11] and 'do not malign anyone'.[12]

Fathers and children

Although the father was the chief authority in the home and his discipline was very strict there are some delightful scenes depicting nobles
relaxing with their children along the river's edge. For example, Ti is
shown with his wife and daughter in a papyrus boat and Mereruka
affectionately holds his son's hand as he helps him catch a hoopoe bird.

The estates of the nobles

The nobles and officials closest to the king were men of great wealth. Their wealth came mainly from the vast estates of rich riverside land which the king granted them. Most Old Kingdom noblemen had more than one estate. Since the noblemen/officials were frequently absent at court or carrying out the king's orders in distant parts of the kingdom, they depended on overseers and foremen to run their estates. The tomb reliefs indicate that their visits to the estates were times of great pleasure and relaxation. They were shown with their families in various forms of relaxation, enjoying country life. Ancient Egyptians were great lovers of nature.

The estates of the nobles comprised:

- the nobleman's airy, brick and timber home surrounded by shady courtyards, gardens, fish ponds and pools
- the homes of estate overseers, scribes and craftsmen
- the simple, one-room, mud-brick homes of the farmers, herders, fishermen, boatmen and papyrus gatherers
- fields of grain and flax, and fruit trees, vines and vegetable gardens
- herds of cattle and oxen, flocks of sheep and goats, donkeys, domesticated water fowl (ducks, geese, cranes) and wild animals (gazelles) as well as family pets such as dogs and monkeys
- marshlands and papyrus thickets along the river's edge filled with a rich variety of bird life

Household and estate activities

The household of the nobleman was a hive of activity, with servants and retainers attending to the noble's every need. For example, Ptahhotep is shown in one tomb scene being pampered by both manicurist and pedicurist while a musician helps him relax and another servant makes sure the air around him is sweet smelling.

Personal attendants

Before the nobleman and his wife started their activities for the day, they paid particular attention to their personal cleanliness and appearance. Men removed body and facial hair with bronze razors, tweezers and scrapers and anointed their bodies with perfumed oils.

In the warmth of Egypt, people were generally lightly clad. The nobleman probably went bare-chested, except for his wide, beaded or jewelled collar (an indication of his high standing) and perhaps several other pieces of bright jewellery. He wore only a broad, pleated, white linen kilt and sandals, and covered his short cropped hair with a wig. In some tomb reliefs the officials (eg, Ptahhotep and Pepiankh) are shown wearing the animal-skin garment of a priest which was one of their roles.

Clothing, jewellery and cosmetics

The nobleman's wife paid particular attention to her hair and cosmetics. She surrounded her eyes with kohl and malachite which served as adornment and protection. In contrast to the more elaborate dress of the women of later periods, upper class women of the Old Kingdom wore simple ankle-length sheaths of linen with broad straps over the shoulders. This simple garment was complemented by beautiful jewellery.

While still young, the nobleman's children wore very little clothing but as they grew older they dressed like their parents. The young boys are identified in the tomb reliefs by their side-lock of braided hair. Mertz suggests that this may have been cut off at the time of circumcision, which was common practice among the ancient Egyptians. Circumcision was associated with the boys' coming of age. Mertz suggests the connection between circumcision and the removal of the side-lock because 'in the texts men often refer to the carefree days of boyhood as the time *before I had cut off the side-lock*.[13]

A statuette of a boy wearing the side-lock of youth

Once the nobleman had completed his toilet he was ready to receive the reports from his overseers and foremen. His scribes were always at hand to write any necessary letters or dispatches and to keep all the estate records.

They would sit cross-legged on the ground with their rectangular wooden palette (containing rush pens and cakes of red and black ink) on one side. On the other side was a pot of water. They diligently recorded their master's words on the roll of papyrus stretched across their knees.

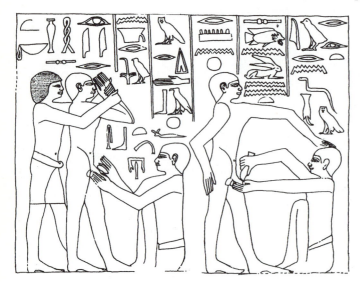

Circumcision

In the various workrooms of the house, servants processed grain into bread and produced beer by fermenting crushed barley and the sweet liquid from dates. Elsewhere, estate workers squeezed extra juice from the recently trodden grapes by twisting a sack attached to two poles. The nobleman would enjoy this wine with one of his three daily meals.

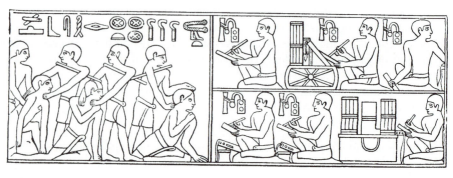

Peasants being brought before the scribes for failure to pay their taxes — from the tomb of Ti

Tomb reliefs showing noblemen sitting in front of tables laden with food offerings indicate that the upper classes ate very well. This is confirmed by three other sources of evidence:

1 The remains of a complete meal found in the tomb of a woman at Sakkara. This meal, set out in bowls and dishes made from alabaster and diorite, had been placed beside her sarcophagus and comprised wheat bread, barley cereal and small cakes, pigeon stew and cooked quail, fish, beef ribs and kidneys, and fruit.

2 Tomb scenes depicting the making of a form of caviar from the ovaries of the bouri fish. After the ovaries were extracted they were salted and dried.

3 Lists of food items inscribed on tomb walls. In one tomb this list mentioned ten types of meat, five varieties of poultry, 16 forms of bread and cake, six kinds of wine and four kinds of beer and 11 varieties of fruit.

Fish and various forms of fowl were particularly popular items on the nobleman's menu and there are numerous tomb scenes showing the way these were caught. The following illustrations show examples of fishing with large and small nets and hand-held lines as well as fowling with clap nets. Some of the wild fowl captured in this way were force fed until they were plump enough to grace the table of the noble.

A woman brewing beer — from the tomb of Meresankh

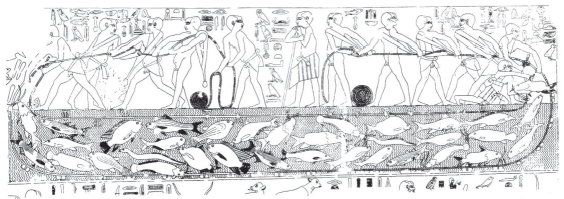

Estate workers fishing with a large net — from the tomb of Ti

Fishing with a line

Fishing with a small net

Estate workers fowling with clap nets — from the tomb of Pepiankh

Furniture and utensils made by estate craftsmen

When the nobleman and his family sat down to eat their sumptuous meals, they sat on chairs, and ate out of bowls using utensils, all of which may have been produced by the craftsmen employed on the estate. For example, a variety of carpentry skills were needed to produce the household furniture, scribal palettes, sennet boards and staffs carried by the noblemen. Evidence of the skill of the Old Kingdom carpenter is seen in the simple yet beautiful carved chairs, tables and beds as well as the various storage chests and headrests. Stone and metal vessels for the serving and storage of food, beer and wine may also have been made by estate craftsmen. The Sixth Dynasty tomb of Ibi at Deir el-

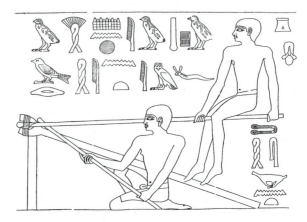

Carpenters making staffs — from the tomb of Ti

Gebrawi shows the hollowing of stone vessels while the craft of the metal worker is frequently represented in Old Kingdom tombs.

Animals such as oxen, cows, sheep and donkeys were an integral part of estate life. Oxen and donkeys were used to draw the ploughs, to trample in the seed, to carry the harvested sheaves to the threshing floor, to thresh the grain and to transport it to storage bins. Although they played an essential part in the agricultural activities and were a source of food, there is evidence that the peasants were very fond of their animals, particularly the cattle. They sometimes gave them names and decorated them during festivals. There are many scenes depicting cattle being hand fed, branded, and even calves being carried across stretches of water. Other reliefs show herdsmen caring for sick animals and helping them give birth. It seems that these simple people may have had some real veterinary knowledge.

Family pets, particularly dogs and monkeys, were featured in many tomb scenes. Adults as well as children seem to have been fond of them. There were several breeds of domesticated dog by the time of the Old Kingdom but the one featured most commonly in the tomb reliefs was the hunting dog. This was a long, lanky dog similar to a greyhound and the hunting dogs still used in parts of Africa today. Monkeys were often depicted sitting under a chair or holding a child's hand. The household pets were often looked after by dwarfs who were frequently employed on the estates in workshops, kitchens and laundries.

The number of cattle and other animals on the estate was carefully recorded by the nobleman's scribes for they were assessed as part of the estate taxes. The amount of grain and flax produced was also assessed for taxation. An occasional tomb scene shows a peasant being dragged before the estate scribes and being punished for failing to pay the correct amount of tax (always paid in produce) or for trying to evade it altogether.

A bull being hand fed

Cattle being driven across the river — from the tomb of Ti

*An official travelling
by donkey*

The nobleman, who made inspections of his entire estate at irregular intervals, was carried from place to place in a carrying chair. Although the tomb scenes record the noble watching the ploughing, sowing and harvesting of crops, he obviously didn't see all of these activities being carried out at one time. It was an artistic convention to show the beginning and end of the agricultural cycle. Peasant farmers are often depicted in these scenes working to the music of a flute, enjoying a drink of beer in the fields and joking with one another. However, their lives were hard and they toiled from morning to night to grow the wheat, barley and flax for the noble's bread, beer and linen clothing.

Harvest in progress

Life for the peasants' children was hard also and yet there are many scenes in the tombs showing them enjoying games such as tug-of-war, wrestling and fencing with sticks.

**Granaries and
workshops**

As well as inspecting the fields, the nobleman probably visited the granaries, shipyard and craftsmen's workshops. Boat building was featured twice in the tomb of Ti who is shown supervising the various phases of shipbuilding — shaping the timber, sawing and drilling the planks, putting the hull together and carving the papyrus-shaped stern. Since many of the craftsmen's tools, including those of the shipbuilder, were made of copper, the coppersmith's workshop would have been a busy place on the estate.

Papyrus products

As the noble was carried along the tow paths beside the larger canals he might have seen fishermen in their papyrus boats engaged in a mock battle, and the papyrus gatherers at the edge of the river filling their baskets with the valuable reed. In the small peasant villages on his estate, the peasants wove the papyrus stalks into mats and the fibres into sandals. These items were exchanged for other necessary goods. The light papyrus skiffs used for fishing, fowling and recreation were made by tying bundles of papyrus together.

A mock fight in papyrus skiffs — from the tomb of Senbi

The papyrus plant was also transformed into the valuable white paper used by Egyptian officials. The long stems of the plant were cut into pieces about 30 centimetres long and the tough outside part was stripped off. The pith was cut lengthwise into thin slices which were then placed side by side on a flat surface. Another layer of thin slices was placed on top of the first layer but at right angles to it. The superimposed layers were either pressed in some way or beaten with a wooden mallet until they became welded together. No adhesive of any kind was used except for the natural starch in the juice which was discharged from the slices when they were pressed or pounded. The surface of the paper was smoothed by burnishing it with a stone or wooden polisher.

After many hours supervising the activities on his estate the noble probably returned to his comfortable home to relax with his family and pets. However, since he had been carried around his estate for hours in a sedan-chair, he may have felt more like enjoying the thrill of a desert hunt. Many tomb reliefs feature the tomb owner accompanied by attendants and his hunting dogs tracking the wild desert gazelles and antelopes. Some of the captured wild animals were taken back to the estate to be domesticated.

Scenes of music and dancing

Perhaps after his evening meal the noble played a quiet game of sennet with his wife or enjoyed the high kicks and acrobatic feats of female dancers as they moved to the rhythm of flutes and clapping hands. Such dancers are featured in the tombs of Ankhmahor and Kagemeni at Sakkara. More conventional dancers (who did not perform acrobatic feats) are depicted in the tomb of Nefer at Giza.

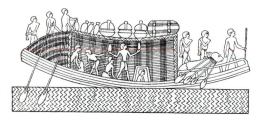

Above: A cargo boat

Right: The type of boat used by officials in carrying out their duties

Boat travel

When it was time for the nobleman to leave his estate and return to Memphis to continue his official duties he travelled in a boat with a deck cabin, a single sail and large oar-shaped rudder. There was always much movement on the river since it was the chief highway of Egypt. Passing cargo boats heading south had their sails filled by the northerly wind. Those heading towards Memphis and Giza, laden with acacia wood, gold and precious materials from Nubia and the eastern deserts and stone from Aswan, were aided by the current.

Mud-brick houses in a modern-day village in Upper Egypt

There was very little difference in the way of life of the peasants from one period to another. In fact, in some of the villages of Egypt today, the lives of the farmers are not too different from those of the ancient peasants. (For more details on the life of the peasant farmer refer to Chapter 16.)

Cult temple and necropolis workers

Old Kingdom cult temples and necropolis sites employed a large range of workers apart from the body of permanent and part-time priests. These included skilled craftsmen, unskilled workers and support personnel as shown in the table below.

Cult temple workers	Necropolis workers
Permanent and part-time priests	Permanent and part-time mortuary priests
Temple dancers, musicians and singers	Architects, overseers and scribes
Scribes	Skilled craftsmen such as masons, sculptors, master artists, tool makers and carpenters
Skilled craftsmen such as sculptors, metal workers, carpenters and jewellers	
Bakers, brewers and butchers	Pyramid workers such as stone cutters, stone haulers, ramp builders, water carriers and tool sharpeners
Peasants and herdsmen	Bakers, brewers and butchers

The activities of the specialist craftsmen can be seen on the tomb walls of many Fifth and Sixth dynasty noblemen such as Ti (Sakkara) and Pepiankh (Meir).

One of the most highly respected craftsmen throughout Egyptian history was the sculptor in the round. These artisans carved in stone and wood, sometimes overlaid with beaten copper and gold. Not only did statues of the gods and ka statues have to be of the highest quality, but those sculpted for the god-king had to reflect his divine nature and power in order to promote and maintain his cult. The skill of the Old Kingdom sculptor can be seen in the magnificent statues of King Khafre.

Skilled craftsmen

Although there were strict conventions followed by the sculptor (pose and proportion), many of the painted ka statues depict individual facial and bodily features. Artists and sculptors were also used to create temple 'decorations'.

Metal workers produced a variety of ritual and funerary objects as well as copper tools used in the construction of the pyramid complexes.

Metal workers and sculptors — from the tomb of Ti

In the tomb of Ti at Sakkara, there are a number of scenes showing metal workers using pipes to blow air into the fires used for smelting, pouring liquid metal into moulds, and beating the metal into shape.

'Pyramid' towns

One of the intriguing questions concerning the hordes of workers involved in the construction of pyramid complexes is 'where did they live?'.

Where did pyramid workers live?

It is believed that many of these people were housed in camp sites and barrack-type towns established close to the construction site. There may have been tens of thousands of labourers and craftsmen who had to be fed and housed at a camp site on the desert plateau. Thousands may have been crowded together in small rooms or cubicles all under one roof.

Although no complete workers' town has been excavated from the Old Kingdom, recent excavations in the low desert area south-east of the Giza plateau have unearthed the remains of a possible 'settlement' site which was used later as a ritual centre. Nearby, the remains of what are believed to be a huge state facility for bread production and a fish processing building have been found.

The huge bakery comprised:

- a rectangular building with pedestals which may have held small silos for grain storage
- an area containing huge vats and bread moulds similar to those shown in Old Kingdom tombs and used in bakeries and breweries. The vats were probably used for mixing the bread dough and the

huge clay pots, up to ten kilograms in weight, were moulds for baking the bread. Bread shown in offering scenes in the tomb of Ti had a conical shape and was probably baked in jar moulds similar to those found at Giza.

It is not known yet whether this bakery serviced a workforce involved with tomb construction or whether it provided food for the whole infrastructure associated with the temples and mortuary cults of kings and nobles. The most commonly-held theory at the moment is that this huge state facility served a ritualistic purpose. Further excavation may throw more light on this question and it may be necessary to change this theory.

Conclusion

The god-king was the capstone of the Egyptian state (society and government). What the king did and said was of the greatest importance to everyone, from the lowliest peasant to the highest official in the land. The king's welfare, both in life and death, was in the hands of thousands of government and household officials. These people made up an extensive civil service or bureaucracy centred on the palace at Memphis.

The high officials to whom the god-king delegated his authority were granted vast estates by him and lived luxurious lifestyles. They were often rewarded with honorary titles such as *friend of the king* and given royal support in the building of their tombs. These nobles/officials were themselves supported by numerous lesser officials, craftsmen, household attendants, peasant farmers and field workers.

> In the Old Kingdom the people were confident (they knew no war or foreign intervention), hard-working and optimistic which was a reflection of a stable and organised government.[14]

Chapter review

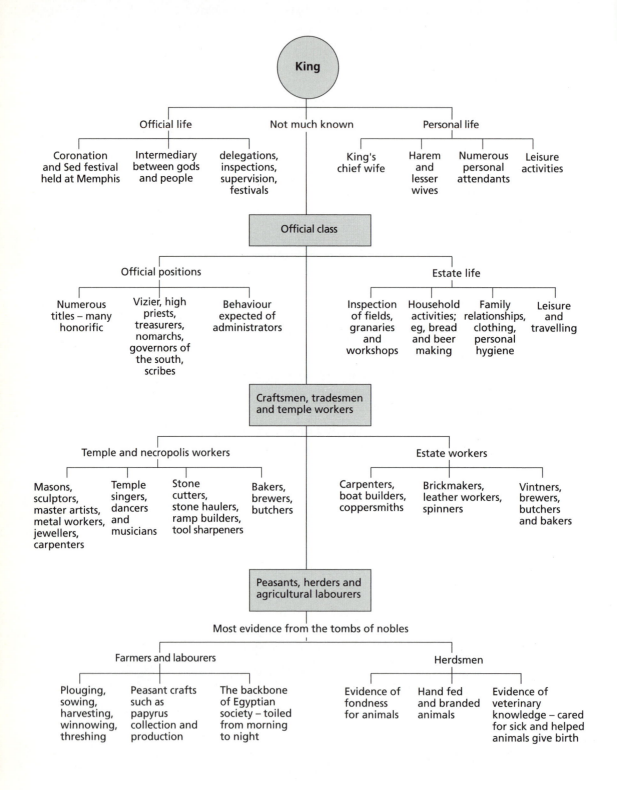

REVISION QUESTIONS AND ESSAY TOPICS

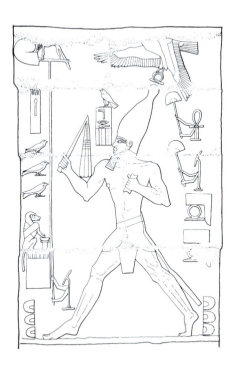

1 Look carefully at the relief on the right and explain what ceremony in the Sed festival is being performed. What was the significance of this ceremony?

2 The figure below shows a number of registers from the tomb of the Fifth Dynasty noble, Ptahhotep. Study them carefully and answer the questions below.

a Describe the way Ptahhotep is depicted in this figure.

b What estate activities are shown? Write a few sentences describing each one.

c What other activities were often shown in Old Kingdom tomb reliefs?

3 **The following extracts come from the *Instructions of Ptahhotep*. Read them through carefully and answer the following questions.**

> *If you meet a disputant in action*
> *A powerful man superior to you,*
> *Fold your arms, bend your back,*
> *To flout him will not make him agree with you*
> *By not opposing him while he is in action:*
> *He will be called an ignoramus*
> *Your self-control will match his pile (of words)*
>
> *If you meet a disputant who is your equal, on your level,*
> *You will make your worth exceed his by silence,*
> *While he is speaking evilly,*
> *There will be much talk by the hearers,*
> *Your name will be good in the mind of the magistrates.*
>
> *If you meet a disputant in action,*
> *A poor man not your equal,*
> *Do not attack him because he is weak,*
> *Let him alone, he will confute himself.*
> *Do not answer him to relieve your heart*
> *Do not vent yourself against your opponent*
> *Wretched is he who injures a poor man,*
> *One will wish to do as you desire,*
> *You will beat him through the magistrate's reproof.* [15]

a What is meant by the line 'If you meet a disputant in action'?

b In a few sentences for each, explain the advice given by Ptahhotep to his son if he should ever find himself in a dispute with:
- an official superior to himself
- a man of equal status
- a poor man?

c What qualities was Ptahhotep hoping to instil in his son?

d The *Instructions of Ptahhotep* also give an idea of the obligations of a husband and wife. What were these obligations?

4 Essay topics

a Describe the main features of the Sed festival and explain why it was so important to all Egyptians. Use the diagrammatic summary on the next page as a guide.

b What do the tombs of the Old Kingdom nobles reveal about the life and work of peasant farmers, herdsmen, craftsmen and household servants?

c Describe a day in the life of a noble and his family.

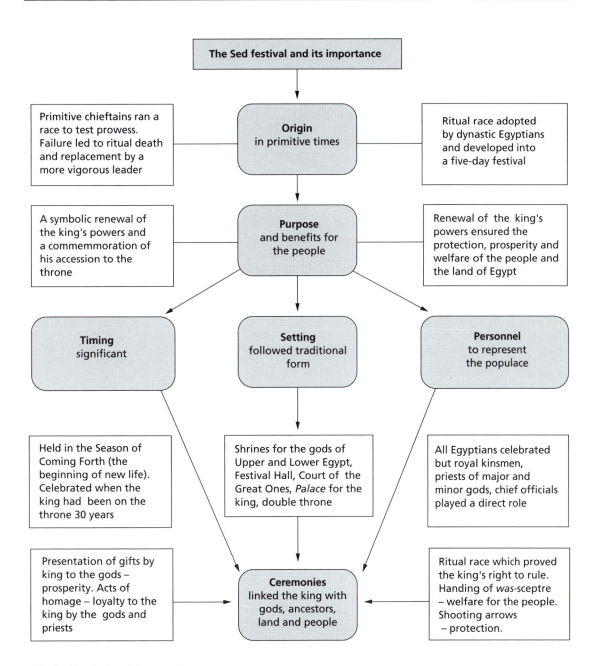

The Sed festival and its importance

Preparing for eternity

Egyptian beliefs about death and the afterlife

From earliest times it appears that the Egyptians believed in some form of life after death. Their beliefs were probably influenced by the nature of the land they lived in — a land in which the sun, the river and the desert were the dominant forces.

Physical forces and the concept of rebirth

The Egyptians observed the sun *die* in the west every day, only to be *reborn* in the east each morning after its passage through the Underworld during the night. They watched as the annual flood revitalised the parched soil and caused the grain to spring from the soil anew each year. Like the morning sun and the grain, they also hoped to be reborn after death.

Since the sun appeared to die in the west, they thought that the land of the dead must also be in the west. For this reason they buried their dead in the desert sands on the western side of the Nile. The desert upland was home to jackals and wolves and these animals who prowled and scavenged near the graves of the villagers, came to be associated with death.

Land of the Dead

These simple beliefs evolved further. The sun god was the most significant god associated with the afterlife of royalty throughout pharaonic history. The Egyptians not only called the sun god by several names but depicted it in many forms, depending on the position of the sun during the day. Also, the sun was believed to travel through the Underworld at night.

The rising sun was referred to as Kheper or Khepri (*He who comes into existence*) and was represented as a scarab beetle pushing the disk of the new sun in front of him. This was based on the Egyptians' observation of the environment. The scarab beetle collects animal dung and shapes it into a ball, pushing the ball of dung along with its hind legs before laying an egg in it and burying it in the hot sand. When it hatches, the beetle larva lives on the dung, before emerging from the sand as an adult. This action of the beetle reminded the Egyptians of the re-emergence or *rebirth* of the sun each morning.

During the day, when the sun god was believed to sail across the sky in its day boat (barque), it was referred to as Re or Re-Horakhte and depicted in its most common form as a king with the head of a hawk bearing the sun disk on its head.

Re-Horakhte in his solar boat

Khepri, represented by a scarab beetle, in the solar barque of the sun god

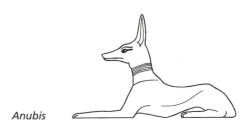

Anubis

Towards evening, when the sun god was believed to be slowly losing its power as it approached the western horizon, it was referred to as Atum and depicted as an old bearded man.

During the night, it was believed to enter the night boat and travel through the Underworld, going through a number of transformations. It was often depicted at this time with the head of a ram.

The god Osiris, who was originally a god of vegetation (particularly grain), was also believed to be the force responsible for the rising Nile and anything that 'came forth from apparent death'.[1] Egyptians later associated life, death and rebirth with the Osirian myth in which Osiris was believed to have been a popular king who was killed and dismembered by his jealous brother Seth. The pieces of Osiris' body were scattered throughout Egypt. Osiris' wife, Isis, and sister, Nephthys, with help from the gods Anubis and Thoth, located the pieces of Osiris' body and reunited them by wrapping them in bandages. Osiris was resurrected to rule in the Underworld as King of the Dead.

Osiris and the concept of resurrection

Jackal and wolf gods were regarded as protectors of the dead during the Old Kingdom. Anubis, the jackal-headed deity, was probably the original funerary god of Upper Egypt. He was the god of embalming, lord of the necropolis (cemetery) and had the title *Prince of Those-who-are-in-the-west* (the dead). Other wolf or jackal gods were Wepwawet and Khentymentyw. These were often confused and worshipped as one god. Osiris also had the title of Prince of the West since he had been killed

Anubis, lord of the necropolis

but had conquered death to become god of the dead. By the latter part of the Old Kingdom it appears that Osiris had absorbed the qualities and role of Khentymentyw as *Foremost-of-the-Westerners.*

The nature of the afterlife

Exactly what form this afterlife took for the ordinary Egyptian is unknown due to the lack of any surviving explanation. What is known from the Pyramid Texts of the Fifth and Sixth dynasties, is that the god-king (and possibly members of royalty) experienced a different afterlife to ordinary men and women. Only royalty could hope to spend eternity with the gods.

The afterlife of royalty

According to the Pyramid Texts, the king could experience:

- an astral afterlife where he would live forever among the *Imperishable Stars* (or circumpolar stars) which, in Egyptian skies, never set and the stars of Orion and Sirius which disappeared for a period during the year
- a solar afterlife where he would be reunited with his father Re, the sun god, and accompany him in his daily travels across the sky.

The following extracts from the Pyramid Texts illustrate both of these views:

> O you who are high exalted among the Imperishable Stars,
> you shall never perish[2]
> You shall live!
> You shall rise with Orion in the eastern sky,
> You shall set with Orion in the western sky, ...[3]

> Re, this Unas comes to you,
> A spirit indestructible
> Who lays claim to the place of the four pillars!
> Your son comes to you, this Unas comes to you,
> May you cross the sky united in the dark,
> May you rise in lightland, the place in which you shine![4]

Evidence from Pyramid Texts

> I am pure,
> I take my oar to myself,
> I occupy my seat,
> I sit in the bow of the boat of the two Enneads,
> And I row Re to the west.[5]

The view that the king would become one of the stars seems to have been held during the early part of the Old Kingdom. However, the most commonly held belief about the afterlife was that the king would spend eternity with the sun god. Because the Egyptians never discarded any of their old beliefs in favour of new ones, a combination of both of these views of eternity is recorded in the Pyramid Texts.

> Be pure; occupy your seat in the bark of Re; may you row over the sky and ascend to the distant ones; row with the Imperishable Stars, navigate with the Unwearying Stars, receive the freight of the Night-Bark.[6]

Just as there were different views about where the king spent the next life, so too were there different ideas about how the king reached the heavens. The spells describe him:

Means of reaching heaven

- ascending a ladder or stairway
- being ferried across in a reed-boat
- breaking the fetters of earth and flying to heaven like a falcon
- being taken by the hand of Nut, the sky goddess
- being lifted up by Shu, the god of air.

A text in the Pyramid of Pepi I says that, as the son of Re, Pepi could raise himself up to heaven.

Towards the end of the Old Kingdom, it appears that the king was associated in the afterlife with the god Osiris as well. However, the early writers of the Pyramid Texts merely describe the dead king as becoming one with Osiris.

Role of Osiris in the Old Kingdom mythology unclear

> O Osiris Pepi, you enfold every god in your arms, their lands and all their possessions.[7]

> O Osiris the king, you have not departed dead, you have departed alive; sit upon the throne of Osiris, your sceptre in your hand, that you may give orders to the living.[8]

Just what the role of Osiris was in the Old Kingdom is not clear.

According to Spencer 'Lack of a consistent point of view (about the afterlife) did not trouble the Egyptians whose ideology was well able to accept the identification of the king or god with several entities at the same time'.[9]

The afterlife of nobles, craftsmen and peasants

Members of the nobility and favoured officials could enjoy immortality only through the beneficence of their lord, the king. They probably hoped that if they served their king faithfully and efficiently during their lifetime they might be called upon to continue this service in the next life as well. Their tombs, built as close as possible to the tomb of their king (at least until the Sixth Dynasty), is evidence of this hope. That they expected their eternal life would be similar to their earthly existence is suggested by the following evidence:

- They built their tombs on the plan of a house.
- They placed household objects in their *home for eternity*.
- They carved and painted scenes from everyday life on the walls of the tomb.

Possible beliefs of lower classes

Craftsmen and peasants probably hoped, by contributing their skills and labour to building the tombs of their lords, filling them with finely crafted objects and producing food for their mortuary cults, that they too would share in an afterlife. 'With these ideas in mind, it became the aspiration of every Egyptian to prepare during his lifetime an adequate place for burial.'[10]

The spiritual aspect of the individual

To the Egyptians of the Old Kingdom, the most important aspect of an individual was his or her *ka* and belief in a *ka* was the most significant influence on funerary practices during the Old Kingdom.

Ka — life force of the individual

The *ka* is a difficult concept to understand. Scholars have interpreted it as the life-force, personality, double or twin, and spirit. Ordinary people were supposed to have only one *ka* but gods and kings had many. The Egyptians believed that the *ka* was born with the child, existed throughout life, guided the person in everything he or she did and remained with the body at death. Without a body (or a substitute life-like statue) the *ka* or spirit had nowhere to rest and ceased to exist. The *ka* could leave the body for a time and move about the tomb but always returned to the body.

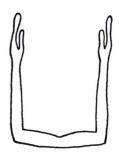

The symbol for the ka (upraised hands)

The belief in the continued existence of the *ka* after death led to the following funerary practices and tomb features:

- Mummification (embalming of the body).
- Inclusion within the tomb (the *house of the ka*) of:
- statues of the deceased in which the *ka* could temporarily reside to accept offerings from the living, or in which it could permanently reside if the body were destroyed. These statues were called *ka* statues
- false or *ka* doors through which the *ka* could pass to accept offerings from the stone *table* placed in front of the door
- *serdabs* or cellar-like rooms enclosing a *ka* statue. From holes in these rooms the *ka* could see the offerings being presented and smell the incense
- *decoration* of the walls with painted reliefs of offerings (food and drink), various forms of food production (agriculture, animal husbandry, fishing, wine making) and other necessities for the continuing existence of the *ka*
- provision in the many storerooms of the tomb of everyday items or models of these which the *ka* would need for eternity.

Associated funerary practices

Another important aspect of the individual was one's name, whether written or spoken. Only by knowing a person's name could one speak well of the deceased. For this reason, Egyptians had their names, titles, achievements and virtues carved in a prominent place in the tomb. On the other hand, an individual could be harmed if someone spoke of him or her in a derogatory way. Removal of a person's name from the tomb was believed to condemn his or her spiritual entities to oblivion. This sometimes happened when an official usurped an existing tomb and inscribed his own name over the top of that of the previous owner.

The importance of a person's name

Towards the end of the Old Kingdom another spiritual aspect of the individual was occasionally mentioned in the texts. This was the *ba* or soul which was believed to be free to leave the tomb, take any form it desired and carry out those activities previously performed by the deceased. At night the *ba* returned to the body. During the New

Ba (soul) not mentioned often in Old Kingdom texts

Kingdom the *ba* was depicted as a human-headed bird. This concept is discussed more fully in Chapter 17.

Funerary practices of the Old Kingdom

Preserving the body for eternity

The Egyptians believed that the *ka* or *life-force* needed the body in which to reside for eternity. For this reason they did what they could, depending on their position in life, to ensure that after death their body survived forever. They did this by:

- embalming the body
- placing amulets on or near the body and writing prayers and magic spells on the walls of burial chambers
- placing bodies in protective coffins and sarcophagi and placing internal organs in canopic chests or jars
- guaranteeing eternal sustenance by providing items of food and drink, either in real or symbolic form in the tomb and as part of the mortuary cult
- performing the *Opening of the Mouth* ceremony to restore the senses to the body
- sealing the body and grave goods in a *secure* tomb.

Predynastic burial practices

In Predynastic times, the inhabitants of the Nile Valley simply buried their dead (in the contracted foetal position) with a few possessions in shallow graves in the desert sands. The body was usually in direct contact with the dry sand which absorbed the moisture in the body fairly rapidly, providing a natural form of preservation. A 3500-year-old body buried in this way, now on display in the British Museum, was discovered by Egyptologists with its hair and skin still intact.

Need for embalming

When these early Nile settlers started wrapping their dead in animal skins or some form of matting, they began the process of insulating the body from the preserving effects of the sand. In their desire to further protect the body and grave goods, they began to build a roof over the grave and to place the body in a form of wooden coffin. However, the more protection they gave to the body, the more quickly it decomposed.

The development of mummification to the end of the Old Kingdom

According to Spencer in his work *Death in Ancient Egypt*, Egyptians of the early dynastic period realised that they would have to find some form of preservation or else their spirit would have nowhere to live in the afterlife. This was the beginning of embalming.

Their first attempts at deliberately preserving the body involved wrapping the corpse in many layers of bandages and placing it in a coffin in the foetal position.

When the Egyptians realised that they could not preserve the flesh they began to soak the bandages in a resinous substance and mould them around the body in such a way as to keep the body's shape and emphasise the individual features. A life-like shell of bandages formed as the resin dried. It appears that the Egyptians who practised this method during the first three dynasties believed that the more bandages they used the greater would be the protection. For example, one mummy found at Sakkara had 14 layers over the chest and eight over the arms and legs. However, the tissues still decomposed under the linen shell. As long as the internal organs were left in the body, no amount of bandaging would prevent the body from rotting.

> The wrapped bodies of the first three dynasties were not truly mummified, since no treatment other than the use of linen bandages and resin was employed.[11]

During the Fourth Dynasty there is evidence that the embalmers began to remove some of the internal organs in order to dry out the body cavity and prevent decomposition of the body tissues. Natron, a salt-like substance used for removing moisture, may have been used at this time.

Evidence for this development comes from three sources.

1 More bodies appear to have been buried in the extended position. Spencer suggests that it was easier to remove some of the internal organs if the bodies were extended rather than contracted.

2 The appearance of recesses built into the southern walls of the burial chambers. These are believed to have held the linen-wrapped organs which the Egyptians hoped would be reunited with the body in the next life. Remains of preserved organs were found in the recess of a tomb in the Meidum necropolis.

3 The discovery, in the tomb of Queen Hetepheres, of an alabaster box-like container with four compartments in which her individually wrapped internal organs had been placed. These were found still soaking in a solution of natron.

This last more sophisticated method may have been used only when embalming royal bodies and those of high-ranking nobles.

During the Fifth and Sixth dynasties the practice of removing and treating some of the organs became more common among the upper classes. In some late Old Kingdom tombs, a pit, cut into the floor on the south-east side of the burial chamber, held the box containing the internal organs. Despite this major step in mummification, the mummies that have survived from the late Old Kingdom are not much better preserved than those from earlier periods.

No further successful developments occurred in mummification at this time. However, the embalming priests adopted ways of making the body more lifelike. For example, they sometimes:

- placed pads of cloth beneath the bandages to fill out the body
- coated the bandages with plaster, carefully following the contours of the face and body

Bandages soaked in resin

Evidence for removal of viscera in Fourth Dynasty

Bodies made more lifelike

- gave the face special attention by painting it green (green was the colour of fertility; and Osiris, the god of the Underworld and of resurrection, was often depicted with a green face) or adding individual features such as a painted moustache or beard.

The embalming process was still at a very primitive stage at the end of the Old Kingdom. The detailed descriptions of mummification found in Herodotus and most modern books describe the process as it was practised at a much later period. Even when mummification was more developed, the survival of a body depended on the degree of care taken by the embalming priests and the importance and wealth of the deceased. In Chapter 18 there is a full description of the process as it was carried out in the latter part of the New Kingdom.

The use of amulets and magic spells

Amulets were protective charms (small images of the gods and sacred symbols) worn by the ancient Egyptians during life and placed on or near the body during mummification and burial. These amulets were often inscribed with magical signs and hieroglyphs.

One of the most common symbols used as an amulet was the scarab, which was associated with the concept of rebirth. The *ankh* (hieroglyphic sign of life) and the *Udjet eye* (Eye of Horus) were two other important amulets.

The ankh or key of life

The significance of the various amulets, particularly those associated with mummification, is fully discussed in Chapter 17 since many thousands of these were found in tombs of the New Kingdom.

During the latter part of the Fifth and the whole of the Sixth Dynasty, magic incantations were inscribed on the walls of royal burial chambers and adjoining passages. These were intended to protect the bodies of the deceased kings and queens and help them on their journey to the next life. Refer to Chapter 5 for details.

Since the magic spells of the Pyramid Texts were the monopoly of royalty, the official class had to resort to a simple warning to those passing by or entering the tomb chapel. By means of this inscription the deceased vowed revenge, in both this life and the next, on any violator of his tomb. For example:

> **Now as for all people ... who shall make a disturbance in this tomb, who shall damage its inscriptions or who shall do damage to its statue, they will fall under the anger of Thoth.**[12]

The Eye of Horus (Udjet)

Another such warning came from a Sixth Dynasty priest named Ankhmahor who threatened to destroy the property of anyone who damaged his tomb. He reminded potential tomb desecrators that he was a very capable lector priest who had a vast knowledge of effective magic.

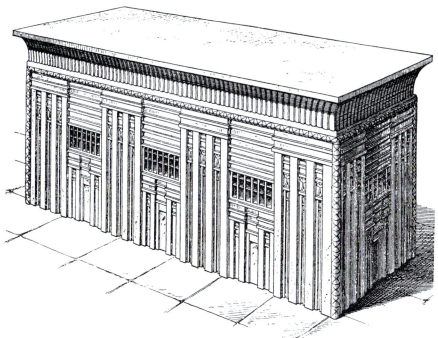

An artist's representation of the sarcophagus of King Menkaure with palace facade decoration

Coffins and sarcophagi

Not only were the rectangular wooden coffins and stone sarcophagi of the Old Kingdom a form of physical protection for the body, but they provided a form of symbolic protection also. For example, both coffin and sarcophagi were identified with:

- the eternal home of the deceased
- the womb of the sky goddess, Nut.

Many sarcophagi were decorated with panelling which looked like the front of a palace or house with a doorway. The doorway allowed the *ka* to leave the coffin to receive offerings. The lids were often shaped like the roof of a house. Sometimes Nut was painted on the inside of the lids.

Royal sarcophagi were made from granite, quartzite and alabaster while those of non-royals were generally of limestone. Inscriptions on the outside of the coffins were quite brief — usually just the owner's name and title, while the inside sometimes featured the traditional list of offerings.

Where canopic jars and chests were found, they were made from stone and lacked any religious texts or symbolic decoration.

Funeral and burial rites

The most informative sources of evidence for the funeral rites carried out during the Old Kingdom are the tomb reliefs of some Sixth Dynasty nobles. The best preserved of these belonged to Pepiankh who was buried at Meir. Another tomb from the Fourth Dynasty (Debehni) shows some aspects of the funeral service. Other information can be conjectured from New Kingdom reliefs of the funeral procession.

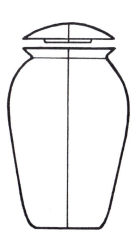

A plain stone canopic jar of the type used in the Fourth Dynasty

The sarcophagus of a Fourth Dynasty noble, in situ

Mourners from the tomb of Idu at Giza

It appears that the deceased was placed in the coffin at home and then taken to a temporary structure referred to as the washing tent. During this initial stage, the body of the deceased was accompanied by a lector-priest (who recited prayers), the embalmer (more important than the lector-priest during the Old Kingdom) and grief-stricken relatives. Among the mourners may have been some professionals (*dryt* mourners) who represented the divine mourners, Isis and her sister Nephthys. In the tomb of Idu at Giza, both male and female mourners appear to be tearing at their hair, beating their heads, fainting and covering themselves with mud. The procession then made its way to the *embalming house* for the mummification of the body.

The tomb scenes then show the coffin, in a papyrus boat, being towed across the river to the *beautiful west*, the land of the dead. Reliefs showing the coffin in a boat may also have represented pilgrimages to Buto and Abydos, centres of Osiris worship. Further prayers and offerings were made by the lector-priest during the river journey.

For the final procession to the tomb, the coffin was either carried by relatives or servants (tomb of Pepiankh) or placed on a sled drawn by oxen (tomb of Idu). A line of servants carried grave goods and led the animals to be slaughtered. Female dancers (*muu* dancers) who performed at the tomb were thought to represent the Egyptians' ancestors. Refer to Chapter 17 for more details on New Kingdom funerals and alternative theories about the *muu* dancers.

The most important burial rite was the *Opening of the Mouth* ceremony. Although 'this important ceremony was not represented in the Old Kingdom' [13] it features prominently in the funeral rites depicted on the walls of New Kingdom tombs. During the New Kingdom this ritual involved a priest or the eldest son holding a chisel-like implement to the mouth of the upright mummy. The purpose of this rite was to restore the deceased's senses so that he or she could take the food and drink and smell the incense offered by the relatives.

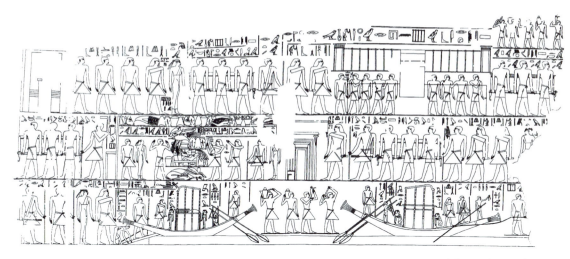

A funeral scene from the tomb of Pepiankh

According to Kanawati, the Old Kingdom version of this rite may have been performed 'upon the tomb owner's statue (*ka* statue) before it left the sculptor's workshop to be placed in the tomb'. [14] In the case of royalty, it may have been carried out on the king's statue in the mortuary temple attached to his pyramid. In royal burials it was important for the heir to the throne to perform this task, just as Horus had done for his father Osiris. Refer to Chapter 17 for details of the ceremony as it was performed during New Kingdom times.

Eternal provisions for the *ka*

Not only did the Egyptians attempt to protect the body as a permanent dwelling place for the *ka*, but they provided the *ka* with items of food, drink and everyday objects. 'Furnish your house in the graveyard and enrich your place in the west' [15] was the advice given by an Old Kingdom prince to his son.

Food and drink for the deceased

In the early dynastic period, the Egyptians believed that they had to provide real items of food and drink for the *ka*. For this reason many of the early tombs had enormous storerooms containing hundreds of stone and pottery jars filled with wine and grain. For example, in King Djoser's Step Pyramid, excavators found 40 000 stone vases. Several early mastaba tombs at Sakkara even included brick granaries for storing large quantities of grain.

Later, the Egyptians began to use substitutes rather than real food and drink. For example:

- they carved reliefs of the tomb owner sitting before a table of offerings
- they depicted servants bringing offerings of food and drink to the deceased and scenes of food, beer and wine production (scenes of agricultural activities, animal husbandry, fishing, fattening of fowl, growing and squeezing grapes making bread and barley beer)
- they placed small models of granaries and loaves of bread in the burial chamber

Substitutes for real food and drink

- they wrote an appeal at the entrance to the tomb requesting those who passed by to make an offering of whatever they could

- they requested that those without anything to offer pray that the deceased be provided with *one thousand loaves of bread, one thousand jugs of beer, one thousand oxen, one thousand fowls and one thousand of every good thing.*

Other funerary goods

Apart from items of food and drink, furniture and jewellery were sealed in the burial chamber for the use of the deceased in the next life. Some of these may have been used by the deceased in his or her lifetime, but most would have been specially-crafted funerary and ritual items. Except for those found in the tomb of Queen Hetepheres, very few of these grave goods have survived from the Old Kingdom.

Those who could afford it provided an estate from which a continual supply of food and drink could be obtained. The deceased hoped that regular funerary offerings of food, incense and prayers, which took the form of a set ritual, would be provided by the eldest son or specially appointed *ka* priests. These mortuary rites were carried out in that part of the tomb complex called the chapel.

In one wall of the chapel was a false door, in front of which the offering ritual took place. It was believed that the *ka* could pass through the doorway from the burial chamber beyond in order to receive the food and drink placed there. Sometimes attached to the chapel was a small sealed room rather like a cellar with two holes at eye level. This is referred to as the *serdab* and enclosed a statue of the deceased in which the *ka* could reside if anything happened to the body. From inside the serdab the *ka* could see all that was happening in the chapel.

A noble sitting in front of an offering table, from the tomb of Ptahhotep

In the case of kings, these rites were performed in a special mortuary temple constructed adjacent to the pyramid. They were far more elaborate than for non-royals and involved a large number of personnel. It has been estimated that somewhere in the vicinity of three hundred people, some permanent and others working on a rotational basis, were employed to provide for the deceased king.

The priests performed two identical rituals, in the morning and evening before the five statues of the king. When each shrine was opened, it was fumigated with incense by a group of priests referred to as the *servants of the god* and sacred formulae were recited. Then another group, known as *the foremost of the royal precinct* unveiled, cleaned, dressed and adorned the statues. Cloth, sacred oil and finally a ritual meal were offered to the deceased king again to the accompaniment of sacred recitations. A libation was poured, after which the liquid was carefully collected and then poured into the drainage system. Ritual equipment was replaced in the sacred chests.

Servant women, representing the various estates of the tomb owner, bringing offerings

Old Kingdom tombs

The importance of the tomb to the ancient Egyptians is expressed in a line written by the Old Kingdom prince, Hardjedef, to his son.

> The House of death (tomb) is for life.[16]

However, not all Egyptians could afford a tomb. During the Old Kingdom, ownership of a tomb, whether pyramid, mastaba or rock-cut in form, was reserved for royalty and the governing class. The rest of the Egyptian population was probably buried in simple graves in the desert close to where they lived.

Ownership of tombs restricted to royalty and official class

Pyramid tombs

The development of pyramid tombs has already been discussed fully in Chapters 4 and 5 and is summarised in the table and diagrams on the following pages.

The development from step pyramid to true pyramid and the position-ing of the mortuary temples during the Third, Fourth and Fifth dynas-ties, appear to reflect changes in beliefs about the afterlife of royalty. It seems that there may have been a move from astral to solar beliefs from the Third to the Fifth dynasties. For example:

Changes in beliefs reflected in tombs

- Djoser's mortuary temple was located on the northern side of his Step Pyramid. This position may have been associated with the circumpolar or *Imperishable Stars*.

- The mortuary temples of the Fourth Dynasty kings were constructed on the eastern side of the pyramids — the side of the rising sun.

- The mortuary temple of Weserkaf, first king of the Fifth Dynasty was located on the southern side of the pyramid where it would receive the rays of the sun all through the day. During the Fifth Dynasty, Re, the sun god was the predominant deity.

Changes in the construction of pyramid tombs

Dynasties	Kings	Pyramid development
Third Dynasty	Djoser	Square-based, six-stepped pyramid developed from a rectangular mastaba. First building constructed of stone — small blocks of limestone. Unique pyramid complex. Mortuary temple and serdab on northern side may have reflected a belief in a stellar afterlife. Decorative and architectural features symbolised the Two Lands and the Sed festival.
	Sekhemkhet Kaban	Similar tomb complexes to Djoser's, but never completed.
	Huni	Pyramid at Meidum started as a step pyramid.
Fourth Dynasty	Sneferu	Completed Meidum Pyramid as a true pyramid. Bent Pyramid started but not completed as a true pyramid. The Northern Pyramid started and completed as a true pyramid. Use of large blocks of stone. Construction of a different pyramid complex. Sneferu was probably the first to build a decorated valley temple and an unroofed causeway. Mortuary temple moved to the eastern side of the pyramid (the side of the rising sun) while entrances still on the northern face — reflected the growing importance of a solar cult while still incorporating aspects of stellar beliefs.
	Khufu	The Great Pyramid of Khufu was a massive true pyramid — symbol of the sun and the largest monument ever constructed for an individual. His mortuary temple differed from that of Sneferu, indicating a possible religious change. Built of massive blocks of limestone with pure white Tura limestone casing. The 'king's' chamber is the only burial chamber within a pyramid at such a height above base level.
	Khafre	His pyramid complex reached the form it was to retain until the end of the Old Kingdom. This is the best preserved of all complexes. Causeways covered.
	Menkaure	Smallest of the main Giza pyramids. Outer casing was to be in granite but unfinished.
	Shepseskaf	Built a huge rectangular mastaba tomb which may indicate an attempt to limit the power of the cult of the sun god of Heliopolis.
Fifth Dynasty	Userkaf (Weserkaf)	Pyramids of Userkaf and his successors were smaller than their predecessors' pyramids and built of inferior materials. Elaborate sun temples reflected the growing importance of the sun cult during this dynasty. It is thought that Userkaf's mortuary temple may have been on the southern side where it would have got the sun all day.
	Sahure	Sahure's pyramid complex included elaborate drainage arrangements and beautiful and detailed reliefs.
	Unas (Wenis)	Unas was the last king of Fifth Dynasty or possibly first king of the Sixth Dynasty. The major development of this period was the inscription of Pyramid Texts (the earliest funerary texts) on the walls of the burial chambers in the pyramids of kings and queens. Unas' Pyramid Causeway is noted for its detailed reliefs.
Sixth Dynasty	Teti, Pepi I, Merenre and Pepi II	Sixth Dynasty pyramids were built of a core of small limestone blocks and rubble with a casing of limestone — evidence of a decline in the revenues available to the kings as well as a decline in their status.

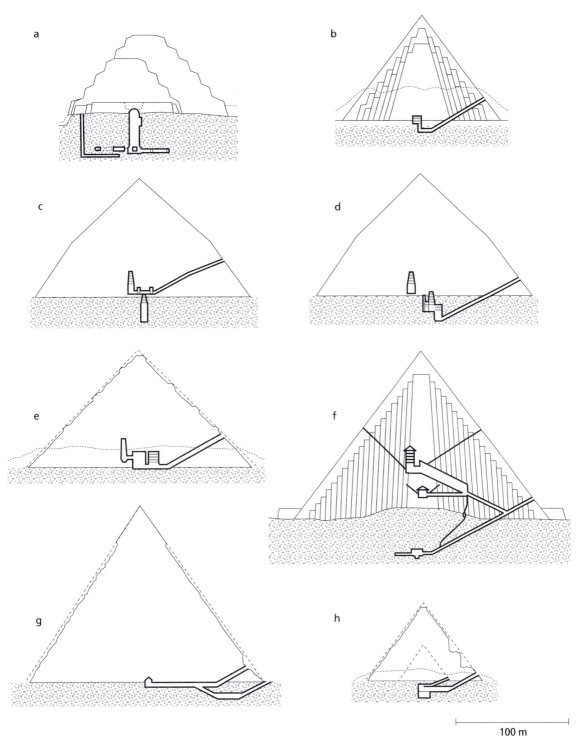

a. Step Pyramid of Djoser   b. Meidum Pyramid   c and d. Bent Pyramid of Sneferu, Dahshur (c. looking south;
d. looking west) f. Great Pyramid of Khufu, Giza   g. Pyramid of Khafre, Giza   h. Pyramid of Menkhaura, Giza

100 m

Sections through the pyramids of the Third and Fourth dynasties

However, Egyptians never discarded earlier religious beliefs. They incorporated them, not only into the new body of belief but continued to feature them in some way in their buildings. For example, the entrances to all pyramids of the Old Kingdom were on the north side, aligned to the circumpolar stars.

Tombs of the nobles and officials

No typical tomb plan in Old Kingdom

The upper class of Egyptians during the Old Kingdom built either mastaba or rock-cut tombs. According to Kanawati 'it is difficult to speak of a characteristic tomb plan such as is found in later periods'[17] because of the range of individual architectural features found in both mastaba and rock-cut tomb.

Some of these individual characteristics reflected the honour in which the king held the noble or official, the wealth of the owner, the type of terrain in which the tomb was built, and the location of the tomb — whether it was built in one of the royal necropolises or in a provincial cemetery.

As the upper classes began to accumulate wealth, they put more effort and expense into the construction of their tombs. The land on which these tombs were built was allocated to them by the king since he *owned* all the land in Egypt. 'The area and location of this land depended on the official's rank, responsibilities, family ties and the place where he held office.'[18] Sometimes the king honoured an official by contributing to the construction of his tomb or presenting him with some essential part of it. The following inscription from the Sixth Dynasty tomb autobiography of Weni illustrates how officials felt about receiving this royal honour.

> When I begged of the majesty of my lord (Pepi I) that there be brought for me a sarcophagus of white stone from Tura, his majesty had a royal seal-bearer cross over with a company of sailors under his command, to bring me this sarcophagus from Tura. It came with him in a great barge of the court, together with its lid, a doorway, lintel, two door-jambs and a libation-table. Never before had the like been done for any servant — but I was excellent in his majesty's heart; I was rooted in his majesty's heart; his majesty's heart was filled with me.[19]

Reasons for changes in tomb construction

Apart from individual differences, there were architectural changes common to particular periods which reflected the need to:

* take extra precautions to protect the body from violation and to keep the funerary items safe from grave robbers
* ensure that the deceased was adequately provided for in the afterlife
* provide a larger public area where the mortuary rites could be carried out.

Developments in tomb construction

Some of these changes in tomb construction from the earliest dynasties to the end of the Old Kingdom included:

* the use of cut stone (limestone) instead of mud-bricks
* experimentation with security measures such as concealed

entrances, deep, rubble-filled vertical shafts, portcullis blocks of limestone and granite plugs

- provision of an increased area for the storage of funerary goods — at first in large superstructures (above ground level) and later in underground chambers
- replacement of simple offering niches and small external chapels with interior chapels which increased in size and complexity
- more elaborate *decoration* of chapel walls and burial chambers.

Mastaba tombs

In the late Predynastic Period, it appears that most people were buried in pit graves of some description. The earlier oval-shaped pits covered with a mound of sand were replaced by rectangular-shaped pits. However, the rectangular shape could only be achieved by lining the walls with sticks and basketwork, smoothing the walls with layers of mud or by building a frame of sticks around the body. As the size of the pits were increased to accommodate more funerary items, the walls were lined with timber and mud-bricks.

Developed from Predynastic pit graves

During the Archaic Period, members of royalty as well as the nobles and officials, began to build large, rectangular mud-brick superstructures on top of their graves. This type of tomb is referred to as a *mastaba*. Modern Egyptians, working on Old Kingdom excavation sites, thought that these mud-brick superstructures looked like the rectangular benches or *mastabas* found outside some Egyptian houses.

At first these superstructures comprised a large number of storage rooms. They were built over the burial chamber which was cut into the rock. The external facades of these mud-brick mastabas were often decorated with a type of panelling similar to that used on the front of houses and palaces (palace-facade panelling).

Because the storerooms in the superstructure were an obvious target for robbers, the builders decided to locate them in the substructure (under-

Storerooms placed underground

The remains of a mastaba with a panelled facade, from Meidum

ground). The rectangular superstructure had a core of rubble which was enclosed by mud-brick walls. The storerooms were adjacent to the burial chamber which, in these early mastabas, was entered by means of a stairway. In the eastern face of the superstructure were two niches with inscribed stelae where relatives could place offerings.

Four developments took place between the early dynastic period and the end of the Fourth Dynasty.

1 For security reasons, stairways to the burial chamber were sealed with huge blocks of limestone. These were lowered into position like the portcullis gate of a medieval castle. Eventually stairways were replaced with deep, vertical shafts which were filled with hard granite plugs and rubble. The entrances to these shafts were in the top of the mastaba.

2 Burial chambers were excavated in the bedrock to the west of the shaft. Sometimes a pit was excavated in the burial chamber to hold the sarcophagus and a recess was built into the wall to hold the canopic chest.

3 The offering niches in the exterior wall of the superstructure, were enclosed fully or partially with brick walls. This created an external chapel where the funerary rites were maintained. However, it became increasingly common for the offering niches to be placed inside the superstructure. This interior chapel was cruciform in shape. Of the two internal niches, the southern most one was reserved for the tomb owner and the other for his wife.

The *false door* or *ka door*, sometimes of wood but usually of stone was an important feature of all chapels. This combined the offering niche and stela. On either side of the door was usually a relief of the tomb owner and above the door the tomb owner and his wife were often shown sitting at a table piled with food offerings.

Sometimes a *ka* statue of the owner was placed in front of the false door as if emerging from the burial chamber.

The remains of a mastaba at Giza

A special chamber, sealed off from the chapel by a wall, was built into the mastabas at this time. These were called *serdabs* and housed a lifelike *ka* statue of the tomb owner which would act as a substitute in case the body was destroyed. The Fifth Dynasty noble, Ti, took extra precautions by building several serdabs, with *ka* statues, within his mastaba chapel.

No tombs built at the time of Khufu featured *ka* statues or serdabs. This is believed to have been due to some religious changes introduced by the king.

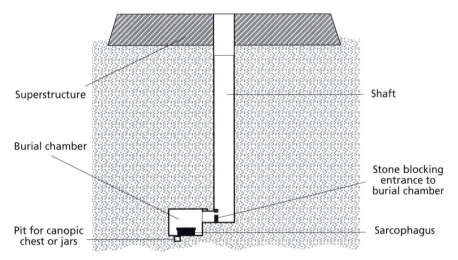

Section of a Fourth Dynasty mastaba

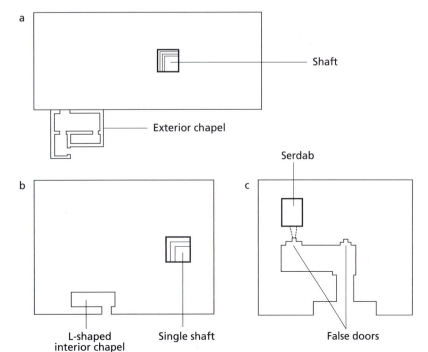

a. Plan of a stone mastaba with exterior chapel and one shaft

b. Plan of a stone mastaba with L-shaped chapel and one shaft

c. Plan of L-shaped chapel with two false doors and a serdab

4   Although mud-brick was still the most common material used in the construction of mastabas at this time, more nobles and officials began to build their tombs in limestone.

Elaborate chapels of the Fifth and Sixth dynasties

The main changes in tomb construction during the Fifth and Sixth dynasties occurred in the interior chapels. Many of them were now constructed in an L-shape. Those of the highest officials, such as Ptahhotep and Mereruka, were elaborate complexes of pillared rooms and porticoes. The walls of these large Fifth and Sixth dynasty chapels were carved and painted with a wider variety of themes than had been possible in the smaller chapels of previous dynasties.

Where the chapel took up the entire area of the mastaba, the entrance to the shaft or shafts leading to the burial chamber was usually in the floor of the chapel. If the chapel occupied only a portion of the mastaba, the shaft was entered from the roof or terrace of the mastaba.

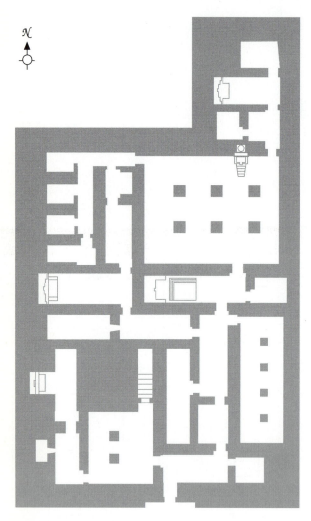

Above: A plan of the elaborate chapel of Mereruka

Right: A wooden false door from a Fifth Dynasty tomb

Rock-cut tombs of the Old Kingdom

> The rock-cut tomb should not be thought of as a later development superseding the mastaba, for the construction of the two types continued simultaneously at different sites.[20]

Most of the rock-cut tombs of the Old Kingdom were located in the provincial areas of Upper Egypt such as Aswan, although the earliest, built for some members of Fourth Dynasty royalty, have been found at Giza.

Rock-cut tombs had a number of advantages over mastabas. For example, there was no need to construct a roof and the special features of mastaba tombs (supporting pillars, huge stone architraves, false doors etc) did not have to be cut in the quarries and transported to the tomb site. They were simply fashioned out of the rock as the tomb was being cut into the cliff face. Rock-cut tombs were more likely to last than the exposed mud-brick and stone mastabas.

Advantages of rock-cut tombs

These tombs tended to follow the same pattern of construction as the mastabas but with some variations in the chapels. Whereas the larger mastabas of the Fifth and Sixth dynasties had chapels comprising many decorated rooms, rock-cut tombs tended to have only one large room. Some of these one-roomed chapels were as large as 180 square metres and featured several rows of non-essential pillars reaching to a height of four metres. Although rock-cut tombs did not require pillars to support the roof, many builders included them in imitation of the mastabas.

Chapels

The other major difference was the serdab. Rather than build a wall of stone to seal off a portion of the chapel to serve as a serdab, the builders of the rock-cut tombs found a satisfactory compromise for the safety of the *ka* statue. Engaged statues (still partially attached to the rock), were carved out of the rock wall. In this way the *ka* of the deceased could emerge from the chambers beyond and safely inhabit the statue to receive the offerings. In some tombs there were as many as 25 of these engaged statues.

Engaged statues

Entrance to the burial chamber was still generally by means of a vertical shaft although this was sometimes replaced with a sloping passageway.

Tomb art

The painted reliefs on the chapel walls of Old Kingdom mastaba and rock-cut tombs were not meant to *decorate*. Their chief purpose was to 'sustain the existence of the tomb-owner by imitating as effectively as possible certain aspects of his life'.[21]

Purpose

Teams of *artists*, under the supervision of a master artist, followed strict guidelines imposed by religious principles. The artist was not expected to produce imaginative or original ideas, but rather adhere to the time-honoured traditions — size, proportion and form of a figure, the themes represented, the use of colour and the arrangement of the scenes into registers (horizontal strips like a cartoon).

Traditional rather than original

The size of a figure usually indicated that person's status. The tomb-owner was always the largest figure in the scene. Sometimes his wife was shown as the same size as her husband but in other scenes she and the children were drawn considerably smaller. Other figures, such as peasants and craftsmen, were shown as even smaller and were frequently arranged in groups to indicate their insignificance.

The artist also followed strict rules with regard to the proportion of each part of the body in relation to the whole figure. To do this accurately, he had to draw a grid on the wall first.

The human body was drawn partly in profile and partly frontal.

Form and proportion of figures

The Egyptian artist drew the head in profile with the eye fully frontal. The shoulders were represented in frontal view and the chest in profile with one nipple shown. The loin and hips were then twisted, revealing the navel and genitals, unless these were hidden under garments. Legs were drawn in profile and, except in rare instances where all toes are shown, are usually viewed from the inner side with both feet showing the big toe. Drawing hands seems to have caused even more difficulties. When the main figure faces right, the preferred direction, holding the staff in the left hand and the sceptre in the right, the hands are usually correctly drawn, but in other situations the left and right hands are confused.[22]

The tomb owner and his wife were always depicted as young and perfect in form while their children, even if grown up, were shown with the plaited side-lock of youth. The use of this idealised form would make it difficult to distinguish one tomb-owner from another if it were not for the accompanying inscriptions which identify them by name.

There were also conventions which had to be followed with regard to the use of colour. For example, women were usually painted in yellow and men in a reddish-brown.

The themes depicted in Old Kingdom tombs were arranged in horizontal strips called registers. The information in consecutive registers was not necessarily related, although similar activities might be grouped together. If a series of related activities such as ploughing, sowing and harvesting were shown then the first of these tasks would appear in the top register. This arrangement of scenes changed during the Middle and New Kingdoms.

Common themes used in tomb 'decoration'

The most common themes represented in Old Kingdom tombs were:
- the tomb owner and his family sitting before a table of food with servants bringing baskets of food to them
- the activities of the agricultural year (ploughing, sowing, harvesting, threshing, winnowing, storing the grain, assessing and recording the harvest) and scenes of animal husbandry
- other activities on the noble's estate such as gathering papyrus, fishing with nets and lines, netting birds, treading grapes, making bread and beer, boat-building and brick-making
- the tomb owner inspecting the craftsmen in the workshops (carpenters, metal workers, and sculptors)
- fowling and hunting scenes (the tomb owner fowling along the

river with a boomerang and hunting in the deserts with lassoes, bows and arrows and hunting dogs)

- the tomb owner and his wife relaxing (playing sennet, listening to music or playing with pets)
- some funerary rites (primarily from the tombs of Sixth Dynasty nobles).

Despite the fact that Old Kingdom artists were expected to follow certain rules in tomb *decoration*, it is possible to see, in some of the small details, evidence of experimentation and individuality. It was in their treatment of animals, birds and vegetation that the Old Kingdom artists showed their best work. These men were obviously great observers of nature since they have accurately captured the lines, colours and markings of the flora and fauna found along the Nile and in the adjacent deserts. Sometimes the peasants are shown in very natural and relaxed poses and with individual features such as bald or thinning hair and sagging breasts. These figures are in marked contrast to the stiff figures of the tomb-owner and his family.

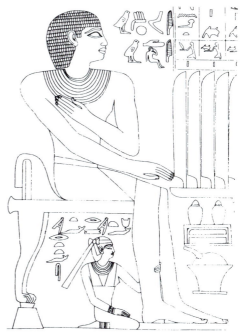

A tomb owner shown as larger than his wife; both bodies are drawn partly in profile and partly frontal

Tombs of lesser officials and workers

Egyptologists excavating on the Giza plateau have recently discovered a large number of tombs and graves which they believe belonged to the overseers and workmen responsible for the construction of the great mastabas clustered around the pyramids. They are located up the slope from an area where excavators have already found a so-called *settlement* site.

Workers' tombs on Giza plateau

The tombs appear to have belonged to men with the title of *overseer of the tomb makers*. These tombs are crowded together and are made from material left over from the construction of the mastabas. Some of the tombs were made from a strange type of mud-brick and appear to have had a reddish-coloured vaulted roof and walls painted in yellow and white. Some of the graves close to the tombs of the overseers had pyramid-shaped, mud-brick tops.

Tomb robbery

Throughout the Old Kingdom, as in all subsequent periods, tomb robbery was a serious problem. The men responsible were often those who had worked on the tombs or who guarded them. No matter what precautions were taken (carefully concealed entrances to deep rubble-filled shafts, passageways plugged with limestone and granite plugs and false burial chambers), very few tombs escaped the attention of those greedy for gold, precious stones and unguents.

Tomb robbers were able to avoid the time-consuming task of breaking through the rubble-filled shafts by:

- piercing the soft limestone blocks of which the tomb was made or with which the tunnels were sealed
- tunnelling from one tomb to another since tombs were generally crowded together. Robbers could tunnel right under the burial chamber and break through into the bottom of the limestone sarcophagus.

They were prepared to risk death if caught but it appears that many got away with their crime.

Conclusion

During the Old Kingdom only kings were believed to spend eternity with the gods. Only members of royalty built pyramids and were protected by the spells and prayers of the Pyramid Texts.

Mastaba and rock-cut tombs were the monopoly of the wealthy nobles and high officials since 'the preparation of a tomb was perhaps the biggest *investment* any Egyptian official made during his lifetime'.[23] The bulk of the Egyptian people were buried in simple pit graves.

Chapter review

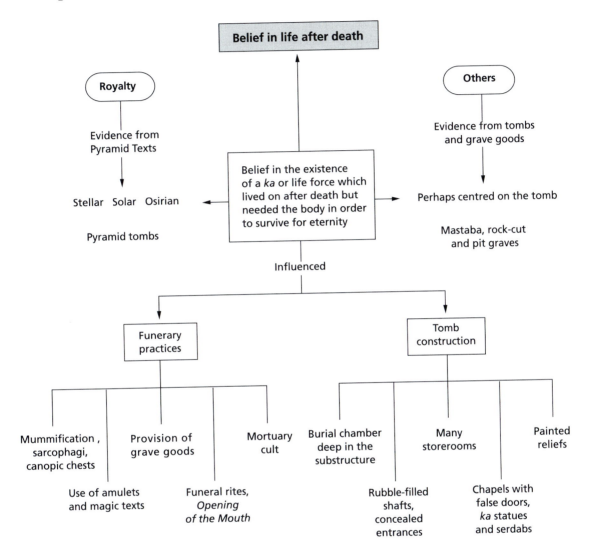

REVISION QUESTIONS AND ESSAY TOPICS

1 From the information provided in this chapter, identify the four illustrations below and explain the significance of each one in the context of Old Kingdom funerary beliefs and practices.

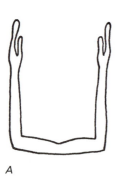

A

B

C

D

2 Read the following six extracts and answer the series of questions under each one.

Extract A

I am pure, I take my oar to myself, I occupy my seat,
I sit in the bow of the boat of the Two Enneads,
And I row Re to the west.[24]

a To what belief about the afterlife does this extract refer?

b What other beliefs were held about the afterlife of royalty during the Old Kingdom?

c What sort of afterlife did non-royal Egyptians envisage for themselves? What evidence do historians have to support this view?

Extract B

Rise up, O Teti!
Take your head,
Collect your bones,
Gather your limbs,
Shake the earth from your flesh!
Take your bread that rots not,
Your beer that sours not,
Stand at the gates that bar the common people!
The gatekeeper comes out to you,
He grasps your hand
Takes you to heaven ....
Rise up O Teti, you shall not die.[25]

a What evidence is there in this extract that only royalty were expected to spend eternity in heaven?

b What funerary belief do the words *Take your head, collect your bones, gather your limbs* illustrate?

c To what does *Take your bread that rots not, your beer that sours not* refer?

Extract C

O flesh of the king.
Do not decay,
Do not rot,
Do not smell unpleasant.[26]

a How did the Egyptians of the Old Kingdom attempt to preserve the body and stop the flesh from decaying and smelling?

b How successful were they?

Extract D

O ye living ... who shall pass by this tomb. So surely as you
wish your gods to favour you, may you say: a thousand of bread and beer, a thousand of
flesh and fowl, a thousand of alabaster and clothing for the ka of the deceased ...[27]

a Where would this inscription be found?

b What was its purpose?

Extract E

Teti's mouth has been parted,
Teti's nose has been opened,
Teti's ears are unstopped. [28]

a   To what important ceremony is this extract referring?

b   What was its purpose?

c   How is it believed to have been carried out during the Old Kingdom?

Extract F

Stand up for me O my father;
Stand up for me O Osiris the king,
For I am indeed your son, I am Horus.
I have come for you in order that I may cleanse you and purify you,
That I may cause you to live and gather together for you your
bones, that I may gather your soft parts for you and collect your dismembered parts for you,
For I am Horus who protected his father.[29]

a   Outline the myth of Osiris.

b   Why is the king referred to here as Osiris?

c   Who was regarded as Horus and what were his funerary duties?

3 Essay topics

a   How did the Egyptians' belief in the existence of a *ka* influence the architecture of the mastaba and rock-cut tombs?

b   Use the information in this chapter to write an account of the death and burial of an Egyptian nobleman or noblewoman. Describe the procedures and ceremonies associated with preserving and protecting the body, the funeral procession and the burial rites.

THREE

The Middle Kingdom

OVERVIEW

The period from the end of the Sixth Dynasty to part-way through the Eleventh Dynasty is referred to as the First Intermediate Period. It appears to have been a time of political and social upheaval and economic distress, resulting in despair and bewilderment. However, the lack of historical documents makes it difficult to gauge the extent of these problems.

Although Wilson refers to this period as 'the first illness', there were some positive developments. There was an increasing awareness of the individual which was reflected in demands for social justice and in the 'democratisation' of funerary practices.

After a century of intermittent warfare between the kings of Herakleopolis (Seventh to Tenth dynasties) and a family of princes from Thebes (Eleventh dynasty), the Two Lands were once again united under one ruler. This was the Theban prince, Mentuhotep (Montuhotep), fourth ruler of the Eleventh Dynasty under whose capable leadership peace eventually returned to Egypt.

He and his immediate successors, ruling from the southern city of Thebes, sent out military expeditions to secure Egypt's borders, resumed mining and quarrying in the Sinai Peninsula and the eastern desert and re-established trading connections with Nubia and the land of Punt. They also carried out a building program mainly in Upper Egypt.

There appears to have been some confusion during the short reign of Mentuhotep III during which his vizier, Amenemhet, took the throne and founded the Twelfth Dynasty. He moved the capital north to a site near Lisht and he and his male successors*, all of whom were called Amenemhet (Ammenemes) or Senwosret (Sesostris), completely reorganised the kingdom. They restored the prestige of the monarchy, extended Egypt's boundaries in Nubia where they built a string of forts, contained Egypt's

---

* The last ruler of the dynasty was a queen, Sobekneferu (Sebekneferu).

enemies in the north-east, promoted trade between Egypt and Sinai, Palestine, Nubia and the Aegean, initiated irrigation schemes in the Faiyum and built their pyramids from the mouth of the Faiyum to the plateau of Dahshur.

Known as the Middle Kingdom, this period was a time of *renaissance*. Although art reached a peak of excellence, the period is generally remembered for its literary contributions to Egyptian culture and is often referred to as a classical period.

The artistic and literary sources reveal a change in the image of kingship from that of the Old Kingdom. The Middle Kingdom image is one of a more fallible ruler, 'a watchful shepherd looking after his flocks', rather than the remote majesty of the Old Kingdom pharaohs.

There were also some significant religious changes at this time, one of which was the emergence of a previously unknown Theban god, Amun (Amen, Amon), after whom Amenemhet I took his name. Another was the predominance of the god Osiris in the funerary cult. Unlike Re, who was associated exclusively with royalty, Osiris appealed to the ordinary Egyptian. Also, anyone who could afford a coffin now had access to the spells and prayers previously reserved for royalty. Pyramid Texts were replaced with Coffin Texts.

The last ruler of the Middle Kingdom was Queen Sobekneferu who reigned for no more than four years. The 60 or so kings who followed her (the Thirteenth Dynasty) ruled for approximately 153 years. Their short-lived reigns and the fact that they left few memorials indicate that Egypt was in decline. It is possible that Egypt experienced similar conditions to those at the end of the Old Kingdom. It was during this so-called Second Intermediate Period, that foreigners from Palestine, called the Hyksos, invaded Egypt, conquered the north and extended their power southward. Refer to Chapter 9 for details on the Hyksos.

Sources of evidence for this period

The chief archaeological sources for this period are the remains of:

* the funerary complexes of the kings in Thebes (Mentuhotep II's tomb and mortuary complex at Deir-el-Bahri) and in the north at el-Lahun, Hawara and Dahshur (Twelfth Dynasty pyramids)
* the mastaba and rock-cut tombs of the nobles, particularly the tombs of the governors of the Oryx Nome at Beni Hasan

- the pyramid worker's town established by Senwosret II at Kahun

- the Nubian fortresses between the First and Second cataracts

- the funerary equipment found in the tombs of royals and non-royals such as the exquisite jewellery and toilet articles belonging to the princesses of the Twelfth Dynasty and the detailed wooden models found in the tomb of the chancellor, Meketre

- the sculptured royal portraits of kings such as Senwosret III and Amenemhet III.

There is a wide range of literary sources from this period including official and private stelae, legal documents, medical and veterinary treatises, wisdom literature, prophecies, sacred dramas and narratives such as the story of *Sinuhe*.

The achievements of the Eleventh and Twelfth dynasties

Background

The breakdown of centralised control of Egypt after the long reign of Pepi II and the resultant rivalry between provincial rulers, affected the supervision and maintenance of irrigation throughout the land. This was probably aggravated by a series of droughts and low Niles together with bureaucratic corruption and negligence. Furthermore, peasant farmers, recruited into local militias, were probably unable to tend their farms adequately and large tracts of land were abandoned. According to the *Admonitions of Ipuwer*,* 'the inundation is disregarded. Agriculture is at a standstill. The cattle roam wild. Everywhere the crops rot.'[1]

Drought, corruption and negligence in maintaining irrigation schemes

As famine and poverty spread, desperate people roamed the countryside causing problems. The nomarch, Ankhtifi, 'found the house of Khuu (in the Nome of Edfu) ... abandoned by him who belonged to it, in the grip of a rebel, under the control of a wretch'.[2] Even farmers were forced to carry a shield with them when they ploughed the fields.

Poverty and abandoned farms

It was not only the poorer classes who suffered. As conditions worsened, essential items such as spices and oils could not be obtained and, as Ipuwer recorded, there was no such thing as clean linen available. Foreign trade, which was a royal monopoly, appears to have declined and items deemed essential for a proper burial were in short supply.

> ... Today there is no trading with Byblos. No one can get pine wood for coffins, funerary materials or the oils for embalming which were once brought from as far afield as Crete. There is a gold shortage, and raw materials for proper burial are exhausted.[3]

As a result, many of the dead were just thrown into the river.

---

* Although Gardiner believes that the *Admonitions of Ipuwer* was written in response to the calamitous conditions of the First Intermediate period, Lichtheim believes that it did not derive from any historical situation.

Social distress

Although the ordinary Egyptians probably blamed the nobles for their situation, there does not seem to be enough evidence to support the view that there was a social revolution in which the old hierarchic order was overthrown. Lichtheim maintains that the ruling families within each nome remained in control, promoting the economic welfare of their local district at the expense of others.

Image of the kingship weakened

During this time of despair and pessimism it seems that many of the old traditions and beliefs were questioned. The literature of the time reflects this.

With the decline in royal power, the image of the kingship was considerably weakened. According to Wilson, 'the First Intermediate Period was the only time in Egyptian history in which the divine king was presented as humanly fallible and errant'.[4] In the *Instructions Addressed to King Merikare*, a Tenth Dynasty king addresses his son, Merikare, and admits that he has done wrong and deserves to be punished by the gods. He then continues with advice on the best way to treat his subjects. As the god-king appeared more humanly fallible, so the nobles and commoners with them were 'levelled up to the plane of the divine ruler'.[5]

Emphasis on individualism

There was a greater emphasis on independence and individualism among the nobles and this was reflected in the funerary beliefs and practices of the time. According to Wilson, there was a gradual 'democratisation' of royal funerary privileges, leading to a reassessment of the individual's place in the universe.

Despite the political upheaval and economic misery of much of the First Intermediate Period, there were some advances, such as demands for social justice and equality. In the story of the *Eloquent Peasant*, the farmer, robbed of his possessions, pleads for justice before the magistrate and does not hesitate to criticise the judge for his failure to make a fair decision.

Chronology of the Eleventh and Twelfth dynasties

Mentuhotep II, the fourth Eleventh Dynasty ruler, from Thebes, was a leader of outstanding military skill. He was able to defeat the Tenth Dynasty rulers of Herakleopolis and bring to an end the disastrous civil disturbances of the First Intermediate Period. Eventually he was accepted as king of Upper and Lower Egypt, the *Uniter of the Two Lands*. It is from the reign of Mentuhotep II (c. 2061–2010 BC), that the Middle Kingdom (Eleventh and Twelfth dynasties) is said to begin.

The table on pages 211 and 212 places the pharaohs of the Middle Kingdom in chronological order and summarises their major achievements.

Kings of the Eleventh Dynasty	Developments and achievements
Mentuhotep II (c. 2061–2010 BC)	Pacified the warring kingdoms and reunited Egypt.
	Kept a close eye on the nomarchs.
	Increased central control.
	Made Thebes the new capital of Egypt.
	Reopened trade routes between Egypt and Nubia; sent mining expeditions to Sinai.
	Constructed a number of public buildings, the majority of which were in Upper Egypt.
	Built his famous mortuary temple at Deir el-Bahri, using innovative architectural features.
	Promoted the local deity, Amun. It would be another 400 years, however, before Amun became the all-powerful god of empire.
Mentuhotep III (c. 2010–1998 BC)	Constructed many buildings in Upper Egypt. Sent an expedition to Punt for incense and to Wadi Hammamat for stone.
Mentuhotep IV (c. 1998–1991 BC) May not have been the son of the previous pharaoh.	Sent a huge stone-quarrying expedition to Wadi Hammamat under the supervision of his vizier Amenemhet (who is believed to have been the next king and founder of the Twelfth Dynasty).

Kings of the Twelfth Dynasty	Developments and achievements
Amenemhet (Ammenemes) (1991–1962 BC) May have seized power from Mentuhotep or was designated as his heir. Believed to have been assassinated.	Moved the capital to Itj-Tawy near Lisht on the border of Upper and Lower Egypt.
	Organised the nomarchs in a feudal system where they owed their allegiance to the king and provided armies for the king's campaigns.
	Built a fortress in the north-east to protect Egypt's boundaries against incursions by people from western Asia.
	Campaigned in Nubia in years 23 and 29, establishing Egyptian control as far as the Second Cataract.
	Built extensively, including a pyramid tomb at Lisht, in the Faiyum area.
	Established a precedent for succession of power by means of a co-regency.
Senwosret (Sesostris) I (1971–1926 BC)	Constructed forts between the First and Second Cataract (eg, Buhen) and implemented a vigorous policy of colonisation in Nubia.
	Exploited the Nubian gold mines.
	Promoted trade between Egypt and Sinai, Palestine, Punt and the Aegean.
	Built throughout Egypt and Nubia.
	Constructed his pyramid at Lisht.
	Continued the practice of co-regency.

(Continued)

Kings of the Twelfth Dynasty	Developments and achievements
Amenemhet II (1929–1892 BC)	Maintained peaceful relations abroad and sent an expedition to Punt. Built his funeral complex at Dahshur.
Senwosret II (1897–1878 BC)	Initiated an irrigation system in the Faiyum. He was the first pharaoh to undertake a systematic exploitation of this region. His successors followed his example. Promoted trade. Built his pyramid complex at el-Lahun and established a workers' town at Kahun, near his pyramid.
Senwosret III (1878–c. 1841 BC)	Reduced the powers of the provincial nobles. Campaigned ruthlessly in Nubia. Built a series of forts around the Second Cataract and confirmed it as Egypt's southern boundary. These forts served as trading stations as well as barriers to the rebellious Kushites from upper Nubia. Campaigned in Palestine. Continued the irrigation and reclamation scheme of his father.
Amenemhet III (c. 1844–1797 BC)	Promoted trade between Egypt and the cities of Phoenicia. Sent out mining expeditions and established mining settlements in Sinai. Strengthened and extended military forts at Semna and Kumma. Reclaimed more land — the area of arable land in the Faiyum reached its maximum. Built a massive 'labyrinth' (over 28 000 square metres) and two pyramids — one at Dahshur and the other at Hawara.
Amenemhet IV (c. 1799–1787 BC) Not much known about him and no evidence of his burial site.	Maintained trade with the Levant (Phoenicia) and mining in Sinai. Built monuments in conjunction with his predecessor.
Queen Sebekneferu (c. 1787–1783 BC) Daughter of Amenemhet III. First female ruler for whom the full titulary of a king is known. No evidence of her burial site.	Completed her father's labyrinth.

Major developments and changes

Not only were there major political and economic changes during the Middle Kingdom, but significant technical, cultural and religious changes as well.

A change in the image of kingship

During the Middle Kingdom there was a change in the nature of the kingship. Whereas the kings of the Old Kingdom had been confident in their divinity, those of the Middle Kingdom present an image of a fallible human with heavy responsibilities and anxieties. The burden of kingship and the need to be ever watchful is depicted in the *Instruction of King Amenemhet I for his son Senwosret I*:

> When you lie down, guard your heart yourself,
> For no man has adherents on the day of woe.
> I gave the beggar, I raised the orphan,
> I gave success to the poor as to the wealthy;
> But he who ate my food raised opposition
> He whom I gave my trust used it to plot.[6]

The sombre portrait head of Senwosret III, with its deep creases at the mouth, furrows in the forehead and hollows under the eyes, seems to confirm the burden of kingship. This may not be a realistic depiction of Senwosret but rather a 'portrait of an age'.[7]

The image of the Middle Kingdom pharaoh was of a shepherd looking after his flocks. Senwosret I, in his building inscription, recorded:

> He appointed me shepherd of this land, knowing him who would herd it for him.[8]

A granite statue of Senwosret III

Shepherd of his flocks

The change in status and power of nomarchs

When Mentuhotep II reunited Egypt, he abolished many of the nomarchs' privileges, discarded some of the provincial governorships and tightened central control by restoring the old positions of vizier and chancellor. The tomb biographies of the Eleventh Dynasty stressed once again the services which the officials carried out on behalf of their rulers.

Abolition of privileges by Mentuhotep

In a wise political move, Amenemhet I, the founder of the Twelfth Dynasty, moved the capital from Thebes to Itj-Tawy (*Binder of the Two*

Lands), some 30 kilometres south of Memphis. As a usurper, he probably wanted to remove himself from a city which had strong ties to the previous dynasty. A more central location would also make it easier to control the country.

Because he needed the support of the nomarchs, he:

Some independence returned to nomarchs

- returned a certain amount of independence to them and reinforced their power by reviving some of the ancient titles
- made new appointments to some of the nomarchies.

Nomarchs in feudal arrangement with the king

However, they were bound to the king in a semi-feudal type of organisation. They owed allegiance to the king and were expected to carry out activities on his behalf and support him with troops if necessary.

Wilson maintains that as the successful Twelfth Dynasty pharaohs demonstrated 'their capacity to be gods',[9] the nobles willingly surrendered to their authority. Tomb inscriptions reflected the advantages that the nobles saw in once again being in royal favour.

Nomarchs still retained considerable power

However, despite the increasing centralisation of authority in the person of the king, these nomarchs were still in charge of their nomes. In their tombs they recorded what they did for the peasants and landowners under their control. There is also evidence from the tombs of their widespread influence and of the resources at their disposal.

For example, in the tomb of Khnumhotep at Beni Hasan, there is a scene recording the arrival of a party of 37 Bedouins from western Asia, bringing gifts of eye-cosmetics and animals for the nomarch. The inscriptions refer to these gifts as tribute.

Bedouins of western Asia bringing gifts to Khumhotep, Nomarch of Oryx Nome

A well-known scene in the tomb of Thehuthotep, ruling noble of the Hare Nome, features the transportation of a colossal alabaster *ka* statue of the noble. This provides evidence for the 'organisation of the government in a Middle Kingdom nomarchy'.[10]

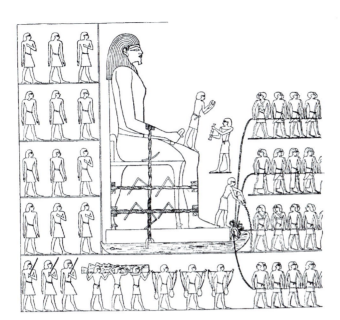

*Transportation of a colossal statue
of the nomarch, Thehuthotep*

Although the Twelfth Dynasty kings, from Amenemhet I to Senwosret II, monitored the activities of their officials, there was always inherent danger to the king from a powerful provincial noble. For this reason Senwosret III is believed to have curbed their powers considerably. Perhaps there had been some attempt to undermine his authority. How he did this is not known but it appears that some of the duties previously carried out by the nomarchs were handed over to three new officials referred to as 'reporters' who resided in the capital. These men headed departments which were responsible for administration in different parts of the country — the north, the south and the 'head of the south' (Elephantine and lower Nubia). These three new administrative departments were under the supervision of the vizier.

Potential danger from powerful nomarchs

The decline in the power of the provincial nobles from the time of Senwosret III is reflected in the size of their tombs. They were smaller than those constructed earlier in the dynasty and the tomb inscriptions were far more modest.

Co-regencies

Amenemhet I, the founder of the Twelfth Dynasty, was not of royal blood and is believed to have usurped the throne on the death of Mentuhotep IV. As a commoner, he resorted to propaganda to justify his claim to rule. In the *Prophecies of Neferti*, written during his reign and designed to promote his achievements, Amenemhet's rule is prophesied.

Propaganda to justify Amenemhet I's reign

> Then a king will come from the South,
> Ameny, the justified, by name,
> Son of a woman of Ta-Seti, child of Upper Egypt.[11]

To make sure of the continuation of his family line, Amenemhet I 'inaugurated a political system which dealt effectively with any attempt to place a rival claimant on the throne after his death'.[12]

Senwosret becomes co-regent

Somewhere around year 20 of his reign, Amenemhet elevated his son, Senwosret, to the position of co-regent and for approximately nine years he ruled alongside his father. Senwosret gained valuable experience as he supervised his father's building activities and led his military campaigns. The co-regency ensured a smooth succession to the throne on the older king's death and the reign that followed was one of great development and stability. Amenemhet I set a precedent which his successors followed.

Trade

Royal monopoly of trade

Foreign trade was a royal monopoly and with the restoration of pharaoh's authority, trading expeditions were once more despatched to Punt, Nubia, Palestine and Syria. Trade was resumed with tropical Africa, via Nubia and there is substantial evidence of trading links with the Minoans of Crete and other Aegean people.

The location of Punt, Wadi Hammamat and the Red Sea

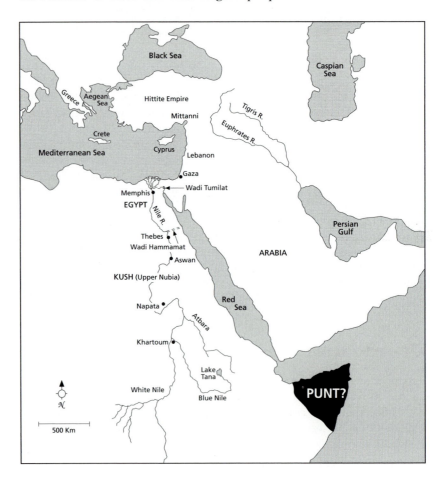

Punt and Nubia

First expedition to Punt under Henenu

During the reign of Mentuhotep III, the great steward, Henenu, who described himself as 'Taxation official, Treasurer of Produce from the Oasis, boat-builder, excavator and expedition leader', led an expedition to Punt. The purpose of his expedition was to bring back fresh myrrh (incense) for the king. Henenu was accompanied by an army of 3000 men who cleared the way for him along the desert route from the Nile Valley to the Red Sea, 'overpowering those hostile towards the king'.[13] The troops also dug numerous wells along the way.

When they reached the Red Sea, the members of the expedition built a ship for the sea journey to Punt, believed to be in the vicinity of present-day Somalia in east Africa. There are no details of his stay in Punt but he was obviously successful, as he recorded in his tomb:

> I executed the command of his majesty, and I brought for him all the goods which I found for him in the region of Gods' land (Punt).[14]

On his return to the Nile Valley through Wadi Hammamat, he cut 'majestic blocks (of stone) for statues belonging to the temple'.[15]

The evidence suggests that during the reign of Amenemhet I, an expedition was sent to the Red Sea to find a more suitable site for a port. Recent excavations at Wadi Gawasis, north of Wadi Hammamat, have revealed the remains of a port and fragments of stelae indicating that there were several expeditions sent to Punt during the reign of Senwosret I. Khentekhtay-wer, an official under Amenemhet II, also left a record of his return from Punt in year 28, on a stela at the Red Sea port.

A new port on the Red Sea

Despite the lack of further information, it is highly likely that the Middle Kingdom pharaohs continued to send their officials to Punt since incense was always in great demand.

To ensure the free passage of trading caravans from tropical Africa and the secure transportation of gold from Nubia, the Twelfth Dynasty pharaohs sent various military expeditions to the south. During the reign of Semwosret I, Ameni, one of the powerful Beni Hasan nobles, recorded that he sailed south with 400 of his best troops 'to bring gold ore for the majesty of the king'.[16] When the tribes from Kush and beyond moved into the area north of the Third Cataract, Senwosret III was forced to carry out at least three campaigns against these groups in years 8, 10 and 16.

Nubian trade supported by military campaigns

Syria, Palestine and the Aegean

During the reign of Mentuhotep II, Chancellor Khety, on an expedition to the Sinai, brought back lapis lazuli as well as galena, a substance widely used in the Middle Kingdom as an eye cosmetic. Since these products came from Afghanistan and western Asia respectively, there must have been some exchange of goods between Egyptian and Asiatic traders in the Sinai.

Amenemhet I resumed relations with the coastal town of Byblos in the Levant. From the time of the Old Kingdom the valuable cedar wood from this area had been in great demand by Egyptian kings as had one of its by-products, resin, used in mummification. It is likely that Amenemhet also made contact with the islands of Crete and Cyprus at this time.

Cedar and resin from Byblos

Evidence of Syrian and Aegean trade

Senwosret I extended his commercial links with Syria as far as Ugarit and his successor, Amenemhet II, also appears to have followed a vigorous trading policy in the north. In a foundation deposit in the remains of the Temple of Montu at Tod, Egyptologists found four copper chests with the cartouche of Amenemhet II on them. The chests were filled with Syrian silverware, amulets of Mesopotamian lapis lazuli and vessels of Minoan (Cretan) design.

There is evidence in the tomb of Khnumhotep, at Beni Hasan, of trade with western Asia during the reign of Senwosret II. Further evidence of trade with western Asia and the island of Crete was found in the pyramid town of Kahun.

The reign of Amenemhet II was a time of prolific trade. Many Palestinian and Syrian sites have revealed Egyptian jewellery, statues, vases, scarabs, seals and other artefacts, while objects with distinctive Aegean designs have been found at other sites along the Nile Valley.

Quarrying and mining

Fine building stones in great demand

To satisfy the building and funerary demands of the Middle Kingdom pharaohs, the Egyptian stone quarries of Wadi Hammamat, Aswan, Hatnub and Tura were worked extensively. Because supplies of gold from the eastern desert had declined by the time of the Middle kingdom, Nubia became Egypt's chief source of gold. The turquoise and copper mines in Sinai were exploited extensively, particularly during the reigns of Amenemhet III and IV.

Amenemhet and the expedition to Wadi Hammamat

When the future Amenemhet I was vizier for Mentuhotep IV, he led a huge expedition to Wadi Hammamat to find 'an august block of pure costly stone which is in the mountain ... for a sarcophagus, an eternal memorial, and for monuments in the temples of Middle Egypt...'.[17] He was accompanied by an army of 10 000 men, 'the choicest of the whole land' as well as 'miners, artificers, quarrymen, artists, draughtsmen, stonecutters, gold-workers, treasurers of pharaoh, of every department of the White House, and every office of the king's house, united behind me'.[18] The task was successfully accomplished. His soldiers descended the mountain with the sarcophagus and 'not a man perished, not a troop was missing, not an ass died, not a workman was enfeebled'.[19] Three thousand sailors from the delta delivered the sarcophagus safely to its destination. To commemorate his achievement, Amenemhet had four rock stelae carved.

Quarrying activities of Senwosret I

The pharaohs of the Twelfth Dynasty continued to quarry stone from Wadi Hammamat. Senwosret I, a prolific builder, is believed by Grimal 'to have extracted sufficient stone blocks for sixty sphinxes and one hundred and fifty statues, numbers that correspond well with his activities as a builder'.[20] There is also a record of at least two expeditions sent by him to the alabaster quarries at Hatnub.

Amenemhet III and Wadi Hammamat

During the reign of Amenemhet III there was a great increase in quarrying projects. In year 19 the king sent a major quarrying expedition to Wadi Hammamat for the purpose of extracting stone for a place or building referred to as *Life of Amenemhet*. Breasted suggests that the stone might have been for his pyramid temple at Hawara. There were three quarry inscriptions associated with that expedition, one of which stated:

> His majesty sent to bring for him monuments from the valley of Hammamat, of beautiful black (basaltic) stone as far as Enekh-Amenemhet, living forever and ever; at the house of Sobek, of Crocodilopolis; ten statues of five cubits ...[21]

The copper and turquoise mines in Sinai were operational throughout the Middle Kingdom. To protect the miners in Sinai from attacks by the Mentjiu nomads, the pharaohs sent out patrols and paid special attention to the northern defences of Egypt. A line of fortresses was built along Egypt's northern boundary, one of which was named The Wall of the Ruler.

Military campaigns to secure Sinai mines

Until the reign of Amenemhet III the miners went out to the Sinai only on a seasonal basis but under Amenemhet and his successor, a construction program transformed the mining areas into permanent fortified settlements. So that they could exploit the copper and turquoise deposits on an unprecedented scale, they built houses for the miners with wells and cisterns at Serabit el-Khadi and enlarged the temple of Hathor, *mistress of turquoise*. Between years 9 and 45 of Amenemhet's reign there were at least 55 texts inscribed at the turquoise, copper and malachite mines of Serabit el-Khadi, Wadi Mahgera and Wadi-Nasb.

Permanent settlements made in Sinai

Nubian fortresses

The reconquest of Nubia had begun under Mentuhotep II, and in year 29 of his successor, Amenemhet I, the Egyptians extended their control in Nubia as far as the Second Cataract. The construction of a number of forts between the First and Second cataracts was already under way by the reign of Senwosret I. Although Senwosret II is believed to have reached as far south as the Third Cataract, Senwosret III confirmed that the Egyptian frontier was to be maintained at the Second Cataract.

Egypt's boundaries set at the Second Cataract

He initiated the construction of a group of forts, including Semna and Kumma, which protected lower Nubia from the kingdom of Kush to the south. This is revealed by their names — *Repelling the Tribes and Curbing the Deserts*. These forts also regulated trade and diplomatic traffic.

He had a formal inscription carved at Semna:

> The southern boundary which was created in the 8th year under the majesty of King Senwosret III to prevent any Nubian from passing it when faring northwards, whether on foot or by boat, as well as any cattle of the Nubians. An exception is a Nubian who shall come to barter at Iken*, or one with an official message.[22]

From these border forts, regular patrols were sent out to check on the activities of the Medjay people south of the Second Cataract and to report on the 'state of the desert'. Regular despatches (Semna Despatches) were sent from the garrison at Semna to Egypt and reported on even the most minor movements of the Medjay people, as the following extract illustrates.

Patrols

Semna despatches

---

* Iken was the name for the huge fortress at Mirgissa at the northern end of the Second Cataract.

> Be informed, if you please, that two males and three female Medjay ... came down from the desert in year 3, third month of the Second Season, day 27. They said: 'We have come to serve the Palace!' They were questioned about the state of the desert. They said: 'We have not heard anything, but the desert is dying of hunger' ...[23]

This marked the beginning of the use of Medjay trackers. Later, Medjay warriors were incorporated into the Egyptian army and used as police in Egypt.

Thirteen forts over 400 kilometres

Amenemhet III expanded and repaired many of the forts constructed by his predecessors. By the end of the Twelfth Dynasty, the Egyptians had built a series of fortresses (approximately 13) between the First and Second cataracts, a distance of 400 kilometres. According to Kemp, these forts reveal the ingenious mind of the Egyptian military architect and the scale of the Middle Kingdom administration.[24]

The site of the Second Cataract and the forts of Semna and Kumma

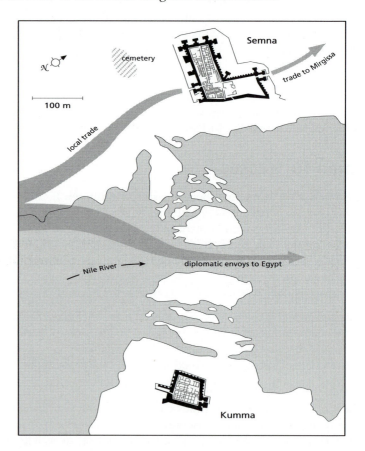

The Nubian forts appear to have been of two types, based on their location and site as well as on the period in which they were built. Those in the first group were built prior to the reign of Senwosret III, on the flat or gently sloping banks of the Nile between the First and Second Cataracts. Their massive walls enclosed a large area. Those in the second group were built after the annexation of the area by Senwosret III, along the 35 kilometre stretch of the Second Cataract, on rugged terrain and rocky promontories. Their fortified area was smaller than the first group.

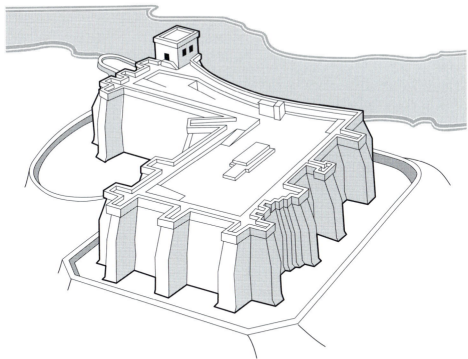

An artist's reconstruction of the fort of Semna at the Second Cataract

Irrigation and reclamation schemes in the Faiyum

Senwosret II initiated a major reclamation and irrigation system in the Faiyum which his successors, Senwosret III and Amenemhet III, continued and expanded.

The Faiyum is a fertile depression in the desert about 80 kilometres south-west of Cairo. The chief feature of the area today, as in ancient times, is a lake (Birket el-Qarun) fed by a 231-kilometre-long channel which diverges from the Nile just north of Asyut. This channel, known as Bahr Yusef, enters the Faiyum basin through the desert hills near el-Lahun. Once in the depression, the channel breaks into numerous smaller channels providing abundant water to the area.

The Faiyum and its fertility

In ancient times, the lake was far larger than it is today and was two metres below sea level. Its marshy shores supported lush vegetation and teemed with wildlife, including crocodiles. From the time of the Old Kingdom, the Faiyum attracted Egyptian royalty who came there to hunt and fish. The area's chief city was Crocodilopolis (modern Medinet el-Faiyum), the cult centre of the crocodile god, Sobek.

Lake much larger in ancient times

The Twelfth Dynasty pharaohs chose to establish their new capital city, Itj-tawy (modern el-Lisht), near the Faiyum, but it was not until the reign of Senwosret II that anything was done about increasing the amount of cultivable land in the area.

The Faiyum

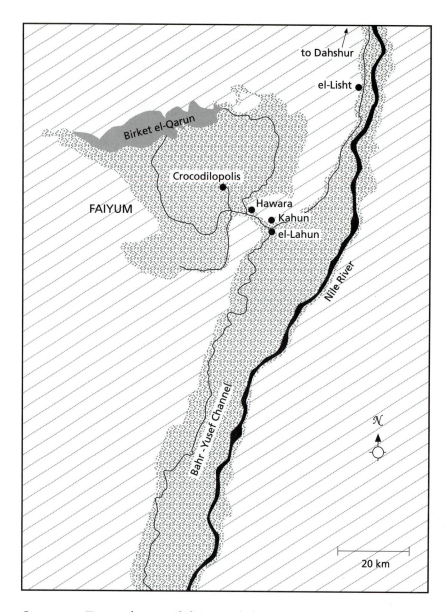

  Fertile land

☐ Desert

Senwosret II saw the possibilities and the means to achieve this and ordered the construction of a barrier across the mouth of the Hawara channel near el-Lahun. This regulated the flow of water from Bahr Yusef into the lake and allowed some of its foreshores to dry out, providing silt-rich land for farming. These newly reclaimed lands were irrigated by a network of canals and protected from future floods by an earthen embankment.

Area of reclaimed land extended by Amenemhet III

Senwosret's successors continued his project. Amenemhet III reclaimed a further 6900 hectares of farming land and continued the construction of the semicircular embankment around the perimeter of the lake which, by the end of his reign, was much reduced in size. Baines and Malek estimate that the Twelfth Dynasty pharaohs added about 117 hectares of arable land to the Faiyum. This ancient irrigation system is still operating in much the same manner today.

Buildings

Apart from the funerary complexes of the kings, not many of the other architectural achievements of the Eleventh and Twelfth Dynasties have survived.

Funerary complexes

The originality of the terraced tomb and mortuary temple of Mentuhotep II, set into the cliffs at Deir el-Bahri, 'remained a Theban phenomenon. His successors (of the Twelfth Dynasty), having moved the capital back to the Memphite region, returned to the Memphite system (pyramids) for their funerary complexes.'[(25)]

The originality of Mentuhotep's Theban funerary complex

The mortuary complex of Mentuhotep II

In the construction of his magnificent funerary complex, Mentuhotep II appears to have:

- modelled it partly on the pyramid complexes of the pharaohs of the Old Kingdom. However, unlike those of the Old Kingdom, his tomb was not enclosed in a separate pyramid — it was within the temple itself
- foreshadowed the mortuary temples of the New Kingdom. Like the *mansions of millions of years* (mortuary temples) of the New Kingdom, Mentuhotep's mortuary temple also served a cult purpose. The chapel cut into the Theban cliffs was not only dedicated to the dead king but to Amun-Re, the new state god.

The figure below shows a possible reconstruction of Mentuhotep's terraced temple underneath which was his tomb. It was once believed that the central building on the terrace supported a pyramid. The most recent work published on this temple, by Arnold, suggests that the walls of the central structure were not strong enough to support a pyramid. According to Arnold, this central structure had a flat top, capped by a cornice. This may have represented the primordial mound on which creation took place.

Views about the central structure

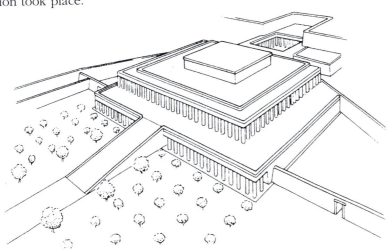

An artist's reconstruction of Mentuhotep's mortuary temple at Deir el-Bahri

**Four stages in
the construction
of the mortuary
temple complex**

Archaeologists have identified what they believe were four stages in the construction of this funerary complex.

1 Early in his reign Mentuhotep defined his temple enclosure with a wall of field stones.

2 Between years 20 and 30, the king built the main enclosure wall. This protected the tombs and chapels of six queens/princesses who were buried on the site. Their decorated chapels were later incorporated into the main temple structure. The main enclosure wall also protected a tomb, referred to today as Bab el-Hosan (*Entrance of the Horse*)*. This tomb was probably intended as the king's original burial chamber but was later turned into a cenotaph tomb 'by sealing a ritual burial inside it',[26] possibly at the time of the king's first Sed jubilee in year 30. A painted statue of the king, wearing a white jubilee cloak and wrapped in linen, was found in the burial chamber. Its black face, curved beard and folded arms also point to its association with Osiris. See the painted sandstone statue of Mentuhotep II later in this chapter.

3 Sometime after year 30 and possibly closer to year 39, when Mentuhotep changed his Horus name to *Uniter of the Two Lands*, the main building phase began. This stage included the erection of:
  - the terrace and central structure
  - a colonnaded ambulatory
  - a peristyle hall
  - a hypostyle hall
  - the chapel to Mentuhotep II and Amu-Re
  - the royal tomb.

4 The last building phase included the construction of the causeway, the inner walls of the forecourt, gateways and the garden in the forecourt.

Refer to the labelled plan and cross section view of the temple shown below for architectural features of the temple and tomb.

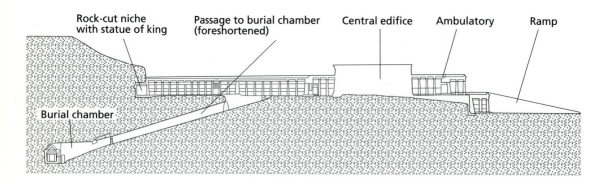

A cross section of Mentuhotep's temple

---

* The tomb was discovered when a horse, ridden by the Egyptologist Howard Carter, caught its foot on the slab which protected this tomb and both rider and horse toppled into a ditch.

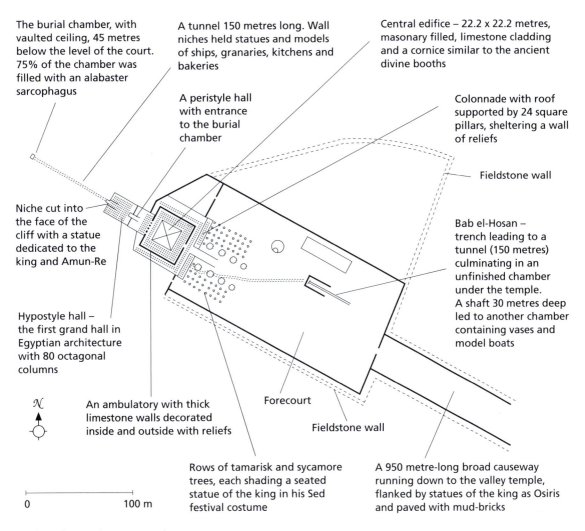

The burial chamber, with vaulted ceiling, 45 metres below the level of the court. 75% of the chamber was filled with an alabaster sarcophagus

A tunnel 150 metres long. Wall niches held statues and models of ships, granaries, kitchens and bakeries

Central edifice – 22.2 x 22.2 metres, masonary filled, limestone cladding and a cornice similar to the ancient divine booths

A peristyle hall with entrance to the burial chamber

Colonnade with roof supported by 24 square pillars, sheltering a wall of reliefs

Fieldstone wall

Niche cut into the face of the cliff with a statue dedicated to the king and Amun-Re

Bab el-Hosan – trench leading to a tunnel (150 metres) culminating in an unfinished chamber under the temple. A shaft 30 metres deep led to another chamber containing vases and model boats

Hypostyle hall – the first grand hall in Egyptian architecture with 80 octagonal columns

𝒩

An ambulatory with thick limestone walls decorated inside and outside with reliefs

Forecourt

Fieldstone wall

0   100 m

Rows of tamarisk and sycamore trees, each shading a seated statue of the king in his Sed festival costume

A 950 metre-long broad causeway running down to the valley temple, flanked by statues of the king as Osiris and paved with mud-bricks

A plan of Mentuhotep's temple

Twelfth Dynasty pyramid complexes

According to Arnold, in his work on Middle Kingdom pyramids, there were two distinct categories of Middle Kingdom pyramid complexes.

Two categories of Middle Kingdom pyramids

1   The pyramids of Amenemhet I and his son Senwosret I, who built their funerary complexes at Lisht. These pharaohs, 'while incorporating innovative elements into their pyramids, were trying to revive the pyramid complex of the late Old Kingdom Memphite tradition'.[27]

2   The pyramids of Amenemhet II (Dahshur), Senwosret II (el-Lahun), Senwosret III (Dahshur) and Amenemhet III (Dahshur and Hawara) did not follow a consistent pattern. They reveal attempts by the builders to experiment with construction techniques, the shape and size of the pyramid enclosures, the orientation of the pyramid, the location of the pyramid entrance, the number of chambers and passages and the position of the burial chamber.

A plan of the pyramid complex of Senwosret I and cross walls

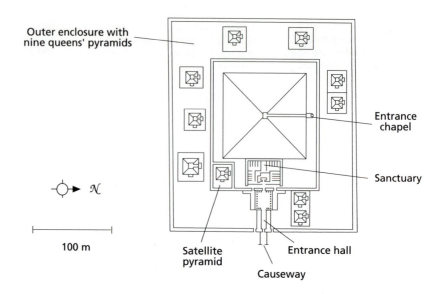

Outer enclosure with nine queens' pyramids

Entrance chapel

Sanctuary

Satellite pyramid

Entrance hall

Causeway

100 m

𝒩

Two pyramids of Amenemhet III

Of this second group, the two pyramids of Amenemhet II, which were completely different in design and layout, were the most innovative. Work on his Dahshur pyramid had to be abandoned because of structural weaknesses. It had too many internal chambers and corridors built without stress-relieving devices. Also the king had the pyramid too close to the valley floor, which led to some subsidence.

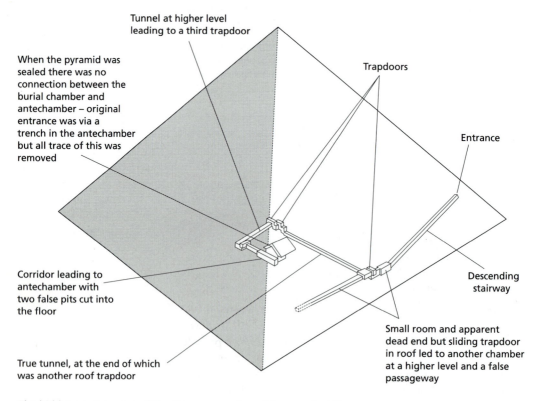

Tunnel at higher level leading to a third trapdoor

Trapdoors

Entrance

When the pyramid was sealed there was no connection between the burial chamber and antechamber – original entrance was via a trench in the antechamber but all trace of this was removed

Corridor leading to antechamber with two false pits cut into the floor

Descending stairway

True tunnel, at the end of which was another roof trapdoor

Small room and apparent dead end but sliding trapdoor in roof led to another chamber at a higher level and a false passageway

The hidden passageways of the Hawara complex of Amenemhet III

His second pyramid, built near that of his grandfather, Senwosret II, incorporated two magnificent technical innovations. These were:

Technical innovations

1 the use of concealed passages closed by sliding stone trap-doors. This was 'a magnificent achievement in the provision of security for the burial chamber'.[28]

2 the burial chamber carved from a single piece of quartzite and set in an open trench prior to the construction of the pyramid.

The labelled diagrams below show the technical skill involved in building these features into the pyramid.

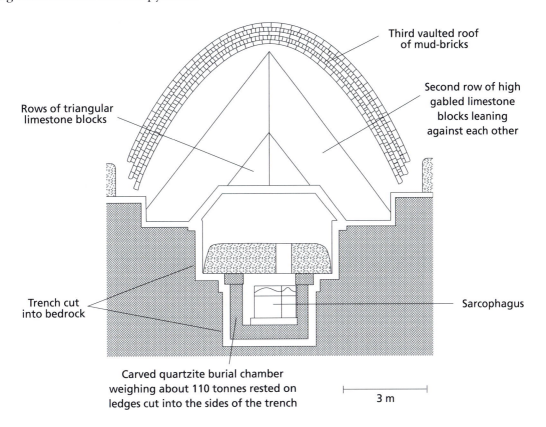

The burial chamber of the Hawara complex of Amenemhet III

Amenemhet's pyramid enclosure, which included the so-called 'labyrinth'*, was the largest of all the Middle Kingdom burial complexes. This building was marvelled at by visitors of the Greek and Roman classical periods such as the historian Herodotus (fifth century BC), the geographer Strabo (first century BC) and the naturalist Pliny (first century AD).

The 'labyrinth'

Grimal believes that this extensive complex of replicated courts and sanctuaries 'was clearly a Sed festival installation comparable to the jubilee complex of Djoser at Sakkara with which Amenemhet's structure had several similarities'.[29] Judging by the description in Herodotus, even given a fair degree of exaggeration, the 'labyrinth' was probably more elaborate than Djoser's Sed court.

---

* A true labyrinth is a maze of nested passages and blind corridors.

**Herodotus' description
of the 'labyrinth'**

I have seen this building, and it is beyond my power to describe; it must have cost more in labour and money than all the works of the Greeks put together ... The pyramids, too, are astonishing structures ... but the labyrinth surpasses them. It has twelve covered courts — six in a row facing north, six south — the gates of the one exactly fronting the gates of the other, with a continuous wall round the outside of the whole. Inside, the building is of two storeys and contains three thousand rooms, of which half are underground, and the other half directly above them. I was taken through the rooms in the upper storey, so what I shall say of them is from my observation, but the underground ones I can speak of only from report, because the Egyptians in charge refused to let me see them because they contain the tombs of the kings, who built the labyrinth, and also the tombs of the sacred crocodiles. The upper rooms, on the contrary, I did actually see, and it is hard to believe that they are the work of men; the baffling and intricate passages from room to room and from court to court were an endless wonder to me, as we passed from a courtyard into rooms, from rooms into galleries, from galleries into more rooms, and thence into yet more courtyards. The roof of every chamber, courtyard and gallery, is like the walls, of stone. The walls are covered with carved figures, and each court is exquisitely built of white marble and surrounded by a colonnade.[(30)]

Unfortunately, nothing remains of this exceptional building except for a few foundations and some fragments of statues of deities, such as Sobek, the crocodile god of the Faiyum. These, together with statues of the king, probably stood in the various courts and sanctuaries.

Queen Sobekneferu is believed to have finished her father's 'labyrinth'.

Other building achievements of the Middle Kingdom pharaohs

**The 'white chapel'
of Senwosret I**

Senwosret I was a prolific builder and there are at least 35 sites from the delta to the First Cataract where the remains of his monuments have been found. The only complete monument from his reign is a beautiful limestone barque sanctuary (the White Chapel) at Thebes. The decorated

*The White Chapel of
Senwosret I at Karnak*

blocks from this building were used by the Eighteenth Dynasty pharaoh, Amenhotep III, for his pylon gateway at Karnak. They were retrieved by Henri Chevier who reconstructed the sanctuary. Today it stands in the open air museum at Karnak and reveals the quality of art of the period. The 18 pillars are carved with the most exquisite hieroglyphs and reliefs of Senwosret in the presence of the gods. Refer to the illustration on page 234.

Developments in literature and art

Literature

A large proportion of the literary works which form the basis of Egyptian civilisation were composed during the Middle Kingdom. This was regarded as a classical age because Egyptian language and literature reached their most 'perfect' forms at this time.

A classical age of language and literature

The questioning of traditional values that followed the distress of the First Intermediate Period contributed to developments in literature. These works 'suggest a series of refinements that combined the Old Kingdom tradition with a more humanitarian sobriety'.[31] Many of these Middle Kingdom literary pieces were used throughout the New Kingdom as exercise models for students.

Used as models for New Kingdom students

The following diagram summarises the main categories of these literary works.

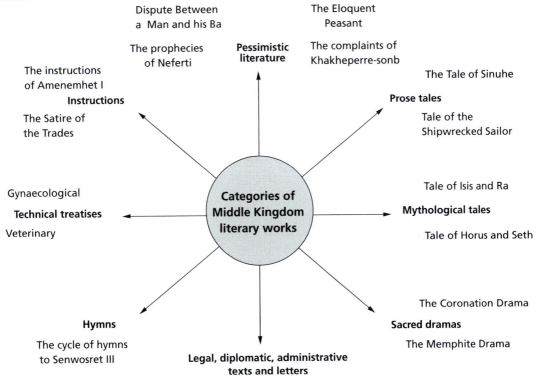

Literary works of the Middle Kingdom

Instructions

This 'genre' of Egyptian literary works developed from those of the Old Kingdom, such as the *Instructions of Ptahhotep*. These usually instructed young men in the attitudes and skills necessary to live satisfactorily in Egyptian society. However, the two mentioned below are slightly different.

The Instructions of Amenemhet I to his son Senwosret I was 'composed to strengthen the dynastic succession'.[32] In this work, the king displays a tone of resentment as he warns his son of the treachery of his subjects.

Warning of treachery by subjects

> Risen as god, hear what I tell you,
> That you may rule the land, govern the shores,
> Increase well-being!
> Beware of subjects who are nobodies,
> Of whose plotting one is not aware.
> Trust not a brother, know not a friend,
> Make no intimates, it is worthless.[33]

In *The Satire of Trades*, a father instructs his son on the advantages of following a scribal profession.

Advice on the advantages of a scribal career

> I have seen many beatings —
> Set your heart on books!
> I watched those seized for labour —
> There's nothing better than books!
> It's like a boat on water.[34]

Pessimistic literature

The works in this category focus on a theme of national and personal disaster and disillusionment. According to Lichtheim these literary pieces were not based on any historical incident. She believes that the authors were simply interested in the themes of social and personal problems.

Themes of national problems

In the *Prophecies of Neferti*, the author discusses the problems that the country faces when the kingship is weak.

> Stir, my heart,
> Bewail this land, from which you have sprung!
> When there is silence before evil,
> And when what should be chided is feared,
> Then the great man is overthrown in the land of your birth.
> Tire not while this is before you,
> Rise against what is before you!
> Lo, the great no longer rule the land,
> What was made has been unmade,
> Re should be made to recreate![35]

Disillusionment with life

The Dispute between a Man and his Ba uses a conversation between a man, disillusioned with life and his *ba* (soul) about life after death. The man wants to die but his *ba* threatens to leave him if he commits suicide. This would be disastrous for the man who, without his *ba* would have no chance of resurrection. The *ba* points out that death is not the wonderful release the man envisages and encourages him to enjoy his life. Eventually, the *ba* agrees to stay with him whatever he chooses to do with his life.

The Eloquent Peasant is 'a plea for justice and a demonstration of the value of rhetoric'.[36] A peasant, named Khun-Anup, on his way to sell his goods, is robbed of everything by a greedy landowner. After ten days of fruitless pleading for the return of his property, Khun-Anup takes his complaint to the high steward of the area, a man named Resni. When Resni hears Khun-Anup's first petition, he informs the king that he has found a peasant 'whose speech is truly beautiful'.[37] The king asks the magistrate to detain the peasant and write down everything he says so that he can read it. The peasant is forced to make nine separate petitions before Resni and each time his words are more eloquent and stirring. Eventually, justice prevails and the eloquent peasant not only has his own property returned to him but is rewarded with the property of the robber.

Pleas for justice

Prose tales

Judging from the numerous copies of *The Story of Sinuhe* found in Egypt, it must have become an Egyptian classic. Whether it was based on the exploits of a real individual is not known. However, it does refer to some historical incidents such as the death, in unusual circumstances, of King Amenemhet I and the military campaigns in Libya led by the co-regent, Senwosret. The story also includes some elements of propaganda to praise the benevolence of Senwosret I.

Story of Sinuhe

Sinuhe was serving with Senwosret I against the Tjemehu Libyans when he heard of the death of Amenemhet I. Believing that there would be upheaval in the capital he fled eastward to Syria. Whether he had some prior knowledge of a plot to kill the king is not known.

He was treated with great hospitality and generosity by 'Ammunenshi, the ruler of Upper Retenu' who offered him refuge in his kingdom. Sinuhe married the Syrian ruler's daughter, was given fertile lands to farm and raised a family. However, as Sinuhe grew older and weaker, he longed to return to the country of his birth and be buried in the Egyptian way. When Senwosret I heard of his condition he sent him a message urging him to return to Egypt.

Sinuhe handed over his possessions to his sons and returned to Egypt where he was treated by the king as a member of royalty. Finally the king ordered the construction of a funerary complex for him 'in the midst of the pyramids'[38] and furnished it with the finest equipment.

> There was no commoner for whom the like has been done. I was in favour of the king until the day of landing (death) came.'[39]

Sacred dramas, mystery plays and hymns

Some of the sacred dramas were composed for special events such as the coronation of a king (eg, the *Coronation Drama* for Senwosret I),

Composed for special religious occasions

while the 'mystery plays' were performed at the great annual religious festivals. One such play, performed at Abydos, focused on the life, death and resurrection of Osiris. Six hymns which made up *The Cycle of Hymns to King Senwosret III*, were found at Kahun, written on a single piece of papyrus. These were meant to be accompanied by an instrument and may have been sung or spoken when the king moved around the country.

Technical treatises

Medical papyri

One of the most important discoveries made during the excavation of the pyramid town of Kahun, were 46 fragments of a medical papyrus (*The Kahun Papyrus*). This is the oldest document on gynaecology found anywhere in the world. It lists symptoms of gynaecological problems and the most effective treatment for them. It also contains descriptions of tests to determine a woman's fertility, pregnancy and the sex of the foetus, as well as describing methods of contraception.

A veterinary papyrus was also found at Kahun which listed the symptoms and treatments for various animal diseases.

Art

The Middle Kingdom was also a time of excellence in art. There were a number of identifiable phases in Middle Kingdom art which coincided with political developments.

During the Old Kingdom a distinctive school of art developed in the royal workshops in the capital of Memphis. The style of tomb decoration and statuary of this period set the standard for all future funerary art.

Provincial art

With the collapse of centralised government during the First Intermediate Period, artists and craftsmen were without their royal and noble patrons. Painting and sculpture declined in quality and developed provincial peculiarities.

> **The sophistication of the Memphite school was replaced with a fresh spontaneous and naive approach .. the figures had a crude vigour.**[40]

The democratisation of funerary beliefs at this time led to a greater demand for burial goods, such as wooden models, and craftsmen moved away from Memphis to the provincial centres.

Theban style

The return of some form of unified government under Montuhotep II at Thebes, resulted in a distinctive Theban style of art. It retained some provincial elements but revealed considerable technical advances. The seated figure of Mentuhotep II with its thick legs and massive feet, shown on page 233, is an example of Theban provincial art.

Return to the Memphite style but with more human elements

When Amenemhet I moved his capital back to the north, the best craftsmen would have followed. Once more in the royal workshops, the Memphite style was adopted, but, as in literature, there was a much more human element apparent in the artistic work of the period. This applied particularly to the realistic sculptured heads of Senwosret III and Amenemhet III.

A black granite statue of Amenemhet III

A painted sandstone seated statue of Mentuhotep II

During the Twelfth Dynasty 'the quality of artistic production for the king and the upper elite reached a high point, that although equalled at other periods, was never surpassed'.[41] This was apparent in the technical excellence of the pieces of jewellery found in the tombs of the princesses Khnumet (daughter of Amenemhet II), Sit-Hathor-Iunet and Sit-Hathor (daughters of Senwosret II), and Mereret (daughter of Senwosret III).

Royal jewellery

Much of the jewellery and toilet articles belonging to these princesses combined beauty, amuletic protection and technical precision. These treasures included:

Beauty, protection and technical precision

- magnificent pectorals of gold cloisonne inlaid with semi-precious stones — lapis lazuli, carnelian, turquoise and garnet.
- a stunning chain, belonging to Mereret, of amethyst beads connecting a number of gold leopard heads, and a girdle belonging to Sit-Hathor of gold cowrie shells and rows of coloured stone 'acacia seeds'
- a mirror from the cache of Sit-Hathor-Iunet (the so-called Treasure of el-Lahun) which is a masterpiece of the goldsmith's craft. The silver mirror disk is attached to an obsidian handle in the shape of an open papyrus which also features the head of the goddess Hathor in gold with inlays of lapis lazuli, carnelian and other stones. Hathor, in her guise as goddess of love and beauty, was particularly revered by women and her image is often found on

the handles of mirrors, used by women to inspect their own beauty. Other toilet articles discovered among the el-Lahun treasure were elegant black obsidian perfume containers with gold rims, a kohl pot, a set of alabaster unguent vases and copper razors with gold handles.

- a magnificent crown worn by Sit-Hathor-Iunet. It was designed to be worn over a wig and was made of a simple gold band with 15 rosettes. Also found were a ureaus inlaid with lapis lazuli, carnelian, green faience and garnets and two feathers and ribbons made of gold.

In architecture, the elegance of the period was reflected in the 'White Chapel' of Senwosret I.

Pectorals belonging to Princess Mereret

Reliefs from the White Chapel of Senwosret I

Religious developments

The emergence of Amun as the new state god

With the political upheaval and decentralisation of the First Intermediate Period, the state cult of Re of Heliopolis declined. There was a tendency to revert to the worship of local gods.

Montu of Thebes

Montu, the falcon-headed war god was the local deity of Thebes, and with the success of Mentuhotep II (*Montu is Pleased*), he increased in importance. At this time, Amun was largely an unknown deity associated with a fertility god, known as Min.*

When Amenemhet I (*Amun is at the Head* or *Amun is in the Front*) established the Twelfth Dynasty, he promoted Amun as the new state god. The name Amun means 'hidden' and as an unseen cosmic god, Amun might be everywhere. Such a god could serve as a unifying force. 'Now at the beginning of the Twelfth Dynasty he was being dragged out of cosmic obscurity to begin his tremendous career.'[42]

---

* Min was depicted with an erect phallus (an ithyphallic god).

Amenemhet I had adopted the throne name of Seketepibre (*He who Appeases the Heart of Re*). This, combined with his birth name, served to announce a religious policy which involved assuring Amun's supremacy by association with the great solar god, Re.

As Amun-Re, he was associated with a consort, the vulture-headed goddess, Mut, and a son, the moon god, Khonsu, as well as a cult centre at Karnak. The following inscription is one of the earliest known which recorded the name of the new state god.

> **Amenemhet I; he made it as a monument for his father Amun-Re, Lord of Thebes, making for him a shrine of pink granite, that he might thereby be given life forever.**[(43)]

'The kings of the Twelfth Dynasty had once again established the supremacy of a state cult.'[(44)] However, it was not until the Eighteenth Dynasty that the cult of Amun-Re reached an unprecedented peak of power and wealth.

Amun-Re, from a wall of the Temple of Karnak

Promotion of Osiris, Min and Sobek

While Amun became the state god of the living, Osiris superseded Re as the pre-eminent funerary god. Originally, Osiris was a god of vegetation and in this role he personified the rebirth of all growing things. In Egyptian mythology, he was regarded as a popular earthly king who brought the arts of agriculture and civilisation to the country before being killed by his jealous brother, Seth. He was resurrected owing to the efforts of his wife Isis, his sister Nephthys, and the gods Thoth and Anubis, and ruled as king of the dead in the Underworld. Refer to Chapter 7 for details concerning the effect of the worship of Osiris on funerary practices.

Osiris as god of the Underworld and resurrection

Abydos became the main cult centre of Osiris since the Egyptians believed that the god's body was buried there. At Abydos, Osiris became assimilated with an earlier god, Khenty-amentiu, known as the *Foremost of the Westerners*. A festival, which re-enacted the god's death and victorious resurrection, was held there annually. During this festival, the statue of Osiris was taken from its temple and carried along a processional way to his mythical tomb. Once he had symbolically overcome his enemies, his statue was returned to the temple. The rites of Osiris carried out at Abydos were not only associated with resurrection, but with the accession and jubilee of the king. For this reason, during the Middle Kingdom, the cult became of paramount importance in maintaining royal power.

Abydos, cult centre of Osiris

Although the two chief gods of the Middle Kingdom were Amun and Osiris, the kings of this period promoted other deities as well, particularly Min and Sobek. Min, the ithyphallic god, has already been mentioned in his early association with Amun. The cult centre of Min was at Gebtu (called Koptos by the Greeks and today known as Qift) at the

Min, patron deity of the eastern desert

entrance to the Wadi Hammamat which connected the Nile Valley with the Red Sea. Because trading and mining expeditions started from this point, Gebtu and Min were important to the people of the Middle Kingdom. Because the eastern desert was his domain, Min was the patron deity of nomads, hunters, miners and travellers. He was propitiated whenever an expedition entered the region.

On a stelae erected by the vizier, Amenemhet (later Amenemhet I), Min was mentioned several times. For example:

> His majesty commanded to erect this stela to his father Min, Lord of the Highlands in this august primeval mountain.[45]

The cult of Sobek

Because of the interest of the Twelfth Dynasty kings in developing and exploiting the Faiyum, they promoted the cult of the local god, the crocodile-headed Sobek with whom they often associated Osiris and Re. Sobek was a god of water and vegetation. The kings built temples to Sobek at various sites in the Faiyum, including Medinet el-Faiyum (Crocodilopolis) and Medinet Madi.

Middle Kingdom Funerary beliefs and practices

During the Middle Kingdom, Egyptians of all classes began to seek an individual eternity and aspired to this through moral behaviour.

New beliefs in an Osirian afterlife

Changes in religious thinking

With the collapse of the Old Kingdom and the decline in centralised control, there was a radical change in religious thinking. Egyptians began to re-evaluate their place in the universe. To the nobles, especially those in the provinces, there was no longer any hope of an afterlife associated with the king. They came to believe that they, like the Old Kingdom pharaohs, could spend eternity in the company of the gods. However, since the sun god Re had been closely associated with royalty, these nobles sought a new god with whom to identify and one who had a wider appeal. Osiris seemed to offer the most comfort as a funerary god.

Widespread appeal of Osiris

> ... he typified to the Egyptians the being who by reason of his sufferings and death as a man could sympathise with them in their own sickness and death ... Originally they looked upon Osiris as a man who had lived on the earth as they lived, who ate and drank, who suffered a cruel death, who by the help of certain gods triumphed over death, and attained eternal life. What Osiris did they could do, and ... as the gods brought about his resurrection so they would bring about theirs, and as the gods made him the ruler of the Underworld, so they would allow them to enter his kingdom and to live there as long as the god himself lived. They believed that all that was done for Osiris would symbolically be done for them and they would be resurrected.[46]

Osirian afterlife and judgment before Osiris

The Osirian afterlife in *Yaru* or the *Fields of Reeds*, which resembled the fertile lands of the delta, appealed more to the ordinary Egyptians than the remote afterlife spent travelling the heavens in the barque of Re.

Although the Egyptians believed that there was now a hereafter for everyone, there was still a royal celestial afterlife.

Associated with the new beliefs in an Osirian afterlife was a preoccupation with social justice and what was regarded as correct behaviour. The Egyptians believed that they would have to satisfactorily pass a judgment before Osiris before entering his kingdom. This was the reason behind the emphasis on charity and good works in the tomb inscriptions of the Middle Kingdom nobles.

The ordinary Egyptians of the Middle Kingdom believed that, as long they worshipped Osiris, behaved correctly during life and followed the correct ritual and burial procedures, they could expect to live forever in the Kingdom of Osiris.

Funerary texts

During the last two dynasties of the Old Kingdom (the Fifth and Sixth), a collection of spells and prayers, to help royalty pass safely to the afterlife, were carved into the walls of the burial chambers of the kings and their queens. The Egyptians believed that thoughts expressed in the written form could become real. These texts were referred to as *Pyramid Texts*.

Pyramid Texts of the Old Kingdom

When the provincial nobles of the First Intermediate Period took over some of the funerary privileges of the earlier kings, they also usurped some of these Old Kingdom religious texts. Those *Pyramid Texts* which contained references to archaic practices were omitted. New texts were added to make them more suitable for non-royals and to reflect contemporary conditions. However, they still provided the protection formerly given only to royalty.

Omissions and additions to the funerary liturgy

Since the First Intermediate Period was a time of economic hardship, most people could not afford to have the texts inscribed on the walls of their tombs. Instead, it became common practice to have them painted on the inside of their coffins. This continued until the New Kingdom. Egyptologists refer to this body of texts as the *Coffin Texts*. About 1200 of these texts have been identified but there was no standard set of them used at this time.

The Coffin Texts included:

Coffin Texts

- a collection of instructions to guide the deceased safely through the Underworld, avoiding the dangers that they believed lay in wait for them. *The Book of the Two Ways* mapped alternative routes that could be taken to the afterlife
- practical aids (spells) to protect the deceased in the afterlife. For example, some spells helped reunite the deceased with loved ones, repel snakes and crocodiles, provide food and drink, and avoid work

Types of spells and instructions

- spells for becoming any god they wished; for example:

  As for any person who knows this spell, he will be like Re in the eastern sky. Like Osiris in the Netherworld.[47]

Lichtheim says that these texts not only reveal the ordinary Egyptians' petty fears but show delusions of grandeur which were out of touch with the reality of their lives. For example, in one of the *Coffin Texts*, the deceased claimed:

> I am lord of the flame who lives on truth; lord of eternity, maker of joy, against whom that worm shall not rebel.

> ... Lord of lightland, maker of light, who lights the sky with his beauty. I am he in his name! Make way for me, that I may see Nun and Amun![48]

Some of the new spells compiled during the Middle Kingdom formed the basis of certain passages in the New Kingdom funerary text, *The Book of the Dead.*

Funerary equipment

Sarcophagi, coffins, canopic jars and chests

Except for royalty and the great nobles, large stone sarcophagi* were not in general use during the Middle Kingdom.

Most well-to-do individuals were buried in two finely painted, rectangular wooden coffins, one fitting inside the other. These were made from imported woods such as cypress. Those Egyptians who were not wealthy had to content themselves with one coffin made from local timber such as sycamore and tamarisk.

Painted wooden inner and outer coffins

In most cases, the sarcophagi and coffins belonging to private individuals were decorated in a similar way. The outer surface was painted or carved with panelling which represented the facade of a house or palace, since the coffin symbolised the dwelling place of the deceased.

House facades, false doors and Udjet-eyes on outer surfces

Alone or in combination with a false door was a pair of sacred udjet eyes at the head end of the eastern side of the coffin. These were in line with the face of the mummy which was placed on its side. The eyes not only protected the mummy, but allowed the deceased to look out. The false door permitted the spirit of the deceased to move in and out of the 'dwelling'. Various versions of offering formulae were painted in horizontal and vertical bands.

The limestone sarcophagi of the two royal women, Kawit and Ashait, found under Mentuhotep II's temple at Deir el-Bahri, were carved with some aspects of the life that the princesses hoped to experience in the hereafter. There were also representations of their personal possessions and of food and drink (livestock and granaries).

The exterior of the limestone sarcophagus of the princess, Kawit

* The word sarcophagus should be used only for outer coffins made from stone.

On the inner surfaces of Middle Kingdom coffins were:

- representations of items needed by the
  person in the next life such as cloth,
  mirrors, furniture, jewellery, tools and weapons. At
  the head of the coffin were depictions of a number
  of ritual objects such as 'the seven oils used in the
  ritual of the *Opening of the Mouth*'[(49)] and headrests.
  Also, models of headrests were placed in the coffin
  near the head of the mummy. Sandals were often
  painted at the foot of the coffin

- vertical columns of Coffin Texts written in cursive
  hieroglyphs (hieratic). These were often accompanied by a text known as the *Book of the Two Ways*
  and a map of the Underworld. A fine example of
  this was painted on the interior of the coffin of
  Sepi, a Twelfth Dynasty noble buried at Bershi.

Detail of the interior of the painted coffin of Sepi, a noble from Deir el-Bershi

Paintings on the lids of coffins from the Middle
Kingdom continued to represent the sky goddess, Nut,
and the interior of the lid was often painted with a
scene of the sun god sailing across the heavens. The
floor of the coffin represented the Underworld.

Detail of the interior of the sarcophagus of Dagi, an Eleventh Dynasty Theban official

For most of the Middle Kingdom period, the heads of mummies were
covered with cartonnage masks* representing the features of the
deceased. Towards the end of the period, these masks were extended
to cover the whole body and were made in two parts, since the mummy
laid on its side. These painted body-shaped (anthropoid) coffins were
originally made of cartonnage and wood and featured a false beard and
ureaus which were the symbols of divinity and kingship. These features
identified the deceased with the mummiform Osiris and reflected the
increasing influence of the god's cult on burial practices. These were the
forerunners of the wooden anthropoid coffins of the New Kingdom.

Cartonnage masks and anthropoid coffins

Since only royalty and the upper classes were eviscerated (ie, had their
internal organs removed during the embalming process) during the Old

---

* Cartonnage was linen stiffened with plaster. This was moulded and painted to form a mask of the deceased.

Kingdom, there are few examples of canopic chests and jars from this period. Those chests that have been found were rectangular in shape, made of stone and lacked any religious texts or symbolic decoration. The plain canopic jars featured stoppers representing the head of the deceased. It was not until the New Kingdom that these stoppers were made in the shape of the four sons of Horus. Refer to Chapter 17.

The canopic jars of Inpuhotep, a Twelfth Dynasty Theban official buried at Sakkara

Funerary stelae, 'soul houses' and wooden models

'Soul houses' replace offering tables

Tomb stelae found in the tombs of the Old Kingdom featured the tomb owner and perhaps his wife sitting in front of an offering table. In the Twelfth Dynasty, stelae were much more religious in nature and often depicted the deceased in the company of a number of gods. For example, a stela belonging to a late Twelfth Dynasty official called Senbi, featured Ptah and Amun-Re. 'For the first time the gods could be represented having direct contact with ordinary people.'[50]

During the Middle Kingdom, the rectangular offering tables in front of the stelae were replaced with what archaeologists refer to as 'soul houses'. The former offering tray became the courtyard of a model house made from pottery. These provide additional information about the domestic architecture of the Middle Kingdom.

Models of everyday activities

For most of the Middle Kingdom period, but particularly in the early phase, collections of painted wooden models were placed in the tombs. These were either hidden in niches cut into the floor or placed beside the coffin. As with the scenes on the walls of Old Kingdom tombs, these models were expected to 'come into existence' by means of funerary formulae and provide the deceased with everything they needed in the next

A model of Meketre inspecting his cattle

life. These collections included detailed models of granaries, livestock, bakeries, butcheries, breweries, craftsmen's workshops (carpenters, metal workers, potters, weavers) and fleets of boats. The most magnificent collection of these models was found in the tomb of Meketre, king's chancellor and steward.

In most tombs there was usually at least one model boat. It was the hope of most people to make a funeral pilgrimage to Abydos, the cult centre of Osiris, before returning to their local area for burial. However, if this could not take place, then a symbolic journey could be undertaken by means of the model boat.

Model boats and the pilgrimage to Abydos

During the Old Kingdom, wall scenes featured young female offering bearers carrying baskets of produce to present to the deceased. These serving girls personified the estates of the tomb owner. Finely detailed models of offering bearers found in Middle Kingdom tombs served the same purpose. The best examples of these come from the model collection belonging to Meketre. One of a pair of servant girls balances a basket of food (cuts of meat, bread and vegetables) on her head and carries a live duck in one hand, while the other girl also carries a duck and a basket containing four wine jars.

Towards the end of the Middle Kingdom, the variety and numbers of wooden models declined. Fertility figurines, miniature images of protective animals and wands and rods, with the supposed ability to ward off evil influences, appeared among the funerary items.

Model of a boat used by Meketre in his official capacity

Mummification

From the evidence of those mummies that have survived, it appears that the most common procedure for treating bodies during the Middle Kingdom included:

- removing the internal organs through an incision in the abdomen
- packing the body cavity with linen
- treating the external tissues with resins and oils.

Common embalming procedures during the Middle Kingdom

There was no attempt to remove the brain. This did not occur until the New Kingdom.

There were still variations in the embalming procedure and a considerable number of bodies suffered decomposition before being treated. Even those bodies belonging to royalty did not necessarily get the best treatment. For example, the Eleventh Dynasty princesses found buried beneath the temple of Mentuhotep II at Deir el-Bahri were not eviscerated. Judging by the state of decomposition of the organs found within the abdomens and chest cavities, their bodies received no internal treatment. It seems that the embalming process was restricted to simply

Variations in treatment

drying out the bodies with natron and treating the outer body tissues with oils and resins. However, even these procedures were not carried out effectively. The bodies were not completely dehydrated before being wrapped, causing rapid bacteriological decomposition. Insect larvae, found within the linen bandages, indicate that the wrapping did not take place quickly enough.

On the other hand, a Twelfth Dynasty noblewoman, named Senebitisi, was given an elaborate embalming treatment. Not only were her viscera removed and the body packed with linen, but the abdominal incision was sealed with a patch of linen soaked in resin. Also, her nostrils were plugged with resin and her eye sockets packed with linen. The remains of her linen-wrapped organs were found in their canopic containers.

The rites that accompanied the embalming procedures, the funeral procession and the rituals performed at the entrance to the tomb (such as the *Opening of the Mouth* ceremony) are discussed in detail in Chapters 7 and 17.

Middle Kingdom tombs

Possible Osirian influences in the royal funerary complexes

Some of the architectural features of the royal funerary complexes seem to reflect the growing emphasis on the cult of Osiris. Lehner refers to some of these in his work, *The Complete Pyramids.*

Burial chambers close to subterranean water

It appears that the pharaohs of the Twelfth Dynasty demonstrated 'a desire to connect to the realm of Osiris'[51] by placing their burial chambers so deep as to reach close to subterranean waters. Some of these burial chambers (eg, of Amenemhet I and Senwosret I) cannot be entered today as they are now underwater.

Two features in the pyramid complex of Senwosret II also point to a connection with the Osiris cult:

Symbols of subterranean islands and mounds

- Sixteen metres below the surface, a horizontal corridor, leading to the burial chamber, is interrupted by a pit or 'well', the bottom of which has never been reached. Was this another attempt to connect with the Underworld? During the New Kingdom, pits or wells like this were often found part-way along the entrance passageways of royal tombs. Some scholars have suggested that these may have symbolised the tomb of Osiris.

- Inside Senwosret's pyramid a passageway loops around the burial chamber. Lehner suggests that this 'circuitous corridor'[52] created a subterranean 'island', an important symbol of Osiris.

Tombs of the nobles

Provincial cemeteries

During the Middle Kingdom some officials continued to be buried in the provincial cemeteries of Middle and Upper Egypt (Beni Hasan, Deir el-Bersha, Meir, Akhmin and Aswan) as they had in the First Intermediate period. However, many others chose to build their tombs in the royal cemeteries of Thebes, Lahun and Dahshur, close to the kings they served in life.

It also became the custom of the elite to build memorial chapels at Abydos, along the processional way to the Temple of Osiris. They hoped that these cenotaphs would assist them in triumphing over death as Osiris had done.

Although some Middle Kingdom tombs were of the mastaba type, most were *saff* tombs* cut into the cliffs bordering the Nile. Although these rock-cut tombs had their own distinctive style, depending on the provincial area, they tended to follow a general pattern which included:

- an imposing facade
- a spacious pillared room cut into the cliff
- a chapel beyond with a false door or niche in the end wall often with a statue of the deceased standing in it
- a vertical or sloping shaft leading to the burial chamber. The entrance to the shaft was either in the floor of the chapel or the pillared hall.

The facade of a rock-cut tomb at Aswan

The steep approach to the rock-cut tombs cut into the cliffs at Aswan

---

* 'Saff' is an Arabic word for 'rows' and refers to the rows of columns or pillars at their doorways.

Provincial variations   The following labelled diagrams show some of the variations found in the tombs of Thebes, Beni Hasan and Aswan.

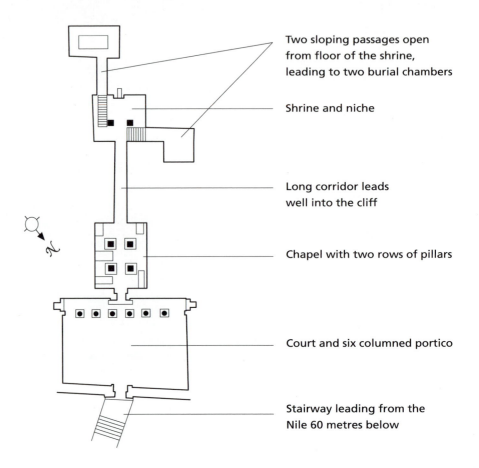

Two sloping passages open from floor of the shrine, leading to two burial chambers

Shrine and niche

Long corridor leads well into the cliff

Chapel with two rows of pillars

Court and six columned portico

Stairway leading from the Nile 60 metres below

A plan of the tomb of Sarenput I at Aswan

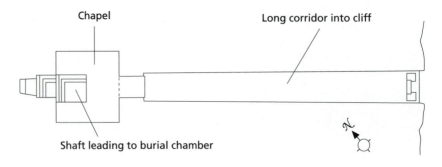

Chapel

Long corridor into cliff

Shaft leading to burial chamber

A plan of the tomb of Antefoker at Thebes

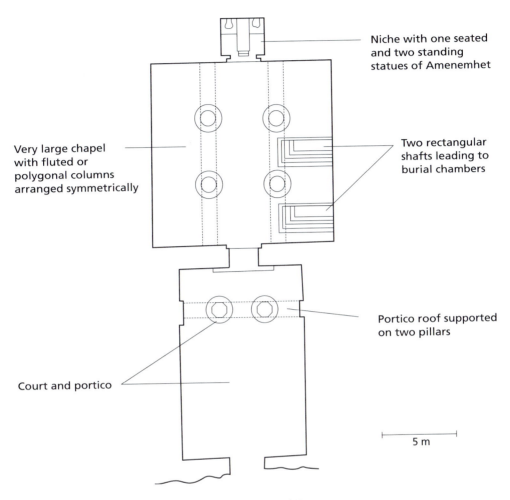

A plan of the tomb of the nomarch Amenemhet at Beni Hasan

The scenes painted on the tomb walls tended to follow the same themes as those of the Old Kingdom — the agricultural cycle, animal husbandry, crafts, fishing and boating. However, there were some themes that were specific to Middle Kingdom tombs. For example, the Beni Hasan tombs of the Oryx nomarchs featured scenes of textile production. One of these nobles also recorded the visit of a group of Bedouins bearing gifts or items of trade. A tomb at Deir el-Bersha features an amazing scene of the transportation of a colossal *ka* statue of the provincial governor. Another specific theme was war. These scenes of fighting and sieges probably reflected the local conflicts that occurred prior to the re-establishment of central control. Scenes of wrestling also featured widely in these tombs as well as games played by girls.

Themes of tomb paintings

With their impressive facades and lack of any real security measures, except for rubble-filled shafts, these rock-cut tombs were an open invitation to robbers. Several mastaba tombs belonging to royal builders and architects incorporated some ingenious security features but these were the exceptions.

Few real security measures

Conclusion

The Twelfth Dynasty pharaohs brought peace and prosperity once more to Egypt. A number of trading expeditions were sent to Punt and trade flourished with Syria and the Aegean area. Mines and quarries were extensively exploited for the metals and fine stones needed for the pharaohs' building projects, particularly the royal funerary complexes between the Faiyum and Dahshur.

Nubia was brought under control and Egypt's southern boundary was set at the Second Cataract. A string of fortresses was constructed along the 400-kilometre stretch of the Nile between the First and Second cataracts. These protected the trade in gold and exotic products and kept the more warlike tribes of Kush in check.

The Faiyum area was developed and agricultural land was increased by an innovative irrigation and reclamation scheme.

The Twelfth Dynasty has often been described as the 'golden age' of Egyptian culture. A number of remarkable literary works were written at this time and royal portraiture and jewellery revealed the craftsmen's absolute mastery of their materials.

Changes in funerary practices reflected the new belief that everyone had the right to an individual afterlife in the Kingdom of Osiris.

After the achievements of the Twelfth Dynasty, the general picture of the subsequent period is one of slow decline. For the next century or so, Egypt was ruled by a series of insignificant kings and there was once again division and disorder (the Thirteenth and Fourteenth dynasties). This provided the opportunity for foreigners from the east (the Hyksos) to invade Egypt.

Chapter review

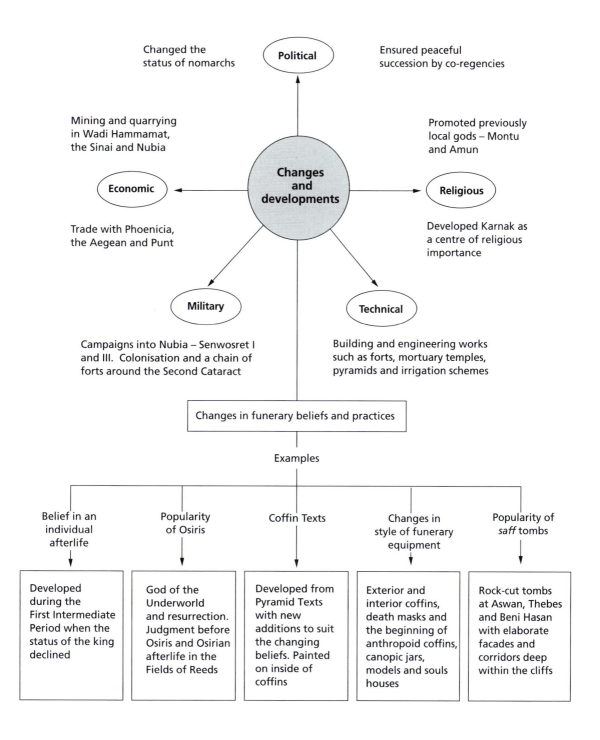

REVIEW QUESTIONS AND ESSAY TOPICS

1 How does the portrait of King Senwosret III shown at the beginning of this chapter reflect the change in the image of kingship during the Middle Kingdom? Why was this image different from that of the Old Kingdom?

2 Analyse the following inscription and answer the questions below.

> My lord ... sent me to dispatch a ship to Punt to bring him fresh myrrh from the chiefs over the desert ... Then I went from Koptos upon the road, which his majesty commanded me. There was with me an army of the south ... The army cleared the way before (us), overpowering those hostile toward the king, the hunters and the children of the highlands were posted as the protection of my limbs ... I went forth with an army of 3000 men. I made the road a river and the desert a stretch of field, for I gave a leathern bottle, a carrying pole, two jars of water and twenty loaves to each one among them every day. The asses were laden with sandals ... Now I made twelve wells in the bush and two in Idehet, 20 cubits in one and 31 cubits in the other. I made another at Iheteb, 20 by 20 on each side.
>
> Then I reached the Red Sea; then I made this ship, and I dispatched it with everything, when I had made a sacrificial offering of cattle, bulls and ibexes.
>
> Now after my return from the Red Sea, I executed the command of his majesty, and I brought for him all the goods which I had found for him in the region of the God's Land. I returned through the valley of Hammamat, I brought for him majestic blocks for statues belonging to the temple.[53]

a Who was the author of this inscription? Which king did he serve and what were his official titles?

b What was the purpose of this expedition?

c Where is Koptos and the Valley of Hammamat?

d Where was the land of Punt?

e What difficulties would the members of this expedition have faced?

f Why was the expedition accompanied by an army of 3000 men?

g What is meant by 'I made the road a river and the desert a stretch of field'?

h What evidence is there that this Punt expedition was successful?

i What other service did the expedition leader carry out for his king before returning to Thebes?

3 The figure at the top of page 249 shows the present-day remains of the mortuary temple of Mentuhotep II.

a Where are these remains located?

b What parts of the original building can be identified from this photograph?

c Which features of this complex were innovatory and which followed the form of the complexes of the Old Kingdom?

d What evidence is there that this building was completed in a number of stages? Why would this have been the case?

4 Identify the objects in the figures below.

(A)

(B)

a   To whom did they belong?

b   Where were they found?

c   What other objects were found with them?

d   Describe the materials from which they were made.

e   What was the significance of the design
     of the object in Figure (A)?

f   What do these objects reveal about art
     in the Middle Kingdom?

5 **Analyse the text below. It comes from the literary genre known as *Instructions*.**

> Do right as long as you are on earth. Calm the afflicted, oppress no widow, expel no man from his possessions ... Do not kill; but punish with beatings or imprisonment. Then shall this land be well established. Leave vengeance to God ... More acceptable to him is the virtue of one who is upright of heart than the ox of the wrong-doer.[54]

a What is the theme of the text?

b How is the advice, to 'do right while you are on earth', associated with the tomb biographies of Middle Kingdom nobles?

c To what funerary practice do the words 'leave vengeance to god' and 'having given satisfaction to the Weary-hearted', refer?

d How does it reflect the changes in funerary beliefs that began during the First Intermediate Period and continued through the Middle Kingdom?

6 **The figures below depict a limestone sarcophagus and painted coffin from the Middle Kingdom period.**

A limestone sarcophagus

A painted coffin

a To whom might each of these objects have belonged. Explain your answer.

b What is the significance of:

   i the scenes carved into the limestone sarcophagus

   ii the painted features on the coffin?

c What other features are likely to have been found on the interior of each of these pieces of funerary equipment?

7 Identify the object in the figure on the right and answer the following questions.

a Where was this model found?

b What was its purpose?

c What other models were found with this one?

d Why was there at least one boat found in a collection of models?

8 Essay topics

a 'He appointed me shepherd of this land, knowing him who would herd it for him.'[55]

To what extent did the kings of the Middle Kingdom fit this image of a shepherd looking after his lands and his flocks?

b Why is the Twelfth Dynasty often referred to as the classical age of Egyptian culture?

c Describe the significance, during the Middle Kingdom, of the cults of Amun-Re, Osiris, Min and Sobek.

d Explain why there was a change in funerary beliefs during the First Intermediate Period and the Middle Kingdom. What were these changes and to what extent were these new beliefs reflected in the burial practices of the time?

FOUR

The New Kingdom

The *New Kingdom* refers to the period from c. 1550–c. 1070 BC. It comprised three dynasties or families of kings — the Eighteenth, Nineteenth and Twentieth dynasties. However, this text focuses only on the New Kingdom down to the death of the Nineteenth Dynasty pharaoh, Ramesses II in c. 1224 BC.

Chapters 9–12 cover the reigns of a series of vigorous, intelligent and ambitious pharaohs who expanded the borders of Egypt, laying the foundations of an empire which extended from Nubia to northern Syria. Chief among these 'warrior' kings were Thutmose I and Thutmose III and associated with both of them was an outstanding woman, Queen Hatshepsut, who ruled Egypt as a king for over 20 years.

These early Eighteenth Dynasty pharaohs promoted Amun as the god of empire. As wealth from booty, tribute and trade began to pour into Egypt, much of it was dedicated to the god whom the pharaohs believed had given them victory. Amun's temple at Karnak became the centre of a massive building program and its priesthood became increasingly powerful.

By the reign of Amenhotep III, Egypt was the unrivalled leader of the known world and was unsurpassed in artistic magnificence.

Chapter 13 covers the dramatic 17-year reign of Amenhotep's son, Akhenaten who initiated a religious 'revolution', focusing on the worship of the Aten or sun-disk. For a time the temples of the other gods were closed and the name of Amun was erased from the walls of temples and tombs. Akhenaten built a new capital city at Amarna (Akhetaten) where he could worship his god freely. His preoccupation with domestic affairs contributed to the loss, during his reign, of Egyptian territory and prestige abroad.

Under Akhenaten's successors, particularly Horemheb, Amun was restored to his place as the chief state god. However, it was not until a new line of kings came to the throne (Nineteenth Dynasty) that Egypt regained some of its prestige and former territory in Syria and Palestine.

Chapter 14 traces the attempts by Seti I and Ramesses II to emulate the deeds of the 'warrior' pharaohs of the early Eighteenth Dynasty and to equal their building achievements. Ramesses II is often referred to as 'Ramesses the Great' because he built on such a colossal scale and because his name is found on more buildings throughout Egypt and Nubia than any other pharaoh in history.

Society changed dramatically in the Eighteenth Dynasty as a result of Egypt's expansion. A new professional army developed; the Egyptians were exposed to foreign products, lifestyles, gods and values; the administration was restructured; the demand for skilled craftsmen increased and the upper classes lived a luxurious lifestyle and built themselves elaborate tombs. However, as in all periods of Egyptian history, agriculture and the work of the peasants was the basis of Egyptian society.

CHAPTER
9

A vigorous new beginning

Liberation and reunification

The Hyksos domination of Egypt

After the brilliance of the Middle Kingdom, Egypt had declined into 'a state of dire havoc and confusion, its rulers murdering and replacing one another with extreme rapidity'.[1] During this time of weak and divided rule (Thirteenth and Fourteenth dynasties), a group of foreigners moved into the delta area from Palestine. Eventually, under the leadership of ambitious chieftains or princes they seized control of the delta city of Avaris and turned it into their stronghold.

The Egyptians referred to these people as *Hikau-khoswet* (rulers of foreign lands) from which the name Hyksos originated. For about 45 years they extended their control over Lower Egypt and in c. 1640, a Hyksos chieftain named Salatis felt strong enough to force the Egyptian rulers out of Memphis. For about 100 years, two dynasties of these foreign kings (Fifteenth and Sixteenth) controlled Egypt as far south as Cusae.

Hyksos expansion

A dynasty (the Seventeenth) of Egyptian princes from Thebes continued to rule in semi-independence but paid allegiance and tribute to the Hyksos kings in the north. The territory controlled by these Theban rulers extended from the Nubian border as far as Abydos.

The Hyksos were able to maintain their dominance for so long because they were militarily stronger than the divided Egyptians. Their chief fighting advantage came from their use of horse-drawn war chariots, unfamiliar to the Egyptians. These chariots gave the Hyksos forces greater mobility and striking power. Other military advantages included their use of:

Fighting advantages

- superior weapons such as bronze swords, scimitars and daggers
- powerful composite bows built up of layers of wood, sinew and horn, glued together. These had far greater striking distance and penetration than the small bows used by the Egyptians

- scaled armour and war helmets, probably made of leather, sewn with gilded metal disks. This was later added to the pharaohs' regalia and is today known as the *khepresh*, the blue war crown
- fortified camps — these made the Hyksos practically invulnerable to the Egyptians with their lesser weapons.

Refer to Chapter 15 for information on the New Kingdom army.

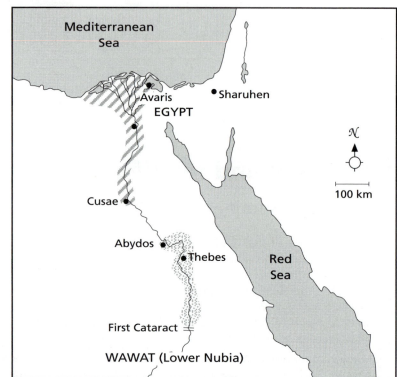

 Hyksos controlled territory

 Theban princes ruled in semi-independence from Hyksos (paid tribute to Hyksos rulers)

The extent of the territory controlled by the Hyksos and the princes of Thebes

Egyptian humiliation

According to Wilson in *The Culture of Ancient Egypt*, the Hyksos invasion of Egypt was a great national humiliation.

> **The proud superiority of Egypt over all her previous opponents was very rudely dashed to the ground, with important consequences to the Egyptian spirit.**[2]

The humiliation felt by the Egyptians is reflected in the lack of contemporary official records.

Bias in the sources

Those Egyptian sources that have survived tend to depict the Hyksos as uncouth barbarians whose rule was totally disastrous for Egypt. Some of these were written on behalf of later kings who defeated and expelled the Hyksos (Kamose and Ahmose) and who repaired the damage supposedly done by them to temples and other buildings (Hatshepsut). Other records were left by historians who lived over a thousand years after the events and must be treated with caution. For example, Manetho, an Egyptian priest in the third century BC, recorded that the

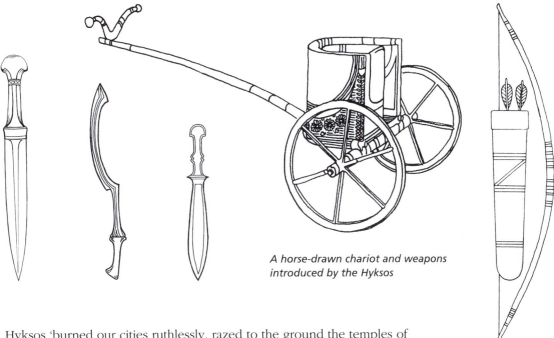

*A horse-drawn chariot and weapons
introduced by the Hyksos*

Hyksos 'burned our cities ruthlessly, razed to the ground the temples of
the gods and treated all the natives with cruel hostility'.[3]

There is another side to the story. It appears that the Hyksos were not
the *ruthless barbarians* and *uncouth savages* described by later Egyptian
writers. Other sources, such as private tomb inscriptions and some of
the material remains of the time, suggest that their administration was
not excessively harsh and oppressive. The Hyksos kings appear to have:

- adopted the traditional titles of the kings of Egypt and even used
  Egyptian names
- included Egyptian officials in their administration
- sponsored the production of typically Egyptian works of art and
  made copies of famous Egyptian literary and medical texts
- modelled their official religion on that of the Egyptians. Their
  Asiatic god, Baal, seems to have been assimilated with Seth, the
  Egyptian god of Avaris. Despite what the records of Hatshepsut's
  time say, the Hyksos seem to have accepted other Egyptian gods
  also. The kings honoured Re, the sun god, by including him as part
  of their throne names (eg, Apophis took the throne name Aweserre)
- introduced many new processes and products which were readily
  adopted by the Egyptians as part of their everyday life. These
  included:
  - the use of bronze rather than copper and the greater use
    of silver in works of art
  - improved methods of spinning and weaving using a
    lighter loom
  - new musical instruments — the long-necked lute, oboe and
    tambourine — and new forms of dancing
  - olive and pomegranate trees.

**Catalyst for
transformation**

The Hyksos' occupation was the catalyst needed for the transformation of the Egyptian state.

For thousands of years the Egyptians, isolated in their fertile valley, had felt safe from the outside world but, with their conquest by the Hyksos, they lost once and for all their feelings of security.

The Egyptian rulers of Thebes realised that if they were ever to free themselves from their Hyksos masters, they would need to become more effective as a military power. At some stage they adopted the horse-drawn chariot, composite bow and other bronze weapons introduced by the Hyksos. This gave them the confidence to begin a war of liberation against the foreigners. Another factor which contributed to their increasing confidence was their employment of sturdy mercenary troops from Nubia. These troops, known as the Medjay, became indispensable to Egyptian kings in their military campaigns over the next few centuries.

The first phase in the war of liberation

King Seqenenre Tao II

As the sources for this period are few and fragmentary, it is not known exactly which of the Theban princes of the Seventeenth Dynasty first took up arms against the Hyksos or why. However, there are two pieces of evidence which suggest that it might have been King Seqenenre Tao II who first came into conflict with the Hyksos king, Apophis:

1   The head of the mummy of King Seqenenre Tao II (who was given the epithet of *the brave*) is covered with wounds which suggest he died on the battlefield. There is a dagger wound behind one ear, his nose and cheek were smashed by a mace-like weapon and the bone above his forehead was apparently cut through with a battle-axe of Palestinian origin.

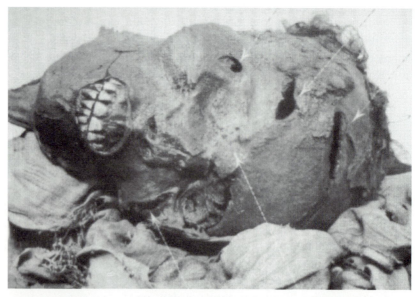

The head of the mummy of Seqenenre Tao II showing the wounds that caused his death

2   A later folk story relates how King Apophis sent an insulting letter
to Seqenenre Tao, complaining that the hippopotamuses of Thebes
were keeping him awake in Avaris. What he meant by this is not
known but it probably had some mythological connotation. The
hippopotamus was an animal sacred to the god Seth whom
Apophis worshipped.

King Kamose of Thebes

**The war of revenge against the Hyksos was successfully launched by
Kamose.**[4]

Kamose was the successor of Seqenenre Tao II and is generally regarded as the last king of the Seventeenth Dynasty. It is uncertain whether
he was Seqenenre's elder son or younger brother. There is no evidence
of his parents, wife or children.

Parentage unknown

From the fragments of two stelae set up by King Kamose at Thebes, we
know that he began a campaign against the Hyksos in the third year of
his reign. At this time, Nubia, which formerly had been a part of Egypt,
was ruled by Nubian princes, allied with the Hyksos.

When Kamose came to the throne in Thebes, he outlined to his council of nobles a plan of action against the Hyksos. His resentment against
the foreigners is apparent in the following extract.

Desire for revenge

> Let me understand what this strength of mine is for! There is one
> prince in Avaris, another in Ethiopia (Nubia), and here I sit associated
> with an Asiatic and a Negro! Each man has his slice of this Egypt, divid-
> ing up the land with me. I cannot pass by him as far as Memphis, the
> waters of Egypt, but behold he has Hermopolis. No man can settle
> down, being despoiled by the demands of the Asiatics. I will grapple
> with him, so that I may cut open his belly! ... My wish is to save Egypt
> and to smite the Asiatics.[5]

Kamose's nobles did not support his idea of an attack. They appear to
have been satisfied with the way things were at the time — 'we are at
ease in our part of Egypt'.[6] Perhaps they felt that their forces could not
fight enemies on two fronts — the Hyksos king in the north and his ally,
the Nubian prince, in the south.

The Theban king obviously ignored his nobles' advice because the text
records that he sailed north with a powerful army on the command of
Amun, the god of Thebes. His troops raided deep within Hyksos-held
territory. Although they failed to take the enemy's stronghold capital of
Avaris, they captured hundreds of Hyksos ships filled with cargoes of
'gold, lapis lazuli, silver, turquoise and countless battle axes of metal,
apart from moringa oil, incense, fat, honey, and ... all their valuable timber and all the good produce of Retjenu (Palestine)'.[7]

**Inroads into Hyksos
territory**

The Hyksos king sent an urgent message to the prince of Nubia for
help, promising him that if they defeated Kamose together, they would
divide up the towns of Egypt between them. However, Kamose inter-
cepted the letter and returned it to Apophis with an account of what his
troops had already done to Hyksos territory in Middle Egypt.

With the annual flood, which made further fighting impossible, Kamose sailed triumphantly back to Thebes. He instructed his chief official to set up an inscribed stela in Karnak Temple recording everything he had achieved.

> The first taste of triumph with the new weapons must have been sweet. Complete victory was soon to come.[8]

It appears from the state of his burial that Kamose died unexpectedly.

Queen Ahhotep

> The Theban royal house, who challenged the power of their over-lords, and initiated the liberation of Egypt from the Hyksos yoke, was not only fortunate in the fire and courage of its kings, it was exceptional for a series of outstanding queens who won the veneration of later generations.[9]

> The Theban saviours of Egypt were a closely knit family in which the women ... played an extraordinarily prominent part.[10]

One of these outstanding queens was Ahhotep, the sister/wife of King Seqenenre Tao II and the mother of King Ahmose, successor of Kamose.

Regent for King Ahmose

It is believed that on the death of Kamose, Ahmose was still a child and that his mother, Ahhotep, ruled as his regent. The evidence suggests that at this critical time she put down a rebellion within the country and may have directed an army.

Two pieces of evidence point to her strength of character and political influence and the respect King Ahmose felt for his mother:

Played a significant political role

1 A stela at Karnak, erected in her honour by King Ahmose, calls on all who read the inscription to respect this great woman whose name is praised in all foreign lands. The stela indicates that Ahhotep made decisions on behalf of the people; gathered together her nobles and united them; looked after her soldiers and brought back refugees and deserters. This 'King's Wife, King's Sister, King's Daughter and respected Mother of the King' pacified Upper Egypt and suppressed its rebels.

Honours bestowed on Ahhotep

2 When Ahhotep's gilded coffin and mummy were found in the nineteenth century, a number of significant items were discovered which point to her status. Amongst her jewellery, which is one of the greatest treasures in the Cairo Museum, was a gold pendant with three large golden flies. During the New Kingdom, the fly was a symbol of bravery and soldiers who had shown courage were decorated with jewellery featuring the golden fly.

Ahmose's ceremonial axe and dagger were also part of her funerary equipment. The bronze axe is particularly informative. On one side it shows the king with Montu (a Theban god of war) and wearing the *khepresh* or war crown, while on the other Ahmose is depicted as a sphinx holding the head of an enemy with symbols of both Upper and Lower Egypt.

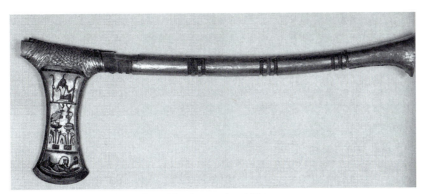

Ahmose's ceremonial axe, found in the tomb of Ahhotep

King Ahmose (Amosis) — the expulsion of the Hyksos and the reunification of Egypt

Ahmose is believed to have been the brother or half-brother of Kamose, although he could have been Kamose's nephew. Although there appears to have been no break in the dynasty, King Ahmose was cited by Manetho as the first ruler of the Eighteenth Dynasty and has been 'hailed by posterity as the father of the New Kingdom'.[11]

Regarded as first ruler of Eighteenth Dynasty

Since Ahmose was a child when he came to the throne, there was probably no attempt to follow up the successes of Kamose against the Hyksos for at least a decade, and during this time the Hyksos may have regained some ground. There appears to have been a certain amount of unrest in Egypt at the beginning of Ahmose's reign and it was probably this situation in which the regent Ahhotep became involved.*

King Ahmose liberated Egypt from the Hyksos. His military successes were recorded in the tomb biography of the marine, Ahmose, son of Ebana, who came from the town of Nekheb (El-Kab). He took part in Ahmose's attack on the Hyksos stronghold of Avaris and accompanied the king on his campaigns into Palestine and Nubia. Ahmose, son of Ebana, also served under two of King Ahmose's successors.

Evidence from the tomb of Ahmose, son of Ebana

Although it is subjective and sketchy, this tomb biography is a most important source, not only for its invaluable information on the defeat and expulsion of the Hyksos, but also for our understanding of the promotion and reward system in the Egyptian army/navy. Refer to Chapter 16 for more details on the career of Ahmose, son of Ebana.

According to this source, King Ahmose conducted a series of campaigns (perhaps three) against Avaris, the Hyksos capital, before it eventually fell to his troops. At one point, the siege, which probably took many years, was interrupted by the need to put down a rebellion in Upper Egypt.

Three campaigns against the Hyksos

Ahmose then drove the Hyksos out of Egypt and campaigned in southern Palestine as far as the city of Sharuhen. According to Breasted, he is believed to have laid siege to the city for approximately six years,

---

* Some historians suggest that the rebellions she crushed may have occurred when Ahmose was absent in Nubia.

after which it was destroyed — 'Pharaoh besieged Sharuhen, and in the sixth year his majesty took it'.[12] This campaign was a warning to the princes of Palestine and Syria that a new force had emerged in Egypt.

The tomb inscription of Ahmose Pen-Nekhbet, another El-Kab noble in the service of King Ahmose, indicates that after the siege of Sharuhen, the king pushed the Hyksos further north into Syria.

Successful Nubian campaign

King Ahmose next turned his attention to Nubia in the south, where he defeated the ruling prince and regained the northernmost part of the country (Wawat) as far south as the Second Cataract. The king was 'joyous with the might of victory, for he had conquered Southerners and Northerners'.[13] However, because he was forced to return there several times to crush rebellions, Ahmose appointed a loyal official as commandant of Buhen. This was the forerunner of the position of viceroy or governor of Nubia.

Internal rebellions suppressed

Despite his successes, Ahmose had to put down several rebellions in Egypt. One of these was led by a man named Teti-en who 'had gathered the malcontents to himself' and because Ahmose would not tolerate any political rivals to his supreme rule, he 'slew him and his servants, annihilating them'.[14] These measures were obviously very effective because there is no evidence of further rebellions during the reigns of Ahmose's successors.

By expelling the Hyksos, Ahmose ended over a century of foreign rule in Egypt and took the first step towards restoring unity and peace to the country. Once again Egypt was ruled by one strong pharaoh.

In return for his military victories, Ahmose dedicated many splendid gifts to the god Amun-Re. A stela found at Karnak provides details of the 'offering tables of gold', dishes and bowls of gold and silver, 'jars of pink granite, filled with ointment', an ebony harp, silver sphinxes, a cedar barge and other precious items presented to the Theban god. [15]

Ahmose also added cedar and limestone features to the Temple of Amun-Re at Karnak and Luxor as well as to the temple of Ptah at Memphis. To honour his grandmother, Tetisheri, 'because he so greatly loved her, beyond anything'[16] King Ahmose and his queen/sister, built her a chapel at Abydos as part of his own cenotaph complex.

Pictorial representation of the expulsion of the Hyksos and the last known royal pyramid

This complex comprised a temple and pyramid, a small temple dedicated to his wife, Ahmose Nefertari, his grandmother's shrine, a rock-cut cenotaph and a set of terraces built against the desert cliffs. These buildings were arranged along a north-east(south-west axis. Recent excavations have located fragments decorated with battle scenes — 'bridled horses, once harnessed to chariots, archers firing bows and Asiatics, with their characteristic beards and long-sleeved garments, fallen in battle'.[17] These fragments show the earliest known representation of horses in Egypt and almost certainly depict the expulsion of the Hyksos.

Ahmose died after 25 years on the throne and was probably buried in one of the small Seventeenth Dynasty mud-brick pyramids at Dra Abu el-Naga on the west bank at Thebes. This was the last royal pyramid built in Egypt.

During his lifetime 'the father of the New Kingdom' was associated with three of the most influential women of the time — his grandmother, Tetisheri, his mother, Ahhotep and his sister/wife, Ahmose Nefertari.

Queen Ahmose Nefertari

Ahmose, like his father before him, had married his sister, Ahmose Nefertari, and it is believed that they had six or seven children — Ahmose-ankh (the original heir), Amenhotep (the eventual successor of Ahmose), Meritamun (the next queen consort), Ahmose-Sipiari, Siamun, Ramose (?) and Sitamun.

From the evidence available, it seems that Queen Ahmose Nefertari was the most able, respected and beloved woman of her time, with a reputation almost without equal in the history of Egypt.

Of all the queens of the New Kingdom, Ahmose Nefertari had the greatest religious status. This was associated with the rise to pre-eminence of the god Amun-Re at the time of her husband's reign.

Great religious status

It seems from a stela (the Donation Stela) found at Karnak, that early in her life she had been granted the title of *second prophet of Amun*. This position appears to have been later transferred to her young son, Ahmose-ankh, when she was further honoured by her husband with the title of *God's Wife of Amun*. The exact duties associated with this priestly office are not known but the title carried with it enormous status.

God's Wife of Amun

Throughout her life, Ahmose Nefertari associated this title above all others with her name. According to the stela, in her role as *God's Wife of Amun*, she was granted vast estates, probably on the west bank of Thebes, labour to work them and a steward (her brother) to administer them for her. As well, she was assisted by a high-ranking woman, known as the *superior of the harem* and *adorer of the god* and a group of court women (chantresses and musicians) who formed part of the *harem of Amun*.

Ahmose Nefertari survived her husband and apparently lived well into the reign of her son Amenhotep I, during whose reign she was further honoured. Both she and her son were later deified and their funerary cults continued until the end of the New Kingdom. Refer to Chapter 15 for more details on the *God's Wife of Amun* and the religious importance of Ahmose Nefertari.

The significance of the Hyksos occupation and the war of liberation

> ... the Hyksos domination provided the Egyptians with the incentive and the means towards *world* expansion and so laid the foundations and to a great extent determined the character of the New Kingdom, or, as it is often called, *the Empire*.[18]

The Hyksos occupation of Egypt had undermined the Egyptians' false sense of security and feelings of superiority and introduced them to new religious beliefs, artistic styles, products and processes which influenced their way of life and culture.

Egypt open to foreign influences

By adopting the foreigners' war chariot and bronze weapons, the native rulers of Thebes were able to free Egypt. Once liberated, the Egyptians took steps to ensure the safety of their country from future invasion, by campaigning beyond the borders of Egypt into Palestine and Nubia. These were the very first steps taken towards establishing an empire.

Egypt was no longer isolated and before long began to play 'a full part in the developments of the eastern Mediterranean'.[19]

Amenhotep I

Extending the boundaries of Egypt in Nubia

Amenhotep I succeeded his father Ahmose and from the evidence (provided once again from the tomb of Ahmose, son of Ebana), the new king began the process of reconquering Nubia and consolidating Egyptian control over it.

Nubia, the land immediately to the south of Egypt, was divided into two parts:

1 Wawat, the northern part of the country, which extended from the border with Egypt (the First Cataract) to the vicinity of the Second Cataract

2 Kush, the southernmost part of Nubia which extended beyond the Second Cataract.

(Refer to the sketch map of Egypt, Nubia and western Asia on page 267.)

The tomb inscription of Ahmose, son of Ebana, recorded that he accompanied King Amenhotep to Kush 'in order to extend the borders of Egypt'.[20] This is the first mention of a deliberate expansionist policy. Large numbers of cattle and 'living prisoners' were transported down river to Egypt and those captives who tried to escape were executed.

The importance of Nubia to the Egyptians

From remotest antiquity, Egyptian trade was chiefly directed towards the lands of the upper Nile and the Sudan, and the pharaohs saw the need to keep this area under control. The reasons for the Egyptians' attraction to Nubia and the decision of the pharaohs to eventually incorporate it into their growing empire were threefold:

1 Enormous quantities of gold, which the Egyptians prized so much, were obtained from the extensive mines of Kush.

2 Taxes in the form of cattle and agricultural products could be extorted from the various native tribes.

3 Nubia was the connecting link between Egypt and the regions of the Sudan and beyond. All the goods which the Egyptians coveted from tropical Africa, such as ivory, ebony, ostrich feathers and eggs, animal skins, cattle, slaves and so on, passed through Nubia.

To ensure the continued supply of these products, the regions of Nubia and all connecting desert routes had to be under Egyptian control. To achieve this, the Egyptian kings of the Middle Kingdom had ordered the construction of a line of fortresses in Nubia, but these had fallen into disrepair during the Second Intermediate Period.

Amenhotep I continued the policy of the Middle Kingdom rulers. He began to rebuild the forts that protected Egyptians living and working in Nubia and to make sure that the flow of gold and tropical products (for which there was an ever increasing demand) was not interrupted.

Middle Kingdom fortresses rebuilt

The commandant of Buhen, appointed by Ahmose I, was now made viceroy of Nubia and given the title *king's son, overseer of southern lands*. In the reign of Thutmose I, Amenhotep's successor, this position was referred to as *the king's son of Kush*, and it became one of the most important offices in the administration of the empire. Refer to Chapter 16 for the role and responsibilities of this important official.

Other aspects of Amenhotep's policy

Although we do not know a lot about the reign of Amenhotep I, it is believed that during his reign art and architecture began to flourish again on a grand scale.

As well as restoring those monuments damaged and neglected during the Hyksos domination, he:

- devoted himself to the building of Thebes as a new capital city
- erected beautiful monuments to the state god Amun-Re at Karnak, 'erecting for him a great gate of twenty cubits (in height) at the double facade of the temple, of fine white limestone of Ayan' [21]
- took the first steps in developing the west bank at Thebes as the site of a vast necropolis (royal cemetery with tombs separated from the mortuary temples)
- founded a special workforce called *workmen of the royal tomb* who lived in their own town at Deir el-Medina. This workforce was responsible for building and decorating all royal tombs. The citizens of this town worshipped Amenhotep I as their founder. He and his mother were deified and worshipped in Deir el-Medina as gods for centuries after their deaths. Refer to Chapter 16 for details on the workmen of the royal tombs

Royal workforce established

- built or repaired temples and chapels at Abydos, El Kab and Elephantine Island.

The succession

Amenhotep had married his sister Meritamun. Whether they had any children is not known but there was certainly no surviving son when Amenhotep, after a reign of approximately 21 years, died.

**Choice of successor
— Thutmose**

Who was to succeed him? It appears that Amenhotep had already selected his successor, a military leader named Thutmose whose mother,
Senseneb, was a commoner. We have no knowledge of Thutmose's
father. He may have belonged to a collateral branch of the royal family
or have been a high ranking noble.

As Thutmose was middle-aged by the time he came to the throne, he
may already have had a wife or was quite possibly a widower. During
his reign, his queen consort was Ahmose. What was her background?

**Theories about
Queen Ahmose**

There are a number of conflicting views about Ahmose:

- Some historians believe she was the younger sister of Amenhotep
  and therefore the daughter of Ahmose and Ahmose Nefertari, or
  else she was the daughter of Amenhotep. In this case, Thutmose
  could legitimately claim the throne because he was married to a
  royal princess.

  Thutmose I appears to have achieved the kingship through his marriage to the hereditary princess Ahmose, the sister and daughter
  respectively, of his two predecessors.[22]

- Others believe that she was perhaps of royal blood but not the
  daughter of Ahmose or Amenhotep.

  Probably his sole title to kingship was as husband of the princess
  Ahmose, a lady evidently of very exalted parentage.[23]

  His chief queen by whom he presumably acquired the kingship was
  another Ahmose who bore the modest title of *King's Sister*, and is
  unlikely to (have been) a child of Amosis (Ahmose), otherwise she
  would have claimed the additional and superior title of *King's Wife*.[24]

- A third view is that she was the sister or half-sister of Thutmose.
  Tyldesley, in her book *Hatshepsut*, suggests that if this were the
  case then 'their brother-sister marriage must have occurred after
  Thutmose's promotion to heir apparent, as such incestuous marriages were extremely rare outside the immediate royal family'.[25]

To ensure his succession, Amenhotep may have associated Thutmose
with him in a co-regency sometime before his death. Co-regencies were
common during the Middle Kingdom and were also a feature of some
of the reigns of the Eighteenth Dynasty.

The beginning of an empire

Thutmose I

Some scholars believe that Thutmose I, and not King Ahmose, was the
real founder of the Eighteenth Dynasty. He was the first in a line of
kings referred to as the Thutmosids, who were:

> ambitious, intelligent and energetic as rulers, vain, self indulgent,
> headstrong, and occasionally ruthless as individuals, but consistent in
> their pious devotion to the god Amun and his fellow deities and in
> their patronage of their country's arts and crafts.[26]

Thutmose I's military achievements

In the early part of his reign, Thutmose I led two important military campaigns (to Nubia and western Asia), during which he displayed exceptional abilities as a military leader.

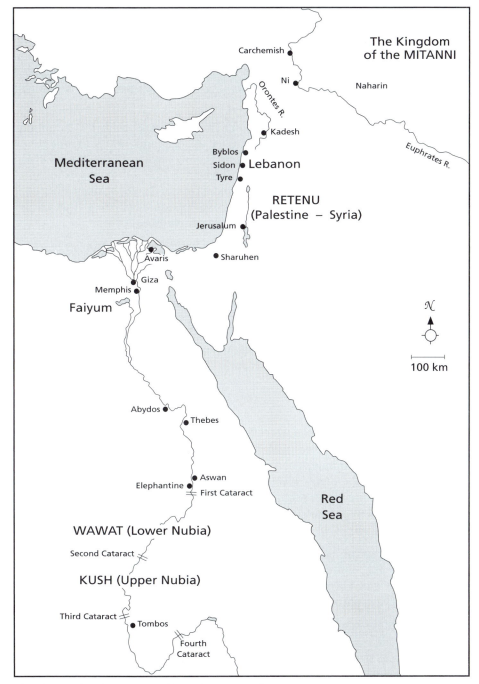

Sketch map showing Egypt, Nubia and western Asia

Nubia

It seems that the Nubian tribesmen took the opportunity of a new king on the throne to rebel against the Egyptians. Thutmose I could not allow this situation to get out of control so he devoted the whole of his second year to the Nubian campaign.

Captain Ahmose, son of Ebana, navigated the king's fleet safely along the Nile and through the rough waters of the cataract regions to 'crush rebellion in the highlands, in order to suppress the raiding of the desert region'.[27] According to Ahmose's biography, when Thutmose faced the Nubians he raged like a panther, piercing the chest of a Nubian chieftain with his first arrow. When the rest of the Nubian rebels attempted to flee 'a slaughter was made among them; their people were brought off as living prisoners'.[28]

Extended borders beyond the Third Cataract

During this year-long campaign, Thutmose personally led his troops well beyond the Third Cataract as far as the island of Argo. This opened the way for the Egyptians to extend their control in Upper Nubia (Kush) as far as the Fourth Cataract. To guard the frontier, Thutmose ordered the construction of a fortress on the island of Tombos. Years later, after his campaign to the Euphrates, an inscription celebrating his victories was cut into the granite cliffs high above Tombos.

Thutmose returned to Thebes with the body of a dead Nubian chieftain hanging upside down at the bow of his flagship for all to see.

Continued fortress construction

It appears that Thutmose had to make another expedition to Nubia several years later during which *wretched Kush* was overthrown. He continued with the building of a string of fortresses in Nubia and established a new administrative system. Although future kings had to make occasional raids into the area, Nubia remained generally stable throughout the Eighteenth Dynasty.

Western Asia

Thutmose also campaigned in the lands of western Asia. He marched through Syria, where the local princes humbled themselves before him and offered tribute. Then he continued as far north as the upper reaches of the Euphrates River. The Egyptian troops, familiar with the Nile which flowed from south to north, were amazed at this great river which they believed flowed upside down. The Egyptians referred to it as 'the inverted river that goes downstream in going upstream'.[29]

Campaigned as far as the Euphrates river

The Egyptian king led his army across the river into the territory of the powerful Mitanni of Naharin. When the Mitannian and Egyptian armies finally met, Thutmose's troops proved to be superior and 'numberless were the living prisoners, which his majesty brought off from his victories'.[30]

In recognition of this great victory, Thutmose ordered the erection of a commemorative stela on the banks of the Euphrates, proclaiming his *mighty deeds to all future generations.* This has not survived but evidence of its existence comes from the records of Thutmose III.

On their way home, the king and his entourage spent some time in northern Syria (at a place called Niy), hunting wild elephants. Thutmose's success at hunting added to the image of the heroic king.

Although Thutmose I campaigned extensively in western Asia he made no attempt to bring the area thoroughly under control by organising a unified administration similar to that set up in Nubia.

The importance of Thutmose I's military campaigns

Nubia, which was the first foreign territory incorporated into the Egyptian Empire, was also the future empire's most valuable territory.

The Syrian campaign showed Thutmose I to be a military leader of exceptional ability. Only one other Egyptian king, Thutmose III, ever reached so far to the north-east.

The first real warrior king

The example set by Thutmose I was followed by Egyptian kings for centuries to come as they realised the benefits of acquiring an *empire*.

The official propaganda described the military achievements of Thutmose I in the following way:

> He brought the ends of the earth into his domain; he trod its two extremities with his mighty sword, seeking battle; but he found no one who faced him. He penetrated valleys which his royal ancestors knew not, which the wearers of the double crown had not seen. His southern boundary is as far as the frontier of this land (Nubia), his northern, as far as the inverted river ...[31]

> I made the boundaries of Egypt as far as that which the sun encircles.[32]

Dedications to Amun-Re at Karnak

To glorify his *father* Amun-Re, who had helped him make 'Egypt the superior of every land',[33] Thutmose ordered superb additions to Amun's *house* (temple) at Karnak. Under the supervision of the king's architect, Ineni, the original Middle Kingdom shrine was enlarged into an enclosed court with columned porticoes and statues of the king in the form of the god Osiris.

Ineni — royal architect

In front of this court, Thutmose ordered the construction of a monumental gateway or pylon. Mounted in slots in the pylon walls were two huge cedar flag masts, the tips of which were sheathed in fine electrum (an alloy of gold and silver). Between the massive towers of the pylons was a 'great door of Asiatic copper wheron was the Divine Shadow inlaid with gold'.[34] This doorway was given the name *Amun Mighty in Wealth* and is an indication of what was to pour into the god's coffers in succeeding years. Later in his reign Thutmose had a second monumental gateway built approximately 13 metres in front of the first. The space between the pylons was roofed over to form a hall.

Additions to Karnak temple

To celebrate his Sed festival Thutmose had erected, in front of the second entranceway, two 20-metre-high obelisks. The pyramidions at the

An obelisk of Thutmose I at Karnak

tip of each red granite obelisk were covered in sheet gold to catch the rays of the sun.

The new architectural trends initiated by Thutmose I set the example for future pharaohs who all added something of their own to honour Amun-Re, the god of the empire.

Funerary developments

Thutmose I set another pattern for future kings to follow by ordering the construction of a rock-cut tomb in the isolated Valley of the Kings.

In the high rugged cliffs behind Deir el-Bahri, the royal architect Ineni 'inspected the excavation of the cliff-tomb of his majesty, alone, no one seeing, no one hearing'. He was 'vigilant seeking that which was excellent'. (35) The royal tomb workers from the village of Deir el-Medina decorated the royal tomb.

The royal family and the succession

Thutmose I and his queen consort, Ahmose, had two daughters — Hatshepsut and Neferubity. The latter died in infancy. It is also known that Thutmose had another wife, Mutnofret, who produced a son named Thutmose after his father.

Offspring of Thutmose I

Three other older princes are known to have been fathered by Thutmose I — Wadjmose, Amenmose and Ramose. Who their mother was is uncertain, but there is enough evidence to suggest that at least Wadjmose and the obscure Ramose were the sons of queen Mutnofret since they were shown associated with her in Thutmose's mortuary temple. Wadjmose and Amenmose appear to have survived into their late teens. After Wadjmose's death, Amenmose was given the title of *great army commander* and was obviously the crown prince for a time. Whether he was the son of Ahmose or Mutnofret is not known.

Tyldesley suggests that 'the princes Amenmose, Wadjmose, Ramose and Thutmose may have been full brothers, possibly born before their father married Ahmose' and that it is highly likely that Thutmose I was a widower at his accession, 'his first wife Mutnofret having borne him several sons before dying'.(36) So, except for Prince Thutmose and Princess Hatshepsut, the offspring of Thutmose I predeceased him.

Accession of Thutmose II

When Thutmose I died about the age of 50, his daughter Hatshepsut may not have been any more than 12 years old. She was married to her half-brother Thutmose who acceded to the throne. He is judged to have been only a young man of about 20 and possibly in poor health.

Thutmose II

At the beginning of his relatively short reign, Thutmose II had to deal with a serious and well-planned rebellion in Nubia. This may have been a way of testing the determination of the new ruler.

A test for the new king in Nubia

An inscription at Aswan describes the outbreak of this rebellion, the king's reaction and the dispatch of an army. Nubian tribesman had attacked one of the forts built by Thutmose I and the 'inhabitants of Egypt (colonists)' were forced 'to bring away the cattle behind this fortress'. The king vowed 'as my father, lord of gods, Amun, lord of Thebes, favours me, I will not let live any among their males'.[37]

The king's army crushed the rebellion and returned with one of the sons of the prince of Kush to be held as a hostage by the Egyptians. The prisoners were brought before Thutmose and the people praised him for having once more taken possession of Nubia. It appears from the inscription that Thutmose II did not accompany the army on this campaign.

A brief reference in the tomb biography of Ahmose Pen-Nekhbet, a general who served a number of kings, suggests that Thutmose II quelled another uprising among the Shasu Bedouin in Palestine. It is possible that this was part of a more extensive campaign into Syria since a fragmentary inscription mentions victories in the land of Niy and horses and elephants presented to the king as a form of tribute.

Possible campaign in Palestine and Syria

Because not much is known about his military exploits and because he did not reign for very long, Thutmose II is usually depicted as being a less effective king than his predecessors. His achievements were overshadowed by those of his immediate successors — his illustrious wife, Hatshepsut, who was about to take centre stage in Egypt for the next two decades, and his son, the great warrior king, Thutmose III. According to Tyldesley, 'we are in danger of underestimating Thutmose II's military prowess, and indeed his entire personality'.[38]

Conclusion

The policies of the first four kings of the Eighteenth Dynasty (Ahmose, Amenhotep I, Thutmose I and Thutmose II) transformed the Egyptian state.

By adopting the superior military weapons of the Asiatics the Egyptians had increased the effectiveness of their army which allowed them to challenge and break the power of the Hyksos and secure Egypt from further external attacks. This new style army included foreign mercenaries such as the Medjay from Nubia.

Campaigns into Nubia extended Egypt's southern frontier beyond the Third Cataract. The construction of fortresses was followed by colonisation and the appointment of a chief administrator with the title of *king's son of Kush* (viceroy). Wealth in the form of tribute and trade began to pour into Egypt from Nubia and tropical Africa.

First steps towards empire

Excursions into Palestine, Syria, and finally Thutmose I's campaign as far as the Euphrates River, secured Egypt's northern frontier, sent a warning to princes in the area and displayed Egypt's new military effectiveness.

Growing importance of Amun-Re

As these kings laid the foundation of an Egyptian Empire, the god believed to be responsible for their successes, Amun-Re of Thebes, became pre-eminent. The god's temple at Karnak was enlarged and embellished as each king dedicated more and more to Amun, his *father*.

In the peaceful conditions that returned to Egypt, art, architecture and trade flourished and Thebes began to grow into a city worthy of being the religious capital of Egypt.

Funerary changes led to the development of a vast necropolis in western Thebes. Amenhotep I was the first king to separate tomb and mortuary temple and Thutmose I set the pattern for future kings to be buried in tombs hidden away in a rugged valley in the Theban hills (the Valley of the Kings).

Chapter review

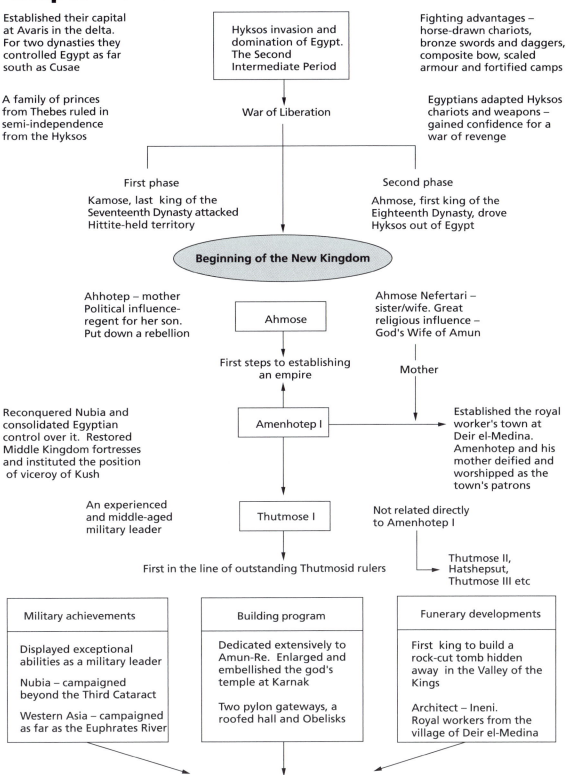

Established their capital at Avaris in the delta. For two dynasties they controlled Egypt as far south as Cusae

Hyksos invasion and domination of Egypt. The Second Intermediate Period

Fighting advantages – horse-drawn chariots, bronze swords and daggers, composite bow, scaled armour and fortified camps

A family of princes from Thebes ruled in semi-independence from the Hyksos

War of Liberation

Egyptians adapted Hyksos chariots and weapons – gained confidence for a war of revenge

First phase
Kamose, last king of the Seventeenth Dynasty attacked Hittite-held territory

Second phase
Ahmose, first king of the Eighteenth Dynasty, drove Hyksos out of Egypt

Beginning of the New Kingdom

Ahhotep – mother Political influence-regent for her son. Put down a rebellion

Ahmose

Ahmose Nefertari – sister/wife. Great religious influence – God's Wife of Amun

First steps to establishing an empire

Mother

Reconquered Nubia and consolidated Egyptian control over it. Restored Middle Kingdom fortresses and instituted the position of viceroy of Kush

Amenhotep I

Established the royal worker's town at Deir el-Medina. Amenhotep and his mother deified and worshipped as the town's patrons

An experienced and middle-aged military leader

Thutmose I

Not related directly to Amenhotep I

First in the line of outstanding Thutmosid rulers

Thutmose II, Hatshepsut, Thutmose III etc

Military achievements	Building program	Funerary developments
Displayed exceptional abilities as a military leader Nubia – campaigned beyond the Third Cataract Western Asia – campaigned as far as the Euphrates River	Dedicated extensively to Amun-Re. Enlarged and embellished the god's temple at Karnak Two pylon gateways, a roofed hall and Obelisks	First king to build a rock-cut tomb hidden away in the Valley of the Kings Architect – Ineni. Royal workers from the village of Deir el-Medina

Achievements set precedents for other New Kingdom pharaohs to follow

REVISION QUESTIONS AND ESSAY TOPICS

1 **Analyse the following extracts and answer the questions below.**

Part of an account of the invasion of the Hyksos, written by Manetho, a priest of the third century BC, and preserved in the writings of the Jewish historian, Josephus.

> By main force they easily seized it (our land) without striking a blow; and, having overpowered the rulers of the land, they then burned our cities ruthlessly, razed to the ground the temples of the gods and treated all the natives with cruel hostility. [39]

An inscription carved on the facade of a temple in Middle Egypt on the orders of Hatshepsut over 150 years after the Hyksos invasion.

> I have restored that which had been ruined. I have raised up (again) that which had formerly gone to pieces, since the Asiatics were in the midst of Avaris of the Delta, and vagabonds were in their midst, overthrowing what had been made, for they ruled without Re ... [40]

The Carnarvon Tablet, copied as part of a schoolboy's exercise from King Kamose's commemorative stela erected after his attempt to free Egypt from the Hyksos.

> His majesty spoke in his place to the council of nobles who were in his retinue: ... 'No man can settle down, being despoiled by the demands of the Asiatics. I will grapple with him, so that I may cut open his belly! ... My wish is to save Egypt and to smite the Asiatics!'.

> The great men of his council spoke: 'Behold, it is Asiatic water as far as Cusae ... we are at our ease in our part of Egypt. Elephantine is strong, and the middle of the land is with us as far as Cusae. The richest of their fields are ploughed for us, and our cattle are pastured in the Delta. Emmer is sent for our pigs. Our cattle have not been taken away ... he holds the land of the Asiatics; we hold Egypt. If someone should come and act against us, then we shall act against him!' [41]

a What are the views expressed by Manetho and Hatshepsut of the Hyksos rulers of Egypt?

b How reliable are these sources for historians? Explain.

c What evidence is there to refute Hatshepsut's claim that the Hyksos ruled without the gods, particularly Re?

d Why were the Hyksos able to 'overpower the rulers' of Egypt so easily?

e What does Kamose mean by 'no man can settle down being despoiled by the demands of the Asiatics'?

f What evidence is there that the rule of the Hyksos was not excessively harsh and that many Egyptians were probably reasonably content under their Hyksos masters?

g What peaceful innovations did the Hyksos introduce into Egypt?

h Comment on the statement that the Hyksos domination was the catalyst for the transformation of change in Egypt.

2 **Carefully study the object in the figure on the right.**

a Identify the object and the person in whose tomb it was found.

b What was the purpose of such an object?

c Why was it given to the owner and by whom?

d What other object, which reflected the conditions of the day and the honour in which this person was held, was found in the same tomb?

3 **The following text is from the translation of the autobiography of Ahmose, son of Ebana, by Breasted. A more recent translation can be found in Lichtheim's *Ancient Egyptian Literature*, vol. II, 'The New Kingdom'. There are some differences in these translations.**

> ... I spent my youth in the city of Nekheb (El-Kab), my father, Baba, son of Royenet, being an officer of the King of Upper and Lower Egypt, Seqenenre, triumphant. Then I served as an officer in his stead in the ship 'The Offering' in the time of the Lord of the Two Lands, Nebpehtire (Ahmose) ... After having set up a household I was transferred to the Northern fleet, because of my valour. I followed the king on foot when he rode abroad in his chariot.
>
> One (pharaoh) besieged the town of Avaris. I showed valour on foot before his majesty. Then I was appointed to the ship 'Shining in Memphis'.
>
> One fought on the water in the canal: Pezedku of Avaris. Then I fought hand to hand, I brought away a hand. It was reported to the royal herald. One gave to me the gold of valour.
>
> Then there was again fighting in this place (Avaris); I again fought hand to hand there; I brought away a hand. One gave to me the gold of bravery in the second place.
>
> One fought again in this Egypt, south of this city (Nekheb, the place where he was buried); then I brought away a living captive, a man; I descended into the water; behold he was brought as a seizure upon the road of this city although I crossed with him over the water. I was announced to the royal herald. Then one presented me with gold in double measure.
>
> One captured Avaris; I took captive there one man and three women, total four heads (people), his majesty gave them to me for slaves.
>
> One besieged Sharuhen* for six years and his majesty took it. Then I took captive there two women and one hand. One gave me the gold of bravery besides giving me the captives for slaves.
>
> Now after his majesty had slain the Asiatics, he ascended the river to Khenthennofer (part of Nubia south of the Second Cataract), to destroy the Nubian Bowmen; his majesty made a great slaughter among them. Then I took captive two living men and three hands. One presented me with gold in double measure besides giving to me two female slaves. His majesty sailed downstream, his heart joyous with the might of victory, for he had seized Southerners and Northerners.

* Breasted argues convincingly for a six-year siege although Lichtheim says that it lasted three years.

There came an enemy of the south (probably a Nubian); his fate, his destruction approached; the gods of the south seized him and his majesty found him in Tinnto-emu (possibly the district of the First Cataract). His majesty carried him off a living prisoner, and all his people carried captive. I carried away two archers as a seizure of the ship of the enemy, one gave to me five heads besides pieces of land amounting to five stat (about one-third of a hectare) in my city. It was done to all the sailors likewise (the whole crew).

Then came that fallen one, whose name was Teti-en, he had gathered to himself rebels. His majesty slew him and his servants annihilating them. There were given to me three heads, fields amounting to five stat in my city.

I sailed the King Zeserkere (Amenhotep I) triumphant when he ascended the river to Kush, in order to extend the borders of Egypt. His majesty captured that Nubian Bowmen in the midst of his army [...] who were brought away as prisoners, none of them missing [...] thrust aside like those who are annihilated. Meanwhile I was at the head of our army; I fought incredibly; his majesty beheld my bravery. I brought off two hands and took them to his majesty. One pursued his people and his cattle. Then I brought off as living prisoner and took him to his majesty. I brought his majesty in two days to Egypt from the upper well (probably the Second Cataract); one presented me with gold. Then I brought away two female slaves, in addition to those which I had taken to his majesty. One appointed me 'Warrior of the Ruler'.

I sailed with King Okheperkere (Thutmose I) triumphant, when he ascended the river to Khenthennofer, in order to cast out violence in the highlands, in order to suppress the raiding of the desert region. I showed bravery in his presence in the bad water, in the passage of the ship by the bend (over the cataract). One appointed me crew commander. His majesty was [...] .

His majesty was furious thereat, like a panther; his majesty cast his first lance, which remained in the body of that fallen one. Then those enemies turned to flee, powerless before his flaming ureaus, made so in an instant of destruction; their people were brought off as living prisoners. His majesty sailed down-river, with all countries in his grasp, that wretched Nubian Bowmen being hanged head downward at the prow of the barge of his majesty, and landed at Karnak.

After these things one journeyed to Retjenu to wash his heart (take revenge or gain satisfaction) among the foreign countries.

His majesty arrived at Naharin; his majesty found that foe when he was planning destruction; His majesty made a great slaughter among them. Numberless were the living prisoners which his majesty brought off from his victories. Meanwhile I was at the head of our troops, and his majesty beheld my bravery. I brought off a chariot, its horses, and him who was upon it as living prisoner and took them to his majesty. One presented me with gold in double measure ...[42]

a   What was the purpose of this inscription?

b   Who was Ebana?

c   What evidence is there in this text that positions were often inherited from a close relative?

d   Find a number of statements which support the view that Ahmose, son of Ebana, was a marine (someone trained to fight on land and sea) rather than a sailor.

e   What evidence is there that during the first attack on Avaris, Memphis, the former capital of Egypt, was recaptured from the Hyksos?

f   What two terms are used in this text for captives?

g   What does the author mean by 'I brought away a hand'?

h   Ahmose, son of Ebana, was decorated with the gold of valour many times. Give three ways by which the kings learned of Ahmose's bravery.

i   What evidence is there to suggest that the capture and destruction of Avaris took many years?

j   Why did Amenhotep I and Thutmose I each hang the body of a Nubian chieftain from the front of his ship on the return journey to Egypt?

k   Why would a king returning to Thebes from a successful campaign, first land at Karnak?

l   What is the chief importance of this inscription to historians?

m   What are its weaknesses as a source of information about the major events of the reigns of Ahmose I, Amenhotep I and Thutmose I?

n   In what way would the account of Thutmose I's Nubian and Syrian campaigns in this text differ from the account recorded by Thutmose himself on the Tombos stela?

4   The alabaster jar shown below belonged to Queen Ahmose Nefertari. It was inscribed with some of her titles:

> The king's Daughter, the Sister of the Sovereign, the God's Wife, the King's Great Wife, the King's Mother, Ahmose Nefertari, may she live forever!

a   Identify each of the kings whose relationship with Ahmose Nefertari is mentioned in this inscription.

b   In what way is the title *god's wife* different from the other titles inscribed on the jar?

c   What is the full title of *god's wife*? Suggest why it might have been first granted to Ahmose Nefertari.

d   According to the Donation Stela what went with this title?

e   What additional religious honours did Ahmose Nefertari receive in the reign of her son and after her death?

5 Write one paragraph about the significance during the first four reigns of the Eighteenth Dynasty of each of the places numbered on the map below.

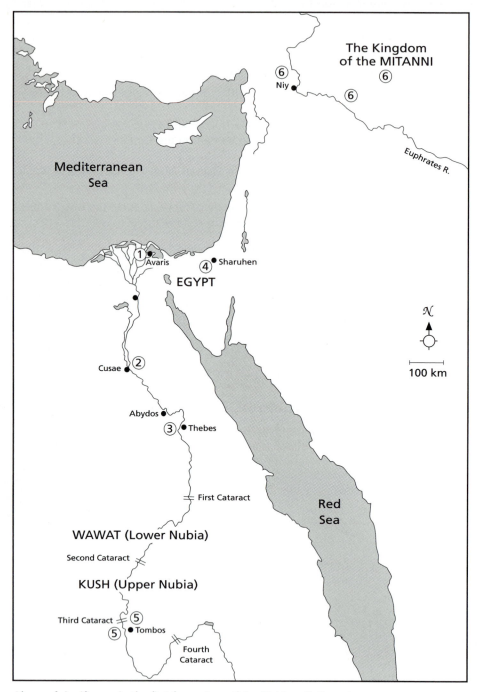

Places of significance in the first four reigns of the Eighteenth Dynasty

'The Female Horus'
— Hatshepsut

After the death of her husband, Queen Hatshepsut became the regent for her nine- or ten-year-old stepson, Thutmose III. However, somewhere between the second and seventh year of her regency she usurped the throne, assumed the title of king and ruled as the senior partner in an official co-regency with Thutmose III.

Why Hatshepsut 'seized' power is open to conjecture, but once she adopted the full regalia and titulary of a king, she set about justifying her actions by:

- focusing on her filial relationship with Amun (divine conception and birth)
- rewriting her past (her selection by Thutmose I as his heir and co-regent)
- associating herself wherever possible with her father and ignoring the reign of her husband, Thutmose II.

Hatshepsut managed to keep complete control over Egypt for nearly 22 years with the support of her close adviser, Senenmut, powerful allies in the bureaucracy and the priesthood of Amun-Re, the god whom she honoured above all others. Her reign marked the beginning of the real power of the priests of Amun. She embarked on a vigorous building program, particularly in Thebes, and expanded trade. Hatshepsut regarded an expedition to the Land of Punt as a highlight of her reign.

Although there is no doubt who was the dominant partner in the co-regency, there is no evidence that Thutmose III resented his stepmother/aunt as has been suggested by some historians. It appears he did not challenge her position when he grew older and instead was kept busy leading a number of military campaigns in Nubia and possibly also several to the north.

Hatshepsut was not the first queen to become a king. Nitocris, Sobeknofru and Twosret each ruled briefly in the turbulent times at the end of the Sixth, Twelfth and Nineteenth dynasties respectively. However, Hatshepsut not only reigned for almost 22 years at a time of internal peace and vigorous growth, but was the first woman to be depicted in official reliefs and statuary as a king (pleated royal kilt, double crown, artificial beard and *five great names*).

Sources of evidence for Hatshepsut's reign

Damaged monuments

Most of the monuments associated with Hatshepsut suffered severe damage during the latter part of the reign of Thutmose III and at the time of Akhenaten. Her inscriptions were selectively erased, her name replaced by those of other kings and many of her statues were smashed to pieces. The reasons behind these actions will be discussed later in this chapter.

Because of the incomplete nature of the sources, there are a variety of interpretations of some of the issues and events of her reign; for example, the reason for her 'seizure' of the throne and her relationships with Thutmose III and her chief adviser, Senenmut.

For some events, there is enough information to build up an adequate picture of what happened (eg, the trading expedition to Punt) while for others, there is only a line in an inscription here and there from which to form an opinion (eg, military campaigns). One thing about which there is no lack of evidence, however, is Hatshepsut's dedication to the god Amun-Re.

Chief source — temple at Deir el-Bahri

Hatshepsut's mortuary temple at Deir el-Bahri is the greatest source of information for her reign. On its walls are inscribed accounts of:

- the trading expedition she sent to the Land of Punt
- the transport of obelisks which were later set up in the Temple of Karnak
- her so-called 'divine' birth and coronation which were intended to justify her co-regency with Thutmose III.

These are described in detail because they emphasise Hatshepsut's close relationship with Amun.

Statues of Hatshepsut, reconstructed from smashed pieces found in a great quarry or pit north of the temple at Deir el-Bahri, show the queen in both male and female guise, as a sphinx and in the form of the god Osiris. These statues once graced the colonnades and terraces of her temple.

Numerous unguent jars, food offerings, models of tools and so on, excavated from the foundation pits on the perimeter of the temple, have provided information about the temple's dedication ceremonies.

This magnificent temple also provides evidence of:

- the ability of the officials (*overseers of works*) employed by Hatshepsut
- the status of Hatshepsut's chief adviser, Senenmut
- the attempted obliteration of her name and achievements supposedly ordered by Thutmose III some considerable time after her death.

Other important sources of information include:

- the surviving pink granite obelisks erected by Hatshepsut at the Temple of Karnak (one still standing and the other lying on its side). The inscriptions on the shafts and bases are further evidence of Hatshepsut's devotion to Amun and her attempts to emphasise the relationship with her earthly father, Thutmose I

- the temple of Speos Artemidos, a small rock-cut temple near Beni Hassan. On its facade Hatshepsut recorded her pride in restoring the sanctuaries destroyed by the Hyksos. The inscription mentions monuments for which there is no other surviving source of information

- the three hundred blocks of red quartzite which originally formed part of the Red Chapel of Hatshepsut at Karnak

- the inscriptions in the tombs of some of Hatshepsut's 'architects' such as Ineni, Thutiy and Puemre. These provide evidence for Hatshepsut's administrative ability and some of the details of the work they carried out for her. Ineni's tomb inscription provides a contemporary comment on the succession of Thutmose III and the regency of Hatshepsut

- the statues of Senenmut and Hapusoneb which record the titles and honours bestowed by Hatshepsut on these important officials and the works carried out by them

- the stela of the noble Djehuty at Dra' abu' negga and the graffito of the noble, Tiy, at Sehel near Elephantine which suggest that Hatshepsut initiated several military campaigns and perhaps even led one herself

- the two tombs built for Hatshepsut (a small cliff tomb made for her as queen consort and an elaborate one built in the Valley of the Kings).

Hatshepsut as queen and regent

As the elder daughter of Thutmose I and his chief queen, Hatshepsut would have been aware of her exalted position from an early age. Her upbringing prepared her for the duties she would one day carry out as queen, and she was probably influenced by the strength of character and status of her female predecessors.

When she married her half-brother, Thutmose II, Hatshepsut was probably very young — perhaps as young as 12, certainly no older than 15.

Although she may have believed, even in childhood, that she deserved to wear the double crown in her own right, there is no evidence that while her husband was alive, she was anything other than a conventional queen consort. There are at least three pieces of evidence to support this statement:

A conventional queen consort

1 There was nothing unusual in her titles — *King's Daughter, King's Sister, God's Wife of Amun* and *King's Great Wife*. She had inherited the important religious title of God's Wife of Amun, which she held until she became king.

2   She ordered the construction of a tomb, suitable for a queen, hidden away in a valley several kilometres from the Valley of the Kings.

3   She is shown on a stela standing 'in approved wifely fashion'[1] behind her mother, the dowager queen, Ahmose, and her husband, Thutmose II who is facing Re.

However, there is one interesting feature of this stela. It was inscribed during the reign of Thutmose II and yet the dowager queen, Ahmose, is referred to as *King's Mother*. Ahmose was the mother of Hatshepsut, not Thutmose II. This piece of evidence has contributed to the theory that perhaps Hatshepsut saw herself quite early on as having a legitimate claim to the throne.

Offspring of Thutmose II and Hatshepsut

Hatshepsut and Thutmose had produced only a daughter, Neferure; although the king had fathered a son by a palace concubine, named Isis. Thutmose II appears to have nominated this son (also named Thutmose), as his heir.

When Thutmose II died prematurely, his son, who was still a small child about nine or ten, 'stood in his place as king of the Two Lands, having become ruler upon the throne of the one who begat him'.[2] In these circumstances the following would be expected to occur:

- Hatshepsut, as the dowager queen, would act as regent for the young king (Thutmose III).

- Thutmose III would be married to his half-sister, Hatshepsut's daughter, Neferure. There is no evidence that this ever occurred.

- When Thutmose III reached an age when he was able to rule alone Hatshepsut would retire from the regency.

Consequences of the untimely death of Thutmose II

When her husband died and Hatshepsut assumed the role of regent, she may still have been in her late teens. Although female regencies were not uncommon in Egyptian history, Tyldesley maintains that this situation 'was unprecedented: Hatshepsut was being called upon to act as regent for a boy who was not her son'.[3] This has led some historians to assume that Hatshepsut would not have tolerated such a situation.

The regency

Whatever Hatshepsut felt about the regency, she took care in the beginning not to overstep her role. She was still referred to by the titles she held as Thutmose II's queen, and was officially depicted on public monuments standing behind her stepson Thutmose III.

Despite her apparent low profile at this time, the evidence points to the fact that from the beginning she was well and truly in full control of the government. Ineni's tomb inscription gives a contemporary comment on Hatshepsut's control of the state:

Hatshepsut's control of the state

> ... the Divine Consort, Hatshepsut, settled the affairs of the Two Lands by reason of her plans. Egypt was made to labour with bowed head for her, the excellent seed of the god ... whose plans are excellent, who satisfies the Two Regions when she speaks.[4]

Hatshepsut obviously had a strong personality and showed herself an efficient administrator. However, she would not have been able to govern the land without the support of a number of loyal officials from the civil, religious and military bureaucracy.

It has been suggested that Hatshepsut spent her regency consolidating her position and gaining support because she had more ambitious plans for herself — to become pharaoh. One of these supporters was Senenmut. Although he had been appointed as the tutor of the princess Neferure during Thutmose II's reign, it was during Hatshepsut's regency that he received his most lucrative posts. Refer to the section entitled 'Senenmut' later in this chapter for further information on the career of this influential official.

Even though Senenmut may have helped her carry out her plans, her strongest support came from the priesthood of Amun-Re and particularly from Hapusoneb, High Priest of Amun, and *Chief of the Prophets of the South and the North*. Hatshepsut held the prestigious position of *God's Wife of Amun* and this may have given her some influence with the priesthood.

Consolidating her position

What evidence is there of Hatshepsut's future ambitions during her regency?

Evidence of future ambitions

- Several inscriptions on the blocks of her Red Chapel at Karnak mention an oracle given to Hatshepsut by Amun in year 2 of her regency. In one, Hatshepsut describes how a 'very great oracle in the presence of this good god, proclaiming for me the kingship of the Two Lands, Upper and Lower Egypt being under the fear of me ... Year 2, 2 Perit 29, the third day of the festival of Amun ...'.[5]

  Another inscription, written in the third person, says 'Thereupon, the majesty of this god gave great oracles, very numerous and very important. After this he placed her before him, taking her up to the Mansion of Maat, she having received the adornments of her majesty.'[6]

  Although an oracle was used to make known what a god's intentions were, the message was translated by the High Priest and coincided with his interests. Also an oracle such as this would not have been uttered without the knowledge of Hatshepsut.

  The problem with this inscription is that it does not name the 'good god' or king in whose reign this pronouncement was made. Should historians take the inscription at face value and assume that the king mentioned is Thutmose III? On the other hand, should it be treated as another example of the fiction about her early years that Hatshepsut recorded on her monuments?

- Robins, in a paper entitled 'God's Wife of Amun', suggests that while Hatshepsut was still only regent she 'used titles modelled on those used by kings'.[7] One of these was *lady of the Two Lands*, a feminine version of the king's title *lord of the Two Lands*.

- Also during her regency Hatshepsut commissioned a pair of obelisks at Karnak (not the two that have survived). This was usually the prerogative of a king. 'She thus reinforced her position as de facto ruler of Egypt by drawing on kingly iconography, titulary and actions.'[8]

Gradual assumption of power

Hers was a gradual evolution, a carefully controlled political manoeuvre so insidious that it might not have been apparent to any but her closest contemporaries.[9]

King of Upper and Lower Egypt

Assumption of power

When and why did Hatshepsut feel the need to change her status from queen regent to king?

The timing of her coronation

There is a difference of opinion among scholars as to the timing of her coronation and adoption of the full titulary of a king.

She was already using her throne name, Maat-ka-re, by year 7. A pottery seal, found in the tomb of Senenmut's mother and dated to the regnal year 7, refers to her as Maat-ka-re.

If the oracle mentioned previously did occur in year 2, then the coronation took place sometime after that. However, on the walls of a temple at Semna in Nubia, which was constructed in the second year of Thutmose III, 'there is a not a trace of Queen Hatshepsut's regnancy (kingship) in the original sculptures'.[10]

Her assumption of power is generally placed somewhere before year 7 and possibly as early as year 2 of Thutmose III's reign. Hayes and Redford support the latter. Hatshepsut probably felt the need to become king before Thutmose III reached an age when he could rule alone. In regnal year 2, the young king would have been only about 12 years of age. Hatshepsut still had time to take a gradual and cautious approach to assuming full kingly powers. Her titulary and statuary seem to support this view. It is therefore probably erroneous to talk about her seizure of power as if it occurred in a dramatic coup.

Reasons for becoming king

Her reason or reasons for wanting to be a ruling king rather than remaining as queen regnant are not known, although there are many opinions.

It is possible that she believed that she had more right to the throne than Thutmose III. Whether this is correct or not there is no evidence to support the picture of a scheming, ruthless and power-hungry queen. If this were the case, as some historians suggest, she would have:

• tried to get rid of Thutmose III and rule alone

• prevented him having any military experience and leading an army

• made sure that he did not share any of her monuments with her.

None of these things occurred and there is no evidence that when he reached maturity, Thutmose III made any attempt to challenge her authority.

Perhaps Hatshepsut assumed kingly powers because she was afraid that the young king might die in childhood (there was a high death rate among young royals) and she was anxious to secure the future for herself and her daughter. It is also possible that she could have feared that some influential individual or group might use the young pharaoh as a pawn in a political struggle.

It is highly unlikely that the question of why she felt the need to become king will ever be answered. However, there is no doubt that both before and after her assumption of power, she had the support of the male elite in the civil and religious bureaucracies. Refer to the section entitled 'Hatshepsut's support base' later in this chapter for information on the men who supported her throughout her reign.

Support of the male elite

Hatshepsut was crowned with full pharaonic powers and took the titles of a ruling king. She was now the Female Horus. Her full titulary was:

Titulary

> Horus: Mighty-of-kas; Two Ladies: Flourishing-in-years; Gold-Horus: Divine-of-Diadems; King of Upper and Lower Egypt, Lord of the Two Lands: Maat-ka-re; Daughter of Re: Hatshepsut Khnemet-Amun.

Officially she ruled jointly (as co-regent) with the young Thutmose III but there is no doubt as to who was the senior pharaoh until at least the twentieth year of their reign.

A female Horus and the gender issue

How was a female king to be described in the texts (official and private) and depicted in statuary and pictorial inscriptions?

Texts

From the time Hatshepsut assumed the role of pharaoh, the scribes responsible for recording her achievements appear to have been baffled as to how to describe a female *Horus*.

Firstly, there were no feminine words for a reigning monarch. So, in most of her inscriptions, Hatshepsut is referred to in both masculine and feminine forms — *Her Majesty, King Maat-ka-re*. Although the scribes often used the feminine pronoun and added the feminine ending for *lord* and *majesty*, sometimes in the middle of a long text *she* and *her* would be replaced with *he* and *his*.

Some confusion in the texts

The record-keepers seem to have decided that where her name was associated with military matters it was more appropriate to use the masculine form. For example:

> I followed the Good God, the King of Upper and Lower Egypt, Maat-ka-re, given life. I saw when he overthrew the Nubian bowman, their chiefs being brought to him as prisoners. I saw when he razed Nubia, I being in his majesty's following ...[11]

Part of the royal titulary which seems to have been regarded as unsuitable for a female ruler was the epithet *mighty bull*. Whereas Thutmose II's Horus name was *Mighty-Bull-Beloved-of-Truth* and that of Thutmose III was *Strong-Bull-arisen-in-Thebes*, Hatshepsut's Horus name was *Mighty-of-kas*.

Images

If Hatshepsut were to be regarded as a true Egyptian king, she had to:

- draw a sharp distinction between her role as a king and that of her previous position as queen regent
- follow tradition and have herself depicted as a conventional king.

In Egypt there was always a clear distinction made between the office of kingship and the individual who held the office. The kingship was represented by a male in full regalia — royal *shendyet*-kilt, ceremonial false beard, folded striped head cloth (*nemes*) and various royal crowns, such as the khepresh or blue war crown. Only in such a guise could a king be shown communicating with the gods.

Depicted as a conventional king

In most of her images (reliefs and statuary) she is shown, like her predecessors and successors, as a male with all the attributes of a traditional king of Egypt. However, there is no suggestion that Hatshepsut was trying to fool her subjects into thinking that their king was actually a man, nor is it likely that in her private life she impersonated a male. The weight of tradition demanded that Egyptians, most of whom could not read, should see their pharaoh depicted in the reliefs and statuary as a king.

However, there appears to have been a period after she became king when she either experimented with a new image suitable for a female king or deliberately proceeded slowly in the adoption of a kingly identity. Tefnin, in his work, *La Statuaire d'Hatshepsout*, suggests that the latter was the case.

A number of statues found at Deir el-Bahri which describe Hatshepsut as king, show her either as a woman or with feminine characteristics. For example:

- One statue in black diorite shows her as a slender female wearing a tight-fitting dress with a soft *hkat* headdress. Although her titles retain the feminine endings, they are those of a king and the symbols of Egypt's enemies are inscribed beneath her feet.
- Another female figure in red granite, wearing the kingly *nemes* headdress with ureaus has the inscription the *Good Goddess, Maat-ka-re, Daughter of Re, Khnemet-Amun Hatshepsut, beloved of Amun who resides in Djeser-djeseru*. This figure has a decoration of Taweret, the hippopotamus goddess of childbirth, inscribed on the back.

  Hayes suggests that these figures may have come from the shrine of Hathor, one of the mortuary deities.
- A limestone statue of her as king, wearing the royal kilt and nemes headdress but minus the artificial beard, has an obviously feminine body (slim, graceful and with breasts). Tyldesley suggests that perhaps this could 'be interpreted as a short-lived attempt to present a new image of the pharaoh as an asexual mixture of male and female strengths'.[12]
- A headless statue from Deir el-Bahri, representing Hatshepsut as a king (nemes, *shendyet*-kilt, and with the symbols of the Nine-Bow people under its feet) reveals 'something of a feminine quality in its slenderness and softly rounded forms'.[13]

Left: The head and shoulders of a red granite statue of Hatshepsut

Right: A limestone seated statue of Hatshepsut with a female body and male accessories

However, most of Hatshepsut's reliefs and statues show her as a male in the full kingly regalia, standing with left foot forward and hands spread in adoration or kneeling before the god (the formal poses of a king). She is also depicted as the conventional sphinx. One of her kneeling statues is so similar to one made for Thutmose III that, apart from the inscriptions, it is difficult to tell them apart.

Hatshepsut had reinvented herself as a traditional king.

> By causing herself to be depicted as a traditional pharaoh in the most regal and heroic form, Hatshepsut was making sure that this is precisely what she would become.[14]

A relief of Hatshepsut as a king kneeling before Amun

Above: Colossal statues of Hatshepsut as a king, offering Nu-jars containing milk or wine

Right: A red granite sphinx of Hatshepsut

Neferure and Senenmut

Neferure

Neferure was probably a very young child when her mother became regent. While still a baby, the young princess was looked after by one Ahmose-Pennekheb who recorded this great honour in his tomb biography. 'I reared her eldest daughter, the Royal Daughter, Neferure triumphant, while she was still a child upon the breast ...'[15] Later, Senenmut, as a steward of Amun, was appointed 'great father-tutor of the king's daughter, Sovereign of the Two Lands, Divine Consort, Neferure ...'.[16] When Senenmut developed a higher profile in the service of Hatshepsut, the role of tutor was passed on to another man, Senimen.

Hatshepsut's plans

Although it is unclear what Hatshepsut's future plans were for her daughter, some scholars suggest that she was planning for Neferure to succeed her as pharaoh. According to Redford, two pieces of evidence support this view.

1 There are several statues of Neferure depicted as a crown prince, wearing the ureaus serpent on her forehead and the artificial ceremonial beard on her chin.
2 A title by which she was known — *Lady of the Two Lands, Mistress of Upper and Lower Egypt.*

God's Wife of Amun

When Hatshepsut became king, she transferred her title of *God's Wife of Amun* to her daughter. This was not unusual, but from this point the references to Neferure, particularly on scarabs, far exceed those referring to many queens and other king's daughters.

Neferure also appeared in offering scenes with her mother, the king. Since a ruling king needed a consort to participate in the religious rituals, Neferure, as *God's Wife of Amun*, may have filled that role. This may be the reason why Neferure, who would have been expected to marry Thutmose III, does not appear to have done so.

Early death

Whatever Hatshepsut's plans were for her daughter, they came to nothing. The last known reference to Neferure was in year 11 and it seems that she died before her mother, probably about the age of 13.

Propaganda and Hatshepsut's right to the throne

To justify her position as a divine ruler in her own right, Hatshepsut:
- made a feature of her divine conception by the god Amun
- rewrote her history so that she was seen as the legitimate successor of her father, Thutmose I.

Deir el-Bahri inscriptions

Inscriptions (text and reliefs) on the walls of her mortuary temple at Deir el-Bahri describe in considerable detail Hatshepsut's divine conception and birth, her appointment as the successor of Thutmose II and her fictitious coronation.

Wherever she could she emphasised her relationship with her heavenly and earthly fathers and recorded those things she did for them.

The account of Hatshepsut's divine conception and birth

There was nothing new in the claims of a pharaoh to be the physical son of the predominant god. For example, each king of the Fifth Dynasty claimed a theogamous birth which resulted from the impregnation of the chief queen by the god Re. Hatshepsut's predecessors in the Eighteenth Dynasty claimed Amun-Re to be their *father*.

However, according to Breasted, Hatshepsut's claims to be the physical daughter of the god Amun, 'was a violent wrenching of the traditional details ... for the entire legend was fitted only to a man'.[17]

According to the Deir el-Bahri inscriptions, Amun prophesied the birth of Hatshepsut at a council of the gods. He then assumed the guise of Hatshepsut's father, Thutmose I, and visited Queen Ahmose as she slept.

The divine conception

> She waked at the fragrance of the god, which she smelled in the presence of his Majesty. He went to her immediately ... When he came before her she rejoiced at the sight of his beauty, his love passed into her limbs ... all his odours were from Punt.[18]

The accompanying relief shows Amun and Ahmose sitting opposite each other in heaven which is symbolised by two female divinities supporting them. Amun holds the *ankh* or key of life to Ahmose's nose and mouth so that she can breathe in the divine essence and conceive the god's child.

The god Amun visiting Queen Ahmose

The queen is then informed by Amun that she has conceived a daughter by him. She is to be named Knemet-Amun Hatshepsut and will 'exercise the excellent kingship in this whole land'.[19]

The name of the god's child

Amun instructs the god Khnum, the creator of flesh, to make the baby and its *ka*** on his potters wheel. The reliefs show Khnum being helped by his wife, the frog-headed goddess, Heket.

The royal baby and its *ka* are depicted in the likeness of a boy, complete with male genitalia.

> Utterance of Amun ... 'Go, to make her, together with her *ka*, from these limbs which are in me; go, to fashion her better than all the gods ..[20]

Queen Ahmose was led off by Khnum and Heket to give birth. She was attended by Bes (the protective deity of the household) and Taueret (the pregnant hippopotamus goddess of childbirth).

The newborn child was offered the symbols of life, power and protection and presented to her 'father' Amun. The next scene shows her being suckled by the heavenly wet nurse, the cow-goddess, Hathor.

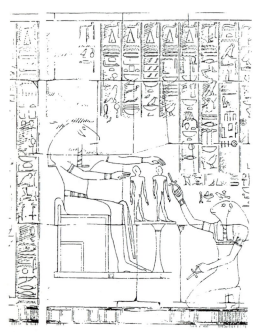

The god Khnum fashioning Hatshepsut and her ka *on the potter's wheel*

Queen Ahmose being led off to give birth

The coronation reliefs

In these reliefs, which were a sequel to the birth scenes, Hatshepsut claimed that she was chosen by Amun and her father, Thutmose I, as his only legitimate successor and crowned by him to share a co-regency.

In the first scenes, the child Hatshepsut is purified, after which Amun 'shows her to all the gods of the South and the North, who come to look upon her, doing obeisance before her'.[21] The reliefs record that as Hatshepsut grew, she became more like a god 'her form was like a god, she did everything as a god ...'.[22]

---

* The royal *ka* was thought to be the personification of kingship. Hatshepsut included it in her throne name, Maat-ka-re and her Horus name, Mighty-of-kas.

She then accompanied her father on a journey through Egypt to attend the shrines of the gods who welcomed her as a future king. The gods supposedly promised her that she would 'restore that which has gone to its ruin ... victual the offering-table of him who begat thee ... embrace many countries'.[23] It is quite possible that as a child Hatshepsut was taken on such a journey, but not for the purpose described in the reliefs.

She is then crowned by the gods — first by Atum at Heliopolis in the north and then by Amun in a similar coronation ceremony at Thebes.

The next inscription refers to her alleged coronation in front of the court. Thutmose I is shown on his throne with Hatshepsut standing in front of him and three rows of 'nobles, companions, officers of the court and the chief of the people'[24] watching the ceremony. The accompanying inscriptions describe her presentation to the court by Thutmose I, who declared:

> **This is my daughter, Khnemet-Amun Hatshepsut who liveth, I have appointed her ...; she is my successor upon my throne, she it assuredly is who shall sit upon this wonderful seat. She shall command the people in every place of the palace; she it is who shall lead you; ye shall proclaim her word, ye shall be united at her command. He who shall do her homage shall live, he who shall speak evil or blasphemy of her majesty shall die.[25]**

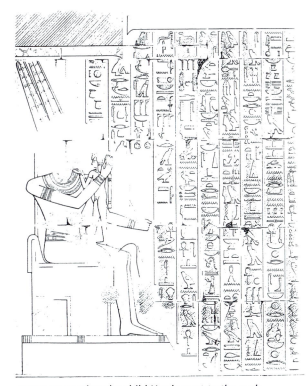

Amun presenting the child Hatshepsut to the gods

Gardiner and Breasted both maintain that this account is purely fictional because:

- it totally ignores the well documented reign of Hatshepsut's husband, Thutmose II

- in the years prior to her regency, Hatshepsut was only referred to as *King's Great Wife*

- the date of the supposed coronation does not tally with the information on her obelisk

- the text was 'taken verbatim from the account of the coronation of Amenemhet III in the Middle Kingdom temple at Arsinoe ...'.[26]

In rewriting her past, Hatshepsut ignored the reign of her husband. She continued the propaganda that she was the legitimate successor of Thutmose I by celebrating her heb-sed or jubilee 30 years after her father's death (that is, early in her reign). To mark her heb-sed, she erected two obelisks at Karnak and on them she continued the theme of her right to the throne.

Another piece of propaganda justifying her right to rule was inscribed on the southern pylon at Karnak where her father is shown calling on the Theban triad (Amun, Mut and Khonsu) to bless his daughter upon her reign.

She also reburied her father in her own tomb in the Valley of the Kings and arranged for him to share in the mortuary services conducted in her Deir el-Bahri temple.

Hatshepsut's support base

At the beginning of her reign, Hatshepsut was supported by a group of officials, some of whom had served her father and others who had been appointed by her husband. Although many of the old guard, like Ineni and Ahmose-Pennekheb, remained loyal to Hatshepsut, they appear to have died early in her reign.

She gradually built up a political support system of officials whose political careers were linked to hers. Hapusoneb was her most influential supporter. He was not only the high priest of Amun but was given the additional title of *chief of the prophets of south and north*. According to Breasted:

> The formation of a priesthood of the whole land into a coherent organisation with a single individual at its head appears for the first time. This new and great organisation, was thus through Hapusoneb, enlisted on the side of Hatshepsut. [27]

Also, at some point during her reign, it is believed Hapusoneb was appointed as vizier, which gave him control of the civil bureaucracy. This powerful official combined both secular and sacred authority.

Other high-ranking officials who served Hatshepsut were:
- Weser-amen, a vizier early in her career
- Thutiy, treasurer, the successor of Ineni as overseer of the double gold and silver houses
- Nehsy, the chancellor who led her famous expedition to Punt
- Thutmose, treasurer
- Inebni, Viceroy of Kush
- Puemre, Second prophet of Amun
- Tiy, treasurer.

However, of all those who served Hatshepsut, it was Senenmut who was her closest adviser. He is generally regarded as the person chiefly responsible for Hatshepsut's success and his career seems to have paralleled her own rise to power.

Senenmut

Senenmut was a controversial figure. He has often been the victim of 'bad press', possibly because he came from a relatively lowly background and yet 'enjoyed privileges and prerogatives never before extended to a mere official'. [28]

Senenmut's private life

Senenmut's parents, Ramose and Hatnofer, were commoners who came from the town of Armant near Thebes. However, the scribal education received by Senenmut indicates that his relatives were from the literate middle class. He is believed to have had two sisters and three brothers but the official named Senimen was not one of his siblings, as was once thought.

His father, Ramose, and six other members of his family died before Senenmut was awarded his first influential post with Hatshepsut, while his mother died well after her son's rise to prominence. The evidence for this was found in his mother's tomb which was located close to the first tomb Senenmut built for himself.

Trial sketches of the head of Senenmut on a limestone flake

In Hatnofer's tomb were seven other bodies — her husband and six unidentified people. Of the mummies, only Senenmut's mother had been carefully embalmed and wrapped in fine linen from Hatshepsut's estate. Also, she had been provided with a complete funerary outfit which included a black-painted anthropoid (human-shaped) coffin, a gold death mask, a magnificent heart scarab set in gold, three papyrus funerary rolls and several silver jugs and bowls. All the personal possessions in the tomb belonged to her.

Although the other mummies were loosely wrapped in bandages, their bodies were not well preserved. Some of their bones were broken or dislocated and there were traces of mud and small stones among the wrappings. Ramose's father had been placed in a painted anthropoid coffin while the others were in plain ones.

This seems to indicate that originally Senenmut's father and six relatives had been given a common burial without any funeral trappings. As Senenmut became more influential, the family fortunes increased and he was able to give his mother a fine burial. At the same time, it appears that he exhumed the bodies of his other relatives, placed them in new coffins and buried them in the tomb prepared for Hatnofer.

Evidence of an increase in family fortune

In her book, *Senenmut*, Meyer maintains that he had no children and in fact remained a bachelor all his life. She bases her view on the following evidence:

- He is shown only with his parents on the funerary stelae in his tombs (he built two).
- He is shown alone, rather than with a wife, in the scenes from the Book of the Dead in his second tomb.
- It was one of his brothers, rather than a son, who carried out the funeral rites for him.

Probably remained a bachelor

Senenmut's official career

We know very little about Senenmut's early career, although a tomb inscription implies that he spent time in the army. At some point in his youth Senenmut entered the service of the Temple of Amun at Karnak and held a succession of positions.

It is not known how he rose to prominence at court and how he won the trust and favour of Hatshepsut but he appears among her officials before the death of Thutmose II. It was at this time that he was appointed as steward and tutor or *great nurse* to her daughter, Neferure.

Meteoric rise to power

His meteoric rise as the queen's most favoured official can be seen in the titles he was given and the offices he held. In his own words, he rose to be 'the greatest of the great in the whole land; one who heard the hearing alone in the privy council'.[29]

Evidence for the status of Senenmut can be found in the inscriptions on:

- a black diorite statue dedicated to Mut which was presented to Senenmut by Hatshepsut and Thutmose III as a token of honour
- the walls and funerary stelae of his tombs
- the rocks at Aswan
- fragments of his smashed quartzite sarcophagus
- stamped pottery funerary cones and name stones from his tombs.

Over 80 different titles appear on Senenmut's monuments although only 20 of these are likely to have been official. The remainder would have been honorary. There is no way of really telling in what order he received these appointments.

His two main titles — *chief steward of Amun* and *chief steward of the king* — indicate that Senenmut was probably a highly competent administrator and financial manager. By means of these two positions, he controlled the estate of Amun (fields, gardens, cattle, peasants), the royal household and the king's estate, which together comprised a large part of Egypt's resources.

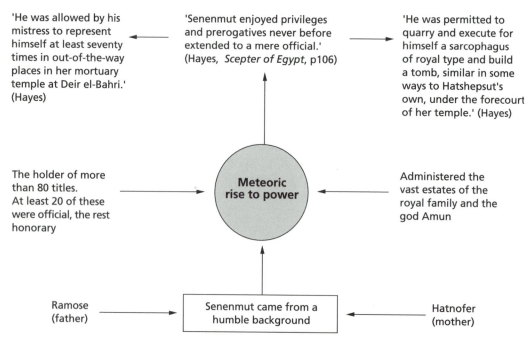

'He was allowed by his mistress to represent himself at least seventy times in out-of-the-way places in her mortuary temple at Deir el-Bahri.' (Hayes)

'Senenmut enjoyed privileges and prerogatives never before extended to a mere official.' (Hayes, *Scepter of Egypt*, p106)

'He was permitted to quarry and execute for himself a sarcophagus of royal type and build a tomb, similar in some ways to Hatshepsut's own, under the forecourt of her temple.' (Hayes)

The holder of more than 80 titles. At least 20 of these were official, the rest honorary

Meteoric rise to power

Administered the vast estates of the royal family and the god Amun

Ramose (father)

Senenmut came from a humble background

Hatnofer (mother)

Senenmut's meteoric rise to power

Another title Senenmut claimed to have held was *controller of works*. In this position he organised and supervised the construction of many of Hatshepsut's buildings 'in Karnak, in Hermonthis, in Deir el-Bahri, of Amun, in the temple of Mut, in Ishru, in southern Opet of Amun (Luxor)'.[30] Also he was commissioned to supervise the cutting of two of Hatshepsut's giant obelisks at Aswan and to see that they were transported safely down river to Thebes. On the cliffs at Aswan he left a record to commemorate this great achievement — 'Came the hereditary prince, count who ... pleases the Mistress of the Two Lands ... Senenmut, in order to conduct the work of the two great obelisks ...'.[31]

On a statue found in the temple of Mut, he maintained also that he was responsible for enlarging and restoring other monuments. Refer to the section entitled 'Hatshepsut's building program' for more information about Senenmut's building activities.

In his position as *overseer of the storehouse of Amun*, he was closely associated with Hatshepsut's great trading expedition to Punt. He would have been involved in the collection and storage of those products brought back from Punt which were dedicated to Amun.

Although Senenmut was not a vizier, his claim that 'I was the one to whom the affairs of the Two Lands were reported, that which South and North contributed was on my seal',[32] indicates that he controlled many of the functions of the vizier.

> **Controller or overseer of works**

> **Overseer of the storehouse of Amun**

Controversies concerning Senenmut

Senenmut appears to have been on the most intimate terms with the royal family. He described how he was 'one who entered in love and came forth in favour, making glad the heart of the king every day' and 'the one whose steps were known in the palace; a real confidante of the king, his beloved'.[33]

> **Relationship with Hatshepsut**

Some scholars have suggested that he may have been more than a close adviser to Hatshepsut — perhaps her lover. Some have gone further and suggested that he may have been the father of Neferure. These views have been based on the great honours which Hatshepsut appears to have given him, such as permission to:

- use over 80 titles
- erect statues of himself, in several of which he is shown embracing the young Neferure, while she leans her head against him. Twenty-five of these statues have survived and most were gifts from the queen
- engrave his name and image in out-of-the-way places in her mortuary temple. Over 60 of these were found and show Senenmut worshipping Amun and Hatshepsut
- excavate a long sloping corridor-tomb, approximately 100 metres in length, under the forecourt of Hatshepsut's temple at Deir el-Bahri
- prepare a quartzite sarcophagus for himself similar to those used by royalty.

Despite these honours, there is no firm evidence that the relationship between Hatshepsut and Senenmut was anything other than one of king and loyal official.

There is still more controversy over the fate of Senenmut, who disappeared from the records some time after year 16 of Hatshepsut's reign. It is not known if he fell out of favour or if he died. However:

- he never occupied the tomb beneath the forecourt of Hatshepsut's temple
- his sarcophagus was smashed to pieces
- some of his statues were deliberately damaged
- his name was chipped out of some of the records
- most of the images of him in Hatshepsut's mortuary temple were hacked out.

What happened to him? Some scholars suggest that Senenmut had a falling out with Hatshepsut. They maintain that she was unaware of Senenmut's engravings in her temple and when she discovered his name and images, she had them destroyed and dismissed him from her services.

Dorman, in *The Monuments of Senenmut*, says such a suggestion is patently absurd. There is no way Hatshepsut would have been unaware of what was going on. In fact, a badly damaged text from Deir el-Bahri indicates that he not only had permission to carve his images in Hatshepsut's temple, but he was permitted to do the same in other temples throughout Egypt.

> **Giving praise to Amun and smelling the ground to the Lord of the Gods on behalf of the life, prosperity and health of the King of Upper and Lower Egypt. Maat-ka-re, may he live forever, by the Hereditary Prince and Count, the Steward of Amun, Senenmut with a favour of the King's bounty which was extended to this servant in letting his name be established on every wall in the following of the King in Djeser-Djeseru, and likewise in the temples of the Gods of Upper and Lower Egypt. Thus spoke the King.**[34]

Dorman also disputes the belief that Hatshepsut had anything to do with the damage to Senenmut's monuments. According to him, 'the amount of damage that can be identified as directed against Senenmut's person is very small indeed'. [35] It seems that his monuments were damaged by different people for different reasons and over an extended period of time.

How or when Senenmut died is unknown but it must be remembered that he was probably an old man by Egyptian standards by year 16.

Hatshepsut's building program

Redford, in *History and Chronology of the Eighteenth Dynasty*, says that Hatshepsut's top priority appears to have been her building program, judging by her repeated references to it.

She outlined her building policy in the text inscribed on the facade of a small rock-cut temple built at Beni Hassan (referred to by the Greeks as Speos Artemidos). From this and other fragmentary evidence, scattered throughout Egypt and Nubia, her building policy appears to have involved:

- repairing temples, chapels and sanctuaries destroyed or neglected during the domination of the Hyksos, such as the Temple of Hathor at Cusae and the Temple of Thoth at Hermopolis. Associated with this was the restoration of some of the cult festivals and processions

- constructing new monuments such as her mortuary temple at Deir el-Bahri; the Red Chapel, obelisks and pylon at Karnak, the barque sanctuary at Luxor and the cliff temple dedicated to the lion goddess, Pakhet, at Speos Artemidos

- completing some of the buildings which were begun during the reign of her husband, Thutmose II.

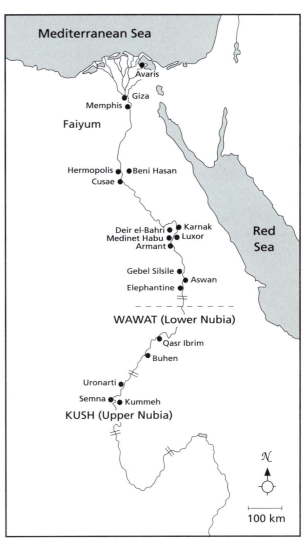

The location of Hatshepsut's building projects

Although most of the chief gods benefited from Hatshepsut's attention, it was her *father*, Amun, who received the lion's share of the new buildings — 'She made them as her monuments for her father, Amun, Lord of Thebes, presider over Karnak'.[(36)] She recorded that she did not sleep because of his temple.

The map on the right shows those places where scholars believe Hatshepsut built, repaired or completed *the houses of the gods*.

Hatshepsut's 'architects'

Who were the men Hatshepsut relied on to carry out her building projects? It is generally believed that Senenmut, Hatshepsut's closest adviser, organised and supervised most of her building works. He certainly claimed that he was responsible for her monuments in Thebes although he does not specify which ones. Gardiner doubts that he was the actual architect. Refer to Chapter 15 for information about Egyptian architects.

Many officials responsible for her building projects

Since Hatshepsut reigned for over 21 years and initiated building projects as far afield as Cusae (Middle Egypt) and Semna (Nubia), there must have been other high officials who claimed that they were responsible for her monuments.

The clues to their identities come from inscribed *name stones** discovered in the foundations of some of the buildings as well as statues, graffiti at excavation sites, reliefs and inscriptions on temple walls, and autobiographical texts in the tombs of officials.

These sources have identified the following officials: Senenmut, Thutiy, Dewaeneheh, Hapusoneb, Puemre, Tetyemre, Ineni and Amenhotep. The table on the next page summarises some of their activities on behalf of Hatshepsut.

Restoration of damaged monuments

Repair to temples destroyed by Hyksos

One of Hatshepsut's main objectives was to restore the monuments damaged and neglected during the reign of the Hyksos kings. In the text on the facade of Speos Artemidos, she claimed to have 'restored that which was in ruins' and to have 'raised up that which was unfinished since the Asiatics were in the midst of Avaris'.[37]

The details of some specific temple rebuilding were given as well. For example, the temple of a local Hathor goddess at Cusae in Middle Egypt had fallen into such ruin that 'the ground had swallowed up its august sanctuary' and 'children played upon its house'. There were no longer any services or processions held there. Hatshepsut recorded, 'I adorned it, having been built anew, I overlaid its image with gold'.[38] At the cult centre of another god, whose name has been lost, Hatshepsut not only rebuilt the temple in limestone but adorned it with alabaster, copper and electrum.

Cult worship re-established

She re-established regular worship at these cult centres, claiming 'the altars are opened ... every one (god) is in possession of the dwelling which he has loved, his *ka* rests upon his throne'.[39] She honoured some of the gods by doubling the offerings and restoring long-forgotten festivals.

A building inscription from western Thebes describes how Hatshepsut also made repairs to the fortress of the necropolis 'according to the ancient plan'.[40]

Construction of new monuments

Djeser-djeseru — Hatshepsut's mortuary temple at Deir el-Bahri

Djeser-djeseru means *holy-of-holies* and it is a shortened version of the name Hatshepsut gave to her mortuary temple — *Mansion of Maat-ka-re-Amun is the Holy of Holies.*

---

* Name stones were sent by the citizens of Thebes as foundation dedications to the officials who were in charge of construction.

Name	Sources	Titles	Building activities
Senenmut	Name stones Statues Graffito Temple walls	Chief steward, who conducted all the works of the king Foreman of the foremen Overseer of all the works of the house of silver Chief of the chiefs of works	Mortuary temple at Deir el-Bahri Buildings in the Temples at Karnak, Luxor, Armant and Ishru Obelisks
Hapusoneb	Name stones Statue	Vizier First prophet of Amun Overseer of the temples	Mortuary temple at Deir el-Bahri Hatshepsut's tomb An unnamed temple, shrines, offering tables
Ineni	Tomb inscription	Overseer of the double gold and silver houses Foreman of the foremen	Not specified
Thutiy	Name stones Temple walls Tomb inscription	Overseer of the double gold and silver houses One who gives instruction to the craftsmen how to work	Mortuary temple at Deir el-Bahri (a 'palace of the god') — an ebony shrine, and temple fittings of precious metals and woods Works in Karnak — obelisks, great doorways and gates of copper and bronze, a shrine of granite and offering tables, and chests of electrum and precious stones
Puemre	Name stones Statue	Second prophet of Amun Foreman of the foremen	Mortuary temple at Deir el-Bahri A great shrine of ebony and a doorway of white limestone Worked mainly under Thutmose III
Amenhotep	Graffito	Chief priest of Khnum	Obelisks
Dewaenheh	Name stones	First herald	Mortuary temple at Deir el-Bahri
Tetyemre	Name stones	Scribe	Mortuary temple at Deir el-Bahri

Officials involved in Hatshepsut's building program

Like her immediate predecessors, Hatshepsut separated her tomb from her mortuary temple. The tomb was excavated in the wild and desolate Valley of the Kings while her temple was built at the base of the Theban cliffs facing the Nile River. Her original plan was to link them by a long underground passage through the mountain so that her burial chamber could be located beneath the mortuary temple.

The site

The magnificence of the site selected by Hatshepsut for her temple is captured in the words of the great archaeologist Edouard Naville, who, in 1894, wrote:

> The tourists who annually swarm into Thebes seldom depart from the ancient city of Amun without visiting the magnificent natural amphitheatre of Deir el-Bahri, where the hills of the Libyan range present their most imposing aspect. Leaving the plain by a narrow gorge, whose walls of naked rock are honeycombed with tombs, the traveller emerges into a wide open space bounded at its furthest end by a semi-circular wall of cliffs. These cliffs of white limestone, which time and sun have coloured rosy yellow, form an absolutely vertical barrier. ... Built against these cliffs, and even as it were rooted into their sides by subterranean chambers, is the temple ...[41]

Inspiration for design

Although the early Egyptologist, Mariette, believed that Hatshepsut's temple was 'an accident in the architectural life of Egypt',[42] the design appears to have been inspired by the adjacent temple of the Eleventh Dynasty king, Mentuhotep I.

Purpose

The temple was built not only for the purpose of carrying out daily offerings to Hatshepsut after her death, but as:

- a dedication to Amun, holiest of the holy
- the focus for the worship of a number of other deities associated with the necropolis and the afterlife — Hathor, Anubis and Re-Horakhte
- a mortuary chapel for her father, Thutmose I.

Its walls also provided Hatshepsut with an opportunity to justify her claims to the throne and advertise her major achievements.

The site of Hatshepsut's temple at Deir el-Bahri

Evidence of the foundation of the temple

Discovered around the boundaries of Hatshepsut's temple area were 14 rock-cut or brick-lined pits containing foundation deposits. These pits, excavated at the time of the laying out of the temple plan, were about a metre in diameter and 1.5 metres deep. They contained a variety of objects which can be categorised as:

- food offerings
- protective amulets and inscribed unguent jars
- models of tools
- examples of furnishings and materials used in the temple construction.

The diagram below itemises these.

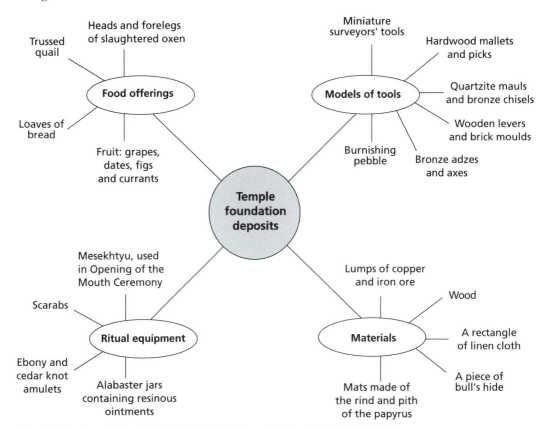

Foundation deposits buried at the site of Hatshepsut's temple at Deir el-Bahri

These deposits have helped historians gain an understanding of the rites carried out at the foundation of this and other temples as well as the variety of craftsmen involved in the temple's construction.

On some of the alabaster unguent jars was the inscription:

> She made as her monument to her father, Amun, on the occasion of stretching of the cord over Amun-Djeser-djeseru, may she live like Re forever! [43]

Stretching of the cord refers to the foundation rites during which the pharaoh ceremonially:

- outlined the projected building by driving stakes at its principal angles and stretching a cord around them
- traced the line of the foundation trenches with a pick
- laid the foundation deposits.

The main architectural features of the temple

The main architectural features of the temple were a long processional avenue, a deep walled forecourt, two broad terraces with colonnades, a ramp and stairway linking the various levels of the temple, a series of chapels and an inner sanctuary cut into the cliffs.

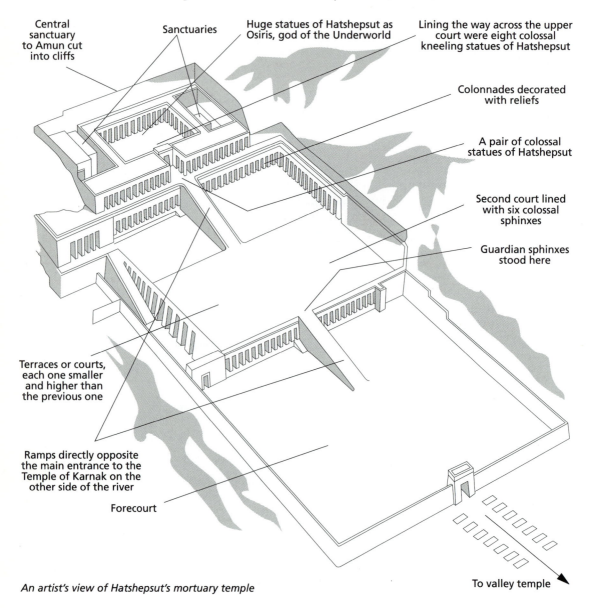

Central sanctuary to Amun cut into cliffs

Sanctuaries

Huge statues of Hatshepsut as Osiris, god of the Underworld

Lining the way across the upper court were eight colossal kneeling statues of Hatshepsut

Colonnades decorated with reliefs

A pair of colossal statues of Hatshepsut

Second court lined with six colossal sphinxes

Guardian sphinxes stood here

Terraces or courts, each one smaller and higher than the previous one

Ramps directly opposite the main entrance to the Temple of Karnak on the other side of the river

Forecourt

To valley temple

An artist's view of Hatshepsut's mortuary temple

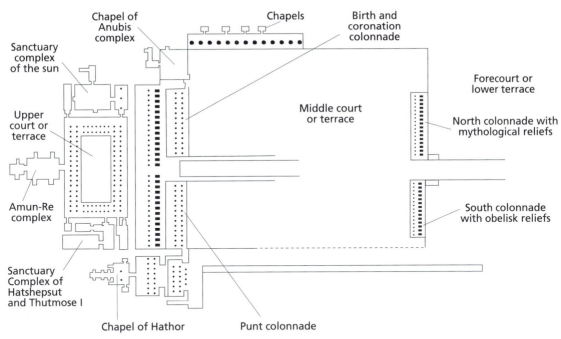

A plan of Hatshepsut's mortuary temple

Hatshepsut's temple at Deir el-Bahri

From a small valley temple on the edge of the cultivated land, a long, walled processional avenue lined with painted sandstone sphinxes, led to the forecourt. It was along this avenue that the portable barque of Amun was carried on the god's annual visit to the temple during the *Festival of the Beautiful Valley*. Refer to Chapter 15 for an account of this festival.

In Hatshepsut's day the forecourt would have been filled with shade trees and pools. The ramp, which connected the forecourt with the second and third courts or terraces, was placed in such a way that it was directly opposite the main entrance to the Temple of Karnak across the river.

At the top of the first section of the ramp, on either side, were small, painted, human-faced limestone lions. These were the guardians of the gateway to the *Underworld*. These lions had the generalised features of Hatshepsut and wore the pharaonic beard and royal ureaus.

Massive sphinxes

The second court or terrace was lined on each side with three colossal red granite sphinxes about 3.5 metres in length and weighing over seven tonnes. Around the walls of this court, reliefs and inscriptions depicting the Punt trading expedition and Hatshepsut's divine birth and coronation were found.

Colossal statues of Osiris

The second ramp led to the uppermost court and colonnade. On all the pillars and in the niches of the colonnade were huge painted limestone statues of Osiris (god of the Underworld) which ranged from twice life size to eight metres in height. Also on this uppermost terrace were 27 free-standing red granite statues of Hatshepsut as a male figure, clad in the costume and equipped with the regalia traditionally associated with kingship.

Leading across the top court towards the sanctuary were huge statues of Hatshepsut as Osiris and eight colossal kneeling statues of her as a king making offerings.

Central sanctuary to Amun

The most sacred part of the temple, the central sanctuary, was cut into the rock of the towering cliffs and was dedicated to Amun. There were other shrines to the gods of the necropolis, Anubis and Hathor and to the sun god Re-Horakhte.

Hatshepsut seems to have had a close association with the goddess Hathor, who was often depicted as a cow or as a woman wearing a horned headdress. Queens of the New Kingdom were frequently shown represented as Hathor (see Chapter 15), but Hatshepsut went even further. She featured Hathor, as the goddess of fertility and motherhood, in her birth scenes (as divine wet nurse) and as the mistress of Punt in her Punt reliefs. A special chapel to the goddess, as the parton deity of the Theban necropolis, was constructed on the upper terrace. It featured many Hathor-headed statues and a cow suckling Hatshepsut.

The rites associated with the mortuary cult of Hatshepsut and her father, Thutmose I, were carried out in two rectangular vaulted chapels. The walls of the lower and middle colonnades of these chapels were used to depict those events in Hatshepsut's life which illustrated her relationship and great devotion to Amun — the birth and coronation scenes, the Punt expedition and the transportation and erection of obelisks at Karnak.

Hathor-head columns at Deir el-Bahri

The inscription in the tomb of Hatshepsut's treasurer, Thutiy, provides evidence for some of the luxurious fittings found in the temple. Refer to the table earlier in this chapter, listing officials involved in Hatshepsut's building program.

Buildings at Karnak
(*the most select of places*)

Throughout her reign, Hatshepsut embellished Amun's temple at Karnak by:

- repairing the Middle Kingdom temple
- adding a great pylon or monumental gate (the eighth pylon)
- constructing a red granite sanctuary for the barque of Amun — the Red Chapel. This building, which incorporated beautiful and significant reliefs, was dismantled sometime after her death. So far, over 300 blocks from the temple have been located
- erecting four obelisks.

Obelisks

Hatshepsut erected four giant red granite obelisks to Amun. The first two were commissioned just before her assumption of full kingly powers while the other pair were dedicated at the time of her heb-sed in year 15.

Obelisks were tall stone shafts tapered towards the top and surmounted by a pyramidion (pyramid-shaped tip) which was usually gilded. During the New Kingdom, they were erected in pairs, usually in front of the temple pylons or gateways.

Hatshepsut's surviving obelisk at Karnak

These stone symbols were based on a later form of the ben-ben stone, on which the creator god, Re/Atum was believed to have first manifest himself. Because the rays of the rising sun were supposed to have fallen on this stone first, it was regarded as the home of the sun god Re. Speaking about her obelisks, Hatshepsut said, 'Their rays flood the Two Lands when the sun rises between them, as he dawns in the horizon of heaven'.[44]

Of the four obelisks erected by Hatshepsut, one pair has entirely disappeared although the pyramidion of one of them is in the Cairo Museum. Of the surviving two, one is still standing at a height of almost 30 metres while its companion lies on its side nearby.

The pyramidion of the fallen obelisk at Karnak

The evidence suggests that Senenmut was responsible for the quarrying and transporting of the first pair, while work on the jubilee obelisks was under the control of an official named Amenhotep.

It is generally assumed that the obelisks described in the scenes at Deir el-Bahri, were the ones cut and transported under the supervision of Senenmut. However, Breasted says that it is impossible to know which of the pairs of obelisks is represented.

On the shaft of the remaining obelisk, Hatshepsut recorded how she had sat in her palace thinking of a way to honour her *father* Amun. She decided 'to make for him two obelisks of electrum whose points mingled with heaven'.[45]

Skill and manpower involved in quarrying

The height and weight of the surviving obelisks reveal the manpower and skill that must have been required to cut 'one block of enduring granite without seam or joining' from the bedrock, drag it to the river, load it on to a specially built ship and ferry it down river to Thebes. It has been estimated that some of these New Kingdom obelisks weighed over 450 tonnes. Since obelisks were always erected in pairs, this task was even more remarkable.

In the case of the second pair, this activity took seven months.

> My majesty exacted work thereon from the year 15, the first of Mechir (sixth month), until the year 16, the last of Mesore (twelfth month) making seven months of extraction in the mountain.[46]

Transporting the obelisks

Before the great blocks could be transported downstream to Thebes, a large vessel, made of 'sycamores from the whole land', had to be built and young men and troops mustered 'in order to load the two obelisks in Elephantine'.[47] The reliefs carved on the lower colonnade of Hatshepsut's temple describe this difficult task. They show the boat carrying the obelisks being towed by three rows of nine barges with each row headed by a pilot boat. Three other escort boats carried temple personnel who performed religious rituals.

Another scene depicts the young recruits waiting at Thebes to unload the obelisks while soldiers, priests and court dignitaries celebrate their arrival.

A partially cut obelisk still lying in the quarry at Aswan

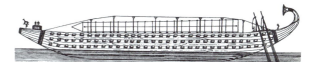

Above: An artist's impression of the barge used to transport Hatshepsut's obelisks

Left: The military escort accompanying the obelisks to Thebes, from the reliefs of Deir el-Bahri

This was not the end of the task. The pyramidions had to be covered with the best electrum (an alloy of gold and silver) that could be found so that when the sun shone on them they could be 'seen on both sides of the river'. Hatshepsut recorded that she 'gave for them the finest electrum which was measured by the heket like sacks of grain'.[48]

Once the obelisks were gilded, inscribed and erected (massive tasks in themselves), Hatshepsut dedicated them to Amun. The dedication is depicted on several of the surviving blocks from her Red Chapel.

Propaganda on the obelisks

The obelisk inscriptions focus on three themes.

1 Hatshepsut's right to the throne:

Amun, the lord of Thebes; he caused that I should reign over the Black and the Red Land ...[49]

2 The glorification Amun:

She made them as her monument for her father, Amun, Lord of Thebes, presider over Karnak ...[50]

I have done this with a loving heart for my father, Amun ... I acted under his command. It was he who led me. I did not plan a work without his doing. It was he who gave directions. I did not sleep because of his temple. I did not stray from what he commanded.[51]

3 Her relationship with her father, Thutmose I:

Her majesty made the name of her father (Thutmose I) established upon this monument ... When the two great obelisks were erected by her majesty on the first occurrence the lord of the gods said 'Thy father, King of Upper and Lower Egypt, gave command to erect obelisks, and thy majesty will repeat the monuments'.[52]

Hatshepsut's tomb

A tomb was prepared for Hatshepsut as the queen consort of Thutmose II in a wadi a few kilometres from Deir el-Bahri. However, when she became king, she ordered her vizier, Hapusoneb, to prepare a much larger and more elaborate one in the Valley of the Kings. He recorded on a statue of himself that he was appointed for this task because of the excellence of his plans.

It is believed that the original intention was to cut a series of sloping passages and stairways through the Theban cliffs in a direct line towards her mortuary temple so that her sarcophagus could lie beneath the sanctuary of Amun, *holiest of holies*. However, when the workmen began excavating they found there were faults in the rock which forced them to change their original plan.

The tomb passages and stairways curve down to her burial chamber, 97 metres below ground level and 213 metres into the mountain.

When the tomb was located and excavated, two magnificent yellow quartzite sarcophagi were found in the burial chamber — one for Hatshepsut and another for her father, whom she apparently reburied in her own tomb. However, neither mummy was found in the tomb. It appears that Thutmose III removed his grandfather's mummy after Hatshepsut's death and reburied it in a more magnificent tomb. Although Hatshepsut's mummy has not yet been discovered, the coffin and perhaps the mummy of Thutmose I were among a cache of royal mummies found in Deir el-Bahri in 1871.

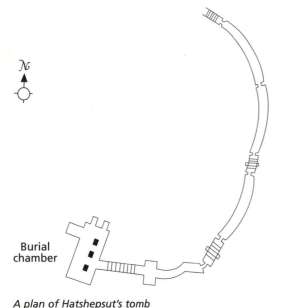

Burial chamber

A plan of Hatshepsut's tomb

Hatshepsut's building program not only expressed her devotion to the gods but gave work to numerous tradesmen and skilled craftsmen and reflected the general prosperity of her reign. Her massive stone buildings 'served as a constant reminder that there was a powerful pharaoh on the throne'.[53]

However, to provide the raw materials for the construction and maintenance of the *mansions of the gods* and to afford the rations needed to pay the workforce, she had to promote trade with foreign lands.

Trade

On the facade of Speos Artemidos, Hatshepsut alludes to her trading activities:

> Roshawet (Sinai) and Iuu (unknown) have not remained hidden from my august person and Punt overflows for me on the fields, its trees bearing fresh myrrh. The roads that were blocked on both sides are now trodden.[(54)]

Although the expedition to Punt was regarded by Hatshepsut as one of her greatest achievements, the evidence reveals that she promoted trade in other areas as well. The autobiographical inscription in the tomb of Thutiy alone points to the raw materials brought to Egypt from the south and north-east — gold, silver, copper, precious stones, ebony and cedar. These products were obtained from Nubia, tropical Africa, Sinai, the Levant (Lebanon) and areas further east. Inscriptions found in Wadi Maghera and at Serabit el-Khadim in the Sinai show that the copper and turquoise mines were extensively exploited during her reign.

Expansion of trade

The trading expedition to Punt

In year 9 of her reign, Hatshepsut ordered preparations to be made for an expedition to the land of Punt, far to the south of Egypt.

Although expeditions had been dispatched to Punt as early as the Fifth and Sixth dynasties, the Egyptians of the Old Kingdom regarded it as a semi-mythical realm. The Middle Kingdom rulers, Mentuhotep III (Eleventh Dynasty) and Amenemhet II and Senwosret II (Twelfth Dynasty) also commissioned expeditions to these distant incense lands. However, because they left no details, Punt remained a place of mystery until the reign of Hatshepsut when the veil was lifted on *God's Land*. Perhaps this is why she claimed that:

A land of mystery

> No one trod the Myrrh-terraces (Punt) which the people knew not: it was heard of from mouth to mouth by hearsay of the ancestors.[(55)]

On the other hand, it was usual for kings to claim that what they had done had never been achieved before.

Hatshepsut considered this expedition so significant that she had it recorded in detail near the birth and coronation reliefs on the walls of her mortuary temple. Although many of the pictures and much of the text are badly damaged, they give some idea of this peaceful trading expedition.

Where was Punt? Many scholars believe it was somewhere in the vicinity of present-day Somalia. Until quite recently, incense trees still grew there and the types of fish and animals featured in Hatshepsut's inscription suggest a location close to the Red Sea, Indian Ocean and the inland tropical areas of east Africa.

Location of Punt

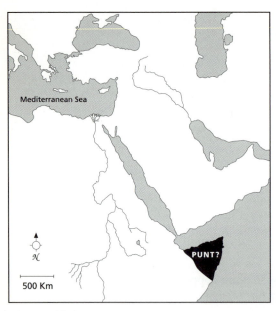

The possible location of Punt

Hatshepsut claimed that in sending this expedition, she was responding to a command 'from the great throne, an oracle of the god himself' which instructed her to seek out the way to Punt so 'that the highways to the myrrh-terraces should be penetrated'. [56] Amun supposedly instructed her to 'establish for him a Punt in his house'.[57]

It is likely that it was Senenmut or Hapusoneb who suggested that an expedition should be sent to bring back myrrh and frankincense trees to plant in the temple of Amun and on the terraces of Hatshepsut's mortuary temple. Incense (*kyphi*) was burned in great quantities in cult temples, particularly during the bathing and purification of the god, and in mortuary temples as an offering to the dead.

Purpose of the expedition

In sending this expedition, Hatshepsut hoped to further honour Amun and maintain the support of his priesthood as well as open up peaceful trade in the area. The Egyptians needed a continuing supply of exotic products, referred to in the Punt inscriptions as 'the marvels of every country'. Those in greatest demand were:

• the precious incense resins and fragrant woods of which there were many varieties. Apart from their use in religious rituals, these were used in mummification, as medicinal aids, for fumigation of houses and for the manufacture of perfumed oils

• ebony; this most prized of timbers was used principally for ritual items such as shrines and tomb furniture, although its bark was considered good for the eyes

• live animals and animal skins. The baboon was a sacred animal of Thoth; apes, monkeys and other exotic animals were kept as pets by the nobility; and African dogs were used for hunting. Panther skins were worn as ceremonial robes by priests and animal skins were used by royalty and nobility as coverings on chairs and stools

• ivory, used in amulets, as inlays for furniture (eg, thrones and chests) and as headrests and gaming pieces

• precious metals such as gold (used in making electrum, ritual and funerary items and jewellery) and antimony, a white metallic element used in alloys and medicine.

The following description of the expedition is based on the reliefs in Hatshepsut's mortuary temple.

The departure of the expedition

Chancellor Nehsi leader

The expedition was organised and led by the *king's messenger*, Nehsi (Nehsy), and accompanied by a small military contingent. It was common practice for a force of soldiers to escort royal expeditions.

It is not known how the members of the expedition reached the Red Sea port from which they sailed south. They probably crossed the eastern desert via Wadi Hammamat and then constructed their ships on the coast of the Red Sea like the officials of the Middle Kingdom. For example, the record of Hennu, chief treasurer of King Mentuhotep III of the Eleventh Dynasty, says 'I reached the sea, and I built this ship and I equipped it entirely ...'.[58]

It is believed that in Hatshepsut's expedition there were five ships, each about 20 metres long with 30 rowers and huge sails. They were laden with jars containing wine and beer, bales of cloth and a variety of gifts to exchange for the products of Punt.

A fleet of five ships

Before their departure from the Red Sea port the members of the expedition sacrificed to the goddess Hathor, the *lady of Punt* so that she might send the wind. There is no record of the journey south.

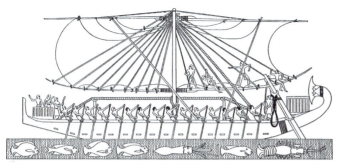

One of the five Egyptian ships in the expedition fleet

The reception in Punt

The next scene shows Nehsi and his escort of soldiers carrying olive branches, ostrich fans, ceremonial axes and standards to show their peaceful intentions to the approaching Puntites.

The native king, Paruhu, with his incredibly overweight or deformed wife, Eti, and three children advanced at the head of their people. It seems that the native people shown in the reliefs were of two types. Some were shown as black- or brown-skinned Africans while others were physically similar to the Egyptians. For example, the chief was painted red and had Egyptian features — goatee beard and aquiline nose.

First contact

The Puntites, probably distrusting the sight of armed men, moved forward somewhat fearfully with their hands uplifted in supplication and with bowed heads. They asked the Egyptians how they had come 'to the land no one knows of' and wanted to know if they had come 'upon the ways of heaven' or 'upon the sea of God's-Land'.[59]

According to the reliefs, the Puntites lived in villages of small conical huts built on piles as protection from wild animals and enemy attacks. Ladders were used to reach the holes which served as doors. The huts were close to the shore, possibly in an estuary of a river, and hidden among trees and exotic plants. Long- and short-horn cattle as well as donkeys are shown grazing beneath the huts.

Puntite villages

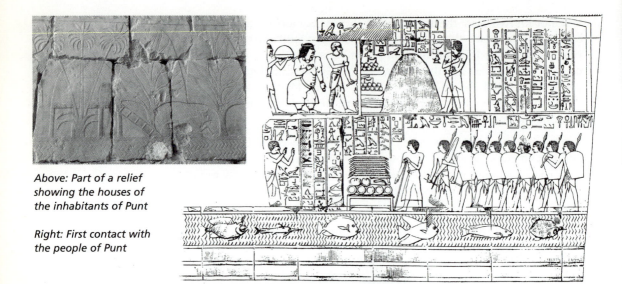

Above: Part of a relief showing the houses of the inhabitants of Punt

Right: First contact with the people of Punt

Close to the beach, the Egyptians set up tables covered with gifts such as daggers, axes, leg bangles, necklaces and large rings. Naville suggests that the jewellery was probably made from glass, glazed metal, bronze or some metal unknown to the Puntites.

Exchange of goods

The reliefs show the people of Punt leading monkeys and panthers and piling up loose myrrh resin in front of Nehsi and the soldiers. According to Naville, fragments of the wall reliefs show 'the cutting of ebony in great quantities'.[60]

Trade appears brisk and satisfactory to both sides although it is obviously one-sided. The items offered by the Egyptians seem to be of markedly lower value than the goods presented by the Puntites. Perhaps the reliefs show only a sample of the Egyptian goods or perhaps the contingent of Egyptian soldiers 'encouraged' the Puntites to trade.

Propaganda — tribute not trade items

However, in the inscription, the goods offered by the Puntites are not described as items of trade but rather as tribute of the princes of Punt to Hatshepsut and the Egyptian items are referred to as offerings for the goddess Hathor, *lady of Punt*. This propaganda may have been intended to equate the expedition with a successful military campaign which usually resulted in the defeated leaders paying tribute to the victors.

Later, in the royal tent, the leaders of Punt are presented with all the good things of Egypt such as beer, bread, wine, fruit and meat.

How long the Egyptians remained in Punt is not known. It is possible that they travelled inland to the land of Irem at some point.

Loading the ships

The next relief depicts the loading of the ships. Fully-grown incense trees in earth-filled baskets, slung on poles and supported by four men, are carried aboard a fully laden ship. They call to each other 'Look to your feet, ye people! behold the load is very heavy!'[61]

The ships are described as being filled with the 'marvels of Punt'. By comparing the translations of Naville and Breasted it is possible to build up a clearer picture of these trade items.

Naville [62]	Breasted [63]
All the good woods of the Divine land	All goodly fragrant woods
Heaps of gum of anti and trees of green anti	Heaps of myrrh resin and fresh myrrh trees
Ebony and pure ivory	Ebony and pure ivory
Pure gold from the land of Amu	The green gold of Emu
Cinnamon wood, khesyt wood, with balsam, resin, antimony	Cinnamon wood, khesyt wood, with Ihmut-incense, sonter incense, eye cosmetic
Cynocephali* monkeys, greyhounds, with the skins of panthers of the south	Apes, monkeys, dogs, and with the skins of the southern panther
Inhabitants of the country and their children	Natives and their children

As would be expected, the inscription concludes with the following comment:

> Never was brought the like of this for any king who has been since the beginning.[64]

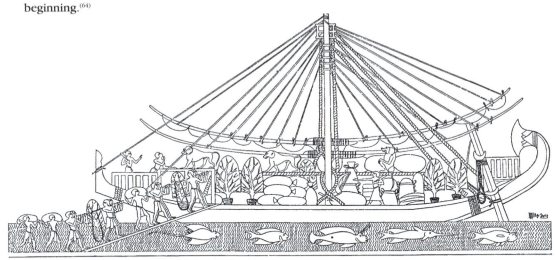

Above: Loading the ships with the products of Punt

Left: Men loading incense trees

---

* Cynocephali were dog-faced baboons.

The return to Thebes

The final scene relating to the actual expedition shows three vessels under full sail on the Nile.

It is highly likely that the cargo was unloaded at a port on the Red Sea and transported through the eastern desert 'upon asses and upon men'[65] as far as Coptos on the Nile for the last leg of the journey by river to Thebes. Their arrival is marked with great celebrations.

Presentation of goods to Hatshepsut

The expedition personnel and a procession of native chieftains from Punt, Irem and an unknown country, called Nemyew, present themselves to Hatshepsut. They are followed by others carrying the products of Punt which include the 31 myrrh trees, a live panther and thousands of small cattle.

In the following scene 'heaps of myrrh in great quantities'[66] are weighed and recorded. This task is supervised by treasurer, Thutiy, on behalf of the queen, while the god Thoth is depicted recording the quantities of the treasures from Punt on behalf of Amun-Re.

Dedication to Amun

The queen, followed by her *ka*, is then shown offering the products to Amun with the words that she has done everything that the god commanded. The inscriptions continue with a speech by Amun praising Hatshepsut and promising success for future expeditions.

Finally, Hatshepsut, from her throne in the audience hall, made a formal announcement of the unprecedented success of the expedition to the assembled court. In front of her stood three men, two of whom have been identified as Chancellor Nehsi, leader of the expedition and Senenmut, Steward of Amun, who was responsible for the financial management of the temple of Amun. Hatshepsut announced that she had followed Amun's instructions and made a Punt for the god in Egypt by planting the trees 'beside his temple and in his garden'.[67]

Above: Products from Punt presented to Hatshepsut

Right: Fully grown incense trees and Egyptians measuring the piles of incense resin brought from Punt

Military campaigns

Scholars once believed there were no military activities during Hatshepsut's reign. Even the eminent historian Sir Alan Gardiner maintained that 'the reign of Hatshepsut had been barren of any military enterprise except an unimportant raid into Nubia'.[68] Wilson believes that Hatshepsut recorded no military conquests because 'her pride was in the internal development of Egypt and in commercial enterprise' rather than imperial expansion like her predecessors.[69]

Erroneous early views

These views are probably based on:

- the lack of monumental reliefs of a military character
- the belief that, as a woman, Hatshepsut would be less aggressive than a man and physically incapable of leading an army.

It must be remembered that many of Hatshepsut's monuments were damaged after her death. Perhaps some of these contained evidence of military campaigns. Despite the lack of official records, there is no reason to suppose that there was any deliberate intention on the part of Hatshepsut to adopt a non-aggressive policy and there 'is nothing in Hatshepsut's character to suggest that she would be frightened of taking the military initiative as and when necessary'.[70] In fact, a number of fragmentary inscriptions do provide evidence of at least four military operations during her reign. When these references are looked at together rather than separately 'the evidence for foreign campaigns is more plentiful than is sometimes thought'.[71]

No evidence of deliberate pacifism

Military activity in Nubia (Kush)

The chief source of evidence for a campaign in Nubia is a graffito written by Tiy, one of Hatshepsut's chief officials and found on the island of Sehel, near Aswan.

Inscription of Tiy

> The hereditary prince and governor, treasurer of the king of Lower Egypt, the sole friend, chief treasurer, the one concerned with the booty, Tiy. He says: 'I followed the good god, the king of Upper and Lower Egypt [Maat-ka-re] may she live! I saw when he overthrew the Nubian bowman, their chiefs being brought to him as living captives. I saw when he destroyed Nubia, I being in his majesty's following ...[72]

The graffito suggests that Hatshepsut led this campaign herself and Tiy says that he was an eyewitness to what happened there.

A second damaged text which throws more light on Hatshepsut's Nubian campaign was found on a stela erected by the scribe Djehuty at Dra abu el-Naga (near Deir el-Bahri). He recorded:

Stela of Djehuty

> I saw the collection of booty by this mighty ruler [Hatshepsut], from the vile Kush who are deemed cowards. The female sovereign, given life, prosperity and health forever.[73]

Whether this is a record of the same campaign reported by Tiy is not known. They may have been entirely separate.

Deir el-Bahri inscription

Another fragmentary text, similar to those inscribed by most pharaohs, was found on the wall of the lower colonnade of Hatshepsut's temple at Deir el-Bahri. It starts with a reference to a previous campaign in Kush led by Hatshepsut's father. It seems that Hatshepsut's campaign may have been connected in some way. If this conventional text was the only description of a military campaign during Hatshepsut's reign then it would be of no great significance. However, in light of Tiy's graffito, it takes on more importance.

> I will cause to sail south ... the chief of Kush whom they brought as a living captive; ... in his moment who seizes without anything being seized from him. She says: 'As Amun lives for me and loves me ... the land in might and valour ... these fortress-towns of his majesty ... the garrisons of the sovereign raged ... as was done by her victorious father, the king of Upper and Lower Egypt, Okheperkare, who seized all lands ... a slaughter was made among them. The number of dead being unknown: their hands were cut off ... she overthrew ... the gods ... likewise: all foreign lands spoke their heart's rage but they turned back on account of the greatness ... the enemy were plotting in their valleys, saying ... overland horses upon the mountains ... the number of them was not known ... Amun, Lord of Karnak who leads me ...[74]

Close to this inscription, Hatshepsut is depicted as a sphinx, the embodiment of royal power, trampling on Egypt's enemies.

Karnak block

Finally, on a broken block at Karnak is a reference to 'the land of Nubia being in submission' to Hatshepsut.

From this evidence, particularly that provided by Tiy and Djehuty, it appears that there was a war in Nubia early in Hatshepsut's reign. She may have led the campaign herself or if not, she was at least at the scene of the hostilities.

Military activity to the north of Egypt

Fragmentary evidence at Deir el-Bahri

Although most of the evidence points to war in Nubia, there are several references at Deir el-Bahri to a campaign in Palestine (Retjenu). This was probably carried out early in Hatshepsut's reign also and may have been a mopping-up operation to consolidate her father's conquests. Conquered chieftains often took the opportunity to rebel when a new Egyptian ruler came to the throne — perhaps this is what happened.

One of the texts, later modified by Thutmose III, says 'her arrow is among the northerners'. Another reference is found in Hatshepsut's coronation inscription. This is in the form of a prediction that she would 'seize the chiefs of Retenu, bearing the sword, the survivals of thy father'.[75] Redford believes that there may be some historical basis in this statement.

References to Thutmose's military activities during Hatshepsut's reign

Thutmose probably received military training from an early age. Hatshepsut may have hoped that when he reached adulthood he would take over the command of the army and lead foreign campaigns. The evidence suggests that this was the case.

Campaigns to the south and north towards the end of Hatshepsut's reign

- A rock inscription at Tombos in Upper Nubia, dated to year 20 of the co-regency, described Thutmose III as 'the good god who overthrows him who has attacked him'.[76]

- In an unidentified campaign, Thutmose is believed to have taken the town of Gaza on the Egyptian–Palestinian border.

- According to Redford, Thutmose conducted a campaign in Nubia just before Hatshepsut's death. A passage on a stela alludes to him having killed a rhinoceros (by archery) in Nubia after he had journeyed to Maw to 'seek him who had rebelled against him in that land'.[77]

There is enough evidence to show that Hatshepsut did not deliberately pursue a policy of non-aggression. In fact, from the Speos Artemidos inscription, it appears that she kept her army in a state of readiness.

> **My troops which were formerly unequipped are now well paid since I appeared as king.**[78]

The evidence suggests that during her reign there were at least four and possibly six military campaigns. Redford, in his *History and Chronology of the Eighteenth Dynasty*, suggests there was:

Summary of campaigns

- a campaign to Nubia, possibly conducted by the queen herself, early in her reign

- an early mopping-up operation in Palestine and Syria

- a campaign, led by Thutmose III, which included the capture of Gaza

- a campaign against Nubia led by Thutmose III shortly before Hatshepsut's death.

None of these campaigns seem to have been of major significance. For this reason, Hatshepsut may have regarded the success of the Punt expedition as an economic triumph equal to the military achievements of her predecessors.

Hatshepsut and the cult of Amun-Re

Although Amun had been worshipped by the rulers of Thebes since the Middle Kingdom, it was during the first half of the Eighteenth Dynasty that this local Theban god became the pre-eminent god of Egypt and its empire. Hatshepsut's immediate predecessors, including her father, had all attributed their successes to Amun.

Hatshepsut as God's Wife of Amun

Hatshepsut's association with Amun began when she was still a young princess. She held the influential position of *God's Wife of Amun* and when she became king she passed this title on to her daughter, Neferure.

During her reign as queen consort of Thutmose II, she appointed Senenmut, the *chief steward of Amun*, as her daughter's steward and tutor.

Support from high priest and steward of Amun

It is highly likely that Senenmut and Hapusoneb, the *high priest of Amun*, helped her to assume the titles and powers of a king. They certainly supported her during her reign.

Hapusoneb was given the additional titles of *chief of the prophets of south and north, overseer of Upper and Lower Egypt, overseer of temples* and *great chief in Upper Egypt.* These titles gave him jurisdiction over all phases of the Amun cult, control of the cults and temples of all the other gods and a position of authority in the civil administration. He was responsible for many of Hatshepsut's building projects, including the construction of her tomb.

While retaining his position as *chief steward of Amun*, Senenmut was also appointed *steward of the king.* As Hatshepsut's closest adviser and confidante, he became in his own words, 'the greatest of the great'. Other titles associated with Amun that Senenmut claimed were *overseer of the administrative offices of the mansion, conductor of festivals, priest of the barque Woser-het-Amun, overseer of the cattle of Amun* and *overseer of the gardens and fields of Amun.* He was responsible for most of the monuments Hatshepsut constructed to honour Amun.

Attributed her birth and coronation to Amun

Hatshepsut reinforced her own position and ensured the continuing success of her reign by attributing everything of importance in her life to her *father*, Amun. She recorded on the walls of her temple that she was conceived by Amun and selected by him to rule as king. According to the propaganda it was Amun who gave her directions and she did everything according to his command.

In her building program she paid particular attention to the god's temple at Karnak. She added a pylon, halls, chapels and four giant obelisks and gave great prominence to the god's sacred barque by building the Red Chapel to house it. The obelisks were erected as enduring monuments to her *father*.

Shared her mortuary temple with Amun

Her own mortuary temple became a cult temple to Amun and was referred to as the *Mansion of Maat-ka-re, Amun is the Holy of Holies.* She planned originally to link her tomb to her mortuary temple via a tunnel from the Valley of the Kings. Her intention was to lie for eternity in a burial chamber directly under Amun's sanctuary, cut deep into the Theban cliffs. Her temple at Deir el-Bahri became the destination for the procession associated with Amun's Festival of the Valley.

Products from Punt dedicated to Amun

Amun also benefited from her trading expedition to Punt. Sacred incense resin and incense trees, to be planted in the temple grounds, were brought back from the *God's Land*. Incense was used extensively in temple worship. Also the lion's share of the other exotic products were dedicated to Amun.

The propaganda in the Punt inscriptions focused on Amun.

- The god commanded the expedition and made her *mistress of Punt*.
- The Puntites praised Amun.
- Amun received the tribute from Punt.
- Amun 'set all the lands beneath her sandals'.[79]
- Amun promised her success for future expeditions.

Hatshepsut also attributed to Amun one of her military successes in Nubia which was recorded on the wall of her temple at Deir el-Bahri.

By glorifying Amun at every opportunity, Hatshepsut contributed to the priesthood's great prestige and influence, which reached a peak under Thutmose III.

A relief of Amun and Hatshepsut from the Red Chapel

Hatshepsut's relationship with Thutmose III

There has been a great deal of conjecture about the relationship between Hatshepsut and her stepson/nephew, Thutmose III.

Although she officially ruled jointly with the young king, there is no doubt that Hatshepsut was the senior pharaoh until at least the twentieth year of their reign.

Her predominance can be understood while Thutmose was still a child and an adolescent, but how did she manage to keep him in her shadow when he was a young man in his twenties?

Because Thutmose had the qualities which later made him one of the greatest kings who ever ruled Egypt and was over 30 years of age when Hatshepsut died, scholars have puzzled over their relationship.

- Was Thutmose III frustrated and resentful towards Hatshepsut for usurping the double crown which should have been his alone?
- Did he accept the situation without too much opposition to her?
- What was he doing while his stepmother/aunt was administering the land?
- What support did he have at the time from among the members of the civil bureaucracy and the priesthood?
- Was he just prepared to bide his time until Hatshepsut died or until an opportunity presented itself for him to overthrow her?

The answers to some of these questions may never be known.

Questions about relationship

Evidence for the relationship

Showed respect but always depicted in front of Thutmose

Even though Hatshepsut was the senior partner, the surviving inscriptions indicate that she accorded Thutmose III the respect to which he was entitled.

They shared monuments and stelae although, throughout most of her reign, her image and name were always in front of his:

- Thutmose appears in the Punt reliefs on the walls of Hatshepsut's temple at Deir el-Bahri. He is shown standing behind the queen dedicating 'the best of fresh myrrh'[80] before the sacred barque of Amun.

- He also appears in the reliefs of the transportation of the obelisks at Deir el-Bahri. In the scene showing the rejoicing of the recruits and soldiers, Thutmose's name is mentioned.

  The acclamation by the recruits of the South and the North, the young men of Thebes ... for the sake of the life, prosperity and health of the King of Upper and Lower Egypt (Maat-ka-re), and for the sake of the life, prosperity and health of the King of Upper and Lower Egypt, Menkheperre (Thutmose III), who giveth life; that their heart may be glad, like Re, forever.[81]

- In a relief on a building inscription in western Thebes, Hatshepsut and Thutmose III are shown worshipping Amun-Re together. Once again, he is standing behind her and there is no mention of him in the inscription.

Both kings are mentioned on a statue of the nobleman, Enebni, and in the tomb of Thutiy. The so-called Mut statue on which Senenmut's titles, responsibilities and honours were inscribed, was presented to him jointly by Hatshepsut and Thutmose III.

Thutmose more prominent in later years

Later in Hatshepsut's reign, Thutmose appears to have taken a more prominent role in public affairs. On a stela found in Wadi Maghera in the Sinai the two kings are shown standing side by side offering to the local gods — Thutmose III to Hathor and Hatshepsut to Sopdu. This was inscribed in year 16 when Thutmose was about 25 or 26.

As leader of an army he posed no threat

The evidence is quite clear about Thutmose's leadership of the army from year 20 and the campaigns into Nubia and possibly Gaza before Hatshepsut's death. Had Thutmose posed a threat to Hatshepsut's security, it is unlikely he would have been given leadership of the army.

Although Thutmose III's private thoughts about his co-ruler will never be known, it appears that he did not challenge Hatshepsut's authority.

Despite the evidence available, some writers still insist that Thutmose III must have been resentful towards Hatshepsut and was only waiting for an opportunity to overthrow her.

  It must have been much against his will that the energetic young Thutmose III watched from the side lines the high-handed rule of the *pharaoh* Hatshepsut and the chancellorship of the upstart Senenmut.[82]

Surely a collision was inevitable between the maturing strength and resentment of the young king and the waning powers of the queen.[83]

However, 'the idea of the antipathy between the two co-rulers needs a thorough re-examination'.[84]

The table below summarises two views of the relationship between Hatshepsut and Thutmose III. The truth probably lies somewhere between the two views; however, it may have been more complex than is often supposed.

View 1	View 2
Thutmose did not like the situation but was incapable of doing anything about it. By the time he was old enough to resent his loss of authority, Hatshepsut controlled the treasury, had full support of the civil service and the high priest of Amun-Re. In other words, the reins of power were well and truly in Hatshepsut's hands.	Thutmose did not feel he had grounds for complaint against Hatshepsut. He may even have welcomed Hatshepsut's guidance when he was young and preferred to show his gratitude by waiting for her death rather than demoting her when he came of age. He would have expected to outlive his step-mother/aunt and then enjoy a solo reign.

Above: A relief from Hatshepsut's temple at Deir el-Bahri showing Thutmose III dedicating to the gods

Left: Hatshepsut and Thutmose III from the Red Chapel

The fate of Hatshepsut and her monuments

Hatshepsut died in year 22 of the co-regency, having reigned for 21 years and nine months. Her age when she died is not known but a statue of her as an elderly woman does exist.

Although her mummy has never been found, there is no evidence to suggest that her death was anything but normal. Despite the lack of evidence, some writers, however, wish to make her end more dramatic.

Wilson and Steindorff and Seele believe that her life came to an abrupt and unnatural end probably during a coup by Thutmose III.

> But at length his hour also struck. ... Thus about 1482 (?) BC she came to what we may well believe was an unnatural end.[85]

Some writers, like Mertz, go even further. For example:

> We are not satisfied with a tame and bloodless ending for the haughty spirit of Hatshepsut. I am personally, if illogically, convinced that Thutmose did away with Hatshepsut. It is highly probable that he did away with her mummy; no trace of it has ever been found.[86]

Mertz also suggests that as Hatshepsut grew older, some of her supporters may have felt that it was time to show their loyalty to Thutmose III.

No evidence of an unnatural death

At the present time there is no evidence to suggest that she was either murdered or deposed by her co-ruler. Redford believes that 'Thutmose had no reason to hasten her death'.[87]

Those historians who subscribe to the theory that Hatshepsut was deposed and murdered also believe that, on assuming sole rule, Thutmose III began a ferocious campaign to completely efface the memory of Hatshepsut.

Damage to monuments

There is no doubt that some time after her death:

- Hatshepsut's names, titles and images were erased from the walls of the temples and replaced with those of her father, Thutmose I, her husband, Thutmose II and her stepson, Thutmose III. Her name was absent from all later lists of kings
- dozens of her statues were smashed and dumped in a pit at Deir el-Bahri, while fragments of many others were strewn over the area
- her giant obelisks in the Temple of Karnak were enclosed behind a wall in order to hide them from sight.

Claims by those who believe in the vengeance of Thutmose III

Many of the secondary sources maintain that the destruction of Hatshepsut's monuments:

- occurred soon after her death — 'It was not long before Thutmose III began to expunge her name wherever it was found'[88]
- was due to vengeance — 'now the king wreaked with full fury his vengeance'[89] and 'The evidence of the vindictive fury of Thutmose III is clear'[90]
- was wholesale — 'wherever the names or representations of Hatshepsut occurred, they were chiselled away'[91] and 'his wholesale destruction of anything Hatshepsut had ever touched'.[92]

These three ideas are not substantiated by the extensive work done at Karnak by C Nims. In his work, *The Date of the Dishonouring of Hatshepsut*, Nims points out that certain architectural features at Karnak make it clear that Thutmose could not have begun the erasures of

Hatshepsut's name until late in his reign. The evidence suggests that the destruction probably occurred after year 42 of his reign — over 20 years after Hatshepsut's death.

> The supposition that the destruction of the queen's monuments was due to the hatred of Hatshepsut by Thutmose must be questioned, for twenty years or more is too long to hold such a grudge before carrying out destructive measures because of it.[93]

Another interesting thing about the destruction of her monuments is its selective nature. Many of the inscriptions have been left partially or wholly intact. Sometimes her name was hammered out in hidden places and sometimes left intact in visible and accessible places. For example, the name and figure of Hatshepsut as queen of Thutmose II were not attacked and images of her *ka* were untouched. This has baffled scholars.

If vengeance did not motivate Thutmose against his stepmother/aunt, why were her monuments destroyed?

Robins believes that Thutmose's actions:

> could be explained by assuming that Hatshepsut had died naturally and that Thutmose felt no resentment against her. He might then have been reluctant to mutilate her monuments; but as time passed by, political expediency might have won over sentiment, and he might finally have agreed that all traces of the unnatural female king should be erased, since they did not conform with maat, the natural order of the world.[94]

Redford says:

> Thutmose was motivated not so much by a genuine hatred as by political necessity. His own legitimacy stood in need of demonstration, and his own links with his illustrious grandfather Thutmose I had to be emphasised. To leave the glories of Hatshepsut's reign open to view would, in any case, invite invidious comparison with his own accomplishments ... He had to assure himself at the outset that his aunt's claims and successes, mutually exclusive as he saw them to his own, would survive in the memory of no one.[95]

Hatshepsut's figure deleted from the walls of her temple at Deir el-Bahri

Redford believes that Thutmose allowed certain of Hatshepsut's images and cartouches to remain because 'she was his own flesh' and she 'had not put him to death, or even deprived him of the crown'. [96] It is more likely that Thutmose had no wish to totally obliterate Hatshepsut's name and images (*damnatio memoriae*), knowing that if he did her spirit would perish forever and she would be condemned to what the Egyptians called *the second death*.

**Some destruction
during the reigns
of Akhenaten and
Ramesses II**

In many of Hatshepsut's reliefs, the figure of Amun has been obliterated. This was obviously not done on the orders of Thutmose III since he continued to glorify Amun and surpassed Hatshepsut in his dedications to this god of empire.

Who would have done this? Towards the end of the Eighteenth Dynasty, a king called Akhenaten introduced the worship of a form of the sun god called Aten. Akhenaten elevated this god to the exclusion of all others and at some point ordered the mutilation of the images of Amun. Furthermore, it is believed that the great king, Ramesses II of the Nineteenth Dynasty also ordered alterations to the inscriptions on Hatshepsut's monuments.

The legacy of Hatshepsut

A legacy is:

• something left to or handed down to someone
• a consequence of some action or event.

In order to understand what Hatshepsut left to her people and what the consequences of her actions were, it is necessary to consider her achievements.

Redford believes that if Thutmose III had left 'the glories of Hatshepsut's reign open to view' it would have invited 'an invidious comparison with his own accomplishments'.[97] If this were one of the reasons for Thutmose's destruction of his aunt's monuments, then he must have believed that her achievements were considerable.

The following diagram summarises Hatshepsut's achievements and her legacy.

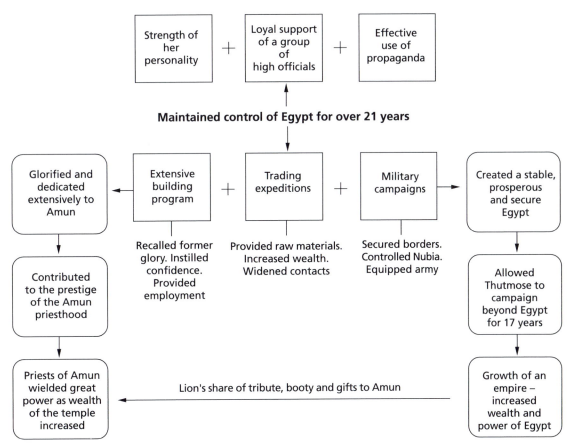

The legacy of Hatshepsut

Conclusion

Despite the absence of Hatshepsut's name from the ancient lists of Egyptian kings, modern Egyptologists have restored her to her rightful place in Egyptian history. Their work has revealed that this 'female Horus' was the one of the most powerful pharaohs of the New Kingdom.

Chapter review

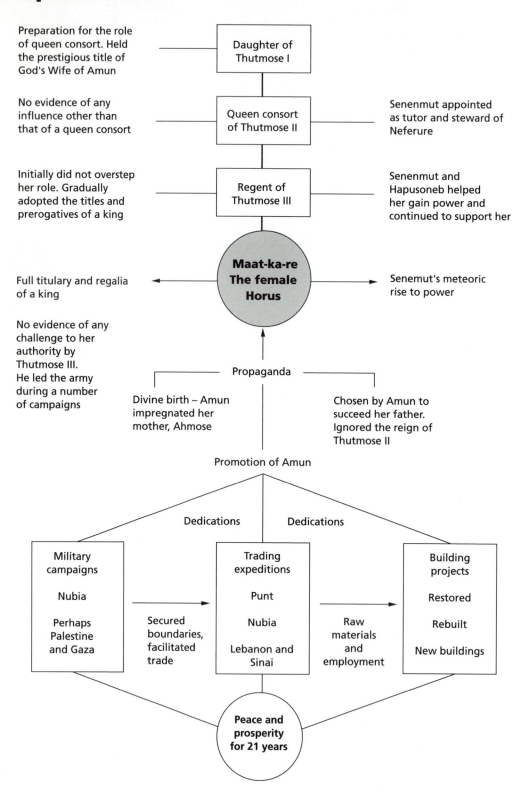

Preparation for the role of queen consort. Held the prestigious title of God's Wife of Amun

Daughter of Thutmose I

No evidence of any influence other than that of a queen consort

Queen consort of Thutmose II

Senenmut appointed as tutor and steward of Neferure

Initially did not overstep her role. Gradually adopted the titles and prerogatives of a king

Regent of Thutmose III

Senenmut and Hapusoneb helped her gain power and continued to support her

Maat-ka-re The female Horus

Full titulary and regalia of a king

Senemut's meteoric rise to power

No evidence of any challenge to her authority by Thutmose III. He led the army during a number of campaigns

Propaganda

Divine birth – Amun impregnated her mother, Ahmose

Chosen by Amun to succeed her father. Ignored the reign of Thutmose II

Promotion of Amun

Dedications   Dedications

Military campaigns

Nubia

Perhaps Palestine and Gaza

Secured boundaries, facilitated trade

Trading expeditions

Punt

Nubia

Lebanon and Sinai

Raw materials and employment

Building projects

Restored

Rebuilt

New buildings

Peace and prosperity for 21 years

REVISION QUESTIONS AND ESSAY TOPICS

1 The 2.5 metre statue of Hatshepsut shown on the right is one of a pair that stood at the gateway leading to the uppermost court of her temple at Deir el-Bahri.

a Apart from the male figure, what features identify Hatshepsut as a conventional king?

b What other kingly regalia did she sometimes wear?

c Why was she often depicted as a sphinx?

d What archaeological evidence is there that Hatshepsut gradually adopted the identity of a king?

e What evidence is there in her full titulary that she did not try to pass herself off as a male?

f Although a mixture of masculine and feminine words were used in the texts to describe Hatshepsut, under what circumstances would she be likely to be referred to in the masculine form?

g Why was it essential for her to be represented in reliefs and statuary as a conventional king?

2 Look carefully at the reliefs shown in Figures A below, and Figure B on the next page. They were found in Hatshepsut's mortuary temple. Answer the questions which relate to each figure.

(A)

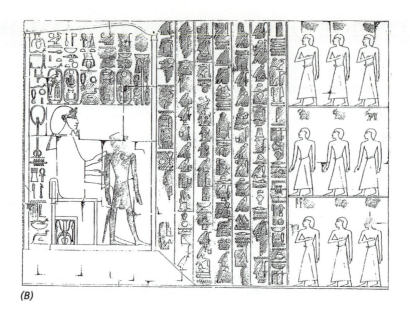

(B)

Figure A

a   Who is the goddess represented in this relief?

b   Why did she often take the form of a cow?

c   Where else and in what form is this goddess represented in Hatshepsut's temple?

d   Who do the infants represent?

e   Of what series of inscriptions does this relief form a part?

f   Describe two previous reliefs in this series.

g   What was the purpose of these inscriptions?

h   Why were they inscribed in Hatshepsut's mortuary temple?

i   What was the significance of the royal ka?

j   What evidence is there that Hatshepsut placed great emphasis on her royal ka?

Figure B

a   Identify the people featured in this relief.

b   What is supposedly happening in this scene?

c   Of what series of inscriptions does this relief form a part?

d   What was the purpose of this inscription?

e   What evidence is there from other sources that the event featured in this inscription is purely fictional?

f   Explain why this relief is partially damaged.

3 **The figure on the right shows an inscribed block of granite from Hatshepsut's Red Chapel. The relief depicts Hatshepsut, as a king, in a ritual race.**

a Where was the Red Chapel originally located and what was its purpose?

b What is the major difference between this image of Hatshepsut and the one on page 319?

c For what important ceremony do these reliefs and inscriptions provide evidence?

d In what year of her reign did Hatshepsut hold this ceremony and what was its original purpose?

e What part did this ceremony play in the propaganda that Hatshepsut promoted?

4 **Each of the texts below are associated with Hatshepsut's building program. Identify each one and answer the questions below**

A The Temple of the Lady of Cusae (the goddess Hathor), which had begun to fall to ruin, the ground had swallowed up its august sanctuary, so that the children played upon its roof, ... I adorned it, having been built anew, I overlaid its image with gold ...

Pakhet, the great (a lion goddess) who traverses the valleys in the midst of the eastlands, whose ways are storm-beaten ... I made her temple with that which was due to her ennead of gods. The doors were of acacia wood, fitted with bronze ... the offering table was wrought with silver and gold, chests of linen and every kind of furniture being established in its place.[98]

B My majesty began work on them in year 15, second month of winter, day 1, ending in year 16, fourth month of summer, last day, totalling seven months of quarry work. I did it for him out of affection as a king for a god. It was my wish to make them for him gilded with electrum.[99]

C 'Most Splendid' the temple of myriads of years; its great doors fashioned of black copper, the inlaid figures of electrum ... the great seat of Amun, his horizon in the west; all its doors of real cedar, wrought with bronze. The house of Amun, his enduring horizon of eternity; its floor wrought with gold and silver; its beauty was like the horizon of heaven. A great shrine of ebony of Nubia, the stairs beneath it high and wide, of pure alabaster of Hatnub. A palace of the god, wrought with gold and silver; it illuminated the faces (of people) with its brightness.[100]

D ... The good god, King Okhepernere (here the name of Hatshepsut was replaced with that of Thutmose II) — appointed me to conduct the work upon his (her) cliff-tomb because of the great excellence of my plans ... I was leader of the works on [ ] in Karnak, in the house of Amun, wrought with gold [ ] ... chief, of silver, gold and black copper; [ ] wrought of copper, the great name upon it was of electrum.[101]

a Where were each of these inscriptions found?

b Which of Hatshepsut's buildings and monuments are referred to in these extracts?

c What do the texts indicate about her building policy and the state of the economy?

5 **The following text comes from the best written source of evidence for the titles, responsibilities and honours awarded to Senenmut.**

> Given as a favour of the king's presence, the King of Upper and Lower Egypt, Maat-ka-re ... to Steward of Amun, Senenmut, triumphant ...
>
> It was the Chief Steward (of the king), Senenmut, who conducted all the works of the king: in Karnak, in Hermonthis, in Deir el-Bahri of Amun, in the Temple of Mut, in Ishru, in southern Opet of Amun in the presence of this august god while maintaining the monuments of the Lord of the Two Lands, enlarging, restoring ... not lax concerning the monuments of the lord of gods, wearer of the royal seal, Prophet of Amun, Senenmut.
>
> ... 'I was the greatest of the great in the whole land; one who heard the hearing alone in the privy council, Steward of Amun, Senenmut, triumphant.'
>
> 'I was the real favourite of the king, acting as one praised of his lord every day, the Overseer of the cattle of Amun, Senenmut.'
>
> ... 'I was one who entered in love and came forth in favour, making glad the heart of the king every day, the companion and Master of the Palace, Senenmut.'
>
> 'I commanded in the storehouse of divine offerings of Amun every tenth day; the Overseer of the storehouse of Amun, Senenmut.'
>
> 'I conducted [ ] of the gods every day, for the sake of the life, prosperity and health of the king; Overseer of the [ ] of Amun, Senenmut.'
>
> 'I was a foreman of foremen, superior of the great, Overseer of all the works of the house of silver, conductor of every handicraft, Chief of the Prophets (priests) of Montu, in Hermonthis, Senenmut.'
>
> 'I was one to whom the affairs of the Two Lands were reported; that which South and North contributed was on my seal, the labour of all countries was under my charge.'
>
> I was one whose steps were known in the palace; a real confidant of the king, his beloved: Overseer of the gardens of Amun, Senenmut.'
>
> ... Given as a favour of the king's presence to the ... Steward of Amun, Senenmut, triumphant, Steward of the female Horus: Wosretkew (Hatshepsut), favourite of Horus: 'Shining in Thebes' (Thutmose III), when maintaining their monuments forever, firm in favour with them every day.[102]

a What was 'given as a favour' to Senenmut by Hatshepsut and Thutmose III?

b What were Senenemut's chief responsibilities as *steward of Amun*?

c What responsibilities did he carry out on behalf of Hatshepsut?

d Why does the title *great father tutor and steward of the Princess Neferure* not appear in this inscription?

e What do the tiles in this inscription tell historians about:
   - Senenmut's abilities
   - his meteoric rise to power
   - his relationship with Hatshepsut?

f What evidence is there in the burials of Senenmut's family of his rise to prominence?

6 **The figure below shows a number of fragments from Hatshepsut's Punt reliefs.**

a   Where is Punt believed to have been located?

b   What evidence is there in these fragments to suggest a coastal tropical location?

c   Why was Hatshepsut encouraged to send a trading expedition to Punt to open the *myrrh terraces*?

d   What other products did the Egyptians seek from Punt? Why were these products in demand? Which of these can be seen in these fragments?

e   Why was the expedition accompanied by soldiers?

f   What evidence is there to suggest that Hatshepsut sent trading expeditions to places other than Punt?

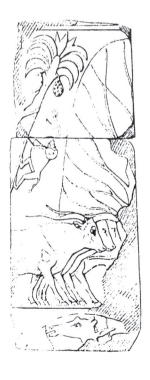
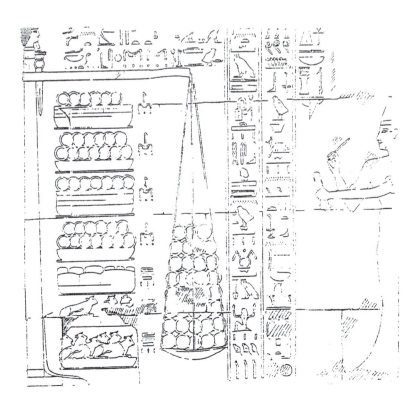

7 **What was the purpose behind the following pieces of propaganda from the Punt inscriptions?**

> The coming of the chiefs of Punt, doing obeisance, with bowed heads, to receive this army of the king; they give praise to the lord of gods, Amun-Re.
>
> Reception of the tribute of the chief of Punt by the king's messenger.
>
> Kissing the earth to Wosretkew (Hatshepsut) by the chiefs of Punt.
>
> ... every country is dominion of her majesty ...[103]

8 **Essay topics**

a Refer to the showing plans and details of Hatshepsut's temple at Deir el-Bahri early in this chapter, and the information in the chapter, to write a description of Hatshepsut's mortuary temple at Deir el-Bahri as it might have appeared to someone eligible to enter the sacred precincts.

b Comment on the statement made by Sir Alan Gardiner that 'the reign of Hatshepsut had been barren of any military enterprise except an unimportant raid into Nubia'. [104] Support your argument with evidence.

c Use the following diagram and the extract from *Images of Women in Antiquity*, to explain how Hatshepsut was able to maintain her power for over 21 years.

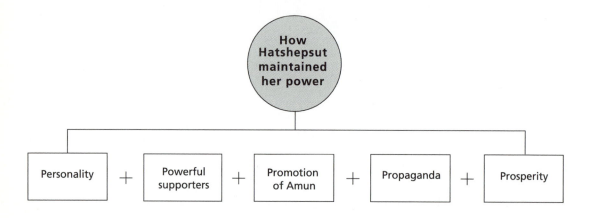

> On a practical government level, we can imagine that she carefully chose the officials who were to serve her and with whom she had to work. Some had previously held office under her husband or even her father, and some were new. Presumably they were all men who were congenial to her and whose fortunes were to some extent linked to hers.[105]

d Write an argument to refute the view that Thutmose III hated Hatshepsut and carried out a vengeful attack on her monuments as soon as she died.

CHAPTER
11

'Valiant like Montu'
— Thutmose III

The image of a warrior king had been slowly developing from the time of Ahmose to the reign of Thutmose I, who set the example for others to follow. It was his grandson, Menkheperre (Thutmose III), who truly epitomised the image of the warrior pharaoh. Many times in the official inscriptions, Thutmose was likened to Montu, the war-god of Thebes — 'Valiant like Montu', 'Lord of power like Montu of Thebes' and 'Montu on the battlefield'.

Soon after assuming sole power, Thutmose III began to build on the foundations of the Egyptian empire laid down by his grandfather, Thutmose I. By means of 17 military campaigns extending over a 20-year period, he established Egypt as the undisputed master of Syria and Palestine. He also fixed the southern border of the Egyptian empire at Napata (Fourth Cataract) in Upper Nubia. During these campaigns he proved himself to be an innovative general and a warrior of great personal bravery. Breasted maintains that he was 'unquestionably the greatest military leader of ancient Egypt'.[1]

However, Thutmose III was far more than this. He was an efficient administrator as well as a statesman. His organisation of the conquered and vassal territories in Syria–Palestine and his use of clemency, diplomacy and threats of force in maintaining Egyptian control, are evidence of this.

To the Egyptians, his success as a king was judged by his service to the gods. Thutmose dedicated enormous wealth, from war booty, tribute and trade, to the chief gods of Egypt, particularly Amun-Re, and built extensively in almost every cult centre along the Nile. Like Hatshepsut, he lavished most attention on Amun's Karnak temple at Thebes.

The evidence suggests that Thutmose was something of a soldier/scholar, admired for his scribal skills and with an interest in botany and history.

Whether he was 'the greatest pharaoh ever to occupy the throne of Egypt' as claimed by Hayes,[2] is difficult to judge, but he was certainly one of the most significant personalities of the New Kingdom.

One of the questions that should be asked is 'would his career have been so brilliant had it not been preceded by the reign of Hatshepsut?'.[3]

Head of a statue of Thutmose III found in a cache at Karnak

333

Chief sources for the period
The Temple of Amun-Re at Karnak

Just as Hatshepsut had used the colonnades of her mortuary temple at Deir el-Bahri to advertise what she considered the major events of her reign, Thutmose III used the walls of the Temple of Amun 'to obtain full publicity for his achievements'.[4] At the same time, he could show his gratitude to Amun by recording what he had dedicated to the god.

The *Annals*

Sometime around year 42 of his reign, Thutmose recorded on the walls of a red granite chamber at Karnak what is referred to as the *Annals*, an account of his 17 military campaigns in Palestine and Syria from year 23 to year 42. This 'forms the most complete account of the military achievements of any Egyptian king'.[5]

Although this account was written retrospectively, it is believed that it was copied from an original leather scroll, kept as a field journal by an army scribe and lodged for safe keeping in the Temple of Karnak. Evidence for the existence of such a document comes from the account of the first campaign:

> Now all that his majesty did to this city (Megiddo), to that wretched foe and his wretched army, was recorded each day by its name under the tile of: [ ] recorded upon a roll of leather in the temple of Amun to this day.[6]

Most of the 223 lines of the inscription record the details of Thutmose's great military victory at Megiddo, in the second year of his sole rule and is the 'earliest full description of any decisive battle'.[7] Historians generally believe that this account is more factual than the official records of most pharaohs. Hayes says that Thutmose III's records, 'for their period, are for the most part moderately phrased and sincere in tone'.[8]

The account of his other campaigns in the *Annals* are more sketchy and seem to focus more on the type and amount of booty and tribute dedicated to Amun from each campaign.

Lists of conquered cities

Associated with the *Annals* is a list of 350 localities subjugated by Thutmose III during his Syrian campaigns. Each of these places is identified and represented as an ellipse containing a bound Syrian prisoner. Accompanying these is a conventional scene depicting Thutmose as a conqueror holding a group of Asiatic prisoners by the hair and smiting them with a mace. On the seventh pylon, constructed by Thutmose, was carved another catalogue of conquered groups from the southern lands (Nubia). However, many of these people are believed to have come under Egyptian control before Thutmose III's reign.

Feasts and offerings

Also linked to his military campaigns are the extensive lists of feasts and offerings dedicated to Amun, inscribed on the back of the south half of the sixth pylon at Karnak.

A piece of propaganda on the exterior wall at Karnak describes the occasion when, via an oracle, Amun-Re chose Thutmose as the future king.

A relief from the Temple of Amun at Karnak
depicting the cities conquered by Thutmose III
in western Asia

Detail of the ellipses containing the names of the
conquered cities

Official stelae

At Napata (Gebel Barkal) in Nubia, near the Fourth
Cataract, Thutmose erected a stela inscribed with
more details of his victory at Megiddo, his other
conquests in Palestine and Syria as well as his successes as far as the Euphrates River. In addition, a
smaller and less complete stela from Armant (near
Thebes), covers much the same ground.

A black granite stela, found near the Festival Hall
at Karnak, was inscribed with a poem, supposedly
written by the priests of Amun to celebrate the military triumphs of Thutmose III. It is a useful supplement to the *Annals*. This hymn of victory was
later adapted by other kings for self-glorification.

Thutmose III smiting his enemies, from the
Temple of Amun at Karnak

Tomb biographies of royal officials

The tomb biographies of Thutmose's chief officials are valuable sources
of information about his military campaigns (Amenemhab), the admin-
istration of Egypt and the role of the vizier (Rekhmire, Vizier of the
South), the wealth that poured into Egypt at this time (Rekhmire,
Menkheperreseneb, High Priest of Amun and Treasurer, and Nehi,
Viceroy of Kush) and Thutmose's buildings (Menkheperreseneb).

Of all of these tombs, that of Rekhmire is the most significant as it contains the fullest account of the administration of Egypt during the New
Kingdom.

Thutmose's early years and co-regency

Thutmose's mother was Isis (Ese), an obscure woman from the royal
harem who appears to have had no royal connections. Her son

ascended the throne at a very early age (perhaps nine or ten) and came under the guidance of his stepmother, Hatshepsut, who ruled first as regent and then shared a co-regency with the young king.

Apprentice priest

During his early years, he spent some time as an apprentice priest in the Temple of Amun at Karnak. It may have been while in the temple that he acquired the scribal skills for which he was noted. Later, he was to record that during his time as an acolyte in the temple he was chosen by means of an oracle from Amun as the future king. This incident supposedly occurred in the colonnaded hall of Thutmose I during a procession of the god. Thutmose probably felt the need to justify his right to rule with a divine oracle because his mother had not been the *king's great wife*.

Military training and sporting ability

According to a stela found in the Temple of Montu in Armant (Hermonthis), Thutmose III learned to know 'all the works of Montu' such as handling the double-curved bow and spear. He claimed that in the presence of the whole army he pierced a copper plate with his arrows and was 'powerful of arm when he (took) the spear'. His personal performance in battle during his more than 20 years of campaigning point to such an education. Also, part of his training would have involved horsemanship and other sporting activities. Evidence of his ability as a sportsman comes from a number of sources, including the temple of Armant and the tomb of Amenemhab. Thutmose shot and killed a rhinoceros during an early campaign in Nubia, led an elephant hunt in northern Syria, supposedly killed seven lions, captured 12 wild cattle and harpooned a hippopotamus.

As he grew older, he accompanied and then led military campaigns, some into Nubia and possibly to the north-east of the delta, around Gaza. These gave him the experience he needed when he was faced with more determined enemies in Syria–Palestine later in his reign.

Played a part in affairs of state

Despite the fact that he was not as prominent as Hatshepsut during their co-regency, he participated in the running of state affairs, dedicated to the gods in his own right and commissioned buildings. An inscription at Karnak, dated to year 15 of his reign (while Hatshepsut was still co-regent) indicates that he was already building extensively at Karnak and making rich offerings to Amun.

> My majesty furthermore gave lands, 2800 stat to be fields of divine offerings, many lands in South and North ... Year 15 of the first month of the third season ... my majesty commanded to found a great divine offering anew ... My majesty furthermore presented to him very many monuments ... many chambers wrought with electrum and black copper, erecting an enclosure a seat ....[9]

Artistic interests

There is even some evidence that Thutmose had an interest in design and actually supplied the craftsmen with designs for some of the furnishings of the Temple of Amun. In year 15 he claimed 'I made it for him out of the conceptions of my heart'.[10] Thutmose III's artistic ability was confirmed by Menkheneseneb, High Priest of Amun. His tomb inscription recorded that ritual items of turquoise and malachite crafted in the workshops of the temple of Amun were made 'after the design of his (the king's) heart to be a monument for his father, Amun'.[11]

During his co-regency, he became a family man with several chief wives, a number of lesser ones and a horde of children. Although Thutmose III would have been expected to marry Neferure, the daughter of Hatshepsut and his half-sister, there is no evidence that he did so. In his tomb he records the names of three wives, Satiah, Merytre-Hatshepsut and Nebetu. Merytre-Hatshepsut was the *god's wife of Amun* when she married Thutmose III. Her mother had also been very high in the cult, holding the positions of *chief adorer of Amun* and *superintendent of the harem of Amun*. Thutmose III also had three lesser wives, whose names, Menhet, Menwi and Merti, seem to indicate that they were possibly the daughters of Syrian princes. Of his sons, it was Amenhotep, the son of Merytre-Hatshepsut, who succeeded him.

Family man

By the time he assumed sole rule Thutmose was a well-educated family man, skilled in military matters.

Thutmose's sole rule

For the first 20 years of his sole reign (between years 23 and 42) Thutmose campaigned vigorously in western Asia, with several expeditions into Nubia as well.

He was able to spend so much of his time beyond the borders of Egypt, fighting his country's enemies and maintaining Egyptian control, because Hatshepsut had maintained a highly effective administration and kept her army fully equipped and ready.

Western Asia at the time of Thutmose III

Syria and Palestine (western Asia), the goal of Thutmose's conquests, comprised over 300 cities, each controlled by a local prince or chieftain. These cities were prosperous since they were on the main trade routes from Egypt and the Mediterranean ports to the great kingdoms in Asia Minor and around the Tigris and Euphrates rivers. They often fought among themselves and made alliances to suit their individual needs at any particular time. They were capable of unity only when faced with a common enemy.

Independent cities of Syria and Palestine

Of all the Syrian cities, Kadesh was Egypt's greatest antagonist. It was a fortress city encircled by thick walls and protected by two branches of the Orontes River.

Kadesh

Surrounding the cities of western Asia were a number of powerful kingdoms, all of which were at some time interested in gaining control over the area — Babylon, Assyria, Khatte (the Hittites) and Naharin (the Mitanni).

At the time of Thutmose III, it was the Mitannian Kingdom from beyond the Euphrates River (Naharin) that competed with Egypt for control of Syria. (In the Egyptian inscriptions, the terms Mitanni and Naharin are synonymous.) Since the time of Thutmose I, when the Egyptians had threatened the borders of Mitanni, this northern kingdom allied itself with some of the Syrian cities such as Kadesh, to ensure that it was not

Mitanni (Naharin)

directly threatened by Egypt. The Mitanni also promoted rivalry between the small city states 'through a subtle game of switching alliances'.[12] They hoped to keep their Egyptian rivals occupied with local Palestinian and Syrian struggles.

Because western Asia was fragmented, it was always difficult to control and it took Thutmose III 17 military campaigns over a period of 20 years 'before his claims in Palestine and Syria could be recognised and the pretensions of the Mitanni checked'.[13]

Western Asia at the time of Thutmose III

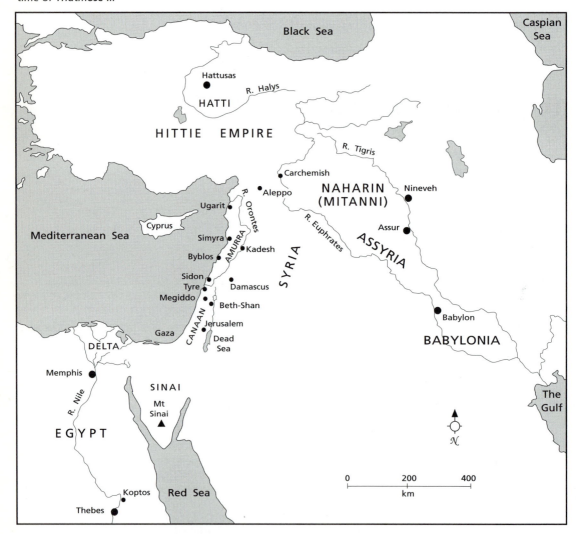

Thutmose's Asiatic campaigns

In year 23 of his reign, shortly after the death of Hatshepsut, Thutmose III embarked on the first and most publicised of his military successes — a campaign against a combined force of Asiatic cities, led by the prince of Kadesh, at Megiddo in Palestine.

The table below shows the likely sequence of Thutmose's 17 campaigns, although the exact chronology is difficult to determine. The campaigns of years 23, 30, 33 and 42 were the most significant. Many of the others seem to have been tours of inspection and shows of force during which he received submission from local rulers and ever increasing amounts of tribute.

The chief military campaigns of Thutmose III

Year	Campaigns
23	Megiddo in Palestine — possibly considered by Thutmose III to be his finest military achievement.
24–28	Three campaigns in Palestine were carried out during this period. They were probably more in the nature of tours of inspection, during which Thutmose seized the wheat harvests and collected tribute.
29	This fifth campaign was against the Prince of Tunip and his allies from Kadesh and Naharin. Thutmose secured the coast around Ullaza, captured Arvad in preparation for his assault on Kadesh and destroyed their wheat fields and orchards.
30	Sixth campaign against the Syrian stronghold of Kadesh.
31	Another campaign in Syria against Ullaza which had re-joined the anti-Egyptian coalition. This campaign resulted in the subjugation of the Phoenician ports.
33	Campaign against the powerful Mitanni in Naharin beyond the Euphrates River.
34–41	Eight more campaigns — against the Mitannian influence in Syria and against the Nubians to the south. Tribute poured into Egypt.
42	The final defeat of Kadesh.

Profile of an ancient military campaign — Megiddo

In most accounts of ancient military campaigns there is not enough information to answer the following questions:

- When did this campaign occur?
- Why was it necessary?
- Where did the major battle or confrontation take place?
- What were the major incidents of this campaign?
- How did the armies of both sides perform, how was victory eventually achieved and how did the victorious army treat the enemy?
- What follow-up actions were taken and what was the significance of the campaign for both sides?

Fortunately for historians, the account of the Megiddo campaign is described in detail in the *Annals* and in the text of the Gebel Barkal stela and these questions can be answered with a fair degree of certainty.

Dates of this campaign

Timing and length of campaign

The *Annals* record that at the end of year 22 of his reign, Thutmose was at the border town of Tharu:

> Year 22, fourth month of the second season, on the twenty-fifth day [his majesty was in] Tharu, on the first victorious expedition to [extend] the boundaries of Egypt with might.[14]

Nine to ten days later, the Egyptian army had reached Gaza:

> Year 23, first (month) of the third season, on the fourth day, the day of the feast of the king's coronation (he arrived) at that city, the possession of the ruler, Gaza.[15]

In a little over two weeks more, the army was camped on the plain south of Megiddo preparing for battle. According to the Gebel Barkal stela, after the battle 'year 23, first month of the third season, on the twenty-first day',[16] Thutmose besieged Megiddo for almost seven months, during which time he carried out other military activities in Syria.

The harvest season

This campaign, like many others that followed, was conducted, according to Breasted, during the Palestinian dry season (end of March–April to October). Thutmose returned to Thebes to dedicate offerings to Amun well into his twenty-third regnal year.

Reasons for this campaign

Revolt of cities of Retenu under leadership of Kadesh

According to the *Annals*, the rulers of Palestine and Syria from 'the city of Sharuhen ... to the marshes of the earth (Euphrates) had begun to revolt against his majesty'.[17] Gardiner believes that these rulers, led by the Prince of Kadesh, 'saw the opportunity of throwing off the yoke imposed on them by the first Thutmose'.[18] He maintains that this rebellion was because 'the reign of Hatshepsut was barren of any military enterprise'.[19] This was not the case, as has already been argued in Chapter 11. It is more likely that the princes of Retjenu (Palestine and Syria) took the opportunity of the death of a pharaoh (Hatshepsut) to test the resolve of the new ruler.

Three-hundred-and-thirty princes from Palestine and Syria, 'every one of them having his own army',[20] formed a confederation under the prince of Kadesh. They centred their rebellion on the fortress city of Megiddo. Their aim was to prevent Egypt bringing Syria under its control and directly threatening their ally, Mitanni. Despite the number of rebellious cities, Wilson points out that some of the armies brought by these minor princes must have been very small since the Plain of Esdraelon below Megiddo could not hold a huge number of men.

Egypt's borders

According to the *Annals*, the god Amun-Re commanded Thutmose to conquer the *wretched enemy* and extend the borders of Egypt.

The choice of Megiddo as the site for the defence of Retjenu

Megiddo itself was a strongly fortified town overlooking the Plain of Esdraelon. The fact that Thutmose laid siege to Megiddo for seven months is evidence of its impregnability.

Strategic site of Megiddo

More important than its fortifications, however, was Megiddo's site. It was the focus of all the major roads north and north-east. The prince of Kadesh had chosen carefully.

> The great commercial road which was the nerve centre of Palestine–Syria entered the Fertile Crescent at Gaza in south-western Palestine and moved north through the Philistine coastland and the Plain of Sharon, broke through the Carmel range to emerge into the Plain of Esdraelon at Megiddo, and then forked for the Phoenician coast, the central valley of Syria, or the hinterland at Damascus. The Megiddo Pass was therefore of high military importance as it continued to be throughout history ...[21]

Choice of route

Eleven days after leaving Gaza, the Egyptian army reached Yehem where the king called a council of war with his army chiefs to discuss the route by which they should approach Megiddo. They had a choice of three approaches:

- The most direct route, but the slowest and most dangerous, would take the army via Aruna and then through a narrow mountain pass before reaching the Plain of Esdraelon.

- The second choice was to approach Megiddo from the south via Taanach.

- The third approach was from the north via Zefti (Dfty).

Thutmose's officers were opposed to the direct route because it meant marching in file, 'horse after horse and man after man', making the vanguard of the army vulnerable to attack as it moved from the confines of

Advice of Thutmose's officers

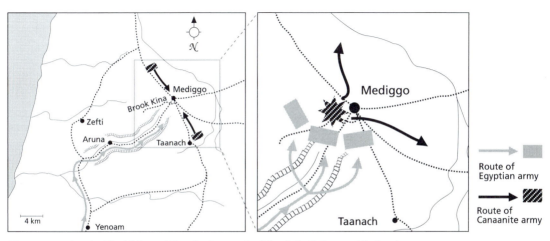

The approaches to Megiddo and the deployment of the Palestinian and Syrian troops

the pass into the open plain. They were concerned that the front of the army would be forced to fight while the rear was 'yet standing yonder in Aruna'.[22]

Thutmose's choice of route

Despite their advice, Thutmose informed them that he would 'proceed upon this Aruna road! Let him of you who wishes go upon these other roads of which you speak, and let him of you who wishes come in the following of my majesty!'[23] He trusted in the support of Amun-Re who had promised him victory and he did not want lay himself open to charges of cowardice by his enemies who might accuse him of setting out on another road because he was afraid of them.

When Thutmose gave the orders for the army to march towards Aruna, he took his place at the head of his troops 'showing the way by his own footsteps'.[24] On the following day, the army, in full battle array and strung out in single file, entered the narrow mountain pass. It appears that at this time they caught sight of the enemy troops — one enemy division in the direction of Taanach and the other to the north. So it seems that the Asiatics expected the Egyptians to arrive by one of the easier routes. Once the front of the army had reached the valley of the Kina, Thutmose's officers appealed to him to wait for the rest of the army to catch up, which he did. Incredibly, there was no opposition to Thutmose as he led his entire army out onto the plain south of Megiddo and set up camp for the night.

Safe passage to the plain of Megiddo

The command was given to his troops to 'Equip yourselves! Prepare your weapons! for we shall advance to fight with that wretched foe in the morning'.[25] The troops were urged to be watchful and 'steady of heart'. It appears that Thutmose had deployed his army in several divisions, for the officer of the watch reported to the king that 'the land is well, and the infantry of the South and North likewise'.[26]

The battle on the Plain of Esdraelon outside Megiddo

On the day of battle, Thutmose had deployed his troops in the following way:

- 'the southern wing of this army of his majesty was on a hill south of the brook of Kina'
- 'the northern wing was at the north-west of Megiddo'.[27]

Pharaoh appears before the army in his chariot

Before the battle, the king paraded at the head of his forces 'in a chariot of electrum, arrayed in his weapons of war like Horus, the Smiter, lord of power; like Montu of Thebes while his father Amun strengthened his arms'.[28]

The size of the enemy force is unknown but judging by the number of chariots seized by Thutmose's troops after the battle (924), its chariotry at least was extensive.

Thutmose, at the head of his army, led the charge. There are no details of the actual fighting. The *Annals* record only that the Egyptians prevailed against the enemy forces who supposedly turned and fled towards the safety of Megiddo, leaving their horses and chariots of gold and silver behind. The inhabitants had locked the gates of the city and those attempting to escape the onslaught of the Egyptians had to be hauled up the walls by whatever could be lowered to them. By this means, both the princes of Kadesh and Megiddo made their escape.

To the disgust of Thutmose, the Egyptian troops began to plunder the abandoned belongings of the enemy, rather than focus on the capture of Megiddo. The king believed that by capturing Megiddo, the Egyptians would have captured a thousand cities, 'because every chief of every country that has revolted is within it'.[29]

Troops' lack of discipline

Instead, the jubilant troops collected as much booty as they could and 'went around counting their portions'.[30] They also cut off the hands of those who 'lay stretched out like fishes on the ground'[31] as proof of their victory.

The siege of Megiddo

Because of the greed of the Egyptian soldiers for booty, Thutmose and his troops were forced to spend almost seven months besieging Megiddo. The city's walls were too strong to be taken by assault, so Thutmose planned to starve the leaders into submission. He ordered his men to enclose the city with trenches and a timber wall which was called 'Menkheperre-is-the-surrounder-of-the-Asiatics'.[32] No one was permitted to leave the city unless they wished to surrender. Famine finally took its toll on those crowded within the walls of Megiddo and they surrendered.

The Gebel Barkal stela describes how the princes sent out 'all their children bearing abundant tribute' while 'they stood on the walls doing obeisance' to Thutmose III and 'seeking that the breath of life might be given to them'.[33]

Treatment of the conquered princes

Thutmose's reaction to their surrender was restrained. Instead of killing the rebellious princes as a lesson for the future, he:

- administered an oath of loyalty by which his opponents promised not to 'return to evil deeds against Menkheperre ... our lord, as long as we live, for we have seen his clemency, when he gave us the breath of life, of his own free will'.[34]

Oaths of loyalty

- gave those within Megiddo permission to return to their cities. Because he had captured their chariot horses, he sent them away on donkeys. It appears that the prince of Kadesh may have already escaped.

Clemency

  By his restraint pharaoh laid the cornerstone of empire for a century.[35]

Spoil from Megiddo

The raising of the siege added to the considerable booty taken from the battlefield. The Egyptians would have plundered the quarters of the prince of Megiddo and seized all that was left behind by the Asiatic princes. The booty collected included:

- prisoners — 340
- hands — 83
- horses — approximately 2238
- chariots — 892 ordinary and 32 wrought with gold and silver mountings
- suits of armour — 200 from the regular army and two fine bronze outfits owned by the princes of Kadesh and Megiddo
- weapons — 502 bows
- tents and gilded tent poles
- domesticated animals — almost 25 000 cattle, sheep and goats.

The Egyptians also harvested the Megiddo wheat crop and, apart from what was eaten by the army, the rest was sent to Egypt.

> Statement of the harvest which was brought to his majesty from the fields of Megiddo: 208 200 fourfold heket of grain, beside that which was cut as forage by the army of his majesty.[36]

The immediate aftermath

Further military activities

It is believed that, during the siege, Thutmose had sent out a number of expeditions to the north, possibly around the Sea of Galilee. After the fall of Megiddo, the Egyptian army moved north towards the city of Tyre, capturing the towns of Yanoan, Nuges and Herenkeru, and he supposedly built a fortress 'among the chiefs of Lebanon' (Tyre) which was called 'Menkheperre-is-the-binder-of-the-Barbarians'.[37]

The *Annals* list further plunder taken from these cities. This included 38 lords of the cities that submitted, '87 children of that foe and the chiefs that were with him, five lords of theirs, 1796 male and female slaves and their children',[38] and rings of gold, finely crafted equipment, furniture and statues.

Return to Thebes

As it was getting close to the rainy season, the king led his victorious army back to Egypt and ultimately to the city of Thebes. There he established, for the first time, *a feast of victory* for his *father* Amun, of five days' duration, to celebrate 'overthrowing of the wretched Retjenu and widening the borders of Egypt in the year 23'.[39]

The importance of the Megiddo campaign

> In the conquest of Megiddo the pharaoh had won at a single stroke all of northern Palestine and the remaining princes of Syria made haste to announce their allegiance by dispatching gifts to the conqueror.[40]

Hostage policy

Thutmose introduced a policy of taking hostages from the defeated princes to ensure their future loyalty. These sons or brothers of the rulers of Retjenu were taken to Egypt to be educated as Egyptians. Thutmose's plan was that these hostages would eventually rule as 'friends of Egypt' in their own cities. There are two clear references to this policy. The first accompanies the lists of conquered cities from the first campaign and describes the children of the 'wretched princes of

Retjenu' whom 'his majesty brought as living prisoners to the city of Suhen-em-Opet', a place of confinement in Thebes.[41] The other reference occurs in the record of the sixth campaign in the *Annals*.

> Behold the children of the chiefs and their brothers were brought to be in strongholds in Egypt. Now, whoever died among these chiefs, his majesty would cause his son to stand in his place.[42]

This proved to be one of the most effective aspects of Thutmose's administration of the empire. Although Thutmose had effectively broken up this coalition of Palestinian and Syrian princes, he ensured their continued submission by making annual tours of inspection of the area and accepting their tribute.

Annual tours of inspection

The king of Assyria was the first of the distant rulers to send gifts to Thutmose, but in usual Egyptian fashion these gifts from 'brother' kings were described in the *Annals* as tribute.

Thutmose's success at Megiddo had ensured that Kadesh and the Kingdom of Mitanni were enemies that would have to be dealt with in the future. However, it was not until year 29 that he felt the need to advance beyond the limits of his first campaign and begin a new phase in his military career.

Enmity of Kadesh and Mitanni

The greatest beneficiary of Thutmose's victories was the temple of Amun and its priesthood. Thutmose introduced new feasts and offerings to the god from this time. He dedicated the three cities of Yanoan, Nuges and Herenkeru to Amun, as well as a large part of the slaves, cattle and costly ornaments taken from Megiddo.

A new phase of Thutmose's military policy — years 29–33

The military campaigns carried out by Thutmose during this period were divided into two parts:

1 an attack on Kadesh — year 30
2 crossing the Euphrates for a direct confrontation with Mitanni — year 33.

Neither of these could have been achieved without considerable preparation, part of which involved securing the coastal area of northern Syria. Thutmose would not have marched against Kadesh and taken on the might of Mitanni without making sure that these cities were firmly under Egyptian control.

Securing the coastal cities

In year 29 (fifth campaign) he took the coastal cities of Ullaza and Arvad and their surrounding areas. These cities were under the control of the prince of Tunip, an ally of Kadesh and Mitanni. The *Annals* describe the capture of Arvad in the following way:

> Behold his majesty overthrew the city of Arvad with its grain, cutting down all its pleasant trees. Behold, there were found the products of all Zahi (the coastline of Phoenicia). Their gardens were filled with their fruit, their wines were found remaining in their presses as water

flows, their grain on the terraces ... it was more plentiful than the sand of the shore. the army were overwhelmed with their portions.

... Behold, the army of his majesty were drunk and anointed every day as at a feast.[43]

Taking into account the difficulties faced by ordinary Egyptian soldiers and their limited daily rations, it is no wonder they revelled in the luxury of this region.

The tribute taken from this area (captives, gold, bronze and copper vessels, animals, lapis lazuli and malachite, 6428 jars of wine, 470 jars of honey, incense, grain and fruit) was loaded onto ships captured by Thutmose and dispatched to Egypt. In the following season, Thutmose returned by sea for his assault on Kadesh.

The attack on Kadesh — year 30

Neither the *Annals* nor the inscription in the tomb of Thutmose's general, Amenemhab (extracts from which are reproduced below), give many details of this campaign.

He arrived in the city of Kadesh, overthrew it, cut down its groves, harvested its grain.[44]

Again I beheld his bravery, while I was among his followers. He captured the city of Kadesh. I was not absent from the place where he was; I brought off two men, lords as living prisoners.[45]

Considering the part played by the prince of Kadesh in organising the rebellion against Egypt in year 23 and the wealth and influence of this city, it is surprising that the records of this campaign are so scanty.

Although the city was plundered and hostages were taken, it is not known to what extent it was destroyed. Thutmose obviously felt confident that Kadesh posed no immediate threat as he prepared to achieve his ultimate aim.

The campaign against Mitanni — year 33

In preparation for this campaign, Thutmose spent the campaigning season of year 31 making sure that the Phoenician coastline was totally secure and setting up supply bases.

Now every harbour at which his majesty arrived was supplied with ... assorted loaves, with oil, incense, wine, honey, fruit — abundant were they beyond everything, beyond the knowledge of his majesty's army ...[46]

As Thutmose's campaigns took him further away from Egypt, it became increasingly important to transport his army by sea and to have provisions available for his troops and garrisons.

He also organised the construction of boats of cedar in the mountains behind Byblos. These were to be used to ferry the Egyptian troops across the Euphrates to Naharin.

I had many ships of cedar built on the mountains of God's Land near the city of the Lady of Byblos.[47]

By year 33, he was ready to begin his campaign against the Kingdom of Mitanni.

After crossing to the coast of northern Syria, the Egyptian army headed north, preceded by the cedar boats carried on ox-drawn carts.

According to the *Annals*, Thutmose went 'north, capturing the towns and laying waste the settlements of that foe of Naharin'.[48] The tomb inscription of Amenemhab recorded that the army fought at least three battles at Senzar, Aleppo and Carchemish. The Gebel Barkal stela continues the account. The army, using the cedar boats, 'crossed the great *Inverted River* in pursuit of that wretched one of Mitanni'.[49] However, the king of Mitanni and his troops had already fled 'in fear' to a remote part of the kingdom.

Crossing of the Euphrates

Thutmose ravaged Naharin. 'I desolated his towns and his tribes and set fire to them. My majesty turned them into ruin-mounds and they will never be re-settled.'[50] He cut down their grain and their orchards and turned the countryside into 'a grass plain'.

Although Thutmose claimed to have taken all their people prisoner, the lists of plunder from Naharin only amounted to three princes, 30 of their wives, 80 men and 606 slaves.

Like his grandfather before him, Thutmose III set up a commemorative stela on the eastern side of the Euphrates. Also following the example of Thutmose I, the king took time out for an elephant hunt at Niy.

Commemorative stela and elephant hunt

> Again I beheld another excellent deed which the Lord of the Two Lands did in Niy. He hunted 120 elephants for the sake of their tusks.[51]

It appears that during the hunt the king was charged by the largest animal and only saved from death by the actions of Amenemhab.

> I engaged the largest which was among them, which fought against his majesty. I cut off his hand (trunk) while he was alive ...[52]

The victorious Thutmose returned to Egypt with the plunder and tribute of Mitanni. Soon after, he received gifts from the rulers of Babylon, Khatte (the Hittites) and Cyprus. These gifts were erroneously referred to in the Egyptian records as tribute.

Gifts from Hittites, Cypriots and Babylonians

Despite his successes, he had not put an end to Mitannian influence in northern Syria, nor had he had his last encounter with the prince of Kadesh. In year 35, Thutmose dealt with a new Mitannian coalition near Aleppo and in year 42, he marched north again to suppress a revolt of Tunip and Kadesh which had the support of troops from Mitanni.

Thutmose's last Asiatic campaign — year 42

Thutmose sailed along the Syrian coast and overthrew the city of Erkatu before turning his attention to Tunip. His plan was to cut Kadesh off from its northern ally. Once he had defeated Tunip, 'harvested its grain and cut down its groves',[53] he moved into the district of Kadesh and attacked a number of towns in the area. He was now ready for the showdown with his long-time enemy, the prince of Kadesh.

Final attack on Kadesh

**Ruse to disrupt
Egyptian lines**

The inscription in Amenemhab's tomb records how the Egyptian infantry and chariotry were deployed outside the city when the prince of Kadesh sent out a mare, which raced among the lines of chariots. The plan was to excite the Egyptian stallions and break the formation, causing chaos in the Egyptian ranks.

Once again, it seems that Amenemhab came to the rescue of the king. He claims to have jumped from his chariot, run after the mare and slashed its belly open with his sword before it could cause too much disruption.

Despite the lack of evidence, it is almost certain that both sides fought fiercely during this battle. There were Mitannian auxiliaries within the city. According to Amenemhab's inscription, this was not a long siege but an assault — 'His majesty sent forth every valiant man in his army, in order to breach the new wall which Kadesh had made'.[54] Amenemhab claimed that he was the first to go over the wall, followed by the other valiant Egyptian veterans.

**Assault on walls of
Kadesh**

The city which had caused so much trouble for Thutmose was at last defeated. That it was a complete victory is shown by the fact that there is no record of further troubles in the north or expeditions to Syria during the remainder of Thutmose's reign.

The Gebel Barkal stela sums up the attributes of this greatest of warrior pharaohs.

> A king is he, mighty of arm, the excellent fortress of his armies, the iron wall of his people. He attacks every land with his sword, without there being millions of men behind him, throwing and striking his target every time he stretches out his hand. His arrows do not miss; mighty of arm, his equal does not exist, Montu, on the battlefield.[55]

An evaluation of Thutmose III as a military leader

When Thutmose III embarked on his extraordinary series of campaigns between years 22 and 42, he was motivated by:

- the need to regain Palestine and southern Syria and to punish the rebellious princes
- a desire to expand Egypt's borders
- an ambition to emulate the exploits of his famous grandfather, Thutmose I.

According to the sources, he achieved all three aims.

Successes, losses and the sources

Thutmose's inscriptions emphasise several times that the accounts of his campaigns are truthful. Although what was recorded may be accurate, it must be remembered that god-kings did not record losses and serious setbacks. Historians are cautious when using official inscriptions. They read between the lines and supplement official records from other sources. Despite the apparent abundance of source material for Thutmose's campaigns, many of the inscriptions are fragmentary and selective, providing more information about the amount of booty and tribute collected than about Thutmose's tactics and strategy.

Thutmose had his setbacks, such as the lost opportunity to take Megiddo which necessitated a long siege for which he had not planned. It is obvious that some of Thutmose's campaigns were less than successful otherwise he would not have had to return several times to recapture areas taken previously. For example, Arvad was captured during his fifth campaign but in the following year Thutmose was forced to punish it again. Also, two years after his supposedly great defeat of the Mitanni and their allies (the eighth campaign), the king returned to northern Syria to once again subdue the princes of that region. Northern Syria was always very difficult to control.

Evidence of setbacks

However, the evidence for his successes includes:

Evidence of successes

- the gifts sent to Thutmose III by the great kings of Babylon, Assyria, Khatte, Cyprus and Crete
- the continued payment of tribute from Syria as recorded in detail in the tombs of Rekhmire, Puemere and Menkheperreseneb
- the lack of any military operations in Syria from year 42 until his death in year 54.

Thutmose as a leader of men

What can be deduced from the sources about his military leadership?

Thutmose not only led his men into battle but also exhibited great personal courage on a number of occasions, which must have filled his men with admiration and confidence. In his tomb inscriptions, his officer, Amenemhab, commented a number of times on the king's bravery. At the time when his men felt apprehensive about taking the narrow mountain road from Yehem via Aruna to Megiddo, Thutmose took the lead — 'None shall go forth in the way before my majesty' and he went forward 'at the head of his army to show the way'.[56] He also led his army into battle at Megiddo.

Personal bravery

However, personal bravery alone does not make a good leader. To what extent he consulted with his officers is not known. The records give one instance, prior to Megiddo, when he asked for their opinion about the best route to take. He did not heed their advice on that occasion because it seems that he was prepared to take a calculated risk in order to surprise the enemy. However, when his officers appealed to him to wait for the rear of the army to catch up, he saw the need to be cautious and agreed.

Consultations with officers

He rebuked his troops when necessary; for example, when their greed to take booty after the battle lost them the chance of capturing Megiddo and the Syrian princes inside the city. On the other hand, he seemed to know when to give his men some leeway; for example, when they were drunk every day after the capture of Arvad.

Ability to handle men

Thutmose as a tactician

Apart from the Battle of Megiddo, there is no other information about the tactics used by Thutmose, so it is very hard to make a fair assessment of his ability.

When Thutmose chose to march towards Megiddo via the Aruna mountain pass, he had already received information that the enemy army was divided, one division south of the Kina Valley and the other near Taanach. He knew that he would be able to surprise them and believed that they were already beaten. When the entire Egyptian army moved out onto the plain and, possibly before they encamped for the night, Thutmose had deployed part of his army to the north-west of the city, with the southern wing one kilometre south of Megiddo. His deployment of the troops allowed him to prevail over the enemy on the day of battle.

Thutmose as a strategist

There is no doubt about Thutmose's ability to plan an entire campaign or series of campaigns to achieve his ends. The best evidence for this comes from those carried out in years 29–33 (the fifth to eighth campaigns).

His strategy for dealing with Kadesh and Mitanni involved:

- campaigning during the harvest season, when his enemies were most vulnerable
- advancing in a methodical way
- transporting his army to the Syrian coastline by sea
- securing the coastal cities to ensure their loyalty
- provisioning the coastal cities with food and other military requirements
- capturing the Syrian strongholds of the interior (such as Tunip and Kadesh) before proceeding further north and east
- building cedar boats at Byblos to be used by the army for crossing the Euphrates River
- ravaging the countryside (harvesting the gain and cutting down the trees) around captured cities to maximise his victories.

Although Thutmose III had emulated some of the deeds of his grandfather (Thutmose I), he far surpassed him in his achievements.

The evidence suggests that Thutmose I's march as far as the Euphrates met with little opposition and was more in the nature of a raid. He did not capture and secure key fortresses along the way. Thutmose III, on the other hand, followed a carefully planned strategy, carried out over a number of years. He faced some serious opposition as he systematically advanced northward making sure of his control of each area before he progressed further.

Thutmose as an organiser

Unlike his grandfather, who made no attempt to bring the cities of northern Syria permanently under Egyptian control, Thutmose implemented a number of effective methods to subjugate and maintain control of the areas he gained. These are summarised below. Thutmose:

- administered oaths of loyalty after Megiddo and possibly readministered these on a regular basis
- set up a system of limited colonisation. The fields around Megiddo were given to Egyptian cultivators
- replaced some princes and took hostages. This was an attempt to ensure permanent loyalty. Children of chiefs were taken to Egypt to be educated. Eventually these pro-Egyptian princes would take the place of their fathers
- carried out frequent parades of power. Occasional shows of force and personal appearances led to a tradition of the 'King's fury'
- imposed an annual tribute. Slaves, grain, cattle, fruit and luxury items were demanded from the vassal princes
- left garrisons in strategic cities and built at least one fortress in Lebanon and there may have been others. Military commanders were left with garrisons to control the surrounding region and to ensure the payment of tribute
- established supply depots in coastal cities. This was essential as the army moved further and further north. These cities had to ensure that they were well prepared for the arrival of the pharaoh
- appointed an *overseer of all northern lands* with his headquarters at Gaza. Djehuty had accompanied Thutmose abroad and remained to administer the conquered territories. This official delegated responsibility to commissioners who were responsible for large areas
- set up a system of envoys and messengers. These men acted as the eyes and ears of the king.

For further information on the organisation of the Egyptian empire, refer to Chapter 15.

From the evidence available, it appears that Thutmose III was certainly 'valiant like Montu' and in Breasted's words, 'unquestionably the greatest military leader of ancient Egypt'.[57]

Methods used to control conquered territories

Thutmose and Nubia

Although there appear to have been several military expeditions to Nubia during Thutmose's co-regency with Hatshepsut, Wawat and Kush (Lower and Upper Nubia) had been substantially subdued during the reigns of his predecessors. The lists of conquered Nubian cities, inscribed by Thutmose III on the walls of Karnak Temple, were those that were already paying tribute.

Two expeditions, late in his sole reign, set the boundary of the Egyptian empire in Nubia at Napata. In year 47 he set up a stela in the temple at

Gebel Barkal, recording his successful Asiatic campaigns. This was probably intended to impress his Nubian subjects. In year 50, the year of his last military campaign, he once again marched south. When he reached the First Cataract he ordered the canal, built by the Middle Kingdom ruler, Senwosret III, to be cleaned out 'after he had found it stopped up with stones, so that no ship sailed upon it'.[58]

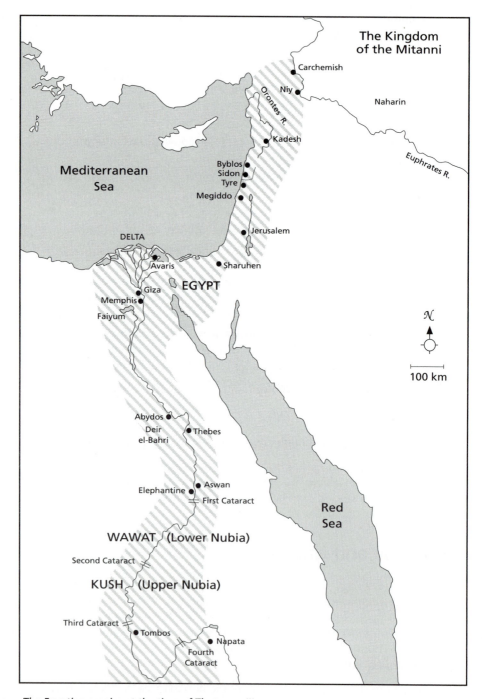

The Egyptian empire at the time of Thutmose III

Three men who helped Thutmose administer his empire

Djeuty

It appears that the first man appointed to serve as *overseer of northern lands* was Djeuty. Although his tomb has never been found and his exploits are only known from a later legend, he was a historical figure as confirmed by funerary items bearing his name.

Overseer of all northern lands

The story associated with him concerns the capture of the Palestinian coastal town of Joppa which was put under siege. This may have occurred before he was made overseer of northern lands. Djeuty, who was besieging Joppa, formulated a plan to trick the ruler of that city. He supposedly invited the prince of Joppa and his retainers to visit his army headquarters. When the Palestinians arrived they were entertained lavishly and all, except the prince, became drunk. When the prince asked to see Thutmose's club, Djeuty knocked him unconscious with it and then tied him up. Djeuty sent a message to Joppa, as if from the prince, announcing that he had captured the Egyptian general and was returning with him and considerable booty. Two hundred Egyptian soldiers hid themselves in baskets and, accompanied by 500 Egyptians acting as prisoners, entered the city. Once inside the walls, the soldiers in the baskets emerged and without too much opposition took control of the city.

Nehi

In the southern lands, Thutmose was ably represented by Nehi, Viceroy of Kush. His tomb records the 'bringing of tribute of the southern countries consisting of gold, ivory and ebony'.[59] Refer to Chapter 15 for information concerning the duties of this important official.

Viceroy of Kush

Intef

The royal herald, Intef, accompanied the king on his campaigns. While abroad, his tasks were:

Royal herald

- to exercise a kind of police control wherever the pharaoh went
- to go ahead of the pharaoh and prepare the residences and palaces for Thutmose's arrival
- to communicate to foreign countries the amount of tribute they were required to pay and verify that they had paid it
- to report to pharaoh anybody who had acted courageously and who deserved rewards.

He also acted as an envoy, reporting to the pharaoh all that he saw and heard. In Egypt he communicated messages from the people to the pharaoh and communicated to the appropriate people commissions given by the pharaoh.

Thutmose and Amun-Re, god of empire

Thutmose attributed all his military successes to Amun-Re.

> His majesty commanded to cause that the victories which his father Amun had given him should be recorded upon the stone wall in the temple which his majesty made anew for his father, Amun, setting forth each expedition by its name, together with the plunder which his majesty brought therefrom. It was done according to all the commands which his father, Re, gave to him [ ][60]

Dedications

The king repaid the god's support by lavishing him with larger offerings, feasts, wealth, lands, slaves and buildings. Some of these gifts are depicted in a relief in a corridor of the Hall of Annals in the Temple of Amun at Karnak. They include obelisks, cedar flagstaves tipped with electrum, a wide range of temple furniture and exquisite vessels and ornaments.

Support for empire by priesthood

Although other gods (such as Ptah of Memphis and Re of Heliopolis) also benefited from the wealth pouring in from the empire and the increased dedications of the king, it was Amun who gained the most. To the priesthood of Amun it was important 'that the domination of the foreigners by Egypt be pushed at all times'.[61] They composed a poem of victory as a constant reminder of the debt of gratitude the king owed Amun. The lines quoted below represent part of the introduction to the poem.

> I gave you valour and victory over all lands.
> I set your might, your fear in every country,
> The dread of you as far as heaven's four supports.
> I magnified your awe in everybody,
> I made your person's fame traverse the Nine Bows.
> The princes of all lands are gathered in your grasp,
> I stretched my own hands out and bound them for you.
> I fettered Nubia's Bowman by ten thousand thousands,
> The northerners a hundred thousand captives.
> I made your enemies succumb beneath your soles.
> So that you crushed the rebels and the traitors.
> For I bestowed on you the earth, its length and breadth,
> Westerners and easterners are under your command.[62]

As well as the gifts and buildings dedicated to Amun, Thutmose recorded that he made every law, regulation and enactment in the interests of Amun.

The king was a pious man and he emphasised to the priests that they must carry out their duties properly. He instructed them 'to be vigilant concerning your duty, be ye not careless concerning all your rules; be ye pure, be ye clean concerning divine things, take heed concerning matters of transgression, guard your heart lest your speech [ ], every man looking to his own steps therein'.[63] This is followed with a request for them to make regular offerings for the king's well-being.

A relief of Thutmose III and Amun from the Temple of Karnak

According to Breasted, 'the beginning of Thutmose's conquests of Asia marks a sudden and profound change in the cult of Amun, occasioned by the enormous and disproportionate wealth which from now on is poured into his treasury'.[64]

The administration of Egypt under Thutmose III

Although, for the first 20 years of his sole reign, Thutmose spent a large part of each year beyond the borders of Egypt, the administration of the country ran smoothly. When Thutmose returned from campaigning each year he appears to have put as much effort into the government of Egypt as he did into his military activities.

Hatshepsut had left an efficient administrative system and many of the officials of the co-regency, such as Puemere, continued to serve Thutmose III. He also had a number of highly competent new appointees (who did not work under Hatshepsut) on whom he could rely to watch over the administration of the land. For example, Rekhmire and Menkheperreseneb.

Competent and reliable officials

The officials on whom the king relied totally were the viziers. Although there was a northern vizier governing from Memphis, and a southern vizier with his headquarters at Thebes, very little is known about the former. It seems that the southern vizier was superior to his northern colleague.

Viziers

During the second half of Thutmose's reign, the southern vizier was Rekhmire, whose tomb in the necropolis at Thebes is the most important single source of information on the government of Egypt during the Eighteenth Dynasty. Rekhmire's tomb included the following valuable information, which is treated in detail in Chapters 15 and 16:

Rekhmire and the evidence from his tomb

- Details about his appointment as vizier.
- Instructions from the king regarding the administration of his office, particularly with regard to justice.
- The duties of a vizier, such as the daily audiences in the vizier's hall, daily conference with the king and daily reports from the treasurer. This is followed by a description of specific duties which include:
  - reception of petitions
  - inspection of taxes. This is the only complete list of the taxes paid by local officials of Upper Egypt
  - reception of the dues to the Temple of Amun
  - inspections of monuments
  - inspections of craftsmen
  - reception of foreign tribute.

Another influential official was Menkheperreseneb. He was the high priest of Amun, *overseer of the houses of gold and silver* (treasurer) and chief 'architect'. In his tomb, Menkheperreseneb is shown in charge of Thutmose's building works at Karnak, and receiving tribute from Asia and treasure from the mines of Africa.

High priest of Amun

Judging by the number of fine tombs in the Theban necropolis, more than 100 high officials must have served Thutmose III. Each one of these officials headed vast bureaucracies of lesser officials and scribes. Refer to Chapter 16 for detailed information about the administration of Egypt.

Thutmose III's building program

> Thutmose built with the same energy as he had fought against Mitanni.[65]

Thutmose's building activities stretched from Kom el Hisn in the delta to Gebel Barkal (Napata) deep in Nubia. His buildings were found at almost every important site along the Nile. Unfortunately, few have survived. The ones we know about are listed in the table below.

Sites in Egypt	Sites in Nubia
Delta — Kom el Hisn and other unidentified sites	El-Dakka
Heliopolis	Quban
Kom Medinet Ghurab	Faras
Dendara	Buhen
Abydos	Semna
Nag el-Madamud	Sai
Thebes	Argo
Armant	Gebel Barkal
El-Tod	
Esna	
Kom Ombo	

Like his predecessors, he devoted most of his efforts to the Temple of Amun at Karnak. Details of these buildings are found on the great Karnak Building Stela. This inscription records those buildings erected by Thutmose after the beginning of his wars of conquests.

Because the colonnaded hall of Thutmose I (built between pylons four and five) was made useless as a ceremonial hall by the erection of Hatshepsut's obelisks, Thutmose partially renewed his grandfather's building and built a new ceremonial hall of his own (the Festival Hall) to the east of that of Thutmose I.

Partial renewal of his grandfather's monument

Only the northern section of his grandfather's entrance hall was rebuilt. This was the place where Thutmose III supposedly had received the oracle concerning his accession to the throne. He replaced the original cedar columns with sandstone ones, approximately 17 metres high. Thutmose recorded that they were 'painted with figures of my father Amun, together with figures of my majesty, and figures of my father (grandfather), the Good God, Thutmose I'. This section was roofed over.[66]

He left the southern section because the bases of Hatshepsut's obelisks took up most of the area. Thutmose simply put a masonry sheathing around her monuments so that only the tops of the obelisks were visible.

Thutmose's Festival Hall
(Menkheperre-is-glorious-in-Monuments)

Immediately after his second campaign (year 24), Thutmose III ordered the construction of a series of colonnaded halls and chambers to the east of his grandfather's hypostyle hall. Thutmose claimed that, although he had to remove a mud brick wall and relocate an ancient shrine to Nun, he did not 'appropriate the monument of another'.[67]

Before the main part of this Festival Hall was completed, he had inscribed on the walls of two of its chambers records of all the exotic plants and flowers that he had collected in Syria during his third campaign (this is often referred to as Thutmose's *botanical garden*; it has been suggested that it may have been his answer to Hatshepsut's depiction of the flora and fauna of Punt) and lists of all his ancestors who had worshipped in this temple. This ancestral chamber, which also contained statues of previous kings, was built as 'monument of his fathers, the kings of Upper and Lower Egypt'.[68] These inscriptions are evidence of Thutmose's intellectual interests as well as his piety and sense of history.

Botanical garden

Hall of ancestors

The enormous, columned main hall was laid out with five aisles. The central nave was supported on sandstone pillars which were tapered to look like the tent poles of the light pavilions used in the Sed festivals. The roof in the centre was higher than at the sides and this provided a clerestory which flooded the entire hall with light.

Features of the Festival Hall

The whole Festival Hall complex and the buildings of Thutmose I were enclosed in a new sandstone wall.

Left: 'Tent-pole' columns and clerestory windows in Thutmose's Festival Hall

Below: Thutmose's Festival Hall

A drawing from the 'botanical garden' reliefs of Thutmose III

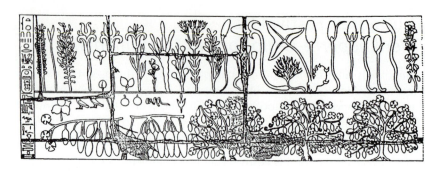

The Temple of Ptah at Karnak

Rest station for the barque of Amun

By Thutmose's reign, this temple in the Karnak precinct had fallen into disrepair. Because it was one of the resting places for the barque of Amun-Re during festival processions, Thutmose rebuilt it. He replaced its brick walls and wooden columns with sandstone and had new doors made from 'cedar of the best of the terraces (Lebanon), mounted with Asiatic copper'.[(69)] He dedicated new temple equipment and commanded that increased offerings be made to Amun and Ptah.

Pylons and obelisks

Like his grandfather, Thutmose built two monumental gateways, referred to now as the sixth and seventh pylons. The latter shows the king in the traditional pose of clubbing his enemies to death. It also records the names of more than 600 cities captured during his northern and southern conquests.

Heb-seds and obelisks

It had become the tradition for Egyptian kings of the Eighteenth Dynasty to erect a pair of obelisks to celebrate their Sed festival. Although a heb-sed was supposedly celebrated after a king had been on the throne for 30 years, this was not always the case (eg, Thutmose I and Hatshepsut). Because of the length of his reign, Thutmose III was able to celebrate many jubilees. There is evidence for four heb-seds with a fifth planned before his death.

From the inscriptional and material remains, it appears that Thutmose III commissioned at least seven obelisks, five of which are known to have been erected at Karnak and two at Heliopolis in the north. Unfortunately, not one obelisk belonging to Thutmose III remains standing at Karnak or anywhere else in Egypt. In both ancient and modern times they were removed to the far corners of the world — London, New York, Istanbul and Rome.

Obelisks commissioned for Karnak

A variety of sources (official inscriptions and the tombs of Puemre and Menkheperreseneb) refer to at least four obelisks erected at Karnak before year 42. The fifth and tallest one (35 metres high), now referred to as the Lateran obelisk and found in Rome, did not have a partner. The record shows that it was a single obelisk 'the first beginning of erecting a single obelisk in Thebes'.[(70)] Thutmose died before this one had been inscribed and erected. It supposedly lay on its side until his grandson, Thutmose IV, erected it 35 years later.

Two more obelisks were erected in front of the pylon of the temple of Re-Atum at Heliopolis and dedicated to Horakhte (a form of the sun god) on his fourth jubilee.

Obelisks at Heliopolis

The harem at Medinet el-Ghurab

At the mouth of the Faiyum, Thutmose III built a huge mud-brick harem palace complex, known as *Mer-Wer*, which housed a community of royal women, children and some male administrators. The complex, which functioned as an independent economic unit, comprised a temple, huge halls, storerooms and living areas (refer to Chapter 16).

The mortuary temple and tomb

Like Hatshepsut's, Thutmose's mortuary temple *(Djeser-Akhet)* was built at Deir el-Bahri, although very little of it has survived. It seems to have been similar in design to that of his stepmother/aunt. Because it was built on higher ground, it may have dominated *Djeser-Djeseru*. After Hatshepsut's death, *Djeser-Akhet* replaced Hatshepsut's temple as the focus for Amun's Beautiful Festival of the Valley.

Djeser-Akhet

Like his predecessors, Thutmose had his tomb excavated into the cliffs of the Valley of the Kings. The decoration of the main hall of his tomb is very unusual. The yellowish-grey walls are covered with black and red drawings and hieroglyphs from the *Book of What is in the Underworld*. This 'decoration' is quite unlike the vivid paintings in most royal tombs. According to Steindorff and Seele ' the resulting impression is much as if the walls of the entire chamber had been tapestried with an enormous inscribed papyrus'.[71]

Unusual decoration of tomb

Although Thutmose's yellow quartzite sarcophagus was found in the burial chamber, his coffin and mummy were missing. A body, thought to be that of this greatest of kings and now in the Cairo Museum, was found in 1889, among a cache of mummies in the tomb of his son, Amenhotep II.

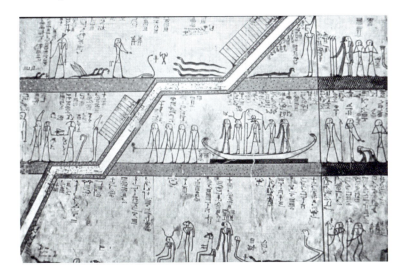

Details of the wall paintings from the tomb of Thutmose III

Conclusion

As well as being a great military leader, administrator and statesman, Thutmose was an energetic builder and a patron of the arts. He showed great piety to both the gods and his ancestors, composed and read literary works, had a keen sense of history and an interest in botany.

His vizier, Rekhmire, recorded that 'there was nothing of which he was ignorant in heaven, in earth or in any quarter of the nether world ... there was nothing he did not know — he was Thoth in everything, there was no affair which he did not complete'.[72]

> If any Egyptian ruler deserves to be honoured by being designated 'the Great', he is a far more fitting candidate than any other ...[73]

Thutmose died in the fifty-fourth year of his reign. He was succeeded by Amenhotep, the son of his second great wife, Merytre-Hatshepsut.

Thutmose's immediate successors — Amenhotep II and Thutmose IV

Amenhotep II — *Powerful Bull, Great in Strength*

In an age when kings advertised their superhuman qualities, 'only Amenhotep II, in his height and physique, and what is known of his character approximates to the quintessence of the hero'.[74]

Most of the Thutmosid kings were on the short and stocky side; Thutmose III, for example, was only about 160 centimetres tall. Amenhotep, judging from his mummy, was tall and well built.

Promoted the image of the superhuman pharaoh

Although his father was almost certainly the greatest military pharaoh who ever sat on the throne of Egypt and also something of a scholar, Amenhotep appears to have been superior in sporting accomplishments and highly competitive. Unlike his father, who often showed clemency to his enemies, Amenhotep II was a ruthless warrior, often resorting to brutality to demonstrate his power.

Historians may be sceptical of some of his exploits, but Gardiner maintains that there are 'examples of his athletic prowess too individual to be rejected out of hand'.[75]

Amenhotep's early years

Amenhotep was born in the northern capital of Memphis and was given the traditional training of a crown prince. Even from an early age it appears that he enjoyed sporting activities. In the tomb of a noble, called Min, Amenhotep is shown as a child being taught how to use a bow and arrow. The text describes him 'enjoying himself by learning about shooting in Pharaoh's Broad Hall of Thinis'.[76]

His ability with horses was already apparent when he was a youth. A stela, erected by him near the Sphinx, describes how 'when he was a lad, he loved his horses, he delighted in them, he was persevering in exercising them and knowing their ways, skilled in training them'.[77] When Thutmose III heard about his son's ability, he gave orders that he be given charge of the best horses from the royal stables in Memphis. Amenhotep was instructed 'to take care of them, to make them obedient, and to give them strong treatment if they (rebelled) against him'.[78]

By the age of 18, 'he knew every craft of Montu with no one like him on the field of combat'.[79] He was renowned for his ability to run, row and use the bow.

While Crown Prince, Amenhotep also held the position of high priest of Ptah of Memphis.

Sporting abilities obvious from childhood

Amenhotep's accession to the throne

For approximately two years, from the age of 18, Amenhotep shared the throne of Egypt with his father. The great general, Amenemhab, records that when Thutmose III died, 'King Akheprure, Son of Re, Amenhotep, given life, was established upon the throne of his father, he assumed the royal titulary'.[80] The new king's official names reflected his strength and physical prowess:

- His Horus name has been interpreted as *Powerful Bull, Great in Strength* or *Strong Bull, Great in Vigour.*
- His Golden Horus name was *He Who Seizes all the Lands by his Strength.*

Throughout his 25-year reign, Amenhotep II continued to emphasise and demonstrate his military and athletic abilities.

Titulary reflected his physical prowess

Amenhotep II shooting arrows through a copper target, from the temple of Amun at Karnak

Amenhotep's campaigns

It is known that Amenhotep led two (possibly three) campaigns into western Asia and appeared in Nubia at least once.

The sources for his Asiatic expeditions (a stela from Karnak, a copy of the same stela found at Memphis and two others found at Elephantine and Amada in Nubia) are fragmentary and make it difficult to clearly follow his campaigns.

Sometime soon after the death of Thutmose III, the cities of Syria revolted against Egypt as a test of the calibre of the new pharaoh. Amenhotep II recorded that during his first campaign he overthrew all those who rebelled against him. He fought a battle at Shemesh-Edam in Northern Palestine, followed by another somewhere near the bend of the Orontes River. On his return journey, the city of Niy opened its gates to him and

Amenhotep in Syria and Palestine

he was forced to punish what is believed to have been the city of Ugarit because the inhabitants were threatening the Egyptian garrison. When he reached the district of Takhsi (near Kadesh) he plundered 30 cities and then forced the inhabitants of Kadesh to take an oath of loyalty.

Amenhotep's second military campaign focused on the towns of Palestine from which he took numerous prisoners and plunder. According to Gardiner, however, the number of captives claimed by Amenhotep for this campaign is far too high.

The surviving records focus on the king's fearless and ruthless exploits. For example:

- When the king was in the vicinity of Katna, north of Kadesh, he saw a number of Asiatic chariots approaching him from the rear. Amenhotep, who 'was equipped with his weapons of war', turned and raced towards them.

  They panicked when they saw him alone among them. Then his majesty felled their commander himself with his battle axe. He carried off this Asiatic at the side of his chariot, and also captured his team, his chariot and all his weapons of war.[81]

Fearless and ruthless behaviour

- At Takhsi, in the region of Kadesh, Amenhotep supposedly captured seven princes with his own hands.

- Further south at Khashabu, he went out in his chariot 'alone and without companion, and returned in a short time bringing sixteen living Maryannu at the side of his chariot, twenty hands at the foreheads of his horses and sixty cattle driven in front of him'.[82]

- In the Plain of Sharon, he also captured a messenger from Naharin with a clay tablet around his neck and took him to Egypt on the side of his chariot.

- On his return to Egypt 'he slew with his own weapon the seven princes who had been in the district of Takhsi' and then 'placed them head downward at the prow of his majesty's barge'[83] for the journey to Thebes. He displayed six of the bodies on the city walls of Thebes while the remaining body 'was taken up-river to Nubia and hanged on the walls of Napata, in order to cause

Brutal treatment of prisoners

to be manifest the victories of his majesty, for ever and ever in all lands and countries of the land of the Negro'.[84]

- Faced with the problem of guarding the booty and prisoners taken during his Palestine campaign, Amenhotep supposedly surrounded them with a trench filled with fire. With only a few retainers, the pharaoh stood guard all night, far from his army.

If these exploits were intended to impress his opponents, he appears to have been successful. The Memphis stela records that when the princes of Naharin, Khatte and Sangar heard of Amenhotep's victories they sent gifts and prayed for peace. The remainder of his 25-year reign was peaceful and tribute continued to pour into Egypt.

Foreign kings and princes sued for peace

Buildings

Like his predecessors, Amenhotep added to the Temple of Amun at Karnak, but claimed in the Armad stela that he was 'a king with heart favourable to the buildings of all gods'.[85]

At Karnak, he repaired the southern section of Thutmose I's hypostyle hall, which had been destroyed by the erection of Hatshepsut's obelisks, and added his name to other existing buildings.

Gardiner says that Amenhotep 'preferred to show his piety to the provinces'[86] dedicating temples at Amada in Nubia, at Elephantine and at sites in the delta.

Provincial buildings

The succession

Amenhotep II's *great royal wife* was Tia, believed to have been his half-sister. She was the mother of prince Thutmose who succeeded Amenhotep on the throne. Aldred suggests that an older son may have shared a co-regency with his father, but died before the king.

In keeping with his sporting image, Amenhotep was buried with his bow with which he was supposedly so proficient.

Thutmose IV

It is generally believed that Thutmose IV (Menkheperure) ruled for less than ten years. However, during his short reign there were two significant developments in religion and foreign policy.

Religious developments

Unlike his predecessors, Thutmose IV seemed to be less concerned with promoting the welfare of Amun and more interested in the cult of the sun god of Heliopolis. Why would this be the case?

Promotion of sun cult at Heliopolis

Thutmose supposedly attributed his accession to the throne to the supreme god of Lower Egypt, Re-Horakhte. According to a stela, erected between the paws of the Great Sphinx at Giza, Thutmose dreamt that

Re-Horakhte promised him the crown if he cleared the sand away from the Sphinx. This human-headed lion was the embodiment of the sun god in one of its many forms.

Breasted maintains that the inscription on the stela was a folk tale written at a later date. However, it may have been based on some incident associated with Thutmose IV who probably hunted frequently in the vicinity of the Sphinx.

> One of those days it came to pass that the king's son, Thutmose, came coursing at midday, and he rested in the shadow of this great god. A vision of asleep seized him at the hour when the sun was at its zenith and he found the majesty of this revered god speaking with his own mouth as a father speaks with his son, saying 'Behold thou me! See thou me! my son Thutmose. I am thy father, Harakhti-Khepri-Re-Atum, who will give to thee thy kingdom on earth at the head of the living. Thou shalt wear the white crown and the red crown upon the throne ... Thou shalt be to me a protector for my manner is as I were ailing in all my limbs. The sand of this desert upon which I am, has reached me: turn to me, to have that done which I have desired, knowing that thou art my son, my protector.'[87]

Although Thutmose IV did not turn away from the worship of Amun, he built fewer monuments in Amun's temple at Karnak than his predecessors. His major contribution was to erect the tallest of Thutmose III's obelisks, which had remained on the ground since that king's death 35 years before. (It should be remembered that obelisks were symbols of the sun god.)

First mention of Aten as a god

Thutmose IV had a large commemorative scarab issued, on which the Aten (the disk of the sun) was referred to as a god who led the pharaoh into battle and helped him win victory. The inscription states that the pharaoh hoped that foreigners, like Egyptians, would serve the Aten forever. This reference to a new and universal aspect of the sun was the forerunner of developments that were to occur in the reigns of his son (Amenhotep III) and grandson (Akhenaten).

Changes in foreign policy

Thutmose's reign was a turning point in terms of the empire. The need for major military campaigns in Syria had ended. All that was necessary in the future were some minor raids to keep the frontiers secure. Diplomacy, rather than war, was employed to deal with foreign powers.

Peace, diplomacy and marriage alliances

The king of Mitanni, Artatama, entered into diplomatic relations with Thutmose IV and an alliance was sealed with the arrival of Artatama's daughter to join the pharaoh's harem. This was a pattern which other eastern rulers followed in the succeeding generations and for nearly half a century there was peace and prosperity in Egypt and its empire.

When Thutmose's son, Amenhotep III, came to the throne, Egypt was on the verge of the most magnificent period in its history.

Chapter review

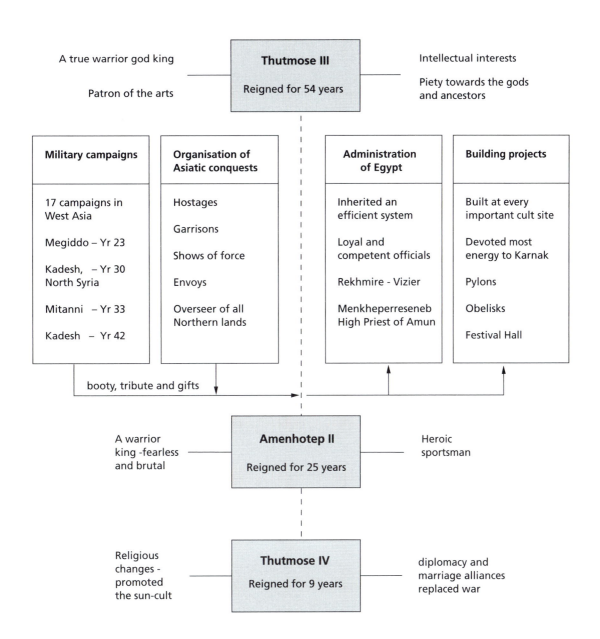

A true warrior god king

Patron of the arts

Thutmose III

Reigned for 54 years

Intellectual interests

Piety towards the gods
and ancestors

Military campaigns	**Organisation of Asiatic conquests**	**Administration of Egypt**	**Building projects**
17 campaigns in West Asia	Hostages	Inherited an efficient system	Built at every important cult site
Megiddo – Yr 23	Garrisons	Loyal and competent officials	Devoted most energy to Karnak
Kadesh, – Yr 30 North Syria	Shows of force	Rekhmire - Vizier	Pylons
Mitanni – Yr 33	Envoys	Menkheperreseneb High Priest of Amun	Obelisks
Kadesh – Yr 42	Overseer of all Northern lands		Festival Hall

booty, tribute and gifts

A warrior
king -fearless
and brutal

Amenhotep II

Reigned for 25 years

Heroic
sportsman

Religious
changes -
promoted
the sun-cult

Thutmose IV

Reigned for 9 years

diplomacy and
marriage alliances
replaced war

REVISION QUESTIONS AND ESSAY TOPICS

1 Read and analyse the following inscription.

The god made the circuit of the hypostyle on both sides of it ... while he searched for [me] in every place. On recognising me behold, he halted!...[I threw myself on] the pavement, I prostrated myself in his presence. He set me before his majesty ... Then they revealed before the people the secrets in the hearts of the gods ...[He opened for] me the doors of heaven; he opened the portals of the horizon of Re. I flew to heaven like a divine hawk ... Re himself established me. I was dignified with the diadems which were upon his head, his serpent-diadem which were upon [my forehead] ...I was presented with the dignities of a god, with ... my diadems.[88]

a Who is 'the god' who made a 'circuit of the hypostyle'?

b What is a hypostyle and to which specific hypostyle is the extract referring?

c Who is the person speaking in this text and what was he doing in the hypostyle? What might the occasion have been?

d Who was it who 'halted' during the circuit?

e What is meant by 'then they revealed before the people the secrets in the hearts of the gods'?

f What is the serpent-diadem?

g What is a word which means a pronouncement by a god?

h Why was this incident inscribed on the temple walls?

2 Complete the following tasks based on Thutmose's Megiddo campaign (year 23).

a When and where were the records of Thutmose's campaign of year 23 inscribed?

b Why are these records so significant?

c What evidence is there to support the statement that Thutmose probably regarded this campaign as his major military achievement?

d Why did the Syrian chiefs and princes choose Megiddo as the place best suited to make a stand against the Egyptians?

e Describe in several sentences the most significant incident that occurred at each of the following places:
   * Yehem
   * Aruna
   * the Valley of Kina
   * the Plain of Esdraelon.

f Why were Thutmose and his troops forced to spend seven months besieging Megiddo? How did the city eventually fall to the Egyptians?

g What was the significance of Thutmose's victory at Megiddo?

3 The figure below shows part of a series of reliefs inscribed on a wall of the Temple of Karnak.

a   What is the name given by Egyptologists to this series of reliefs?

b   In what part of the Temple of Karnak were these reliefs found?

c   When were they inscribed?

d   Why were they inscribed?

e   What do they reflect about the person who chose to have them inscribed?

4 Compare the three extracts below and then answer the following questions.

From the *Annals*:

His majesty arrived at the city of Niy, going southward when [ ] his majesty, having set up a tablet in Naharin, extending the boundaries of Egypt.[(89)]

From the Gebel Barkal stela (Nubia):

Another instance of the victory which Re ordained for me: he repeated for me a great deed of valour at the lake of Niy. He let me meet droves of elephants, and my majesty fought them in a herd of 120.[(90)]

From the tomb inscription of Thutmose's general Amenemhab:

Again I beheld another excellent deed which the Lord of the two Lands did in Niy. He hunted 120 elephants, for the sake of their tusks and — . I engaged the largest which was among them, which fought against his majesty; I cut off his hand (trunk) while he was alive before his majesty, while I stood in the water between two rocks. Then my lord rewarded me with gold ...[(91)]

a   During which of Thutmose's campaigns did this incident occur?

b   What is the connection between the two statements, 'having set up a tablet in Naharin' and 'repeated for me a great deed of valour at the lake of Niy'?

c   What is the major difference between these three records? Why does the third extract contain more details than the second text?

5 An extract from the Poem of Victory:

> ... I came to let you tread on Djahi's* chiefs
> I spread them under your feet throughout their lands...
> I came to let you tread on those of Asia,
> To smite the Asians' heads in Retjenu ...
> I came to let you tread on eastern lands,
> To crush the dwellers in the realm of God's land† ...
> I came to let you tread on western lands
> Keftiu, Isy# are in awe of you ...
> I came to let you tread on lowlanders.
> Mitanni's regions cringe in fear of you ...
> I came to let you tread on islanders,
> The sea-borne people hear your battle cry ...
> I came to let you tread on Nubians;
> As far as Shat you hold them in your grasp ...[92]

a Who wrote this poem and for what purpose?

b Which of these areas did Thutmose conquer?

c Explain why the others are included in this poem of victory?

6 Identify the following text:

> He could not be approached in fleetness. Strong was he of arms, one who never wearied when he took the oar; but rowed at the stern of his falcon-boat as the best of two hundred men. After casting off, when they had finished half an iteru they were worn out and their bodies exhausted, nor could they draw breath any more. His majesty, however, was mighty under his oar of twenty cubits (about ten metres) ... He did this also: he drew three hundred stiff bows, comparing the workmanship of the artisans who had made them ... He entered his northern garden and found set up for him four targets of Asiatic copper of a span (7.5 centimetres) in their thickness and with twenty cubits between one pole and its fellow. Then his majesty appeared in a chariot ... he seized his bow and grasped four arrows at once. He rode northward shooting at them ... His arrows came forth from the back of one of them while he attacked another.[93]

a To which pharaoh does this text refer?

b Where was it found?

c What was the purpose of recording this information?

d What evidence is there that there could be some truth in these claims?

e Provide evidence from other sources to show that this pharaoh promoted the warrior image?

7 Essay topic

Comment on the statement that Thutmose III was responsible for creating the Egyptian Empire.

---

* Djahi is thought to have been the coastal part of Palestine.

† God's land refers to lands to the south and east of Egypt; for example, Punt.

The Keftiu were the people from the island of Crete.

CHAPTER
12

'The Dazzling Sun-disk'
— Amenhotep III

During the reign of Amenhotep III, Egypt reached a 'zenith of magnificence'.[1] Amenhotep has been described by various authors as Egypt's *Sun-King* and as *Amenhotep the Magnificent*. In the records of his own day he was referred to as *The Dazzling Sun-disk*.

He reaped the benefits from the conquests of his predecessors, Thutmose III, Amenhotep II and Thutmose IV. At his accession, Egypt was the unrivalled leader of the known world.

Amenhotep III ruled his empire through diplomacy rather than force and his messengers travelled freely throughout the kingdoms and states of the East. He communicated and exchanged gifts with the great kings of Babylon and Naharin (Mitanni).

The incredible wealth pouring in to Egypt at this time, through trade and tribute, enabled Amenhotep to initiate the greatest building boom of the Eighteenth Dynasty — from the delta to Nubia. Like his predecessors he lavished most of his attention on the city of Thebes and dedicated vast wealth to the god Amun. Amenhotep III built temples at Karnak and Luxor and constructed an enormous mortuary temple and a magnificent complex of palaces on the west bank of the Nile. The southern capital had never experienced such a period of prosperity.

It was a time of great artistic flowering. Craftsmen displayed 'a confident and complete command of their medium, which was never again equalled in the 1500 years Egypt's pharaonic culture survived'.[2]

Court life was fashionable and elegant and Amenhotep surrounded himself with a group of brilliant administrators. One of these was Amenhotep, son of Hapu, *King's Scribe of Recruits*.

Amenhotep as a young man

Throughout his reign Amenhotep was supported by the *Great Royal Wife*, Queen Tiye, whose influence on the government of Egypt was not only considerable but unquestioned.

Chief sources for the period

The major written sources of evidence for the reign of Amenhotep III are the inscriptions on:

Stelae

- stelae found at Thebes, the First Cataract, Konosso, Semna and Bubastis in the delta. The most important of these stelae is the so-called Building Inscription which originally stood in Amenhotep's mortuary temple and recorded the king's building works in honour of Amun-Re. The stela suffered severe damage during the reign of Amenhotep's son, Akhenaten. The other stelae are part of the official propaganda regarding a Nubian campaign in regnal year 5

Scarab bulletins

- commemorative scarabs. Although small seal scarabs, inscribed with a few words, were used by earlier kings for commemorating important events, Amenhotep III issued large scarabs, inscribed with 'a whole narrative or its equivalent'.[3] He used them for spreading information (the official propaganda) throughout Egypt and the provinces. These large scarabs, produced in their hundreds, recorded some of the events he considered important in his reign such as his marriage to Tiye and the Mitannian princess, Gilu-khepa. They were also used to promote the image of the sporting pharaoh

One of a series of 'bulletin' scarabs commemorating the building of a lake for Queen Tiye

Temple walls

- the walls of the temples of Amun-Re at Luxor and Karnak and the Temple of Soleb in Nubia. On the walls of the Luxor temple, which in itself is testimony to the scale and magnificence of Amenhotep's building program, is an account of Amenhotep's divine birth. This appears to have been copied from the birth scenes of Hatshepsut. Amenhotep's pylon at Karnak (the third pylon) which now forms the back wall of the great hypostyle hall of Seti I and Ramesses II, records details about the building of the pylon. The Temple of Soleb in Nubia provides evidence of the cult of the king, established by Amenhotep III, and supplements other information on his building projects

- a statue of one of the most famous of Amenhotep's officials — Amenhotep, son of Hapu

- the tomb walls of Amenhotep's chief officials such as Ramose, *Vizier of the South*

Amarna Letters

- clay tablet letters, inscribed in a cuneiform script (the language of international communication). In 1887 a cache of 377 clay tablets was found in the remains of the city of Akhetaten (El Amarna). These so-called 'Amarna Letters' were communications from foreign kings (Babylonian, Mitannian and Assyrian) and despatches from Syrian, Phoenician and Palestinian princelings and governors to the Egyptian court. They were addressed to Amenhotep III and Akhenaten and are the chief source for information on foreign affairs of the period. This discovery was of far greater historical significance than the tomb of Tutankhamun. Unfortunately these letters present a one-sided view of the situation in the East as there are very few replies from the Egyptian pharaohs.

Amenhotep's accession and marriage to Tiye

Amenhotep was the son of Thutmose IV and Queen Mutemweya, who some historians have suggested may have been the daughter of Artatama, the king of Mitanni. Since the name of the Mitannian princess married to Thutmose IV is not mentioned in the records, there is little evidence for this belief. Aldred maintains that she was an Egyptian and came from an influential military family from Akhmin, 240 kilometres north of Thebes. His mother's non-royal background may have prompted Amenhotep to record an account of his divine birth similar to that of Hatshepsut.

King's Mother, Mutemweya

When Thutmose IV died Amenhotep was only a young boy, possibly around twelve years of age, perhaps even younger. Aldred believes that he couldn't have been more than nine. His mother, Queen Mutemweya, probably acted as his regent. There are two pieces of evidence which point to this.

Possible regency

1 One of Mutemweya's epithets was *All that she says is done for her*. This suggests that she may have had some considerable influence during Amenhotep's early years.

2 In the tomb of Hekareshu, *Overseer of the Royal Nurses*, there is a picture a young Amenhotep on his throne with Queen Mutemweya standing behind him with her hand affectionately around his shoulder.

Possibly soon after Amenhotep's accession to the throne or even as part of his coronation ceremonies, the young king was married to Tiye. To

Marriage to Tiye

Green steatite head of a youthful Queen Tiye

announce this important event, Amenhotep ordered the first set of commemorative scarabs to be inscribed and circulated around the kingdom.

> **Live Mighty Bull, Shining in Truth; Establisher of Laws, Quieter of the Two Lands, Great in Strength, Smiter of the Asiatics, Good God, Ruler of Thebes, Lord of Strength, Mighty of Valour, Nebmare, Amenhotep (III), who is given life and the Great King's Wife Tiye, who liveth. The name of her father is Yuya, the name of her mother is Thuya. She is the wife of a mighty king whose southern boundary is as far as Karoy and northern as far as Naharin.**[4]

According to Breasted this was the first time that a queen's name was inserted into the royal titulary, a practice which was followed by Akhenaten.

Historians have pointed out that the so-called *Marriage Scarab* emphasised Tiye's non-royal background by referring to her parents simply as Yuya and Thuya with no titles. Aldred questions this view and provides evidence for believing that her family was an important and influential one from the town of Akhmin. He goes even further and suggests that Tiye's father, Yuya, may have been the brother of Queen Mutemweya.

Tiye's father was referred to as *Father of the God*, a term used for the father-in-law of the king. He was a prophet and *overseer of the cattle of Min*, the local god of Akhmin and at some stage in his career he held the position of *commander of chariotry*. Thuya, the mother of Queen Tiye was high in the cult of Amun. She was *superior of the harem of Amun* at Thebes and *superior in the harem of Min* at Akhmin. Amenhotep honoured his queen's parents by allowing them to be buried in a richly endowed tomb in the vicinity of the Valley of the Kings.

Inlaid ebony head of an aging Queen Tiye

The representations of Tiye indicate that she had a rather exotic appearance and this has led historians to suggest that her family originally came from Nubia.

No matter what her background, she became *great royal wife* and appears to have had Amenhotep's affection and confidence. He was very rarely represented without her and right from the beginning of his marriage he associated her name with his on official inscriptions. In statuary she was depicted often on an equal level (size) with her husband and in the tomb of one of Amenhotep's nobles, she was represented as a sphinx. Such an image was usually reserved for kings.

It seems that he trusted her input in state matters and she was respected by foreign rulers for her diplomatic skills. Her influence over domestic and foreign policy continued during the reign of her son, Akhenaten. Refer to the following chapter.

Throughout his reign, Amenhotep publicly honoured his chief queen who was described as *lady of delight who fills the palace with love*. In year 11, he commissioned a final issue of commemorative scarabs, to inform his people of the construction of a pleasure lake for Queen Tiye, in her city of Djaruka.

> His majesty commanded to make a lake for the Great King's Wife, Tiye, in her city of Djaruka. Its length is 3700 cubits, its width 700 cubits. His majesty celebrated the feasts of the opening of the lake, in the third month of the first season, day 16, when his majesty sailed theron in the royal barge: 'Aten-Gleams'.[5]

According to the scarab inscription, the construction of the lake (400 metres wide and 1.6 kilometres long) took only 15 days. Gardiner finds this hard to believe. Amenhotep also dedicated a temple to Tiye at Soleb in Nubia.

It is believed that Tiye and Amenhotep had seven children — two boys and five girls. The eldest son and heir was named Thutmose. As was the custom for the heirs to the throne during the Eighteenth Dynasty, he became the High Priest of Ptah at Memphis. He was probably destined to marry his sister, Sitamun, the eldest princess; however, he died prematurely. A second son, named after his father, eventually came to the throne as Amenhotep IV (Akhenaten).

Sitamun's name appeared frequently in the inscriptions and about year 30 or 31 she was given the title of *king's great wife*, the same status as her mother. It is not known whether her father actually married her or not, but the title of *king's great wife* meant that she played a prominent role at state and religious functions. Some historians, such as Hayes, maintain that she had a physical relationship with her father and bore him several children (Smenkhkare and Tutankhamun). There is absolutely no proof of this. Another of Amenhotep's daughters, Isit, also held this title.

The remaining three princesses were Henet-to-neb, Nebet-ah and the youngest, probably born late in Amenhotep's reign, Baketaten.

Promotion of the image of the superhuman warrior king

It was essential that early in his reign, Amenhotep, like his predecessors, promote an image of himself as the superhuman, all-conquering warrior king.

The scarab bulletins

Amenhotep advertised his abilities as a great hunter of wild animals in a series of commemorative scarabs issued in years 2 and 10 of his reign.

The wild bull scarab

The earlier series of scarabs claim that, during a hunting trip, probably somewhere in the delta, the young king rounded up a total of 75 wild bulls with the help of a detachment of soldiers.

> His Majesty appeared in his chariot with his whole army behind him. The commanders and enlisted men of the entire army, with the young recruits, were commanded to keep watch over the wild cattle. Behold His Majesty ordered that these wild cattle be driven within a walled enclosure. His Majesty proceeded against all these wild cattle. Tally thereof: 170 wild bulls. Tally of His Majesty's bag in the hunt of this day: 55 wild bulls ... His majesty four days ... tally of these cattle which he captured in the hunt: 20 wild cattle. Total 75 wild cattle.[6]

Aldred suggests that since this event occurred when the king was very young, it seems more likely to have been a military operation with the king in attendance.

Larger scarabs, issued eight years later, recorded that in the first decade of his reign 'his majesty brought down with his own arrows ... fierce lions, 102'.[7] This seems more credible than the previous claims about the wild bulls.

Military propaganda

Owing to the exploits of his predecessors, 'the era of warring in Asia and extending the boundaries of Egypt (was) over'.[8]

There was only one minor revolt in Nubia, which occurred in the fifth year of Amenhotep's reign. The people of the district of Ibhat, south of the Second Cataract, occasionally raided southern Egyptian settlements and it was decided to teach them a lesson.

Promotion of the warrior image

This minor police action, under the leadership of the king's viceroy of Kush, Merimose, was exaggerated into a major victory for the king even though he was only a youth. When the number of the dead and captured (1052) are taken into consideration, the true nature of this affair can be gauged.

Amenhotep III had no opportunity to play the warrior-king but the official records still depicted him as the all-conquering pharaoh. For example:

- His marriage scarab, issued when he was barely a teenager, describes him as *smiter of Asiatics*.
- On a victory tablet set up in his mortuary temple, he is shown driving in his chariot over conquered Syrians with the words 'smiting Naharin with his mighty sword'.[9] There is no evidence of any campaign undertaken in western Asia during his reign.
- The stela at the First Cataract shows the king killing two Nubians. The text described him as leading his troops to victory and like 'a fierce-eyed lion, he seized Kush'.[10]
- The Konosso inscription adds that 'his majesty returned, having triumphed on his first victorious campaign in the land of Kush'.[11]

- A further stela from Bubastis records that during the Nubian campaign 'his majesty smote them himself with the baton which was in his hand'.[12]
- The Semna inscription informs its readers that 'the might of Nebmare took them (rebels in Nubia) in one day, in one hour, making a great slaughter'.[13]

Foreign policy

Even though Amenhotep had to deal with a minor incident in Nubia in year 5 and maintained a military presence in western Asia (forts and garrisons), he governed his empire by a policy of diplomacy. This involved:

- communicating by letter with the great kings of Mitanni, Babylon and Assyria, with the vassal princes of Syria and Palestine and with Egyptian officials
- negotiating alliances with the rulers of the north-east
- adding foreign princesses to the royal harem
- exchanging gifts with brother kings
- employing highly trusted envoys who travelled throughout the east.

Letters

It is interesting to note the forms of address used by the vassal princes of Palestine and Syria when communicating with Amenhotep III. These differ markedly from the forms used by the great kings of Babylon and Mitanni.

Excessive flattery by vassals

Letters from the vassal princes usually began with:

> To the king, my lord, the Sun-god from heaven (name of the vassal prince) thy servant, the servant of the king, and the dirt under his two feet, the ground which he treads. At the two feet of the king, my lord, the Sun-god from heaven, seven times, seven times I fall, both prone and supine.[14]

Such excessive flattery was usually followed by a complaint or explanation of some incident and a plea for the pharaoh's understanding and action.

Complaints and pleas

> Behold I am a faithful servant of the king, and I have not rebelled and I have not sinned, and I do not withhold my tribute, and I do not refuse the requests of my commissioner. Now they wickedly slander me, but let the king, my lord not impute rebellion to me!

> ... Further if the king should write for my wife, how could I withhold her? If the king should write to me, 'Plunge a bronze dagger into thy heart and die!', how could I refuse to carry out the command of the king?[15]

Letters between brother kings

Communications with free and independent rulers, who were categorised as *great kings* and *lesser kings*, were quite different, particularly if they had negotiated a marriage between one of their daughters or sisters and the Egyptian king. In these cases the pharaoh was usually referred to as *my brother*.

> To Nimmuraria (Amenhotep III) the great king, my brother, my brother-in-law, who loves me, and who I also love, speak as follows;[16]

Most of the communications from *brother kings* to Amenhotep were written in a friendly but self-assured tone. However, they reveal that the relationship between Amenhotep and these kings was 'built upon a purely materialistic foundation'.[17]

Diplomatic marriages

Diplomatic marriages were not only a means of maintaining friendly relations, but a way of obtaining luxury goods. Foreign princesses were sent to Egypt with rich dowries and accompanied by caravans full of luxurious gifts. Their fathers expected valuable items, particularly gold, in return.

There was a continuing obligation on the *brother* kings, to write letters inquiring about each other's welfare. Judging by the complaints of the Babylonian king, Kadashman-enlil, Amenhotep did not write frequently enough and occasionally treated him with less respect than he deserved. It seems that Amenhotep took six years to reply to one Kadashman-enlil's letters and failed to write when he was ill.

Business transactions

In addition, a regular exchange of 'gifts' was expected after the marriage. This was nothing more than trade carried on between two rulers and often involved bitter complaints and considerable haggling. These kings did not hesitate to reprimand each other for some failure to live up to their side of the transaction. Even if one of the kings died before a promised transaction could be completed, the other demanded satisfaction from the successor. Amenhotep III had promised Tushratta of Mitanni two solid gold statues, but died before they could be delivered. Akhenaten did not honour his father's promise and when reprimanded, delivered two wooden statues covered with gold. This incident caused much bitterness.

One-sided marriage arrangements

Marriage arrangements were one-sided. No Egyptian princess was ever sent to a foreign court. Perhaps the Egyptian pharaohs at this time regarded themselves as pre-eminent among their *brother* kings. Despite persistent requests from the King of Babylon, Amenhotep replied, 'never has the daughter of an Egyptian king been given to anyone'.[18]

Foreign wives and the king's harem

From year 10 it appears that the king 'gave himself over to the pleasures of the harem'.[19] Apart from his *great royal wife*, Tiye, Amenhotep is known to have married at least seven foreign princesses from areas such as Mitanni, Babylon, and Syria.

In year 10, the Mitannian princess, Gilu-khepa, arrived in Egypt with an extensive entourage of 317 ladies-in-waiting. This may have been the first of these diplomatic marriages and was celebrated with a special issue of large scarabs. Tiye's status and the affection that Amenhotep appears to have had for her, were not affected by this or later marriages. In fact, her name with those of her mother and father were included on the scarab 'newsletter'.

Arrival of Gilu-khepa

> Year 10 under the majesty of ... the Son of Re, Amenhotep, Ruler of Thebes, who is granted life and the Great King's Wife, Tiye, who liveth; the name of whose father was Yuya, the name of whose mother was Thuya. Marvels brought to his majesty ... Gilu-khepa, the daughter of the chief of Naharin, Shuttarna and the chief of her harem ladies, 317 persons.[20]

Further marriages occurred. Amenhotep married the sister of the Babylonian king, Kadashman-enlil, and some time later requested the king's daughter as well.

A great deal of haggling took place between these two kings over the proposed marriage. The Babylonian king had agreed to send his daughter in return for a huge shipment of gold to complete a palace he was building.

Babylonian princesses

> Now as for the gold about which I wrote you, send very much gold, as much as possible, now quickly, (even) before your (return) messenger reaches me ... that I may carry through the work I have undertaken. If during the harvest ... you send the gold for which I sent to you, then I will give you my daughter ...[21]

Kadashman-enlil warned Amenhotep that if the gold arrived late, he would not send his daughter to Egypt. Apparently negotiations went on for some time and the Babylon king seemed to be having second thoughts about his daughter's marriage when he wrote:

> Indeed, you want my daughter in marriage, but my sister, whom my father gave you is with you there, but no one has seen her (recently), or knows whether she is alive or dead ...[22]

Eventually Amenhotep must have satisfied Kadashman-enlil's demands, for the princess joined the Egyptian king's harem.

The daughter of King Tarkhundaradu of Azarwa, in Asia Minor, also married Amenhotep.

Towards the end of his reign, Amenhotep arranged with the new Mitannian king, Tushratta, to marry his daughter, Tadu-khepa. Like the other kings, Tushratta also wanted gold in return for his daughter's hand — 'let my brother send me exceeding much gold, without measure ... for in my brother's land gold is as plentiful as dust ...'[23]

Marriage arrangements with Tushratta of Mitanni

It is not known whether the aging pharaoh actually married Tadu-khepa, because when she is next heard of it is as the wife of Amenhotep IV (Akhenaten).

It increased Amenhotep's status and power to have his harem full of the royal daughters of the most powerful rulers in the east. However, the

Foreign concubines

king also demanded on his representatives abroad to find beautiful women to be sent as concubines. The following extract is taken from instructions he sent to a prince in Palestine.

> I have sent you this tablet to inform you that I am sending you Colonel Khanaia ... to procure fine concubines: Silver, gold, linen garments ... various precious stones, chairs of ebony, and sundry other fine things: total value, 160 deben. Total: 40 concubines; 40 pieces of silver being the cost per woman. So send very fine concubines in whom there is no blemish.[24]

Results of his foreign policy

Amenhotep's foreign policy had two important results:

1 Egyptian society became more cosmopolitan as increasing numbers of foreigners came to Egypt to trade and settle. The regular trade and exchange of gifts between rulers familiarised Egyptians with the skills of foreign craftsmen, and local arts and crafts were greatly influenced by those of the east. Refer to Chapter 15 for more details.

2 Because there had been no need to make a show of force in western Asia during Amenhotep's reign, a certain amount of complaisance crept in to the administration. Towards the latter part of his reign there were some disturbances in northern Syria. These minor outbreaks were to escalate during the reign of his successor when a number of Syrian princes began to seek their independence. This was to prove dangerous, since a new force had appeared on the scene in Asia Minor — the Hittites.

Administration of Egypt

For the first part of his reign, Amenhotep lived in the northern capital of Memphis and so it is not surprising that a large number of his chief officials came from Lower Egypt (the delta and Memphis areas). When he moved his residence to Thebes, these men accompanied him so that he continued to have a group of dedicated and highly competent administrators around him.

Chief officials

The diagram on the next page shows some of the brilliant officials who made Amenhotep III's reign the high point of the Eighteenth Dynasty. The fathers and relatives of most of these men had held important official posts also.

Coveted title of
king's scribe

Apart from the chief officials mentioned on the next page there were others, of more humble background, who were given the coveted title of *king's scribe* because of the roles they played in the household of the king and queen. For example, Kheruef, was *King's First Herald* and *Steward of the House of the King's Great Wife Tiye* and Nefersekheru was *Steward of the House of Nebmare-the-Dazzling-Sun*.

The influence and wealth of these officials is reflected in the size and richness of their tombs.

Amenhotep's chief officials

Vizier of the south
Ramose

Responsible for the day-to-day running of the vast palace complex, the smooth operation of the bureaucracy and all construction work in the south.

Scribe of recruits
Amenhotep, son of Hapu

Although a recent *portfolio*, this position was one of the most important during Amenhotep's reign. He was in charge of all the country's manpower.

Superintendent of the
treasury – Sobekhotpe

His family had controlled the treasury for three generations. He was responsible for the acquisition of all precious metals and involved in all mining operations.

Viceroy of Kush
Merimose

Responsible for government of Nubia as well as being responsible for the gold mines of the Sudan.

Chief steward
Amenhemet *Surer*

The men who were chief stewards in Memphis and Thebes were extremely powerful since they were responsible for all the king's possessions, which at this stage were enormous.

High Priest of Amun
Ptahmose

Ptahmose had been mayor of Thebes and vizier before becoming high priest of Amun and first prophet of Upper and Lower Egypt.

Overseer of granaries
Khaemhat

Responsible for all grain growing and collection of harvests in Egypt and the empire. He had control of enormous numbers of field scribes, police and tax collectors.

Amenhotep, son of Hapu, Scribe of Recruits and Overseer of all Works of the King

Amenhotep, son of Hapu, often referred to as Huy, was possibly the most outstanding official in an outstanding reign. From contemporary and later sources he appears to have been regarded as one of the truly great New Kingdom personalities.

Revered for centuries

Later generations revered him as a sage. Wise sayings attributed to him were translated by the Greeks 1200 years after his death and he was worshipped as a god during the Ptolemaic period.

He was a member of an old family of nomarchs from Athribis in the delta and was related to Ramose, the *Vizier of the South* and another Amenhotep, *Chief Steward* in Memphis. Amenhotep, son of Hapu, never held any of the highest positions in the state and was always shown as a royal scribe and yet his reputation surpassed all others at this time.

His official career was recorded on a statue which was placed in the Temple of Amun at Karnak on orders of the king.

The inscription outlines the various promotions he received from Amenhotep III:

1 *inferior royal scribe*

2 *superior royal scribe of recruits*

3 *minister of all public works.*

As inferior royal scribe (undersecretary of the king), Amenhotep, son of Hapu, 'was introduced into the divine book' (the temple library collection) and became very familiar with the 'excellent things of Thoth' (hieroglyphic passages).[25] His advice was sought on all sacred matters.

Titles and roles

His next appointment was as *scribe of recruits*. This semi-military position was one of the most important during Amenhotep III's reign as it involved the recruitment and supervision of manpower throughout the country. The person who held this office had to be brilliant at logistics, because he was responsible for:

• recruiting the work gangs necessary for quarrying and building activities

• levying and despatching army divisions

• providing manpower for the garrisons of the empire

• manning the customs posts on the Nile mouths in the delta.

As *chief of all works*, his third promotion, he 'did not imitate that which had been done before'.[26] For example, he supervised the quarrying, transportation, sculpting and erection of a massive statue of the king which was 'immense in width, taller than his column, its beauty marred the pylon'.[27] For this massive undertaking he had the army under his control.

Amenhotep, son of Hapu, was also responsible for the estates and possessions of the king's eldest daughter, Sitamun, and played an important role in the Sed festivals of the pharaoh.

Amenhotep III honoured him with a statue in the Temple of Amun at Karnak, a mortuary temple in western Thebes, as

Amenhotep, son of Hapu, as an aged man

magnificent as those of the kings nearby and a permanent endowment for the maintenance of his mortuary cult.

> Hear the command which is given to furnish the ka-chapel of the hereditary prince, the royal scribe, Amenhotep, called Huy, Son of Hapu, whose excellence is extolled, in order to perpetuate his ka-chapel with slaves, male and female, forever; son to son, heir to heir, in order that none trespass upon it forever.[28]

He lived to be 80 years of age.

The greatest building boom of the Eighteenth Dynasty

'Goods that cannot be counted, silver, gold and all kinds of costly stones in their millions'[29] poured into Egypt from the empire. These enabled Amenhotep to inaugurate a massive building program which earned him a reputation for magnificence.

> It pleased his majesty's heart to make very great monuments, the likes of which had not existed since the beginning of the Two Lands.[30]

Although all pharaohs made this claim, it was probably closer to the truth in the case of Amenhotep III than for any other king of the Eighteenth Dynasty.

The work which continued throughout his reign, included new buildings as well as renovation of monuments that had fallen into disrepair.

The four major features of his buildings were:

1 enormous size and massive statuary

2 lavish use of rich materials

3 quality of design

4 precision of workmanship.

Not only are these features evident in the surviving monuments, but Amenhotep left a detailed description of some of his works on a black granite stela, three metres high, originally set up in his mortuary temple.

The Temple of Luxor

The Temple of Luxor (*southern Opet or southern harem*) was Amenhotep's greatest building achievement and 'has the distinction of having been planned as a unit and three-quarters constructed by a single king'.[31]

It was designed by the architects Suti and Hor and built for the celebration of the Opet festival. During this annual celebration, the statues of the Theban trinity of Amun, Mut and Khonsu were taken from their shrines in Karnak to the *southern harem*. Refer to Chapter 15 for details of the Opet festival. The temple was linked with that at Karnak by an avenue of stone, ram-headed sphinxes one and a half kilometres in length.

Above: The remains of the forecourt of Luxor temple, built during the reign of Amenhotep III

Left: The remains of the processional colonnade of Luxor temple, built during the reign of Amenhotep III

The temple was built of sandstone and originally decorated with gold, silver, lapis lazuli and coloured glass.

> ... of fine sandstone, wide, very great and exceedingly beautiful. Its walls are of fine gold, its pavements of silver. All its gates are worked with the pride of lands. Its pylons reach to the sky, its flagpoles to the stars.[32]

Its main features included:

- a large, airy court with 96 graceful papyrus-bud columns and a central colonnade which 'surpasses any previously attempted'. 'In their proportions and spacing, the towering shafts are as noble as any which Egyptian architecture has produced'[33]

- a vestibule with a podium for holding the barque of Amun during its stay in Luxor and subsidiary chapels which provided resting places for the barques of Mut and her son Khonsu

- an inner sanctuary with a stone canopy over a balustrade which supported a colossal statue of Amun and numerous storage rooms for the emblems, equipment, garments and offerings used in the cult

- a series of reliefs, depicting Amenhotep's divine birth, on the walls of the so-called *birth chamber*.

The building was still unfinished at the end of Amenhotep's reign.

The third pylon at Karnak

Amenhotep commissioned a great triumphal gateway to be built for the Temple of Amun at Karnak. Because the king intended this two-tow-ered, monumental entrance to be the final western facade of the temple, he had a canal built from the Nile to the gateway. This ended in a docking and turning basin for ships. The pylon was:

> ...worked with gold throughout, with the god's shade in the likeness of a ram, inlaid with real lapis lazuli and worked with gold and costly stones. The like has never been made. Its pavement was made pure with silver, the portal in its front firmly set; (there are) stelae of lapis lazuli, one on each side. Its twin towers reached to the sky, like the four supports of heaven.[34]

Seventy years later it was covered by the hypostyle hall of Seti I and Ramesses II.

Amenhotep's mortuary temple

Judging from the two gigantic statues of the king (both over 21 metres high) which once stood at its main entrance, Amenhotep's mortuary temple was probably the most impressive ever built in western Thebes. These statues are all that remains of the temple but the building stela recorded that it was very large and wide and built of:

> ... fine white sandstone, wrought with gold throughout; its floor is adorned with silver, all its portals with electrum ... It is numerous in royal statues of Elephantine granite, of costly gritstone, of every splendid costly stone, established as everlasting works ... It is supplied with a 'Station of the King', wrought with gold and many costly stones. Flagstaves are set up before it, wrought with electrum ... Its lake is filled with the great Nile ...[35]

Colossal statues from Amenhotep III's mortuary temple

The *House of Rejoicing* — the palace at Malkata

One kilometre to the south of his mortuary temple, Amenhotep built a palace complex which covered 32 hectares. It was originally called the *Radiance of the Aten* but after his first jubilee it was renamed the *House of Rejoicing*. Unlike his temples, the palace complex was built of mud-brick and timber. It was gaily coloured and its white-washed, plastered walls were decorated with natural scenes. Refer to Chapter 16 on the palaces of royalty.

The complex comprised:

- several palaces for the king, Queen Tiye, Sitamun and Amenhotep IV (Akhenaten)
- quarters for his other wives
- a great hall of the vizier
- audience rooms
- administrative offices for such things as the royal archives
- private apartments and villas for high officials
- a temple to Amun
- quarters for palace workers and servants
- gardens and courtyards and close by a great pleasure lake built for Queen Tiye.

Also, to celebrate his various heb-seds he built a festival hall at Malkata.

Other buildings constructed by Amenhotep III are shown in the chart on the next page.

Art during the reign of Amenhotep III

The statues, tomb reliefs, jewellery, household furnishings and personal possessions produced for the court and the families of pharaoh's officials reveal a high standard of technical excellence, combine beauty and elegance and show a lively imagination and a love of novelty.

It appears that a new trend towards naturalism in art, influenced by contact with the east, was beginning at this time although it did not yet exhibit the exaggerated naturalism of the Amarna Period which followed.

In the latter part of Amenhotep's reign, there appears to have been two schools of artists working in Thebes — those following the more traditional style and others (more progressive) tending towards the style later inaugurated by Akhenaten. The exquisite reliefs in the tomb of Amenhotep's vizier, Ramose, are evidence of this. The work is done in both 'the style of the high Eighteenth Dynasty and in the somewhat eccentric style of Akhenaten's reign'[36] and it is interesting to compare the scenes on the left and right sides of the doorway.

A drawing of Ramose after a relief in his tomb. The figure features the prominent lips and jaw of the 'Amarna' style of representation

Other buildings constructed by Amenthotep III

Place	Name	Description
Karnak	Temple of Montu, the falcon-headed god of the Theban area	Built to the north of the Temple of Amun. Included a quay, long entrance flanked by sphinxes and a pair of obelisks over 18 metres high. Constructed of sandstone, with electrum, gold, copper, lapis lazuli, turquoise and bronze. The amounts of metal and precious stones used in this temple alone are staggering. Only the ground plan now remains.
Karnak	The building sacred to Mut, consort to Amun	Built of sandstone half a kilometre south of the Temple of Amun beside a crescent-shaped lake. In this shrine, Mut took the form of the lion-headed Memphite goddess of war and pestilence, Sekhmet. Over six hundred statues of Sekhmet were found here but not all may have been there originally. Since a plague was raging through the east at the time, this building may have been intended to propitiate Mut as Sekhmet. A gateway facing the precinct of Mut was flanked with two enormous statues of Amenhotep. This gateway was never decorated and was torn down by the end of the century. All that remains of his colossal statues is a single gigantic foot.
Western Thebes	The 'viewing place' or *maru*	Built as a place of relaxation for the god Amun. It included gardens and a pond and like all his other buildings was made from opulent materials.
Western Thebes	An artificial harbour	Constructed a huge basin, connected to the Nile by a canal for merchant ships. On its western side lay docks, warehouses and a settlement, plus the palace. It is not known for sure if this was the same as Tiye's pleasure lake.
Soleb, Nubia	Temple to Amun and Nebmare the living god	Built of white sandstone, with gold and silver throughout. Two great obelisks were erected on either side.
Sedeinga, Nubia	Temple to Tiye	In this temple Tiye was represented as a god.

Other temples were built to Ptah at Memphis (the castle of Nebmare), to Re-Horakhte at Heliopolis, Thoth at Hermopolis, Khnum at Elephantine and Nekhbet at el-Kab.

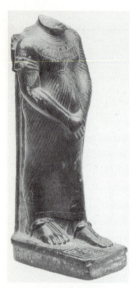

A headless statuette of Amenhotep III carved in serpentine, showing a marked feminine quality

A statuette of Amenhotep III, found at Thebes, shows that in the latter part of Amenhotep's reign artists were beginning to adopt the style which characterised the Amarna Period. Unlike the traditional representations of an Egyptian king, the statuette depicts Amenhotep as a fat old man, wearing a fringed and pleated overgarment, normally worn only by women.

The jewelled casket of Thuya

The cult of the king and the rise of the Aten

The most striking feature of religion during the early Eighteenth Dynasty was the dominance of the cult of Amun over all others. Not only did the kings ascribe their military successes to the support of Amun, but they filled the god's treasury with untold wealth and endowed the temples with vast tracts of land and captives. The priests of Amun had played a part in deciding who sat on the throne by giving or withdrawing the support of their god and the kings had adopted as one of their titles, *son of Amun*. According to Redford:

> **Amun's cult and his priesthood had become an association wherein political power seekers could fulfil themselves.**[37]

Throughout his reign, Amenhotep, like those before him, showed his devotion to Amun but there is evidence that he was concerned about the status of the kingship. It has been suggested that he may have believed that the temples and estates of Amun 'had received enough of the riches of empire to pose a threat to the king in certain circumstances'.[38]

Promotion of the Aten and its links with royalty

Amenhotep began to promote the interests of a form of the sun god called the Aten (the physical disk of the sun). He also associated the Aten with a cult of the king, possibly because:

- the sun god, Re, had been the prominent deity in earlier days when kings had exercised absolute power

- the Aten, as a symbol of divinity, had been associated with royalty since the Middle Kingdom. Under Amenhotep's predecessors the Aten had graduated to a god in its own right.

For the first time temples were built for this god within the precinct of Amun at Thebes and at Heliopolis. Also, Amenhotep:

- was referred to as the *Dazzling Sun-disk*

- called his palace complex at Malkata (before year 30 of his reign) *Radiance of the Aten* or *Splendour of Aten* and gave the same name to the state barge and to a regiment in his army

- built a temple in Nubia called *Gem Aten*

- named his youngest daughter by Queen Tiye, Beketaten and possibly a son by another wife, Tutankhaten. Refer to Chapter 13 for discussion of the question of Tutankhaten's parents.

A drawing based on a painting in the Temple of Soleb in Nubia showing Amenhotep III worshipping himself

Unlike other kings who became gods when they died, Amenhotep was deified during his lifetime and statues of him were worshipped in a number of temples. A relief in a temple at Soleb in Nubia depicted him worshipping and making offerings to an image of himself as a god.

Although these measures may have countered the power of Amun's priests, they 'were not directed against the cult of Amun or any other god but were part of a wider struggle being waged by the crown'.[39]

The latter part of Amenhotep's reign

After 25 years of residing in the northern capital of Memphis, Amenhotep and the court moved to Thebes where they took up residence in the palace at Malkata. The king remained there for the next 13 years of his life.

Amenhotep's three jubilees

Amenhotep celebrated three Sed festivals, in years 30, 34 and 37. On these occasions the pharaoh was ritually rejuvenated and his kingly powers renewed. The statuette shown on the right was made around year 30 and shows the rejuvenated Amenhotep with a child-like appearance.

The Sed festivals were traditionally held in Memphis, but the evidence suggests that Amenhotep celebrated his jubilees at Thebes. Aldred suggests that the king may have held his heb-sed in both the northern and southern capitals.

The evidence for these festivals comes from a number of sources, but it is difficult to put together a continuous account because the references to them are fragmentary.

A jubilee figure of Amenhotep III with a child-like appearance

Evidence

Amenhotep's leading officials proudly recorded in their tombs the part they played in the Sed ceremonies.

- The most detailed account of the Sed rites of year 30 are found in the tomb reliefs of Kheruef, who was *palace controller* during the celebrations. He recorded that Amenhotep delved into the archives to discover the way the Sed ceremonies were carried out in remote antiquity and that the king followed the most ancient form of the service described in *the writings of the ancients*. His tomb also showed the participation of Queen Tiye in the guise of Hathor, Tiye's daughters shaking sistra, Asiatic princesses pouring libations and high officials rowing the king's barge and towing the boat of Sokar, the god of death and resurrection associated with the necropolis of Sakkara.

- Khaemhat, *Overseer of Granaries*, recorded in his tomb that in year 30, in preparation for the king's jubilee, he presented to the king an enormous amount of grain collected as taxes. He also participated in the celebrations as *priest of Anubis*.

- In the tomb of the *Chief Steward*, Amenemhet Surer, are representations of the royal statues that were prepared for the Sed festival.

- *Overseer of the Treasury*, Sobekhotep, in preparation for Amenhotep's third jubilee, led an expedition to obtain turquoise from the mines of Sinai.

- Merimose, Viceroy of Kush, participated as one of the *controllers of the double throne* with Nefersekheru who also played the part of a *custodian of the boundary markers in the broad hall*.

Dated jar labels as evidence

Excavated from the rubbish mounds on the site of the Malkata palace, were thousands of broken pottery jars with labels written in black ink. The jars were used to store supplies of food, drink and other goods, used on special occasions such as the king's jubilees. The jar labels or dockets were usually dated and described the contents, where they came from or who donated them to the king. Enormous supplies of food and drink were required for the Sed festivities and came from the royal estates, donations by high officials and from as far afield as Syria.

Talatat and temple reliefs as evidence

Fragmentary scenes on the temples at Karnak and Soleb in Nubia as well as on carved talatat* found at Karnak, supplement the previous evidence. The participation of Queen Tiye and her daughters is shown on the walls of the temple at Soleb while the talatat depict the foreign emissaries who travelled to Egypt for the jubilee and the tribute that they presented to the king.

The Theban celebrations were held in Amenhotep's Malkata palace in western Thebes.

---

* Talatat is an Arab word for inscribed blocks of stone with standard dimensions of 52 by 26 by 24 centimetres.

Foreign princesses making libations during Amenhotep's jubilee. This relief, from the tomb of Kheruef in the Theban necropolis, illustrates the high quality of the art of the period

The question of a co-regency

The purpose of a co-regency was to prevent dynastic strife at the death of a king by establishing an approved partner on the throne. This practice was common during the Middle Kingdom but there is some controversy over whether it happened during the Eighteenth Dynasty.

The question of whether Amenhotep shared his throne for a time with his son Amenhotep IV (Akhenaten) has been hotly debated in scholarly circles. The evidence for a co-regency is incomplete, yet scholars on both sides argue persuasively for acceptance of their view.

Opposing views

Redford, author of *The History and Chronology of the Eighteenth Dynasty* and *Akhenaten the Heretic King*, is the most critical opponent of the idea. He believes that Amenhotep IV (Akhenaten) came to the throne after his father's death.

Aldred, in *Akhenaten King of Egypt*, argues in favour of a co-regency that lasted for at least ten years. He uses the Tomb of Ramose to present his case for a co-regency and the royal mummy no. 61070 (believed to be that of Queen Tiye) as evidence.

Others who argue in favour of a co-regency use a number of objects inscribed with the names of both kings, scenes of both Amenhotep and Akhenaten in the tombs of officials at Thebes and Amarna and a letter from Tushratta, King of Mitanni.

However, taken as a whole, the evidence for a co-regency is inconclusive. If Amenhotep III and his son shared some time on the throne together, it was likely to have been in the last few years of Amenhotep's reign when he was in very poor physical health.

Amenhotep's illness and death

Amenhotep's physical condition in the latter part of his reign reflected his life of ease and luxury. He is shown on a stela as fat and lethargic and in a scene from the tomb of Kheruef, he appears weak and sickly. He was probably ill in year 36 when his brother-in-law, Tushratta of Mitanni, sent him a cult statue of the goddess Ishtar in the hope that she would be able to heal him.

> ... may my brother honour her, in joy send her back, and may she return. May Ishtar, mistress of heaven protect my brother and me ...[40]

Despite this 'brotherly' help, Amenhotep died at Malkata sometime in year 38. An examination of his mummy revealed that at the time of his death he had been obese and bald, with severely abscessed teeth.

Condolence message from Tushratta

When Tushratta of Mitanni received news of his *brother's* death, he sent a message of condolence to Amenhotep's successor and widow.

> When I was informed that my brother Nimmuria (Amenhotep III) had gone to his destiny, then I wept on that day. I sat here day and night; on that day I partook neither food nor drink, for I was in sorrow.[41]

Conclusion

The significance of the reign of Amenhotep, *The Dazzling Sun-disk*, is summarised in the three views expressed below.

> Amenhotep III and the Egypt he ruled, never had been, nor would be again, in such a position of absolute power in the world.[42]

> Amenhotep's reign was an autumn of richness and luxury, controlled by taste and high standards of fine craftsmanship.[43]

> When Amenhotep died he took with him an Egypt of political and religious certainties, a state that had regained strength and respect at home and abroad.[44]

Chapter review

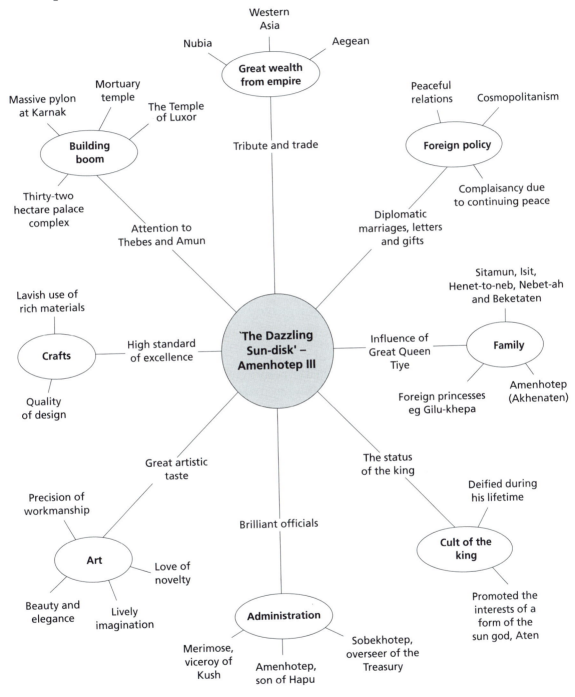

Western Asia

Nubia   Aegean

Great wealth from empire

Mortuary temple

Massive pylon at Karnak   The Temple of Luxor

Building boom

Peaceful relations   Cosmopolitanism

Foreign policy

Tribute and trade   Complaisancy due to continuing peace

Thirty-two hectare palace complex

Attention to Thebes and Amun

Diplomatic marriages, letters and gifts

Sitamun, Isit, Henet-to-neb, Nebet-ah and Beketaten

Lavish use of rich materials

High standard of excellence

Crafts

`The Dazzling Sun-disk' – Amenhotep III

Influence of Great Queen Tiye   **Family**

Amenhotep (Akhenaten)

Quality of design

Foreign princesses eg Gilu-khepa

Great artistic taste   The status of the king

Deified during his lifetime

Precision of workmanship

Art   Brilliant officials   **Cult of the king**

Love of novelty

Beauty and elegance   Lively imagination

Administration

Promoted the interests of a form of the sun god, Aten

Merimose, viceroy of Kush   Amenhotep, son of Hapu   Sobekhotep, overseer of the Treasury

REVISION QUESTIONS AND ESSAY TOPICS

1 **What do these two pieces of evidence (the statuary on the right and the scarab inscription below) indicate about the status of Queen Tiye?**

Year 10 under the majesty of (full titulary) the Son of Re, Amenhotep (III), ruler of Thebes, who is granted life and the great King's Wife Tiye, who liveth; the name of whose father was Yuya, the name of whose mother was Thuya.

Marvels brought to his majesty ... Gilu-khepa, the daughter of the chief of Naharin, Shuttarna, and the chief of her harem ladies, 317 persons.[45]

What other evidence can be used to assess her status?

2 **Read the following extract carefully and answer the accompanying questions.**

... But if you do not ... send the gold so that I cannot carry through the work I have undertaken, why should you send anything at a later date? When I have finished the work I have undertaken, why should I want gold? Even if you should then send 3000 talents of gold, I would not accept it, but would return it to you; nor would I give you my daughter in marriage.[46]

a Who is the author of this letter?

b What is the purpose of this letter?

c What does this letter reveal about the relationship between the sender and the recipient?

d How do you know that this letter was not sent by Amenhotep III?

e What does it reveal about the foreign policy of Amenhotep III?

3 **Identify the object in the figure on the right and answer the following questions.**

a   Which goddess does this figure represent?

b   What qualities did this goddess supposedly possess?

c   Where was this statue, and others like it, found?

d   Why was it placed at this ancient site?

4 Identify the temple remains shown in the figure on the right. Draw up a table similar to the one below and fill in the appropriate information about this building.

Name and location of building	
Its purpose	
Materials used in its construction	
Architectural features	

5 The following extract is from an inscription belonging to an official in Amenhotep's administration.

My lord again showed favour to me ... he put all the people subject to me, and the listing of their number under my control, as the superior King's scribe over recruits.[47]

a What is the name of this official?

b Where was this inscription found?

c What is meant by 'My lord again showed favour to me'?

d Why was the position held by this official so important?

e What other activities did he carry out for the king?

f What evidence is there that this official was greatly honoured by Amenhotep III?

g On what was his later reputation based?

6 Note the association of the object in the figure below with the inscription of one of Amenhotep's chief officials.

Appearance of the king upon the great throne, to receive the report of the harvest of the South and the North.

Communication of the report of the Year 30 in the presence of the king, consisting of the harvest of the great inundation of the Jubilee which his majesty celebrated by the stewards of the estates of Pharaoh together with the chiefs of the South and the North ...

Reward of the Stewards of the estates of pharaoh ... together with the chiefs of the South and the north after the statement of the overseer of the granary concerning them, 'They have increased the harvest of Year 30'.[48]

a Identify the object in the figure.

b Where might it have been found?

c What type of information might the hieratic inscription contain?

d How might an object like this contribute to our knowledge of Amenhotep's reign?

e What is the association of an object like this with the extract from the tomb of one of pharaoh's officials?

f In whose tomb was this inscription found?

g What position in pharaoh's administration did he hold?

h Why was the harvest of year 30 so important?

i Why was Amenhotep so pleased with this official and those who worked for him?

7 Essay topics

a Explain the status, influence and significance of each of the following women associated with Amenhotep III.

- Mutemweya
- Tiye
- Sitamun
- Gilu-khepa and Tadu-khepa
- the sister and daughter of Kadashman-enlil.

b What was Amenhotep's relationship with Amun?

c To what extent did Egypt reach the 'zenith of magnificence' during the reign of Amenhotep, *The Dazzling Sun-disk*?

Akhenaten and the Amarna interlude

Introduction

The 17-year reign of the pharaoh Akhenaten (Amenhotep IV) is referred to as the Amarna Period after the name of the present-day village where the remains of Akhenaten's capital city were discovered.

This was a brief but dramatic period in Egyptian history. During his reign, Akhenaten:

- initiated a religious 'revolution' which focused on the sole worship of the sun-disk known as the Aten. Aten worship became a personal cult of the king. The temples of the other gods were for a time closed and their priesthoods disbanded
- built a new capital city dedicated to the Aten which he named Akhetaten (*Horizon of the Sun-disk*). This was located midway between Memphis and Thebes at a site never before claimed by any other god
- developed a very distinctive style of art which reflected the new iconography (symbol) of the Aten and the role of the king and his family in its worship
- contributed to the loss of Egyptian prestige and power abroad.

Because of the nature of the surviving written and archaeological sources 'it has proved impossible to write a history of Akhenaten's reign which does not embrace an element of historical fiction'.[1] The inscriptional and artefactual evidence are easily misinterpreted. In some cases, according to one Amarna scholar, the 'evidence has been over-interpreted'.[2]

There is a great deal of doubt and confusion about some of the events and individuals of this period. For example, leading Amarna scholars cannot agree on whether Amenhotep III and his son Amenhotep IV (Akhenaten) shared a co-regency and if so, how long it lasted. The question of a co-regency affects the interpretation of other events in this period.

Also there are various theories proposed by Amarna experts about the fate of Akhenaten's queen, Nefertiti, after year 14 of his reign. Some suggest she died before Akhenaten. Others believe she fell out of favour or

A summary of Akhenaten's reign

Controversial issues and questions

395

was disgraced and forced to live elsewhere. One interesting theory is that she was really the co-regent, Smenkhkare, and another that she ruled as regent for the child pharaoh Tutankhamun until he was old enough to rule alone. Each scholar's interpretation depends on the pieces of evidence he or she considers most significant.

Other questions that have puzzled scholars include the following:

- What motivated Akhenaten 'to step outside the mentality of his time'?[3]

- Were the gross distortions in the figures of Akhenaten, particularly in the earlier part of his reign, a reflection of his unusual physical appearance or in some way a reflection of his religious ideas?

- Why, after year 5, did he desecrate the name of the god Amun wherever it appeared? Was it the act of a religious fanatic or did Akhenaten have some political or economic motive?

- Was Ahkenaten uninterested in what was going on in his empire and solely responsible for its disintegration?

- Who were the parents of Smenkhkare and Tutankhamun?

Unless new evidence comes to light, the answers to these and many other questions about the Amarna Period will be based on conjecture.

Sources of evidence for the reign of Akhenaten

Inscribed blocks of stone from Akhenaten's sun temples

Because of the heretical nature of Akhenaten's reign, most of his monuments were destroyed or dismantled soon after his death. Fortunately for historians, thousands of untouched, inscribed and decorated blocks from Akhenaten's sun temples were used by the pharaoh Horemheb as filling for his pylon gateway at the temple of Karnak. Ramesses II also used many of these blocks as the core of his entrance pylon at Luxor temple and in buildings elsewhere. Since these inscribed blocks remained hidden until recently, they were not distorted or corrupted by those who came after Akhenaten.

A talatat showing one of the king's escorts at his jubilee held in year 3

Tens of thousands of these small blocks (52 by 26 by 24 centimetres), called *talatat* in Arabic, have been collected and provide glimpses of:

- rituals associated with the worship of the Aten and the king's jubilee

- Akhenaten and his family

- processions featuring officials, priests and the army

- palace scenes and foreign emissaries bearing tribute.

Remains of the city of Akhetaten

When Akhenaten decided to build a new capital in Middle Egypt called Akhetaten, he ordered 14 stelae to be carved into the cliffs on both sides of the Nile to set the boundaries for the city. Despite considerable weathering, two of the stelae have provided historians with details about the choice of the site and the dedication of the city.

Excavations have laid bare the outlines of many of the buildings of this short-lived city. They include:

- sun temples
- palaces
- roads
- administrative buildings
- police and military barracks
- houses of important government officials
- residential areas
- a workmen's village outside the city.

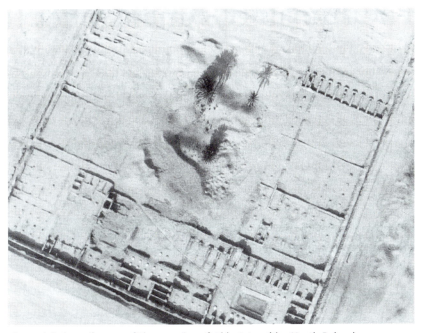

An aerial view of some of the remains of Akhetaten (the North Palace)

Tombs at Akhetaten and Thebes

Despite the fact that the tombs prepared for Akhenaten, his family and some of his chief officials in the cliffs behind Akhetaten were unfinished when the city was abandoned and were defaced soon after, they have provided evidence of:

- the life of the royal family in Akhetaten

- architectural features of the city
- the art of the period
- Akhenaten's view of his god.

The Theban tomb of the vizier, Ramose, shows the transition that occurred in religion and art in the first few years of Akhenaten's reign.

The Amarna letters

Refer to Chapter 12.

Summary of events during the Amarna Period

The following chart summarises what is known at this point about the order of major developments during the 17-year reign of Akhenaten.

Possible sequence of major events in the reign of Akhenaten (Amenhotep IV)

Date	Developments
Years 1–4 Amenhotep IV	• Amenhotep IV proclaimed a new version of the solar god Re-Horakhte. • He ordered the decoration of his father's pylon gateways at Karnak in the traditional form. • The name of Re-Horakhte was enclosed in double cartouches and a new icon (the rayed sun-disk) was inscribed on the temple pylons. • A decree was issued, announcing the erection of four sun temples near the enclosure of the god Amun-Re at Karnak. • Amenhotep IV held a jubilee (Sed festival) in year 3.
Years 5–8 Akhenaten	• The king had produced three daughters by year 5. • Akhenaten announced the founding of a new capital city dedicated to the Aten half-way between Memphis and Thebes. • He changed his name from Amenhotep IV to Akhenaten, and ordered the closure of Amun's temple. • The city of Akhetaten became the religious and administrative centre of Egypt by year 8.
Years 9–11 At Akhetaten	• Akhenaten changed the name of the Aten and purged any reference to other gods except Re — no plurality of gods. • Maat (truth) was no longer represented as a woman. • Three more daughters fathered by Akhenaten. By year 9 he had six daughters.

Years 12–17 At Akhetaten	• A great reception of foreign ambassadors from Asia, Africa and the Aegean held at Akhetaten in year 12.
	• The Queen Mother, Tiye, visited and possibly lived at Akhetaten.
	• The Egyptians were faced with problems in Syria and Palestine and a plague, originating in the kingdom of Mitanni, spread to Egypt.
	• About year 14, both Queen Tiye and Akhenaten's second daughter, Meketaten, died.
	• After year 14 there were no more references to Nefertiti and soon after Kiya, another wife, died or retired.
	• Akhenaten's eldest daughter took the role of the queen and in year 15 was married to Smenkhkare.
	• Between years 14 and 17, intensification of attack on Amun.
	• Co-regency between the heir, Smenkhkare and Akhenaten.
	• Possible death of Akhenaten in year 17.

The early years

Amenhotep IV, the second son of Amenhotep III and Queen Tiye, was probably born in the northern capital of Memphis where the court resided until the last decade or so of his father's reign.

Apart from the fact that he was born at the height of the Egyptian Empire and brought up in an environment of luxury and elegance, very little is known about the young prince's childhood and youth. This is not surprising since information about royal sons is generally lacking in the sources and Amenhotep was not expected to rule since he had an older brother, Thutmose.

No evidence of his childhood and youth

However, when Thutmose died at a very early age, Amenhotep still appears to have been kept in the background. He was 'conspicuous by his absence from the monuments of his father',[4] who for some reason seems to have overlooked him and kept him away from the activities of the court. The evidence seems to suggest that he was close to his mother, Tiye.

It is possible that on his brother's death he inherited the title of *high priest of Ptah*, commonly held by the crown prince. Aldred suggests that it may have been Ptah's other role as *greatest of the craftsmen* that influenced Akhenaten's interest and flair in art and sculpture.

Whether the priests of the sun god at On (Heliopolis) had any influence on Amenhotep's religious beliefs is not known. Redford says there is no evidence that he ever resided or was educated at Heliopolis. However, it is possible that he spent some time there because of the number of Heliopolitan officials who later made up his entourage.

Possible influence of priests of Heliopolis

Amenhotep lived in Thebes during the last ten years of his father's reign. There, the court occupied the new palace (*House of Rejoicing*) at

Malkata on the west bank close to his father's mortuary temple. The only firm evidence that Amenhotep lived there comes from the seal of a wine jar found in the palace which mentions *the estate of the true king's son, Amenhotep*. By this time he might have already been married with his own quarters in the palace.

The young Amenhotep would have been familiar with the developments in the solar cult that had taken place during the reigns of his grandfather and father. It would have been surprising if he had not been influenced by them.

Unlike his predecessors he did not boast of his sporting abilities. He appears to have had poetic tendencies and was fascinated with nature.

It must have been with some apprehension that the officials who had served Amenhotep III waited to see how this young and unknown pharaoh would administer Egypt and its empire.

Accession to the throne and marriage to Nefertiti

Amenhotep IV at his coronation, with the goddess Maat representing 'an eternity of rule'

It is thought that Amenhotep IV was about 16 or 17 when he came to the throne. A wall relief from the tomb of Ramose, Vizier of the South, shows the young king, wearing the blue Khepresh crown of coronation and enthroned under a canopy with the goddess Maat.

Did he share the throne for a time with his father and if he did, how long did the co-regency last? These are two of the most debated questions among Amarna scholars. Despite the lack of hard facts and the ambiguous nature of much of the evidence, scholars have managed to present convincing arguments both for and against a co-regency.

In his work, *History and Chronology of the Eighteenth Dynasty of Egypt*, Redford argues that Amenhotep III did not share a co-regency with his son. He believes that Amenhotep IV succeeded his father on his death and ruled alone for 17 years.

On the other hand, Aldred, in *Akhenaten, King of Egypt*, argues persuasively not only for a co-regency but for one lasting for 12 years. 'Disturbing as this conclusion may be, we shall have no option but to accept it.'[5] Hayes, author of *Scepter of Egypt*, agrees with Aldred: 'Amenhotep III seems to have survived his son's elevation to the throne by as much as ten or twelve years'.[6]

Other scholars are prepared to accept a co-regency of no more than two years since Amenhotep III's health was failing by about year 36 of his reign and he may have wanted to secure the throne. However, all that can be said at the present time is that the evidence for a co-regency is inconclusive.

Nefertiti

It is believed that Amenhotep IV (Akhenaten) was already married to Nefertiti when he came to the throne. There are no details about the queen's background or parents but it is generally believed that she came from a family that was well known at court. It has been suggested that she might have been the daughter of Ay, thought to be the brother of Queen Tiye.

Ay came from the same town as Queen Tiye's family and held the same titles as Tiye's father. Since a son often inherited his father's offices, the evidence suggests that Ay was Yuya's son. Although inscriptions associated with Nefertiti and her sister Mutnodjmet never name their parents, it is possible that Ay was their father. Mutnodjmet was featured in the original tomb prepared for Ay and his wife Tey. However, Ay's wife, Tey, was not Nefertiti's mother. She had the tile of royal nurse. Perhaps Tey was Ay's second wife and was Nefertiti's stepmother or perhaps she had been a nurse in an important family in which Nefertiti was the daughter.

Possible parentage

Despite Nefertiti's obscure background, there are more images of her as queen, wife and mother than any other woman of the New Kingdom.

The earliest depiction of her is the one found in Ramose's tomb. At this early date the young king and queen are represented in the traditional artistic form with the wife standing demurely behind her husband. There appear to be no children at this time. However, after the birth of her first daughter, Meritaten, Nefertiti is shown officiating as the king's equal and from this time she is treated as the king's partner, not only in their family life but in religious and political life as well. They were hardly ever shown apart and she is described in the records as 'possessed of charm', 'sweet of love' and one who makes others happy by the sound of her voice.

Earliest representations of Nefertiti

From the magnificent bust of Nefertiti in the Berlin Museum, she appears to have been a great beauty and is usually depicted wearing the elegant and distinctive crown which she initiated for herself — the tall straight-edged blue headdress perhaps an echo of the blue *khepresh* or war crown frequently worn by the king. This was just one of the many indications of her great status.

Even in the early years when the couple were still living at Thebes, Nefertiti was depicted in kingly style on the walls of temples and in statuary. In one scene she is shown as a warrior king subduing the enemies of Egypt in female form and in another she is depicted wearing a version of the kingly *atef* crown. Samson believes that Amenhotep IV was emphasising her equality with him in the rule.

Evidence of Nefertiti's regal status will be presented throughout this chapter. There is also an outline of her religious and political status in Chapter 15 — Prominence of royal women.

A bust of Nefertiti

Religious revolution — the cult of the Aten

Akhenaten did not invent the sun-disk

It is often thought that Akhenaten invented the life-sustaining sun-disk (Aten) as a philosophical concept and that he stood out from those who preceded him by his radical thinking. This was not the case. As Redford maintains, 'changes had been building up for generations'[7] and according to Gardiner, 'revolution was already in the air'[8] in the reign of his father, Amenhotep III.

Changes in the solar cult in the decades before the reign of Amenhotep IV (Akhenaten)

The worship of the sun god had been associated with royalty since the Old Kingdom and the Aten (sun-disk) was regarded as a physical aspect of the sun god.

During the Eighteenth Dynasty there were a number of changes in the solar cult.

Universality of Re

1 Re was seen as more than just a sun god. He was the universal god — *the sole god who has made himself for eternity* and as such embodied all the other gods in his being. He was described in the hymns carved into rock-cut tombs, as *Re of the Disk*.

Thutmose III was described as *Re, the Lord of Heaven, the Lord of Upper and Lower Egypt when he rises, The Aten when he reveals himself.*

2 Thutmose IV, Akhenaten's grandfather, developed a closer relationship with the Aten than his predecessors. For example, on a commemorative scarab, he was described as *The Disk in his Horizon.* He also recorded that he fought 'with the Aten before him' and hoped that the conquered foreigners would, like the Egyptians, 'serve the Aten forever'. There was a tendency during the reign of Thutmose IV to describe the sun-disk as a god in its own right rather than as the physical aspect of Re.

3 It was during the reign of Akhenaten's father, Amenhotep III, that the sun-disk:

Association of sun-disk with the king

- became increasingly associated with royalty and particularly with the status of the king
- developed into a god with its own temples and priests
- began to be credited with the creative powers of Re.

Amenhotep III was known as *The Dazzling Sun-disk* and he gave the name *Radiance of the Aten* to his state barge and to his Malkata palace in western Thebes.

Priests and shrine to Aten at time of Amenhotep III

It appears that at some time during Amenhotep III's reign, a shrine to the Aten was built near the Karnak temple of Amun-Re and that a priesthood was established. Ramose, a priest of Amun, also had the title of *Steward in the Temple of the Aten* and another official, named Pen-buy, bore the title of *Scribe of the Treasury of the Temple of the Aten*.

A hymn to the sun god, inscribed in the tomb of Amenhotep's architects, the twins, Suty and Hor, describes the Aten as *the one who created everyone and made their life*.

4 Throughout this period the sun god was depicted in the traditional form of a falcon-headed man with a sun-disk on its head or as a winged sun-disk.

So in the generations before Amenhotep IV's (Akhenaten's) accession to the throne there was already:

- the concept of one universal, creative sun god (Re-Horakhte) and the expression of this doctrine in the form of a hymn

- a new deity called the Aten possibly with its own sanctuary and priests

- a close association of the Aten with the pharaoh.

Changes prior to the accession of Akhenaten

It is quite probable that prior to his accession, the young Amenhotep, aware of the changes that had occurred in the solar cult under his predecessors, 'had religious ambitions of his own'.[9]

Stages in Akhenaten's religious revolution

From the table near the beginning of this chapter it can be seen that there were a number of definite stages in the development of the king's religious ideas.

Stage 1

In the first months of his reign the king announced a new form of the solar god which had been growing in popularity during the reigns of his immediate predecessors. This god was Re-Horakhte, *The Great Sun-disk, The Fashioner of Brightness* and *The Living Disk who Brightens the Land with its Beauty*.

Re-Horakhte — part of an inscription of Amenhotep IV

In this proclamation, known only from a very damaged text found on two talatat blocks, he stated that his new god was unique. The Aten was a living, self-created god represented only by the light that radiated from the sun-disk. Other gods were worshipped as images or statues made by craftsmen from descriptions kept in books in the temple archives.

At this stage his new supreme god was still represented by the falcon-headed man in a kilt with the sun-disk on his head. In the initial decoration of his father's pylons, Amenhotep IV and his god were depicted opposite each other across a table of offerings. Redford points out that already, in this earliest form, there is evidence of a close relationship with the king. In some scenes the falcon-headed god was shown with the same pot-belly as the pharaoh.

Stage 2

Possibly in his second or third year, Amenhotep IV introduced some major changes. These may have coincided with his jubilee which for some reason he held in his third year.

Icon — disk with arms

The anthropomorphic god (falcon-headed man) was replaced with an icon. The disk remained but took on another form. The Aten was now represented as a large disk with a ureaus and arm-like rays ending in hands. In some depictions the hands hold ankhs and offer this symbol of life to the king. In other scenes the hands are open to accept the king's abundant offerings.

The god's name was now enclosed in two cartouches (showing it was a heavenly king) and accompanied by the new title *Aten the Living, the great, Who is in Jubilee, Lord of Heaven and Earth.*

Karnak pylons carved with new icon

This new icon, with its accompanying double cartouches and new epithet, was inscribed on the Karnak pylons and on the walls of the new sun-temple complex that the king was building at east Karnak. However, an interesting feature of the reliefs is the dominance of Amenhotep IV in relation to the symbol of the sun-disk. The king's figure is large and occupies the centre of the scene.

The significance of these changes is obvious.

- By choosing an icon rather than an anthropomorphic form for his god, Amenhotep IV was breaking with the tradition of cult images and the ritual associated with them. He was also pointing out that his god *built himself by himself* without the involvement of any human hand.

- The size and position of the image of the king in the scenes was an affirmation of the king's divinity — the manifestation of the sun-disk on earth. The king became the focus of worship since only he could have a relationship with the Aten.

Despite his announcement of the supremacy of the Aten, Amenhotep IV built his new sun-temples just outside the temple enclosure of the great Amun-Re at Karnak. At this stage in the development of Amenhotep's religious ideas, there was no break with any other god and the worship of the Aten was carried on side by side with that of Amun.

The royal pair on the palace balcony at Thebes, from the tomb of Ramose

Stage 3

From years 5 to 9, Amenhotep's belief that the sun-disk was the one and only god, was implemented with greater intensity. He decided to build a cult centre which belonged exclusively to Aten and about the same time took actions against the other gods. The chief focus of his attack was the great god of the Egyptian empire, Amun. As evidence of his break with Amun he changed his name from Amenhotep (*Amun is Satisfied*) to Akhenaten (*He Who is Serviceable to the Aten*). Akhenaten ordered the closure of all the temples of other gods and the erasure of the gods' names from the walls of temples and tombs. The mortuary gods such as Osiris were no longer mentioned in the texts and the Osirian funerary rites no longer practised. The plural word *gods* was never used again during Akhenaten's reign.

The sun-disk as the 'only' god

Closure of temples

Akhenaten's view of the Aten

Akhenaten's view of his god is revealed in the beautiful Hymn to the Sun-disk which was found inscribed in the tomb of Ay, one of his officials. The ideas expressed in this hymn, which may have been written by Akhenaten, are not new. A similar hymn to Amun included many of the same sentiments. However, there is one major difference — in Akhenaten's hymn there is no mention of other gods.

Hymn to sun-disk

According to the hymn, the sun-disk is:

- the creator of all life:

  You made the earth as you wished, you alone, all people, herds, flocks, all upon earth that walk on legs, all on high that fly on wings. You made millions of forms from yourself alone, towns, villages, fields, the river's course.[10]

- a universal god:

  The lands of Khor (Syria) and Kush, the land of Egypt, you set every man in his place ... Their tongues differ in speech, their character likewise; their skins are distinct, for you distinguished the peoples.[11]

- the sustainer of life:

  Your rays nurse all fields, when you shine they live, they grow for you.

  Who makes seed grow in women, who creates people from sperm, who feeds the son in his mother's womb ... When he comes from the womb to breathe on the day of his birth, you open wide his mouth to supply his needs ...

  When the chick in the egg speaks in the shell, You give him breath within to sustain him.[12]

- a source of power and beauty:

  When you have dawned in eastern lightland, you fill every land with your beauty. You are beauteous, great, radiant, high over every land.[13]

- a remote, heavenly king:

  Though you are far, your rays are on earth. Though one sees you, your strides are unseen.[14]

Despite the great beauty of this hymn, Redford maintains that Akhenaten's god was cold and lacking in compassion. Although the Aten created and sustained life, 'no text tells us that he hears the cry of the poor man, or succours the sick, or forgives the sinner'.[15]

The sun-disk was not a god to which the ordinary Egyptian could relate and this was intentional. Akhenaten's god could only be worshipped directly by the 'beautiful child of the disk' and his 'great queen whom he loves'.

Akhenaten's relationship with the Aten

Evidence for Akhenaten's relationship with his god, comes from the hymns and prayers inscribed on the tomb walls of the king's courtiers, Ay, Any, Meryre, Apy, Mahu and Tutu. These praise the Aten, the king and the queen. The following diagram summarises Akhenaten's relationship with his god.

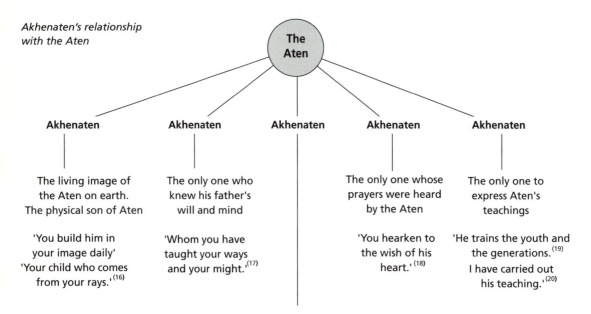

Akhenaten's relationship with the Aten

The Aten

Akhenaten

The living image of the Aten on earth. The physical son of Aten

'You build him in your image daily' 'Your child who comes from your rays.'[16]

Akhenaten

The only one who knew his father's will and mind

'Whom you have taught your ways and your might.'[17]

Akhenaten

Akhenaten

The only one whose prayers were heard by the Aten

'You hearken to the wish of his heart.'[18]

Akhenaten

The only one to express Aten's teachings

'He trains the youth and the generations.[19] I have carried out his teaching.'[20]

Akhenaten's relationship with the Aten, 'reaffirmed the divinity of kingship'.[21]

Features of the cult

Akhenaten's reforms created an exclusive cult with almost nothing left from the traditional forms of worship.

- There were no other gods but the Aten.
- Unlike other chief deities, the Aten was not associated with a divine family such as Amun, Mut and Konshu; Osiris, Isis and Horus and Ptah, Sekhmet and Nefertum. However, it appears that Aten, the creator, was linked in a triad with his creation, Akhenaten (the male principle) and Nefertiti (the female principle).

- An abstract symbol, the rayed sun-disk replaced the vast collection of anthropomorphic deities that existed in the complex universe of the ancient Egyptians.

- There was no mythology associated with the Aten. All the ancient myths associated with the afterlife and the magical texts from the *Book of the Dead* disappeared.

- The Aten, as a living god, had no cult statue which required the daily attention of the priests. The only daily ritual was the essential food offerings.

- Since there was no cult image of the god there was no need for processional festivals such as the Opet and Valley festivals.

- Although there was a hierarchy of priests (*servants of the disk in the Mansion of the Disk*), only the king communicated directly with the Aten. The other priests ministered to the cult of Akhenaten, the image of the disk on earth.

Akhenaten attempted to simplify the solar cult but what he 'left to Egypt was not a *god* at all but a disk in the heavens'.[22]

Removal of all traditional cult forms

Effects of Akhenaten's religious changes

Akhenaten's religious revolution had an effect on:
- temple architecture, decoration and ritual
- art
- the king's jubilee
- the site and layout of the new capital city of Akhetaten
- the economy
- funerary practices
- the social life of the ordinary Egyptians.

Temple architecture, decoration and ritual

Since there was no longer an anthropomorphic image of the god in the new cult, there was no need for a place to house the statue and its ritual paraphernalia. The traditional roofed temple with its dim interior and dark windowless sanctuary was replaced with a temple open to the sky so that the living disk could be seen throughout the day.

No innermost sanctuary

Open to the sun

Architectural features of Akhenaten's sun temples

The sun temple complexes built by Akhenaten (the Gempaaten at east Karnak and the Great Temple of the Aten at Akhetaten) appear to have followed the same architectural form. Their main features were:

- a series of open courts each with a great altar as its focal point
- roofed colonnades around the perimeter of the courts
- hundreds of stone offering tables
- storage rooms, possibly for the storage of the abundant supplies of food offerings needed daily
- colossal statues of the king
- reliefs of the offering ritual and the king's jubilee.

It is almost certain that all of Akhenaten's sun-temples were oriented to the rising sun.

The sun-temple complex at Thebes

Evidence from the talatat point to the existence of four sun temples built to the Aten at Thebes in the early years of Akhenaten's reign.

1 Gempaaten — *The Sun-disk is Found*

2 The Mansion of the Ben-ben Stone

3 Rud-menu — *Sturdy are the Monuments of the Sun-disk Forever*

4 Teni-menu — *Exalted are the Monuments of the Sun-disk Forever.*

Royal building decree

According to a quarry inscription at Gebel es Silsila, Ahkenaten ordered his army commanders to levy a huge workforce for 'cutting out sandstone, in order to make the great sanctuary of Herakhte'[23] at Thebes. The king's highest officials were in charge of transporting the stone.

> This great undertaking was set in train almost as a national enterprise, with an energy that had hitherto been devoted to foreign campaigns ...[24]

Features of the Gempaaten

The Gempaaten was a rectangular enclosure approximately 300 by 200 metres enclosed with a mud-brick wall. The figure below shows a part of the roofed colonnade around the perimeter of the central court and the site of a number of colossal statues of the king. These statues were in the strange and slightly grotesque style of the early part of the reign. See below for a possible explanation of this style of art.

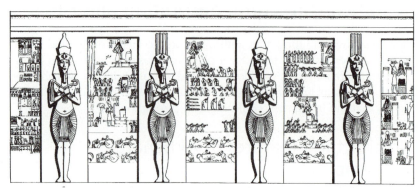

The likely appearance of the south colonnade of the Gempaaten at Thebes

Apart from the Gempaaten, there is no firm evidence of the purpose or location of the other three cult temples.

The Great Temple of the Aten at Akhetaten

The House of the Aten was a vast rectangular enclosure comprising several temples and six open courts laid out in a processional plan.

At its western end was the colonnaded House of Rejoicing which opened into a large court with lustration basins and an offering place. A series of five other courts followed, each with altars and storage rooms for cult equipment. The last court was the Gem-aten with a huge altar in the centre and 365 tables for offerings arranged on each side to represent Upper and Lower Egypt.

Separated from the Gem-aten by an avenue of sphinxes was the Mansion of the Ben-ben which was the holy of the holies. It featured a raised podium for offering to the Aten and a colossal statue of the king.

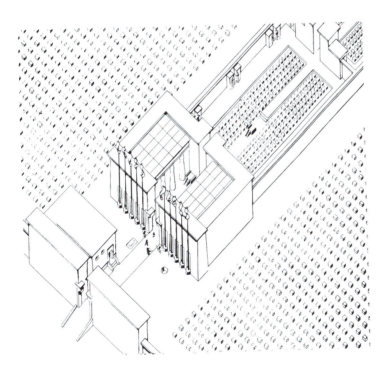

An artist's impression of the entrance to the Great Temple of Aten at Akhetaten

Decoration of the sun temples

The two main themes inscribed on all Aten temples were:

1 the offering ritual
2 the Sed festival and other royal activities.

Scenes of the offering ritual

In these scenes, the king and queen, alone and together and sometimes with one daughter, officiate before an altar.

In the Mansion of the Ben-ben at Karnak, Nefertiti (who is referred to as Nefer-neferu-Aten — *Beauty of the Beauties of the Aten*) is shown alone with her arms raised to the Aten, making offerings to the god, a role traditionally reserved for the king. In other representations she is shown holding a replica of the goddess Maat which was normally the king's offering in the temple. Her name was written in full with that of the god.

Other scenes of the offering ritual show processions of servants carrying food to temples and palaces, and vast quantities of beer, bread, fowl, meat, oil, honey and other commodities on tables, altars and in storehouses.

Scenes of royal activities

Royal activities (such as the Sed festival) and public appearances of the king (such as chariot drives and presentations of rewards to officials) were depicted on the Gempaaten. In all of these scenes there are bowing courtiers adoring the royal couple, as well as military personnel. See below on the religious significance of these scenes.

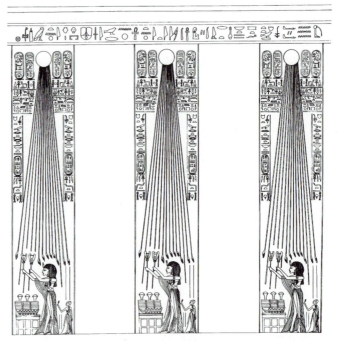

Nefertiti offering to the Aten, from the Ben-ben colonnade

The offering ritual

The offering ritual, held in the open, was conducted by the king who was the only one eligible to deal directly with the Aten.

Reliefs show the king riding to the temple of Aten in his chariot, accompanied by his family, officials and soldiers. He is welcomed by a priestly cortege who accompany him to the open-air shrine which is crowded with courtiers and servants carrying containers of foodstuffs on their heads, reciting the benediction 'O thou beautiful child of the Sun-disk! May the Sun-disk favour thee'. Rows of offering stands are covered with fowl,

Massive quantities of food and drink

bread and wine and behind each one stands a priest, a *Servant of the Disk in the Mansion of the Disk in Akhetaten* or an official/servitor who raises a censor to the king with one hand and pours a libation with the other with the request that the sun-disk favour the king and keep him healthy.

Akhenaten was assisted in the ritual by Meryre I, the *Great Seer of the Aten* whose job was to hand the ritual equipment to the king and burn incense in front of him. Meryre's appointment to this position is record-ed in his tomb and the text explains why he was given this role.

Role of great seer

> Said the king, living in truth, Lord of the Two lands: Neferkheperure-Waenre, to the *Great Seer* of the Aten, Meryre: 'Behold I am appoint-ing thee for myself, to be the *great seer* of the Aten in the temple of Aten in Akhetaten, saying: 'O my hearer of the call who hears my teaching. As for any commission with which thou art charged, my heart is satisfied therewith'.[25]

Because the king was the living image of the Aten on earth, he had his own hierarchy of priests — *prophets of Neferkheperure Waenre*. Their task was to wait upon the king when he performed the cult ritual.

Since the purpose of the food offering was to emphasise the role of the Aten and his son in nourishing and sustaining the land, there were reg-ulations concerning the temple offerings. These included the amount of food and drink dedicated each day and the annual taxes imposed on officials and institutions for the continuing provision of these supplies. As recorded in the tomb of Parennefer, *Steward* and *King's Cup Bearer*, 'the corn imposts of every other god are measured by oipe, but for the disk they are measured in superabundance'.[26] This meant that other temples suffered as more and more goods were earmarked for the wor-ship of the Aten. Parennefer warned those officials who did not fulfil their obligations to the Aten, that they would answer to the king.

Regulations regarding offerings

Akhenaten offering to the Aten, from the tomb of Panehsy, Chief Servitor (priest) to the Aten at Akhetaten

A bust of Akhenaten from the Gempaaten

A colossal statue of Ahkenaten from the Gempaaten

The new iconography and Amarna art

With the pre-eminence of the Aten, came a change in temple and funerary art. The two most obvious changes were in:

- the proportions of the human figure, particularly that of the king
- the composition of scenes which included the royal family.

Images of Akhenaten

Early in his reign, the images of Akhenaten were grossly exaggerated, although later in his reign they were less extreme. He was represented with:

- a large head, long neck, narrow face and chin, pouting lips and elongated eyes
- a narrow upper torso
- a lower torso of obviously feminine proportions — prominent buttocks, swelling thighs, drooping belly and no evidence of genitals
- short lower legs.

As no artist would have represented the king in this way without royal approval, Akhenaten must have been making a statement of some kind.

Some scholars believe that because Akhenaten was described over and over as 'living in truth', the art at this time became more realistic and the images in some way reflected what he looked like. Robins says 'there is no reason to suppose that art under Akhenaten became any more realistic than it had traditionally been'.[27] She thinks these images are a reflection of the king's religious convictions.

If Akhenaten was making a religious statement with these exaggerated images, what was it? Perhaps the following extracts from hymns and prayers to the king can provide a clue.

> **You are mother and father of all that you made.**[28]

Since Akhenaten believed he was the living image of the Aten, perhaps he had himself depicted in an androgynous form to incorporate both male and female aspects of the creator.

There are constant references to Akhenaten as Hapy, the Nile.

> **Hapy flowing daily who nourishes Egypt.**[29]
>
> **This thousand fold Hapy who flows every day.**[30]
>
> **He inundates the hearts, and all lands are in festivity because of his rising.**[31]

Hapy brought fertility, abundance and prosperity to Egypt and was always shown as a male with drooping stomach, female breasts and no genitals. The depiction of Akhenaten 'recalls the way in which fecundity figures are depicted'.[32] The suggestion of fertility is also obvious in the images of Nefertiti where the focus is on the pubic area.

Ordinary people also tended to be depicted in the new style but with less exaggeration than royalty. To accommodate the change in figure proportions (long neck and pendulous stomach), the artists added two more squares to the grid system which they traditionally used to guide them in representing figures.

Composition of scenes featuring the royal family

The composition of the scenes of the king's public and private life also 'encode a statement of belief'.[33] The images of warm family life, the window of appearances and the chariot drives were all religious icons.

Religious icons

Wherever Akhenaten and Nefertiti appear together, standing under the rays of the Aten, the image created is one of a divine triad — creator god and the male and female aspects of the cosmos. Robins believes that when a child was added to the scene, this represented 'the continued powers of creation'.[34]

According to Kemp, other scenes of Akhenaten and his family were intended to show them as 'a loving group so perfect as to warrant veneration'.[35] Evidence of this veneration comes from the tombs and houses of Akhenaten's nobles. Not only did they address their prayers to Akhenaten and Nefertiti, but they are also shown worshipping before them. Domestic stela of the divine couple and the Aten, as well as statues of the king, have been found in the remains of the homes of the Amarna elite.

Ideal family

A family scene — 'manifesto' of the solar cult

Royal procession

Another religious icon was the royal procession with the king and his family in their chariots, attended by retainers and bodyguards running alongside in a bowed position. This icon served two purposes:

1 It identified the movements of the king with the cycle of the sun-disk across the sky during the day.

2 It was the equivalent of the previous processions of the gods during important festivals, such as the Opet.

A royal chariot drive between the palace and the Great Temple of the Aten, from the tomb of Panehsy at Amarna

Was Amarna art a radical break from tradition?

Traditional aspects of Amarna art

Although Amarna art was distinctive because of the new themes used in the 'decoration' of temples and tombs and the change in the proportions of the human figure, it did not depart from the traditional form in any other way.

According to Robins, in *Egyptian Painting and Relief*, size was still used to denote importance, artists still used registers to depict different aspects or phases of an event, groups were still shown as rows of overlapping figures and the importance of balance was recognised.

The influence of the new doctrine on the Sed festival (king's jubilee)

Akhenaten celebrated a Sed festival in his third year on the throne instead of after the customary thirty years. His reasons for this are not known. Those who support the theory that he shared a co-regency with his father suggest that this Sed may have corresponded to one of his father's jubilees.

Omissions from Sed festival

Although it seems that he followed the traditional form of the festival, his new doctrine required that some changes be made. For example, nowhere are the great gods — Amun, Ptah, Thoth and Osiris mentioned. Although the standards of these gods are shown being carried by the priests, statues of them are absent from the individual shrines in the Court of the Great Ones. Instead, in each roofless shrine is a statue of the king under the rays of the sun-disk.

The traditional hymn to Hathor was retained but the names of the other gods mentioned in it were removed.

An unusual aspect of these proceedings was the prominent role played by Nefertiti. In one procession scene she is shown in a palanquin surrounded by kingly symbols in the manner of a pharaoh. Her carrying chair was carved with striding lionesses and sphinxes in her own image, similar to that of Akhenaten.

Prominence of Nefertiti

From these and other reliefs, there is no doubt about Nefertiti's religious status even at this early stage.

The influence of the sun cult on the site and layout of Akhetaten

Sometime in year 5, it is believed that the king announced his decision to build a new city dedicated to the Aten. According to Gardiner this was 'doubtless promoted by the recognition that the cults of Aten and Amun-Re could no longer be carried out side by side'.[36] Although there is no evidence of any civil strife at this time, Akhenaten later recorded that he had heard 'evil words'.

Decision to move from Thebes

> As my father Aten lives! If [...] even though it be more evil than what I heard in the 4th year, than what I heard in the [year], than what I heard in the 1st year, than what my father Nebmare [heard, or than] what Menkheperure heard ...[37]

Whether these so-called evil words were associated with opposition to his projects from some of his officials or from the priests of Amun is not known. It may have had some connection with his decision to abandon Thebes.

The site of Aten's cult centre

The king had already built sun temples to Aten at the cult centres of Amun at Thebes, of Ptah at Memphis and of Re at Heliopolis. Perhaps he believed that the Aten deserved a special city of its own, built on a site which had never been associated with any other god.

Such a site was found almost midway between Memphis and Thebes, near modern El Amarna. The king recorded that the Aten had revealed it to him, 'no official proposed it, nor any man in the entire land'[38] and claimed it was where the god had appeared *for the first time* (at creation).

Site midway between Memphis and Thebes

It is possible that on one of his river journeys between Memphis and Thebes, Akhenaten had noticed the site and how the morning sun, rising over a break in the eastern hills, formed the hieroglyph for *horizon*.

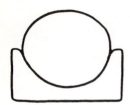

The hieroglyph for 'horizon'

It is interesting that he named his new city Akhetaten which meant *Horizon of the Aten* and built his tomb in the wadi over which the morning sun rose.

The site for the king's new city was a plain about 13 kilometres long and five kilometres wide, surrounded by a crescent of hills which were interrupted in places by wadis. On the opposite side of the river was an area of fertile land, large enough to support a substantial agricultural population. Akhenaten claimed both sides of the river for the Aten and delineated the area with boundary stelae cut into the surrounding cliffs. These stelae were originally between three and nine metres high, flanked by statues depicting Akhenaten and Nefertiti holding narrow tablets inscribed with the names of the Aten and themselves. The two eldest royal daughters, Meritaten and Meketaten were also featured on the stelae.

Foundation ceremony

According to the inscriptions on his boundary stelae, Akhenaten visited the site in year 5 and conducted a foundation ceremony from an altar specially erected for the occasion. After making a great offering to the god, the king called his followers before him — 'royal courtiers, the great ones of the palace, the army officers and the entire entourage'.[39] Akhenaten explained how the Aten had led him to the site promising that it would belong to him 'as a horizon of the disk for ever and ever'.[40] and outlined the extent of the proposed city.

> I have demarked Akhetaten on its south, on its north, on its west, on its east.[41]

> Now as for the area within the four landmarks ... it belongs to my father Aten, whether mountains, or cliffs, or marshes or uplands, or fields, or waters, or towns, or shores, or people, or cattle, or trees, or anything which Aten, my father, has made ...[42]

Oath to never extend the city

He swore an oath that no one, not even the queen, could convince him to build Aten's city anywhere else and that he would not extend the city beyond these original boundaries.

> I shall not pass beyond the southern landmark of Akhetaten towards the south, nor shall I pass beyond the northern landmark of [Akhetaten towards the north].[43]

> As for the middle landmark which is upon the eastern mountain of Akhetaten, it is ... as far as I make a stand; I shall not pass beyond it ... The middle landmark which is upon the western mountain of Akhetaten is made over against it, opposite.[44]

Plans for the city

The king then:

- announced that Aten's city would be the new capital where he would hold audience for people from all over Egypt
- listed some of the buildings he planned to erect on the site so that the city would be a true monument to the Aten
- indicated that he intended Aten's city to last forever, by announcing that the royal tombs would be built in the eastern hills and that if he happened to die elsewhere, his body was to be brought back to Akhetaten for burial. The same applied to his family.

In the following year, the king returned to the site and although surveyors and builders had been working at a feverish pace, he had to stay in a 'pavilion of woven stuff'.[45] He inspected and confirmed the boundaries and ordered the cutting of eleven more boundary stelae, making fourteen in all. It was a further two years before the city was fully occupied and functional.

Layout of Akhetaten

Since the site had never been occupied, the city could be planned with no constraints. The main public buildings (religious and administrative) were located in what is referred to as the Central City. From this nucleus the city spread along the river with satellite suburbs to the north and south and various palaces and retreats towards the limits of the city.

Nucleus of administrative and religious buildings

Apart from the corridor of royal and administrative buildings there appears to have been no real planning in the suburbs. The impression gained from the excavations is one of a series of joined villages composed of houses, both rich and poor, interlocked in complex patterns.

The following figures show the layout of Akhetaten and the buildings which archaeologists identified in the central city.

The site of Akhenaten's capital, Akhetaten, as delineated by 14 boundary stelae

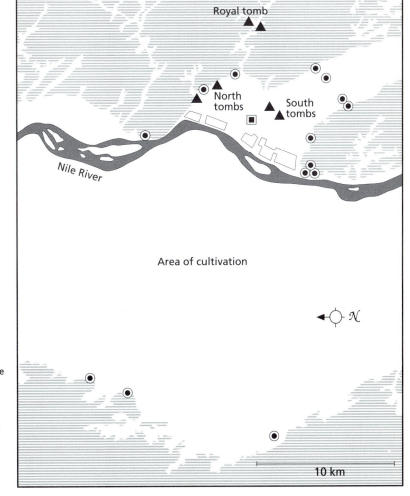

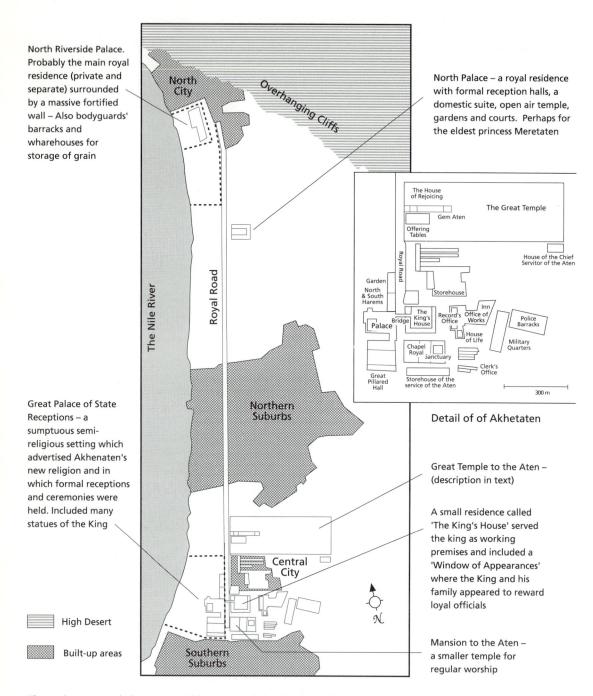

North Riverside Palace. Probably the main royal residence (private and separate) surrounded by a massive fortified wall – Also bodyguards' barracks and wharehouses for storage of grain

North Palace – a royal residence with formal reception halls, a domestic suite, open air temple, gardens and courts. Perhaps for the eldest princess Meretaten

North City

Overhanging Cliffs

The House of Rejoicing

Gem Aten

The Great Temple

Offering Tables

House of the Chief Servitor of the Aten

Royal Road

Garden

North & South Harems

Storehouse

The Nile River

Royal Road

The King's House

Bridge

Record's Office

Office of Works

Inn

Police Barracks

Palace

House of Life

Military Quarters

Chapel Royal

Sanctuary

Clerk's Office

Great Pillared Hall

Storehouse of the service of the Aten

300 m

Great Palace of State Receptions – a sumptuous semi-religious setting which advertised Akhenaten's new religion and in which formal receptions and ceremonies were held. Included many statues of the King

Northern Suburbs

Detail of of Akhetaten

Great Temple to the Aten – (description in text)

A small residence called 'The King's House' served the king as working premises and included a 'Window of Appearances' where the King and his family appeared to reward loyal officials

Central City

N

High Desert

Built-up areas

Southern Suburbs

Mansion to the Aten – a smaller temple for regular worship

The main structural elements at Akhetaten and the details of the central city

This spread of domestic and public buildings provided Ahkenaten with an 'arena of royal display'.[46] As he and his family made their way 'in procession' from the chief royal residence in the north city to the central city and back again via an eight-kilometre road (the royal road) there was plenty of opportunity for public adulation of the living image of the Aten. According to Kemp, these excursions by the royal couple, their daughters, retainers and bodyguards, were used to fill the vacuum left by the lack of religious festivals and processions previously celebrated, such as the Opet and Valley festivals associated with Amun.

Further opportunities for the royal couple to display themselves, receive blessings and accept praise were provided by the *windows of appearances*. These were architectural features built into some of the Amarna buildings from which the king and queen bestowed gold collars on worthy officials.

The villas of Akhenaten's nobles, the workers' village and the tombs in the eastern cliffs are described in Chapters and 16 and 17.

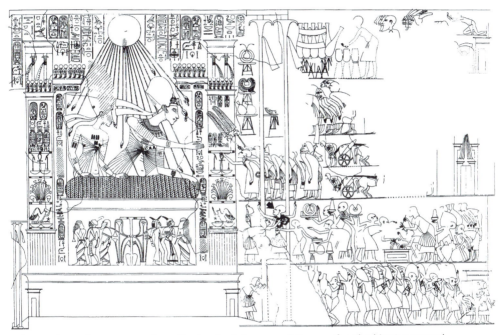

The window of appearance from the tomb at Amarna of Parennefer, the king's personal attendant and cupbearer

The sun cult and the economy

For centuries the Egyptians had a system in which religion, politics and economics were integrated. By focusing on 'the one god', building a new capital dedicated to the Aten, Akhenaten altered the economy and turned the whole system upside down.

Integration of economy, politics and religion

Early in his reign, Akhenaten (Amenhotep IV) had issued orders for a massive mobilisation of workers, officials and troops to quarry and transport stone and build four sun temples in Thebes. In year 3 he held a jubilee in which enormous amounts of commodities were required from all over the country. The amount of revenue and labour required for these projects was not unusual. However, within two years of his jubilee and before his Theban sun temples were completed, Akhenaten announced that he was planning to build a new capital and transfer the seat of government to a remote and isolated site in Middle Egypt.

At the same time, he officially broke with Amun by changing his name from Amenhotep IV to Akhenaten (*He Who is Serviceable to the Sun-disk*). This was followed by the closure of Amun's temples and the erasure of the god's name from all public places. To what extent he suppressed the worship of other gods is not really known.

It is possible that Akhenaten had an economic motive for his actions at this time. He was about to embark on a massive building project and needed revenue. Also a continuing source of income was required for the lavish offerings to be dedicated to Aten. If Akhenaten closed the temples and disbanded their priesthoods he would be able to take control of the temple estates and revenues.

Closure of Amun's temple, the richest establishment in Egypt

Amun's establishment was the richest in Egypt and the greatest single employer of labour. Huge estates all over the country were cultivated by small farmers, agricultural labourers, temple agents and even officials who rented out temple property. Numerous scribes were employed to carry out administrative and financial tasks and the temple maintained a fleet of ships and massive storehouses and granaries. These resources could now be redirected to Akhetaten and the temples of Amun and the other gods began to fall into disrepair.

Economic problems caused by closure of temples

Not only did the closure or restriction of temple activities adversely affect individuals but 'the abandonment of the system of divine estates led to the ruination of a whole system of production and distribution without providing any new structure to replace it'.[47]

Even work on Akhenaten's sun temples in Thebes ceased and the workforce employed on these, as well as many of the craftsmen responsible for cutting, decorating and furnishing the royal and private tombs at Thebes, were transferred to Akhetaten. Those workmen who were immediately set to work on the royal and noble tombs east of Akhetaten, were housed in a specially built workers' village outside the city. Refer to Chapter 16 for details on this village. It appears that the army was also used as a labour force on much of the Akhetaten construction work.

Effects of diversion of resources

As more and more of the country's resources were transferred to Akhetaten and the king and his court isolated themselves in the new capital, 'the once thriving religious and administrative centres of Thebes and Memphis stood idle. Government offices had been virtually shut down, and the sons of illustrious houses that had served pharaoh well suddenly found themselves bereft of function.'[48] Also, effective government at the local level became difficult and bureaucratic corruption increased.

The 'construction of the new city and new temples was to the detriment of the economy in general and to the temple-based economy in particular'.[49]

Changes in funerary practices

Osirian burial practices prior to Akhenaten's 'revolution'

Prior to the reign of Akhenaten, Egyptians believed that when they died they faced a judgment before the god Osiris. This involved declaring before each of forty-two gods that they had committed no sin, after which they were led into the hall of Osiris by Anubis, the jackal-headed god of embalming and the necropolis. Near to Osiris stood the goddesses Nephthys and Isis and the god Horus. Then the deceased's heart had to be weighed on the scales of truth against a feather (*ma'at*) and the judgment was recorded by Thoth. If the judgment was favourable the deceased were escorted before the throne of Osiris who announced that they were true of heart and could pass into the afterlife.

Royalty expected to spend eternity travelling with the sun god, Re, across the heavens during the day and through the Underworld of Osiris during the night. The dead king supposedly joined the crew of the sun god's boat which included other gods such as Horus, Seth and Thoth. During the nightly journey through the Underworld, the sun god brought light to the region and fought off the enemy serpent, Apopis. At dawn the following day, the deceased king emerged from the eastern horizon and travelled for the next 12 hours with the sun god's boat and its celestial crew.

Views of the afterlife

Most ordinary Egyptians preferred the idea of an afterlife spent in the *Fields of Reeds*, the kingdom of Osiris, a land somewhat like the lush Nile delta. There they continued an ideal rural existence and helped the sun god's boat on its nightly journey.

To help them through the ordeal of death, the Egyptians had special texts inscribed and painted on the walls of their tombs and on special papyrus rolls which were buried with the body. The scenes of the judgment, the sun god's journey and life in the Osirian Fields of Reeds were recorded on the tomb walls.

Funerary texts prior to Akhenaten

In the new doctrine of the Aten, the sole god, all these aspects of the funerary beliefs were eliminated. The afterlife was no longer peopled with a host of gods. The new doctrine focused only on the life-giving aspects of the disk as it travelled alone across the daytime sky. There was no journey by the sun through the Underworld and there was no kingdom of Osiris.

By day the sun drew the deceased's *ba* (or soul) from his body to stay near the altar of his temple but at night there was nothing 'as their maker rests in lightland'.[50] The living and the dead merely slept in the cold darkness.

The afterlife according to the new doctrine

Only the king, who was *the beautiful child of the disk* knew the mind of his heavenly father and received favours from him. In the doctrine of the Aten all that people could hope for was that their *ka* would survive because of their dedication to the king. They could no longer look forward to the judgment before Osiris, being welcomed into the afterlife by the gods and spending eternity continuing their lives in the Fields of Reeds.

The traditional funerary formulae were not appropriate to the new doctrine. Only by addressing their praise and prayers to the king and the Aten could Akhenaten's courtiers look forward to a favourable life in the next world.

The extract below, which illustrates this hope, is from a prayer to Akhenaten found in the tomb of one of his courtiers, Ay.

> I live by worshipping his *ka*,
> I am sated by attending him;
> My breath, by which I live is this north wind ...
> Neferkheperure, Sole-one-of-Re.
> Grant me a lifetime high in your favour!
> How happy is your favourite, O Son of the Aten!
> All his deeds will endure and be firm.
> When the *ka* of the Ruler is with him forever ...
> ... Grant me to kiss the holy ground
> To come before you with offerings
> To Aten, your father, as gifts of your *ka*.
> Grant that my *ka* abide and flourish for me,
> As when on earth I followed your *ka*,
> So as to rise in my name to the blessed place,
> In which you grant me to rest, my word being true.
> May my name be pronounced in it by your will,
> I being your favourite who follows your *ka*
> That I may go with your favour when old age has come.[51]

The royal family became the focus of funerary themes

A totally new and limited number of funerary themes, which focused on the royal family in various domestic and public situations, now appeared on the tomb walls. Refer to the figures showing the royal family in this chapter, and to Chapter 17 for more details of Amarna tombs.

Effects of the religious changes on the ordinary Egyptian

Although statues of the king and domestic shrines to the Aten and royal family were found in the homes of the wealthy nobles, the religious changes did not affect the personal worship of ordinary Egyptians.

No effect on the worship of ordinary people

Throughout Egyptian history the common people were, to a certain extent, isolated from what went on in the great cult temples. They worshipped a variety of household gods and rarely, if ever, entered the outer court of the temples. When the workers' village at Amarna was excavated, it was found that right through Akhenaten's reign the inhabitants had continued to worship Hathor, Bes, Taweret and a cobra deity, Renenutet.

The greatest effect the closure of the cult temples had on the ordinary people was the ceasing of the annual festivals and processions of the gods in which they had participated. These had always been an important feature of their social life.

Dissatisfaction with lack of festivals

To the people, the Aten was a remote god associated exclusively with the king. 'The failure to set up a program of celebration and feasting with its popular appeal'[52] would have contributed to the dissatisfaction of the populace.

Personnel at Akhetaten

Akhenaten's family

By year 9 Akhenaten had six daughters (Meritaten, Meketaten, Ankhesenpaaten, Nefernefruaten, Neferneferure and Setenpenre) by his beloved queen consort, Nefernefruaten Nefertiti.

Daughters and secondary wives

Despite his apparent affection for Nefertiti, Akhenaten had other wives, one of whom was Kiya. Also the king had taken into his harem the Mitannian princess, Tadukhepa, originally sent to marry his father. Some scholars have suggested that Tadukhepa might have been the same person as Kiya but there is no evidence for this.

Like many royals, Kiya's background is unknown but it is likely that she came from an official family with royal links. She was described as the much beloved wife of the king. This was an acknowledgment of her position as a secondary wife who had produced children by Akhenaten, and that she was probably the mother of a son. She appears to have been a favourite for a reasonably long time as her 'name was associated with both the early and late forms of the name of the Aten'.[53] Also her status is indicated by the sun-shade temple that Akhenaten built for her in the Maru-Aten (a royal retreat comprising two large walled enclosures, lakes, gardens and shrines, to the south of the city), chapels for her cult near the Great Aten Temple and her opulent funerary equipment.

Thomas suggests that Kiya is a likely candidate for the mother of the princes, Smenkhkare and Tutankhaten (Tutankhamun) who in turn succeeded Akhenaten on the throne. This will be discussed later.

From year 12 it appears that the widowed Queen Tiye and her youngest daughter, Baketaten, set up residence in Akhetaten.

Detail from a talatat showing 'the favourite', Kiya

Akhenaten's courtiers

Some of the men who followed Akhenaten from Thebes to Akhetaten appear to have come originally from Heliopolis. For example, Maya, who was made *General of the Army of the Lord of the Two Lands* had been a steward in Heliopolis and as *Scribe of the Elite Troops* may have been in charge of the labour force which quarried the stone for the sun-temples in Thebes. Bek, also from Heliopolis, was a sculptor and worked on the king's sun-temples. Pawah was the High Priest of the Sun in Heliopolis. Parennefer, the King's Cup Bearer, had been at Thebes also.

Nobles from Heliopolis

New 'faces'

However, most of the king's courtiers in Akhetaten were new faces. Even Ay, *Favoured of the Good God, Fan Bearer on the King's Right Hand, True King's Scribe and God's Father, Commander of Chariotry*, is absent from sources before the move to Akhetaten.

Information concerning these officials comes from their tombs and houses in Akhenaten. They are identified in the figure below.

Akhenaten's courtiers

Why did Akhenaten rely on new men? During the reign of Akhenaten's predecessors, most of the able administrators came from the ranks of those who had a close association with the royal family. In some cases the mothers of these men were royal wet nurses, royal favourites or high in the cult of Amun. These palace children were brought up at court and formed an influential peer group from which future administrators were chosen. Also, many of these men followed their fathers, grandfathers or uncles into high-ranking positions. By the time Akhenaten came to the throne the upper ranks of the bureaucracy must have wielded great power.

For those scholars who support the view of a long co-regency between Amenhotep III and Akhenaten, the explanation would be that the 'old guard' remained in Thebes to continue to serve Amenhotep III while Akhenaten took courtiers of his own choosing to Akhetaten. On the

Reasons for new 'faces'

* Some individuals held several positions.

other hand, if there was no co-regency or only a brief one, perhaps Akhenaten, aware of a certain timidity in his own character and a weakness of resolve, may have been afraid or resentful of the power of these 'old guard' officials.

It appears from the scenes on the tomb walls of these Amarna nobles that most of them at some stage received the gold of honour and a fine tomb from Akhenaten. According to Breasted, 'it is clear that Akhenaten was holding all his great officials faithful to his reforms, only by such means'.[54]

Parennefer, below the palace balcony, receiving the gold collars

Perhaps there were a few sincere men (such as Ay and Pentu, who were the only men prominent in the years after his death) who shared Akhenaten's passion for the new doctrine. However, most of them probably only paid lip service to the new faith and when the king died they 'hastily abandoned his teaching and returned to the comforting beliefs in the many gods who offered help to man in life and beyond death'.[55]

Reception of foreign ambassadors and the visit of Tiye

According to the evidence from the tombs of Huya and Meryre II, a magnificent reception for foreign dignitaries was held in Akhetaten in year 12. Representatives from Nubia, Libya, Punt, Palestine, Syria, the Aegean, Naharin (Mitanni) and Khatte (Hittites) came to the new capital with tribute and gifts for the Egyptian king.

Foreign dignitaries at Akhetaten

> Year 12, second month of the second season, day 8. Live my father, Aten, given life forever and ever; live the King of Upper and Lower Egypt, Akhenaten and the great King's Wife, Nefernefruaten-Nefertiti, living forever, at the arrival [ ] the tribute of Kharu and Kush, the west and east [ ] united in one head, the isles in the midst of the sea [ ] on the side [ ] , the tribute [ ] the great storehouse of Akhetaten for receiving the impost of [ ] that he may give to them the breath of life.[56]

The purpose of this event is not really known.

Aldred and others who support the view of a long co-regency between Amenhotep III and Akhenaten, believe that it was associated with the accession of Akhenaten to sole rule. Perhaps the death of Amenhotep III was also the reason for the visit to Akhetaten and eventual residence there of Queen Tiye at this time.

Purpose

On the other hand the reception could have been instigated by Queen Tiye, who was aware of the apathy of her son towards the empire and the problems that were occurring in Egypt's Asiatic territories. Refer to the section entitled 'Foreign affairs' later in this chapter.

Visit of Queen Tiye

The international reception is recorded in the tomb of Meryre II. This evidence is supplemented by scenes in the tomb of Huya, Queen Tiye's chief official (Steward of her House, her Treasury and her Harem) who accompanied her to Akhetaten. He was given the Gold of Honour by Akhenaten and permission to build a tomb in the eastern hills which also contains scenes of the festivities associated with Tiye's visit.

Akhenaten and Nefertiti arriving at the tribute reception in year 12

The king and queen are shown being carried in their ceremonial lion chairs to a special reception area which is believed to have been set up in the desert, east of the city. There a platform and shaded pavilion had been erected for the king, queen and six princesses to view the proceedings and receive the foreign representatives. This is the last time we know of that Akhenaten, Nefertiti and their six daughters were shown together. It is a very informal scene with the younger princesses playing with a pet gazelle, and the king and queen holding hands.

It appears that apart from the royal family, everybody else present had to stand in the scorching sun. The representative from Assyria later complained of this to his king, Ashurballit I, who wrote to Akhenaten about his lack of consideration.

Why are my envoys kept standing in the open sun? They will die out in the open sun. If it does the king good to stand in the open sun, then let him stand in the open sun himself and let him die himself.[57]

Scenes from the reception of tribute in year 12, from the tomb at Amarna of Meryre II, Overseer of the Royal Harem

The delegations from the various nations approached the royal dais carrying ornate weapons, vases and bowls of gold and silver, rings of gold, logs of ebony and elephant tusks and leading exotic animals, cattle, chariots, slaves and prisoners. The captives from Asia were a sign of the trouble brewing in Egypt's empire.

The festivities included music, dancing, fencing, boxing and wrestling and gave Akhenaten another opportunity to present *shebu* collars of gold to worthy officials. During the visit of Tiye and her youngest daughter Baketaten, Akhenaten honoured his mother by dedicating a sun-shade temple (*Shade of Re*) to her, accompanying her on a visit to the Great Temple of the Aten and entertaining her at family banquets.

Festivities

Foreign affairs

Akhenaten's apparent lack of interest in military affairs is believed to have led to the loss of Egypt's lucrative Asiatic Empire. However, Gardiner maintains that Akhenaten was not solely responsible for the loss of Egyptian prestige abroad. His father, Amenhotep III, was equally to blame. Gardiner also believes that scholars need to reconsider the accusation that Akhenaten threw away the empire built up in Western Asia by Thutmose III. In fact he questions whether the Egyptians actually had an empire in western Asia.

Was Akhenaten to blame for the loss of empire?

Was Akhenaten:

- uninterested in what was going on in his empire
- solely responsible for its disintegration?

There are a number of factors to consider with regard to the loss of Egyptian control over western Asia during this period.

- Egyptian control in Palestine and Syria had always been difficult to maintain. The dissensions between states and their periodic attempts to revolt from Egypt and seek independence meant that the pharaoh had to make frequent shows of strength. Even the great Thutmose III had to conduct numerous campaigns in the area to bring it under control.

Difficulties of maintaining control in Syria

  Towards the end of the reign of Amenhotep III, a few local Syrian princes, remote from Egyptian control, began to seek their independence and yet, neither Amenhotep nor Akhenaten appeared at the head of an army to put down rebellion among some of their own dependencies. It was inevitable that even those who remained loyal to Egypt 'should eventually wonder what benefit they derived from their dependence on the Egyptian empire'.[58]

- A new force had appeared in Asia Minor during the reign of Amenhotep III. The Hittites, under their young, energetic and ambitious king, Suppiluliumas, had awoken to new life. Suppiluliumas, who was one of the great strategists in the ancient world, involved himself in the internal dissensions of Egypt's ally Mitanni and the power politics of the states of northern Syria. This brought him dangerously close to a confrontation with Egypt.

Appearance of Hittites

Akhenaten, who appears to have been essentially a timorous man, hesitated in dealing with the rapidly developing crises in western Asia. 'Akhenaten's hesitancy and lack of foresight lost him the initiative.'[59]

Evidence of actions taken by Akhenaten

The evidence, from the Amarna Letters, the Buhan stela and the art of the period, though limited, seems to indicate that Akhenaten's reign was not totally devoid of military activity and that he continued the diplomatic policy of his father with regard to western Asia.

One-sided view of Amarna Letters

Unfortunately, the Amarna Letters present an incomplete and one-sided view of the situation. There are virtually no records of the replies sent by Akhenaten or his general, Maya, to the letters and despatches from the vassal princes, governors and officials in Syria and Palestine. Only six of the surviving letters are from an Egyptian pharaoh.

Evidence that Akhenaten did take some action

The *letters* 'show only interrupted glimpses of the shifting historical scene and the characters who played their parts in it'.[60]

Depending on the chronological order in which scholars arrange these letters, so the interpretation of events in western Asia changes. For example, Aldred says:

> The many letters of Rib-Addi, for instance, have been used to tell a story of the progressive decline of Egyptian power in Asia, whereas the course of events, by rearrangement of the sequence, could be shown to have been an ebb and flow rather than a constant retreat.[61]

The letters seem to indicate that the Egyptian king did not respond to many of the requests made by Syrian princes for Egyptian troops. However, there is evidence that:

- Akhenaten issued orders to local princes concerning the need to be alert in protecting their territory
- the king's commands were being implemented
- some limited military aid, such as a brigade of archers to one vassal ruler and chariots to another, was provided by Akhenaten in response to requests
- Akhenaten wrote a letter on behalf of the anxious Rib-Addi of Byblos to the ruler of Sidon.

Campaign in Nubia

The inscription on a fragmentary stela from Buhan (Nubia), suggests that Akhenaten ordered at least one military campaign in Nubia. The stela records that when a minor rebellion broke out among some southern tribes, Akhenaten ordered the viceroy of Kush to move against them. During this campaign, over 145 Nubians and 361 head of cattle were captured and a number of captives were impaled on stakes.

There is further evidence that Akhenaten:

- used Nubian contingents for garrison duty in his Asiatic dependencies
- deported numbers of troublemakers from Asia to Nubia

- continued his predecessors' practice of implanting Egyptian-type towns in Kush.

Redford maintains that Akhenaten's policy in Nubia may have been 'unoriginal but it was pursued with determination and intelligence'.[62]

Amarna art provides evidence that:

Evidence of
military presence

- Akhenaten regarded his army highly. Soldiers are evident in most of the reliefs depicting important events of his reign

- the king is frequently represented wearing the *khepresh* or war crown of a warrior king

- Asiatic and Nubian captives are still shown around the royal dais and under the *window of appearance* when Akhenaten and Nefertiti appeared to the people during reward ceremonies

- during Akhenaten's first Sed festival, *the sons of the chiefs of every foreign land* presented their tribute

- foreign kings and princes still sent their gifts and in fact appeared in Akhetaten in year 12 for a huge reception of foreign ambassadors.

Akhenaten and the Kingdom of Mitanni (Naharin)

Since the time of Thutmose IV, Egypt and Mitanni had been on friendly terms. This cordial relationship was cemented by the marriage of Mitannian princesses to several Egyptian kings.

Of all the great kings of the east, Tushratta of Mitanni seems to have had the closest relationship with Egypt during the reign of Amenhotep III. After Amenhotep's death, Tushratta sent a letter to Akhenaten, saying that he was ten times closer to him than he had been to his father.

Akhenaten's treatment of Tushratta

However, it appears that Akhenaten treated the Mitannian king with a certain amount of indifference. According to the correspondence from Tushratta, Akhenaten refused to honour his father's promises to send gifts to the king, failed to answer Tushratta's letters and even kept a Mitannian messenger waiting at the Egyptian court for four years before giving a reply to one piece of correspondence. Why he behaved this way is not known.

Akhenaten also seems to have had no interest in Tushratta's internal problems. The Mitannian king was faced with two palace revolutions during his reign and a government in exile was set up to oppose him. The Egyptian government's lack of concern for the fortunes of Tushratta allowed the dynamic young Hittite king, Suppiluliumas, to exploit the situation.

Hittite attack on Mitanni

He undermined the relationship between Egypt and Mittani by writing to Akhenaten congratulating him on his accession and by sending him appropriate gifts. Redford suggests that Akhenaten may have signed a treaty with him despite strong objections from some of Egypt's allies. Suppiluliumas also supported the Mitannian prince-in-exile and launched a surprise attack on Tushratta, forcing the king and members of the Mitannian court to abandon their capital. Tushratta was later assassinated and with his death, the great power of Mitanni ceased.

Appeals from northern Syria for help

The Hittite king then attacked those cities which had been in alliance with Mitanni. These former vassal states of Mitanni did not like the idea of becoming part of the Hittite empire and had formed an alliance against Suppululiumas. Several leaders wrote to Akhenaten pleading for help. Based on the former *brotherhood* that had existed between the kings of Mitanni and Egypt, they hoped that Akhenaten would send a military force to support them. One of these letters, sent by the ruler of Qatanum, states:

> All these kings are indeed servants of my lord! If the king my lord so desires, he marches out; but they say the king my lord will not march out. So let my lord dispatch archers, and let them come (alone).
>
> Let my lord's ministers say what shall be their tribute and they shall pay it.[63]

Another letter concludes:

> ... and if my lord does not wish to march forth, then let him send one of his commissioners with troops and chariots.[64]

Before any letter could reach Egypt, Suppululiumas swept into northern Syria, attacking those cities which failed to give him allegiance. This area remained in the hands of the Hittites for the next 170 years.

Possible reasons for the king's actions

Akhenaten took no action to help these former vassals of Mitanni. Why? Perhaps, as Redford suggests, Akhenaten would have had to send a force of at least 1000 men to make any impression against the Hittites. This he was not prepared to do in the light of instability in his own dependencies. On the other hand, perhaps the Egyptian king, preoccupied with his new god, considered that the affairs of these northern Syrian cities were of no concern to him.

Suppululiumas refrained from threatening any of Egypt's dependencies at this stage, but formed a friendly alliance with Aziru, prince of Amurru, Egypt's northernmost dependency. The princes of Amurru had been playing a double game with Egypt for some time.

It was not until the reign of Tutankhamun, that Hittite and Egyptian forces came into direct conflict.

The disintegration of Egypt's empire in central Syria

Double game played by leaders of Aziru

The leaders of the Egyptian dependency of Amurru, Abd-Ashirta (during the reign of Amenhotep III) and his son, Aziru (during the reign of Akhenaten), carved out an independent state for themselves at the expense of the weaker states around them. However, at the same time they continued to write friendly letters to the pharaoh, assuring him of their loyalty.

The Hittites found Prince Aziru an effective tool in undermining Egyptian power in central Syria and they supported him in his endeavours. The chief areas which he coveted were the wealthy city-states of the Phoenician coast — Simyra, Sidon, Tyre and Byblos. In his letters to Akhenaten, Aziru denounced the loyal leaders of these cities as traitors and enemies of Egypt. A warlike desert tribe called the Habiru also helped him seize control of Egypt's coastal dependencies.

Akhenaten and his father before him had been warned about the actions of Abd-Ashirta and Aziru by the loyal ruler of Byblos, Rib-Addi, but they took no action against them. Rib-Addi's impassioned despatches form a large part of the collection of the Amarna Letters.

Appeals for help from Byblos

The first coastal city to fall to Aziru was Simyra, the headquarters of Egyptian administration. Aziru had blockaded and destroyed it when its inhabitants refused to accept him as governor. The elders of the city of Tunip had sent a letter warning Akhenaten that this would happen.

> Who would have formerly plundered Tunip without being plundered by Thutmose III? When Aziru enters Simyra, Aziru will do as he pleases, in the territory of our lord the king; and on account of these things our lord will have to lament. And now Tunip, thy city weeps, and her tears are flowing, and there is no help for us. For twenty years we have been sending to our lord the king, the King of Egypt but there has not yet come to us a word - no, not one![65]

Letter after letter was sent to Akhenaten by the leaders of the cities threatened by Aziru, but they received no support as he continued to escape justice. The leaders of Sidon, realising that the Egyptian king would send no help, joined forces with Aziru who then attacked Tyre. Byblos was next.

No Egyptian help for vassal states

Aziru's treatment of Rib-Addi of Byblos, who had been pleading with Akhenaten for 15 years to take action, was the most notorious. The wily and persuasive Aziru convinced the Egyptian army commander in Galilee that Rib-Addi was a traitor to the Egyptians and the pharaoh's mercenaries attacked the city of Byblos. However, the old ruler's loyalty to the pharaoh seems never to have faltered despite Akhenaten's lack of response to his pleas for help. It has been suggested that Aziru may have had a friendly agent at the court of Akhenaten who kept from the king much of what was happening in Syria.

When Akhenaten was informed that Rib-Addi had been put to death, he sent a strongly worded letter to Aziru, ordering him to come to Egypt for investigations. The king also listed other complaints made against Aziru and demanded that he rebuild the city of Simyra that he had earlier destroyed. Aziru delayed appearing in Egypt, using the excuse that the Hittites were threatening Amurru. When he sent Akhenaten eight ship-loads of timber, plus hostages, the king relented and gave him a year's grace. Aziru played on this lack of resolve by Akhenaten and continued his double game, even going so far as to entertain the Hittite king's envoys.

Aziru used Akhenaten's lack of resolve to his advantage

Eventually Akhenaten sent his envoys to accompany Aziru to Egypt where he was kept for a long time. However, such was Aziru's power that he continued to influence affairs in central Syria. The successor of Rib-Addi in Byblos wrote to Akhenaten that:

> Aziru committed crimes even after the king had interviewed him, a crime against us! He has sent his men to Etakkama, and he has smitten all the lands of Amki, the king's lands; and now he has (even) sent his men to take possession of the lands of Amki.[66]

When Aziru was eventually released from Egypt and returned to Syria, he became a vassal of the Hittites. He was forced to pay an annual tribute and forbidden from pursuing an independent foreign policy.

Obviously Suppiluliumas' power was greater than that of Akhenaten.

Problems in Palestine

In Palestine, the situation was not much better. The petty princes who ruled in this area had made frequent attempts to gain their independence from Egypt even during the reigns of kings stronger than Akhenaten.

Akhenaten's hesitancy to take military action encouraged some of them to rebel and allowed the Habiru and Suti Bedouin, warlike desert tribesmen, to overrun the countryside and seize towns for themselves.

Those vassals who remained loyal to Egypt, such as Abdi-Khepa of Jerusalem, were attacked and plundered by the Habiru. Abdi-Khepa appealed to Akhenaten to 'care for his land'.[67] He warned the king that 'the Habiru are plundering all the lands of the king' and 'if no troops come in this very year, then all the lands of the king are lost'.[68] He continued, 'if there are no troops in this year, let the king send his officer to fetch me and my brothers, that we may die with my lord the king'.[69] Abdi-Khepa asked Akhenaten to send as few as 50 soldiers to help him.

Loss of Jerusalem and Megiddo

His appeals were in vain and the Habiru continued to plunder the countryside. It is not known whether Abdi-Khepa and his brothers escaped from Jerusalem or died when the city fell. Megiddo was also taken.

What sort of man was Akhenaten that could see his empire crumbling and not lift a finger to save it?

Was there a communication problem?

If he were an idealist and pacifist how could he watch the slaughter of so many subjects and betray those so faithful to him? The king's reaction may never be known but one possible explanation is that the true situation in Syria was never revealed to him. The workings of a complex bureaucracy do not always allow for good communication and are sometimes screens for truth. The writers of the Amarna Letters complained that they were being misrepresented by the pharaoh's officials. One of these officials was Tutu who claimed, 'As for the messengers from foreign lands, I was the one who communicated their affairs to the Palace'.[70] Perhaps Tutu did not pass on all of the foreign messages to the king, preferring to deal with some of them himself.

Even so, allowing for poor communication, for deception and for any amount of red tape, Akhenaten failed to take action on evidence that would have had his ancestor, Thutmose III, dashing for the field with an army behind him.

Complaisance during the reign of Amenhotep III and inertia and internal distractions during the reign of Akhenaten contributed to the loss of Egypt's control over Syria and Palestine.

Complaisance and inertia

The last years of Akhenaten's reign

The evidence for the events of the last three years of Akhenaten's reign, years 14 to 17, are fragmentary and in some cases of dubious reliability. This makes it difficult to put events in sequence and to build up a picture of what happened. Each Amarna scholar has tried to fit the fragmentary pieces of the puzzle together, resulting in a variety of theories. Unfortunately, most of the important pieces of information are still missing.

Lack of evidence

Deaths in the royal family

In year 14, Meketaten, the second of Akhenaten's daughters, died. A tomb was hastily prepared in a side chamber of the king's tomb and the tragedy was recorded on the walls. The scenes show a grief-stricken Akhenaten and Nefertiti holding onto one another as they view their daughter's body. Because a royal baby, held by a nurse, was also shown in the tomb scenes, Aldred maintains that the princess died in childbirth. However, Redford says that this was impossible as Meketaten was only about eleven when she died.

Meketaten

The royal family mourning the death of Meketaten

It appears that Queen Tiye also died about this time. The last record of her was in year 14 when she accompanied Akhenaten to the Great Aten Temple, recorded in Huy's tomb. She would probably have appeared in the scenes on the walls of her grand daughter's tomb had she been alive.

Younger princesses

Since there is no evidence of the three younger princesses after their appearance at the international reception in year 12, it is believed that they had died also.

Before year 15, Kiya also disappeared from the records. Since the name of the eldest princess, Meritaten, was inscribed over that of Kiya at the north palace and Maru-Aten, it is assumed that the king's favourite had died also.

**Plague from
Western Asia**

What caused so many royal deaths at this time? The most likely cause was a plague which had been devastating areas in western Asia. It supposedly started in Mitanni and spread to coastal Syria. There is evidence from the Amarna Letters that it had broken out in Simyra, the Egyptian headquarters in the Levant and had spread to Byblos. It would have been difficult for Egypt to escape the ravages of this epidemic since traders, officials and soldiers moved back and forth between Egypt and the Syrian coast. It is possible that some of the delegates attending the reception in year 12 carried the plague.

There is a belief that as a result of these tragedies, Akhenaten became more desperate in his destruction of Amun's monuments. In this latter part of his reign he even removed the *Amun* part of his father's name from articles belonging to Queen Tiye, including a magnificent gilded shrine made for her burial.

The promotion of Meritaten and the appearance of Smenkhkare

**Meritaten as
king's favourite**

About years 14 and 15, Akhenaten's eldest daughter, Meritaten, became more prominent. She was given the rank of favourite of the king and *Mistress of his House* and was shown performing certain religious rituals.

Meritaten's status is revealed in the correspondence sent to Akhenaten from the king of Babylon, Burnaburiash, and the ruler of Tyre, Abi-Milki. In their letters they refer to her as 'your daughter Mayati' and 'Mistress of your house'. Burnaburiash speaks of her as though she were the queen consort.

**Marriage to
Smenkhkare**

From year 15 she is shown in the company of a young man, named Smenkhkare. He appears to have been her husband, to have filled the role of co-regent and to have been held in great affection by Akhenaten. Who was he and what had happened to Queen Nefertiti? These questions have posed the greatest puzzle for historians.

The identity of Smenkhkare and the fate of Nefertiti

Harris and Samson both believe that the royal youth known as Smenkhkare did not exist and that the co-regent with whom Akhenaten shared his last three years was in fact Nefertiti.

Nefertiti does disappear from the records about the same time as the appearance of the youthful co-regent.

On what evidence do Harris and Samson base this view?

1 About year 15, Nefertiti's title of *Great Royal Wife* was given to her eldest daughter, Meritaten. Samson says that this was the practice carried out prior to a queen assuming kingly titles, as in the case of Hatshepsut and Tawosret.

2 In a scene from these later years, Nefertiti is shown pouring a libation to Akhenaten. A similar scene featuring Queen Tawosret and her husband King Seti II, suggests that this may have indicated that both kings were ailing and the wives were asking for long or eternal life for their husbands. Samson says that 'if Akhenaten was ailing at this time, then the gradual changes being made in the names and titles of Nefertiti may well have been a natural progression in his plans to establish her officially as his co-regent'.[71]

3 On a broken stela Akhenaten's two names were accompanied by a co-regent with two names, one of which was 'Nefernefruaten, Beloved of ...'. This was Nefertiti's name and she had always been described as beloved of Akhenaten. The name in the other cartouche was Ankhkeprure.

Samson maintains that after Akhenaten's death, the co-regent's name (Nefertiti) was changed to Ankhkeprure-Smenkhkare, 'beloved of Aten'.

4 As a co-regent with Akhenaten, Nefertiti would need a consort. This explains the elevation of Meritaten to the position of *great royal wife*.

This view is not supported by other Amarna scholars. According to Redford:

> While the theory is well-reasoned and ingenious, it glosses over and raises too many difficulties. The fact that Nefertiti and Smenkhkare share a sobriquet in common is not significant ... There is upon closer examination, a slight but consistent difference in the writing of the epithet when applied to Smenkhkare, in contrast to the ubiquitous spelling when seen in Nefertiti's cartouche.[72]

Aldred agrees that the arguments put forward by Harris and Samson are ingenious but totally unacceptable in the light of other evidence.

What other evidence?

*   Nefertiti's ushabti.
*   The body of a young male king found in Tomb 55 in the Valley of the Kings.

The ushabti of Nefertiti

Ushabtis were small figures of the deceased person or other people such as servants which were placed in the tomb with the mummy. These figures were expected to answer the call of the deceased and perform tasks for them in the afterlife. In the case of royalty, these ushabtis were made after the person had died, during the 70 or so days of the embalming process.

The remains of a ushabti of Nefertiti reveal that:

- she had not changed her name or held kingly titles when she died. The inscription on the ushabti says *The heiress, high and mighty in the palace, one trusted of the King of Upper and Lower Egypt Neferkheprure, Waenre, the Son of Re, Akhenaten, Great in his lifetime, the Chief Wife of the King, Nefernefruaten-Nefertiti.* Had she been a co-regent, she would have been depicted in kingly garb but the ushabti is in female attire.

- she died before her husband. As part of Akhenaten's new doctrine, the Osirian funeral practices were ignored. No longer was a dead person's name followed by the term 'justified'. This benediction was missing from Nefertiti's ushabti. However, immediately after Akhenaten's death, 'justified' was again added to funerary equipment, including some belonging to Akhenaten. According to Aldred, 'it seems improbable therefore that Nefertiti could have died after Akhenaten'.[73]

Tomb 55

The mystery of Tomb 55

The Harris/Samson theory ignores the evidence in Tomb 55.

In 1907 a small, incomplete and badly damaged tomb was found in the Valley of the Kings. The coffin, obviously prepared at the height of the Amarna period, still contained a mummy although it had suffered some desecration. The excavators also found canopic jars and the remains of funerary equipment inscribed with the names of Akhenaten, Tiye and Amenhotep III, and clay seals featuring the cartouche of Tutankhamun.

To whom did this tomb belong? Unfortunately all evidence of the name of the occupant of the coffin had been removed.

The damaged inscription at the end of the coffin revealed that it had been prepared for a royal woman during the earlier part of Akhenaten's reign and that she had a close relationship with the king. At a later date the feminine inflections in the inscription had been altered to masculine forms without too much change to the original text. This indicated that the male for whom this coffin was altered had also had a close relationship with Akhenaten. Two further clues were found. Part of the original inscription had been replaced with the words 'Son of Re' followed by a cartouche; and on a gold fragment, which appeared to have been dislodged from the coffin, were the words 'beloved of Waenre' (part of Akhenaten's titulary).

Other modifications made to the coffin included the addition of sceptres, a ureaus and beard. The fact that a ureaus had to be added meant that the woman for whom it was originally made was not entitled to wear the royal cobra. This narrowed down the identification of the original owner of the coffin to one of the young princesses or Kiya, Akhenaten's secondary wife. The coffin had been altered for a king.

After extensive medical and scientific investigation of the mummy during the 1960s and 1970s it was determined to be a young male who had died about the age of 20. When a comparison was done with the mummy of Tutankhamun, it was found that the occupant of Tomb 55 had the same blood type (A2 with serum antigen MN) which indicated a close relationship, possibly that of brothers. A reconstruction of the skull of the mummy revealed a striking similarity to Tutankhamun and Queen Tiye.

Evidence for the existence of a young male Amarna king

Pending any further discoveries, the evidence suggests that the occupant of Tomb 55 is Smenkhkare, the 'shadowy figure who played an ill-defined role as co-regent of Akhenaten'[74] in the last years of his reign.

Tomb 55 was obviously a secondary burial. It is believed that it once contained the mummies of other Amarna personalities, removed from their tombs in Akhetaten when the court moved back to Memphis at the time of Tutankhamun. The evidence in the tomb suggests that some time later the tomb was entered again and the other bodies removed.

Who was Smenkhkare?

It is generally accepted that Smenkhkare and Tutankhaten (Tutankhamun) were brothers, born about ten to 12 years apart.

An inscription from the reign of Akhenaten described Tutankhaten as *king's son of his body*. Since Tutankhaten was the son of a king, so too was Smenkhkare. Also, Akhenaten would not have taken Smenkhkare as his co-regent if he had been of lesser status than Tutankhaten.

Which king was their father? Amenhotep III or Akhenaten? The generally accepted view is that they were the sons of Amenhotep III and Tiye. However, this would only have been possible had there been a relatively long co-regency between Amenhotep III and Akhenaten. The evidence in favour of Tiye and Amenhotep is provided later in this chapter (Tutankhamun). It is possible too, that the princes were the sons of one of Amenhotep's secondary wives. If Akhenaten was their father, the most likely candidate for mother was Kiya.

Parentage

Smenkhkare ruled for only three years and is believed to have survived Akhenaten by less than a year. Nothing more is heard of Meritaten after this time.

What happened to Nefertiti?

Aldred believes that Nefertiti died about the same time as so many other members of her family (year 14) and was buried as the beloved *great wife* of Akhenaten in the royal tomb at Akhetaten. This would explain why her eldest daughter was elevated to the position of *great wife* prior to her marriage to Smenkhkare.

Some scholars, like Redford, believe that she was alive during the last years of her husband's reign but that she was less prominent in public life than she had been earlier.

Hayes believes that she became estranged from Akhenaten and retired to the Northern Palace. This view is supported by Desroches-Noblecourt who goes further and suggests that she deserted the heresy and promoted the young Tutankhaten as an alternative ruler. This is not generally accepted.

Samson proposes the theory that Nefertiti as Smenkhkare survived her husband and ruled as regent for the boy king, Tutankhamun, who succeeded to the throne after the death of Akhenaten. She points to a statue in the Berlin museum of the aging Nefertiti wearing a pharaoh's crown, to support her view.

The death of Akhenaten

The last date we have for Akhenaten was year 17. There is no record of his death but he was buried in the tomb in the royal wadi east of the city he built for his 'father' the sun-disk.

Although his sarcophagus was viciously destroyed sometime after his death, fragments have survived. In keeping with his doctrine of 'one god', figures of Nefertiti replaced the protective goddesses (Isis, Nephthys, Selket and Neith) normally found at each corner of the sarcophagus (see Chapter 17 for details about this practice).

No mummy ever found

Akhenaten's mummy has never been found. It was probably destroyed during the reign of Horemheb who attempted to remove all evidence of Akhenaten and everything associated with the Aten cult.

> The historian of ancient Egypt would sacrifice much to be able to examine the authentic mummy of Akhenaten, and replace the many conjectures about him with even a few hard facts.[75]

Conclusion

The doctrine of the Aten was short-lived. Akhenaten's ideas were rejected soon after his death, his monuments were destroyed and he disappeared from the later king lists.

Much of what has been written about him and his reign is subjective, not only because most of the important pieces of information are missing but because of the background and beliefs of the scholars themselves.

Every scholar has formed his or her own theory about what happened and has a personal opinion of Akhenaten the individual. These opinions range from *humanist* to *religious fanatic* and everything in between.

Views of Akhenaten, the individual

Some, like Gardiner, see him as 'self-willed but courageous',[76] while others, such as Kemp, perceive him as a tragic figure who saw 'the irrelevance of much of the thought of his day'[77] but was unable to find anything acceptable to put in its place. Some probably agree with Thomas that he did not have the 'strength, perception and tolerance to carry out his policy successfully'.[78]

Hayes describes him as a remarkable and sensitive man who was more concerned with 'matters of the mind and spirit — chiefly of his own mind and spirit',[79] and Aldred points out that his monuments reveal a man who was 'humane and sympathetic'.[80]

On the other hand, Redford is decidedly negative. Not only is he contemptuous of Akhenaten and his immediate circle of sycophants who lived in an environment of 'refined sloth', but is damning of a cult which expected people to stand in the open sun of Egypt for hours on end. 'I cannot conceive of a more tiresome regime under which to be fated to live.'[81]

The Amarna aftermath

Following the death of Akhenaten and Smenkhkare, Tutankhamun, a child of about nine years of age, came to the throne and ruled for approximately nine years. With his death, the Eighteenth Dynasty officially came to an end.

Tutankhamun, Ay and Horemheb

He was succeeded by the elderly official Ay who had been prominent at Akhetaten and his death, after a short four-year reign, brought the so-called Amarna Period to a conclusion.

The reign of Horemheb was really a transition from the Eighteenth to the Nineteenth Dynasty.

Tutankhamun (Tutankhaten)*

Prior to the discovery of his tomb by Howard Carter in 1922, Tutankhamun was only known as a shadowy figure caught up in the intrigues and confusion associated with the end of Atenism and the reinstatement of Amun as chief god.

After the excavation of his tomb, he became a household name but unfortunately his enormous treasure revealed very little about his life or the important events of his reign. It did, however, provide evidence of the luxurious lifestyle of the upper classes and confirmed many of the New Kingdom burial rites and practices.

Little historical evidence from Tutankhamun's tomb

Tutankhamun's parentage and accession to the throne

Although a fragmentary inscription found at Hermopolis, referring to Tutankhaten as *king's son of his body*, identifies him as a prince, there is no satisfactory documentary evidence which identifies his parents.

Evidence of parentage

The majority of scholars tend to support the theory that he was the youngest son of Amenhotep III and Queen Tiye. There are several pieces of evidence which support this theory.

Amenhotep III and Tiye?

1 There is a striking resemblance between Tutankhamun (mummy and face mask) and Queen Tiye (images).

2 On a stone lion originally placed in the Nubian Temple of Soleb is an inscription in which Tutankhamun refers to Amenhotep III as his father. Some scholars, however, believe that this should not be taken literally.

* Tutankhamun was born Tutankhaten and for the first half of his life was referred to by his Atenist name.

3 In the tomb of Tutankhamun there were two miniature coffins side by side, one of which contained a small golden statuette of Amenhotep III wrapped in linen while the other held a lock of Queen Tiye's hair.

4 Queen Tiye's youngest daughter was called Baketaten and Tutankhamun was named Tutankhaten at birth.

However, if Tutankhaten (who came to the throne at age nine) was the youngest child of Tiye, born two years after Baketaten, the queen would have been about 48 years of age. When Tiye's body has been identified beyond all doubt, careful analysis might throw some more light on the matter. If he was the son of Amenhotep III, there must have been a long co-regency between his father and brother (Akhenaten).

Amenhotep III and a secondary wife?

Another theory is that Tutankhaten and Smenkhkare were the sons of Amenhotep and a secondary wife. Some scholars have suggested that Tutankhaten may even have been the son of Sitamun, the daughter of Amenhotep and Tiye, who married her father late in his reign. However, although Sitamun held the title of *Great King's Wife* from about year 31 of her father's reign, it is unlikely that this involved a physical relationship.

Akhenaten and Kiya?

It is possible that Tutankhaten was the son of Akhenaten and his secondary wife, Kiya, and that Amenhotep and Tiye were his grandparents.

Early years

Tutankhaten was brought up under the Atenist religion and probably spent his youth between the palaces of Thebes and Akhetaten. If he was the son of Tiye, he would have accompanied his mother to his brother's capital when he was three and later spent time there with Tiye. It appears that after Tiye's death the young prince lived in Akhetaten but whether he was looked after by Nefertiti, as suggested by some scholars, is not really known. Probably just before his accession to the throne he was married to Ankhesenpaaten, the third daughter of Nefertiti and Akhenaten, who was several years older than him.

Marriage to Ankhesenpaaten

Conjecture by Desroches-Noblecourt

Desroches-Noblecourt, in *Tutankhamun — Life and Death of a Pharaoh*, suggests that Tutankhaten became a pawn in a power game. She maintains that there were a number of people and groups with vested interests in promoting young prince Tutankhaten as the future king even before the death of Akhenaten. According to her theory, the priests of Amun believed that with a young king on the throne they would be able to regain their power. Perhaps at the death of Amenhotep III (assuming there was a long co-regency) they had already decided to choose Tutankhaten as his father's heir and ignore Akhenaten. Desroches-Noblecourt goes further and suggests that the priests might have tried to gain the support of Nefertiti who may have realised that her husband's heresy was leading the country to disaster. Believing that the supporters of Amun might carry out violent reprisals when Akhenaten died, Ay, Nefertiti and possibly Horemheb, general of the northern armies, might have decided to implement a plan to save the Egyptian crown and protect their own interests. With Tutankhaten established on the throne, Ay would be in a very powerful position.

Redford, in his work *Akhenaten — The Heretic King*, disputes the view of 'a party with vested interests, an Amun priesthood, waiting in the wings breathing fire and slaughter against the innocent Aten-worshippers. There was no such professional clergy to speak of in the 14th century BC.'[82]

Opposition to the view of a vengeful Amun priesthood

After the deaths of Smenkhkare and Akhenaten, possibly in the same year, the nine-year-old Tutankhaten was crowned in the temple of Karnak at Thebes.

If there was to be a return to the pre-Amarna conditions then Tutankhaten's coronation should announce the reinstatement of Amun as the supreme state god. For this reason it was important that the ceremony be held at Thebes (rather than at Memphis) so that Amun could bestow on Tutankhaten the right to rule on the throne of his ancestors. During the coronation ceremonies, Tutankhaten was referred to as Tutankhamun and assumed the throne name of Nebkheprure. While the young king was still in Thebes, a statue of a larger than life-size Amun, protectively holding Tutankhaten by the shoulders, was placed in the Temple of Karnak.

The boy-king, Tutankhamun, wearing the studded blue war crown or khepresh

The nine-year-old king then returned to Akhetaten where it seemed he lived for the first three years of his reign. Redford maintains that during this time there was a certain hesitancy about what to do, judging by the fact that while the cult of the disk continued, the young king was given the Horus-name *Propitiating the Gods*.

It is believed that in the third year of his reign the court moved from Akhetaten. According to those who believe that Nefertiti was Tutankhaten's regent, this move may have coincided with her death. It is probable that the court spent some time in Thebes before taking up residence in Memphis. This move from the isolation of Akhetaten gave Ay and Horemheb the opportunity to implement a more realistic policy — one marked by tolerance. This would restore the confidence of the people since there seems to have been a breakdown in morale during the latter part of Akhenaten's reign. It is possible that the Egyptian people believed that the gods had withdrawn their support from them as the temples throughout the land fell into disrepair and suffered desecration.

Tutankhamun's restoration program

Ay was Tutankhamun's regent and adviser until he was old enough to rule alone and 'much of the course charted during the new reign was undoubtedly of his design'.[83] He was helped in his task of governing the country on behalf of the young king by Horemheb, *Lieutenant of the Entire Land* and responsible for foreign affairs, Maya, Treasurer and *Master of Works* and Huy, *Viceroy of Kush*.

A statue of Amun protecting Tutankhamun

These men realised that for economic and social reasons the temples throughout the land had to be reopened and the old gods and cults reinstated. This would immediately restore the confidence of the people.

Change of name

To lead the way in this process, the king and his queen changed their birth names from Tutankhaten and Ankhesenpaaten to Tutankhamun and Ankhesenamun. Despite the change of names and the fact that Tutankhamun took 'counsel with his heart in seeking all sorts of effective ways ... (to benefit) his father Amun',[84] the young king and his queen did not turn away from the Aten.

There were no reprisals against the temples and priesthoods of the Aten at this time. In fact the cult continued for another ten years side by side with the reinstated cults of all the older gods. In this transition period there seems to have been a mixture of Aten and Amun references. For example, in a new version of a Hymn to Amun, the god is described as *dazzling and brilliant*, a *master of brightness* whose *sun-rays inundate all the lands* and who *shines in his disk*.

Both cults operated side by side

On some of the furniture found in Tutankhamun's tomb, the king is described as the *son of Amun* and the *eldest son of the sun-disk in heaven*. The cartouches on the throne enclosed the Amun names of the king and queen as well as featuring the sun disk icon. On a set of sceptres buried with him was the name Amun while a smaller set, found alongside, was inscribed with the name of Aten.

The Restoration stela

Influence of Horemheb

It is believed that Horemheb was the author of a royal edict, issued on behalf of the king, known as the Restoration stela. The relief on this large quartzite block, erected in Amun's temple, depicted Tutankhamun's offering to Amun and his wife Mut.

The stela recorded the deplorable conditions existing in the country at Tutankhamun's accession.

> The land was in confusion, the gods forsook the land ... If one prayed to a god to ask things of him [in no wise] did he come ...If an [army] was sent to Djahi to widen the frontiers of Egypt it met with no success at all.[85]

The inscription also outlined the solutions that were needed to be carried out in order to suppress evil in the land, restore order, make Egypt 'flower again' and please Amun.

According to the stela, Tutankhamun built many statues of the chief gods. One of the epithets given to him — *The king who spent his life making images* — indicates the scale of his activities. To satisfy Amun, 'an august image' of the god was made of pure gold inlaid with precious stones. It was supposedly the largest statue ever made. Only slightly smaller was another statue dedicated to Ptah of Memphis.

Activities on behalf of the gods, particularly Amun

Numerous statues of Amun with the features of the young king were set up around Thebes. To emphasise the return to orthodoxy, the king was shown with Amun and Mut as the *divine son*. In none of these official stone portraits was the young queen shown with her husband, as her mother Nefertiti had been during the reign of Akhenaten.

The stela records that the king rebuilt the god's barges in cedar wood covered with gold and repaired damaged temples and ordered the restoration of their revenues. 'All the imposts of the temples have been doubled, tripled, quadrupled in silver, gold, lapis, every kind of august costly stone, royal linen, fine linen, olive oil, gum.'[86]

Tutankhamun established new priesthoods, the personnel of which were selected from 'children of the notables of their towns, each the son of an eminent man whose name is known'.[87] Male and female slaves were recruited for the temple as well as musicians, singers and dancers from palace personnel who were paid out of the royal revenues. Work was resumed on the Temples of Luxor and Soleb and the Avenue of Sphinxes which had been discontinued during the reign of Akhenaten.

Although his restoration program benefited all of the older Egyptian gods, Ay and Horemheb saw to it that most of Tutankhamun's building activities were devoted to the temple complexes at Thebes. The young king endowed the Temple of Amun with a pictorial representation of the majestic Opet festival held in the early months of the flood. The walls of the temple depict the procession of the cult figures of Amun, his wife Mut and their son Khonsu from Karnak to the Temple of Luxor. Refer to Chapter 16 for details of the Opet festival.

Ay and Horemheb did not hesitate to take the credit for these buildings when they in turn came to power. Like many rulers before them they obliterated the cartouches of Tutankhamun and replaced them with their own.

Foreign policy under Tutankhamun

Horemheb was concerned with the country's military strategy and the defence of Egypt's frontiers. He seems to have strengthened Egypt's hold over her Palestinian vassals after the lack of interest shown by Akhenaten, and to have collected the taxes owed by the Palestinian cities. However, the scenes in his tomb at Memphis, which show all the Asian races bringing tribute to the pharaoh, are not entirely accurate.

Horemheb and Palestine

The area of most concern to the Egyptians at this time was Syria. The Hittites had defeated a Mitannian army and assassinated Egypt's ally, King Tushratta, causing the Mitannian kingdom to crumble. This created a power vacuum in central Mesopotamia and a serious threat to those states in Syria whose rulers were vassals of the Egyptian king.

Desroches-Noblecourt maintains that although there was a gradual weakening of Egypt's control over her protectorates in Syria during Tutankhamun's reign, there is no evidence of any real war.

On the other hand, Redford and Aldred believe that Egypt joined forces with Assyria to prevent Suppiluliumas, king of the Hittites, from threatening the pharaoh's vassals in northern Syria. They made a two-pronged attack on the Hittite-held centres in Syria.

Losses in Northern Syria

The Egyptians besieged the city of Kadesh and the Assyrians crossed the Euphrates River. The Hittites, although taken by surprise, pushed back the Assyrians and then marched to Kadesh to relieve the siege. Although the Egyptians had retreated, the Hittites crossed into the northern part of the Egyptian *empire*, attacked the cities and carried off Egyptian prisoners.

Evidence from Hittite records

There is no Egyptian record of this setback; the sources are entirely Hittite. Egyptian military reverses were always depicted in the monumental inscriptions as victories for the king and this was no exception. The usual head-smiting scene and list of conquered cities was carved into one of the walls of Amenhotep's pylon. A painted chest found in Tutankhamun's tomb shows the young king in the traditional warrior-king pose — standing in a chariot, reins tied around his waist and shooting arrows at the Asians who are being trampled by the king's chariot.

Order maintained in Nubia

The few police actions necessary in Wawat and Kush (Lower and Upper Nubia) were carried out by Tutankhamun's viceroy, Huy. Again the decorative chest found in Tutankhamun's tomb seems to suggest that these raids were much larger operations and that the king was responsible for their success. Huy's beautifully decorated tomb shows his investiture as viceroy by Tutankhamun and his presentation to the king of the tribute from Nubia. Refer to Chapter 15 for details.

The sudden death of Tutankhamun and its significance

Tutankhamun died suddenly somewhere between the age of 18 and 20. It is impossible to say with any certainty whether the king died from a sudden illness, an accident or murder, although a recent re-examination of his mummy has revealed a skull wound near his left ear. This wound is similar to that inflicted by an arrow. Could he have died during a hunting expedition or a military skirmish?

Cause of sudden death?

His death caused serious problems in Egypt. According to the Hittite records, the young pharaoh died about the time the Egyptian army returned from their military loss in Syria and this twofold tragedy threw the people into a panic. Their concern was understandable since he left no heir and there appears to have been no relative from another branch of the family to inherit the throne. Who would succeed Tutankhamun?

The question of succession

It appears that Ay had convinced Tutankhamun to designate him as heir to the throne if the young king should die without surviving children. Several scenes from the Temple of Amun show the elderly Ay, who held the title of *King's Eldest Son*, standing in the manner of a son and heir behind the king.

However, according to the Hittite records, the young widow, Ankhesenamun, sent a letter to the Hittite king asking for one of his sons to be sent to Egypt to share her throne.

Ankhesenamun's request for a Hittite husband

> My husband is dead and I have no son. People say that you have many sons. If you send me one of your sons he will become my husband for it is repugnant for me to take one of my servants (subjects) to husband.[88]

Because such a thing had never happened before, the Hittite king was suspicious and sent his chamberlain to investigate. This caused the queen to write another letter, complaining:

> Why do you say, 'they are trying to deceive me'? If I had a son should I write to a foreign country in a manner humiliating to me and my country?[(89)]

This was an unprecedented act. Did she instigate this herself or was she encouraged to do it and if so, by whom? Who was the 'servant' whom she considered it distasteful to marry? Desroches-Noblecourt believes it was probably Horemheb, *Scribe of Recruits* to whom she referred in her letter; or could it have been her elderly relative, Ay? Since Ay already had a wife, Tey, who was portrayed in his tomb, this is unlikely.

During the time it took to embalm Tutankhamun, emissaries travelled backwards and forwards between Egypt and the Hittite capital. Eventually the Hittite king agreed to send his son, Zannanza, to Egypt with a large entourage. Redford maintains that what happened next 'was an act of state'.[(90)] Some scholars believe that Horemheb gave orders to his *police* to murder the prince before he reached Egypt but there is no clear evidence that Horemheb was directly involved.

The Hittite king invaded Egyptian territory in Palestine in retaliation and Horemheb went to the front to organise Egypt's defences.

Death of the Hittite prince led to conflict

In the meantime, the young king had to be buried. Ay, in the role reserved for the heir to the throne and wearing the traditional animal skin, officiated at the funeral. Evidence of Ay performing the *Opening of the Mouth* ceremony is found on the walls of Tutankhamun's burial chamber. Ay then ascended the throne.

What happened to Ankhesenamun? Did she share the throne with Ay as co-regent. A scarab ring with the joint cartouches of Ay and the young queen is the only evidence for this. From this time she completely disappears from the records. With Tutankhamun's death the Eighteenth Dynasty officially came to an end.

End of the Eighteenth Dynasty

According to Howard Carter the best thing that Tutankhamun ever did was to die because his burial treasure provides evidence of the art, culture and burial practices of the Eighteenth Dynasty.

Ay's shortlived reign

During Ay's short four- or five-year reign, he continued the policy of rehabilitating Amun and abandoning the extreme aspects of the Atenist religion. The building projects begun at Karnak under Tutankhamun were continued, although Ay's name replaced that of his predecessor.

Abandoned extreme aspects of Aten religion

Aldred suggests that, since there were no remaining members of the royal line, Ay, who apparently had no sons, accepted Horemheb as his co-regent.

Ay finished his tomb in the western branch of the Valley of the Kings and the paintings in the tomb show that Tey, Nefertiti's nurse, was still

Ay's wife at this time. Both the tomb paintings and Ay's red sarcophagus were deliberately damaged. Perhaps this occurred during the later campaign of vengeance carried out by Horemheb on all those closely associated with the heretic, Akhenaten.

Horemheb

Horemheb was 'one of the most enigmatic power-wielders of the New Kingdom'.[91]

Early career

The only surviving evidence of Horemheb's early career comes from the inscriptions in the magnificent tomb which he was building in the Memphite necropolis at Sakkara during the reign of Ay.

Early years in the army

He seems to have spent his early years in the army but it is doubtful if he was ever at Amarna during the reign of Akhenaten and Smenkhkare.

About the middle of the reign of Tutankhamun he seems to have been given the title of *royal lieutenant* with responsibility for foreign affairs in the north. It appears that he was selected also by Tutankhamun to lead a punitive expedition to Nubia to coincide with the appointment of the new viceroy. His tomb depicts the occasion in the usual propagandist way.

Promotions

According to his own account, he played a key role in the rehabilitation of the country after the Amarna interlude, initiating the reforms of Tutankhamun. He next appears as *chief overseer of the army* during the reign of Ay and is shown in his tomb receiving rewards and presenting captives to the king.

Heir apparent and accession to the throne

According to an inscription in Horemheb's Sakkara tomb, it seems that Ay appointed him as heir apparent.

> When his Majesty appeared on the throne for the reception of tribute, and the tribute of the North and South was brought in, the Heir Apparent, Horemheb, was standing beside the throne, thanking god for his Majesty.[92]

In his rather ambiguous coronation inscription, Horemheb claimed that he had 'acted as vice regent of Egypt over a period of many years'.[93] and that an oracle from the god Amun had sanctioned his right to the throne of Egypt.

Marriage to Mutnodjmet

Before his accession to the throne he married Mutnodjmet, Nefertiti's sister or half-sister. Some historians believe that they were both daughters of Ay. If this were the case, such a marriage would have strengthened Horemheb's claim to the throne.

Perhaps Horemheb had been planning his accession to the throne for a long time. If so:

- Did he have anything to do with the death of Ay and Ankhesenamun's disappearance?
- Did the priests of Amun help him seize the crown as Desroches-Noblecourt claims?

On Ay's death, Horemheb was crowned at Karnak by the priests of Amun during the great Feast of Opet. The priests placed the crowns upon Horemheb's head and granted him his pharaonic titulary — *Djeser-khepru-Re, Chosen of Re*. His rule was legitimised by Amun. According to Gardiner, 'no act could better have signalled the end of the Amarna period and the beginning of an orderly and auspicious reign'.[94]

Crowned at Thebes by priests of Amun

Horemheb as pharaoh

When Horemheb came to the throne, his chief aims appear to have been:

- to restore law and order, eradicate bureaucratic corruption and improve the lot of the lower classes
- to disassociate himself from the Atenist heresy and promote the view that he was the legitimate successor of Amenhotep III.

Aims

Horemheb's Edict of Reform

It is believed that after his coronation Horemheb made a grand tour of his kingdom. It may have been as a result of what he saw and heard at this time that he issued a decree known today as his Edict of Reform. In it he outlined his plan for restoring the welfare of the Egyptian people.

This important record, of which one-third is now lost, was inscribed on a stela and erected at Karnak. It recorded:

- the widespread corruption prevalent among high officials, particularly those in the judiciary
- the exploitation of the poorer classes by tax collectors, who operated with the full knowledge of royal inspectors
- the abuses by soldiers such as robbery and extortion of goods from the peasants.

Problems to be addressed

In his edict, Horemheb promised to redress the situation and return Egypt to an earlier standard of behaviour.

In order to reform the judiciary he toured Upper and Lower Egypt looking for men of good character who were good judges of people and who were prepared to follow the laws. He laid down strict guidelines for them to follow, similar in some ways to those in the Instructions to a Vizier, recorded in the tomb of Rekhmire (see Chapter 15).

Reforms

To remove the temptation for local officials to extort extra taxes from the peasants, Horemheb remitted the tax on mayors and town councils and revived the practice of giving a monthly banquet to treasury officials.

Soldiers who had stolen property from the peasants were forced to return it and the king eased the peasants' destitute conditions by remitting their taxes. Horemheb imposed extremely harsh penalties on dishonest soldiers and officials, such as mutilation (their noses cut off) or exile (to Sinai). He made regular tours of inspection throughout the land to see that his orders were carried out. By the end of his reign he had re-established the government of Egypt on sound lines.

Destruction of all reminders of the Aten heresy

Even though he had risen to power during the reigns of his Amarna predecessors, Horemheb blamed the deplorable state of the country on them. He attempted to remove all evidence of their reigns and set about destroying everything associated with the Aten cult.

It is highly likely that Horemheb did not attempt to obliterate all traces of the Aten religion until the death of his wife Mutnodjmet in the fifteenth or sixteenth year of his reign. 'Her departure from the scene must have cut the last links with the personalities of Amarna.'[95]

His first action was to attribute to himself all the recent monuments of Tutankhamun and Ay, hammering out their names and replacing them with his own. This was not an unusual practice.

Destruction of the monuments of Akhenaten, Tutankhamun and Ay

Then he began the wholesale dismantling and destruction of the buildings and sites dedicated to the Aten. The city of Akhetaten was razed to the ground so that not a single block of stone remained on another, every stela and piece of statuary was smashed and the royal tomb was desecrated. The site became a quarry for later kings.

The sun temples at Karnak, Memphis and Heliopolis were dismantled. According to Redford, Horemheb's wrecking crews at Karnak followed a careful plan.

> First, any mud-brick construction within the Gempaaten was demolished and the rubble flattened. Then the legs of the colossal statues around the outside of the court were smashed and the upper parts of the images allowed to fall forward on their faces into the courtyard. Next, the roofing blocks of the colonnade were taken off and thrown into the court, and the piers demolished one by one. The dismantling of the talatat-wall, with its still-fresh reliefs, followed immediately, section by section.[96]

A stream of workmen, each carrying an inscribed block (talatat) moved from the slowly disappearing Gempaaten to the construction site of Horemheb's pylon. Tens of thousands of these inscribed blocks from Akhenaten's temples were used for the foundations and core of the three pylons which Horemheb added to the Temple of Amun. Other blocks were carried further afield.

Whether Horemheb ordered the desecration of the tombs of many of those associated with the heretical family, cannot be firmly established; however, we do know that:

- the tomb of Ay at Thebes was sacked — the sarcophagus was smashed and Ay's names obliterated

- Akhmin, the birthplace of Ay and his family, was also a focus of persecutions
- the tomb which Tutankhamun had used as a hiding place in Thebes for what remained of the royal burials at Akhetaten (the so-called Tomb 55) was attacked. The protective bricks supporting the coffin of what some historians believe are the remains of Smenkhkare, were destroyed
- Huy, the Viceroy of Kush and other nobles who remained faithful to Akhenaten's successors, had their tombs desecrated in some way. In the tomb of Huy, Tutankhamun's portrait and name were chiselled out and several images of Huy were mutilated.

Why was the tomb of Tutankhamun left untouched? Perhaps those who carried out the destruction believed that, as Tutankhamun was the first king to restore the worship of Amun, mutilation of his tomb might bring down the wrath of the god.

Tutankhamun's tomb untouched

No part of Egypt escaped the attention of Horemheb's agents. While single mindedly destroying all reminders of the cult of the sun-disk and those associated with it, they restored the name of Amun.

Horemheb's efforts were so effective that in the king lists of the Ramesside period, he was recorded as the successor of Amenhotep III. The number of years from the reign of Akhenaten to the death of Ay were added to the reign of Horemheb, so that in the king list Horemheb was accredited with a reign of 59 years.

Shown in the records as the successor of Amenhotep III

Horemheb's chosen successor

An important part of Horemheb's reforms was a much needed revitalisation of the army with more opportunities for advancement. This gave Pramesse, a member of a military family from the delta, an opportunity to rise first to the top of the military hierarchy and then to the highest ranks of Horemheb's government. Eventually, he became the pharaoh's vizier and trusted supporter and was given the highest religious rank in the land, that of *primate of all Egypt*.

Pramesse, later Ramesses I

As Horemheb was in his sixties and childless, he turned to the trusted and able Pramesse to act as his deputy and then bestowed on him the title of *hereditary prince in the entire land*, confirming Pramesse as his successor.

When Horemheb died, he was buried in a partially completed tomb in the Valley of the Kings, instead of in the large and beautifully decorated tomb he had prepared at Sakkara during the reigns of Tutankhamun and Ay. Queen Mutnodjmet, who died about year 15, was buried in his Sakkara tomb alongside his first wife, who had been a chantress of Amun. It appears that Mutnodjmet died in childbirth after many unsuccessful pregnancies.

In his Theban tomb, Horemheb had his walls painted with a new funerary theme — *The Book of the Gates* and this became one of the major themes found in the tombs of Nineteenth Dynasty pharaohs. Pramesse succeeded to the throne of Egypt as Ramesses I, ushering in the Nineteenth Dynasty.

The beginning of the Nineteenth Dynasty

Chapter review

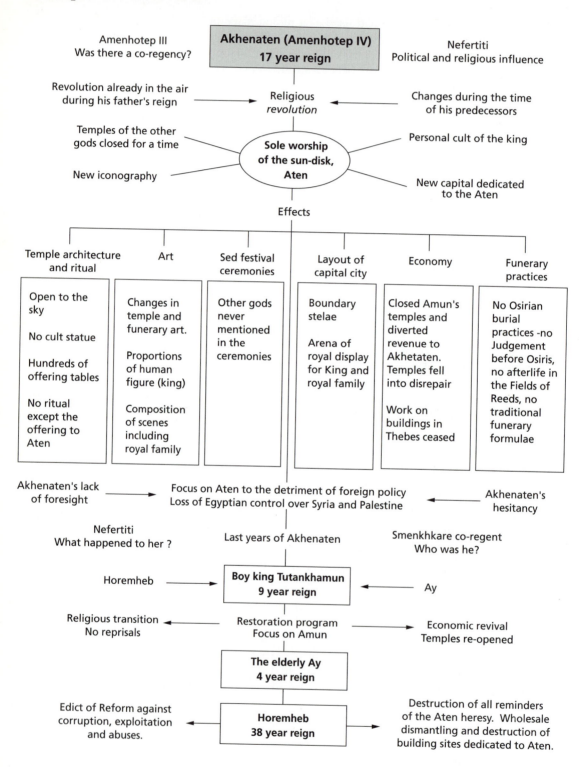

Amenhotep III
Was there a co-regency?

**Akhenaten (Amenhotep IV)
17 year reign**

Nefertiti
Political and religious influence

Revolution already in the air
during his father's reign

*Religious
revolution*

Changes during the time
of his predecessors

Temples of the other
gods closed for a time

**Sole worship
of the sun-disk,
Aten**

Personal cult of the king

New iconography

New capital dedicated
to the Aten

Effects

Temple architecture and ritual	Art	Sed festival ceremonies	Layout of capital city	Economy	Funerary practices
Open to the sky No cult statue Hundreds of offering tables No ritual except the offering to Aten	Changes in temple and funerary art. Proportions of human figure (king) Composition of scenes including royal family	Other gods never mentioned in the ceremonies	Boundary stelae Arena of royal display for King and royal family	Closed Amun's temples and diverted revenue to Akhetaten. Temples fell into disrepair Work on buildings in Thebes ceased	No Osirian burial practices -no Judgement before Osiris, no afterlife in the Fields of Reeds, no traditional funerary formulae

Akhenaten's lack
of foresight

Focus on Aten to the detriment of foreign policy
Loss of Egyptian control over Syria and Palestine

Akhenaten's
hesitancy

Nefertiti
What happened to her ?

Last years of Akhenaten

Smenkhkare co-regent
Who was he?

Horemheb

**Boy king Tutankhamun
9 year reign**

Ay

Religious transition
No reprisals

Restoration program
Focus on Amun

Economic revival
Temples re-opened

**The elderly Ay
4 year reign**

Edict of Reform against
corruption, exploitation
and abuses.

**Horemheb
38 year reign**

Destruction of all reminders
of the Aten heresy. Wholesale
dismantling and destruction of
building sites dedicated to Aten.

REVISION QUESTIONS AND ESSAY TOPICS

1 Analyse the following quarry inscription.

First occurrence of his majesty's giving command to [ ] to muster all the workmen from Elephantine to Samhudet and the leaders of the army, in order to make a great breach for cutting out sandstone, in order to make the great sanctuary of Herakhte in his name: 'Heat-Which-is-in-Aten', in Karnak. Behold, the officials, the companions, and the chiefs of the fan-bearers, were the chiefs of the quarry-service, for the transportation of stone.⁽⁹⁷⁾

a What evidence is there that this inscription was carved very early in Akhenaten's reign?

b For what building project was the sandstone being quarried?

c Who was Herakhte?

d What evidence is there that this was regarded by the king as a great national enterprise?

e What part did the leaders of the army play in this enterprise?

f What part were the officials and courtiers of the king expected to play?

g What other important buildings were located at Karnak?

h Describe the 'great sanctuary of Herakhte' that the king built at east Karnak.

I What evidence is there that an important festival was celebrated there in the early years of Akhenaten's rule.

2 Write a caption for each of the following figures of Nefertiti and show how they provide evidence of her regal status during the reign of her husband.

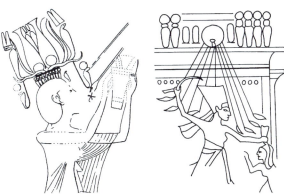

3 **Provide evidence to support each of the following statements.**

a Akhenaten did not invent the life-sustaining sun-disk.

b The ideas expressed in the Hymn to the Aten were not new.

c Akhenaten's relationship with the Aten reaffirmed the divinity of kingship.

d The androgynous representations of Akhenaten are more likely to have been a religious statement than an indication of some physical affliction.

e Akhenaten had a strong economic motive for closing the temples, particularly of Amun, after year 5.

4 **How did the scenes of Akhenaten, Nefertiti and their children at the *window of appearances* and in chariot drives:**

a serve as religious icons?

b attempt to keep the nobles and common people satisfied?

5 **Identify the event depicted in the scene below.**

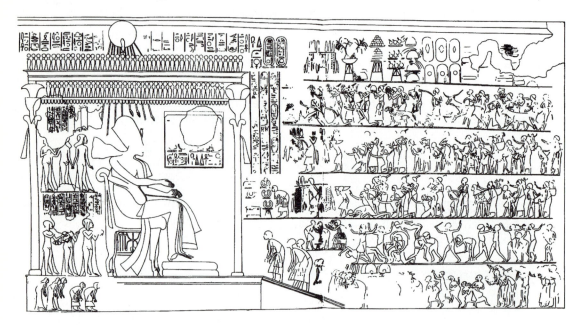

a Give this scene a title.

b In what year was this celebration held?

c What information does this appear to provide about:
  • the royal family
  • the relationship between Akhenaten and Nefertiti
  • foreign affairs at this time.

6 **Look at the limestone statue of Akhenaten and Nefertiti reproduced on the right and answer the following questions.**

a What evidence is there that this statue was probably made later rather than earlier in Akhenaten's reign?

b Where would this statue have been originally located and why would it have been found in this location?

c What is the association between this statue and the inscriptions below?

> May I be one who may adore his majesty; may I be his follower. Grant that I may be satisfied with seeing thee.[(98)]

> May he see thee forever and ever; may he endow thee with jubilees like the numbers of the shore … and for the Great King's Wife, his beloved … May she be by the side of Waenre (Akhenaten) for ever and ever …[(99)]

7 **Carefully read the words of Howard Carter, written sometime after he discovered the tomb of Tutankhamun in 1922.**

> As self-respecting historians, let us put aside the tempting 'might have beens' and 'probablys' and come back to the cold hard facts of history. What do we really know about this Tutankhamun with whom we have become so surprisingly familiar? Remarkably little, when you come right down to it. In the present state of our knowledge we might say with truth that the one outstanding feature of his life was in fact that he died and was buried.[(100)]

Draw up a table of two columns with the headings:
- Known facts about Tutankhamun
- Conjecture (guesswork) based on inconclusive evidence.

Fill in the columns based on the information available so far.

8 **The three figures on page 454 are associated with the reign of Tutankhamun.**

a What features in Figure A indicate that Tutankhamun's reign was a transition period?

b Identify the deities in Figure B. In what ways does this relief differ from the former representations featuring Akhenaten?

c What do these figures indicate about state religion at this time?

d Explain who later ordered the obliteration of the names in Figure C and the reason behind this destruction.

e What other destruction occurred at this time?

f How did this campaign of destruction allow historians to bring Akhenaten, the heretic king, to life after approximately 3300 years?

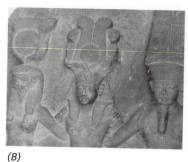

(B)

9 Identify and analyse the following document extracts.

(C)

His majesty took council with his heart how he might expel evil and suppress lying. The plans of his majesty were an excellent refuge, repelling violence ... and delivering the Egyptians from the oppressions which were among them. Behold, his majesty spent the whole time seeking the welfare of Egypt and searching out instances of oppression in the land ... Came a scribe of his majesty. Then he seized palette and roll; he put it into writing according to all that his majesty, the king himself said.

... I have improved this entire land — I have sailed it as far as south of the wall ... I have learned its whole interior, I have travelled it entirely in its midst ... and I have sought two officials, perfect in speech, excellent in good qualities, knowing how to judge the innermost heart, hearing the words of the palace, the laws of the judgment-hall.

... Now, as for any official or any priest concerning whom it shall be heard saying: 'He sits to execute judgment among the official staff ... and he commits a crime against justice therein'; it shall be against him a capital crime.[101]

a   Who was the author of this document?
b   By what name is this document known today?
c   What is the general theme of these extracts?
d   What were the conditions existing in Egypt at the time this document was recorded and why was the country in this state?
e   What actions, mentioned in these extracts, did the author of the document take?
f   What other measures did he implement?
g   What punishments did he impose on those who did not abide by his regulations?

10 Essay topics

a   In what ways did the sun-temples and the tombs of Akhenaten's officials reflect the king's new doctrine?
b   Comment on the following statement.

Akhenaten's apparent lack of interest in military affairs is believed to have led to the loss of Egypt's lucrative Asiatic empire.

CHAPTER
14

A change of dynasty
— Seti I and Ramesses II

A new era began with the accession to the throne of the former general, Pramesse of Avaris in c. 1307 BC. He became King Ramesses I and was followed on the throne by his son, Seti I, and his famous grandson, Ramesses II, under whom the dynasty reached its peak.

Although Thebes remained the religious and cultural capital, the kings of the Nineteenth Dynasty administered the country from the royal residence in the delta which Ramesses II extended into a vast administrative complex, called Pi-Ramesse (Per-Ramesse).

Seti I and Ramesses II regained some of Egypt's empire in Syria and Palestine as they followed the example of the warrior pharaohs of the early Eighteenth Dynasty. They also inaugurated a massive building program throughout Egypt and some of their works, such as the Temple of Abydos initiated by Seti, rivalled those of Amenhotep III in form and decoration. The sheer size of Ramesses II's buildings and statuary surpassed anything that had been done before. However, decades of extravagance by Ramesses II depleted the national resources and the monuments of his successors reflected this.

Ramesses II, who reigned for over 66 years, outlived each prince chosen as his successor. He was finally succeeded by his thirteenth son, the elderly Merenptah. During his reign, the warlike *Sea People* from all over the Mediterranean moved into the area west of the delta, posing a threat to Egypt's security. Merenptah's successful defence against the Sea People delayed a full-scale invasion for another 45 years.

From the death of Merenptah to the end of the dynasty (17 years) four pharaohs ruled in quick succession — Amunmesse (perhaps a usurper), Seti II, Ramesses-Siptah (a minor) and his mother, Queen Tewosret. However, the sequence of their reigns and their exact relationship to one another have not been established conclusively. It is generally believed that the last pharaoh of the dynasty was Tewosret, wife of Seti II, who, like Hatshepsut, took the throne for herself with the full titles of a pharaoh. With her death the Nineteenth Dynasty came to an end.

Sources for the Nineteenth Dynasty

The cult and mortuary temples at Abydos, Karnak, Luxor, western Thebes, Abu Simbel, Beit el-Wali and elsewhere in Nubia and their monumental inscriptions are the chief sources of information for the reigns of Seti I and Ramesses II. These have to be carefully analysed as they present the official propaganda about such achievements as:

- military campaigns — Seti's campaign in Syria and the Battle of Kadesh between Ramesses II and the Hittites
- diplomatic negotiations — the treaty signed between Ramesses II and the Hittites and the celebration of the marriage of Ramesses and the Hittite princess
- mining operations — Seti's provision of a well and compound for workers mining gold in the desert.

Victory stelae, such as those set up on behalf of Seti I at Beth-Shan are another form of official record.

Clay tablets, inscribed in cuneiform, found in the Hittite capital of Hattusas (Bogazkoy) present the other side of the picture — the Hittite version of the Battle of Kadesh and the treaty with the Egyptians, the haggling that went on over marriage negotiations between the daughter of the Hittite king and Ramesses II, and letters about royal visits to Egypt.

Letters and reports, such as those passed between the king's officials and between officials and the royal workmen at Deir el-Medina, provide an interesting insight into Nineteenth Dynasty administration.

Unlike Eighteenth Dynasty tombs, there are very few scenes of daily life found in the tombs of Nineteenth Dynasty nobles. Despite the minimum number of scenes showing the tomb owner carrying out his official duties, some contain biographical details such as the account of the appointment of Nebwenenef as high priest of Amun by Ramesses II.

Margin notes
Monumental inscriptions

Cuneiform records from Hattusas

Official reports

Tomb biographies

Ramesses I

Qualifications as successor

The choice of Pramesse (Ramesses I) as Horemheb's successor was based on three qualifications — his ability, loyalty and line of heirs. To the childless Horemheb the latter qualification was very important.

With his military background and the opportunities that opened up for him under Horemheb's administration, Pramesse advanced through the military hierarchy and eventually held the second highest position in the land, that of vizier. In each of his positions he had proven himself highly competent and loyal to his pharaoh.

By the time Horemheb died, Pramesse, who had been designated as his successor, was an elderly man with a middle-aged son and grandchildren — an established dynasty.

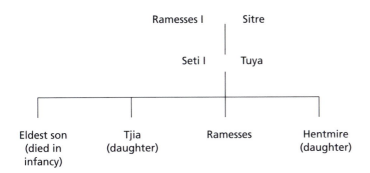

The family tree of Ramesses I

Ramesses I, the founder of a new line of kings, chose to model his names and titles on those of Ahmose, the founder of the Eighteenth Dynasty.

From the outset, the elderly Ramesses shared his pharaonic duties with his son, Seti, who described himself at this time as the star beside his father, Re.

Shared rule with his son

There were no events of great historical importance during the short 16-month reign of Ramesses I. However, the building project which he initiated at Karnak, the show of force in Palestine led by Seti and the adoption of a policy of honouring many gods, set the pattern for his successors.

Seth, the ancient god of the delta was elevated to a more prominent position in the Egyptian hierarchy of gods and honours were given to Re, Ptah and Mut. Although Ramesses and Seti were keen to prevent any one cult having precedence over another, they continued to show official respect for Amun. At Thebes they began the conversion of the open area between the pylons of Amenhotep III and Horemheb into a huge columned hall. Although initiated by Ramesses I, this massive hypostyle hall was not completed until the reign of his grandson, Ramesses II.

Balanced policy with regard to the gods

Seti, as *commander of the troops*, was probably hoping for an opportunity to reclaim the part of Syria which had once been under Egyptian influence. However, during his father's reign, his military activities were restricted to protecting Egypt. He 'subdued the land of Fenkhu' and 'repulsed for him (Ramesses I) the dissidents from the desert'.[1]

When Ramesses died after such a short time on the throne, his tomb in the Valley of the Kings was unfinished and had to be hurriedly made ready for his burial. When Seti came to the throne, he honoured his father by:

Death after 16 months on the throne

- building a chapel for him next to his own magnificent temple at Abydos
- providing a sanctuary for the cult of Ramesses I in his own great mortuary temple in western Thebes.

Seti I (Sethos) — *Bringer of Renaissance*

Seti's ambitions

Modelled himself on Thutmose III and Amenhotep III

According to Kitchin, Seti I's overriding aim was the renewal of Egypt which he hoped to achieve by following the examples of the great Eighteenth Dynasty pharaohs Thutmose III (conqueror) and Amenhotep III (builder). His royal titulary is evidence of this. He adopted the throne name of *Men-ma-re* which Kitchin maintains was a cross between that of Thutmose III (**Men**-*kheper-re*) and Amenhotep III (*Neb-ma-re*). His Two Goddesses' attribute was *Bringer of Renaissance (rebirth), Strong-armed, Subduing the Foe.*

His ambitions seem to have been:

* to restore those areas of Syria which had been part of the Egyptian empire by following the military strategy of Thutmose III
* to equal in magnificence the buildings of Amenhotep III.

Seti's military campaigns

Aim to conquer Kadesh

Seti's ultimate military objective was to conquer the lands of Kadesh and Amurru, but he knew that if he were to achieve his objective he would have to follow the three-step strategy used by Thutmose III. This was:

* to gain a firm hold on Palestine
* to control the seaports along the Phoenician coastline
* to launch his attack on central and northern Syria from the coast.

During the first six years of his reign he achieved his objective. However, the records on the walls of the Temple of Karnak, which provide an overview of his campaigns, make it difficult to build up a clear chronological picture, particularly with regard to his activities at Kadesh.

Campaigns in Palestine and Phoenicia

Rebellion of Shoshu Bedouin

As had often happened in the past, when a new king came to the throne of Egypt, the local princes in Palestine took the opportunity to rebel. According to the records at Karnak, the Shosu Bedouin of southern Palestine had revolted, 'they have taken to cursing and quarrelling ... they disregard the laws of the palace'.[2] The hostile Bedouin chief of Hammath, further north, had captured the Egyptian garrison towns of Beth-Shan and Rehob.

So in year 1, Seti was given the opportunity for which he had been waiting — to lead his well-drilled army out of Egypt. The record on the wall of the hypostyle hall at Karnak reveals his pleasure at taking up arms.

> His Majesty was glad on account of it ... rejoicing to begin battle, he delighted to enter into it.[3]

He moved with the three divisions of his army against the poorly-armed Shosu Bedouin near Gaza and then 'dispatched the First Division of Amun, *Mighty of Bows*, against the town of Hammath; the First Division of Re, *Abounding in Valour*, against the (captured) town of Beth-Shan; and the First Division of Seth, *Strong of Bows*, against the town of Yenoam'.[4]

After erecting a victory stela at Beth-Shan, he may have re-established Egyptian control over the southern part of the Phoenician coast before returning in triumph to Egypt.

During the next three years he led several more campaigns during which:

- he dealt with disturbances in Galilee caused by the Apiru
- he secured the province of Upi in southern Syria
- he marched up the Phoenician coastline taking control of the seaports of Tyre, Sidon, Byblos and Simyra
- he organised the shipment to Egypt of precious cedar from Lebanon which was to be used for Amun's barge and flagstaffs.

Victory in Palestine and southern Syria

He erected three more stelae at Beth-Shan, Tell es-Shihab and Tyre describing his triumphs.

Seti had reaffirmed Egypt's hold on her possessions in Palestine and southern Syria, had control of the Phoenician coastline and had cut off the Hittite-controlled territory of Amurru from the sea. He was now prepared to launch an attack on Amurru and Kadesh and face the opposition of the Hittites who 'were more formidable than the doughy Mitanni of Thutmose III's day'.[5]

Threat from Libya

There is some confusion in the sources as to the chronology of Seti's campaigns in Syria but Kitchin believes that the king's attempt to take Kadesh was interrupted by the need to deal with the Libyans who were threatening Egypt from the west.

The Libyans were being pushed eastward as they were displaced by groups of *Sea People* moving into the coastal areas of north Africa. This movement was part of a general upheaval throughout the Mediterranean area at this time.

Influx of *Sea People* pushes Libyans towards the delta

Seti and his forces dealt with the Libyans so effectively that they were not a serious threat to Egypt for about another 115 years.

Campaign against Amurru and Kadesh and conflict with the Hittites

In year 5 or 6, Seti probably launched his attack on Amurru and Kadesh from the Phoenician coastline, following the strategy of Thutmose III. The reliefs on the walls of the hypostyle hall at the Temple of Amun depict the storming of Kadesh. For this important victory, Seti honoured

Erected a victory stela in Kadesh

the gods Montu, Seth and Amun by erecting a stela inside the city of Kadesh. Seti was the first pharaoh for over 100 years to bring Kadesh under the control of the Egyptians.

However, the king's triumph was shortlived because the young Hittite king, Muwatallis, did not stand by and watch territory held by the Hittites for two generations fall under the control of the Egyptians.

Possible agreement with Hittites

It appears that Seti, satisfied that he had proved himself as a warrior, may have signed a peace treaty with the Hittites. Although this was not mentioned in the Egyptian records, Seti seems to have agreed to stop further attacks on Amurru and Kadesh in return for Hittite acceptance of Egyptian control over Palestine and the cities along the Phoenician coastline. Seti knew when to withdraw from the area.

A copy of a relief showing Seti I fighting in northern Syria

Actions in Nubia

In year 8, according to a rock inscription in Nubia, Seti ordered military action against a group of nomadic people called the Irem who roamed between the wells and oases beyond the Third Cataract in Nubia. These tribesmen seemed to have planned a raid on the Nile Valley to seize cattle, crops and land if possible. It appears that Seti did not lead this campaign himself.

The results of Seti I's military actions

Between years 1 and 8, Seti carried out five campaigns by which he:

- showed his own potential as a military leader
- revived the image of the warrior pharaoh which had developed in the early part of the Eighteenth Dynasty
- satisfied his honour by being the first pharaoh to capture the formidable city of Kadesh in over a century
- secured Egypt's borders
- proved that Egypt was once again a force to be reckoned with, by subduing rebellious tribes and cities in Palestine and restoring much of Egypt's former territory along the Phoenician coast.

Building, quarrying and mining

To fulfil the second of his ambitions — to emulate the building activities of Amenhotep III — Seti directed his many capable officials to oversee the construction and decoration of:

- a magnificent pure white limestone temple at Abydos
- a great columned hypostyle hall at Karnak
- a glittering summer palace at Avaris
- new work on the sanctuaries of Re at Heliopolis and Ptah at Memphis
- his mortuary temple and tomb in western Thebes.

Since his extensive construction program required massive amounts of building material, he initiated expeditions to locate better supplies of fine stone and gold and attempted to improve the conditions of the quarry workers and miners who laboured in the intense heat of the desert.

Much of the initial building work was supervised by the vizier Nebamun but after year 10, Paser became Seti's vizier of the south and took over the tremendous task of construction work in Thebes. The viceroy of Nubia, Amen-em-ope, was responsible for the vital gold supply needed for the *mansions of the gods*.

Crown Prince Ramesses not only visited most of his father's building sites but was put in charge of the 'multitude of works' commissioned by the king at Aswan such as 'very great obelisks, and great and marvellous statues'.[6] This project involved the construction of huge barges for transporting the obelisks and black granite statues down river. Ramesses also spent much of his time at Abydos, supervising the work on his father's cenotaph temple and the preparation of a huge gold statue of the king for the sanctuary.

Seti often left his palaces in the north (Memphis and Avaris) to travel south, to celebrate one of the great festivals and check on the progress of his temples and tomb. It was during two of these visits, in years 6 and 9, that he took a personal interest in the welfare of his quarrymen and transport force and personally investigated the conditions of the gold miners in the desert near Edfu.

Because of his non-royal background, Seti was probably more aware than most kings of the hardships under which his workmen and supervisors laboured. He attempted to encourage them and make their work a little easier. According to a quarry inscription at Silsila, Seti ordered that those involved in quarrying and transporting sandstone should have their rations substantially increased.

> Now His Majesty increased what was issued to the army-force (of 1000 men), in terms of ointment, beef, fish and plenty of vegetables without restriction. Every man of them had 20 dbn (2 kg) of bread daily and a bundle of vegetables, a portion of roast meat and two sacks of grain monthly.[7]

As a result, 'they worked for him with a loving heart'.[8]

Second of Seti's aims

Chief officials in charge of building

Seti's interest in the welfare of quarry workers

To speed up the delivery of gold from the mines to the treasury of the temple he was building at Abydos, Seti took a personal interest in improving the conditions of the mine workers as well.

The mines were located at Wadi Mia, 60 kilometres from the Nile in the eastern desert, an area where water supplies were limited and the heat intense. In year 9, Seti decided to experience these conditions for himself.

Seti's personal experience

> ... his majesty inspected the desert lands as far as the mountains, for his heart desired to see the mines from which the fine gold is brought. After his majesty had gone up for many miles, he halted on the way to take counsel with his heart. He said: 'How painful is a way that has no water! What are travellers to do to relieve the parching of their throats? What quenches their thirst, the homeland being far away and the desert wide? Woe to the man who thirsts in the wilderness!'[9]

He sent workers to find a place in the mountains suitable for digging a well 'in order that it might uplift the weary and refresh the heart of him who burns in the summer heat'.[10]

Search for water and provision of wells

Because the gods had 'made water come forth from the mountain',[11] Seti ordered the construction of a settlement for the mine workers and gave directions to the stone cutters to build a temple in the sandstone cliffs. He dedicated this Temple of Wadi-Mia or Al-Kanais to Amun, Re, Ptah, Osiris, Isis, Horus and Menmare (Seti).

On its walls he recorded his impressions of the terrible conditions under which these men had worked before his arrival, an account of his successful exploration for water in the area and a formal dedication of the well and the temple.

The Temple of Osiris at Abydos

Abydos a holy site

From Predynastic times, Abydos had been a holy site. It was supposedly the place where the head of the dismembered Osiris had been buried and where Egypt's earliest kings had built their cenotaphs. Seti claimed that he built his temple cenotaph there in response to an oracle.

Gardiner suggests that Seti's construction at Abydos may have had something to do with his name which was associated with the god Seth, the murderer of Osiris. Perhaps the temple was an attempt to placate Osiris and his priesthood.

A national shrine

Not only did Seti dedicate the temple to the triad — Osiris, Isis and Horus — but to the great national gods, Amun of Thebes, Ptah of Memphis and Re-Horakhte of Heliopolis. He also dedicated it to the service of the deified king (Seti) and to the remote kings of the past whose tombs were nearby.

According to Breasted, the Abydos temple is 'perhaps the noblest monument of Egyptian art still surviving in the land'.[12]

Unlike most temples, which are rectangular, this remarkable temple was L-shaped. It was made from fine quality white limestone and featured seven beautiful chapels located behind a columned hall. Each chapel was fitted with a door of electrum and decorated with exquisite reliefs showing Seti offering to each of the gods mentioned above. Inscribed on each door was a dedicatory formula similar to the following:

> He made it as a monument for Horus residing in the House of Menmare, making for him a Great House of Gold that he may be given life.[13]

These reliefs, with their delicacy, pure lines and technical perfection, are in the best artistic tradition of Amenhotep III. Gardiner finds this surprising since Egypt was 'on the threshold of a period of undisputed decadence' (the reign of Ramesses II).[14]

Other features of the temple included:

- a number of rooms to the rear of the chapels with unique reliefs from the legend of Osiris. It is likely that the rituals associated with the worship of Osiris were performed there

- a gallery in which Seti listed the kings of Egypt from the time of Menes to his own reign. This king list did not include the names of Hatshepsut, Akhenaten, Tutankhamun and Ay because Seti recorded only those kings whom he considered legitimate rulers of Egypt

- a small limestone chapel dedicated by Seti to his father, Ramesses I.

Behind the temple was a subterranean cenotaph, referred to as the Osireion, where each year a festival was held to celebrate the death and resurrection of Osiris.

A painted relief from the Temple of Abydos, showing Seti raising the Djed pillar

The facade of the Temple of Abydos

Temple endowments

The Abydos temple was:

- provided with gold from the desert mines south-east of Edfu
- assured of revenue from estates in Nubia
- equipped with priests
- protected by royal edicts from interference by future kings and government officials.

A painted relief from the Temple of Abydos, showing Seti offering to Horus

Part of Seti's endowment to the temple was the appointment of a special troop of gold washers. The inscriptions on the wall of the desert temple at Kanais declared that 'they and their dependants are exempt (from taxes) as children of my House, as dependents of my temple'.[15] A warning, against any interference with their work by officials or future kings, ended with a curse on those who might violate his royal edict:

Royal edicts to protect endowments

> The gods shall punish him who spoils my plans; they shall deliver him to the slaughterhouse in *dat* (the Underworld) … As to anyone who shall be deaf to this decree, Osiris shall be after him, Isis after his wife and Horus after his children, and all the great ones, the lords of the necropolis, will make their reckoning with him.[16]

Seti established estates in Nubia for the provisioning of the Abydos temple and its staff. To protect these estates he issued an even more harshly-worded royal edict. In the version inscribed on a cliff south of the Third Cataract, he threatened government officials and workers on the estates with severe punishments if boundary markers were moved, if estate workers were moved to another project or if cattle were allowed to wander away. The punishments for offenders included amputation of the nose and ears, flogging — 'two hundred blows and five pierced wounds',[17] payment of compensation and forced labour on the estates. The harshness of these punishments was reminiscent of punishment imposed by Horemheb for lawlessness.

Harsh punishments for offenders

The Temple of Abydos was unfinished when Seti died but was completed by his son, Ramesses II, who added another hall. Unfortunately, he walled up six of Seti's original seven doorways and the reliefs carved on Ramesses' orders lacked the delicacy of those of his father.

The great columned hypostyle hall at Karnak

This awe-inspiring building was initiated at the beginning of the dynasty and during Seti's reign the northern half of the great hall, including the nave, was completed. The project was finished during the long rein of Ramesses II.

The hall in its finished state had 134 columns. The taller columns (26 metres high) that formed the two central rows, had open papyrus capitals while the smaller side columns (13 metres high) had capitals of closed papyrus buds. The difference in height between these central and side columns allowed for clerestory windows to admit light into the dim interior.

Some of the massive columns in the hypostyle hall at Karnak

The mortuary temple and tomb in western Thebes

From a few fragmentary inscriptions it is known that Seti's mortuary temple was called *Temple-of-the-Spirit-of-Seti-Merenptah-in-the-House-of-Amun-in-the-West-of-Thebes*. It was built of fine white sandstone 'with doors of real cedar, wrought with Asiatic copper, made high and large' and with a wide hall for the appearance of 'his august image at his beautiful Feast of the Valley'.[18]

Seti's tomb is one of the most impressive in the Valley of the Kings. It is approximately 100 metres long and is decorated with high quality raised reliefs. According to Hornung, in *The Tomb of Pharaoh Seti I*, the king began a new tradition in tomb decoration. The reliefs began at the entrance and continued all the way to the burial chamber.

The zodiac on the ceiling of Seti's tomb

Buildings in Lower Egypt

Seti built extensively in Lower Egypt as well as at Abydos and Thebes. In the delta city of Avaris he constructed a summer palace and at Memphis and Heliopolis added substantially to the ancient temples of Ptah and the sun god, Re. An inscription at Aswan indicates that he 'filled Heliopolis with obelisks'.[19]

Conclusion

When Seti I died at about the age of 50, the country was prosperous and firmly administered. Egypt once again had an empire, although not as extensive as previously, and Seti's buildings rivalled the best of those built by Amenhotep III.

The new dynasty had begun well and a king now came to the throne who would carry on the New Kingdom tradition of the superhuman pharaoh.

Ramesses II — the archetypal pharaoh

Kitchin, in his work *Pharaoh Triumphant*, refers to Ramesses II as the 'archetypal' pharaoh because he is a 'symbol of the proud majesty of Egypt through the ages'.[20] However, the length of his reign (67 years), the size and number of his monuments and his 'craze for self advertisement'[21] do not necessarily make him the greatest pharaoh in Egyptian history. An evaluation of his achievements is found towards the end of this chapter.

Ramesses, the crown prince

Unlike most Egyptian crown princes, about whom there are few records, Ramesses' early years are well documented. He was brought up in a military tradition and at the age of ten was granted the title of commander-in-chief of the army by his father, although this did not carry with it any real powers.

Well documented early years — military experience

Seti appears to have considered Ramesses old enough at 14 or 15 to accompany the Egyptian army on a number of campaigns. Although the adolescent was kept in the background on each of these occasions, his small figure, depicted as a combatant, was added later to Seti's Karnak inscription. He was with his father at Kadesh when, for a short time, the Egyptians once again controlled this strategic Syrian city.

When the prince was in his mid-teens, his father presented him to the court as prince regent, leaving no doubt about the succession. Ramesses later recorded this event on a wall in the Temple of Abydos.

> He (Seti I) said concerning me: 'Crown him as king, that I may see his beauty while I live with him'. Thereupon approached the courtiers, to set the double diadem upon my head. 'Place for him the crown upon his head', so spake he concerning me, while he was upon earth. Let him organise this land, let him administer [—], let him show his face to the people.[22]

Also, according to Ramesses' Abydos inscription, his father apparently set him up with 'household women, a royal harem, like the beauties of the palace' and chose several wives for him.[23]

His chief wife, Nefertari — 'the one to whom beauty pertains', was barely a teenager. She was not of royal blood but seems to have come from one of the Theban royal families. The epithet 'beloved of Mut'*, often attached to her name, seems to point to her Theban origin. Since Seti and his family came from the delta region in Lower Egypt and had no ties with royalty, it would have been politically shrewd to arrange a marriage of the crown prince with the daughter of a noble family from Thebes. Nefertari's name also conjured up the image of her famous namesake, Ahmose Nefertari whose Theban family founded the glorious Eighteenth Dynasty.

During the latter part of Seti's reign, Ramesses acted as his father's deputy and worked alongside Paser, the vizier, making tours of inspection up and down the Nile Valley, supervising some of his father's building projects and searching the quarries at Aswan for granite suitable for great statues and obelisks.

Three years before his father's death, the 22-year-old prince successfully put down two minor wars — one in Nubia and one against Sherden pirates, who were raiding the delta area. It was these same Sherden captives who, forced into the Egyptian army, later accompanied Ramesses on his own Syrian campaigns.

A statue of the youthful Ramesses II

Ramesses' first three years on the throne

When Seti died, Ramesses was about 25 years of age, with two chief wives, Nefertari and Istnofret, and a large number of children. Kitchin estimates that Ramesses had probably already fathered somewhere between 17 and 27 children by his wives and harem women. Nefertari had borne him his first and third sons, Amen hir-wonmef and Pre-hir-wonmef, while his second and fourth sons and eldest daughter, born to Istnofret, were Ramesses, Khaemwaset and Bint-Anath. Many more were to come in the years ahead.

A family man

The young king took the throne name of Usi-ma-re, *Strong in Right is Re.* Two years later he added Setepenre, *Chosen of Re*, to Usi-ma-re.

After sailing to Thebes with the body of his father and presiding over his burial, Ramesses II:

Activities in Thebes after Seti's burial

- celebrated the Opet festival
- appointed Nebwenenef as high priest of Amun
- laid the foundations for his own mortuary temple, the Ramesseum, on the west bank
- ordered the continuation of work on the hypostyle hall at Karnak and additions to the Temple of Luxor — a forecourt, pylon and obelisks.

Ramesses was accompanied to Thebes by Nefertari who appears to have played an active part in the events of year 1. She is shown officiating with Ramesses at the investiture of Nebwenenef and was also depicted on a rock shrine at Gelel el-Silsila appeasing the gods. This

* Mut was the divine consort of the Theban god Amun.

Nefertari's status

was a task usually reserved for the king in his role as intermediary between the gods and the people. One of her titles, *mistress of the Two Lands*, was a female version of the kingly epithet, *lord of the Two Lands*. Even at such a young age, the chief consort had considerable status and was playing a significant role in public life.

When Ramesses and the court reached Abydos on their return journey to Memphis, the king 'turned aside to see his Father, Osiris, traversing the waters of the Abydos canal to make offerings to Wennufer (Osiris) with every good thing that his spirit loves'.[24] Ramesses was shocked at the condition of his father's temple which had not been completed before his death.

> The Temple of Menmare had its front and rear still under construction
> ... its monuments were unfinished, its columns were not set on the
> platform, its statue was upon the ground, without being fashioned in
> accord with the regulations of the House of Gold.[25]

He was also upset by the dilapidated state of the cemetery containing the cenotaphs of former Egyptian kings.

Promise to complete Seti's temple and restore ancient tombs

The king summoned the court, the chief officials, all the *chiefs of works*, the army commanders and the *keepers of the house of rolls*[26] to listen to his plan to restore the ancient tombs and complete the temple of his father.

> Said his majesty to them; ... 'It is a happy example, to provide for them
> that have passed away, excellent to behold good ... the thought of the
> son that he should incline his heart after his father. My heart leads me
> in doing excellent things for Men-mar re (Seti I). I will cause it to be
> said forever and ever: "I was his son who made his name live".'[27]

Planned a new city in the delta

He then returned north to organise the building of a new city based on the summer palace at Avaris which he planned to call Pi-Ramesse *Great in Victories*.

The king's building activities required massive amounts of gold; however, it appears that by the time of Ramesses, the gold supplies in the eastern desert of Upper Egypt were diminishing. This meant that more gold had to be mined in the Nubian area of Akuyati. In year 3, Ramesses, like his father, commissioned a well to be dug in the area after the viceroy of Kush had confirmed that half of the gold workers sent into that region had died from thirst.

> It has been in this difficult state regarding water since the time of God:
> people die of thirst there. Every previous king has wanted to open up
> a well there, but with no success.[28]

Initiated a search for water in the Nubian desert

Apparently Seti had failed in an attempt to find water in this area despite his success in Wadi Abbad, but Ramesses was more fortunate. He sent a letter to the viceroy ordering him to 'send a survey party halfway to Akuyati'[29] and to spend a month searching for a source of water. Eventually a dispatch from the viceroy announced that water which 'spurted out just as a god would do it'[30] had been found at a depth of about six metres.

By year 4, Ramesses had set his initial building program in motion but his real ambition was to dislodge the Hittites from Amurru and Kadesh and recapture all of Egypt's former possessions in Syria. Only by achieving this would he, like his father, prove that he was the equal of the great Eighteenth Dynasty warrior kings — Thutmose I and Thutmose III.

> The Egyptians were always trying to reassert the past in a world that would not stand still.[31]

Ramesses the warrior

In order to recapture Egypt's former territories in western Asia, Ramesses, like Thutmose III, planned to take one step at a time. Firstly he had to make sure of the coastline, retake Amurru, capture Kadesh, and then move inland and north beyond Aleppo.

Military ambitions

The campaign against Kadesh — year 5

> There is no episode in Egyptian history which occupies so much carved space in Egyptian temples.[32]

There are two distinct versions of the campaign against Kadesh. Historians refer to as the *Bulletin* (official report with its accompanying reliefs) and the *Poem* (the heroic role of the king with a narrative introduction and ending). Each of these accounts was carved numerous times on the walls of Ramesses' temples — the Bulletin seven times and the Poem eight times.

Sources — the *Bulletin* and the *Poem*

Despite the fact that parts of the Bulletin and Poem 'leave the realm of the possible and become entirely fanciful',[33] it is possible to work out the main features of the campaign from the Egyptian point of view. To get a fairer picture of what happened, the Hittite records also need to be consulted.

The combined sources provide information on:
- Hittite preparations
- Ramesses' army en route
- Ramesses' inadequate intelligence system
- emergency measures taken by Ramesses and the surprise attack by the Hittites
- Ramesses' personal bravery and the arrival of a relief force
- the flight of the Hittite chariotry
- the stalemate and a peace proposal.

Ramesses' first Syrian campaign and Hittite preparations for further conflict

In year 4, Ramesses embarked on his first Syrian campaign, against Amurru. He led his troops through Palestine and along the coast of Phoenicia, securing the northern coastal cities before turning inland towards Amurru, taking its king, Benteshina, by surprise. After several months, Amurru became once more an Egyptian vassal. Ramesses returned to Egypt to prepare for the attack on Kadesh in the following season.

Amurru captured in year 4

When news of Benteshina's defeat reached Muwatallis, the Hittite king, he began massive preparations to prevent Ramesses taking any more Hittite-held territory in northern Syria. He recruited troops and chariotry, not only from his own kingdom, but from numerous allies.

> He left not a country which was not brought together with their chiefs who were with him, every man bringing his chariotry, an exceeding great multitude without its like.[34]

According to the Egyptian sources, which may have been exaggerated, Muwatallis' force consisted of approximately 2500 chariots, each with three men, and 37 000 infantry. Kitchin believes that this army could have been twice the size of the Egyptian force.

The Egyptian army en route

In the second month of year 5, Ramesses, with several of his sons, the vizier, his bodyguard and four military divisions, left Pi-Ramesse bound for Kadesh.

The divisions of the Egyptian army

It appears that the king and his bodyguard marched ahead with the Division of Amun, followed in order by the Division of Re, the Division of Ptah and bringing up the rear, the Division of Seth.

Although the Bulletin does not mention another Egyptian force, the Poem and reliefs describe a special force of recruits which was detached from the main army and sent, via the coast of Amurru, to Kadesh.

> ... his majesty had made a first battle force from the best of his army, and it was on the shore of the land of Amor.[35]

Within a month of leaving Egypt, Ramesses and his troops arrived in the vicinity of Kadesh.

Ramesses' inadequate intelligence system

When the king and the Division of Amun were close to Shabtuna, south-east of the Orontes river, two Shosu tribesmen requested an interview with the king. They said that their tribal chiefs had sent them to offer to become 'the servants of pharaoh' and to abandon their allegiance to the Hittites because Muwatallis was 'too fearful of Pharaoh to come southward'.[36] When questioned about the location of the Hittite forces, the Shosu told Ramesses that they were in the land of Aleppo, north of Tunip. This was approximately 200 kilometres to the north.

Ramesses tricked by Hittite allies

Without any further cross-examination of the Shosu, and 'lulled into a complacency, bordering on outright carelessness',[37] Ramesses pushed ahead, crossed the Orontes and marched unknowingly into a trap.

Ramesses caught in a trap

While the king and the Division of Amun set up camp on the north-west of Kadesh, the troops in the Division of Re had forded the Orontes and were making their way across the plain. However, the other two divisions were still miles away to the south.

In the meantime, a squad of Ramesses' scouts had come upon two Hittite spies in the area, whom they brought before the king. The reliefs show these spies being beaten to divulge the whereabouts of the Hittite king and his army. Ramesses is shocked to hear that the enemy are 'concealed behind Kadesh', just over three kilometres away 'already equipped with their infantry and their chariotry, and with their weapons of war' and 'ready to fight'.[38]

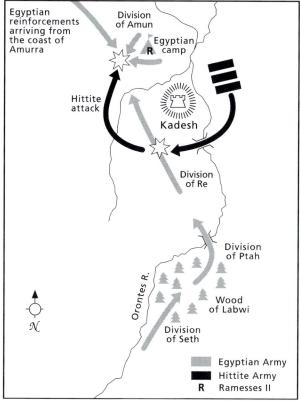

Troop movements in the Battle of Kadesh

Emergency measures and a surprise attack

After reprimanding his 'governors of foreign countries' and the 'chiefs of the land of pharaoh'[39] for failing to discover the whereabouts of the enemy, the king sent his vizier to the commander of the Division of Ptah with orders to hurry to the king. The Division of Seth was still too far away. He also directed members of the royal family, led by his son, Pre-hir-wonmef, to flee to safety.

As he was discussing emergency measures with his generals, the enemy chariots appeared. They had rounded the south of Kadesh and cut their way through the unsuspecting Division of Re as it crossed the plain. 'They charged into his majesty's army as it marched unaware',[40] and drove the shocked Egyptian troops towards Ramesses' camp.

Surprise charge by Hittite chariotry

The troops with the pharaoh (Army of Amun) panicked and were thrown into confusion. It appeared that Ramesses was about to face a disaster on a huge scale.

Personal bravery of the pharaoh and the arrival of relief troops

Despite the propaganda in the records of Ramesses' superhuman courage and prowess in averting disaster all on his own, the king does appear to have shown considerable personal bravery.

Determined not to go down without a fight and unable to rally his cowardly troops, the king seized his coat of mail, jumped into his chariot and, accompanied only by his retainers and bodyguard, charged at the enemy.

Ramesses saved by relief force from Amurru

The king was saved by the arrival from the west of the youthful force that he had sent to the coast of Amurru. The only account of the part played by these troops is found in the text accompanying the monumental reliefs of the battle.

> The arrival of the recruits of Pharaoh from the land of Amor. They found that the force of Kheta had surrounded the camp of his majesty on its western side ... Then the recruits cut off the foe belonging to the vanquished chief of Kheta, while they (the foe) were entering into the camp, and Pharaoh's officers slew them.[41]

Flight of the Hittite chariotry

The Hittite chariot commanders pulled back to regroup before another attack on the Egyptians. They probably hoped to finish them off before the arrival of the rest of the army (Divisions of Ptah and Seth). This lull in fighting gave Ramesses a chance to reorganise his troops and to take the offensive. According to the reliefs, the Egyptians were ready for the next onslaught and drove the enemy back to the river.

Offensive taken by Ramesses

> He overthrew them prostrate upon their faces, and hurled them down, one upon another into the waters of the Orontes ... His majesty was behind them like a fierce-eyed lion.[42]

Hittite chariotry pursued to the Orontes River

On the other side of the river, the Hittite king, Muwatallis, with his huge force of infantry, had been waiting to order his troops into action. When he saw his retreating chariotry struggling to cross the river, he knew that Ramesses had the upper hand for the moment and that he would need to reassess the situation in the light of his losses. He had not anticipated the arrival of the support force from the west.

The two intact Egyptian divisions finally arrived and the troops from the armies of Amun and Re, who had fled in panic, returned to the camp. Ramesses supposedly reproved their indiscipline and cowardice.

> What about you, my captains, soldiers,
> My charioteers, who shirked the fight? ...
> Have I not done good to any of you,
> That you should leave me alone in the midst of battle?
> You are lucky to be alive at all.[43]

Stalemate and a peace proposal

It appears that on the following day the battle was indecisive. The Hittites and their allies had suffered severe losses in chariotry in their previous encounter with the Egyptians. However, their infantry was far superior to that of the Egyptians and it seems that Ramesses' troops would have been unable to make much headway against them.

Indecisive battle on following day

Perhaps on the basis of Seti's willingness, 15 years earlier, to agree to a treaty maintaining the status quo, Muwatallis sent an envoy to Ramesses with a peace proposal. There is no evidence of what this proposal entailed. Kitchin maintains that it is highly unlikely that Ramesses would have agreed to make no further effort to reclaim the cities of northern Syria.

It appears that the Egyptian king called his commanders together and read the letter to them. They were unanimous in their acceptance of peace — 'very excellent is peace —. there is no blame in peace when you make it'.[44] Ramesses and his army then made their long way back to Egypt.

The aftermath of the Kadesh campaign

Attacks and territorial losses

Despite his limited military success in breaking out of the Hittite ambush at Kadesh, Ramesses actually suffered a political defeat. Muwatallis was still in control of Kadesh and in the following weeks, the Hittite king re-took Amurru and sent its Egyptian vassal, Benteshina, into exile.

Before Ramesses reached Egypt, Muwatallis marched south and occupied the whole of the Egyptian province of Upi. The Egyptians took no counteraction.

Hittites extended control into Egyptian territory

Some of the groups within Palestine saw recent events as a sign of weakness on the part of Egypt and many local rulers failed to pay their tribute. Nomadic tribes raided Egyptian territory and new kingdoms across the Jordan River refused to recognise pharaoh's rule.

Ramesses' massive advertising campaign

On his return to Egypt, Ramesses proceeded to magnify a military set-back into a stunning personal victory, the fictional details of which were repeated over and over again on the walls of his Egyptian and Nubian temples.

In Egyptian dogma it was unthinkable for a pharaoh to be defeated or to fail. The official records always focused on the superior wisdom, superhuman exploits and personal bravery of the king, with help from the gods. The vile and wretched enemy, whether successful or not, was always depicted as cowardly and terrified of the pharaoh. For these reasons, it is often difficult for historians to separate propaganda from fact.

In the case of Ramesses II, self-glorification went far beyond anything recorded by previous pharaohs. The *Annals* of the great conqueror Thutmose III were restrained compared with those of Ramesses II.

Official Egyptian propaganda

The following extracts and labelled copy of one of the temple reliefs illustrate some of the official propaganda of the Kadesh campaign.

> No officer was with me, no charioteer
> No soldier of the army, no shield-bearer;
> My infantry, my chariotry yielded before them,
> Not one of them stood firm to fight with them ...
> ... My numerous troops have deserted me,
> Not one of my chariotry looks for me:
> I keep on shouting for them,
> But none of them heeds my call.

> I know Amun heeds me more than a million troops ...
> ... I found the mass of chariots in whose midst I was
> Scattering before my horses;
> Not one of them found his hand to fight,
> Their hearts failed in their bodies through fear of me ...
> ... And the wretched chief of Khatti stood among his troops and chariots,
> Watching his majesty fight all alone ...
> Stood turning, shrinking, afraid ...
> ... They found all the foreign lands I had charged
> Lying fallen in their blood;
> All the good warriors of Khatti,
> The sons and brothers of their chiefs.
> For I had wrecked the plain of Kadesh,
> It could not be trodden because of their mass ...

> You have saved your soldiers, your chariotry;
> You are Amun's son who acts with his arms,
> You have felled Khatti by your valiant strength.
> You are the perfect fighter there is none like you,
> A king who battles for his army on battle day ...[45]

> Thereupon the forces of the Foe of Khatti surrounded the followers of his majesty who were by his side. When his majesty caught sight of them he rose quickly, enraged at them like his father Mont. Taking up weapons and donning his armour he was like Seth in the moment of his power. He mounted Victory in Thebes, his great horse and started out quickly alone by himself ... He heeded not the foreign multitude; he regarded them as chaff. His majesty charged into the force of the Foe of Khatti and the many countries with him ... His majesty slew the entire force ... their infantry and their chariotry falling on their faces one upon the other. His majesty slaughtered them in their places; they sprawled before his horses; and his majesty was alone, none other with him.[46]

Military improvements

After his return from Kadesh, Ramesses rebuilt his battered army, made changes in military leadership and improved his intelligence service. He also initiated a program to protect the western delta region from the Libyans. He strengthened already existing settlements along the desert margins from Memphis to the sea and built a series of fortresses along the coast for about 300 kilometres. These were about two days' march or one day's chariot ride apart.

An improved army and fortresses to protect the delta

A copy of one of the many reliefs describing the Battle of Kadesh

Further offensives in Palestine and Syria — years 7–17

Between years 7 and 8, Ramesses and his son, Amen-hir-wonmef, successfully subdued Canaan and eastern Palestine and then retook the province of Upi.

In the following year the king marched north, bypassing Amurru and Kadesh. He moved deep into Hittite-held territory, the first Egyptian king to do so for 120 years. By taking the towns of Tunip and Dapur, Ramesses cut off Kadesh and Amurru from their Hittite overlords. It was during this campaign that the king, with scant regard for his own safety, supposedly led his troops against the enemy without his protective coat of mail.

Campaign into Hittite-held territory

Surprisingly, there was little reaction from the Hittites. It appears that there was a crisis over the succession. Muwatallis had died and his son, Urhi-Teshub, by a palace concubine, ascended the throne as Mursil III. However, Muwatallis' brother, Hattusil, seems to have been something of a threat to the young king who was not inclined to leave his kingdom to lead an army against the Egyptians. Mursil III delegated his Syrian viceroy, the king of Carchemish, to deal with any new Egyptian attacks in Syria.

Unfortunately for Ramesses, his successes were short-lived. As soon as he returned to Egypt, emissaries from Hattusas and Carchemish convinced the rulers of Tunip and Dapur to return to Hittite allegiance.

In year 10, Ramesses once again attacked the towns of northern Syria but as in the previous year, the captured cities returned to their former allegiance as soon as the Egyptian forces went home.

How long he continued these campaigns in Syria is not known but Kitchin believes that, despite Ramesses' stubbornness and persistence, he must have realised eventually that he could not hold the area permanently. He probably began to wind down his campaigns between years 11 and 17.

Failure to permanently hold northern Syria

Ramesses the diplomat

The Egypto-Hittite Treaty

Year 18 of Ramesses' reign was a turning point in Egypto-Hittite relations. A conflict between Mursil III and his uncle, Hattusil, the brother of Muwatallis had come to a head. Hattusil had seized power and Mursil was sent into exile, first to Syria and then to Cyprus, from where he escaped and made his way to Egypt. The news that he was at the court of Ramesses alarmed Hattusil who demanded his extradition. Ramesses refused to hand him over.

Hattusil was in a dilemma. He could not force the issue with Egypt since he was being threatened on the east by the Assyrians. They had recently moved westward and taken over the kingdom of Hanilgalbat (the

'There shall be no hostilities between them forever. The great chief of Khatte shall not pass over into the land of Egypt, forever, to take anything therefrom. Ramesses, the great ruler of Egypt, shall not pass over into the land of Khatte to take anything therefrom, forever.'

'If another enemy comes against the lands of Usermare-Setepnere (Ramesses) ... and he shall send to the great chief of Khatte, saying: "Come with me as reinforcement against him", the great chief of Khatte shall come and ... shall slay the enemy ... or he shall send his infantry and his chariotry. Vice versa.'

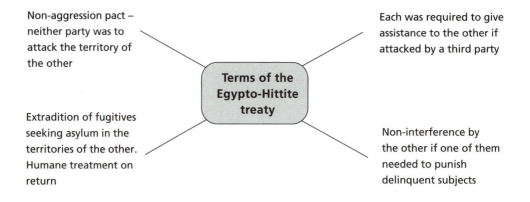

Non-aggression pact – neither party was to attack the territory of the other

Each was required to give assistance to the other if attacked by a third party

Terms of the Egypto-Hittite treaty

Extradition of fugitives seeking asylum in the territories of the other. Humane treatment on return

Non-interference by the other if one of them needed to punish delinquent subjects

'If any great man shall flee from the land of Khatte and he shall come to Usermare-Setepnere, the great ruler of Egypt, from either a town or a district, or any region of those belonging to the land of Khatte ... then the great ruler of Egypt shall not receive them but ... shall cause them to be brought to the great chief of Khatte. They shall not be settled. Vice versa.'

'If Ramesses, the great ruler of Egypt, be provoked against delinquent subjects when they have committed some other fault against him, and he comes to slay them, then the great chief of Khatte shall act with the lord of Egypt (in harmony with him). Vice versa.'

The terms of the Egypto-Hittite treaty
(Extracts from Breasted, *Ancient Records of Egypt*, Vol. III, pp. 168-171)

remnant of the Mitannian empire) which had provided a buffer zone for the Hittites. Hattusil must have considered that a treaty with Egypt would be preferable to making peace with the Assyrians.

Although nothing is known of the negotiations leading up to the signing of the treaty between Ramesses II and Hattusil, they must have been lengthy and involved. It was not until year 21 that Hittite envoys arrived in Egypt with the silver tablet on which the terms of the treaty were engraved in cuneiform.

Hattusil opens negotiations with Egypt

There are two surviving Egyptian copies of the original treaty (stelae in the Temple of Karnak and the Ramesseum) and one Hittite copy (a clay tablet found in the remains of the Hittite capital of Hattusas).

The terms of the treaty

The diagram on page 476 summarises the main points of 'the good treaty of peace and of brotherhood, setting peace between them forever'.[47]

Mutual non-aggression and defensive pact

The signing of the treaty was accompanied by an exchange of letters and gifts between Hattusil and Ramesses and their chief queens, Padukhepa and Nefertari.

> Says Naptera (Nefertari) the great queen of Egypt to Padukhepa, the great queen of Khatte, my sister, thus, with you my sister may all be well, and with your country may all be well. Behold, I have noted that you my sister, have written me about the matter of peace and brotherhood between the great king of Egypt and his brother the great king of Khatte. May the sun god (of Egypt) and the storm god (of Khatte) bring you joy and may the sun god cause the peace to be good ... In friendship and sisterly relation with the great queen of Khatte now and forever.[48]

Even Ramesses' mother, Tuya sent a letter to the Hittite queen.

The significance of the treaty for Ramesses

By the terms of the treaty, Ramesses had lost his chance to capture Kadesh like the Eighteenth Dynasty warrior pharaohs whose victories he tried to emulate. There would be no more opportunities to win military glory in northern Syria. However, 'from now on suspicion and uncertainty about Syria would cease; what was Egyptian would stay Egyptian'[49] like the valuable Phoenician coastal cities. Ramesses could devote the second half of his reign to diplomatic ventures, honouring the gods, building on a massive scale and celebrating his numerous Sed festivals.

Situation in Syria stabilised

Marriage links with the Hittites

After a decade of stability, Hattusil proposed a marriage between his eldest daughter and Ramesses as a way of further cementing their relationship. The Hittite princess was to be accompanied by a magnificent dowry. However, it took two years of haggling and negotiations before the marriage occurred in year 34.

Proposal for diplomatic marriage

At one point in the negotiations Ramesses wrote a letter to Queen Padukhepa complaining about the delay. In her answer she implied that Ramesses was more interested in the dowry than in her daughter.

> ... that you my Brother, should wish to enrich yourself from me ... is neither friendly nor honourable.[50]

Eventually the haggling ceased. The Hittite princess with an escort of soldiers, members of the court and 'splendid gifts before them, of silver and gold, marvels many and great'[51] plus slaves, chariots and 'cattle, goats, rams by the myriad'[52] started their long journey south. They were to be met by an Egyptian military escort at the border of Amurru. Finally after a journey of almost 1350 kilometres, the princess arrived in Pi-Ramesse with troops from both lands mingling together.

Marriage celebration in Egypt

In the celebrations that followed in year 34, the Hittite princess became 'great king's wife, mistress of the two lands: Matnefrure (*she who sees the beauty of Re*), daughter of the great chief of Khatte'.[53]

In the official propaganda (marriage inscription) carved into the walls of the temples at Karnak, Elephantine, Abu Simbel and others, this marriage was just another of Ramesses' victories.

Visits from Hittite royalty

In the years to follow, the Hittite crown prince, Hishmi-Sharruma, visited the Egyptian court at Pi-Ramesse and although there is no firm evidence, it is believed that the Hittite king himself also came on a state visit. He was certainly invited by Ramesses who offered to meet his Hittite counterpart in Palestine and escort him to Egypt personally.

Possible visit of Hittite king to Egypt

Two pieces of inscriptional evidence point to the invitation by Ramesses and the possible visit by Hattusil.

> ... may my Brother carry out this good suggestion to come and see me. And then we may see each other face to face at the place where the king sits enthroned.[54]

> The great chief of Kheta sent to the great chief of Kode:
> Equip thyself that we may proceed to Egypt,
> That we may say: 'the behest of the god comes to pass'.[55]

At some later date a second Hittite princess was sent to Egypt to marry Ramesses.

Ramesses the builder

Cartouches of Ramesses everywhere

If a pharaoh's greatness was gauged by the number and sheer size of his monuments, then Ramesses would be one of the greatest.

His name is found on more buildings throughout Egypt (Pi-Ramesse, Memphis and Thebes) and Nubia than any other pharaoh in Egyptian history. Although most of these buildings were initiated by him, he claimed some of the buildings of other kings as his own also.

From the material and inscriptional remains, it appears that Ramesses' major building achievements were:

Major building projects

- the completion of a town Seti I was building at Amara-West (Nubia) to be the new southern capital. It was known as Ramesse-Town and was strategically located on the route from the Sudan

- the twin temples at Abu Simbel (Nubia) — the Great Temple dedicated to Re-Horakhte, Amun-Re, Ptah and the cult of Ramesses, and the Small Temple dedicated to Hathor and Nefertari

- the temple at Derr (Nubia) dedicated to Re, Amun and the cult of the king

- the temple of Re and the deified Ramesses at Wadi es-Sebua (Nubia)

- the temple of Ptah and Hathor and cult of Ramesses at Gerf Husein (Nubia)

- the temple of Amun-Re at Beit el-Wali (Nubia)

- the Ramesseum — Ramesses' mortuary temple at western Thebes

- the completion of Seti I's mortuary temple at Qurna in western Thebes which he also dedicated to his grandfather, Ramesses I

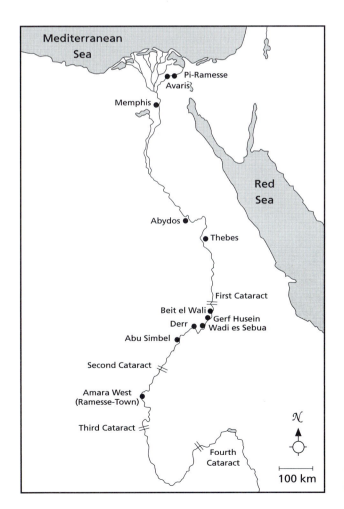

The locations of Ramesses II's building projects in Nubia

- the addition of an outer peristyle courtyard and two pylon towers at Luxor Temple at Thebes. To do this he destroyed a beautiful chapel built by Thutmose III

- the completion of the southern section of the hypostyle hall in the Temple of Karnak at Thebes. Although the conception was his father's, the dedicatory inscriptions are largely those of Ramesses. He also added a courtyard and pylon to the temple

- the completion of Seti I's cenotaph temple at Abydos

- Ramesses' temple at Abydos

- the addition of a forecourt and pylon to the temple complex of Ptah, the god of Memphis, and the addition of another temple within the enclosure. Most of Ramesses' buildings at Memphis have disappeared and historians have to rely on inscriptions from elsewhere to identify them

- the temple to Thoth at Memphis and restoration of the Sphinx

- the enlargement of the palace at Avaris and the construction of the new capital of Pi-Ramesse, built around the palace.

Enormous size

Ramesses built on a colossal scale. One of the statues in the Ramesseum was said to weigh 1000 tons and the gigantic seated statues of the king at Abu Simbel are 21 metres high.

Lacking in artistic quality

However, his monuments, unlike those of Amenhotep III, 'attempted to impress by overpowering size, without concern for artistic quality'.[56] Compared with the delicate reliefs carved into the walls of the Temple of Abydos at the time of his father, the work of Ramesses was crude.

His desire for speedy results forced him to ransack many of the monuments of previous periods to obtain building blocks already cut to size. It was during his reign that the last remaining traces of the buildings of Akhenaten were removed and the stone from the demolished sites used for his own projects. Size and quantity were Ramesses' 'major criteria of artistic effectiveness'.[57]

Parts of a fallen colossus of Ramesses in the court of his mortuary temple (the Ramesseum)

Although many of Ramesses' temples were traditional in their layout and form, he did introduce some changes. For example:

- When Ramesses enlarged the complex at Luxor built by Amenhotep III, he changed the axis of the temple. The change in alignment seems to have been caused by 'the difference in the angle between the points of observation of the heliacal rising of Sirius (by which the temple was traditionally oriented) in the two different reigns'.[58]

Change in temple alignment and layout

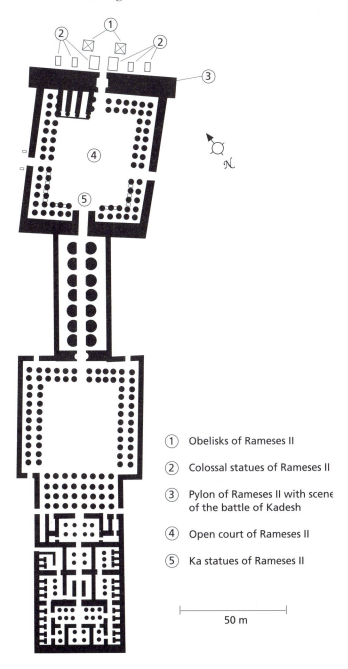

① Obelisks of Rameses II

② Colossal statues of Rameses II

③ Pylon of Rameses II with scene of the battle of Kadesh

④ Open court of Rameses II

⑤ Ka statues of Rameses II

50 m

Ramesses' additions to the Temple of Luxor

The exterior of the Temple of Luxor, showing the pylon, obelisk and colossal statues of Ramesses II

Speos style of temple used in Nubia

- In his mortuary temple, the Ramesseum, the king introduced some novel aspects. He replaced the traditional broad open courts in front of the temple proper (eg, Hatshepsut's mortuary temple) with a huge pylon entrance, two colonnaded open courts and a hypostyle hall similar to that at Karnak.

- Because the cliffs in Nubia sloped down to the river, Ramesses built his seven Nubian temples in the *speos* and *hemispeos* style. A speos temple is cut out of the rock cliffs while in a hemispeos form, only the rear of the temple (sanctuary and columned hall) is cut out of living rock, while the courtyard and pylons are built in the usual way. The temples of Abu Simbel are examples of the former while the temple at Wadi es-Sebua is of the latter form.

Ramesses built twin speos temples at Abu Simbel in adjacent sandstone bluffs. The larger of the two was dedicated to the deified Ramesses — Re of Ramesses, Ptah of Ramesses and Amun of Ramesses — while the smaller one was built for Queen Nefertari as the goddess Hathor. The Great Temple of Ramesses extended about 60 metres into the cliff, while that of Nefertari was cut about 26 metres into the bluff.

They were positioned so that the rising sun would illuminate their facades every day and twice a year the rays of the sun would penetrate the sanctuary and shine on the statue of Ramesses, uniting him with the sun's disk.

These temples, begun early in Ramesses' reign were not completed until year 24, when they were dedicated. However, there is no record that Queen Nefertari was present at the inauguration; her place was taken in the ceremonies by her daughter Meryetamun. Perhaps she had died or was too sick to make the long trip to Nubia.

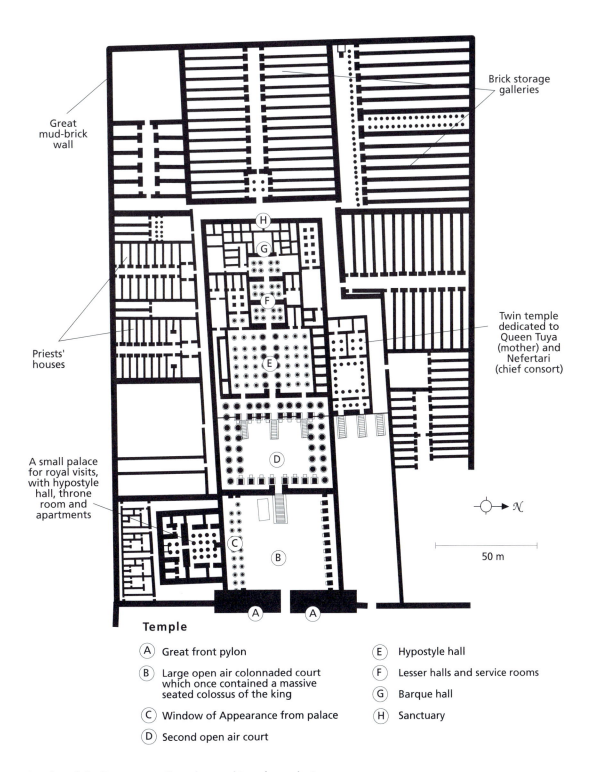

Great
mud-brick
wall

Brick storage
galleries

Priests'
houses

Twin temple
dedicated to
Queen Tuya
(mother) and
Nefertari
(chief consort)

A small palace
for royal visits,
with hypostyle
hall, throne
room and
apartments

N

50 m

Temple

(A) Great front pylon

(B) Large open air colonnaded court
which once contained a massive
seated colossus of the king

(C) Window of Appearance from palace

(D) Second open air court

(E) Hypostyle hall

(F) Lesser halls and service rooms

(G) Barque hall

(H) Sanctuary

The plan of the Ramesseum, the palace and temple precinct

The remains of the Ramesseum temple and brick storage galleries, taken from the air

Cult of the king

- In his temples, Ramesses 'sought to anchor the restored monarchy firmly in the centre of Egyptian religious faith and practice'.[59]

  - To emphasise the divine status of the king, he erected colossal statues of himself outside each temple pylon, in the colonnaded courtyards or carved directly out of rock cliffs. The statues of Nefertari at Abu Simbel are as large as those of her husband and indicate the religious status of the queen.

  - He dedicated his temples to a large range of gods — Re, Amun, Ptah, Re-Horakhte, Seth, Hathor, Nephthys, Udjo and even the Canaanite goddess, Anath.

Ramesses has often been praised for his concern for the Egyptian workmen involved in his projects — providing wells for those working in the desert gold mines and providing for all the needs of the special workforce at Deir el-Bahri who worked on the royal tombs (*servants in the House of Truth*). However, he appears to have had a different attitude to the Apiru (from Asia) working in the brickfields in the delta and the southern Libyans who were taken in raids on the oases of the western desert to work on his Nubian temples.

The great temple at Abu-Simbel

*Above: Nefertari's temple
at Abu-Simbel*

*Left: A colossus of Ramesses
with Nefertari, from Luxor*

Because of the length of Ramesses' reign, the number of men who contributed to his monumental building program must have been enormous. The most noteworthy of these were:

**Administrators in
charge of building**

* Paser — southern vizier

* Amen-em-inet — chief of works of all royal monuments,
  especially the Ramesseum

* Panhesy and Suty — chiefs of the treasury

* Iuny, Hequanakht, Paser (not the vizier), Huy and Setau
  — viceroys of Kush (Nubia)

* Bakenkhons — high priest of Amun and overseer of
  works at Luxor.

A new capital city — Pi-Ramesse,
Great in Victories

There were a number of personal, diplomatic and religious reasons why
Ramesses decided to extend the summer palace built by Seti I at Avaris,
into a new capital city to rival Memphis and Thebes.

**Reasons for a new
capital city**

* Ramesses' family came from the area around Avaris
  in the Nile Delta.

* The king wanted a centre which was more convenient
  in dealing with Egypt's Asiatic territories.

* Building a city in the delta allowed Ramesses to distance
  himself from Thebes and reinforce royal links with Heliopolis
  and Memphis.

Because of the dampness of the delta region, many of the buildings constructed at Pi-Ramesse have disappeared.

The palace

All that remains of the great palace which was the nucleus of the city, are some lengths of mud-brick walls, glazed tiles and the bases of four throne platforms. Fortunately the ancient scribes left a clue to the appearance of this magnificent palace:

> **Beauteous of balconies, dazzling with halls of lapis and turquoise.**[60]

Beautiful glazed tiles excavated at the site have also provided a clue to the decoration of the palace. It appears that the public rooms, such as the throne room and audience halls, were decorated with faience tiles in browns, yellows and blue, with touches of red, black and white. These glazed tiles covered much of the throne platforms, stairs, ramps and balustrades. On the steps and floors the tiles featured the subject people and traditional enemies of Egypt. On either side of the stairway leading to the throne were lions devouring the heads of kneeling captives.

Decorative themes

The decorations on faience tiles found in what would have been the private apartments of the palace were similar in subject matter to the paintings found in the palaces of Akhetaten and Malkata — waterlilies, fish, rosettes, birds and animals. Nude ladies of the harem and the household god, Bes, also featured in the decorations.

The city plan

The city built by Ramesses around the extended palace comprised:

- military barracks — 'marshalling place of your chariotry, mustering place of your infantry, the mooring for your marines'[61]

① Palace
② Princes
③ High Officials
④ Temple of Amun
⑤ Jubilee halls
⑥ Temple of Ptah
⑦ Temple of Uto
⑧ Temple of Re
⑨ Temple of Astarte
⑩ Temple of Seth
⑪ Workshops
⑫ Glaze works
⑬ Stores

Military

Town

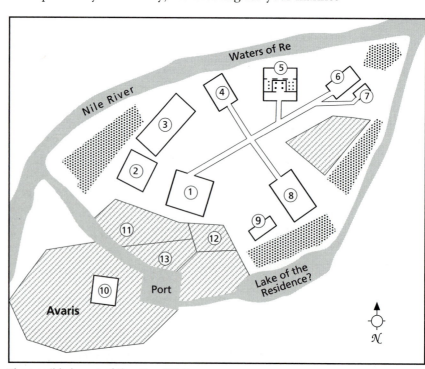

The possible layout of the city of Pi-Ramesse

- temples to Seth, Ptah, Amun and Re
- a jubilee hall for the celebration of Ramesses' 14 Sed festivals
- administrative buildings and offices of the highest officials
- a glaze factory
- a recreational lake
- a royal zoological garden (remains of the bones of African animals were found here).

Features of the city

Life in Pi-Ramesse

Life in Ramesses' capital was described in one composition in the following way.

> I have come to Pi-Ramesses and find it beautiful, unlike any other, fashioned after the pattern of Thebes. Re himself founded it ... The fields around it are filled with good things. There is fresh food every day. Its meadows are green with grass, its banks bear dates, its melons are abundant on the sands ... Its granaries are so full of barley and emmer that they almost reach the sky. They also have onions and leeks to eat, as well as lettuce from the gardens, pomegranates, apples and olives, figs of the orchard, sweet wine that tastes better than honey ... The Shi-hor branch of the Nile produces salt and the *her*-canal has natron. Its ships go out and come back so that supplies are brought every day ... The young men of *Great in Victories* are dressed up every day, with sweet oil upon their heads and newly dressed hair. They stand beside their doors, their heads bowed down with flowers ... The ales of *Great in Victories* is sweet ... The singers of *Great in Victories* sing very sweetly, being trained in Memphis.[62]

Ramesses' family

Ramesses had been provided with a harem and several wives from the age of 15 and already had a large family when he ascended the throne. During his long reign, he had eight principal wives and numerous lesser wives, as well as an enormous harem. It is little wonder that he produced well over 100 children. However, it appears that many of them died in infancy and some of those who survived adolescence died in their early twenties.

Over 100 offspring

Sons and heirs

There is not a great deal known about most of the royal princes or the part they played in their father's administration. It appears that most, if not all, of his first 14 sons accompanied him on his various military expeditions and some of them held titles such as *general-in-chief of the army, first brave of the army* and *first charioteer of the army*.

Military experience and priestly offices

A number of them held high priestly offices. For example, Ramesses' fourth son, Khaemwaset was the high priest of Ptah at Memphis and his sixteenth son, Mery-Atum was the high priest of Re at Heliopolis.

Ramesses outlived many of his children and heirs. He was forced to name five different sons as heirs-apparent* throughout his reign. The following table names Ramesses' sons by Nefertari and Istnofret, at least four of whom are known without doubt to have become heirs-apparent.

Name	Mother	Birth sequence	Designated heirs-apparent
Amen-hir-wonmef (later changed to Amen-hir-khopshef)	Nefertari	Eldest of Ramesses' sons	First heir-apparent (1) Had died by year 20 of Ramesses' reign
Ramesses	Istnofret	Second born	Third heir-apparent (3) From years 25–50 of Ramesses' reign
Khaemwaset	Istnofret	Fourth born	Fourth heir-apparent (4) From years 50–55 of Ramesses' reign
Merenptah	Istnofret	Thirteenth born	Fifth heir-apparent (5) and eventual successor of Ramesses II
Set-hir-khopshef*	Nefertari	Seventeenth-born	Second heir apparent (2) From year 21 to year 25 or 26 of Ramesses' reign

The role of Khaemwaset

Of all of Ramesses' sons, apart from his eventual successor, Merenptah, the most well-known was Khaemwaset who was learned in history, theology, magic and the scribal arts. He played an influential role in:

- the administration of Ptah's estates and the cult of the Apis bull, Ptah's sacred animal, for 40 years
- the restoration of the monuments of his ancestors
- his father's first five jubilees — announcement from Memphis and proclamations throughout Egypt.

High priest of Ptah and builder of the Serapeum

As *sem* priest of Ptah, Khaemwaset was responsible for the cult of the Apis bull. Only a bull with exactly the right markings could become the Apis bull and when it died it was mummified and buried with great ritual in a special tomb at Sakkara. Then the search would begin for the next Apis bull. During his tenure of office, Khaemwaset initiated the building of the famous Serapeum or communal burial vault of the sacred bulls. This was a vast underground gallery with individual chambers for the deceased bulls, and for over 1300 years the burial of these bulls followed the pattern set by Khaemwaset.

Historian and first Egyptologist

This fourth son of Ramesses and Istnofret also desired 'to restore the monuments of the kings of Upper and Lower Egypt, because of what they had done, the strength of which was falling into decay'.[63] As a historian, Khaemwaset supervised the restoration of many of the famous monuments erected by his ancestors over 1000 years earlier. He placed an inscription on each one, indicating the king responsible for its construction and informing future generations how he, Prince Khaemwaset had 'set forth a decree for its sacred offerings, ... its water ... endowed with a grant of land, together with its personnel'.[64]

---

* In his work *Pharaoh Triumphant*, Kitchin states that Set-hir-khopshef (perhaps son number 17) was for a short while heir-apparent. However, in his article in *KMT*, Kitchin questions whether Set-hir-khopshef was really a much younger son elevated over many senior princes. He suggests that Ramesses had again changed his first son's name as there was a religious shift from Amun to Set.

When he died in year 55 of his father's reign, it is believed that Khaemwaset was buried in a tomb in the vaults of the sacred bulls in the Memphite necropolis.

What of the other sons? In 1988, an American Egyptologist, Dr Kent Weeks, working in the Valley of the Kings made a startling discovery — a tomb which he believed might have been the burial place of some of Ramesses' sons. When the tomb complex, numbered KV 5, came to light in 1995 it was found to contain six antechambers, more than 60 chapels along five corridors and two other suites. It is possible that in the years to come, excavators will find the actual burial chambers and perhaps the remains of a number of Ramesses' sons. The hieroglyphs above some of the surviving fragments of wall paintings indicate that Ramesses' first, second, seventh and fifteenth sons were buried in this tomb. Perhaps there were others. So far, KV 5 is the biggest and most complex royal tomb ever found.

Tomb complex of Ramesses' sons recently discovered

Royal women

Of all the women in Ramesses' life, his mother, Tuya and his first principal wife, Nefertari, appear to have been held in great affection by the king and to have been given the highest honours. Others, such as his associate wife, Istnofret, and the Hittite princess, Matnefrure (Maat-Hor-Neferure), were also held in high esteem and their names appear on monuments and stelae. The table on page 490 gives details of these women.

Queen Nefertari, from her tomb

Nefertari with Ramesses, on a wall at Luxor

An evaluation of Ramesses II

Ramesses has often been likened to one of his own colossal statues, striding through Egypt, larger than life. It is easy to see why many early Egyptologists and Victorian travellers referred to him as Ramesses the Great. This was probably due to:

Labelled by early travellers as the 'Great'

Royal women

Name	Relationship	Details
Tuya	Ramesses' mother	Tuya survived the death of her husband, Seti I, by 22 years. Ramesses was devoted to his mother and recognised her publicly. He erected statues to her at Pi-Ramesse, in the Ramesseum, and at Abu-Simbel; he built her a small temple on the north side of the Ramesseum which she shared with Nefertari and gave her a lavishly decorated tomb in the Valley of the Queens.
Hentmire	Sister/wife	Ramesses took her as one of his official wives but she played only a modest role.
Nefertari	First principal wife	Nefertari was Ramesses' chief consort until at least year 24, after which she is heard of no more. She appeared beside him on state and religious occasions. In year 1 she accompanied him to Thebes for the burial of his father, and also to Abydos. By year 3 she was shown in monumental scale on the interior face of the new Pylon at Luxor. There is no datable reference to her between years 3 and 21 but she is known to have sent official letters and gifts to the Hittite queen in year 21. Because there is no record of her at Abu-Simbel when the massive twin temples were dedicated, she is thought to have died in year 24. She shared a small temple with Tuya in the Ramesseum and her tomb in the Valley of the Queens is the finest yet discovered.
Istnofret	Associate queen with Nefertari and then principal wife some-time after year 24	Between years 24 and 34 Istnofret was shown on a number of rock stelae in the quarries of Aswan and Silsila with her sons Ramesses (heir-apparent), Khaemwaset and young Merenptah and her daughter, Bint-Anath. She probably died about year 34.
Bint-Anath	Daughter/wife	Ramesses' eldest daughter (by Istnofret). Firstly, associate queen with her mother and then chief queen associated with Nefertari's daughter Meryetamun. Bint-Anath bore her father, Ramesses, a daughter. She survived her father's death and later became one of the consorts of her brother, King Merenptah.
Meryetamun	Daughter/wife	Eldest daughter of Nefertari. She died before her father.
Nebttawy	Daughter/wife	The last of Ramesses' daughter/queens. Took her place alongside her father in the last two decades of his reign.
Maat-Hor-Neferure	Foreign wife	Hittite princess who married Ramesses in year 34. Later retired to the harem at Mer-wer.
?	Foreign wife	Sister of Maat-Hor-Neferure.

- the sheer size and number of his buildings and statues
- his cartouches found inscribed everywhere, their hieroglyphic characters 'conveying by sheer force of association the name and style of Ramesses'[65]
- the epic accounts (*Poem* and *Bulletin*) of his Battle of Kadesh, adorning the walls of every major temple in Egypt and Nubia, which presented the official view of Ramesses II (propaganda)
- the great length of his reign and the number of his offspring
- the fact that his successors modelled themselves on him, with so many of them adopting his name. The term 'Ramesside' is used to describe the late New Kingdom period (Twentieth Dynasty).

In the early twentieth century, Ramesses II seems to have been regarded by Egyptologists as the boastful and 'overadvertised hero of Kadesh, a megalomaniac builder' and an unbridled despot.[66]

In the 1950s Wilson held a somewhat similar view:

> The fact remains that the arrogant bellowing of victory comes as an insincere ostentation similar to the bloated bulk of Ramesses' monuments or to his shameless appropriation of the monuments of his ancestors ... Blatant advertising was used to cover up the failure to attain past glories.[67]

However, most scholars today hold a more balanced view of Ramesses II. This is due to:

- the availability of evidence provided by recent intensive studies of the inscriptional and archaeological sources
- a fairer judgment of him against the ideals of his own culture rather than against the social values of the twentieth century.

Ramesses must be considered in the context of his time

Was Ramesses a great pharaoh?

An Egyptian pharaoh was supposed to be:
- the intermediary between the gods and the people
- the defender and protector of his people
- the source of prosperity and upholder of order and justice.

The divine responsibilities of a king

Ramesses conscientiously sought to carry out these pharaonic ideals.

Intermediary between the gods and people

Ramesses II appeased, praised and cajoled the gods to assure the welfare of the Egyptians. In the service of the gods:
- he outdid all pharaohs in the vastness of his temple-building program, even if his monuments lacked the artistic quality of those of previous pharaohs
- he promoted all the major gods
- he conscientiously conducted religious rites and took part in the major festivals throughout Egypt.

Attempts to please the gods

Defender and protector of his people

Ramesses attempted to defend his 'empire' from assaults by the Hittites in Syria, tribesmen in Palestine and the Nubians of Irem. Also, he tightened up security in the delta region by constructing a string of desert fortresses against incursions by the Libyans.

Ramesses recognised the need for making peace with the Hittites. Although he was sometimes demanding and overbearing in his initial letters to the Hittite court, when he was reprimanded for his attitude, he wisely used restraint and sent conciliatory letters. He eventually earned a reputation as a valuable and trustworthy ally.

The Egyptian people expected their god-kings to have superhuman prowess and to display great personal courage. The official versions of military campaigns were always the same — an exaggeration of the part played by the pharaoh, acting alone with only the help of the gods, with no mention of failings or mistakes.

Promoted the expected image

In the monumental inscriptions, Ramesses went to great pains to promote the image of himself as a great warrior king in the mould of the pharaohs of the early Eighteenth Dynasty.

Although he provided the Egyptian people with the image they expected, Ramesses was not a military leader of the calibre of Thutmose III, whose exploits he had tried to emulate. For example:

- In his ambition to recover the territory claimed by the Thutmosid kings in Syria, he did not respect the agreement his father Seti had made with the Hittites.
- Owing to his youthful enthusiasm and impetuousness, Ramesses failed to carry out careful reconnaissance which placed himself and his army in acute danger at Kadesh in year 5.
- He did not fulfil his aim of capturing Kadesh and driving the Hittites back to Asia Minor.
- His behaviour at Kheta in northern Syria was foolish. He supposedly fought without his coat of mail three times in order to impress his troops.
- His pride and stubbornness resulted in 20 years of wasted effort and resources as he led his armies into Syria year after year with no permanent result.

However, he did show great personal courage at Kadesh.

Source of prosperity and an upholder of order and justice

The country was prosperous and well-governed

The fact that Egypt was able to sustain Ramesses' incredible building program for such a long time is evidence of the country's prosperity and order. The tombs, temples, stelae, papyri and letters confirm that the country buzzed with activity.

Ramesses chose his administrators wisely and did not hesitate to promote men from outside the narrow circle of Thebes and Memphis. He earned a reputation for firm government, treating his Egyptian workers fairly and establishing high standards of honesty.

> He has avoided deceit and expelled lying from the land, while his laws are firm in the administration of the regulations of the ancestors ...[68]

Since Egypt was prosperous, peaceful and secure during Ramesses' long reign, his subjects would have been in no doubt that he was doing what was necessary for their welfare and that the gods were well pleased.

Hayes and Kitchin sum up Ramesses' reign in the following way:

More balanced modern views

> Though his victories on the battlefield were sometimes inconclusive ... and the works of architecture and sculpture with which he flooded the land more notable for their size and quantity than for their beauty, Egypt prospered at this time and the empire survived in the midst of dangers as serious as any which it had to face.[69]

> If a ruler's greatness be measured by the prosperity, balance and relative contentment of a nation's society, then in that sense Ramesses was 'great', and not so merely on his role of impetuous warrior or tireless builder ... He was by no means Egypt's greatest king although he must still rank overall as one of the leaders; and even now remains in some measure an 'archetypal' pharaoh, symbol of the proud mastery of Egypt through the ages.[70]

The death of Ramesses II and his immediate successors

Ramesses died in his sixty-seventh year on the throne and was buried by his thirteenth son and heir, Merenptah.

Despite his age when he came to the throne (somewhere between 60 and 70), Merenptah faced a number of potentially dangerous external threats with vigour and determination.

The reign of Merenptah

By year 6 of his ten-year reign, the elderly king had:

• prevented a threatened revolt in Palestine

• defeated a force of Libyans and Mediterranean people who attempted to invade Lower Egypt, seeking land

• ruthlessly suppressed a revolt in Nubia which was planned to coincide with the Libyan invasion.

Under the control of Merenptah, Egypt's empire was still firmly intact, peace with the Hittites was maintained and the country continued to be governed effectively.

However, after Merenptah's death, there were dynastic problems and four kings, one of whom was a usurper, ruled in quick succession. The last ruler of the dynasty was the female pharaoh, Tewosret. Like Hatshepsut, she had been the regent for her step-son and on his premature death she seized power for herself. Unlike Hatshepsut, however, her reign was short-lived (two years) and the Egypt that she ruled was beginning to face serious problems. With her death in 1196 BC, the Nineteenth Dynasty came to an end.

Succession problems

Tewosret

Chapter review

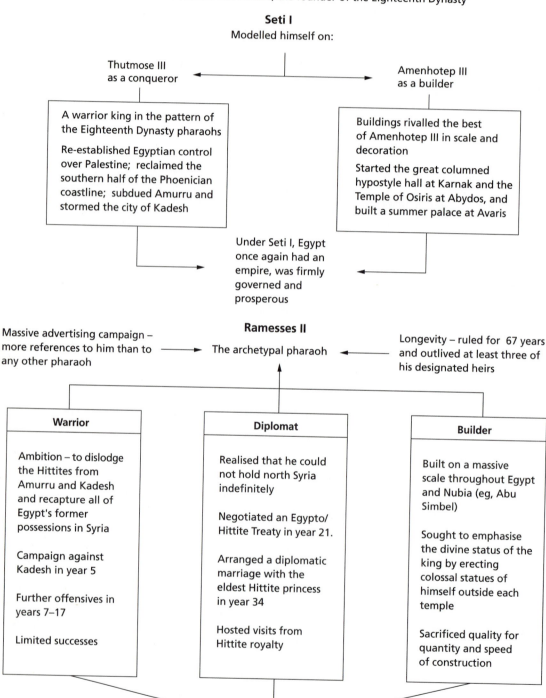

Ramesses I

Modelled himself on Ahmose, the founder of the Eighteenth Dynasty

Seti I
Modelled himself on:

Thutmose III
as a conqueror

Amenhotep III
as a builder

A warrior king in the pattern of the Eighteenth Dynasty pharaohs

Re-established Egyptian control over Palestine; reclaimed the southern half of the Phoenician coastline; subdued Amurru and stormed the city of Kadesh

Buildings rivalled the best of Amenhotep III in scale and decoration

Started the great columned hypostyle hall at Karnak and the Temple of Osiris at Abydos, and built a summer palace at Avaris

Under Seti I, Egypt once again had an empire, was firmly governed and prosperous

Massive advertising campaign – more references to him than to any other pharaoh

Ramesses II

The archetypal pharaoh

Longevity – ruled for 67 years and outlived at least three of his designated heirs

Warrior

Ambition – to dislodge the Hittites from Amurru and Kadesh and recapture all of Egypt's former possessions in Syria

Campaign against Kadesh in year 5

Further offensives in years 7–17

Limited successes

Diplomat

Realised that he could not hold north Syria indefinitely

Negotiated an Egypto/Hittite Treaty in year 21.

Arranged a diplomatic marriage with the eldest Hittite princess in year 34

Hosted visits from Hittite royalty

Builder

Built on a massive scale throughout Egypt and Nubia (eg, Abu Simbel)

Sought to emphasise the divine status of the king by erecting colossal statues of himself outside each temple

Sacrificed quality for quantity and speed of construction

Not the greatest Egyptian pharaoh, but the 'symbol of the proud mastery of Egypt through the ages'

REVISION QUESTIONS AND ESSAY TOPICS

1 **The following extracts come from a dedication inscription and decree carved in the rock walls at Wadi Mia (Kanais) during the reign of Seti I (Menmare).**

A ... I will make for them the means to sustain them, so that they may bless my name in the future, in years to come; that generations yet to be may come to glory in me for my energy. For I am indeed considerate and compassionate towards travellers. ...[71]

B Amun give him eternity.
double him everlastingness;
Gods who are in the well,
give him your span of life!
For he opened the way for us to go,
that had been blocked before us.
Of which we said, 'If we pass it we are safe',
we now say, 'If we reach it we live'.
The difficult way that troubled us,
it has become an excellent way.[72]

C ... Another good deed has come into my heart by God's command also: To found a town with a sanctuary on this spot, bearing the great name of my fathers (the gods). May they make my name flourish throughout the eastern lands ... Amun is in it, Re is within it; Ptah and Osiris are within its great hall, and Horus, Isis, and Menmare (Seti), they are the Ennead in this temple.[73]

D The troop of gold-washers that I have appointed for the House of Menmare shall be exempted and protected. It shall not be approached by anyone in the whole land, by any controller of gold, by any inspector of the desert. As to anyone who shall interfere with any of them so as to put them in another place, all the gods and goddesses of my House shall be his adversaries.[74]

a To which of Seti's achievements do extracts A and B refer?

b What other project did Seti carry out in the same area?

c What task was carried out by the workers in the desert south of Edfu? Describe the difficulties that these labourers would have worked under before year 9 of Seti's reign?

d With what important project, initiated by Seti in another part of Egypt, was their work associated? Refer to extract D.

e What does extract C indicate about Seti's religious policy?

f What benefits did Seti hope to gain from these constructions in Wadi Mia (Kanais)? Provide supporting evidence from the sources.

2 The figures below show scenes from Seti's temple at Abydos.

(A)

(B)

a Abydos was the cult centre of which god?

b Suggest two reasons why Seti I might have felt the need to build a magnificent temple cenotaph at Abydos.

c List several design features of Seti's temple at Abydos.

d Which goddess is depicted in Figure A?

e Where in the temple would this relief have been found?

f What other gods were depicted in the temple?

g How does this confirm the information in the previous extracts about Seti's religious policy?

h How does Figure B show Seti's great reverence to his royal ancestors?

i How did Ramesses II, when he became king, show his devotion to his father at Abydos?

j What evidence is there at Abydos that Ramesses II shared his father's reverence for his royal ancestors?

k How do Ramesses' building activities at Abu Simbel and Pi-Ramesse show that he followed the religious policy of his father?

3 To what particular incidents in Ramesses' campaign against Kadesh do each of the following quotes refer?

A   Now the two Shosu who said these words to his majesty said them falsely ...[75]

B   Now the vile Foe of Khatte had come and brought together all the foreign lands as far as the ends of the sea.[76]

C   He crossed the ford of the Orontes with the first army, 'Amun-gives-victory-to-Usermare-sotpenre' ...[77]

D   The camp of his majesty's army was pitched there and his majesty took his seat on a throne of fine gold ... Then came a scout in his majesty's retinue bringing two scouts of the Foe from Khatte.[78]

E   Then they came forth from the south side of Kadesh and attacked the army of Re in its middle as they were marching unaware ...[79]

F   Thereupon the forces of the Foe from Khatte surrounded the followers of his majesty who were by his side.[80]

G   Then his majesty drove at a gallop and charged the forces of the Foe from Khatte ...[81]

H   The arrival of the recruits of Pharaoh from the land of Amor.[82]

I   My majesty caused the forces of the Foe from Khatte to fall on their faces, one upon the other ... into the water of the Orontes.[83]

J   He sent his envoy with a letter in his hand addressed to the great name of my majesty ...[84]

4 Study the figure below carefully and identify the following:

a   The Egyptian camp.
b   The Hittite spies being beaten for information.
c   The Egyptian governors and commanders being informed of their failed intelligence system.
d   Ramesses' horse, Victory-in-Thebes.
e   The attack of the Hittite chariots.
f   The arrival of the Egyptian support force.

Drawing of a relief of the Battle of Kadesh, from Luxor Temple

5 Draw up a table similar to the one below and fill in the relevant information in point form.

Regnal year	Ramesses' military achievements	Ramesses' diplomatic achievements

6 **Identify the buildings of Ramesses to which each of the following extracts refer and explain how each one was identified.**

    A   Ramesses II has made a temple excavated in the mountain of eternal workmanship in Nubia ... for the King's Great Wife, Nefertari, beloved of Mut, forever and ever ... Nefertari ... for whom the sun does shine.[85]

    B   Ramesses made it as a monument for his father Amun-Re, Lord of Thebes, making for him the 'Temple-of-the-Spirit-of-Ramesses-Meriamom-in-the-House-of-Amun' of fine white sandstone. Its beauty reaches to the height of heaven; over against Karnak; its august columns are of electrum, made like every place that is in heaven.[86]

    C   Lo his majesty ... the champion of his father Wennofer (Osiris), by making him an august temple.[87]

    D   I have enlarged thy house in Memphis, protected with everlasting works, with excellent labour, in stone wrought with gold and genuine costly stones. I constructed thy forecourt on the north with an august double facade before thee ... I made for thee an august temple in the midst of the enclosure. Thou god, whom I have fashioned, art in its secret chapel, resting upon its great throne.[88]

7 **Study the two glazed tiles below.**

a In which of Ramesses' buildings would these tiles have been used?
b In which particular part of the building complex would each tile have been found? Give reasons for your answer.
c What other information is available to help Egyptologists build up a picture of this building and its immediate surroundings?

8 **Essay topics**

a To what extent did Seti I live up to his epithet *Bringer of Renaissance*?
b What does the surviving evidence reveal about the status of the various women in Ramesses' life?
c Explain why Ramesses has gone down in history as 'Ramesses the Great'. How accurate is this description with regard to the major aspects of his foreign and domestic policy?

CHAPTER
15

Egyptian expansion and its effects on New Kingdom society

The Eighteenth Dynasty, particularly from the time of Thutmose I to Amenhotep III, was marked by successful military campaigns abroad and prosperity and stability at home.

The Egyptian armies, led by a number of warrior-kings, brought Syria, Palestine and Nubia under Egyptian influence and control. As a result, great wealth poured into Egypt in the form of booty, tribute and increased trade.

More than any other pharaoh of this period, it was Thutmose III who made Egypt, for a time, the greatest power in the ancient world. However, it was Amenhotep III, three generations later, who reaped the material (wealth) and diplomatic (peaceful relations) benefits from the campaigns and conquests of his predecessors. He ruled Egypt at the height of its magnificence.

During the brief Amarna Period, Egypt not only lost prestige abroad but its entire Syrian province. It was not until the early Nineteenth Dynasty, that Egypt again produced kings in the warrior image — Seti I and Ramesses II who re-established some of Egypt's former prestige and power in the countries to the north.

Although the territories brought under Egyptian *control* are referred to as an *empire* (a modern concept), some scholars such as Gardiner doubt whether the vast area under Egyptian influence could ever have been called an empire.

During the period of the so-called empire, the Egyptians:

- devised a variety of ways for maintaining a hold over their foreign conquests
- dealt with the pressure on their northern provinces from two other dominant powers in the region — the Mitanni and the Hittites
- made extensive political and commercial contacts with other states in the Near East, east Africa and the Aegean region.

Wilson, in *The Culture of Ancient Egypt*, maintains that the period between Thutmose III and Amenhotep III marked a transitional stage in Egyptian society and its culture. At this point, Wilson believes that the simple agricultural and introverted society of the Nile Valley changed forever.

> **Under the shock of empire, changes became so rapid that the old sanctions of life could no longer hold society within its distinct integrity.**[1]

The diagram below summarises the changes that occurred in Egyptian society as a result of the acquisition of the so-called empire during the Eighteenth and Nineteenth dynasties.

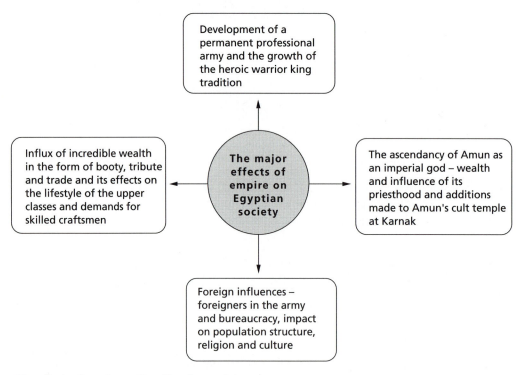

Development of a permanent professional army and the growth of the heroic warrior king tradition

Influx of incredible wealth in the form of booty, tribute and trade and its effects on the lifestyle of the upper classes and demands for skilled craftsmen

The major effects of empire on Egyptian society

The ascendancy of Amun as an imperial god – wealth and influence of its priesthood and additions made to Amun's cult temple at Karnak

Foreign influences – foreigners in the army and bureaucracy, impact on population structure, religion and culture

The effects of empire on New Kingdom society

The growth and organisation of the Egyptian empire

At the beginning of the Eighteenth Dynasty, the need to drive out the Hyksos from Egypt and the Kushites from Lower Nubia led the Egyptians to create buffer zones in southern Palestine and the Second Cataract region. These were the first steps to further conquests.

As the Egyptians expanded further into Palestine and Syria, they came into contact with other powerful forces to the north and east such as the Mitanni and the Hittites. Threats from these sources, plus the periodic rebellions in Egypt's Palestinian and Nubian territories, meant that the Egyptian army always had to be prepared for rapid military action.

Areas of Egyptian control and influence during the New Kingdom

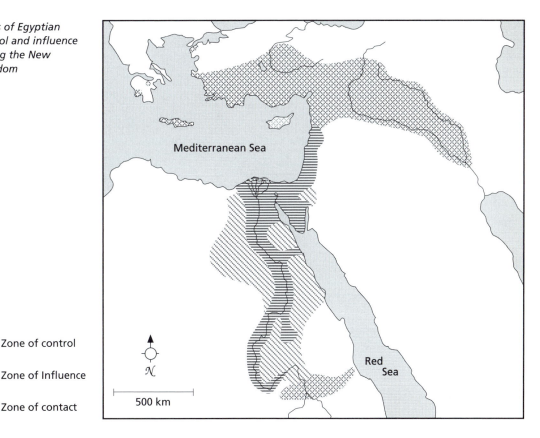

Zone of control

Zone of Influence

Zone of contact

500 km

Egypt's expansion was based on more than just a need for security. Aldred suggests that for some pharaohs, 'the taste for warfare and the pre-emptive strike, provoked by the Hyksos wars, had developed into an appetite for imperial adventures'.[4]

There is evidence to suggest that some of the early Eighteenth Dynasty pharaohs carried out a policy of deliberate expansion. Amenhotep I 'ascended the river to Kush, in order to extend the borders of Egypt'[5] while Thutmose I 'made the boundaries of Egypt as far as that which the sun encircles' and 'made Egypt the superior of every land'.[6]

Deliberate expansion

Two further references to a policy of expansion are found in the annals of Thutmose III on the walls of the Temple of Karnak.

> On the 25th day his majesty was in Tharu on the first victorious expedition to extend the boundaries of Egypt with might...[7]

> ... departure from this place in might ... in power, and in triumph, to overthrow that wretched enemy, to extend the boundaries of Egypt, according to the command of his father Amun-Re...[8]

The erection of victory stelae on the Euphrates in the north by Thutmose I and III and at Napata in the south by Thutmose III, marked the pharaohs' extensions of Egypt's borders to their furthest limits. Thutmose III also compiled a catalogue of towns and people subjugated in his Palestinian and Nubian campaigns and had them recorded on the walls at Karnak.

A catalogue of captured cities, symbolised by short-haired Nubians and long-haired Syrians

Need to maintain pharaoh's warrior image

Owing to the activities of these early Eighteenth Dynasty pharaohs, an image of the king as a warrior and conqueror developed. The prestige and power of later rulers were dependant on maintaining this image of a successful military leader. This meant that some show of strength was needed, whether the pharaoh was a true warrior-king or not, and usually this took the form of a raid or minor campaign at the start of a reign. Refer to the section titled 'The king as a warrior', later in this chapter, for more details on the image of the warrior-king.

The economic motives for gaining and maintaining control of areas beyond Egypt's borders were significant. The lands of Wawat (Lower Nubia) and Kush (Upper Nubia) and the coastal area of Phoenicia were sources of products highly valued by the Egyptians.

Access to valuable resources

Nubia was not only rich in gold, but was the connecting link between Egypt and tropical Africa, the source of ivory, ebony, leopard skins, ostrich feathers, incense, cattle and slaves. The pharaohs of the New Kingdom believed that the vital trade in gold and exotic products could only be maintained if the whole of Nubia and all connecting desert routes were controlled by Egypt.

As the pharaohs' political and commercial relationships with the powerful kingdoms of western Asia expanded, gold became an even more valuable commodity. It played an important part in the pharaohs' diplomatic negotiations with their *brother* kings. This partly explains why so many New Kingdom pharaohs were forced to personally lead or direct campaigns in response to local rebellions and incursions from native tribes in Nubia.

The Egyptians had been interested in the resources of southern Syria since the time of King Sneferu of the Fourth Dynasty. Byblos was the source of the cedar so valued by the Egyptians, particularly for ship building. Thutmose III recorded that he 'had many ships of cedar built on the mountains of God's Land near (the city of) the Lady of Byblos'.[9]

The prosperous cities of northern Syria dominated the vital trade routes leading to Asia Minor and the great empires on the Tigris and Euphrates rivers. The importance of maintaining control over these areas was obvious to the Egyptian kings, the priests (particularly those of the imperial god Amun) and members of the official class, all of whom benefited by conquest.

The wealth that flowed into Egypt enabled the kings to enhance their status by generous endowments to the gods, rewards to officials and massive building programs. The imperial god Amun-Re, who was credited with each victory of his *son*, the god-king, was rewarded for his divine help. Amun's priests expected and received the lion's share of the booty from each campaign. The official class, both civil and military, not only shared in the wealth that flowed into Egypt, as their tombs testify, but had more opportunities for advancement. The power and lifestyle of many people depended on the growth and maintenance of the empire.

Benefits to ruling classes

Four factors which motivated the Egyptians of the New Kingdom to conquer and maintain control of Nubia and Palestine/Syria were the need to:

• maintain a sense of security

• gain access to valuable resources

• enhance the warrior image of the pharaohs

• preserve the interests of the ruling classes.

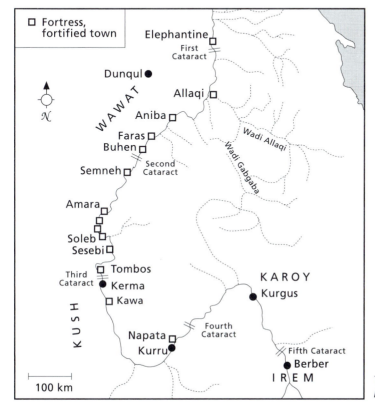

The location of the chief Egyptian fortresses in Nubia

Hostages

The organisation of the empire

Nubian territories

Nubia (Wawat and Kush) was brought under permanent Egyptian control by the time of Thutmose I.

Egyptianised Nubians

The early Eighteenth Dynasty kings carried on the policy of the Middle Kingdom kings by repairing and constructing a number of Nubian fortress towns along the Nile.

The Egyptians also implemented a policy of taking hostages. The sons of chiefs were carried off to Egypt and brought up at the court of the pharaoh. This policy served two purposes:

1 It kept rebellious chiefs in check.

2 It provided future Egyptianised officials and rulers for the conquered territories.

Some of these former hostages became administrators, scribes and deputies to the viceroy while others, who succeeded their fathers as chiefs, administered the Nubian communities and liaised with the Egyptian officials.

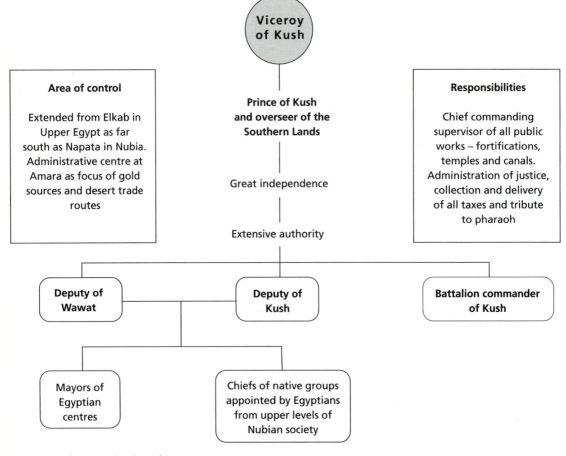

Egyptian administration in Nubia

The Egyptians drafted numerous Kushites into their armies, particularly those units serving in Egypt's Asiatic territories.

The administration of the Nubian province under an Egyptian viceroy of Kush (see the section titled 'The viceroy of Kush' later in this chapter) was generally sound and as a result the country developed and its people eventually became completely Egyptianised. The structure of the administration is shown in the diagram on page 504.

Viceroy of Kush

Despite Nubia's well-ordered administration, the authorities were faced with periodic disruptions, particularly from groups in the areas around the Fifth and Sixth cataracts. The Egyptians would tolerate no interference to the supplies of gold coming from the mines of Kush nor to the exotic products from east Africa, so regular patrols and occasional military campaigns were carried out in these areas.

Sometimes the Nubian people had to be reminded of the power of the Egyptian king. The following extract describes how Amenhotep II achieved this. The king had returned from a campaign in Asia with the bodies of seven princes whom he had killed himself.

Reminders of pharaoh's powers

> He hanged six of these fallen ones on the face of the wall at Thebes, and the hands as well. Then the other fallen one was taken up river and hanged on the wall at Napata (Nubia), to show his majesty's victories for ever and ever in all lands and in all the countries of the negro ...[10]

Palestine and Syria

Palestine and Syria were composed of numerous independent states, each with its own princely ruler. The area was politically disunited as the princes bickered with and intrigued against one another. However, whenever they joined together they could be formidable opponents.

Politically disunited

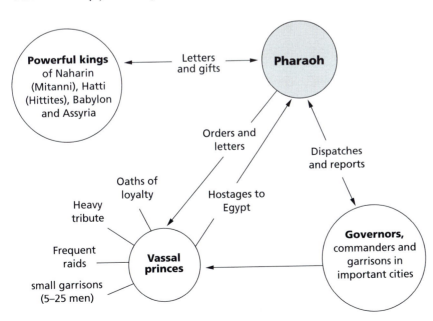

Means used by Egypt to control its Syrian and Palestinian conquests

The Egyptian kings who conquered these states, knew that it would be impossible to organise a unified administration similar to that set up in Nubia. Such an organisation would require far more military and administrative resources than the Egyptians had available. Other methods had to be found.

The following diagram shows how the Egyptians maintained control over the vassal princes of Palestine/Syria.

Oaths of loyalty and tribute

Many of the princes were permitted to retain their authority, as long as they recognised the pharaoh as their lord. Oaths of loyalty were demanded, they had to agree to pay regular quotas of tribute, to supply any Egyptian troops marching through their territory with all the necessities, and to serve in the pharaoh's army when needed. Stern warnings were given to those who might consider rebellion or defection. However, it would have been politically naive of the Egyptians not to have taken extra precautions to make sure that these princes continued to show proper respect for the pharaoh's authority and to supply the required tribute.

Egyptian commanders and garrisons

The conquered cities and towns of the *Northlands* were grouped into three *provinces*, of Canaan, Upi and Amurru. There were also the cities along the Phoenician coast from Tyre to Ugarit. These provinces were administrated by governors whose task was to keep an eye on the vassal princes. These administrators were assisted by the presence of Egyptian commanders and a garrison of archers and charioteers in important towns and at fortified military stations. Smaller garrisons of from five to 25 men acted as local police and performed intelligence services.

To make doubly sure of the allegiance of these Syrian princes, the Egyptians took members of their families as hostages. These young men were brought up in the Egyptian capital. When a vassal prince died or rebelled, these Egyptianised Syrians were sent back to their original cities to rule in their father's place.

Despite the precautions taken by the Egyptians, they were forced to make frequent raids against rebellious states. Uprisings against Egyptian authority often occurred when a new pharaoh came to the throne.

Royal envoys and couriers maintained contact between the Egyptian court and the vassal princes. They carried orders from the pharaoh and letters from the Asiatic princes.

The collection of clay tablets found at Amarna included letters from the princes of Byblos, Tyre, Jerusalem and Megiddo, who:

- gave praise and assurances of loyalty to the pharaoh
- made complaints about the intrigues of neighbours
- requested assistance
- criticised the failure of the Egyptians to send help.

The Egyptians often ignored petty quarrels between states, provided they did not disrupt trade and the rulers continued to pay the tribute they demanded.

The development of a permanent professional army

In earlier periods of Egyptian history, each nome (province) had its own militia. This was conscripted from local able-bodied men who served seasonally and then returned to their homes. In times of national emergencies these local militia were organised under a commander chosen to meet the emergency and were provided with weapons from the royal armoury.

During the wars against the Hyksos at the end of the Seventeenth and beginning of the Eighteenth dynasties, the Egyptians adopted the superior weapons that had been introduced by the Asiatic invaders — new types of bronze swords and daggers, bronze and leather armour, the powerful compound bow and, most important of all, the horse-drawn chariot. It was also about the time of the war of liberation against the Hyksos that the Egyptians used the Nubian *Medjay* troops as mercenaries. The Medjay became indispensable to the Egyptians in the following centuries.

Changes in weapons introduced by Hyksos

Mobile warfare based on chariots, the use of the Nubians and a new patriotic fervour transformed the Egyptian state into a military power.

Chariots

The campaigns against the western Asiatics in the early Eighteenth Dynasty and the need to leave garrisons to control conquered territory led to the development of a permanent professional army by the time of Thutmose III. This was based on a continuous levying and training program. At this stage the army was composed of a nucleus of native Egyptians organised into two divisions — the *Division of Amun* from Thebes and the *Division of Re* from Heliopolis. However, this force was increasingly augmented by mercenary troops from surrounding countries.

Mercenaries

As the early patriotic fervour waned, continued service away from home was not seen as desirable, particularly by the lower classes. The Egyptian forces were strengthened more and more with captives and mercenaries, such as:

- the Medjay and Nehsiu from the south
- the Shasu from the east
- the Merwesh from the west
- the Sherden of the *Sea Peoples*.

During the Nineteenth Dynasty, a division of 5000 troops might include only 1900 Egyptians as against 3100 mercenaries.

The fighting forces and military bureaucracy

At the head of the armed forces was the pharaoh, who frequently led the army in person, in keeping with the New Kingdom image of the warrior-king (refer to the section titled 'The king as a warrior' later in

Commander-in-chief

this chapter). However, he often delegated the position of commander-in-chief to the crown prince. During the Amarna period, a non-royal, Horemheb, held the position. A war council assisted the pharaoh with tactics and strategy.

The Egyptian military organisation included:

- the fighting force with its hierarchy of field officers
- the military administration with highly placed officers in charge of recruits, supplies, communications, accounts, records and other operations.

Army divisions

By the reign of Ramesses II, the army was divided into four divisions, each of 5000 men and named after one of the chief gods — Amun, Ptah, Re and Seth. Each division was composed of smaller units of about 250 men, possibly led by a standard bearer. Not very much is known of their structure although some of their names have survived — *Amun protects his soldiers, Beauty of the sun-disk* and *Squadron of the Pharaoh*.

Charioteers

The elite members of the army were the charioteers, whose barracks were the royal stables. Each chariot, drawn by a pair of horses, was manned by two men — the driver, whose manoeuvring of the chariot during battle was vital, and the fighter who was armed with a spear, bow and arrows. The highest officers in the chariotry were the royal charioteers. They were distinguished, well-educated men of high birth, including the sons of the pharaoh.

The infantry comprised units of spearmen, archers, axe-bearers, clubmen and slingers, each with its hierarchy of officers.

Within the army at any one time there were three groups based on differences in skill and experience:

- an elite group of first class warriors
- a corps of seasoned soldiers
- the newest recruits.

As well, there were the necessary scouts, spies and messengers who made up the intelligence branch of the army.

Military training included route marches and sometimes mock combats, often performed in front of the court.

Egyptian soldiers

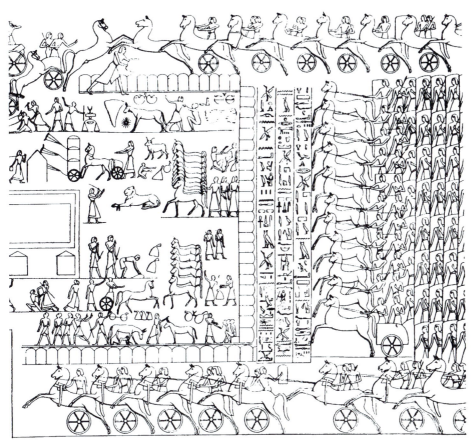

An Egyptian chariotry force and fortified camp

The army on campaign

The evidence suggests that after a pharaoh decided to send an army abroad, he consulted with his war council of senior officers concerning a plan of action. However, he was not obliged to follow their advice.

The first task was to call up the troops and issue them with weapons. According to the pictorial representations, this was a solemn affair supervised by the pharaoh himself. The infantry, dressed only in loincloths, advanced in turn to a group of scribes who issued them with a variety of weapons including sickle-shaped swords with long handles, javelins, bows and quivers of arrows. The scribes scrupulously recorded the name of each man and his equipment. At the time of Thutmose III, the infantry appear to have been very lightly clad but by the reign of Ramesses II they were issued with short-sleeved coats of mail and helmets.

Issuing weapons

The order of march appears to have been as follows:

- part of the infantry, in ranks seven or eight deep
- trumpeters
- officers of the king's personal staff
- a chariot bearing the standard of Amun-Re, the sacred ram crowned with the sun disc

Order of march

- two parasol bearers on foot
- the royal chariot, driven by the king himself
- more infantry
- chariotry
- supplies carried by asses and wagons.

Detailed written accounts (Thutmose III) and the pictorial representations (Ramesses II) provide evidence of soldiers on the march, in camp, and storming a fortified town, as well as in the midst of battle.

Rations

Throughout the campaign the soldiers and subordinate officers were provided with rations of grain, bread, beef, cakes, vegetables and wine.

Booty

Ordinary soldiers also received some share of the booty. In the Egyptian account of the Battle of Megiddo, Thutmose III's troops 'went around counting their share of the plunder as the defeated troops lay stretched out like fish on the ground'.[11]

Egyptian soldiers in the midst of battle

Captives depicted on the walls of the temples of Thebes

Some of the difficulties faced by soldiers and subordinate officers are described in an extract at the end of this chapter. Although it is prejudiced there is probably some truth to it.

On the return journey, high-ranking prisoners marched in front of the pharaoh's chariot. Generally their arms were bound and they were led by ropes around their necks.

Captives

Celebrations for the success of the pharaoh began as soon as the army re-entered Egypt, with some of the prisoners being ceremonially put to death by the priests. Later, at a dedication ceremony, the fate of the rest of the prisoners was decided and the booty was consecrated to the various gods. The pharaoh acknowledged his father Amun-Re for his victory and presented him (via his priests and temples) with the lion's share of prisoners and booty.

The army during peace time

Some troops were left behind to garrison foreign cities and states. These soldiers and officers were maintained at the expense of the conquered people.

Of those who returned home, some, particularly the mercenaries, were quartered in the capitals and residence-cities throughout Egypt. Others were settled as military colonists on farms which their families could inherit so long as a male descendant remained available for military service. These troops were rapidly mobilised when the need arose. Any peasants who had been drafted returned home to resume work on the land.

Garrisons and military colonists

In times of peace both the infantry and chariot forces were employed on public works, accompanied trading and mining expeditions and acted as bodyguards for the king during important festivals.

Akhenaten's military guard

Promotion and rewards

There were always opportunities for men of initiative, courage and loyalty to be promoted within the Egyptian army and those who showed outstanding bravery or merit might be rewarded with the *gold of valour* (a necklace of gold decorations presented in public ceremonies), as well as land and slaves.

Gold of valour

An ordinary soldier in the infantry might hope to advance to the position of standard bearer and then further to become commander of archers.

Rewards of land, slaves and titles

On retirement, successful field officers often continued to hold important positions within the bureaucracy, such as chief of police or chief steward of the royal estates. Others retired in great comfort. The military careers described below illustrate promotion and reward within the military organisation.

Ahmose, son of Ebana, started his military career as a young marine during the reign of King Ahmose I. After his marriage, he was promoted to the king's northern fleet because of his bravery. His services to the king during the first attack on the Hyksos capital of Avaris, earned Ahmose another promotion to a ship called *Shining-in-Memphis*. He accompanied the king during his siege of Sharuhen in Palestine and his campaign against the Nubians.

During the reign of Amenhotep I, Ahmose, son of Ebana, sailed with the king to Nubia where he fought at the head of his army. He was once again rewarded and promoted to a position called *warrior of the ruler*. Ahmose survived to serve Thutmose I as crew commander in Nubia and leader of the troops in the king's campaign against the Mitanni.

He ended his days under Thutmose I as a man of great position and wealth, with many slaves and land holdings.

> **I have been rewarded seven times with gold in the sight of the whole land, with male and female slaves as well. I have been endowed with many fields.**[12]

A favoured officer under Thutmose IV, called Horemheb (not the later pharaoh), included among his titles *overseer of the buildings of Amun, overseer of the priests in Upper and Lower Egypt and overseer of fields.*

Didou, an ordinary soldier during the reign of Ramesses II, held the posts of commander of the deserts west of Thebes, king's messenger, standard bearer of the king's bodyguard, captain of the ship *Mery Amun* and chief of police. He also received the gold of valour several times.

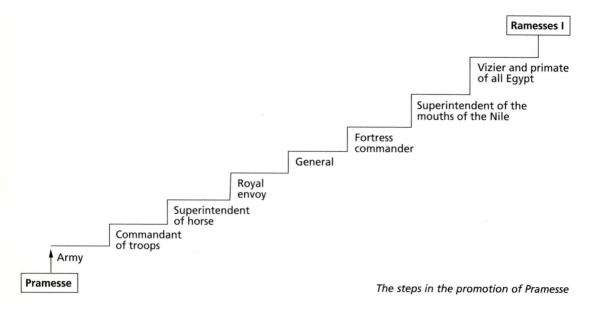

The steps in the promotion of Pramesse

Nebamun, a standard bearer in the army of Ramesses II, was honoured by the king on his retirement. He was assigned the job of chief of police at a ceremony attended by the pharaoh himself, and given a vast estate which was granted immunity from payments demanded by officials on behalf of the king. He was further honoured with a burial at the pharaoh's expense.

The diagram below shows the promotion of Pramesse through the military and civil hierarchy. Pramesse later became the pharaoh Ramesses I.

Changes to the image of the pharaoh

The prestige of the Egyptian kings, which had suffered as a result of the Hyksos domination, was restored with the success of Ahmose over the invaders in c. 1532 BC. However, the Middle Kingdom image of the good shepherd looking after his flock was replaced with the image of a divine war lord — a warrior god of heroic proportions.

The warrior god-king

The king as a god

From earliest times, the Egyptian king was believed to be:

- the earthly form of the falcon god Horus (Lord of Heaven, Lord of the Horizon, the Distant One)
- the son of Re, the sun god
- Horus and Osiris — the king became Horus, the son, when he ascended the throne and Osiris when he died.

During the New Kingdom, the pharaoh was regarded also as:

- the son of the imperial god Amun-Re
- the incarnation of a warrior god like Montu or Seth.

Thutmose IV wearing his blue war crown (khepresh) in his war chariot, guided by the falcon-headed god, Montu — from a relief on the king's chariot

He was often depicted at this time wearing the feathers of Amun and in battle with the wings of Montu.

Incarnation of Montu

The king's relationship with his *father*, Amun-Re, is illustrated in the birth scenes on the walls of the temple of Hatshepsut at Deir el-Bahri and on the temple constructed by Amenhotep III at Luxor. These scenes depict the divine marriage between Amun (in the guise of the pharaoh) and the queen consort, the conception and finally the birth of the royal child which takes place in front of a large number of the gods. Amun recognises the child, promising it *millions of years like Re.*

One of the responsibilities of the god-king was to defend the land against physical threats and confront evil or chaotic forces. The tradition of the pharaoh as a *smasher of heads* continued during the New Kingdom. The towering king was shown striding forward, grasping in his left hand the hair of a captive or captives while the mace-head or scimitar in his right hand was about to beat out the enemy's brains. No one could hope to resist the divine ruler and survive.

A scene from the divine birth reliefs at Luxor showing Queen Mutemweya, the future mother of Amenhotep III, being impregnated

Ramesses II killing a Syrian victim while a god hands him a sickle-sword

The king as a warrior

Most pharaohs of the New Kingdom were war leaders. Some were true warrior-kings who extended the boundaries of Egypt north and south. Others directed or participated in campaigns only in the first few years of their reigns. However, this was enough to maintain Egyptian power abroad and to reinforce the tradition of the warrior-king who had divine support and approval. Almost all New Kingdom pharaohs took an interest in the recruiting and arming of their troops, whether they personally led them or not.

Superhuman qualities

Except in the case of Hatshepsut, the court writers and artists of the day focused on the superhuman qualities of the god-king. No matter what the abilities of the individual pharaoh or the incidents of history, the pharaoh was always shown larger than life in the midst of battle. Alone in his chariot, he had the reins fastened around his waist so that both hands were free for the fight. He was vastly outnumbered but needed no help from his forces. His arrows always found their mark and the enemy was utterly powerless against him.

The warlike image of the New Kingdom pharaohs was reflected in their names and titles. They include such descriptions as:

Warlike image

- *Mighty in Strength* (Thutmose III)
- *Who Conquers all Lands by His Might* (Amenhotep II)
- *Great in Strength, Smiter of Asiatics* (Amenhotep III)
- *Strong-armed, Subduing the Foe, Mighty of Bows in all Lands* (Seti I)
- *Protector of Egypt who curbs the foreign lands* (Ramesses II).

This image was further enhanced by:

- the king's constant association with Montu, the war god of Thebes
- the addition of the blue war crown (*khepresh*) to the collection of royal regalia. This blue leather crown covered with gold studs was not only worn into battle but whenever the pharaoh wanted to emphasise his warlike powers and military feats

Warlike regalia

- the addition of the scimitar (a sword-like weapon with a curved cutting edge) to the other sceptres — the pastoral crook and the whip or flail
- decoration which featured Negroes and Asiatics on the base of the king's throne or footstool (under the pharaoh's feet).

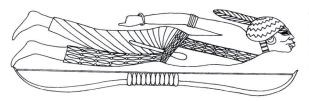

A drawing from a relief on the ceremonial footstool of Tutankhamun depicting some of the enemies of the king

The following extracts describe the superhuman actions of the pharaohs Thutmose III, Amenhotep II and Amenhotep III.

Thutmose III:

A king is he, mighty of arm, the excellent fortress of his armies, the iron wall of his people. He attacks every land with his sword, without there being millions of men behind him, throwing and striking his target every time he stretches out his hand. His arrows do not miss; mighty of arm, his equal does not exist, Montu, on the battlefield.[13]

Amenhotep II:

Then his majesty saw a few Asiatics coming in chariots, at the gallop. Now, his majesty was equipped with his weapons of warfare; his majesty became terrible like the strength of Seth in his hour. They panicked when they saw his majesty alone among them.[14]

Amenhotep III:

The Good God ... lord of the sword, mighty in dragging them alongside his chariot, annihilating the heir to the wretched Kush, taking their princes prisoner. The Good God, Golden Horus, shining in the chariot, like the rising of the sun; great in strength, strong in might, mighty hearted like him who dwells in Thebes, mighty Montu; smiting Naharin with his mighty sword.[15]

The depiction of the pharaoh as a warrior god reached its ultimate form under Ramesses II. (Refer to the extract at the end of this chapter.)

The heroic image was also repeated in the records of the pharaoh's hunting forays against lions, wild cattle and even elephants. The pharaoh, always looking magnificent in his chariot, disposed of the wild beasts charging at him. No one could equal his prowess with the bow.

Sporting prowess

Thutmose III claimed to have hunted 120 elephants, captured a herd of 12 wild bulls in the space of an hour and to have killed seven lions 'in the completion of a moment'. Amenhotep II, 'like Montu in his strength', shot at four copper targets six centimetres thick, the arrows completely passing through them. 'Such a feat had never been accomplished nor heard of before.'

Many of these warrior-kings were associated with outstanding queens who played a prominent role in public life.

Prominence of royal women

One feature of the imperial age of Egyptian history was the prominence of women. In a sense this was not new. Egyptian queens had been important factors in the Old Kingdom ... The Eighteenth Dynasty, however, surpassed previous ages in the acknowledged influence of women.[16]

The status of New Kingdom queens

Queen consort and queen mother

Of all the royal women, the most important was the queen consort. If she happened also to be the mother of an heir-apparent, her status was further enhanced.

Although queens in all periods of Egyptian history were regarded very highly, 'New Kingdom queens were more visible than ever before with increasing emphasis on individuality and divinity'.[17]

The Eighteenth Dynasty was notable for a number of exceptional and influential queens. One took over the reigns of government in a time of crisis, another ruled as a king for 20 years, others held honoured positions in the Amun and Aten cults, while another was held in high regard by powerful foreign kings.

Influential queens

From the evidence available, the most noteworthy among the Eighteenth Dynasty queens were:

- Ahhotep — mother of King Ahmose
- Ahmose Nefertari — wife of King Ahmose and mother of King Amenhotep I
- Hatshepsut — Daughter of Thutmose I, wife of Thutmose II and co-ruler with Thutmose III
- Tiye — wife of Amenhotep III and mother of Akhenaten
- Nefertiti — wife of Akhenaten.

Religious status

Association with female deities

Since the kingship was regarded as a divine office, it is highly likely that the position of queen consort was also believed to be divine. In the Eighteenth Dynasty most queens were identified with the goddesses Maat and Hathor. Evidence from the regalia worn by queen consorts seems to confirm this. For example, the cow horns and solar disk of Hathor were now incorporated as part of the queen's vulture headdress.

Queen Tiye was presented as the incarnation of Hathor at her husband's jubilee and was worshipped in the form of Hathor in the temple dedicated to her by her husband at Sedeinga in Nubia. King Ramesses II built a great temple for the goddess Hathor at Abu Simbel and dedicated it to his chief queen, Nefertari.

Images on temple walls of Hathor and Isis wearing the regalia of a queen further emphasised the link between New Kingdom queens and these female deities.

Ahmose Nefertari

Of all the queens of the Eighteenth and Nineteenth dynasties, Queen Ahmose Nefertari had the highest religious status. She was the first queen to be given the title of *god's wife of Amun* or *divine consort of Amun*. This title had been originally held by the high priestess of Amun whose marriage to the god was believed to have ensured the continuance of the work of creation. The importance which Ahmose Nefertari attached to this position of god's wife of Amun is indicated by her use of this title, above all others, before her name.

God's wife of Amun

The appointment of Queen Ahmose Nefertari to this position was accompanied by the foundation of the *harem of Amun* which was under her control. This harem was composed of a body of priestesses and a choir of singers and musicians to which most of the high-ranking court women belonged. An account of the foundation of this harem of Amun has been found on three inscribed fragments from a destroyed temple at Karnak. The inscription is referred to as the Donation Stela and records what goods and services Ahmose Nefertari was to receive in her capacity as god's wife or divine consort.

The deified Ahmose-Nefertari with her son Amenhotep I

She inherited a large and wealthy estate and the labour to work it. A male high steward (her brother) was appointed to take care of any administrative details. To assist her in her religious duties, a female *supervisor of the harem* was appointed. The woman who held this title was also very influential in court circles. The list of goods Ahmose Nefertari was to receive included treasures of gold, silver, copper, and supplies of grain. This arrangement or contract was witnessed by the high dignitaries of Thebes and the court. The position of *second prophet of Amun* was to go to her son. The female descendants of Ahmose Nefertari were entitled to inherit this position with all its wealth and power.

Evidence that in her priestly role she was involved with her husband's building projects, comes from a number of stone quarries and a stela at Abydos. It appears that when King Ahmose planned to build a cenotaph to his grandmother, he gained approval for the plans from the God's Wife, Queen Ahmose Nefertari. The enormous number of objects dedicated by her are further evidence of her ritual importance.

Deification

Ahmose Nefertari was later deified and worshipped as *Mistress of the West*. She and her son, Amenhotep I, became the patron deities of the royal necropolis and were worshipped by the royal tomb workmen and their families in Deir el-Medina. Her cult continued there throughout the New Kingdom.

Nefertiti

There is no doubt about the religious status of Queen Nefertiti. She played a vital role in the Aten ritual during the brief Amarna Period. There is evidence of this even in the early years when she and her husband, Akhenaten, were still in Thebes. After the court moved to Akhetaten, her status increased and her role became more central. This is reflected in the Amarna temple inscriptions and in the tombs of Akhenaten's courtiers (refer to Chapter 13).

It appears that the couple's roles in the worship of the Aten were interchangeable. For example, when they were shown making offerings together, sometimes the king offered flowers while Nefertiti poured the libations or vice versa. Sometimes they both hold up the *sekhem* sceptre in recognition of their equal authority.

The Amarna nobles directed their prayers for blessings in the afterlife to the Aten, the king and his queen. Sometimes Nefertiti, in the manner of a king, was shown officiating alone. In one scene her arms are raised to the god as she offers up a statuette of the goddess Maat which was traditionally the king's offering in the temple. In another scene she performs the ritual of *purification* in the libation ceremonies to the god. This was normally the act of the king or a priest.

In the inscriptions, her name was linked closely with that of the Aten. For example:

- the hieroglyphs of the god's name were written so that they faced her name
- accompanying her name was the description *adoration by all the people of the Aten*. The words *adoration* or *praise* were usually reserved for a god or pharaoh
- the usual phrase *He who found the Aten* became *She who found the Aten*.

Political status

Chief queens of the New Kingdom were more prominent in public life than in any previous period. For example, they accompanied their husbands on tours of inspection, attended royal audiences, were present at the investitures of important officials and at presentations of rewards, and attended dedication ceremonies and annual festivals. A number of queens, particularly during the Eighteenth Dynasty, played more significant political roles than others.

Nefertiti worshipping the Aten

Ahhotep

Ahhotep, the mother of Ahmose (regarded by many scholars as the founder of the Eighteenth Dynasty) provided an example of strength that was followed by future queens. She took over the reins of government on the sudden death of her husband, Seqenenre Tao II, and ruled as regent for her son during the last years of the Hyksos domination of Egypt. She seems to have wielded some real political power. According to a stela erected by Ahmose at Karnak, Ahhotep rallied the Theban troops, eliminated rebels, brought back fugitives and pacified Upper Egypt:

Regent for Ahmose

> King's Daughter, respected Mother of the King, who is in control of affairs, who unites Egypt. She has assembled her notables with whom she has assured cohesion: she has brought back its fugitives, she has gathered its dissidents; she has pacified Upper Egypt, she has put down its rebels; the King's wife, Ahhotep who lives![(18)]

Hatshepsut

The most outstanding queen of the Eighteenth Dynasty was Hatshepsut, the daughter of Thutmose I. She ruled first as the queen of Thutmose II and then as regent for the child-king Thutmose III:

Pharaoh Hatshepsut

> The God's Wife Hatshepsut governed Egypt, and the Two Lands were under her control. People worked for her and Egypt bowed her head.[(19)]

Somewhere between years 2 and 7 of her regency she decided to govern as a pharaoh in her own right. She was crowned king and co-ruler with Thutmose III, although there is no doubt as to who was the dominant partner. From this time, she emphasised her position as king by being depicted in royal male attire, including the artificial beard.

The strength of Hatshepsut's personality was illustrated in her ability to maintain the support of powerful political allies for over 20 years and to keep Thutmose, the future empire-builder in the background for so long. The prosperity of Egypt increased substantially under her rule.

Support of powerful allies

Tiye

Another queen who had a high public profile was Tiye, the wife of Amenhotep III (refer to Chapter 12). Although she was a commoner, she was granted many titles usually reserved for those of royal blood. She was also:

High public profile

- the first queen consort to have her name associated with that of her husband on official inscriptions
- depicted in a number of statues (eg, the colossal pair of statues now in the Cairo Museum) as being on an equal level with her husband
- represented in the tomb of a noble as a female sphinx, trampling female Asiatic and Nubian captives underfoot. The sphinx was a representation usually reserved for kings.

Tiye was consulted on internal and external affairs relating to the state. She is believed to have influenced her husband in diplomatic matters and corresponded with foreign rulers who apparently respected her political skills.

Communication with foreign rulers

When Amenhotep III died, Tushratta, the king of Mitanni wrote a letter of condolence to her. Further correspondence from Tushratta to Akhenaten indicates that Tiye had some influence over her son and was capable of mediating between the two rulers.

> Whatever your father Nimoria (Amenhotep III) said and wrote to me, Tiye, spouse of Nimoria the great and beloved, your mother, knows everything relating to this. Ask your mother, Tiye, about these matters.[20]

Nefertiti

There are more images of Nefertiti performing public duties than of any other queen. Although Queen Tiye was greatly revered and honoured, even outside the frontiers of Egypt, she was never shown on temples or pylons, or in statuary and other forms of art in the way Nefertiti was.

Political partner to Akhenaten

There is no doubt about Nefertiti's political status. Akhenaten treated her as a real partner, not only in their family life but in their public life as well — they were hardly ever shown apart. In most scenes she participated with her husband as his equal. Sometimes she is even shown officiating alone.

Depicted in role of king

She was featured in the inscriptions in a role normally reserved exclusively for pharaohs (refer to Chapter 13). For example:

- She was depicted as a *warrior-king* subduing the enemies of Egypt. In her particular blue crown, she was shown striding forward towards captives, grasping them by the hair and swinging a scimitar over her head. Throughout the whole of Egyptian history only pharaohs were shown in this conqueror's role.

- She featured prominently in Akhenaten's Sed festival in Thebes. She was carried in a palanquin, the state carriage of the day, surrounded by kingly symbols in the manner of a pharaoh. While Akhenaten's carrying chair was carved with striding lions and sphinxes, that of Nefertiti was carved with striding lionesses and sphinxes mounted in her own image. She was surrounded also by courtiers and officials.

- She was shown handing out the treasured gold collars to those who had performed outstanding service to her husband. Traditionally a queen stood behind her husband on these occasions.

- There are many scenes at Akhetaten of her driving her own chariot in kingly fashion.

- Her full name, *Nefernefruaten Nefertiti*, was placed in the double cartouche used only by kings and regnant queens such as Hatshepsut.

A number of scholars believe that these examples of Nefertiti's unique status provide evidence that Akhenaten intended Nefertiti to be his successor. According to this theory, while at Thebes, Akhenaten emphasised her equality with him and later, at Akhetaten, she became his co-ruler. Whatever the truth of this matter, the public profile of Nefertiti was exceptional.

Ankhesenamun

Ankhesenamun, who was the daughter of Akhenaten and the wife of Tutankhamun, wrote a remarkable letter to the great Hittite king, Suppilulimas, after her husband's untimely death. Since there was no male heir to the throne, the young widow was faced with a crisis of succession. She requested that Suppilulimas send one of his sons for her to marry and to share the throne of Egypt with her. Such an act was unprecedented.

An unusual request

> My husband is dead and I have no son. People say that you have many sons. If you send me one of your sons he will become my husband for it is repugnant for me to take one of my servants (subjects) to husband.[21]

The suspicious Hittite king who sent one of his officials to investigate, received another strong letter from Ankhesenamun.

> Why do you say, 'they are trying to deceive me?' If I had a son should I write to a foreign country in a manner humiliating to me and my country?[22]

Royal and non-royal queens and the succession

Although some of the principal wives of New Kingdom pharaohs were of royal birth, others were not. Those who were the daughters of a king and his principal wife often married their brothers or half-brothers. Such royal daughters included Ahhotep, Ahmose Nefertari, Hatshepsut and possibly Ankhesenamun. This form of marriage was probably regarded as the ideal because the gods (Geb and Nut, Osiris and Isis, Nephthys and Seth) practised brother-sister unions. Such marriages would have emphasised the king's divinity and set him apart from his subjects.

Brother-sister marriages among royalty led some scholars to conclude that the throne of Egypt was transmitted through the female line. According to this theory, a future king would have to marry his *heiress* sister or half-sister in order to legitimise his position on the throne.

Heiress theories

Another succession theory suggests that the woman who became queen was not necessarily a king's daughter but a female descendant of Ahmose Nefertari who held the religious title of god's wife of Amun. Ahmose Nefertari was the first royal daughter and queen to hold this position and was legally able to pass it on to her female heirs. However, neither of these heiress theories can be substantiated by the evidence available.

There appears to have been no obligation on the part of the king to marry his sister and many rulers of the Eighteenth and Nineteenth dynasties married women of non-royal birth. Also, there was no continuous line of queen consorts who held the position of god's wife of Amun. In fact, this position seems to have declined in political importance after the death of Hatshepsut and some notable queens, such as Tiye, never held the title. Other queens who are believed to have used the title, were granted it in the reigns of their sons (Tiaa, mother of Thutmose IV and Mutemweya, mother of Amenhotep III). The title disappeared for over 80 years until the beginning of the Nineteenth Dynasty.

Intervention of the god Amun in the succession

In some cases, when a chief queen was neither the daughter of the previous king nor had held the title of god's wife, the god Amun is supposed to have intervened to legitimise her offspring. The Egyptians believed this could occur in two ways:

1   The god, in the guise of the king, took the queen as his divine consort and impregnated her as in the cases of Ahmose, queen of Thutmose I and Mutemweya wife of Thutmose IV.

2   Sometimes Amun intervened in the succession by pronouncing an oracle, as in the case of the future Thutmose III whose mother, Isis, was supposedly a royal concubine.

There does not seem to be enough evidence to support the belief that the right to the throne, during the New Kingdom, was transmitted from one *heiress* to the next.

Backgrounds of non-royal wives

How then was a woman of non-royal birth chosen as king's great wife or queen consort? Although this question cannot be satisfactorily answered, there does seem to be some similarity in the backgrounds of those non-royal queens about whom we have some information.

It seems that many of the mothers of non-royal queens played some part in the hierarchy of the cult of Amun. For example, the mother of Meritre-Hatshepsut (second principal wife of Thutmose III) was an *adoritrice of the god* while Tuya, the mother of Queen Tiye, was a *superior of the harem of Amun at Thebes* and *superior in the harem of Min* at Akhmin. It is possible that others, such as the mother of Sitiah (first principal wife of Thutmose III), were royal nurses. Some of the fathers of non-royal queens appear to have held high positions in the chariotry forces. For example, the father of Queen Meritre-Hatsheptut, was possibly Yey, a commander in the chariotry; the father of Tiye was Yuya, commander of chariotry; and the father of Tuya, the principal wife of Seti I, was Raia, lieutenant of chariotry.

Honours bestowed on queen consorts and dowager queens by their husbands and sons

Examples of respect for mothers and wives

The respect and love felt by many New Kingdom pharaohs for their chief queens and their dowager queen-mothers is reflected in the great honours they bestowed on them. For example:

• Ahmose built a cenotaph at Abydos to honour his grandmother, Tetisheri, and had the achievements of his mother, Ahhotep, immortalised on a stela at Karnak.

• Amenhotep I honoured his mother, Ahmose Nefertari, by building her a separate mortuary temple at Thebes and permitting her to be buried in his own tomb.

- Thutmose I had a statue of Ahmose Nefertari erected at Karnak even though he was probably not directly related to her.

- Amenhotep III is supposed to have built a great pleasure lake for Queen Tiye, *Lady of Delight who Fills the Palace with Love*, on which they sailed together. He honoured her with a vast estate at Djaruka which provided her with more personal income and also dedicated a temple to her in Nubia (refer to Chapter 12).

- Akhenaten's devotion to Nefertiti was depicted in the hundreds of affectionate scenes carved and painted of them together at Akhetaten (refer to Chapter 13).

- Ramesses II honoured his mother, Tuya, during her later years by placing statues of her in the Ramesseum at Thebes, in the capital of Pi-Ramesse and alongside those of himself and Queen Nefertari at Abu Simbel. He also dedicated a small temple to her near the Ramesseum and prepared a lavish tomb for her in the Valley of the Queens.

- Above all others, Ramesses II honoured his beloved wife Nefertari with temples, statues and a beautiful tomb in the Valley of the Queens (refer to Chapter 14).

Royal daughters

Kings' daughters were held in very high esteem and had a privileged position in New Kingdom society. There is evidence of kings' daughters accompanying their parents on their tours of inspection and at dedication ceremonies. Amenhotep III's youngest daughter, Beketaten, accompanied her mother, Tiye, to the dedication of a new building in Akhetaten. When the two great temples at Abu Simbel in Nubia were to be dedicated by Ramesses II, his eldest daughter, Meryetamun, accompanied him on the 3200 kilometre return journey.

When a king married his own daughter, she was expected to play a prominent role at state and religious functions. In the case of the pharaohs Amenhotep and Akhenaten, these marriages were not necessarily of a physical nature although Ramesses' marriages to his daughters Bint-Anath and Meryetamun may well have been.

Political and religious roles

Kings' daughters also played significant roles in the religious establishment, particularly the cult of Amun-Re. Some, like Hatshepsut and her daughter Neferure, were honoured with the title of *god's wife of Amun*. In the Nineteenth Dynasty, Tjia, the daughter of Seti I, was *chantress of Amun* attached to the cult of Amun in Pi-Ramesse. She was linked also with the cults at Memphis and Heliopolis. During the brief Amarna Period of the Eighteenth Dynasty, Akhenaten's young daughters were shown taking part in the Aten ritual with their mother Nefertiti.

The ascendancy of Amun and the influence of his priesthood

More than any other deity Amun was the creation of political circumstances.[22]

The rulers of Thebes had worshipped the god Amun since the Middle Kingdom (Eleventh and Twelfth dynasties) when he replaced the local god Montu. Amun was a god of air and was referred to as the *Hidden One*. He was depicted in human form with a headdress of tall ostrich feathers.

Gained prominence with expulsion of Hyksos

When the princes of Thebes successfully expelled the Hyksos from Egypt and reunited the Two Lands once more, it was their god Amun who was given the credit.

At first Amun was primarily a war god. Then, so that he would have no real rival in Egypt, his priests, had early on, associated him with the sun god Re, the creator god who was also the protector of royalty. Amun-Re, as he was now called, absorbed all the characteristics of the solar god, and a sun-disk was added to his feathered headdress.

A new myth of creation was formulated in which Amun-Re became the invisible but all-powerful creator of mankind and Thebes became the site of the original mound of earth that had emerged from the waters of chaos at the time of creation. It was on this mound that Amun-Re created

Above: Amun, depicted as a ram with its horns curved downwards

Left: One of the many reliefs from the walls and columns of the Temple of Karnak showing Amun wearing the double plumed headdress

the world. In this Theban view of creation Amun was linked to Mut, the vulture goddess, and Khonsu, the moon god (their son) in a divine triad. As a creator god, Amun was sometimes depicted in the form of a ram with its horns curved downwards.

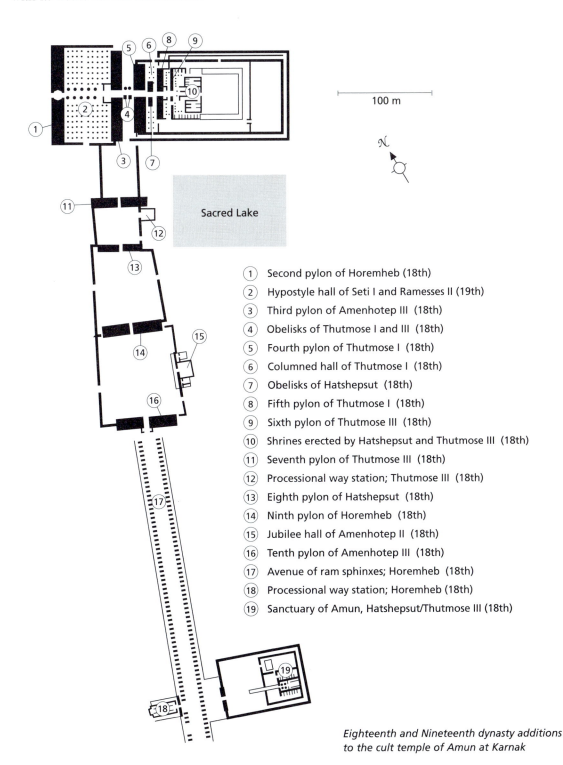

100 m

N

1. Second pylon of Horemheb (18th)
2. Hypostyle hall of Seti I and Ramesses II (19th)
3. Third pylon of Amenhotep III (18th)
4. Obelisks of Thutmose I and III (18th)
5. Fourth pylon of Thutmose I (18th)
6. Columned hall of Thutmose I (18th)
7. Obelisks of Hatshepsut (18th)
8. Fifth pylon of Thutmose I (18th)
9. Sixth pylon of Thutmose III (18th)
10. Shrines erected by Hatshepsut and Thutmose III (18th)
11. Seventh pylon of Thutmose III (18th)
12. Processional way station; Thutmose III (18th)
13. Eighth pylon of Hatshepsut (18th)
14. Ninth pylon of Horemheb (18th)
15. Jubilee hall of Amenhotep II (18th)
16. Tenth pylon of Amenhotep III (18th)
17. Avenue of ram sphinxes; Horemheb (18th)
18. Processional way station; Horemheb (18th)
19. Sanctuary of Amun, Hatshepsut/Thutmose III (18th)

Eighteenth and Nineteenth dynasty additions to the cult temple of Amun at Karnak

Responsibility for growth of empire

Amun-Re was believed to be responsible for leading the Egyptian armies to victory in western Asia and Nubia, thus laying the foundation of the empire.

It was Amun who *permitted a campaign*, who *gave his sword to pharaoh*, whose standard the soldiers followed into battle and who brought victory to the king, *his son*, giving him the strength of thousands of men and protecting him in the midst of battle.

As Egypt's supremacy in western Asia became well-established from the middle of the Eighteenth Dynasty, the priests of Amun-Re emphasised the universal creative nature of their god. He was not only regarded as supreme in Egypt but throughout the empire.

Cult centre at Karnak

Amun had evolved from a local god to an imperial god during the first half of the Eighteenth Dynasty and Thebes became the religious centre of Egypt and the empire. The Theban cult centre of the god was the great temple complex at Karnak, although other temples to Amun were built throughout Egypt.

Additions to Amun's temple

The pharaohs of the New Kingdom did not forget the debt which they believed they owed the god Amun-Re. Each king of the Eighteenth and Nineteenth dynasty, except Akhenaten, added a new building, colonnade, court, columned hall, obelisk, pylon or sphinx-lined avenue to the original Temple of Amun built in the Twelfth Dynasty (refer to the temple plan shown on page 525). The pharaohs attempted to outdo their predecessors and, in fact, some kings put their names to the unfinished work of others. Occasionally the monument of one ruler was dismantled or incorporated in the building of another.

Along with additions to the Karnak temple, the New Kingdom pharaohs endowed vast wealth, estates and numerous captives to the god and his temple.

The following *hymn of Amun to the king*, presumably written by the priests, reminded the kings what they owed the god.

> When I turn my face to the South, I work a wonder for you:
> I make the princes of the wretched Kush come to you,
> Carrying all their tribute on their backs.
> When I turn my face to the North, I work a wonder for you:
> I make the countries of the ends of Asia come to you,
> Bearing all their tribute on their backs.
> They themselves present their children to you,
> In order that you may give them the breath of life.[24]

The priesthood of Amun (Amun-Re)

From the time of Hatshepsut, the status of Amun was raised above all other gods and his priesthood acquired great religious, economic and political influence.

High priest of Amun

The position of high priest or first prophet of Amun was a political appointment. Until the time of Ramesses II the person appointed by the pharaoh was someone who had a high profile and a distinguished career at court. A number of high priests held the position of vizier or at least had the powers that went with the vizierate; for example, Hapusoneb in the reign of Hatshepsut and Ptahmose in the reign of Amenhotep III. The exception to this was Bakenkhons, appointed by Ramesses II. He had entered the temple in his youth, passed through successive grades of the priesthood, holding the positions of third and second prophet before being rewarded with the prestigious position of high priest.

The high priest was not only the king's representative in the cult of Amun, but he eventually claimed the right to supervise the cults of other gods such as Ptah of Memphis and Re of Heliopolis, frequently holding the title of *overseer of prophets of all the gods of Upper and Lower Egypt.*

He led a hierarchy of permanent and part-time priests, some of whom, from time to time, held important posts within the pharaoh's household and the government bureaucracy. The permanent priests were referred to as second, third and fourth prophets. Below them in importance was a college of *god's fathers*. The body of part-time priests or *pure ones* served in the temple three times a year and then returned to their own profession or craft inside or outside the temple precincts.

A hierarchy of priests

Although the high priest was the pharaoh's representative in securing the favours of the god, it is likely that he only officiated on special occasions and during festivals. He probably left the daily rituals to his immediate subordinates.

The economic and political influence of the priesthood

Part of the booty taken during military campaigns, a large proportion of the annual tribute from subject rulers, raw materials acquired through trade, and personal gifts from other kings went into Amun's treasury. Although the temples and priesthoods of the other great gods also received these benefits, Amun-Re received by far the lion's share. This powerful civilian priesthood controlled one of the largest and richest establishments in Egypt.

Wealth from empire

Huge estates all over Egypt and some in conquered territory were cultivated either by temple labourers, temple agents or rented out to officials and small farmers. The temple also owned huge herds of animals, extensive vineyards, beehives, and fishing and fowling rights along the river.

Estates

The priesthood controlled mining deposits from which many of the raw materials used in the temple workshops came, and collected taxes in the form of grain, beer, wine, metals and other goods from all over Egypt. These products were transported in the god's own fleet of ships and stored in massive warehouses within the temple precincts.

Mines and ships

At the end of the Nineteenth Dynasty, the Temple of Amun-Re at Thebes owned approximately 90 000 slaves, 500 000 head of cattle, 400 orchards, 80 ships and 50 workshops as well as receiving revenue from 65 towns in Egypt and Palestine/Syria. The king, by royal decree, also granted the priesthood of Amun special privileges such as exemption from certain taxes.

Labour force

The Temple of Amun-Re was the greatest single employer of labour in the country. As its wealth increased, so too did the number of temple staff which the priesthood controlled. As well as singers, musicians and dancers, there was a huge body of scribes employed to carry out the daily administrative and financial affairs of the god. Enormous numbers of slaves, agricultural labourers, unskilled workmen and skilled craftsmen worked on the temple estates, in the workshops, slaughterhouses,

Pharaoh	Official	Titles associated with the estate of Amun
Hatshepsut	Senenmut	Chief steward of Amun, overseer of the granaries of Amun, overseer of the fields of Amun, overseer of the cattle of Amun, chief of the weavers of Amun and overseer of all works for the god
	Duaueheh	Overseer of the estate of Amun
	Nebamun	Counter of grain in the granary of divine offerings
Thutmose III	Baki	Chief servant who weighs the silver and gold of the estate of Amun
	Amenemhet	Agent of Amun
	Sennufer	Overseer of the gold-land of Amun
	Amenhotp	Overseer of the magazines of Amun
	Dhutnufer	Scribe of the counting of grain in the granary of divine offerings of Amun
	Nebseny	Overseer of goldsmiths
	Amenmosi	Necropolis stonemason of Amun
	User	Weigher of Amun, overseer of the ploughed lands of Amun
	Dhout	Head of the makers of fine linen of the estate of Amun
	Simut	Overseer of works of Amun-Re at Karnak
	Pairi	Overseer of the peasants of Amun
Amenhotep III	Senenre	Overseer of sculptors of Amun
Late Eighteenth Dynasty	Neferronpet	Scribe of the treasury in the estate of Amun-Re
	Nekht Dhout	Overseer of carpenters on the northern lake of Amun
Ramesses II	Hori	Head of the outline-draughtsmen in the house of gold on the estate of Amun
	Amenemha	Herdsman of Amen-Re
	Penernutetb	Chief watchman of the granary of the estate of Amun
	Simut	Counter of the cattle of the estate of Amun
	Nekhtamun	Chiseller of Amun

bakeries, breweries, storehouses and temple treasury as well as on the temple's fleet of ships. Even traders were employed to exchange some of the temple's surplus produce.

Some of the wealth of Amun and the personnel employed by the temple can be gauged by titles found in the tombs of a number of the New Kingdom officials (see the table on page 528).

The power and influence of the priesthood was further enhanced by Amun's contribution to the warrior image of the pharaohs. The great conqueror, Thutmose III, had the following words inscribed on the Temple of Tiraqa:

> I have achieved this according to that which was ordained for me by my father, Amun-Re, Lord of the Thrones of the Two Lands, who leads my majesty on the good road by means of his excellent plans.[25]

The priesthood also played a part in the succession of the pharaohs. This was especially the case when there was a controversy, a question of legitimacy or the introduction of 'new blood' into the royal line.

The god's approval of a particular monarch was often made known via the 'miracle' of an oracle. This occurred during one of the public appearances of the god when the portable barque of Amun was taken from its sanctuary and carried on the shoulders of the priests. A slight dipping of the shrine in the direction of a particular individual indicated the god's choice of the next monarch.

A drawing of a relief on the wall of the Temple of Karnak showing priests carrying the barque of Amun during the Opet festival

Both Hatshepsut and Thutmose III claimed to have been divinely chosen in this way, while the commoner, Horemheb, had his position as pharaoh validated by holding his coronation as part of Amun's Festival of Opet. Other important political decisions were made through oracular judgments during the two chief festivals of Amun — the Opet and Valley festivals.

The pharaohs often associated their Sed festival and mortuary cult with Amun. During the Sed festival, 'which had no historical connection with either Thebes or its gods',[26] the pharaoh built a special festival hall or palace. Thutmose III built his within Amun's complex at Karnak and Amenhotep III went even further. For his second Sed jubilee, he built a palace on the west bank at Thebes in the form of a temple, which he called *The Temple of Amun in the House of Rejoicing*. 'Amun had been inserted to play the dominant role'[27] in Amenhotep's jubilee.

New Kingdom pharaohs dedicated their own mortuary temples, on the west bank at Thebes, to 'a specific form of the god Amun with whom they became fused ... Each of the mortuary temples was really an Amun temple'.[28] As part of the annual Valley festival, the image of Amun was transported across the river where it spent the night at the mortuary temple of the reigning king.

Festivals dedicated to Amun

The Opet and Valley festivals, dedicated to Amun and held annually at Thebes, reinforced the dominance of the temple and its priesthood. The pharaoh and his court travelled upriver from the capitals of Memphis (Eighteenth Dynasty) and Pi-Ramesse (Nineteenth dynasty) to Thebes to play a vital role in these festivals.

The Opet festival

Time and place

In the second month of the season of inundation, the images of the gods Amun, his *wife* Mut and son Khonsu, were taken from their sanctuaries at Karnak to begin a processional journey to the Temple of Luxor (southern Opet) three kilometres to the south. Amenhotep III had built the Temple of Luxor on the site of a small Thirteenth Dynasty temple as a 'monumental setting for the culmination of the rites of Opet'.[29]

The god's statues, housed within portable barques, left the temple of Karnak on the shoulders of the priests. They were accompanied by *ka* statues of the king.

Processional ways

During the reign of Hatshepsut, the journey to Luxor was via one of the sphinx-lined processional ways with the return journey by river. By the late Eighteenth Dynasty both legs of the journey were by water.

The great golden barge (*Userhat*) of Amun was accompanied by members of his *family*, the king's flagship (rowed by officials), and a flotilla of smaller craft. The barges and boats were towed by ropes hauled by gangs of officials, soldiers and peasants on the river banks.

Accompanying the glittering flotilla were priests, musicians, singers and crowds of ordinary Egyptians from all classes of society. It is likely that many of the people who celebrated this festive holiday came from areas beyond Thebes. It was one of the few occasions when they might catch a glimpse of the gods' barques and for some it was an opportunity to present pleas before them.

Rites at Luxor

When the barques of Amun, Mut and Khonsu reached Luxor Temple, the images of the gods were placed together in the sanctuary. Some scholars believe that the rites conducted during this time renewed the sacred *marriage* of Amun and Mut, who like their human counterparts then celebrated a divine *honeymoon*.

The presence of *ka* statues of the king and an inscription from the time of Amenhotep III, seem to suggest that the rituals conducted in the darkened, incense-filled chambers in the presence of Amun, focused on the transformation of the king. Amenhotep described Luxor Temple as:

> His place of justification in which he is rejuvenated. The palace from which he sets out in joy at the moment of his Appearance, his transformation visible to all.[(30)]

During the mid-Eighteenth Dynasty, the festival lasted about ten or 11 days but by the time of Ramesses II, the celebrations went on for more than three weeks. At the end of this period the gods returned to their *homes* at Karnak. Once again the procession was an occasion of great festivity for the ordinary people.

Length of festival

A relief from Luxor Temple showing a scene from the Opet festival procession

During the reign of the heretic pharaoh, Akhenaten, the public worship of Amun was forbidden. After his death, when Amun was reinstated, Tutankhamun ordered an account of the Opet festival to be carved into the walls of the Temple of Luxor.

The Valley festival

In the tenth month at the time of the full moon, Amun crossed the river in his golden barge, accompanied by the king and the high priest to celebrate the *Beautiful Feast of the Valley*. Although less opulent and of shorter duration than the Opet, the Valley festival was of great significance to those who had family members buried in western Thebes.

Time and place

The god's destination was the bay of cliffs at Deir el-Bahri, the site of the mortuary temples of Mentuhotep (Eleventh Dynasty) and Hatshepsut (Eighteenth Dynasty). Deir el-Bahri lay in a direct line from Karnak. After crossing the Nile, the god's barque and its priestly bearers, accompanied by soldiers, musicians and dancers, proceeded by canal to the edge of the desert and then via one of the temple causeways to Deir el-Bahri.

The original route was later extended to allow Amun to visit the mortuary temples of previous kings and finally to *rest* for the night at the temple of the reigning pharaoh. An inscription on the wall of the Ramesseum, describes it as the 'resting place of the Lord of the Gods in his beautiful Feast of the Valley'.

Celebrations

During the festivities, lavish offerings were made to Amun, and gifts, such as fine linen garments, were presented to those who participated.

In the evening, families wound their way in a torchlit procession to the Theban necropolis. In the tomb chapels, cut into the desert cliffs, they honoured their ancestors and gave thanks to Amun. The celebrations and singing continued throughout the night. On the following day Amun returned to Karnak.

Control over the influential priesthood of Amun

Although the priesthood of Amun was very influential, the kings of the Eighteenth and early Nineteenth dynasties were able to maintain control over them.

The king not only appointed the high priest of Amun but usually chose one of his trusted officials for the post. Occasionally he appointed a nonentity who owed everything to the king's favour.

In the early Eighteenth Dynasty it appears that the Second Prophet of Amun may have been a close relative of the king or his chief queen, and a female member of the royal family was appointed as the *god's wife of Amun*.

When it appeared to some pharaohs that the power of Amun and his priests could jeopardise their absolute control, they discreetly placed more emphasis on the cults of Re and Ptah in Egypt. Some also promoted a royal cult, particularly in Nubia, in order to re-emphasise the importance of kingship (see below).

For a short time, under Akhenaten, the Amun cult was prohibited altogether. Later, Ramesses II balanced the power of Amun's priests by openly linking himself with Re and Ptah as well as Amun.

The cult of the king

King more closely associated with other gods

Although the pharaohs were regarded as divine, it was not until the time of Amenhotep III that a cult of a living king was instituted. It may have seemed to Amenhotep that the powerful role of Amun threatened his absolute authority so he 'sought to redress the balance, firmly but discreetly'.[31] He did this in three ways:

1 By continuing a trend which was under way during the reigns of his father and grandfather — identifying the Aten or sun-disk (an aspect of the sun god Re) with the cult of the king.

2 By linking himself with the gods in the temples of Nubia. The temple of Soleb in Nubia was dedicated to the divine Neb-ma-re (Amenhotep III) and on a relief from that temple, the king is shown making an offering to himself.

3   By erecting colossal statues of himself and placing them in front
of the temples. These statues embodied some divine aspect of
the king. They were placed in such a way that they could be
honoured by the common people (the common people did not
usually enter the temple, so for them to worship the king and be
reminded of his divinity, huge statues had to be placed outside
the temple pylons). The giant statue outside Amun's temple at
Karnak was called *Neb-ma-re, Montu* (the war god) *of Rulers.*
Another was referred to as *Neb-ma-re, Ruler of Rulers.*

Amenhotep III did not direct any of these measures against the cult of
Amun but his son and successor, Akhenaten, did.

Seti I and Ramesses II continued the cult of the king as instituted by
Amenhotep III. Ramesses affiliated his own cult with that of Amun at
Thebes while in his temple at Abu Simbel in Nubia, he was depicted
and worshipped as a form of the sun god, Re. Also in Nubia he dedicated a temple at Aksha to his divine kingship. In all the Nubian temples which Ramesses built to Amun, Re and Ptah, it was actually the
image of himself as a god which was in the sanctuary.

Like Amenhotep III, he erected colossal statues of himself in front of the
great temples throughout Egypt and gave them names which reflected
some divine aspect of the kingship such as *Montu in the Two Lands* and
Ruler of Rulers.

These New Kingdom pharaohs attempted to set the monarchy in the
centre of Egyptian religious practice.

Influx of incredible wealth

According to the Egyptian records, all the wealth that entered Egypt as
a result of the growth of the empire was listed as *tribute*. Tribute is a
payment made by one prince or state to another as acknowledgment of
submission and subject status. However, the official Egyptian propaganda referred to booty taken during campaigns, products of normal
international trade, and gifts from powerful kings as tribute.

Definition of tribute

Many of the scenes of foreign tribute found on the walls of monuments
and in the tombs of the Egyptian officials show people who were never
subject to Egypt, such as the Keftiu from the Aegean (possibly the
Minoans of Crete) and the Hittites. These people were shown kneeling
before the Egyptian king and making offerings. Other scenes depict foreign princes not directly under Egyptian military and political control, kissing the ground in front of the good god 'with their tribute on their backs'[32]
asking that they be given the breath of life by the Egyptian pharaoh.

**Propaganda in
the texts**

Booty

Some idea of the amount of booty taken during the many military campaigns of the New Kingdom pharaohs can be gained from the two
examples on page 534.

Booty collected by Thutmose III's army after the Battle of Megiddo	Plunder taken from Palestine and Syria (Retjenu) by Amenhotep II in year 2 of his reign
captives — 340 horses — over 250 chariots, some worked with gold — 924 fine bronze suits of armour — 2 ordinary suits of armour — 200 bows — 502 silverwork tent poles — 7 cows — 1929 goats — 2000 sheep — 20 500[33]	captives of officer rank — 550, and their wives — 240 vessels of fine gold — 6800 copper — 50 000 horses — 210 chariots — 300[34]

Tribute

The Theban tomb of Amenhotep-Huy, Viceroy of Kush at the time of Tutankhamun, contains some of the best evidence on the presentation of tribute to an Egyptian pharaoh.

Tribute from Wawat and Kush (Nubia)

The beautiful tomb paintings show the princes of Wawat and Kush who accompanied Huy to Thebes to pay their tribute in person. These Nubian princes and nobles wore animal pelts hanging down their backs and ostrich feathers set into headbands over short wigs. At least one of these young men from Wawat had been brought up at the Egyptian court with Tutankhamun. These high-ranking Nubians were accompanied by a princess in a shaded, ox-drawn chariot driven by a female slave. Behind her were bound captives with their wives and children, giraffes and fat oxen with curiously shaped and decorated horns.

Nubian princes presenting tribute to the viceroy, Huy

Servants carried the tribute which consisted of gold rings and bags of gold dust, carnelian and red jasper; finely made furniture of precious woods, elephant tusks, giraffe tails for decoration and whisks, ebony boomerangs, shields covered with animal skins, a gold plated chariot and bows and arrows. The showpiece of the entire tribute was a gold model of a Nubian landscape.

Paintings in the tomb of officials, such as Sobekhotep, show bearded Syrians, in their heavily embroidered gowns, bowing before the king and presenting their precious offerings of gold, silver and stone vessels, weapons and slaves. Although most of the vessels were of fine Asiatic workmanship, the rhyton (drinking cup), of Minoan design, carried by one of them, indicates that there was substantial trade between the Syrians and the Aegean cultures.

Tribute from Syria and Palestine

Tribute bearers from Syria

The chief items of tribute from Syria and Palestine included:
- a part of the yearly harvest. A portion was used to feed the Egyptian garrisons and the rest was shipped to Egypt
- male and female slaves who were used in the mines of Sinai, in the stone quarries and on major construction works
- valuable metals (such as copper, lead and silver) and semi-precious stones (such as lapis lazuli and rock crystal)
- finely crafted vessels
- great herds of all kinds of animals
- timbers which were extremely valuable in an almost treeless Egypt.

On the Barkal Stela, Thutmose III declared:

> Every year there is hewed [for me in] Djahi genuine cedar of Lebanon which is brought to the court ... without passing over the seasons thereof, each and every year. When my army, which is in garrison in Ullaza comes [they bring the tribute] which is the cedar of my majesty's victories. I have not given [any] of it to the Asiatics, for it is the wood that [Amun-Re] loves.[35]

Trade

Crete (Keftiu)

In the records, the Egyptian pharaohs claimed to have control over all foreign countries. To maintain this fiction, all trade goods arriving in Egypt were shown as tribute from foreign rulers. For example, in the tomb chapel of Menkheperresonb, High Priest of Amun during the reign of Thutmose III, Syrians and Cretans were described as tribute-bearers when in fact they were traders. From other sources it appears that the Cretans often used Syrians as middlemen in their trading negotiations.

Punt

What often appears on tomb walls as tribute from Nubia was in fact part of the regular trade between Egypt and tropical Africa. Although the Egyptians made contact with the land of Punt during the Old Kingdom, it was not until the reign of Hatshepsut that there is evidence of a major trading expedition. Punt was never under Egyptian control and yet goods brought back from that country were referred to as tribute to Hatshepsut.

Gifts from brother kings

The great kings of Babylon, Naharin, Hatti and Assyria communicated regularly with the kings of Egypt and accompanied their letters with valuable gifts.

Treaties between the Egyptian kings and these rulers were often cemented by royal marriages for which enormous dowries were paid to the pharaoh. Following the treaty between Ramesses II and Hattusil of the Hittites:

Men from tropical Africa with goods to present to the pharaoh, from the tomb of Sobekhotep. For ease of transport the gold has been cast into rings

Keftiu traders (from Crete) with copper ingots, a conical cup, a gold vase and a leather-sheathed dagger, from the tomb of Mekheperresonb

> He (the Hittite King) caused his eldest daughter to be brought, with
> splendid *tribute* set before her, of gold, silver, much bronze, slaves,
> spans of horses without limit, and cattle, goats, rams by the myriad.
> [such were] the dues they brought for Ramesses II.[36]

Massive building programs

Each pharaoh of the New Kingdom initiated an ambitious building program aimed at honouring the gods, glorifying his or her (Hatshepsut)
own achievements and ensuring a continued existence in the hereafter.
The wealth that flowed into Egypt from its empire made this possible

Purpose of building program

Apart from the time, physical resources and human effort spent on the
construction of the royal tombs, most of the New Kingdom's vast wealth
was poured into the building, restoration and decoration of cult and
mortuary temples.

The cult temple was the *house* of a particular god or gods such as the
Temple of Amun-Re at Thebes and the Temple of Ptah at Memphis. It
was the place where the god lived and where priests or servants looked
after his or her daily needs which were similar to those of humans —
to be cleaned, provided with food and drink, to be clothed and to enjoy
a holiday.

Cult temple

Most Egyptian cities had a cult temple. The larger administrative and
religious centres had many. For example, at Thebes during the New
Kingdom, the huge complex of which the Temple of Amun-Re was the
centre, included several other temples — the Temple of Mut, Temple of
Montu, the Temple of Khonsu and the temple of Ptah. Several kilometres away at Luxor there was another great temple to Amun-Re, his wife
Mut and son Khonsu.

Mortuary temples were the places where the funerary rites of Egyptian
rulers were performed and where special groups of mortuary priests
provided for the continuing sustenance of the deceased. Usually the
New Kingdom mortuary temples were dedicated to Amun as well as to
the king and so they also played the part of a cult temple.

Mortuary temples

Originally these mortuary temples had been attached to the tombs of
the pharaohs but during the New Kingdom they were separated from
the royal burials, which were hidden away, in the Valley of the Kings.
Most of the enormous New Kingdom mortuary temples were built some
distance away on the flat plain closer to the Nile. Apart from the
Ramesseum of Ramesses II and the temple of Ramesses III at Medinet
Habu, very few of these have survived. Fortunately, the magnificent
mortuary temple of Hatshepsut, constructed at the base of the Theban
hills at Deir el-Bahri, is still standing.

Temple architecture

> With the New Kingdom the Egyptian temple comes of age ... The
> scale of temple building by individual kings can be regarded as an indi-
> cator of wealth and royal power during their reigns with high points
> under Amenhotep III and Ramesses II ...[37]

Size and materials

The temples built for the rulers of the New Kingdom were designed for impressiveness (height and bulk) and durability. These qualities are found in the remains of:

- the soaring temple pylons and obelisks (some as high as 27.5 metres and weighing 320 tonnes) erected at Karnak by Thutmose I, Hatshepsut and Thutmose III
- the gigantic hypostyle hall at Karnak, with its 134 columns, built by Seti I and Ramesses II
- the columned inner court of the Temple of Luxor (Amenhotep III)
- the 21-metre-high colossus of Memnon (all that remains of the mortuary temple of Amenhotep III)
- the huge rock-cut temple of Ramesses II at Abu Simbel with its four colossi, each 20 metres high
- the Ramesseum (the mortuary temple of Ramesses II), with its gigantic statues
- the massive temple/palace complex at Medinet Habu (Ramesses III).

The pharaohs lost no opportunity to emphasise the size of their monuments. On the temple walls and the shafts of the obelisks they declared, for example:

> ... its towers reach heaven and mingle with the stars.

> ... their height pierces to heaven.[38]

Use of stone

Unlike the temples of the earlier periods, those of the New Kingdom were built almost exclusively of stone, particularly of sandstone brought from Gebel es-Silsila near Aswan. This new development in building was recorded by Thutmose III at Karnak.

> Lo my majesty found this temple built of brick ... My Majesty ordered that the measuring cord be stretched anew over this temple, it being erected in sandstone.[39]

Brilliantly coloured

The use of stone enabled the pharaohs to decorate the walls and columns with carved and brilliantly painted scenes and hieroglyphs. These sandstone temples blazed with colour — blues, greens, yellows and reds.

Some idea of other raw materials used in these temples can be gauged from the inscriptions of Hatshepsut and Amenhotep III. Hatshepsut recorded that the doors of her mortuary temple at Deir el-Bahri were

Precious materials

made of black copper inlaid with electrum, the floors of the shrine to Amun were of gold and silver, the stairs leading to the shrine were of alabaster and the shrine itself was made from the finest Nubian ebony.

The Temple of Luxor, built by Amenhotep, was:

> ... of fine white sandstone, made very wide and large and its beauty increased. Its walls are of electrum, its floor is of silver, all the portals are wrought with [gold].[40]

Amenhotep's pylon at Karnak was:

> ... a very great portal ... wrought with gold throughout. The Divine Shadow, in the shape of a ram, is inlaid with real lapis lazuli wrought with gold and many precious stones ... Its floor is adorned with silver, towers are over against it. Stelae of lapis lazuli are set up, one on each side. Its pylons reach heaven like the four pillars of heaven, its flagstaffs shine more than the heavens, wrought with electrum.[41]

The enormous mortuary temple of Amenhotep, which was dedicated to Amun also, 'was an everlasting fortress of fine, white sandstone, wrought with gold throughout'. Its floors were of silver, its doors of electrum and it was filled with numerous statues 'of elephantine granite, of costly gritstone' and 'of every splendid, costly stone'.[42]

Temple layout

A major development in cult temple design during the New Kingdom was the adoption of a standard plan, comprising:

Standard temple plan

- a massive pylon gateway which was used as a billboard for royal propaganda'[43]

- a large open colonnaded courtyard to which there was limited access to the public during important festivals

- a hypostyle hall of numerous columns which acted as a screen for the innermost part of the temple

- the barque sanctuary where the image of the god was kept and there were storerooms for cult equipment

- a sacred lake close to the houses of the priests, the storehouses and the area where the god's food was prepared.

20 m

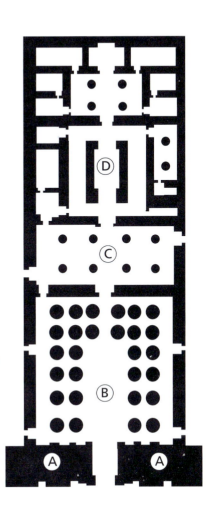

Ⓐ Pylon gateway

Ⓑ Colonnaded courtyard

Ⓒ Hypostyle hall

Ⓓ Barque sanctuary

The plan of the temple of Khonsu

Multiple elements at Karnak

Often it is difficult to see this standard plan in the remains of the New Kingdom temples because pharaohs repeated this design by adding another courtyard or pylon in front of the existing ones. The temple of Amun at Karnak is an example of multiple elements. For example, it has numerous pylons or entrance gateways.

Although New Kingdom mortuary temples were similar in design to cult temples, they were often quite different at the rear. Instead of a single sanctuary there were often suites of rooms dedicated to Osiris, god of the Underworld and Re, the sun god, both of whom were associated with the afterlife. Also, a central apartment was usually dedicated to Amun with another chapel to the king and his or her royal ancestors.

Above: The resting place of the divine barque.

Right: Temple pylons

There were some exceptions to the standard New Kingdom plan. For example, the mortuary temple of Hatshepsut at Deir el-Bahri; the Great Aten Temple at Akhetaten built by Akhenaten, the Cenotaph Temple of Osiris at Abydos started by Seti I and completed by Ramesses II, and the rock-cut temples at Abu Simbel built by Ramesses II as part of the royal cult of the king.

Processional ways

Another important feature in the design of temple complexes — the processional way — was introduced during the New Kingdom. The Egyptians celebrated numerous religious festivals during the year (54 in the reign of Thutmose III). During these celebrations the gods visited neighbouring temples. Processional ways were constructed along the route of these divine *visits.*

Great attention was paid to the construction of processional ways. They were generally paved with stone and lined on both sides with ram or human-headed sphinxes. At frequent intervals along the avenue were small shrines with stone pedestals for resting the god's barque. These *rest houses* also gave the priests, carrying the barque on their shoulders, a breathing space.

The two most important festivals held in Thebes, the Opet and Valley festivals, started from the Temple of Amun at Karnak. At these times Amun visited Luxor Temple (Opet) and the mortuary temples of the pharaohs on the west bank (Valley).

The diagram below shows the processional ways built from the Temple of Amun at Karnak.

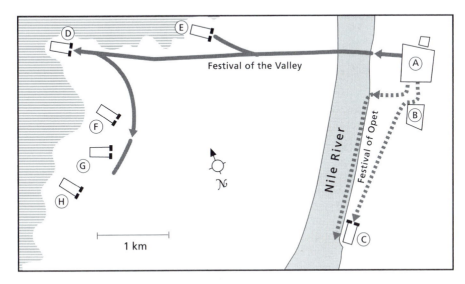

Ⓐ	The Temple of Amun at Karnak	Ⓕ	The Ramesseum – Mortuary Temple of Ramesses II
Ⓑ	Enclosure of the temple of the godess Mut	Ⓖ	Mortuary Temple of Amenhotep III
Ⓒ	Luxor Temple	Ⓗ	Medinet Habu – Mortuary Temple of Ramesses III
Ⓓ	The Mortuary Temple of Hatshepsut at Deir el-Bahri		
Ⓔ	The Mortuary Temple of Seti I		High desert

The main processional ways during the New Kingdom

Part of a processional avenue with ram-headed sphinxes

Temple symbolism

Mansion of the gods

The Egyptians believed that the temple was not only the *house* or *mansion* of the god but symbolised the conditions that existed at the time of creation.

The temple as a house

**Symbolism of
the First Time**

Like domestic houses, temples were built with entries (pylon and forecourt), reception areas (hypostyle halls), storerooms (side rooms for the god's treasures and possessions such as clothing and insignia), areas for the preparation of food (bakeries, breweries and butchery), areas for washing and purification (wells and sacred lakes), and living and sleeping rooms (the god's inner sanctuary).

The temple as the island of creation

According to the various Egyptian myths, at the time of creation an island or primeval mound emerged from the waters of chaos which covered the earth. On the highest part of this mound the first god appeared and built a sanctuary of reeds.

Every Egyptian temple was believed to represent this original island of creation and its layout and architectural features replicated in stone the physical features of the island and the original reed sanctuary. By building all their temples in this way, the Egyptians believed that the right order of things, established at the beginning, would continue forever.

- The enclosure wall of the temple was built with alternating convex and concave courses to produce a wavy impression which symbolised the waters that surrounded the island of creation.
- The pylon which formed the gateway to the temple represented the towers of woven reeds which guarded the entrance to the first sanctuary. It also provided a barrier to the chaos outside.
- The hypostyle hall was composed of an enormous number of columns, far in excess of the number needed to support the roof. These columns, with their capitals in the shape of papyrus reeds, lotus buds and palms were meant to represent the lush vegetation on the island of creation. At the bases of the columns other forms of vegetation and animal life such as frogs and grasshoppers, were carved into the stone. The decoration of the columns also featured the bindings which held together the original bundles of reeds of the Predynastic sanctuary.
- The ceilings of the temple halls and rooms were decorated to represent the sky above the mound — golden stars on a blue background.
- The god's sanctuary at the far end of the temple was always built higher than all other parts of the temple in an attempt to reproduce the primeval mound with its reed sanctuary on top. This change in floor level was achieved by selecting a site with a gradual incline or by building a series of pavements at different heights.

The ceilings of the halls and courts became progressively lower until reaching the small, unlit sanctuary which retained the shape of the earliest reed shrines.

The combined effect of the rising floor level, lower ceilings and increasing gloom created a sense of mystery.

- The darkness of the sanctuary was symbolic of the darkness out of which the mound and the creator god emerged.

- The sacred lake symbolised the primordial waters of Nun out of which the Egyptians believed the world was originally created.

The temples were also aligned east-west or vice versa so that the sun, rising or setting between the twin pylons made the hieroglyph for *horizon* and also shone along the axis of the temple to the sanctuary.

The base of a temple column featuring the vegetation of the primeval marshes.

The wavy brick enclosure wall symbolising the waters that surrounded the original island of creation

Other New Kingdom building projects

Despite their overriding concern for projects dedicated to the gods, particularly the imperial god, Amun, and to life in the hereafter, New Kingdom rulers were responsible for a number of civic and military building projects. Unfortunately, the evidence for many of these is very scanty.

Refer to the chapters on each of these pharaohs for further information about their building programs.

The architects

Once a pharaoh decided on a particular building project, he or she appointed an official to be in charge of architecture. The evidence suggests that the man chosen was not an architect by profession although he would have been from the educated elite.

From educated elite

A New Kingdom copy (the Berlin Leather Roll) of a Middle Kingdom text outlines the appointment of an anonymous architect.

> The Royal Seal-bearer, Sole Companion, Overseer of the Two Gold Houses and the Two Silver Houses, a Privy Councillor of the Two Diadems: It is your counsel that carries out all the works that my majesty desires to bring about. You are the one in charge of them, who will act according to my wish ... Order the workmen to do according to your design.[44]

Overseers of all the king's work

In this example the architect is not given a title which specifically mentions building. However, in most cases, the men associated with the major buildings of the New Kingdom had as one of their many titles — *overseer of works* or *overseer of all the works of the king*. Their other titles indicate that they held influential positions at court or within the religious and civil bureaucracies.

Ineni, whose career spanned the reigns of kings from Amenhotep I to Thutmose III, is best remembered as the architect of the alterations made to Karnak Temple by Thutmose I and the construction of the king's tomb in the Valley of the Kings. Although he appears to have been responsible for the new trends in architecture, his principal function was as an administrator of the vast grain supplies of Amun.

The construction of Hatshepsut's magnificent temple at Dei el-Bahri was, at various stages, under the supervision of:

- Hapusoneb — vizier, high priest of Amun and overseer of all the priests of Upper and Lower Egypt.
- Senenmut — steward of Amun, steward of the king
- Thuty — treasurer
- Dewa-enheh — first herald
- Puy-en-Re — second prophet of Amun
- Tety-em-Re — scribe.

All of these men, in addition to their other duties, functioned as Hatshepsut's *overseer of works* or *overseer of all the works of the king* (architect).

Sobk-mose, one of Amenhotep III's architects, was the king's treasurer as well as *overseer of works (in) southern Opet* (Luxor). Three of Ramesses' architects — Bakenkhons, Iuny and Aebsed (held the positions of high priest of Amun, viceroy of Nubia and first king's cup bearer respectively.

Judged on their ability as a good official

These men were judged and appointed, not on their ability as architects, but as good officials. They organised building projects in the same way they organised quarrying expeditions and irrigation works. They employed surveyors who measured and laid out the site, draughtsmen who drew up the plans and builders who supervised teams of masons, sculptors and artists, as well as gangs of unskilled workers.

There were obviously men of genius among these so-called architects but they were generally not free to create. They followed the will of the king who in turn interpreted tradition.

The increased demand for artists and craftsmen

During the New Kingdom there was an ever-increasing need for highly trained artists and craftsmen with the skill and imagination to meet the demands of the kings as they initiated their massive building projects, dedicated ever more luxury items to the gods and filled their tombs with the finest funerary objects. The upper classes also became more demanding, as their tastes became more sophisticated, their lifestyles more opulent and their tombs more elaborate. There was also a need for craftsmen to meet the needs of the king's armies for equipment such as chariots and weapons.

Demand for luxury items

Most of the skilled craftsmen and artists were employed by the pharaoh or the temples. Some were employed in the workshops on the estates of the nobles. Those who worked on the excavation, carving and painting of the royal tombs in the Valley of the Kings and the Valley of the Queens were a special group. They and their families lived apart from others in the workers' town of Deir el-Medina near the royal necropolis.

Employment

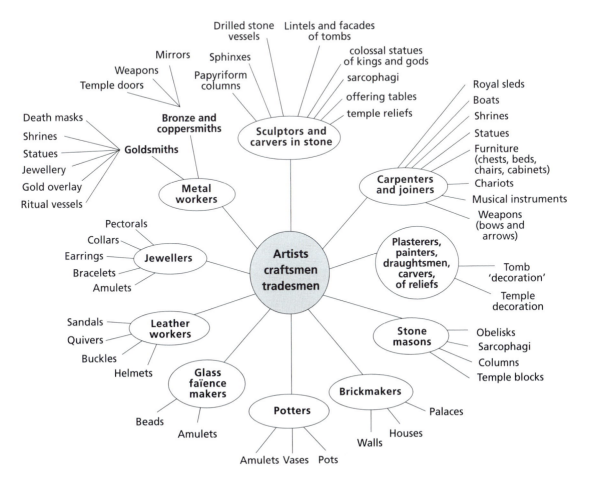

The range of skilled craftsmen and unskilled workers employed in the temple workshops and on the large estates

Evidence of skill

The items found in the tomb of Tutankhamun and pictured on the walls of the Theban tombs of the nobles illustrate the beauty and technical excellence achieved by these New Kingdom artists and craftsmen. The working and living conditions of these workers are discussed in Chapter 16.

Foreign influences

As the pharaohs' armies moved south as far as the Fourth Cataract and north-east to the Euphrates, Egypt's former superior isolationism came to an end.

Exposure to foreign goods and lifestyles

The Egyptians were exposed to foreign products, lifestyles, gods and values as administrators and garrisons took up residence in conquered territory and as envoys moved constantly between the major cities. Egyptian and foreign ships sailed between the Nile Delta and the coasts of Phoenicia and the Aegean, and thousands of foreigners, either voluntarily or by force, settled in Egypt.

Foreigners in Egypt

During the New Kingdom, there were many foreigners living permanently in Egypt. The majority of these were from Palestine and Syria. Many had been brought to the Nile Valley as hostages, war captives or slaves. The records from the reign of Amenhotep II show that in his ninth year alone he brought back over 90 000 captives.

Voluntary and involuntary residents

Some had moved to Egypt voluntarily to engage in trade or crafts and took up residence in the larger cities like Memphis where there was a substantial foreign quarter adjacent to the port. Towards the end of the Nineteenth Dynasty, others moved into Egypt as a result of the pressure on their own lands from the *Sea Peoples*.

The royal harems

As the pharaohs' influence and control spread beyond the borders of Egypt, the number of foreign princesses and concubines entering their harems increased.

Foreign queens and concubines

Although some of these women were given to the pharaoh by Syrian rulers and chieftains as a sign of submission, others were used as diplomatic pawns to seal alliances between the pharaoh and the great kings of Naharin (kingdom of the Mittani), Hatti (kingdom of the Hittites) and Babylon. For example:

- Three of the wives of Thutmose III — Menway, Mertit and Menhet — appear to have come from Palestine or Syria. An inscription from year 24 of Thutmose's reign listed 'the daughter of a chief' among the tribute from Retjenu.
- Thutmose IV married the daughter of the Mitannian king, Artatama, as a sign of peace between the two peoples.

- Amenhotep III continued the alliance by marrying the daughters of two more Mitannian kings — Gilukhepa, the daughter of King Shuttarna and Tadukhepa, the daughter of King Tushratta. He also married the daughters of successive Babylonians kings — Kurigalzu II and Kadashman Enlil I, as well as a princess from Anatolia.

- Ahkenaten married the Mitannian princess, Tadukhepa, who had been sent to Egypt to marry his father, as well as a Babylonian princess.

- Ramesses II married several foreign princesses but the most noteworthy was the daughter of the Hittite king, Hattusilis. This marriage in year 34 of Ramesses' reign celebrated the stability of the alliance between Hatti and Egypt which had been signed in year 21.

Although Egyptian kings accepted, as wives, the daughters of their 'brother' kings, they did not offer their own daughters in return.

Despite the number of foreign wives in the households and harems of the pharaohs, it appears that none, except for the daughter of the Hittite king, who married Ramesses II, was ever given the honour of *king's great wife* or *king's principal wife*.

Employment of foreigners

Some captive foreigners were put to work as slaves or servants in the Sinai turquoise mines, on the vast estates of the nobles and on the lands belonging to the temples. A group of prisoners of war, captured by Thutmose IV, was presented by him to the priests who were to maintain his mortuary temple. Foreigners were also employed in the households of the nobles and within the harems of the royal family.

Places of employment

Household slaves had opportunities to make themselves indispensable to their masters. Some rose to high positions, a few even reaching the position of butler and chamberlain in the royal households.

Households

Foreigners also joined the army. It became increasingly necessary for the Egyptians to rely on mercenaries to man their armies because lower class Egyptians regarded the army as an undesirable career. Also, many drivers in the Egyptian chariotry divisions were of Asiatic descent. Those who had entered Egypt as captives saw the army as a way to advance their position in society. The soldiers in Akhenaten's bodyguard were mainly Libyan and Nubian while Ramesses employed men from the ranks of the Shardana to protect him. Others, like the Medjay (desert Nubians) were used as police.

Army

At the beginning of the New Kingdom the official class was almost entirely Egyptian but increasingly, reliable foreigners, usually Asiatics, worked their way into important posts in the government. These Asiatics were from urban cultures and many were familiar with the way bureaucratic scribal government worked.

Bureaucracy

Foreign impact on religion, lifestyle and art

Religion

Far-reaching influence of Amun-Re

Amun-Re and other Egyptian gods, particularly those associated with the cosmic forces (eg, sun and air), were elevated to universal gods who were believed to have concern for people beyond the Nile Valley. Sanctuaries and temples were built to these gods in Syria and Palestine.

Foreign deities accepted

Foreigners to Egypt brought their own gods with them. The Syrians and Palestinians worshipped Baal, Astarte, Anath, Baalat and Qedesh. Towards the end of the Eighteenth Dynasty, Baal and Astarte (worshipped in Egypt as a goddess of healing) had their own priesthoods.

Egyptians resident in Asia not only paid respect to the local deities but some went so far as to address their mortuary prayers (recorded on stelae) to them.

This interchange of deities was achieved by identifying certain Asiatic gods with particular Egyptian gods — Hathor with Baalat, Seth and Montu with Baal or Teshub (a Hittite god) and Re with Shamash. These Asiatic gods also entered the literature of the period and some Egyptians even incorporated them into their names; for example, Baal-khepeshef.

Daily life

Domestic architecture

Some aspects of Egyptian domestic architecture were influenced by foreign styles. One of the houses excavated at Tell el-Amarna did not have its external staircase supported by a blank wall, which was typical of Egyptian architecture. Instead, it was supported by a square pier, common in Cretan houses. Its gardens also were laid out in the more informal random way of the Aegean societies.

Fashion

As riches poured in from the lands to the north-east, the Egyptians developed a more luxurious lifestyle. Fashions in dress changed from the simple styles of earlier times. The plain shift was replaced with pleated robes, wigs became larger and elaborately coiffed, and the decorated earrings fashionable in Asia were worn by upper-class women.

Music

New varieties of musical instruments (long-necked lutes, oboes and tambourines) and forms of dance were also introduced from the lands to the east, possibly by women like the 270 *entertainers* captured by Amenhotep II during his Syrian campaign.

Art

Influence of foreign craftsmanship

The enormous amount of booty and tribute which came from Palestine and Syria revealed a high quality of craftsmanship. These foreign items had a great influence on Egyptian art. Aspects of Babylonian and Aegean art were also adopted by the Egyptians.

There was a greater use of bronze and silver (not found in Egypt) in works of art and the more natural and lively feeling expressed in Egyptian art from the time of Thutmose IV and Amenhotep III, which owed much to foreign influence. Wilson, in *The Culture of Ancient Egypt*, believes that the exaggerated naturalism of the Amarna Period had already appeared about 40 years previously and was due to foreign influences.

In the century that followed the reigns of Hatshepsut and Thutmose III there were more changes in artistic forms than there had been in the preceding thousand years.

> ... the methods of presentation began to throw off the shackles of old tradition and to move in new directions ... strange ornamentation was imitated and foreign forms were adopted, so that the rich Egyptian treasury of patterns was greatly enhanced by accretions from without.[45]

Changes in the structure and size of government

After the expulsion of the Hyksos and the reunification of the country into one kingdom, there was a need to restructure the administration. More changes occurred as Egypt gained and organised its empire. For example, the civil, military and religious bureaucracies developed extensive hierarchies as the demand for officials at all levels increased. Within this reorganised administration there was much that was traditional[46] as well as some features that were new.

Development of extensive bureaucracies

The administration and the king

At the head of this vast administration was the god-king 'by whose guidance men live'.[47] As a god, the king was totally responsible for the welfare of his people and was expected to maintain the order of things that had been established at the time of creation. As well as defending his people, his divine responsibilities involved:

- performing sacred rituals in all the temples of the land. On the walls of temples both inside and outside of Egypt the king was shown making offerings to the gods, being blessed by them, taking part in all the great religious festivals and personally conducting foundation and dedication ceremonies.

- upholding rightness and dispensing justice (*ma'at*) by *creative utterance* and understanding. The court eulogists of the New Kingdom never ceased to praise each pharaoh for his divine wisdom. The following extract was written in praise of Thutmose III:

> Every speech of thy mouth is like the words of Harakhti; thy tongue is a balance: more accurate are thy lips than the tongue of the balance of Thoth. What is there that thou dost not know? Who is there that is as wise as thou? What place is there which thou hast not seen. ... Authority is in thy mouth and perception is in thy heart; the activity of thy tongue is the Temple of Ma'at (goddess of Truth) ... All is done according to thy will, and whatever thou sayest is obeyed...[48]

- sustaining life by controlling the waters of the Nile, thus ensuring the fertility of the soil and the prosperity of the country. 'He is one who makes the Two Lands more green than a high Nile. He has filled the Two Lands with strength and life.'[49]

During the New Kingdom, as in all previous periods, the connection between the king and the provision of water was stressed. For example:

- Of Thutmose III it was said, 'if thou sayest to the waters, "Come upon the mountain" a flood floweth directly at thy word for thou art Re'.[50]
- Seti I supposedly divined water in the eastern deserts. 'He drew water from the mountains far away from the people.'[51]
- Ramesses II was regarded as being able to make it rain as far away as the Land of Hatti.

Support of a select band of officials

No matter what divine powers the king was believed to possess, in practice he relied on the support and cooperation of others to run the country. He appointed a body of competent and dedicated officials to whom he delegated authority and made known his wishes.

Government in Egypt was by royal decree, the system of administration was the sum of these decrees.[52]

Refer to Chapter 16 for more details on the role and daily life of the pharaoh.

The king's men

Hierarchical administration

A small group of powerful officials, reporting directly to the king, maintained control of the four major divisions of the administration of Egypt — the civil government, the religious government, the administration of the army and navy and the royal domains (the court and the royal estates).

Official titles

Responsible to each of these heads of department were deputies and officials of high status who in turn were supported by vast bureaucracies of minor officials, scribes, priests, police, mayors, village chiefs and so on. These men, most of whom were buried in the Theban necropolis, had some of the following titles:

- *vizier of Upper Egypt*
- *overseer of the treasury*
- *viceroy of Kush*
- *overseer of works*
- *overseer of the granaries of Upper and Lower Egypt*
- *overseer of the treasury*
- *overseer of cattle*
- *first, second and third prophets of Amun*
- *great commander of soldiers*
- *chief steward of the king*
- *overseer of the granary of Amun*
- *overseer of the royal harem*

- *scribe of the pharaoh's fields*
- *scribe of recruits*
- *harbour master in the southern city.*

Many of them also had the title of *royal scribe*.

Every part of the administration was hierarchical, which meant that each official was answerable to someone above him and responsible for someone below him.

Although it was possible for a man of reasonably humble background to rise to the top of the bureaucracy and to gain a position of influence with the pharaoh, there were considerable barriers to this promotion.

Barriers to promotion

Literacy was the essential requirement for any position of responsibility and the number of high positions available at any one time was reduced by the practice of giving some officials a number of important roles. For example, Hapusoneb held the positions of vizier of Upper Egypt and high priest of Amun during the reign of Hatshepsut. Treasurers were often also overseers of all the works of the king. There was a tendency for positions of importance to be monopolised by a small, elite group.

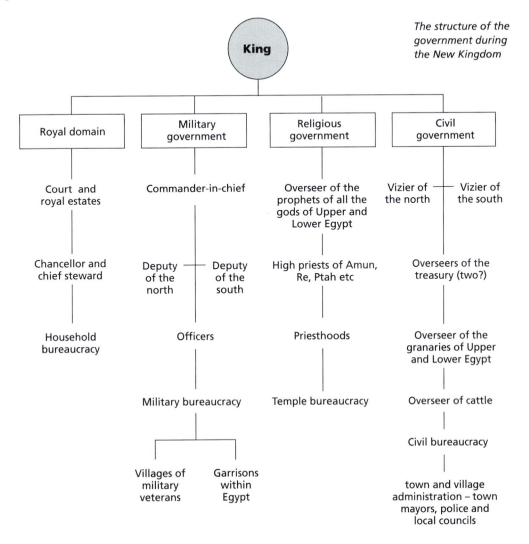

The structure of the government during the New Kingdom

Hapusoneb had been preceded in the job of high priest of Amun by his grandfather and great-grandfather. Rekhmire, Vizier of Upper Egypt under Thutmose III, followed his uncle and grandfather in that office.

There are many other examples of high administrative positions being held by members of the same family for generations.

Top jobs

The most powerful officials in the administration were the viziers of Upper and Lower Egypt, king's son of Kush (viceroy of Nubia), overseer of the treasury, high priest of Amun and commander-in-chief of the army, the latter being held by either the king or crown prince.

The vizier

The vizier was the most important of all the pharaoh's officials. He headed the vast bureaucracy necessary to govern Egypt efficiently during the New Kingdom. Those appointed to the position of vizier during the New Kingdom had to be men of great ability since the office of vizier was 'the pillar of the whole land'.[53]

By Eighteenth Dynasty there were two viziers

Originally there was only one chief minister but by the time of the Eighteenth Dynasty there seem to have been two viziers — the *southern vizier* who governed from Thebes and the *northern vizier* who governed from Memphis. Although very little evidence is available about the affairs of the northern viziers, the documentary and pictorial evidence for the duties and responsibilities of the Theban viziers is quite extensive.

Pre-eminence of southern vizier

It appears that during most of the New Kingdom the position of the southern vizier was superior to that of his colleague in the north, since Thebes was the religious capital (the centre of the worship of the imperial god, Amun, and the site of the royal necropolis).

One of the best known of the southern viziers was Rekhmire, who served both Thutmose III and Amenhotep II. Although Rekhmire was supported by a vast bureaucracy of scribal officials, his job was the most demanding in the country. He described himself as the king's 'very own skipper who knew no sleep by night as by day'.[54]

Since the time of the Old Kingdom, the behaviour expected of viziers and other officials had been outlined in tomb inscriptions (eg, the *Instructions of Ptahotep*). During the Eighteenth and Nineteenth dynasties a text known as the *Installation of the Vizier* was found carved in the tomb chapels of a number of notable viziers of the Theban area. The best known is from the tomb of Rekhmire. A part of the text was found also in the tomb of the vizier, Paser, who served under Seti I and Ramesses II.

These texts, which were associated with the ceremonial appointment of a vizier, were divided into two parts:

1 advice from the king

2 a survey of the vizier's duties.

The installation of the vizier, from the tomb of Rekhmire

Advice from the king

Thutmose III was aware of just how difficult the job was when he addressed the incoming vizier with the words:

> As to the vizierate, it is not sweet, indeed but it is bitter as gall. For the vizier is hard copper enclosing the gold of his master's house.[55]

Role as chief judge

The king outlined the code of behaviour which he expected his highest official to follow. Although it is unlikely that all officials acted according to the principles laid down, it seems that the ideas of justice, charity, understanding and kindliness were fairly generally accepted.

The king instructed his vizier, in his role as chief judge in all civil cases, to accept all petitioners and to do everything to allow a man to plead his innocence. There should not have been any cause for anyone to complain that the vizier prevented them from pleading their case or that he was biased. Everyone could expect to be treated equally, 'the man you know and the man you do not know',[56] 'whether he be mayor or district governor or common person'.[57]

The king further instructed his vizier to dismiss a petitioner only after considering everything he had to say. When the vizier finally decided to dismiss the petitioner he had to give his reasons for doing so, because the 'petitioner prefers the consideration of his utterance to the judgment on the matter about which he has come'.[58]

The incoming vizier was reminded that it was inappropriate for the vizier to 'lose his temper with a man improperly'[59] and that he should not act according to his own wishes 'in matters about which the law is known'.[60] Finally, the king stressed that when making judgments, the vizier should take into account the records of other cases preserved in the archives or 'hall with records of all judgments'.[61]

Duties of the vizier

The text in the tomb of Rekhmire not only gives details on the duties of a vizier but the way he should dress, who should attend him and how he should present himself when making judgments. Although the list of duties seems extensive, the text does not cover all the activities supervised by the vizier. Tomb paintings, which illustrate other activities supervised by Rekhmire, are used to supplement the text.

The vizier was in total control of the civil administration. He:

Extensive list of duties

- maintained law and order in civil cases and presided over the highest court of justice in the land
- supervised the king's residence
- assessed and collected taxes
- appointed and supervised officials

- received tribute and met deputations from foreign countries
- supervised the vast temple workshops and the estates of the capital
- controlled all public works
- supervised the royal necropolis
- controlled the movement of all traffic up and down the Nile
- maintained all records and control of the archives
- equipped ships and despatched agents when the king was on campaign.

Daily reports to king

Every day when the king was in residence, the vizier presented himself to get his orders and to report on the state of the country. He then met with the *overseer of the treasury* who informed him that all matters were 'in a good state and prosperous'.[62] Once the treasurer reported that all the strongrooms had been sealed and re-opened at the correct hour, the vizier sent someone to open all the doors of the palace. He was kept informed of everything that was taken in and out of the palace.

Much of the vizier's time was spent in his audience hall making judgments on a large range of issues. He could be called upon to make a ruling on a tax question, a dispute over a property boundary or contract, an accusation against an official, 'a case over any deficiency of divine offerings' or 'anyone who plunders a nome'.[63]

Despatches

He had to read reports from district assessors and administrators, from his agents on the state of the delta and northern fortresses, and from stewards on the condition of the royal estates. Although he sent frequent despatches to his agents in the provinces, he often made personal tours of inspection to check the granaries and the state of the country's water resources and irrigation works. 'It is he who should examine water supplies on the first day of every ten-day period.'[64]

Vizier and the Temple of Amun

The vizier held regular meetings with the officials in charge of public works, particularly those involved in the construction of the royal tomb. It was the vizier's responsibility, for example, to make sure that the workmen from Deir el-Medina, who were employed on building and decorating the royal tombs, were kept supplied with equipment and rations. The foremen of the work gangs reported directly to the vizier.

The vizier also visited the workshops attached to the Temple of Amun, where skilled craftsmen manufactured equipment for the palace and the king's tomb. On a visit to these temple workshops, Rekhmire is described as 'seeing all the crafts and letting every man know his responsibilities in the execution of every occupation'.[65]

The scenes in Rekhmire's tomb also show him 'receiving tribute from the foreign southern land, together with the tribute of Punt, the tribute of Retjenu, the tribute of Keftiu together with the plunder of all foreign lands'.[66]

A New Kingdom vizier shouldered enormous responsibilities. Fortunately, he was supported by officials such as the *overseer of the treasury*, the *overseer of the granaries of Upper and Lower Egypt, the chief steward* and the *overseer of works*, each one of whom was at the top of a hierarchy of lesser officials.

Refer to Question 9 at the end of this chapter for more of the text of the *Installation of the Vizier*. Scenes from the tomb of Rekhmire are found in Chapter 16.

The viceroy of Kush

This important official had great independence since he controlled the lands from Elkab in Upper Egypt to the southern frontier of the empire (which at the time of Thutmose III was near Napata). He was responsible for:

Responsibilities

- the protection of his province from internal uprisings and external threats
- the construction of temples, fortresses, canals and storehouses
- the administration of justice
- the delivery of all payments (taxes and tribute) from his province at the right time. Gold, cattle, female slaves, ebony, ivory and other exotic goods were shipped to Thebes and often presented to the king by the viceroy in person.

The wall paintings in the tomb of Huy, the viceroy of Kush at the time of Tutankhamun, provide a detailed account of his administration in the provinces of Kush and Wawat (Nubia).

The investiture of Huy, Viceroy of Kush during the reign of Tutankhamun

Prior to his appointment as viceroy, Huy had held the following positions — *scribe of the correspondence* in the service of a previous viceroy of Kush (Merimose), *sovereign's messenger in all foreign lands, divine father* and *fan-bearer on the king's right, superintendent of Amun's cattle in the Land of Kush* and *superintendent of the lands of gold of the Lord of the Two Countries*. So, as well as holding a position of great prestige and power at court, he had diplomatic experience and a wide knowledge of Nubia, its organisation and its particular problems.

Tutankhamun presided over Huy's elaborate investiture, during which he was handed the ring of office and possibly also the vizier's seal. Once invested he took ship for Nubia.

The ship used by Huy, Viceroy of Kush

Huy appears to have been an enterprising viceroy judging by the way he established stable government, subdued and captured rebels, exploited the resources of Nubia and collected the exotic products of the Sudan and central Africa for his king.

The procession of ships laden with tribute, rebel captives and princely Nubian hostages down river to Thebes and the presentation of this rich tribute to the king are all recorded on the walls of Huy's tomb. Some of these scenes are reproduced in the section on tribute and at the end of this chapter.

The overseer of the treasury

Responsibility for finances

The man who held this position looked after all aspects of the economy. This was particularly difficult since Egyptian business was carried on by the system of barter. The treasurer was directly responsible for:

- the calculation of taxes (based on the height of the inundation, the yearly agricultural yield and the wage structure)
- the amount to be paid to workers on the royal estates
- the economic affairs of the temples (which owned the largest amount of land throughout Egypt, after the king)
- payments to the army
- the distribution of tribute paid from foreign princes and plunder collected during military campaigns.

All payments were collected and distributed in kind (goods of one form or another). Peasants paid a proportion of their crops as tax while craftsmen paid their tax in the form of a piece of handiwork. The royal storehouses were filled with an assortment of objects and products including perishable food items which had to be distributed as soon as possible after collection.

The number of people working for the treasury was extremely large as were the number of documents and records which had to be kept. The Egyptians were conscientious in keeping the details of exactly how much and what type of payment was received, from whom it was collected, when it came in and how it was used.

First prophet of Amun, and the priesthood

Like the civil administration, the religious establishment was hierarchical. During the New Kingdom, the high priest or first prophet of Amun was *overseer of prophets of all the gods of Upper and Lower Egypt*. The man appointed to this position by the king, usually had a high profile career at court or in the civil bureaucracy. This was a political appointment. Refer to the section titled 'The ascendancy of Amun and the influence of his priesthood' earlier in this chapter for more details about the priesthood of Amun.

The highest ranking priests (first, second, third and fourth prophets) held their positions permanently while those lower on the scale served in the temple on a part-time basis. All priests came from the educated elite and many of them were appointed to a priestly position previously held by one of their close relatives.

Extensive record-keeping necessary

The part-time priests, lived for three months of the year in the temple and for the remaining nine months carried on with their ordinary life. Some of them specialised in liturgy, medicine, law, mathematics, geometry, astronomy and astrology and so on. 'Religious beliefs and practices permeated every aspect of life in ancient Egypt.'[67]

Not only did they attend to the needs of the gods, but because the temples were centres of higher learning, they taught the knowledge and skills associated with their professions. Any boy wishing to enter the religious or civil bureaucracy attended a temple school from about the age of 14. Much of this learning probably occurred in the *house of life* where scholarly books were stored and sacred writing was carried out.

The temples as centres of education

While in the service of the temple, priests had to maintain ritual *purity*. They did this by bathing in a sacred lake several times a day, shaving their heads and bodies daily, giving up sexual intercourse and wearing only the finest linen garments.

When taking part in any one of the numerous rituals they wore a variety of garments, wigs, pectorals and masks. There appears to have been a fairly standardised daily ritual performed in the cult temples throughout Egypt. These ceremonies, depicted on the walls of the temples, show the god-king, as the representative of every Egyptian, performing rituals associated with both Re and Osiris.

Daily temple ritual

The daily ritual comprised two services, both of which focussed on the pharaoh or the high priest who deputised for him. The pharaoh could not perform these rituals in every cult temple throughout Egypt, so the high priests acted as his proxy. The two services were:

1 the *rite of the house of the morning*
2 the daily service.

The *rite of the house of the morning*

As soon as the god-king arose each morning he was ritually bathed with water from the temple's sacred lake. This water symbolised the primordial waters of Nun out of which the Egyptians believed the world was originally created. With this water the pharaoh was *reborn* each morning.

Two priests, wearing the masks of the ibis-headed god Thoth and the falcon-headed god Horus, anointed the king with precious unguents, placed his robe on him and then presented him with the royal insignia. The priests then led him to the sanctuary where the statue of the god was enclosed.

The daily service

Once the king or high priest broke the seal of the sanctuary, he lay face down before the shrine and recited the hymn of morning worship to awaken the god. He then purified it, held it in his arms, fed it, rouged its cheeks and clothed it in fresh coloured robes and royal emblems. During each of these phases, ritual formulae were recited. After replacing the god's statue in the shrine and sealing the doors, the king or high priest walked backwards, removing his footprints with a palm leaf. At midday and in the evening, more food was laid before the god. After each of these rituals, the food was removed and divided up among the priests as part of their daily food allowance.

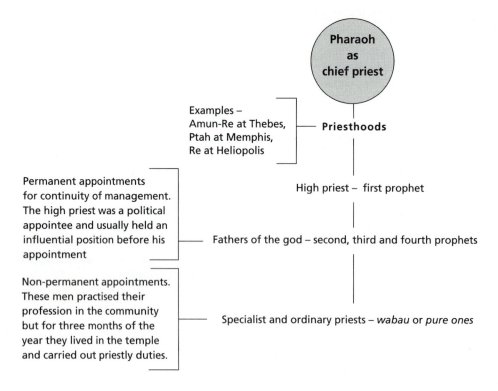

The hierarchy of priests

Specialist priests

The lector priest specialised in the knowledge of the sacred writings and was often skilled in magic. It was he who read or spoke the prayers and spells during festivals and funerals.

The *sem* priest, who was always depicted wearing a leopard-skin garment, was the chief funerary priest and conducted the rites at the entrance to the tomb.

Lector and sem-priests

The *overseer of the secrets of the place* was the senior priest in the *per-nefer* or *house of vitality*, where embalming was carried out. The chief embalmer was the *controller of the mysteries* and his assistant was referred to as *god's spell bearer*. These priests were identified with the great mortuary god, Anubis.

Embalming priests

Priest-doctors were often associated with the cult of a god of disease and healing. For example 'doctors could be priests of Sekhmet, goddess of disease and epidemics',[68] of Thoth, the god of scribes, who knew the healing formulae, or of Isis, who reassembled her husband's body when it had been mutilated.

These medical priests used a combination of religion (prayers and rituals), magic (spells and incantations) and knowledge of anatomy and drugs (hands-on treatment) for most illnesses or accidents. Medical papyri (the Edwin Smith and Ebers papyri) describe a variety of symptoms, diagnoses and treatments. An extract from the Edwin Smith Papyrus, which dealt with 48 types of injuries to the head, face, neck, chest and spine, is found at the end of Chapter 17.

Medical priests

Scribes

The extensive bureaucratic system depended on the services of scribes (those who could read and write the hieroglyphic and hieratic script). They were employed at all levels — in the palaces, in the temples, in all departments of the administration, in the army and by the nobles on their estates.

Vital role at all levels of society

Scribes regarded their profession as superior to most others. Their training gave them the opportunity to move up the official ladder and to occupy a place in society which gave them many advantages.

> Set your sight on being a scribe; a fine profession that suits you. You call for one; a thousand answer you. You stride freely on the road. You will not be like a hired ox. You are in front of others.[69]

Scribes were often able to avoid disagreeable duties. They were not subjected to hard physical labour, they were not conscripted for the army and it seems that they may have had special advantages with regard to taxation — 'There is no tax levied on him who works in writing; he has no levies (to settle)'.[70]

The men who reached the higher positions could expect to live a good life. One senior official, Nebmare-nakht, *Chief Overseer of the Cattle of Amun*, tried to impress this on his apprentice.

Rewards for a scribe

I instruct you ... to make you become one whom the king trusts; to make you gain entrance to treasury and granary. To make you receive the ship-load at the gate of the granary. To make you issue the offerings on feast days. You are dressed in fine clothes; you own horses. Your boat is on the river; you are supplied with attendants. You stride about inspecting. A mansion is built in your town. You have a powerful office, given you by the king. Male and female slaves are about you. Those who are in the fields grasp your hand, on plots that you have made. Look I make you into a staff of life! Put the writings in your heart, and you will be protected from all kinds of toil. You will become a worthy official.[71]

Promotions possible for a scribe

Some of the responsible and influential positions in the administration to which a scribe could aspire were:

- *scribe of the treasury*
- *scribe of recruits*
- *scribe of the granary*
- *scribe of pharaoh's despatches.*
- *scribe of the divine offerings of Amun*
- *scribe of the royal workmen*
- *scribe of pharaoh's fields*

Amenhotep, son of Hapu, as a young scribe

Two men who became influential and wealthy in the service of the pharaohs of the Eighteenth Dynasty were Menna, the *Scribe of Pharaoh's Fields* and Nebamun, *Scribe in the Granary of the Divine Offerings of Amun*. In their tombs at Thebes are some of the most beautiful and informative scenes yet found in New Kingdom tombs, showing them inspecting the royal and temple estates under their supervision. Both officials are shown arriving for the inspections in their fine chariots which they leave in the care of servants while they walk through the fields. Menna is depicted sitting on a stool under a canopy, inspecting his workmen while a servant offers him a cool drink. Other scribes attached to the estate are shown recording the amount of grain which has been harvested for tax purposes. Nebamun inspects cattle as they are paraded before him while one of the estate scribes is about to record the numbers and type of cattle and another conducts a goose census.

It appears from the following extracts that scribes who were employed as supervisors on the large estates were diligent in carrying out their master's work. Sometimes, however, they may have gone too far in exercising their authority.

I am carrying out every order given me by my lord with excellent attention and the hardness of copper. I shall not let my lord be dissatisfied with me.[72]

There is none among them (the workers) who will denounce me to my lord over rations or unguent. I am controlling them with excellent attention.[73]

Rewards for service

A scribe carrying out a goose census, from the tomb of Nebamun

The members of the Egyptian upper class held their official positions by the good grace of the pharaoh. Throughout their careers, their main aim was to gain and retain the pharaoh's esteem and to reap the rewards which he frequently gave to those who pleased him. These rewards could be in the form of promotions, estates in various parts of the country, captives from the pharaoh's successful military campaigns, the *gold of valour* or a site on which to build their tomb.

Officials' desire to gain esteem of the king

Pharaoh's rewards

The gold of valour was not a simple decoration, but valuable pieces of gold jewellery, sometimes in the form of collars, which were bestowed on officials in public ceremonies.

The evidence seems to show that the king allocated a site for each of his officials in a cemetery close to where the official carried out his duties. The size of the site and its location would depend on the official's rank. Occasionally the king went further and honoured his favourites by providing a significant part of their tomb (eg, lintels or sarcophagus) or with a complete tomb. This was the greatest honour that could be bestowed on an official.

The lifestyle of these officials is discussed in Chapter 16.

The official, Ay, being congratulated after receiving collars of gold and a pair of gloves from Akhenaten

Conclusion

The growth of the so-called Egyptian Empire of Nubia (Wawat and Kush) and Palestine/Syria was the work of a number of outstanding warrior pharaohs who led a new style Egyptian army. The tradition of the heroic warrior-king supported by the imperial god, Amun-Re was established in the early Eighteenth Dynasty and maintained throughout the New Kingdom period.

The valuable resources of Nubia and Asia which came to Egypt in the form of tribute, booty and trade satisfied the needs of various groups in Egyptian society for wealth, position and power. It was in the interest of these groups to make sure that the empire was maintained.

Chapter review

Increased size of civil service. New positions such as the viceroy of Kush

Attention focused on continual foreign perils

Increased use of mercenaries in Egyptian army

Army career offered chances for promotion

The growth of the tradition of pharaoh as a warrior-god

Military hierarchy and more officials in civil administration

Development of a permanent professional army

Military successes; pharaoh champion of his people

Amun elevated to status of an imperial god

Captives used in mines, quarries and the army

Changes in structure of government

Changed status of New Kingdom pharaohs and their queens

Foreigners employed in government

Amun, bringer of victory to his son, pharaoh

Captives employed on royal, temple and officials' estates

Changes in population structure

Effects of the empire on Egyptian society

The ascendancy of Amun and the prominance of his priesthood

Influence of Amun on the succession to the throne

Wider contacts led to adoption of new ideas and goods

Amun's priesthood received lion's share of booty and tribute

Educated foreigners found among the official class

Foreign influences in art, religion, fashion and entertainment

Influx of great wealth – booty, trade, tribute and gifts

Vast temple estates and captives to work them

Foreign gods – Baal, Astarte. More eroticism in art

Influence on decoration

Massive building program of Eighteenth and Nineteenth Dynasties

Opulence and luxury

Luxurious life-style of royalty and official class seen in their tombs

New temples to the gods built in Nubia and all over Egypt

Additions to Amun's cult temple at Karnak

Mortuary temples, tombs and palace complexes for kings

REVISION QUESTIONS AND ESSAY TOPICS

1 **The following extract, which refers to Ramesses II, comes from a monumental inscription carved into the walls of the temples of Abydos, Luxor, Karnak, Abu Simbel and the Ramesseum.**

His Majesty was a youthful lord,
Active and without his like;
His arms mighty, his heart stout,
His strength like Mont in his hour.
Of perfect form like Atum,
Hailed when his beauty is seen;
Victorious over all lands
Wily in launching a fight
Strong wall around his soldiers,
Their shield on the day of battle;
A bowman without his equal,
Who prevails over vast numbers.
Head on he charges a multitude,
His heart trusting his strength.
Stout-hearted in the hour of combat,
Like the flame when it consumes.
Firm-hearted like a bull ready for battle,
He heeds not all the lands combined;
A thousand men cannot withstand him,
A hundred thousand fail at his sight.
Lord of fear, great of fame,
In the hearts of all the lands;
Great of awe, rich in glory,
As is Seth upon his mountain;
[Casting fear] in foreigners' hearts
Like a wild lion in a valley of goats.
 ... Who saves his troops on battle day,
Greatly aids his charioteers;
Brings home his followers, rescues his soldiers,
With a heart that is like a mountain of copper.[74]

a What was the purpose of this monumental inscription?

b In what ways is this extract typical of royal inscriptions of the New Kingdom? Use examples from the extract to illustrate your answer.

c How were New Kingdom pharaohs shown pictorially in the monumental inscriptions to emphasise their warrior image?

2 **The extract below, on the poor conditions endured by Egyptian soldiers, comes from a papyrus entitled *A Schoolbook*. This was used by scribal teachers not only to urge their students to work hard at their studies but to praise the scribal profession at the expense of other professions.**

Come, [let me tell] you of the woes of the soldier, and how many are his superiors: the general, the troop commander, the officer who leads, the standard bearer, the lieutenant, the scribe, the commander of fifty, and the garrison-captain. They go in and out in the halls of the palace, saying: 'get labourers!' He is awakened at any hour. One is after him as (after) a donkey. He toils until the Aten sets in his darkness of night. He is hungry, his belly hurts; he is dead while yet alive. When he receives the grain ration, having been released from duty, it is not good for grinding.

He is called up for Syria. He may not rest. There are no clothes, no sandals.

The weapons of war are assembled at the fortress of Sile. His march is uphill through mountains. He drinks water every third day; it is smelly and tastes of salt. His body is ravaged by illness. The enemy comes, surrounds him with missiles, and life recedes from him. He is told: 'Quick, forward, valiant soldier! Win for yourself a good name!' He does not know what he is about. His body is weak, his legs fail him. When victory is won, the captives are handed over to his majesty, to be taken to Egypt. The foreign woman faints on the march: she hangs herself on the soldier's neck. His knapsack drops, another grabs it while he is busy with the woman. His wife and children are in their village; he dies and does not reach it. If he comes out alive, he is worn out from marching. Be he at large, be he detained, the soldier suffers. If he leaps and joins the deserters, all his people are imprisoned. He dies on the edge of the desert and there is none to perpetuate his name.[75]

a   What is the theme of this passage?

b   List the members of the military hierarchy mentioned in this extract.

c   With what animal is the lot of the ordinary soldier compared? Why?

d   According to the author of this extract, what were the conditions suffered by the ordinary soldier during a campaign?

e   Why was it unlikely that a soldier would desert despite the harsh conditions of army life?

f   Explain why the difficulties faced by the ordinary soldier, mentioned in this papyrus, are likely to be exaggerated.

g   What did the soldier receive from the government when he was demobilised?

h   What are mercenaries? Why did the number of mercenaries in the Egyptian army steadily increase in comparison to the number of native Egyptian soldiers?

3 **The relief shown in Figure A on the following page was carved into the walls of the Temple of Karnak during the Eighteenth Dynasty while the relief shown in Figure B was inscribed on the walls of the large temple at Abu Simbel during the Nineteenth Dynasty.**

a   For which two great warrior pharaohs were these images inscribed?

b   What is depicted in each inscription and what else might have been shown on the adjacent parts of the temple walls?

c   From which areas did the people shown in Figure A come and what might have been their fate after they were taken to Egypt?

d   From which areas did the people shown in Figure B come?

e   Which of the areas under Egyptian control was the most stable throughout most of the Eighteenth Dynasty? Why was it vital for the Egyptian government to keep control of this area?

f   Which area proved the most difficult to control? Explain why.

g   Choose one area which was part of the Egyptian empire and explain how the pharaohs maintained control over it.

A

B

4   The scenes in the figures on the following page were painted on the tomb walls of high-ranking officials of the Eighteenth Dynasty.

a   What is the common theme of these two paintings?

b   What two groups of people, under the control of the Egyptians, are represented? Provide evidence for your answer?

c   What items are shown being presented to the Egyptian king or his representative?

d   In what form was gold usually transported to Egypt?

e   Gold was extremely valuable to the Egyptians because of its incorruptible qualities. Suggest three important uses for gold during the New Kingdom.

f   What other items, not shown in these paintings, were regularly presented to the pharaoh?

g   Were the items shown in these scenes classified as booty, trade or tribute? Provide an explanation for your answer.

h   Explain how the flow of incredible wealth into Egypt during the Eighteenth and Nineteenth Dynasties:

•   increased the power and prestige of the king

•   contributed to the influence of the priests of Amun.

5 Imagine yourself in the place of a high official at the court of an Eighteenth Dynasty pharaoh. Delegations have arrived from Nubia and Syria to present their tribute to the king. You are an eye-witness to this exciting event. Describe what you see as each group of tribute bearers comes forward.

6 **The three letters below are part of the collection of cuneiform tablets found at Tell el-Amarna and now known as the Amarna Letters. The letters quoted here were written to and received from Amenhotep III.**

From Biridiya, prince of Megiddo in northern Palestine, to Amenhotep III:

To the king, my lord, and my Sun-god, say: Thus Biridiya, the faithful servant of the king. At the two feet of the king, my lord, and my Sun-god, seven and seven times I fall. Let the king know that ever since the archers returned (to Egypt), Lab'ayu has carried on hostilities against me, and we are not able to pluck the wool, and we are not able to go outside the gate in the presence of Lab'ayu, since he learned that thou hast not given archers; and now his face is set to take Megiddo, but let the king protect his city, lest Lab'ayu seize it ... let the king give one hundred garrison troops to guard the city, lest Lab'ayu seize it.[76]

From Lab'ayu, prince of Shechem, in the central Palestinian hill country, to Amenhotep III:

To the king, my lord and Sun-god: Thus Lab'ayu, thy servant, and the dirt on which thou dost tread. At the feet of the king, my lord, and my Sun-god, seven times and seven times I fall.

I have heard the words which the king wrote to me, and who am I that the king should lose his land because of me? Behold I am a faithful servant of the king, and I have not rebelled and I have not sinned, and I do not withhold my tribute, and I do not refuse my commissioner. Now they wickedly slander me, but let the king, my lord, not impute rebellion to me! ...

Further, the king wrote concerning my son. I did not know that my son associates with the 'Apiru and I have verily delivered him into the hand of Addaya.

Further, if the king should write for my wife how could I withhold her? If the king should write to me, 'Plunge a bronze dagger into thy heart and die!', how could I refuse to carry out the command of the king?[77]

From Amenhotep III to Milkilu, prince of Gezer, in southern Palestine:

To Milkilu, prince of Gezer. Thus the king. Now I have sent thee this tablet to say to thee: Behold, I am sending to thee Hanya, the commissioner of the archers, together with goods, in order to procure fine concubines (ie *weaving women*): silver, gold, (linen) garments, *turquoise*, all (sorts of) precious stones, chairs of *ebony*, as well as every good thing, totalling 160 deben. Total: 40 concubines: the price of each concubine is 40 (shekels) of silver. So send very fine concubines in whom there is no blemish. And let the king, thy lord, say to thee, 'This is good. To thee life has been *decreed*.' And mayest thou know that the king is well, like the Sun-god. His troops, his chariots, his horses are well. Behold the god Amun has placed the upper land and the lower land, the rising of the sun, and the setting of the sun under the two feet of the king.[78]

a What do the first two letters indicate about the situation in Palestine?
b What were the grievances of Biridiya?
c What was his request to Amenhotep III?
d What was the reason for Lab'ayu's letter to the Egyptian king?
e How did he emphasise his loyalty to Amenhotep?
f Which of the two princes seems the more genuine in his letter? Why?
g What methods, used by the Egyptians to control the vassal Palestinian princes, are mentioned in the first two letters?

h   What was the purpose of the letter from Amenhotep to Milkilu?

i   What were the products sent by Amenhotep to Gezer? Where did some of these come from?

j   What does the third letter show was one of the Egyptians' main motives for gaining and maintaining an empire?

k   What did Amenhotep III mean when he said 'Behold, the god Amun has placed the upper land, the lower land, the rising of the sun, and the setting of the sun under the two feet of the king'? Why did he feel obliged to end his letter this way?

7   The figures below would be found in any one of a number of cult temples throughout Egypt.

a   In which part of the temple would each one be found?

b   What did Figures A and B symbolise?

c   Describe two temple rituals which would be associated with Figure C.

A

B

C

8 **To whom does the following extract refer and what does it tell you about the responsibilities of the person concerned?**

He is the god Re whose beams enable us to see. He gives more light to the Two Lands than the sun's disc. He makes the earth more green than the Nile in flood. He has filled the Two Lands with strength and life. He is the Ka (the kingdom's life force). He is the god Khnum (a creator god) who fashions all flesh. He is the goddess Bast (cat goddess who was supposed to defend Re) who defends Egypt. Whoever worships him is under his protection; but he is Sekhmet the terrible lion-goddess, to those who disobey him. Take care not to defy him.[79]

9 **The text below comes from the *Duties of a Vizier* found on the walls of the tomb of Rekhmire, vizier during the reign of Thutmose III.**

Now he should go in to greet the Lord ... every day when the affairs of the Two Lands have been reported to him in his house. He should go into the Great House (the palace) when the overseer of treasurers stands at the northern flagstaff ... Then the overseer of treasurers should advance to meet him and address him as follows: 'All your matters are in a good state and prosper. All functionaries have reported to me as follows ... "The King's House is in a good state and prospers." ... then the vizier should send (someone) to open every door in the King's House to allow all that should enter to come in, and all that should go forth likewise. It is his agent who should arrange that it should be properly recorded in writing.

Let no official have the power to judge in his (the vizier's) hall. If an accusation should occur against one among the officials belonging to this hall, then he should have him brought to the judgment hall. It is the vizier who should punish him in return for his wrongdoing.

It is his agents who should bring mayors and district governors to the hall of judgment. ... Now as to the behaviour of the vizier in judging in his hall, if anyone (officials) is not efficient in carrying out any duty, he should judge him in the affair, and if he is not able to remove the guilt in hearing the details about it, then an entry should be placed in the criminal register which is kept in the Great Prison. So too if he is not able to remove the guilt of his agent. If their misdeeds occur a second time, a report should be made setting out that they are in the criminal register, and stating the matter on account of which they are placed in the register according to their offence.

Any document for which the vizier may send from any hall (court), provided they are not confidential, should be taken for him along with the register of their curator, on the seal of the judges and the scribes attached to them, who were in charge of them. Then he should open it (the document) and after he has seen it, it should be taken back to its place, sealed with the vizier's seal. Now if he asks for a confidential document, let it not be released by the (archival) curators. But in the case of any agent sent by the vizier about it on behalf of a petitioner, he (the curator) should let it go to him.

Now anybody who petitions the vizier about lands, he (the vizier) should order him (to appear) before him over and above listening to the overseer of farm lands and the assessor of the land register; he may grant a delay of two months on his behalf for his lands in the South and in the North; but for his lands which are in the neighbourhood of the Southern City (Thebes) or of the Residence (palace), he should grant a delay for him of three days.

... It is he (the vizier) who makes distribution of the land in the form of plots of land. In the case of any petitioner who says, 'Our boundaries are shifted,' then it should be seen that it has happened under the seal of an official. If it has happened, the he (the vizier) should take away the plots of the (district) assessor who had them (the boundaries) shifted ... Any petitioner of the land should be reported to him (the vizier) after he has put (his affair) in writing.

... It is he who appoints from the magistrates those who are to be the administrators of the North, the South, the head of the South and Tjau-wer. They should report to him whatever has happened through them at the beginning of each season, and they should bring him the written accounts thereof (of what has happened) through them and their assessors.[80]

What do these extracts reveal about:

a the vizier's responsibility with regard to the palace
b the treatment of officials who did not carry out their duties properly
c the procedure when an Egyptian petitioned the vizier concerning a land problem
d the Egyptians as record keepers.

10 Essay topics

a What were the reasons behind the establishment of the Egyptian Empire? How was the Empire maintained?
b Read the following hymn and explain what part the Egyptians of the New Kingdom believed the god Amun and his priesthood played in Egyptian imperialism.

I gave you valour and victory over all lands
I set your might, your fear in every country.
The dread of you as far as heaven's four supports.
I magnified your awe in every body,
I made your person's fame traverse the Nine Bows.
The princes of all lands are gathered in your grasp.
I stretched my own hands out and bound them for you.
I fettered Nubia's Bowman by ten thousand thousands,
The Northeners a hundred thousand captives.
I made your enemies succumb beneath your soles,
so that you crushed the rebels and the traitors.
For I bestowed on you the earth, its length and breadth,
Westerners and Easterners are under your command.[81]

Why was it important to the priests of Amun that Egypt's domination of foreigners be pushed at all times?

Everyday life in New Kingdom Egypt

Sources of evidence

Royalty and the official class

Although there appears to be a great deal of inscriptional and archaeological evidence for the public lives of the New Kingdom pharaohs, there is not much known about their private lives.

The kings' chief duty — propitiating the gods on behalf of the people — is well attested but evidence for the two most important ceremonies in their lives, their coronation and jubilee (heb-sed) festivals, is fragmentary. Although there are numerous scattered references to these celebrations, there is no source which describes the ceremonies in full. The most informative sources from the New Kingdom are the reliefs of the coronation of Hatshepsut on the walls of her temple at Deir el-Bahri, the jubilee festival of Amenhotep III on the walls of the Temple of Khonsu, Amenhotep's jubilee in the tomb of Kheruef, *King's First Herald* and the jubilee of Amenhotep IV (Akhenaten) on the talatat blocks at Karnak.

Evidence for coronation and Sed festival

Since the kings' official residences, harems and 'resting houses' were built mostly of mud-brick, little has survived. However, some inscriptional and archaeological remains provide evidence of their layout, decoration and functions.

Remains of palaces

The incredible luxury in which Egyptian royalty lived can be gauged by the objects found in the tomb of Tutankhamun. However, it must be remembered that many of these objects were manufactured specifically for funerary purposes.

Funerary furniture

Scenes of family life were found on the walls of the temples and tombs at el-Amarna. However, the brief reign of Akhenaten was unique and these images might not reflect the private lives of pharaohs generally.

The tombs in the Theban necropolis are the best source of information for the public and private lives of officials from all ranks of the civil administration, the priesthood, the pharaoh's household and the army.

Apart from scenes of an obvious funerary nature, there was usually some scene in each tomb which reflected the duties carried out by the official at the height of his career. For example:

- The tomb of a vizier usually showed him judging cases; supervising workshops in the Temple of Amun, overseeing the building of temples, receiving tribute, reporting to the king, checking on the state of the granaries and receiving reports from his officials throughout the country.

- An overseer of the treasury might be shown receiving gold from Nubia, and supervising the weighing of precious metals and their transformation into jewellery and other items in the workshops.

- An overseer of granaries would have included in his tomb some scenes showing scribes and surveyors measuring the fields and recording of the harvest, as well as of the storage and shipment of grain.

- The scenes in the tomb of an army commander might show him taking part in a campaign, aspects of camp life and soldiers being drilled.

- A viceroy would have himself depicted receiving tribute from foreign lands.

Artists, craftsmen and unskilled workers

New Kingdom sources of evidence for the working and living conditions of Egyptian craftsmen and unskilled workers fall into five general categories.

Deir el-Medina

1　The remains of the worker's village at Deir el-Medina is the best source of evidence for all aspects of the public and private life of a group of workmen in the New Kingdom. Large quantities of official records, biographical inscriptions, private letters, literary texts and graffiti written on papyri, ostraca (flakes of limestone and broken pottery on which things were written) and tomb walls have provided historians with a wealth of information about this special group of workmen. Their houses, tombs, household objects and tools supplement the written records. However, because this was a special community the conditions which existed there may not have been typical of this class.

A workers' village at Amarna

2　The workmen's village just outside Akhenaten's capital at Akhetaten (el-Amarna) was rich in archaeological remains which throw some light on the life and economy of this settlement. Unlike Deir el-Medina, this site did not produce much in the way of written records.

3　The reliefs and paintings on the tomb walls of officials such as Rekhmire, Nebamun and Apuky illustrate some of the craftsmen's techniques, tools and finished products. Unfortunately, these scenes show only a selection of the jobs carried out in the best workshops.

Funerary objects

4　The objects found in the tombs at Thebes and other New Kingdom sites show the high standard of workmanship achieved by many of

Rural activities related to food production	Transportation and markets	Professions and industries	Tomb owner and his family	Sports and recreation

Harbour scenes; loading and unloading cargo boats

Exchange of goods – food, clothes, sandals and tools

Ceremonial barges, sedan chairs and chariots

Intimate family scenes

Estates – houses, gardens, estate workers and pets

Aspects of officials' careers, carrying out tasks for the king and receiving promotions

Agricultural activities associated with the growing of grain, flax, fruit and vines

Methods of irrigation

Animal husbandry

Domestication of wild animals and force feeding of fowl

Fishing with spears and nets

Assessment of taxes

Scribes at work in the fields, temples, workshops and vizier's court

Skilled craftsmen such as goldsmiths, bronze workers, jewellers and sculptors, carpenters in their workshops

Raw materials, tools, equipment, processes and finished items

Tradesmen such as tanners, weavers, brickmakers and food processors at work

Fowling in the marshes with boomerangs

Hunting in deserts with bows and arrows, on foot or from chariots.

Adults playing board games such as sennet and youths shooting with bows and arrows, throwing, wrestling and fencing with sticks

Banquets with fashionably dressed and coiffeured guests, abundant food and drink, music and dancing

Everyday life depicted in the tombs of the nobles

these specialist craftsmen. The domestic and funerary goods found in the tomb of the pharaoh Tutankhamun illustrate the technical skill of those employed in the royal and temple workshops.

5 A literary piece called the *Satire of Trades*, which originated in the Middle Kingdom, was used in the schools of the New Kingdom to convince trainee scribes of the superiority of their profession. It did this by ridiculing the various trades. Although it was prejudiced and probably based on the worst possible examples, it may have contained some elements of truth.

Literature

Peasants and agricultural labourers

Because they were illiterate, the farmers, who formed the largest group in society, left very few records about their lives. A picture of the life of people on the land has to be surmised from:

Tomb scenes

- the paintings and inscriptions in the tombs of their masters, the official class of the Eighteenth Dynasty. Some of these tombs — those of Menna (Scribe of Fields), Nakht (Scribe of the Granaries), Rekhmire (Vizier) and Khaemhet (Overseer of Granaries) were found at Thebes. Others, like that of Paheri (Mayor of Nekheb and Iunyt) were located in the provinces. The rural activities depicted in the tomb scenes generally represent what was best for the tomb owner in the next life and so often show the farmers in an ideal situation and happy in their work

Farming tools

- the remains of tools, equipment and even models of the people involved in their day-to-day jobs (ushabtis)

- the many passages used by scribes as exercises for their students. These passages were deliberately prejudiced to convince the young students of the benefits of a future in the bureaucracy. The passages emphasise the difficult and often miserable life experienced by the peasant farmer.

The diagram on the previous page shows some of the details of everyday life depicted in the Eighteenth Dynasty tombs of the official class.

Royal life

Coronations and jubilees

The coronation was possibly the most important ceremony in the life of the king and his people. The Egyptians believed that their god-king maintained *ma'at* (the right order of things that was established at the time of creation). Therefore, the death of a king could lead to disorder and chaos and only when the new king was officially installed on the throne was divine order re-established.

Importance of coronation for the Egyptian people

Place

This ceremony was traditionally held in the northern capital of Memphis, although several New Kingdom pharaohs (Amenhotep IV/Akhenaten and Tutankhamun) were crowned in Thebes. The numerous monumental reliefs show the pharaoh, as the son of Amun-Re, being crowned by his *father* in heaven in front of the assembled gods. The actual ceremony, which began on the first day of the season of inundation, lasted many days. It was conducted in the temple by priests wearing masks representing the gods. The rituals were carried out in two sanctuaries which symbolised the primitive temples of the north and the south.

Time

A priest, in his leopard skin garment, invested the king with all his powers and duties by presenting him with the crowns and other royal insignia. Each of the crowns — the Red Crown of Lower Egypt, the White Crown of Upper Egypt, the Double Crown of the Two Lands, the blue leather *Khepresh* or war crown, the *Atef* Crown, the plumed diadem, the *Seshed* headband, and a variety of linen headdresses — were placed on the king's head in succession. He then received his *great name*, the titulary of five names selected by the priests of the House of Life.

The king left the chapel, wearing the Khepresh, the animal tail of the archaic chieftains and sandals, on the soles of which were images of Egypt's traditional enemies — Nubians, Syrians, Libyans and Bedouins.

The coronation ceremony was probably performed again in front of an assembly of nobles and high officials. At this time priests performed a ritual entwining of the plants of Upper and Lower Egypt. Finally, the newly crowned king performed a symbolic circuit of the *White Walls* of Memphis.

The crowns, which did not belong to individual pharaohs but to the throne, were returned to the temple where they were kept. This explains why no crowns, except the Seshed band (worn in death) were found in the tomb of Tutankhamun.

Marks of royalty

The royal headdresses

Surmounted by the uraeus or cobra. Depicted on statuettes and coffins. No actual crown found except the seshed headband

The sceptres

The crook (heka) and the flail (nekhekh) carried on ceremonial occasions. Two pairs of sceptres – one small set with the name of Aten and a larger set with the name of Amun – an indication of the transitional period in which Tutankhamun lived

The animal tail

Archaic symbol of a primitive chieftain worn by pharaohs on ceremonial occasions. Attached to a girdle around the waist of the mummy

Marks of royalty

Items worn, carried or used by Tutankhamun in his official capacity

State chariots

Used by the king during festival and jubilee processions. Covered in gold and semi-precious stones and decorated with traditional scenes

The throne

Decorated with winged serpents wearing the Double Crown of Egypt. Shows a domestic scene of Tutankhamun and his young wife with the Aten disk shining on them – from the Amarna Period, although both the Aten and Amun form of the king's name is used

State barge

Used during festivals such as the Opet from Karnak to Luxor. A brightly painted model with central cabin, tall mast and smaller deck cabins

Purpose of Sed festival

The jubilee or Sed festival (heb-sed) was also a great moment in the life of the king and his subjects. It was usually held for the first time when the king had been on the throne for 30 years. Thereafter it was held every three years. The chief purpose of the celebration was to ritually renew the powers of the reigning king so he could continue to rule effectively. It also commemorated the king's accession to the throne by recreating the coronation ceremony.

Like the coronation, the Sed festival was usually held in Memphis. However, several New Kingdom pharaohs held a version of their jubilee in Thebes (eg, Amenhotep III) and Ramesses II celebrated his jubilees at the delta capital of Pi-Ramesse.

Thutmose III and Amenhotep III celebrated three heb-seds and Ramesses II, who ruled for 67 years, is believed to have celebrated 14 jubilees. Even though some New Kingdom pharaohs did not reign for 30 years, they still celebrated a Sed festival (eg, Akhenaten). The ceremonies associated with this significant event in the life of the pharaoh are described in more detail in Chapter 6.

Journeys and public appearances

The king's chief duty was to show gratitude to the gods, which he performed by:

> ... restoring what had fallen into decay, building new shrines, reconstructing and strengthening the walls surrounding them, filling them with statues, renewing their furnishings and sacred boats, erecting obelisks, heaping the altars and offering tables with flowers and generally outrivalling all his royal predecessors ... Even after the king had showered gifts upon the gods ... he must take the personal trouble to supervise the execution of his orders and, when the work was completed, ceremonially consecrate the temple and dedicate it to the gods.[1]

Movement of the king throughout the year

He also conducted tours of inspection, led expeditions, received visiting ambassadors, presided over investitures and attended many of the numerous religious festivals along the Nile. This meant that throughout the year the king moved from one royal residence to another (Thebes, Memphis and Pi-Ramesse). These were occasions of great pomp and ceremony.

> ... the splendour of his surroundings displayed to advantage the splendour of the king himself.[2]

Nile voyages

The constant movement of the pharaoh and his entourage from one capital to another involved 'mobilising a regular convoy' of boats, which were like floating houses.[3] The royal ship of state was probably towed by one or two vessels with enormous rectangular sails and a large complement of rowers. On the journey to Upper Egypt and Nubia, these boats hoisted their sails since the prevailing wind was northerly. On the return voyage they were rowed, the current helping them along.

Preparations for king's arrival

Long before the king's arrival at one of his palaces or 'rest houses', officials and servants were involved in preparations on a grand scale. The following extract gives some idea of the amount of food necessary for a welcoming banquet.

> Get on with having everything ready for Pharaoh's (arrival) ... have made (ready) 100 ring-stands for bouquets of flowers, 500 food-baskets. Foodstuff, list, to be prepared: 1000 loaves of fine flour ... 10 000 *ibshet*-biscuits; 2000 baskets at 300 cuts ... Milk, 60 measures; cream, 90 measures; carob beans, 30 bowls. Grapes, 50 sacks; pomegranates, 60 sacks; figs, 300 strings and 20 baskets...[4]

The list also specified amounts of vegetables, meats, drinks, incense and oils. Sometimes the local mayor was called on to organise the provision of extra supplies.

By the time the king left his royal barge, the streets of the capital were probably lined with people ready to acclaim their ruler and enjoy the spectacular procession to the palace. On these occasions the king was outfitted magnificently. The clothing and jewellery found in the tomb of Tutankhamun — royal robes with gold sequins, rosettes and beadwork, a buckle of sheet gold, pairs of gold sandals, rings, necklaces and bracelets in gold, turquoise, lapis lazuli and carnelian — are evidence of this magnificence.

Nefertiti carried in a palanquin during a Sed festival

King Horemheb in a carrying chair supported by soldiers

On ceremonial occasions the pharaoh was carried in a richly decorated palanquin or sedan-chair resting on the shoulders of courtiers or soldiers, and accompanied by fan-bearers. Their job was not only to fan the king but to wave small floral bouquets around him to sweeten the air. At other times he rode in his spectacular gilded chariot, drawn by two splendidly harnessed and plumed stallions controlled by drivers, perhaps of Asiatic descent. The palanquins or chariots of the king's chief consort, family and members of the court followed. Armed Egyptian soldiers and foreign mercenaries protected the royal entourage and cleared the way through the crowd of onlookers. During religious festivals, such as the Opet, the procession of the king would have been even more spectacular.

Akhenaten and Nefertiti in a chariot, drive to and from the temple

Investitures

Investitures of the king's chief officials and tribute presentations were elaborate affairs. They were often held in an open courtyard with the king and his chief queen enthroned under a rich canopy on a specially constructed and decorated platform. Often, presentations of the gold of valour were carried out from the *window of appearances* in the palace.

Royal palaces and life at court

The pharaohs' palaces, royal lodges and harems reflected the opulent tastes of the New Kingdom but were also designed to incorporate the Egyptians' love of nature.

Decoration of royal residences

These cool retreats featured lakes, pools, columned courts and huge gardens of sweet-smelling trees and flowers. Inside, the natural theme was continued. For example, in one of the wings of the royal residence at Akhetaten, the walls were covered with glazed tiles inlaid with flowers — lotus garlands, water reeds, cornflowers, persea fruit and daisies. The floor was painted in the form of a pool full of fish and lotus flowers, with ducks, butterflies and dragonflies flying overhead. In a room in the small northern palace at Akhetaten, murals over three metres high and on all four walls, featured life in the papyrus marshes around the river — shimmering water, tall green stems with feathery tops, opening lotus blossoms, nesting and darting small birds (ducks, kingfishers and pigeons). This room would have provided a cool, peaceful and private sanctuary from the heat of the day.

The decoration in the great Malkata palace complex in western Thebes, built by King Amenhotep III, also featured vividly coloured scenes from nature. The palace in Ramesses' capital of Pi-Ramesse shone with brilliant colours and vivid scenes. It was described as 'dazzling, with halls of lapis and turquoise'.[5]

The Malkata palace complex covered over 32 hectares. It comprised not only the king's palace but a palace for Queen Tiye; the domains of his eldest daughter, Sitamun; the harem or *secluded place* for his Egyptian and Asiatic wives and numerous concubines; private apartments and villas for his chief officials; servants' quarters and a great pleasure lake. The public areas of the royal residences included a central audience hall, throne room and balconies for royal appearances.

Size of the Malkata palace

Wall decoration from the palace of Amenhotep III at Malkata

Evidence of the ornate and luxurious furnishings of royal residences comes once again from the tomb of Tutankhamun. The beds, couches, chairs and chests were made from cedar, ebony, ivory, gold and woven cord, inlaid or painted with traditional scenes. Beautiful alabaster vases and lamps complemented the furniture.

Everything associated with the king's life at court would have followed strict rules. As a god, his day probably started like that of every other god in the land, with a ritual bathing and anointment with precious unguents. Then he would either make sacrifices and listen to prayers by the high priest or else officiate at the temple in the *rite of the house of the morning*.

Although he was regarded as a god, the king was a hard-working ruler. He listened to daily reports from his vizier on the state of the kingdom and made his wishes known, held audiences, and read despatches from his officials and dictated replies.

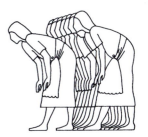

The bowing pose of Amarna courtiers, officials and priests

Court etiquette

Although there is little evidence of the ceremonies of the Egyptian court, strict etiquette would have applied to the order in which officials were presented to the king and the method of presentation. The reliefs show that when high officials and priests approached the king they bowed respectfully, either with their arms by their sides or raised in praise. Any communication with the king would probably have been preceded by a reference to his divine nature.

Private lives of royalty

Not much is known of the private lives of the New Kingdom pharaohs. Most of the evidence available comes from the wall decorations in the tombs of the Amarna nobles which show intimate scenes of Akhenaten and his family dining together, being entertained by musicians and enjoying a family outing in their chariots.

Some of the objects from the tomb of Tutankhamun feature scenes of the king enjoying the company of his young wife, Ankhesenamun. Although these scenes were probably part of the symbolism of rebirth, they provide a glimpse into the private life of the queen and her husband, as in the scene that shows Tutankhamun sitting on an elaborately decorated chair with his feet on a footstool while Ankhesenamun anoints him with precious unguents.

In the hot, dry climate of Egypt and especially during the fly-ridden summers, it was important to keep the skin oiled and the eyes protected. A large number of magnificent unguent, oil and cosmetic containers, as well as elaborate fly whisks and ostrich feather fans, were found among Tutankhamun's funerary items.

Tutankhamun giving audience to Huy

Akhenaten and his family and Queen Tiye, having a family meal

An ebony and gold chair inlaid with ivory, from the tomb of Tutankhamun

A magnificent unguent jar featuring papyrus and lotus plants, from the tomb of Tutankhamun

The kings probably spent their leisure time in much the same way as the nobles — at banquets, being entertained by musicians and dancers, playing games of sennet and taking part in hunting expeditions into the deserts and the papyrus marshes.

Queen Nefertari playing draughts (or sennet)

New Kingdom pharaohs constantly emphasised their sporting prowess, particularly with the bow. Accompanied by attendants, they drove their own chariots into the desert to hunt for gazelle and wild cattle. During their military campaigns abroad they indulged in more dangerous activities such as hunting elephants and lions.

Sporting activities

A number of single-occupant chariots, a riding crop and glove, many bows, arrows and throwing sticks, found among Tutankhamun's possessions, indicate that the young king was probably trained in chariot handling and participated in hunting activities. It should be remembered, however, that some of these items in the tomb would have served a ritual purpose.

The royal harems

New Kingdom pharaohs had numerous secondary wives (both Egyptian and foreign) as well as concubines but only a select number of women travelled with the king as he moved about the country on official business. The rest, together with their many children, nurses and personal attendants, were housed in special harem/palaces attached to the royal residences which the king visited only occasionally.

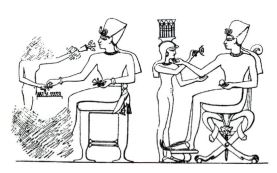

Ramesses III being entertained by the ladies of his harem

Harems functioned as independent economic units, with their own lands, labourers and administrators, some of whom appear to have been married men. The evidence suggests that the harem established by Thutmose III at a site called Mer-Wer (Ghurab) in the Faiyum, was not only a recreational centre for the king but an important centre for weaving and textile manufacture. Although it is not known whether the royal women at Mer-Wer were actively engaged in manufacturing cloth, it appears that they supervised and trained the textile workers and stored cloth and garments in the harem storehouses. The women, in this harem at least, do not appear to have wasted their days in idle luxury.

The harem also had the potential for intrigue and conspiracy, as secondary wives and kings' favourites sought to promote the interests of their own sons.

Royal children

There is little evidence of the names, early life and role of royal princes before the Nineteenth Dynasty, whereas the names of many royal daughters are found in the records. Even so, little is known about the lives of these princesses.

Royal nurses and tutors for princesses

Only the highest ranking men and women were appointed as nurses and tutors for the kings' daughters. Evidence for the type of education they received is very scanty. The survival of several ivory writing palettes belonging to the daughters of Akhenaten indicate that royal daughters learnt how to read, write and paint in watercolours.

A relief showing the young Amarna princesses riding in their own chariots indicates that they were brought up to be independent and given similar training to royal princes in the handling of horses. Horsemanship was possibly taught to them by Ay, *Overseer of the King's Horses*.

Princes and milk brothers

Royal princes were looked after by high-ranking wet-nurses. There is evidence that some princes formed close associations with their *milk brothers*, who became their companions throughout adult life.

In keeping with the military nature of the period and the emphasis on sporting prowess, young princes were probably taught at an early age to ride, handle horses and chariots, swim and use a bow and arrow.

They accompanied their older male relatives on hunting expeditions into the desert and would have been expected eventually to display their own skill and courage in facing a wild animal alone.

An essential part of their education was to learn to read and write, so, like the young Thutmose (the future Thutmose III), they attended schools, either in the palace or the temple. Perhaps some also became apprentice priests. One of the sons of Ramesses II, Khaemwaset, was outstanding in all the scribal arts and was interested in religion. He eventually became a high priest (*sem* priest) of Ptah at Memphis.

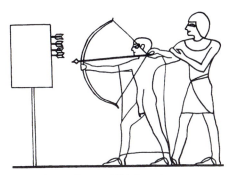

Amenhotep II as a child, learning how to shoot

When a royal prince, particularly the crown prince, reached adolescence, he served an apprenticeship in the army under the supervision of veterans especially chosen for the job. In military competitions a royal prince was expected to exhibit great skill in all the arts of war.

Even at an early age, a prince often accompanied his father on his campaigns. At 14 years of age, Ramesses II played a minor role in his father's campaign in Libya and a year later was present at the storming of Kadesh. When he became king, Ramesses took his own son, Khaemwaset, on his Nubian campaign even though he was only five.

A wealthy elite

Within the Egyptian official class there were many levels of wealth and influence. The great nobles/officials who ran the administration and led the armies became extremely wealthy during the New Kingdom. Their tombs in western Thebes testify to this.

As Egypt prospered under the empire, these nobles and their families indulged themselves in extensive estates in different parts of the country with beautiful villas, gardens and pools; town houses; numerous household officials and servants; costly food and wine; fashionable clothes, finely-made jewellery and expensive unguents, perfumes and cosmetics; fine chariots and splendid boats.

Luxurious lifestyle

The extent of their wealth can be gauged by the record left in the tomb of an unnamed dignitary who lived during the reign of Amenhotep II. It appears that at the start of each new year it was the custom for officials to present gifts to the king. This anonymous official presented the following items to Amenhotep II:

- carriages made of silver and gold
- ivory and ebony statues of the king with a variety of robes
- collarettes and jewels of all kinds
- weapons — 140 bronze daggers, 360 bronze swords, 220 ivory whip-handles inlaid with ebony, 680 shields made from the skin of rare animals, coats of mail and hundreds of leather quivers
- numerous vases of precious metal and carved ivory.

Examples of wealth

The following extract from a Nineteenth Dynasty papyrus further illustrates the life of luxury lived by many of these high-ranking officials.

> Thy raiment is of linen, thou ridest in a chariot, a golden handled whip in thy hands, and thou holdest new reins. Thou art drawn by colts from Syria and negroes run before thee to clear the way. The boat thou boardest is of fir wood, decorated from stem to stern. Thou comest to thy fine mansion which thou hast built for thyself. Thy mouth is filled with wine and beer, with bread and meat and cakes. The oxen are dismembered and the wine unsealed. Sweet strains of song echo in thine ears. The scent maker spreads over thee the odour of sweet resin, and the chief gardener comes to offer thee garlands. The chief hunter brings thee quails from the oases and thy chief fisherman presents thee with fish. From Syria hath thy vessel brought thee all manner of precious cargo. Thy stalls are full of calves and thy women spin to much profit. Thou art secure and thine enemies are brought low.[6]

Of course not all officials were as fortunate as these two.

Country villas and town houses

It is difficult to form an exact picture of the houses of the wealthy. All residences, from palaces to peasant's houses, were constructed predominantly of mud-brick and virtually nothing of these has survived. Also, scenes in tombs and on illustrated papyri, which feature domestic architecture, can be misleading. Egyptian artists gave no indication of the size of different parts of the house and often showed both sides of the house together. Sometimes what looks like a second or third storey is in fact different parts of a single storey house.

Interpretation of scenes difficult

> When an Egyptian artist ... had to draw a great building or a garden ... he wished to show every part of it ... He considered his duty accomplished when he had placed all the details before the spectator, but he did not care whether the spectator understood how these details fitted together ... the Egyptian artist had no sense of proportion between different parts of the representation.[7]

Several examples of country villas and town houses belonging to the wealthy classes can be found on the illustrated funerary papyrus of Nakht, *Royal Scribe and General* at the end of the Eighteenth Dynasty; in the Theban tomb of Djehutnufe, *Royal Scribe and Overseer of the Treasury* under Amenhotep II; in the remains of the town of Akhetaten (el-Amarna) and in the tombs of the nobles of the Amarna period.

Features of a country villa

A country villa appears to have had some of the following features:

- one or two storeys
- smooth whitewashed mud-brick walls
- projecting wooden (or sometimes stone) doorways and window frames
- doors placed at one end of the main wall
- windows on the second floor with what appears to be a balcony

- a flat roof with triangular constructions which caught the cool north wind and forced it into the upper storey. In some cases the upper storey was left open for air circulation
- a main family room in the upper storey
- walled gardens planted with fig trees, date palms and pomegranates, and vine-covered arbours
- fish ponds and pools.

Three views of the house of Meryre at Akhetaten

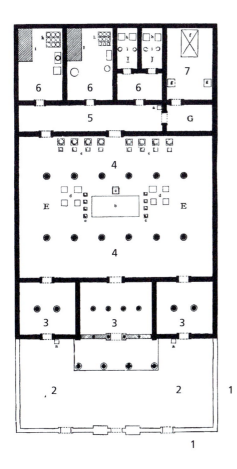

1 wall

2 a courtyard in which servants are shown sweeping and sprinkling water

3 the front of three small rooms including a central vestibule (with a porch) which led to the main hall beyond — side rooms perhaps for porters

4 the large dining hall with chairs, basin with jug and water, tables laden with food and flowers and huge wine jars appears to be ready for a banquet

5 a small courtyard

6 kitchens and bakery

7 the owner's sleeping quarters with his bed and tables for holding basins of water

In this house there were no women's quarters since Meryre was not married.

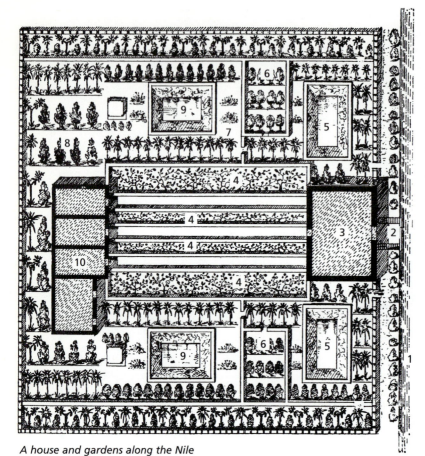

1   canal

2   doors in high wall

3   porter's lodge

4   vineyard though which
    paths lead to the house
    at the back of the garden

5   fish ponds

6   an enclosed area possibly
    containing rare trees

7   palm garden

8   other fruit and shade
    trees such as fig and
    sycamore

9   pool with lotus and
    papyrus plants and
    wild birds

10 house at the far end
    of the garden

A house and gardens along the Nile

A scene in the tomb of Djehutnufe shows a section through what appears to have been a three-storey house in the city of Thebes. It is difficult to know whether it is really multi-storeyed or whether the artist was trying to show different parts of the house which were all on the same level. This Theban home had a ground floor or basement area in which domestic activities (making bread and cloth) were carried out. The family's living area was above the street level. On the next floor the owner, Djehutnufe, appears to have had his working area. Storage bins and a kitchen were located on the roof. The number of people in the illustration — scribes, spinners, weavers, grinders, bakers, butchers and servants running to and fro with refreshments, indicates that these town houses may have been rather cramped.

Watering a noble's garden

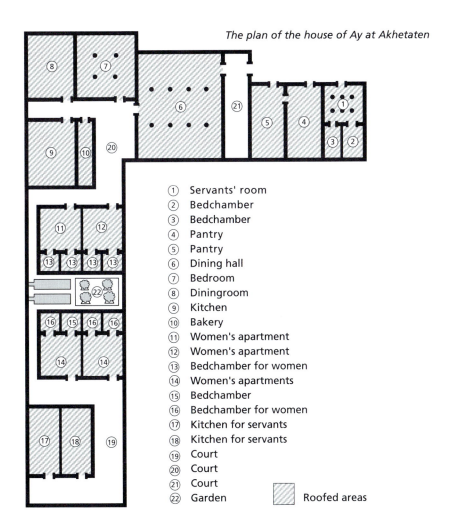

The plan of the house of Ay at Akhetaten

1. Servants' room
2. Bedchamber
3. Bedchamber
4. Pantry
5. Pantry
6. Dining hall
7. Bedroom
8. Diningroom
9. Kitchen
10. Bakery
11. Women's apartment
12. Women's apartment
13. Bedchamber for women
14. Women's apartments
15. Bedchamber
16. Bedchamber for women
17. Kitchen for servants
18. Kitchen for servants
19. Court
20. Court
21. Court
22. Garden

Roofed areas

Unlike Thebes and Memphis which would have been crowded, bustling cities during the New Kingdom, the planned city of Akhetaten had plenty of space for building. The homes of the officials who served Akhenaten were large one-storey complexes which featured a vestibule with an antechamber for the porter, a central hall for dining, other rooms for more intimate family gatherings and use during hot weather, bedrooms for family and guests, bathroom and toilets in the owner's bedroom, a number of courtyards, separate women's quarters, kitchens, storerooms and servants' quarters.

Features of Amarna villas

These houses, although built of whitewashed mud-brick, had stone door-frames and wooden pillars, staircases and roof supports. The interiors were brightly coloured, glowing with blues, greens, reds and yellows. Ceilings were usually in a bright shade of blue while friezes of flowers (lotus flowers were popular) and birds decorated the tops of the walls which were probably hung with coloured matting. The floors were often plastered and painted in designs and/or covered with rugs.

The furniture in upper class homes was elegant and practical — high-backed chairs and stools, often inlaid with ebony and ivory, and with lion's paw legs; folding stools; couches piled with cushions and chests for holding clothes. In the dining rooms, stands were used for holding food and jars of wine, while jugs of water and basins were provided for washing hands after eating.

A nobleman's household

The noble's family probably comprised his wife, his sons and their wives and children, unmarried daughters and sisters and possibly widowed relatives.

Polygamy and monogamy

For a long time it was thought that the Egyptians were polygamous, but the evidence suggests that only the most wealthy could afford more than one wife. 'The overwhelming majority of Egyptian men remained monogamous, officially restricting themselves to one wife at a time ...'[8] Also, many of the women previously classified as concubines were in fact unmarried women in the household. This is not to suggest, however, that upper class men did not have concubines.

Apart from his family and concubines, a nobleman's household included a wide range of supervisors, servants and slaves. Among the supervisors were estate stewards and bailiffs, scribes, and overseers of the household, storehouses, bakery and slaughterhouse.

Household personnel

There was a significant difference in the status of servants and slaves. Free servants could leave their master's employ at any time, set up their own households, go into business and inherit property. Slaves, who were mostly foreigners, could be sold or hired out and were often treated harshly. There is evidence that if they tried to run away they were pursued and punished severely.

Some of the servants and slaves employed in a wealthy household included:

- cup-bearers (*wedpou*), who supervised the meals and waited on the master and his guests
- listeners, who were always ready for their master's call
- followers (*shemsou*) who attended the lord when he left the house. One was a sandal carrier and the another carried a roll of matting, the lord's staff and a fly whisk. When their master stopped to carry out a task, these servants placed the mat on the ground, handed him his staff, kept the flies away and washed his feet
- barbers, hairdressers, manicurists, chiropodists and experts who looked after toiletries, cosmetics and perfumes. Upper-class Egyptians took their personal hygiene very seriously and paid great attention to their appearance
- nurses to look after the children
- gardeners
- porters who guarded the gates
- bakers, brewers and butchers. Bread and beer were the staples of the Egyptian diet. A huge variety of bread was baked and beer,

made from barley and dates, was drunk at every meal. Although meat was not necessarily eaten every day, the slaughterhouse was an important feature of the wealthy household

- some tradesmen, particularly on country estates where equipment had to be made and repaired
- musicians
- a host of slaves, from stable hands to pretty slave girls who waited on tables and entertained their master.

Upper-class women

The picture of women presented in New Kingdom literature, painting and sculpture reflects 'male ideals concerning women and their place in society'.[9] They are always depicted as young and beautiful and are shown in relationship to their fathers, husbands and sons, playing a supportive but subordinate role. However, legal documents and correspondence reveal a different picture from the passive supporter featured in art and literature.

Idealised view of women

In theory at least, Egyptian women of all classes were the equals of men in the eyes of the law. A woman could:

Legal rights

- inherit, purchase, lease and sell property
- continue to administer her own property even when married
- hire or buy slaves
- make a legal contract, go to court as a plaintiff or defendant and give evidence
- live alone without the protection of a male guardian
- retain her property if divorced and claim a share of any joint property, except in the case of adultery.

A married woman was more respected than an unmarried one. She derived her status from her husband's position within society and this status increased with motherhood. The more children she had, the greater her standing in the community and the happier her husband would be since a man 'was saluted on account of his progeny'.[10] The birth of a boy further enhanced her status, because a son provided support for his parents in their old age and played an important role in his parents' funeral ritual.

Status associated with marriage

After motherhood, a woman's chief duty was to look after the home. No matter from what class she came, a woman's most coveted title was *mistress of the house*.[11] When she performed this role well she had the respect of her husband, as the following extract from *The Instructions of Ani* shows.

Do not control your wife in her house,
When you know she is efficient;
Don't say to her: 'Where is it? Get it!'
When she has put it in the right place.
Let your eye observe in silence,
Then you recognise her skill;

> It is joy when your hand is with her,
> There are many who don't know this
> If a man desists from strife at home,
> He will not encounter its beginning.
> Every man who founds a household
> Should hold back the hasty heart.[12]

The wives of high officials, however, had no need to perform any of the usual domestic tasks. They had numerous slaves and servants to do these for them, including wet-nurses to breast-feed and attend to their children. Their chief task was to supervise the running of the household.

No careers available for women in the civil bureaucracy

Very few women learned to read and write and those who did had no chance of entering the male-dominated civil bureaucracy. 'After all the upper class wife derived her status from her husband's position in the community and she had no need to work to increase either her social standing or her personal wealth.'[13] Her duty was to support her husband in his career. The evidence does suggest, though, that it was acceptable for a wife to stand in for her husband if he were absent.

Temple positions

The only activity outside the home in which high-ranking women were involved was associated with the temple. Except for *mistress of the house*, the most common title associated with upper class women was *musician*.

In the first half of the Eighteenth Dynasty, some women were appointed to the *Harem of Amun* as honorary priestesses, musicians and singers. Later, they could choose to become part of the 'musical troop of the temple' of Amun, Mut or Khonsu. Women could also carry out the duties of mortuary priests.

Because our sources of information about women reflect a male perspective, we know very little about their private lives and the things which really concerned them.

Family relationships

Through their writings, statues and paintings, the Egyptians have revealed their ideal of marriage and family life. It appears that 'the bond between husbands and wives and their children was long-lasting and profound'.[14] Scenes from the tombs of the officials show wives tenderly embracing their husbands, sharing a meal or playing a game of sennet with them, accompanying them on fowling trips, and socialising at banquets. Even though these scenes may have been associated with ideas about rebirth, it seems that couples expected to share the next life together also.

Husbands and wives

A Nineteenth Dynasty text, written by a widower to his dead wife, reveals the ideal of a marriage relationship. The rest of this text is found at the end of the chapter.

> I was a young man when I married you, and I spent my life with you.
> I rose to the highest rank but I never deserted you from my youth to
> the time when I was holding all manner of important posts for
> Pharaoh (Life, Health, Strength): nay rather I always said to myself 'She
> has always been my companion'.[15]

The writer seems to be suggesting that not all men would have behaved as he did. Although consideration of one's partner was highly regarded in a relationship, some marriages ended in divorce.

Divorce

Either husband or wife could initiate a divorce, but most of the evidence suggests that more often than not it was the man who repudiated his wife. Incompatibility, infertility or love for another, particularly a younger woman, might be cited as reasonable grounds for divorce. In these cases the woman returned to her father's home with all her possessions and a share of the joint property of the marriage. Under no circumstances could a woman commit adultery and remain married. She would be divorced immediately, socially disgraced and lose her legal rights to all property.

> Men were ... expected to respect another man's sole right of access to his wife and indulging in sexual relations with a married woman was frowned upon ... in cases of adultery the woman was clearly seen as the temptress corrupting a weak but essentially innocent man.[16]

Parents and children

The Egyptians loved children and hoped for large families. Although boys were favoured, parents were caring and affectionate to all their children. Scenes in many of the tombs show parents and children enjoying each other's company.

Nakht and his family fowling

In a tribute to the devotion of mothers, Ani, a minor official of the Eighteenth Dynasty, instructed his son to support his mother in her old age:

> Double the food your mother gave you,
> Support her as she supported you;
> She had a heavy load in you,
> But she did not abandon you.
> When you were born after your months,
> She was yet yoked (to you)
> Her breast in your mouth for three years.
> As you grew and your excrement disgusted,
> She was not disgusted, saying "What shall, I do!"
> When she sent you to school.
> And you were taught to write,
> She kept watching over you daily,
> With bread and beer in her house.[17]

The mother's father took a great interest in the welfare of his daughter's sons, and young men were often appointed to positions owing to the influence of their maternal grandfathers.

Women were frequently honoured by their sons in their tombs, and on funerary stelae it was the custom to trace the descent of the dead man through his mother.

Grooming and personal hygiene

Hygiene and climate

Upper-class Egyptians paid particular attention to their appearance and personal hygiene. Frequent washing, removal of body hair, oiling and perfuming the skin, and protecting the eyes were all a response to the hot, dry climate of Egypt.

Hair and wigs

Both men and women kept their natural hair short, wearing elaborate wigs on social occasions. They also went to a great deal of trouble to remove body hair with tweezers, knives and hooked razors. Barbers and hairdressers were important members of the noble's household.

Only the upper classes could afford the imported, scented unguents used for moisturising and perfuming the body. They were obviously considered just as important in the next life judging by the numbers of elaborate containers found among the funerary items of the wealthy.

Cosmetics

Cosmetics were used by both men and women to enhance their looks, 'convey a message of high social status' and protect them from the harsh sunlight.[18] Black kohl (made from galena — mineral-lead) and green powder (made from malachite) were used by the Egyptians to highlight their eyes and protect them from glare, dust or insects.

The Egyptians had numerous recipes for problems such as body odour, bad breath, wrinkles and baldness. For example, an early Eighteenth Dynasty medical papyrus (the *Ebers Papyrus*):

- suggested that body odours could be alleviated by rubbing a mixture of roasted ostrich egg, tortoise shell and gall nuts (from the tamarisk tree) into the skin
- recommended a mouth wash made from goose grease, milk and bran and a mouth freshener of cinnamon, myrrh and frankincense
- promoted a daily facial cream to remove wrinkles, made from ground rush-nuts, 'frankincense gum, wax and balanites oil'[19]
- suggested, as a cure for baldness, a mixture of the fat of a variety of animals — lion, hippopotamus, crocodile, cat, snake and ibex.

Meals and family entertainment

Evidence of family meals limited

The evidence suggests that the Egyptians really enjoyed their food. However, although there are many scenes of food production, preparation and presentation, there are none showing a family meal in progress, except for one featuring Akhenaten and his family.

Breakfast was not a family affair. The noble/official ate his food while dressing and it appears that his wife was also offered food while having her hair done. Whether the members of the family gathered together for the other two meals is not known.

The Egyptian upper class ate well — meat, game, fowl, fruit, vegetables, cakes and bread. Beer was the main beverage, although wine was consumed at social gatherings.

Banquets

It appears that the upper classes took the opportunity whenever possible to entertain guests at dinner parties or banquets. In the tombs of the Old Kingdom, the owner, his wife and family are often shown quietly enjoying food, music and dancing. However, by the New Kingdom these occasions had taken on the form of proper banquets. Despite the differences of opinion about the significance of these banqueting scenes in tombs, they do provide evidence for the social habits and fashions of wealthy Egyptians.

Preparations for a banquet were extensive. These included slaughtering and cooking an ox, roasting fowl (such as ducks and geese which had been fattened for weeks), and preparing special sauces and other delicacies. As flowers and perfume played a very important part in any banquet, floral garlands and sweet-scented pomades were prepared for the guests.

Preparations

It is possible to build up a fairly clear picture of these social occasions from the paintings in the tombs of Nebamun and Nakht, as well as from a number of literary sources.

Features of a an upper-class banquet

If the guests were important officials, the host probably met them at the door. Otherwise, young servant girls, dressed in little more than a girdle and necklet, greeted the guests and presented them with lotus flowers and perfumed incense cones which were worn on the head. During the night, these cones melted, and the scented oil ran down over the guests' wigs and clothing. The servants would renew them during the evening.

Presentation of flowers and perfume cones

The banquet was the perfect place for these officials and their wives to show off the latest fashions. Both sexes wore finely pleated, flowing garments of the sheerest white linen, either tied under the bust (for women) or around the waist with a sash of the same material (for men). The white robes were a perfect foil for their colourful and expensive bracelets, earrings and necklets and their long curled wigs. Their elaborate leather slippers were probably removed before entering the house as a mark of respect to the host.

Important guests were shown to high-backed chairs, others to low stools, while some had to be satisfied with mats or cushions. The seating was arranged around tables laden with food. Sometimes the men and women sat separately, sometimes together. This may have indicated the difference between single and married women.

Seating arrangements

A banquet scene from the tomb of Nebamun

Drunkenness

Serving girls circulated among the guests, offering them food and bowls of the finest wines. Perhaps the guests urged each other to 'celebrate the joyful day' and to 'cast behind thee all cares and mind thee of pleasure'[20] and offered health to each other's *ka*. Some, like the woman in the scene in the tomb of Paheri, might have called to the servants to 'give me eighteen cups of wine. I want to drink to drunkenness, my throat is as dry as straw'.[21] It was quite normal for the evening to become disorderly as men and women drank to excess. Drunkenness was tolerated and there are scenes showing both men and women vomiting and being carried from the room.

Musicians and dancers from the tomb of Nakht

Music and dancing

Apart from conversation and gossip, the guests were entertained by musicians playing the harp, lyre, lute, flute, castanets and tambourines. A singer might urge the guests to 'follow thy heart and thy happiness as long as thou art on earth'.[22] Female dancers performed sensual movements, sometimes combined with acrobatic feats. While some of the entertainers were professional, others were probably members of the noble's household.

Quieter forms of entertainment were also enjoyed by the upper classes. A family might take a boating or fishing trip on the canals or lakes of their estate, gather in the shade of the trees in their garden and listen to music, or play one of the several popular board games, like sennet and draughts. Many rectangular boards, divided into squares, have been found among funerary items. In some of the tomb paintings, husbands and wives are shown playing board games together.

A guest who has had too much to drink

Women playing a board game, from the tomb of Khabeki

A noble hunting in the desert

Hunting in the desert and marshes

Hunting for pleasure was the prerogative of the pharaoh and the nobility. During the Old Kingdom, hunting wild animals in the deserts was done on foot but by the Eighteenth Dynasty chariots were used. Nobles with their specially bred hunting dogs, were accompanied by professional hunters and attendants who carried the nobles' equipment. They ambushed gazelles, bulls, lions, hyenas and ostriches and attacked with bows and arrows. Sometimes animals were rounded up with lassos or trapped with nets to be kept for breeding or domestication. Wealthy Egyptians kept menageries of animals on their estates.

While scenes of hunting tended to disappear from the tomb walls after the reign of Thutmose III, the theme of fishing and fowling in the marshes continued to appear in many of the well-decorated tombs of the Eighteenth Dynasty. The noble, watched or helped by various members of his family speared fish and used a throwing-stick, similar to a boomerang, to catch water birds such as geese.

Fishing and fowling

Travelling and visiting estates

High-ranking officials travelled extensively between their numerous estates, between capitals and provincial cities and even beyond the borders of Egypt. Most of these journeys were taken by boat and/or chariot.

Frequent journeys by ship

Since most of these officials controlled and supervised widely dispersed estates, they were obliged to make personal tours of inspection from time to time. On these occasions they probably travelled in a boat similar to the one used by the viceroy of Kush which was:

> ... a long, crescent-shaped vessel rising clear out of the water at both bow and stern, and with an enormous sail attached by numerous ropes to a single mast. Instead of a central rudder, a pair of rudders were set against the hull slightly forward of the stern, and fastened to great posts to port and starboard respectively. The passengers quarters were in a big cabin amidships, with an extension in the form of a shelter for the horses, and two smaller cabins were placed at bow and stern.[23]

The use of chariots

Once an official arrived at the wharf of his estate, he made the rest of the journey by chariot, drawn by two horses. Dykes, built up when canals were dredged, served as roads for chariots, cattle and pedestrians.

The tombs of Menna, Nebamun and Paheri show these officials driving their own chariots as they supervised the activities on their estates. Running ahead of the noble's chariot were several grooms, ready to look after the horses when their master continued on foot. Following behind were a number of servants, who carried everything the lord needed when he stopped to rest or consult with his bailiffs and scribes. The *shemsou* (servants) set up elaborate booths with a seat and refreshments for the lord while he conducted his business. The scenes in Paheri's tomb seem to indicate that he spent quite a lot of time in the fields and his presence appeared to spur on the labourers. A text describes him as 'seeing all the activities going on in the fields'.[24]

Cargo boats

High-ranking officials had a fleet of boats to collect and distribute the produce from the estates under their control and some had their own trading boats which made the long trips to Nubia and Byblos. The boats used by Hatshepsut in her voyage to Punt were examples of these trading vessels.

Artists, craftsmen and unskilled workers

The status of artists and craftsmen

The numerous artists and skilled craftsmen employed by pharaohs, temples and wealthy individuals were, for the most part, anonymous.

Many of the officials buried in the Theban necropolis filled their tombs with images of artists and craftsmen carrying out their work. However, the tomb owners did not record the names of any of the talented individuals who produced the luxury, ritual and funerary items used and dedicated by the official class. On the other hand, these officials promoted their own role in 'seeing all the crafts (and) letting every man know his responsibilities in the execution of every occupation'.[25]

Only occasionally can we catch a glimpse of an individual artist and learn his name. Of the approximately 288 known tombs belonging to Eighteenth and early Nineteenth Dynasty officials in the Theban necropolis, only a handful belonged to artists and craftsmen such as portrait sculptors (Nebamun and Ipuki), master draughtsmen (May and Peshedu), master stonemasons (Amenmose) and goldsmiths (Neferronpet and Nehem'away). The existence of these tombs points to a hierarchy of craftsmen. Others who ranked highly were jewellers, silversmiths, bronze workers, coppersmiths, stone vase makers, master carpenters and painters. Lower down the scale were plasterers, stone workers, leather workers, weavers and brick makers.

According to the *Satire of the Trades*, the working conditions of craftsmen and tradesmen were far inferior to those of scribes. However, the negative aspects of the occupations mentioned in this text were exaggerated so that young students would aspire to a scribal career.

A glimpse into a royal and temple workshop

The joint tomb of Nebamun and Apuki, sculptors to Amenhotep III, has some of the best preserved scenes of a royal workshop. In the paintings, a superintendent is shown watching a scribe weighing thick rings of gold on a set of scales. Close by, wood carvers, using a chisel and adze, are shaping symbols (a *djed* for stability and a *tyet* for protection) to be fitted into a catafalque* by cabinet makers. Other craftsmen are engaged in hammering out and chasing gold and metal vessels, chiselling a sphinx and making jewellery. Finally, two workers hold out a number of finished products (jewellery, a wooden chest, a scribe's palette and metal vessels) for inspection by the supervisor.

Scenes from the tombs of Apuki and Nebamun

The walls in the tomb of the vizier, Rekhmire, feature a wide variety of crafts and trades carried out in the workshops attached to the Temple

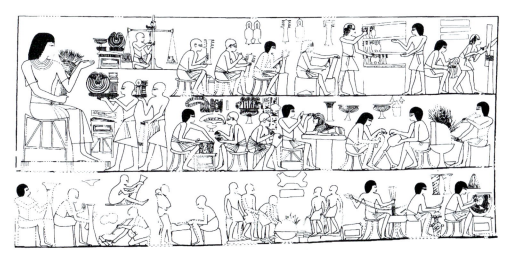

Craftsmen in a royal workshop, from the tomb of Ipuki and Nebamun

* A catafalque was a decorated wooden support for a coffin.

of Amun at Karnak. Rekhmire was responsible for the raw materials that entered the temple workshops and the finished products that were destined for the palace, the king's tomb or the temple. The craftsmen pictured are goldsmiths, bronze workers and coppersmiths, masons, sculptors, carpenters, jewellers, stone vase makers, leather workers and brick makers.

Unfortunately, the workshop scenes in both of these tombs are not totally realistic. For example:

Lack of realism in tomb scenes

- Not all stages in the manufacturing processes are shown. The tomb artist was selective in his choice of activities and techniques to be portrayed.

- It is unlikely that all of these crafts were carried out in the one workshop. It is more likely that there were separate workshops and that the supervisor inspected each in turn.

- Although the royal and temple workshops appear to be clean and orderly, most real workshops would have been bustling, noisy, dirty, crowded and very hot.

However, the scenes in these tombs do throw some light on the techniques and tools used by the New Kingdom craftsmen and some of these are described below.

Work techniques

Sculptors

The Egyptians were masters at working in granite, basalt, limestone, quartzite, schist and diorite. A sculptor employed by the king or the temple also had to have extensive knowledge of Egyptian mythology, religious ritual and forms of worship, the conduct of festivals, the characteristics of the gods and the attributes of kingship. An artist, who believed his knowledge and skill placed him 'above the common herd', recorded that he 'knew the proper attitude for a statue (of a man) ... how a woman holds herself ... the way a man poises himself to strike with the harpoon ... the way a spearman lifts his arm, the tilt of a runner's body' and 'the secret of making inlays that fire cannot melt and water dissolve'.[26]

Sculptors, from the tomb of Rekhmire

In the tomb of Rekhmire there are scenes showing masons squaring a block of limestone and sculptors using chisels and mallets to shape a colossal red granite statue of Thutmose III. Also being chiselled were a white limestone sphinx and an offering table. Other workers are shown polishing and grinding the statues (using hard diorite stones and sand) and preparing to paint the figures. Finished sculptures, especially those carved from limestone, were usually painted. On the back of a standing statue, a draughtsman outlines the hieroglyphs to be engraved. Once these were carefully cut into the stone, a painter would fill them with brilliant colours. Obviously these activities did not all occur simultaneously.

Goldsmiths

Because of its imperishability, gold was particularly valuable for funerary and ritual items. Gold arrived at the temple and palace workshops in the form of nuggets or rings and was carefully weighed. Scribes kept a strict record of how much gold was handed out to the craftsmen so that they could check this later against the weight of the finished product. The metal rings were often weighed against a weight in the shape of the head of Maat, the goddess of truth. The scenes from the tombs of Rekhmire and Nebamun/Apuki show this strict security measure.

This precious metal was used in jewellery, for making vessels and for gilding fine wooden objects (gold leaf or foil). In Rekhmire's tomb the workmen are shown using pounders to beat out sheets of gold which were then raised into various types of decorative vessels (vases, bowls and jugs). The skill of New Kingdom goldsmiths in making objects from sheet gold is best seen in the funeral mask of Tutankhamun.

The importance of gold for ritual items

Once an object was hammered into shape, other craftsmen used a pointed bronze tool to chase (punch) a design or dedicatory text into it. When several parts of an object had to be joined (brazed), such as a handle that had to be attached to a pot, charcoal furnaces were used. The heat from these furnaces was increased by the use of blowpipes. Brazing was a very skilful operation which required speed and accuracy to prevent the bronze tongs, used to hold the vessel, from melting. An even more difficult form of brazing was used in jewellery making.

The inscription accompanying the scenes in Rekhmire's tomb refers to the goldsmiths and silversmiths as:

> making all sorts of vessels for the god's limb (the person of the king), making very many ritual jugs in gold and silver in all kinds of workmanship which will last forever.[27]

Goldsmiths and jewellers often worked together fitting the lapis lazuli, turquoise, carnelian and faience beads into the gold settings. In the tomb of Rekhmire, a worker is shown drilling holes into stone beads with a bow drill while another strings them together.

Using a blowpipe to increase the heat in a furnace, from the tomb of Rekhmire

Copper and bronze smiths

The work of copper and bronze smiths was also shown in Rekhmire's tomb. An inscription says that the copper came from Asia as a result of Thutmose III's victory over that area and that it was to be used for casting monumental bronze doors for the Temple of Amun at Luxor.

Ingots of copper and tin (from which bronze was made) were smelted in large furnaces. These were fuelled with charcoal and the heat was controlled by means of foot-bellows. The men operating these held ropes which were pulled to refill the bellows once the operators had trodden the air from them.

Furnaces for melting metal, from the tomb of Rekhmire

Handling molten metal must have been extremely difficult, as it had to be poured quickly into the moulds. This involved careful preparation by the master smith to make sure that there was just enough molten metal to fill the mould in one pouring.

There is evidence of two types of casting or moulding. The molten bronze for the huge temple doors mentioned in Rekhmire's tomb was poured into pottery moulds. Sometimes stone moulds were used. The use of pottery or stone moulds was the most common method.

Another method of casting was the lost-wax technique. The object to be made was first modelled in wax and then covered in clay. When the clay was heated, the wax melted, leaving a rigid clay mould into which molten metal was poured.

Carpenters

The Tomb of Rekhmire

In a scene in Rekhmire's tomb, carpenters are shown building and decorating a shrine similar to one found in Tutankhamun's tomb. These workmen are depicted sawing planks, assembling the shrine, shaping and painting the protective symbols (*djed* pillars) with which to decorate it, and fitting these symbolic forms into position.

Types of timbers used

According to the text accompanying the images, carpenters made 'furniture in ivory and ebony, in sesnedjem-wood and meru-wood, (and) in real cedar from the heights of the terraced hills (Lebanon)'.[28]

Other scenes illustrate the making of:

* chairs with woven rush seats
* the framework of a bed, ready to have the cords for the string base woven into it
* chests about to have strips of various wood veneers and ivory glued to their surfaces.

A carpenter using a bow-drill on a chair, from the tomb of Rekhmire

A carpenter with his tools, from the tomb of Rekhmire

Carpenters used axes, pull-saws, adzes, chisels, bradawls, bow-drills and stone polishers. With these simple tools they produced work of the finest quality.

Tools

The scribe in *Satire of Trades*, however, didn't think too highly of carpentry as a profession.

> The carpenter who wields an adze,
> He is wearier than a field labourer:
> His field is his timber, his hoe the adze.
> There is no end to his labour,
> He does more than his arms can do,
> Yet at night he kindles light (ie, he goes on working).[29]

Leather preparation, from the tomb of Rekhmire

Leather workers

Leather making had been an established craft since the early dynastic period. Some of the items made from leather during the New Kingdom were sandals, ropes, satchels for carrying papyrus rolls, whips, reins, helmets, quivers and small, round shields. Some of these items were elaborately embossed with foreign designs.

Hides were stretched on a board and then left to soak in a jar of oil. When the tanned hide was almost dry it was hammered and scraped until all the oil was absorbed into the skin, giving it suppleness and durability. The leather was then cut into the shapes required.

Processes shown in the tomb of Rekhmire

The tomb makers of Deir el-Medina

On the west bank of Thebes, close of the Valley of the Kings, was the small settlement of Deir el-Medina. It was a special community, comprising the families of the craftsmen and workers who were responsible for the construction of the royal tombs.

This community of royal tomb builders (*servants in the Place of Truth*) was probably first established under the pharaoh Amenhotep I (c. 1527–1506 BC). He and his mother, Ahmose Nefertari, were later worshipped as the patrons of the village. However, the village itself may not have been built until the reign of Thutmose I. For approximately 300 years the inhabitants of this segregated community excavated the kings' tombs from the barren cliffs and carved and painted the interiors with funerary scenes.

A special community

The men who lived in Deir el-Medina were predominantly stonemasons, plasterers, draughtsmen, sculptors, painters and carpenters. Each of them specialised in different phases of tomb construction. They tended to pass their skills on to their sons who hoped to inherit their father's position in the work gangs.

The personnel in the teams or gangs included master craftsmen, skilled workers, apprentices and labourers.

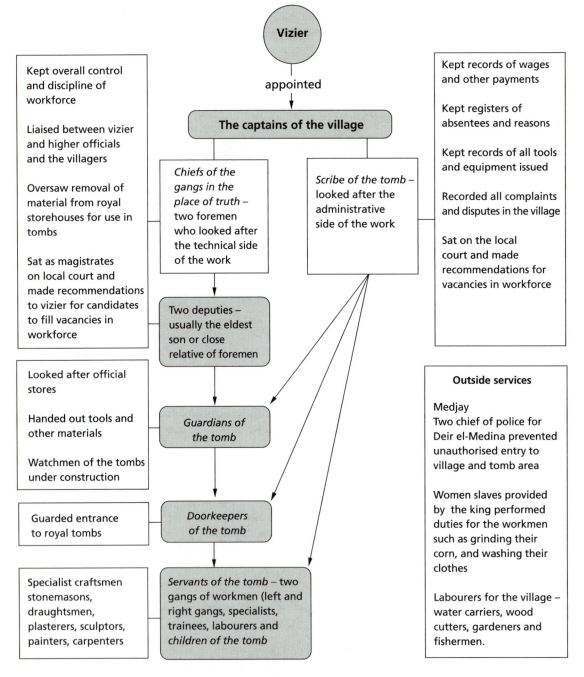

The organisation of the workforce from Deir el-Medina

Working conditions

The written evidence from Deir el-Medina provides a more realistic and detailed account of working conditions for men of this class than do the scenes on the tomb walls.

Organisation of the workforce of Deir el Medina

The workers were organised into two gangs — one worked the left side of the tomb while the other worked the right side. The size of the gangs varied from time to time. Each gang was supervised by a foreman and these two men, together with a scribe, made up the captains of the village. Certain selected workmen were chosen to act as *guardians of the tomb* and *doorkeepers of the tomb.* These royal workmen and their families were supported by other workers from outside the village.

Two gangs of workers

The diagram on the previous page shows the way the workforce in Deir el-Medina was organised and the responsibilities of each group.

Working hours

The men worked in four-hour shifts for eight days straight, in the Valley of the Kings. During this time, they camped near the tombs, after which they returned to the village and their families for two days.

Since the Egyptian month was made up of 30 days, the men had six free days a month. This, of course, did not include special festival days and the frequent absences about which there is substantial evidence.

Attendance

The *scribe of the tomb* kept a careful register of those men who did not turn up for work and the reasons given by them for their absences. The most frequent excuses were:

- scorpion bites and eye diseases
- family events and crises such as births and deaths
- brewing beer for a festival
- hangovers
- doing personal work for their superiors
- building houses.

A worker also had a valid excuse if either his wife or daughters were menstruating because 'coming in contact with a man whose female relations were bleeding could be considered undesirable'.[30]

Kitchin, in his book *Pharaoh Triumphant, The Life and Times of Ramesses II*, quotes a document which was probably the scribe's attendance sheet. It records the absentee's name, the date and the reason why he was missing from work.

> Pendua: 1st month of Inundation, Day 14 — (out) drinking with Khons...

Haremwia: 3rd of Inundation, Days 21 and 22 — with his boss (foreman); 2nd of Winter, Day 8 — brewing beer; 3rd of Summer, Days 17, 18, 21 — ill.

Huynefer: 2nd of winter, Days 7, 8 — ill; 3rd of Summer, Days 3, 5 — eye trouble; Days 7, 8 — ill.

Amenemwia: 1st of Winter, Day 15 — mummifying Harmose; 2nd of Winter, Day 7 — absent; Day 8 — brewing beer; Day 16 — strengthening the door...

Seba: 4th of Inundation, Day 17 — a scorpion bit him.

Khons: 4th of Inundation, Day 7 — ill; 4th of Winter, Day 8 — attending his god; 1st of Inundation, Day 14 — his feast; Day 15 — his feast (a birthday hangover?).

QeAnuy: 1st of Winter, Day 24 — fetching stone for Qen-hir-khopshef; 2nd of Winter, Day 7 — ditto; Day 17 — absent; Day 24 — absent with scribe.[31]

Provision of equipment

Careful records kept by scribes

Although many of the workmen had their own tools, they did not use them when working for the king. Tools were issued from the government storehouse when required. The scribe kept a careful record of every piece of equipment distributed to the workers and every tool handed back to be sharpened or repaired.

Since much of the work was done deep within the tomb, the workers were provided with lamps. These consisted of wicks made from greased pieces of twisted linen placed in pottery bowls which were filled with salted oil. The salt prevented the wicks from smoking. Not only would smoke have made it difficult for the workers to see but it would have damaged the paintings. Wicks were issued daily and it seems from the evidence that the men went through an enormous number of them each day.

Account of wicks issued from the storehouse in the 3rd month of Summer, [Day...]: 528 wicks. Account of consumption rendered this day: 118 wicks.[32]

Pay

Monthly rations

Wage slips have been found among the remains at Deir el-Medina and they show that the workmen were paid in the form of monthly rations of emmer wheat flour (for making bread) and barley (for making beer). These payments were authorised by the vizier and paid through the royal treasury. A bonus of meat, salt and oil was generally paid on festival days.

Sources of additional income

The foremen and scribe received the highest wages, followed by the guardians and doorkeepers. However, the craftsmen were amply paid most of the time. They also had opportunities to supplement their income by doing extra jobs for their superiors and making funerary equipment for their colleagues. In addition, the men received deliveries of vegetables, fish, water, wood and pottery from suppliers outside the village.

Opportunities for promotion

The members of the work gangs were usually recruited from the sons of workmen. Since families were large, not every son was fortunate enough to become a member of one of the gangs. Those who missed out had to seek work elsewhere.

Competition for vacancies in the workforce was fierce. Although these positions were theoretically filled by the vizier, it was the foremen and scribe who made the recommendations. This situation often led to bribery and it was not unusual for a man to give gifts to his superiors in order to ensure his son a position.

Competition for positions

Although the position of foreman was not strictly hereditary, the chiefs often made their sons deputies in order to give them a greater chance to inherit the position. For example, a draughtsman, called Amennakht, was promoted by the vizier to the position of scribe and for the next six generations a member of his family held this important position.

Positions tended to be hereditary

Work-related disputes

There is evidence that the captains of the village did not always get along with each other. For example, a foreman by the name of Paneb threatened his colleague, Hay, that he would get him in the mountains and kill him. His threat was not carried out but the situation indicates that relations were not always smooth. This was not the only occasion on which Paneb threatened to kill someone. He threw stones at the house of a chief workman called Neferhotep and said 'I will kill him in the night'.[(33)]

A draughtsman-painter named Prehotep sent the scribe an angry note because he felt he had been treated unfairly. 'What's the meaning of this rotten way you've treated me? I am to you just like a donkey.'[(34)]

Workmen were far from happy if they thought others were not doing their job properly. For example, a draughtsman complained about the laziness of someone called Ib who took the whole day to get water for the workmen.

The foremen and even the workmen often sent notes reminding the vizier that their rations were overdue or that they were short of essential supplies needed to complete a tomb. On one occasion, when the workmen did not get their rations on time, they refused to work and actually staged a sit-down demonstration, supported by the foreman and the chief of police. Mentmose, the police chief, advised them to:

> Go up, collect your tools, lock your doors and bring your wives and your children. And I will go in front of you to the Mansion of Menmaetre (Temple of Seti I) and install you there in the morning.[(35)]

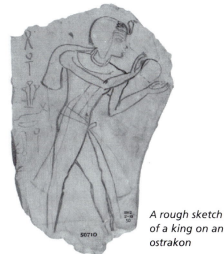

A rough sketch of a king on an ostrakon

Techniques used in the construction of a royal tomb

When a new king came to the throne, the royal tomb workers rejoiced because it meant the start of a new project. They would have no trouble getting rations and supplies and if the king wanted his tomb completed quickly, more men would be recruited. Once a royal commission, headed by the vizier, had chosen a suitable site in the Valley of the Kings and a plan was drawn up, the quarrying began.

Masons

The stonemasons used copper or bronze spikes which, when pounded with a wooden mallet, would split the rock. The limestone debris was removed from the site in baskets and deposited on the valley floor. The workmen and their superiors used these limestone chips for keeping records, making rough notes, sending messages, scribbling and drawing.

Plasterers

Draughtsmen

As the quarrymen and stonemasons excavated further into the cliff, the plasterers followed, smoothing down the walls with a layer of gypsum and whitewash. The draughtsmen outlined the layout of the text and pictures in red ink. Any mistakes or improvements were marked in black by the master draughtsman. The scenes to be inscribed and/or painted featured mainly funerary themes such as the journey of the sun god Re, (with whom the king was associated) through the Underworld at night and his rebirth every morning to begin his journey across the sky by day. Refer to Chapter 17 for examples of the skills of the craftsmen of Deir el-Medina.

Sculptors and painters

The sculptors and painters followed. In some areas, the quality of the stone did not favour reliefs and so the scenes were simply painted on the plaster surface. Where the carving of reliefs was possible, the sculptors used bronze chisels. The reliefs were then painted, using natural oxides (red, brown and yellow), derivatives of copper (blue and green), whitewash and soot. These were ground and then mixed with water and occasionally gum.

When a king died, the workmen had to stop what work they were doing and concentrate on making the tomb as presentable as possible before the funeral.

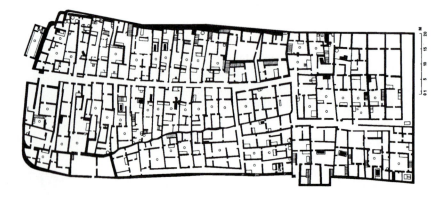

A plan of the workers' village at Deir el-Medina

Life in Deir el-Medina

This purpose-built village was protected by its own police force since the location of the royal tombs had to be kept secret and the men who worked on them had to be protected. The police station was located outside the village walls.

Village police force

Village houses

At the time of Ramesses II, the village contained about 70 houses within an enclosure wall and approximately 40 outside the wall. There was one main street and a number of side alleys, which some archaeologists believe may have been covered.

The mud-brick and stone houses, which opened straight onto the street, generally followed a similar pattern. However, there were variations according to status within the community.

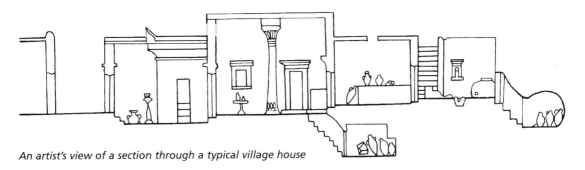

An artist's view of a section through a typical village house

The white, one-storey houses had flat roofs made from palm trunks and leaves which were covered with plaster. The evidence suggests that doors may have been painted red. Texts, also written in red, were written above some of the doorways and these have enabled archaeologists to identify individual home owners. A stairway at the back of the house provided access to the roof which acted as a cool terrace during the warm evenings. Outside each house stood a large water-storage jar which was filled from the community well outside the northern gate of the village. Water carriers who did not live in the village kept the well full. They carted water from the Nile River a few kilometres away.

Most of the sparsely furnished houses consisted of four rooms with a walled courtyard at the back where the cooking was done. The entrance hall contained niches for offering tables, stelae and the busts of ancestors. It also featured a large brick structure which may have been an altar or a *bed* where the women of the family gave birth. The next room had a brick platform around the walls which acted as seating during the day and beds at night. The ceiling of this room was higher than the rest and light filtered in through small high windows. In most homes the floor was of hard-packed earth but wealthier inhabitants plastered their floors as well as the walls. In some houses, remains of cellars have been found beneath this room. Side rooms were probably used as sleeping quarters, for storage and as work areas.

Village women

Except for a few old men and invalids, it was the women who carried on all the activities associated with daily life during the eight days the men were away. They were often required to answer requests for more food to be sent to the mountain camp. For example, a workman called Nebneteru sent the following message to his mother:

> **Have brought to me some bread, also whatever (else) you have by you, urgently, urgently!**[36]

As well as looking after their many children, the women supplemented their meagre issue of clothing by spinning, weaving and dressmaking. Slaves, provided by the government, alleviated their housework somewhat by grinding corn and carrying out other menial tasks. There was also a regular laundry service provided by workers from outside the community. These washermen were assigned a certain number of households to service.

It appears that some of the women in Deir el-Medina could read and write. This is not surprising in a village with a high number of skilled and educated personnel. Notes about female matters (dressmaking advice, laundry lists) and letters by workmen to their wives and mothers are evidence of this.

A woman's importance in the community was recognised by law. If she inherited property she was left in control of it even after marriage and she was entitled also to a third of the marital property. She was also permitted to leave her property to whomever she wished. There is evidence of a woman disinheriting her children because they did not look after her when she grew old.

If she divorced her husband she retained control of her private property. Although the one who left the marriage had to pay the other compensation, the amount expected from a wife to her husband was less. The only exception was if the husband accused the wife of adultery.

A letter found in the village described a situation involving a woman and her married neighbour who were having an affair. This almost led to an ugly incident as supporters of the wronged wife took matters into their own hands. Fortunately the police arrived before the pair were attacked by the incensed mob

Neighbourhood squabbles and court cases

In a community as small and confined as Deir el-Medina disputes often broke out. Although there were serious offences committed such as theft and violence, the majority of disputes which led to court cases concerned failure to pay for goods and services. In fact, the evidence seems to suggest that the villagers went to court over very trivial matters such as the failure to pay for a pot of fat and the sale of a lame donkey. Perhaps a good court case alleviated the boredom of the daily routine.

One notorious case concerned the foreman Paneb. He was accused of robbing private tombs, using government equipment and employees for work on his own tomb, threatening members of the community and making sexual assaults on several married women. Paneb was eventually removed from office.

The local court, called the *kenbet*, was composed of the foremen, deputies, scribes and some highly regarded senior villagers. It dealt with all civil cases and some minor criminal ones. Very serious cases were referred to the vizier's court.

Recreation

Life in the village was not all work. Religious festivals and family celebrations gave people the chance to relax and have fun. The evidence suggests that they needed little excuse for a party and that on these occasions there was a plentiful supply of beer and wine.

During one of the yearly feasts to their patron, the deified king Amenhotep I, 'the gang made merry before him for four full days, drinking with their wives and children — sixty people from inside (the village) and sixty people from outside'.[37]

Scenes from the villagers' tombs show members of the family amusing themselves at a game of draughts and the numerous ostraka reveal that many villagers sketched and read popular stories. One of the largest ostraka ever found had the complete version of the story of Sinuhe (see Chapter 8) written on it.

Religion

The painted scenes in the workmen's tombs and the number of village and household shrines and stelae indicate that the villagers had a strong personal devotion to the gods. Their tombs, cut in the cliffs above the village, feature Osiris and Isis as well as the deified Amenhotep and his mother Ahmose Nefertari (refer to Chapter 17). Village shrines were dedicated to Amun, Hathor, Thoth and Meretseger, the snake goddess of the peak which dominated the west bank.

Two particularly popular deities with the villagers were Taweret, the hippopotamus goddess of childbirth and Bes, the bearded dwarf, god of fertility, dance and music. This latter god was depicted on amulets (protective charms) and frescoes found in the houses.

Stelae placed in the home or in special chapels were dedicated to deceased members of the village and family ancestors.

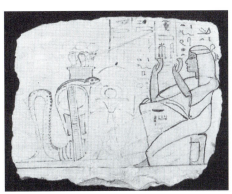

A workman from Deir el-Medina worshipping the snake goddess, Meretseger

A workers' village at Amarna (Akhetaten)

Another workmen's village from the Eighteenth Dynasty has been excavated just outside the capital city of the heretic king, Akhenaten. This village was built in a secluded valley, close to the eastern cliffs of Amarna.

Government planned village

Unlike the village of Deir el-Medina, where numerous texts provided evidence of daily life, most of what is known about the activities in this workers' village comes from archaeological remains. It appears that the village was planned and partially built by the government to house a special group of workers. Who were they?

Aldred suggests that when Akhenaten decided to build a new capital city at Akhetaten, 'part of the labour corps in the Place of Truth (Deir el-Medina) — which was concerned with the cutting, decorating and furnishing of the royal tombs, was transferred to Akhetaten ... '.[38] This seems a reasonable conjecture since the village was secluded, guarded and close to the southern group of tombs (of high-ranking officials).

Size of the village

House plans

The village, laid out in a square, was enclosed by a mud-brick wall. The 68 houses were identical in size, except for a larger one which housed the official in charge of the workers. A typical house had four areas — outer hall, living quarters, bedroom and kitchen with access to the roof. There is some evidence that an upstairs room with special wall paintings 'was the focus for domestic femininity'.[39] The homes were built from two types of bricks — the usual mud-bricks and a type made from pebbly, desert clays quarried just outside the village. This suggests that the government supplied the mud-bricks for the wall and some of the houses but when they became scarce, because of the amount of building going on in Akhetaten, the workers were forced to find their own building material.

This village had no well and like Deir el-Medina, water had to be carried from the river several kilometres away.

An interesting discovery made by the excavators indicates that these necropolis workers may have developed a lucrative sideline to supplement their income — pig raising. Grain-fed pigs, kept in specially constructed pens, were slaughtered at about one to two years of age. Butchers salted the meat, packed it in pottery jars and sold it to the inhabitants of Akhetaten. This appears to have been a well-organised operation.

Religion

During the life of this village, Egypt, at an official level, experienced a brief religious revolution. Akhenaten promoted the worship of only one god (Aten), yet the remains in the village indicate that on a personal level, the inhabitants continued to worship Hathor, Bes, Taweret and a cobra deity, Renenutet.

The village survived beyond the death of Akhenaten

Although the village had a fairly brief existence, it did continue to be occupied after the death of Akhenaten and into the reign of Tutankhamun. Workers were still building family chapels outside the village during the reign of the boy king. The texts found in these chapels reflect the religious transition that was occurring at the time. Short prayers, to both Amun and Aten, were written on the walls.

It has been suggested that the workers remained at Amarna 'perhaps looking after the tombs, either until their precious contents were removed, or perhaps just in case a further turn in history brought the court back again'.[40]

Peasant farmers and agricultural labourers

Agriculture was the most important activity in ancient Egypt and the peasant farmer was the backbone of society. Every other class depended on the never-ending toil of the farmer for its survival. Even life in the hereafter (*Fields of Reeds*) was believed to be based on agriculture.

Backbone of society

The Egyptian peasant was not a slave but a free tenant farmer who worked the lands of the pharaoh, the nobles and the temples. As well as peasants, there were slaves (captives) working on many estates as field labourers.

Although the Egyptian farmer was favoured by nature, life on the land was hard. This was recognised by the wealthier classes who, in order to avoid having to work in the *blessed fields* of the next life, placed small statuettes (*shabtis*) in their tombs to do the work for them. Despite their recognition of the farmers' back-breaking work and the frustrations they must have experienced, the officials continued to represent rural life in an idealised form. They depicted the peasants as good-natured, happy people who joked and sang as they worked.

Idealised view of peasants in the tombs

The tombs of Menna (*Scribe of Fields*), Nakht (*Scribe of the Granaries*) and Khaemhet (*Overseer of Granaries*) show the conventional and somewhat idealised picture of rural life. A more interesting picture of peasants at work comes from the provincial tomb of Paheri (*Mayor of Nekheb and Iunyt*), because the scenes are accompanied by remarks supposedly made by some of the labourers.

The cycle of farming activities

The farming calendar was geared to the annual flooding of the Nile. Before the river level began to rise, the farmers and their families prayed to Hapi, god of the Nile, for a 'good' flood. If the rise was insufficient 'the people dwindle, a year's food supply is lost'.[41] (Refer to Chapter 1 for the complete Hymn to Hapi.)

Akhet — the season of inundation

The season of flood began about the nineteenth of July. As the Nile began to rise, the farmers moved their cattle to higher ground and fed them by hand with fodder already in storage. This was a time for repairing equipment and making objects for use in the household.

> (Comes) the inundation and soaks him ... he attends to his equipment.
> By day he cuts his farming tools; by night he twists rope.[42]

The central authorities could demand the services of the peasants at this time to labour on large-scale constructions such as temples.

Perit — the season of coming forth

**Labour-intensive
period**

Perit began about the fifteenth of November and was the most labour-intensive part of the year. The people worked frantically to get the land and the irrigation system back to normal after the flood so that planting could take place before the soil dried out. This called for emergency procedures, involving the cooperation of a large part of the community working under centralised control.

Preparation for ploughing and planting included:

- digging out the canals and smaller channels to their proper depths
- repairing the dykes and rebuilding embankments to their proper heights
- getting the water sluices functioning properly
- re-establishing the boundaries of the estates by surveying and planting markers
- spreading the freshly-deposited Nile mud.

When all these tasks had been done it was time to begin the ploughing as the elder brother points out in *The Tale of the Two Brothers*.

> **Let us prepare our team of oxen for ploughing, for the waters have uncovered the earth and the ground is ready for the plough ... Next morning at daylight they walked out into their fields with their seed and began to plough.**[43]

**Evidence from the
tomb of Paheri**

On the walls of Paheri's tomb, six men are shown ploughing by hand followed by a younger man casting seeds into the furrows. Others use a plough drawn by two teams of oxen. The texts suggest that the men are enjoying their work because the weather is fine and cool and 'The year is good, free from difficulties; all crops flourish and the calves are better than anything'.[44] However, when they see Paheri watching from his chariot they feel guilty about not working fast enough. 'Hurry up, leader; drive on the cattle. See! The mayor stands, looking on.'[45]

Hoes were used to break up the heavy, sticky clods of earth left by the plough and to cover the seed. Hoeing was exhausting work and one labourer, depicted in Paheri's tomb, shows a slight trace of irritation with his workmate who is obviously taking too long. He urges him to 'buck up the work so that you let us go home in good time'.[46]

At the end of the day, the farmer unyoked his animals and carrying his plough and hoe, drove the oxen home. There was probably some truth in the scribe's statement that if the farmer left his equipment and animals in the fields overnight:

> **Comes dawn, he goes to make a start and does not find it in its place. He spends three days searching for it; he finds it in the bog. He finds no hides on them; the jackals have chewed them. He comes out, his garment in his hand, to beg for himself a team.**[47]

Even when sowing was completed the farmer could not sit back and, as Herodotus records, 'wait for the harvest'.[48] He had to: water the fields by shadouf or, more laboriously, by filling jars and watering by hand; clear wind-blown sand from canals and fields; and deal with the birds that ate the newly sown seed, young grain and fruit. Birds were either scared or snared. Small boys spent their days in the fields and gardens scaring the birds with loud noises. When flocks of birds were particularly troublesome, they were snared in nets and traps. This was a very simple method. A large net, supported on poles, was placed over a tree, allowing room for the birds to perch on the branches. When a large number had settled, children crept close and knocked the poles out. The net collapsed and the entrapped birds were collected and caged.

Constant work throughout Perit

Occasionally the farmers were faced with plagues of insects, particularly the voracious locusts. The only way to deal with this catastrophe was by praying to the gods.

Shemu — the season of harvest

This extremely busy time began around the sixteenth of March. The grain had to be harvested, threshed, winnowed, measured and transported to storage bins. Of all the agricultural scenes depicted on the walls of tombs, these are the most common.

Most common tomb scenes

At this time, the farmers once again felt the heavy hand of the central authorities as the pharaoh's officials carried out the annual census and tax assessment. The peasants' master, or his agent, appeared on the estate 'accompanied by a swarm of scribes, surveyors, servants and representatives of the civil authority'.[49] It appears, from the tomb of Menna, that when these officials arrived, the tenant farmers greeted them with gifts and refreshments.

Tax-men and surveyors, from the tomb of Menna

Before the harvesting began the surveyors measured the fields. In the tomb of Menna, two of them, using a rope knotted at intervals, are shown measuring the standing crops. They are accompanied by scribes who record the results on their palettes. The scribes then worked out and recorded the number of bushels of grain that the farmer's fields would produce. This formed the basis of the tax assessment.

Because cobras were often found among the ripened grain, the Egyptians believed that the cobra-headed goddess, Renenutet, had to be placated with offerings before the harvest began. The help of the gods was also sought to prevent thunderstorms from destroying the crop before it could be harvested.

The farmers spent weeks harvesting and threshing the grain, starting at daybreak and finishing at dusk. These activities are shown in considerable detail in the tombs of Menna and Paheri.

Methods of harvesting the grain

Reapers, working in pairs, harvested the barley with sickles. This was done by holding the grain with one hand and cutting off the heads, leaving the stalks. Since the heads only were taken to the threshing floor, this was a very efficient method. The stalks were recovered later for such things as basket-making, brick-making and as fuel for firing pottery kilns.

Gleaning

In the tomb of Paheri, wall paintings show the reapers being followed by two young girls, carrying baskets. Their job was to pick up anything that was dropped or left behind by the reapers. This was known as gleaning and it seems that certain families, in order to supplement their meagre rations, were given the right to glean in particular fields.

Gleaning was a job which often led to minor conflicts. In the tomb of Menna, two girls are shown pulling each other's hair. The text accompanying the scene in Paheri's tomb shows that the gleaners are not at all happy with the reapers. The older girl grumbles because the reapers did not let enough barley heads fall to the ground.

> Give me a handful, or you will make us come (again) in the evening. Don't repeat the malicious acts of yesterday, today.[50]

Men harvesting with sickles and young girls gleaning, from the tomb of Paheri

Unlike grain, flax was harvested according to its use. For example, a young plant was used for making fine linen thread, the stalks of an older plant were used for courser thread and the seed-heads of a mature plant were used for producing linseed oil.

Paheri's tomb paintings show three men and a woman harvesting flax by pulling the whole stalk from the ground, roots and all, while an elderly man bundles and ties the stalks together. These are carried to another old workman who combs (strips) the seed heads with a special instrument operated with his foot. He and the harvesters joke with each other. The old man urges them to bring him 11 009 bundles to comb and they reply, 'Don't gabble you bald old man of a fieldworker'.[51] These interchanges seem to illustrate a cheerful attitude to life.

Grain being carried in a pannier to the threshing floor. The scene also shows two gleaners fighting, peasants relaxing in the shade of a tree, and an old man, from the tomb of Menna

Once the grain was harvested, it was taken by labourers carrying panniers (large baskets on carrying poles) to the threshing floor. There was a sense of urgency to remove the harvested grain as quickly as possible to avoid losses from thieves and flocks of birds. In Paheri's tomb, the texts seem to indicate that the urgency is more about completing the threshing and winnowing before the river begins to rise. An overseer raises his stick and shouts to the labourers to 'Buck up, move your feet, the water is coming and reaches the bundles (of barley)'.[52] The labourers complain that it's too hot for them to hurry and that they have been working non-stop all day. It is highly unlikely that the flood was imminent.

At the threshing floor, workers forked over the ears of grain and a team of oxen, urged on by whips, trampled the grain from the chaff. Men, with their hair covered to keep the chaff out, used wooden scoops to toss the grain in the air so the lighter chaff would blow away. The grain was collected in special measuring containers while a team of scribes and supervisors recorded the amount harvested and checked it against their original assessment.

Winnowing and threshing, from the tomb of Paheri

The sacks of grain were carried to the granaries on the estate or to an open enclosure to await shipment, possibly for the settlement of taxes. In his tomb paintings, Paheri's labourers load seven barges with sacks of grain under the watchful eye of the mayor who urges them to hurry. One of the men complains:

> Are we to spend all day carrying barley and white emmer? The granaries are full, the heaps overflowing their mouths, the barges are heavily loaded with grain bursting out. Yet we are made to go even faster. Are our hearts of copper?[53]

Harvesting and treading grapes

The vintage

Harvesting and processing of grapes

Although the main Egyptian drink was beer, wine was a favourite with the upper classes. Some of the steps in the process of wine making are depicted in many Theban tombs. The grapes were harvested by hand (no knives were used) and carried in rush baskets to huge vats into which they were emptied. At least six men crushed the grapes with their feet and the juice was poured into open pottery jars for the first stage in the fermentation process. After the skins and stems of the grapes were given another squeezing in a bag press, the wine was poured into other jars and sealed.

Difficulties faced by the peasant farmer

Seasonal misfortunes

Not only could life be made very difficult for the farmer by an overzealous scribe but he had to face the possibility of seasonal catastrophes (low flood levels, drought, famine, plagues) as well as heavy taxation and the annual corvee.

The misfortunes faced by farmers are outlined by a scribe in the *Lansing Papyrus* (refer to the extracts from this papyrus in Question 13 at the end of this chapter). Although many of the problems are exaggerated, there is probably an element of truth in the scribe's account.

The annual corvee

Since the Egyptian way of life was based on successful farming which in turn depended on a 'good' Nile flood, careful management of the land and water supplies was essential. Centralised management was particularly helpful when catastrophes, such as drought, affected the annual harvests.

To carry out large-scale water and land management as well as deal with the emergency tasks immediately after the flood, the government conscripted labour. This was called the corvee. Gangs of men were put to work, sometimes far from their homes, under the authority of a high local official who coordinated their activities. Although most men were eligible for this duty, some were exempt because of their special rank or occupation. A wealthy man could pay for a substitute to take his place in these gangs. So the bulk of those who were conscripted were the farmers, field workers and slaves. This was the worst aspect of a farmer's life.

Yearly conscription of peasants

Taxes

No peasant looked forward to the arrival of the tax collector at harvest time. Not only did the farmer pay a large portion of his harvested grain but he was also taxed on any yearly increase in livestock (eg, cattle, geese). For this reason, a yearly census was carried out. The produce of the farmer's orchards, gardens and vineyards was also taxed. Once the tax had been paid, there was very little left for the farmer's basic needs.

Form of taxation

From the evidence in a number of tomb scenes which show farmers being punished for dishonesty, and the example cited by the scribe in the *Lansing Papyrus*, it appears that some peasants tried to cheat the tax collector. To a certain extent this was overcome by the New Kingdom practice of measuring the height of crops and assessing the amount of tax payable before the crops were harvested.

Cattle herders

Herds of cattle were found on every estate. Even peasants had their own animals for ploughing and threshing. Cattle were raised not only for their meat and milk and as beasts of burden, but for ritual purposes.

In many tombs, officials are shown inspecting and counting their cattle and overseeing the branding of their animals. However, only an overseer of cattle would show details of stables, fodder preparation and cattle feeding (eg, Haty, *Counter of Cattle of the God's Wife of Amun*).

The herders who looked after the cattle lived a harsher life than the farmers. As they moved constantly with their herds in search of the best grasses, they had to safely negotiate swamps and crocodile-infested waters. During the flood, they hand fed the cattle in their stables. The cattle byre was the herder's home.

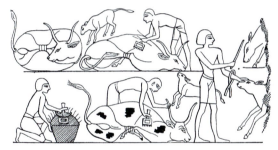

Branding cattle, from the tomb of police captain Nebamun

> Now when it had dawned and another day had come ... he took bread for himself for the fields, and he drove his cattle to let them eat in the fields. He walked behind his cattle, and they would say to him: 'The grass is good in such and such a place'. And he heard all they said and took them to the place of good grass that they desired.
>
> Now when many days had passed ... he returned to his house... Then he drank and ate and went to sleep in his stable among his cattle.[54]

The herders guarded their animals closely as they were punished severely if any were stolen, seized by a crocodile, or died of disease. When the time came for the cattle inspection and census, the herdsmen were expected to bring in a herd larger than the previous year.

> Thus the cattle he tended became exceedingly fine, and they increased their offspring very much.[55]

Life in a peasant village

For most of the year the farmers probably lived fairly independent lives in their mud-brick villages, without too much interference from the authorities.

The houses in these peasant villages varied in size depending on the number of people in the extended family. Because mud-bricks were easy to make and use, additions to the basic dwellings were simple to build. Each family probably had a small vegetable garden and a few domesticated animals.

A woman bartering goods, from the tomb of Ipuy

Peasant women

It is highly likely that marriages were arranged with close relatives to keep what little property the peasants had within the family. As in most classes, the woman's chief duty was in the home but some are shown helping their husbands in the fields — gleaning, harvesting flax, winnowing, carrying baskets to the storehouses and providing refreshments.

Within the village, women probably exchanged goods with one another, and to supplement the family income they could set up a stall in the local market. There they could convert any surplus beer, bread, vegetables or fish into other items needed by the family. The tomb of Ipuy depicts such a market scene.

A fishing scene, from the tomb of Ipuy

Although the peasants worked hard, they are also shown relaxing and enjoying themselves — snoozing under a tree, playing their flutes, refreshing themselves with a drink of beer and joking with their companions. Boating and fishing were other popular activities.

Annual religious festivals gave them the opportunity to take a break from the seasonal routine. During these holidays they probably took the opportunity to view the glittering religious processions and even possibly catch a glimpse of the king.

Conclusion

The great nobles and lesser officials who ran the civil, military and religious bureaucracies on behalf of the king shared in the great wealth that poured into Egypt during the *empire*. Their tombs in western Thebes provide evidence of their luxurious lifestyle.

Demands for more magnificent buildings, beautifully decorated tombs and finely crafted household and funerary items led to an increase in the number of skilled craftsmen. Less skilled workers such as brick-makers, leather workers and weavers were also in great demand. As in all areas of Egyptian government and society, there was a hierarchy of craftsmen and their living conditions varied accordingly. Compared with many other craftsmen, the workmen of Deir el-Medina were probably better off. Their tombs indicate that they had a good standard of living.

The whole of Egyptian society was dependant on the back-breaking toil of the peasants and agricultural labourers. Evidence found in the tombs of the wealthy elite indicate that the upper classes appreciated the invaluable role played by this group.

Chapter review

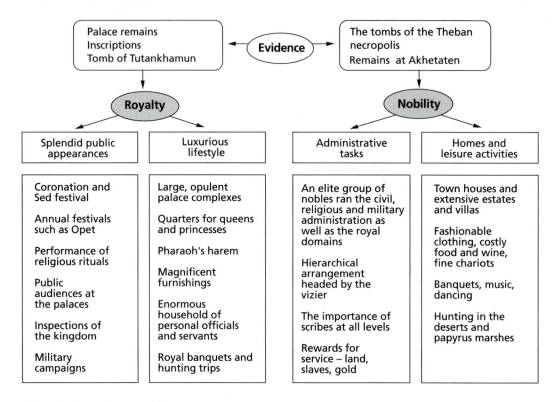

Lifestyle of royalty and nobility

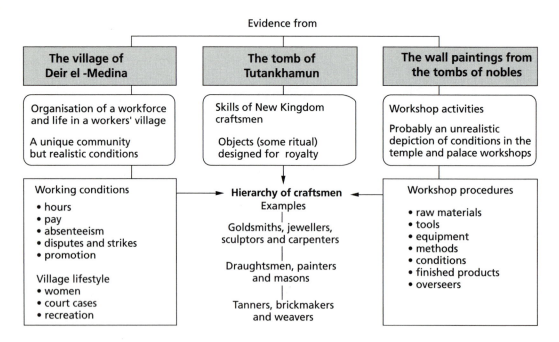

New Kingdom craftsmen

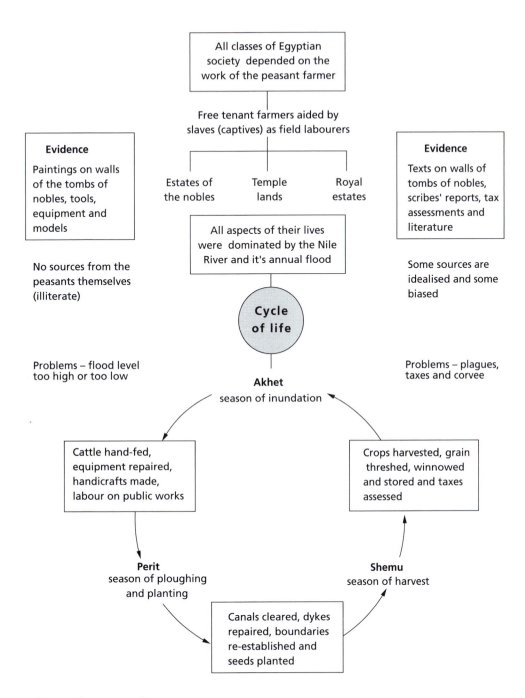

The Egyptian peasant farmer

REVISION QUESTIONS AND ESSAY TOPICS

1 The items shown below were found in the tomb of Tutankhamun.

An ebony and ivory gaming set, from the tomb of Tutankhamun

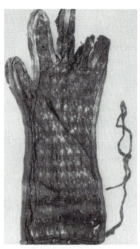

A riding glove, from the tomb of Tutankhamun

a   What do they appear to reveal about the life of a New Kingdom ruler?

b   What else do the contents of Tutankhamun's tomb seem to indicate about the lifestyle of royalty?

c   Why is it necessary to be cautious when making generalisations about the items found in a royal tomb?

2 Look carefully at this line drawing of the Theban house of Djehutnufe and answer the following questions.

a   Identify the activities that are being carried out in this home.

b   What is a problem faced by historians when interpreting scenes depicting domestic architecture?

3 **The following line drawing illustrates the visit of an Egyptian family to the country house of friends.**

a What evidence is there in the drawing that this visit marks some important event in the life of the family (a family festival)?

b What evidence is there that this family enjoyed:
- privacy
- nature
- places to escape the heat of the day?

c This is a smallish country house. What additional features would be found in the larger country villas of the wealthiest nobles?

d What forms of recreation would the members of this family and their friends be likely to enjoy?

4 **The following Nineteenth Dynasty text was written by an official to his dead wife.**

I was a young man when I married you, and I spent my life with you. I rose to the highest rank but I never deserted you from my youth to the time when I was holding all manner of important posts for Pharaoh (Life, Health, Strength): nay rather I always said to myself 'She has always been my companion'. When any one came to talk to me of you, I would not heed the advice he gave me about you, saying instead, 'I will do your pleasure'. Moreover, when I was responsible for training the officers of Pharaoh's infantry and cavalry, I caused them to come and prostrate themselves before you, bearing rich offerings of every kind to lay at your feet. Never have I concealed from you anything I have gained until this very day ... No man has ever seen me playing you false, like the peasant who sneaks into another's house. I never had my scents, cakes and garments taken to the house of another, saying instead, 'My wife is there', for I would do nothing to distress you. When you fell sick and suffered your illness, I summoned a master physician who gave you treatment and did everything at your behest. When I accompanied Pharaoh on his journey to the south, see how I behaved towards you — for eight months I neither ate nor drank as befitted a man of my rank. When I returned to Memphis, I begged leave of Pharaoh and I went to your dwelling place (tomb), and there I wept much before you with my kinsfolk. And now behold I have spent three years alone and yet I frequent no other house, though such a man as I could do so if he would ...[56]

What does this extract suggest about:

a the relationship between the writer and his wife

b the behaviour of many high-ranking officials

c the lifestyle of the wife of an important official?

5 **The following song was possibly performed at upper class social functions such as banquets.**

Celebrate the joyful day!
Let sweet odours and oils be placed for thy nostrils,
Wreaths of lotus flowers for the limbs
And for the bosom of thy sister, dwelling in thy heart
Sitting beside thee.
Let song and music be made before thee.
Cast behind thee all cares and mind thee of pleasure,
Till cometh the day when we draw towards the land
That loveth silence.
Put myrrh on thy head, array thyself in fine linen
Anointing thyself with the true wonders of god
Adorn thyself with all the beauty thou canst.
With a beaming face celebrate the joyful day and rest not therein.
For no one can take away his goods with him,
Yea, no one returns again, who has gone hence.[57]

a What is the message in this song?

b Provide evidence from the song to support the view that this might have been sung at banquets.

6 **Compare the extracts below. What do they reveal about Egyptian medicine?**

a Extract from the *Edwin Smith Medical Papyrus*:

Instructions: a gaping wound in his head, penetrating to the bone,

You should palpate his wound, [though] he shudders greatly. You should cause him to lift his face. If it is difficult for him to open his mouth, and his heart is weary to speak; if you observe the spit upon his lips, not falling to the ground, while he gives blood from his nostrils and ears, and he suffers a stiffness in his neck and is not able to look at his shoulders and breast; then you say concerning him:

'One having a gaping wound in his head, reaching to the bone, perforating the suture [ ] of his skull, the mandible is contracted; he gives blood from his nostrils and ears; he suffers a stiffness in his neck:

An ailment with which I will contend.'

Now if you find the cord of that man's mandible — his jaw — is contracted, you should have made for him something hot, until he is comfortable, so that his mouth opens. You should bind it with fat, honey and lint, until you know he has made a decisive point.

If you then find that the man has developed fever from that wound ... you should lay your hand upon him. Should you find that his face is wet with sweat, the ligaments of his neck are tense, his face is ruddy, his teeth [and] his back ..., the odour of the box of his head is like the urine of goats, his mouth is bound, his eyebrows are drawn ... you should say concerning him:

'One having a gaping wound in his head, reaching to the bone, perforating the suture [ ] of his skull, he has developed *tiz*, his mouth is bound, he suffers a stiffness in his neck:
An ailment not to be treated.'[58]

b   Extract from the *Ebers Medical Papyrus*:

Prescription to cause a woman's uterus to go to its correct place: tar that is on the wood of a ship is mixed with the dregs of excellent beer, and the patient drinks this.[59]

c   Secondary sources — A. R. David, *The Ancient Egyptians, Religious Beliefs and Practices* and P. Montet *Everyday Life in Egypt*:

Pharmaceutical treatments were also offered — aromatic oils and pleasant substances were believed to attract good gods and to repel evil ... some medicines contained disagreeable substances such as dung or urine, in the hope that these would expel the evil from the patient. The treatment of some complaints involved the use of *transfer* ... one example was the migraine headache, when the head of the sufferer was rubbed with that of a fish, to transfer the pain.[60]

Every temple contained statues or stelae with a reputation for healing. The surface of stelae of this type was engraved with the figure of a naked child Horus standing on a crocodile and holding serpents in his hands ... On the back or the base was engraved the legend of how, while his mother was away, the divine child was bitten by a snake in the swamps of Akhbit. On hearing his mother's cries, the lord of the gods had bidden Thoth to cure the injury. Alternatively the text might tell how the goddess Bastet was cured by Re of a scorpion's sting; or how Osiris was ... miraculously preserved from the jaws of a crocodile ... Each statue and stelae stood upon a pedestal in the middle of a basin full of water, connected by a channel to a second pool cut in the lower level of the pedestal. When anyone had been bitten, water was sprayed over the statue or the stela and thus became impregnated with the virtues of the magical texts and legends engraved thereon. It was then collected from the lower pool and given to the injured person to drink. 'The poison does not enter his heart, it does not burn in his breast, for Horus is his name and his father's name is Osiris and his mother is called Neith who weeps.'[61]

7   **Examine the reproductions below of wall paintings from the tomb of the Eighteenth Dynasty vizier, Rekhmire and answer the questions that follow.**

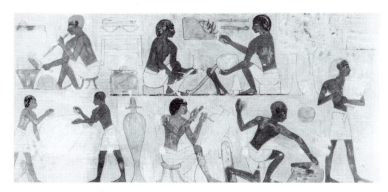

a   Identify the crafts and list the associated activities depicted in these wall paintings.

b   Why were the skills of these craftsmen so highly regarded during the New Kingdom?

c   Explain why sculptors would have been near the top of the hierarchy of craftsmen.

d   Why did Rekhmire's tomb contain so many scenes of craftsmen in their workshops? What other scenes would be depicted in the tomb of a vizier?

e   How did the growth of the Egyptian empire affect the demand for skilled craftsmen?

8 Examine the reproduction on the right and answer the questions below.

a   Where would this wall painted relief have been found? Provide reasons for your answer.

b   What was the title given to the group of people responsible for this wall *decoration*?

c   To which high official were they directly responsible?

d   List the specialist craftsmen involved in creating this scene. Briefly describe the task of each craftsman.

e   What other workers were associated with the construction of the place in which this painting was found?

9 Describe life in the village of Deir el-Medina from the perspective of a wife of one of the royal tomb makers.

10 The three extracts below come from a work entitled *The Satire of Trades*.

The jewel-maker bores with his chisel
In hard stone of all kinds;
When he has finished the inlay of the eye,
His arms are spent, he is weary;
Sitting down when the sun goes down,
His knees and back are cramped.

The potter is under the soil,
Though as yet among the living;
He grubs in the mud more than the pig,
In order to fire his pots.
His clothes are stiff with clay,
His girdle is in shreds;
If air enters his nose,
It comes straight from the fire.
He makes a pounding with his feet,*
And is himself crushed;
He grubs the yard of every house
And roams the public places.

* The clay was initially pounded with the feet. Then it was moulded by hand.

I'll describe to you the mason:
His loins give him pain;
Though he is out in the wind,
He works without a cloak;
His loincloth is a twisted rope
And a string in the rear.
His arms are spent from exertion,
Having mixed all kinds of dirt ...[62]

a   What is the attitude of the writer to trades other than the scribal profession?

b   What is meant by:
   • *when he has finished the inlay of the eye*
   • *he grubs the yard of every house*?

c   Explain why the mason works in near nudity.

d   According to the writer, what hardships do these craftsmen/tradesmen suffer in carrying out their jobs?

e   What evidence is there from these extracts that the writer has ranked these crafts or trades?

11 Study the two registers below from the tomb paintings of an Eighteenth Dynasty official, then answer the questions that follow.

a   Identify the official in whose tomb this scene was found. What role did he play in the bureaucracy?

b   Provide this scene with a title or caption.

c   Starting from the bottom register, identify and describe the main tasks being carried out by the peasants and field labourers as well as the tools and equipment being used by them. Don't forget to describe the smaller figures and those in the background since they add a realistic touch to this scene.

d   How accurate are the depictions of peasants shown in the tombs of officials?

12 The scene below shows Nebamun (Police Chief of Western Thebes) supervising estate activities. In the far top corner, he is shown making offerings before a temple. What else is happening in this scene?

13 The following extract is from a story called *The Misfortunes of the Peasant.*

Let me expound to you the situation of the peasant, that other tough occupation. (Comes) the inundation and soaks him [], he attends to his equipment. By day he cuts his farming tools; by night he twists rope. Even his midday hour he spends on farm labour. He equips himself to go to the field as if he were a warrior. The dried field lies before him; he goes out to get his team. When he has been after the herdsman for many days, he gets his team and comes back with it. He makes for it a place in the field.

When he reaches his field he finds [it broken up]. He spends time cultivating, and the snake is after him. It finishes off the seed as it is cast to the ground. He does not see a green blade. He does three ploughings with borrowed grain. His wife has gone down to the merchants and found nothing for (barter). Now the scribe lands on the shore. He surveys the harvest. Attendants are behind him with staffs, Nubians with clubs. One says (to him): 'Give grain.' 'There is none.' He is beaten savagely. He is bound, thrown in the well, submerged head down. His wife is bound in his presence. His children are in fetters. His neighbours abandon them and flee. When it's over, there's no grain.

If you have any sense, be a scribe. If you have learned about the peasant, you will not be able to be one. Take note of it![63]

a   Who is the author of this text?

b   In this extract the author describes the major agricultural tasks carried out by the farmer during the three seasons. Which sentence best describes the chief activity carried out by the farmer during *Akhet*, *Perit* and *Shemu*?

c   Why does the farmer *have to go out to look for his team* of oxen? Where have they been?

d   Why does the author compare the peasant farmer to a warrior?

e   According to the author, what problems does the farmer face during the year? List these.

f   Which part of the extract seems to be the most exaggerated? Explain.

g   Why was this extract written in a deliberately biased way?

h   How does this view of peasant life compare with that presented in most of the tomb paintings?

14 Essay topics

a   What can be learned about the life of the Egyptian nobility in New Kingdom times? Refer to specific tombs. In your answer consider such aspects as:

   • activities associated with the careers of particular officials

   • relationships between men and women

   • types of houses

   • recreation and leisure activities.

b   Discuss the importance to historians of the excavation of the village of Deir el-Medina.

c   Why are scholars chiefly dependent on the wall paintings and texts found in the tombs of the nobles for evidence about the life of the New Kingdom peasant farmer? How reliable are these tombs as sources of information? What information do the tombs provide about the conditions under which the peasants lived?

New Kingdom funerary beliefs and burial practices

Sources of evidence

The tombs of the kings, queens and officials of the Eighteenth and Nineteenth dynasties are the chief source of information for New Kingdom funerary (mortuary) beliefs and burial practices.

The wall paintings provide details of the Egyptians' beliefs about the judgment of the dead, the Osirian and solar afterlife and funeral rituals. Differences in the funerary themes in tombs of the first half of the Eighteenth Dynasty, the Amarna Period and the Nineteenth Dynasty, indicate some change in funerary beliefs.

Paintings

Those mummies that have survived provide evidence of New Kingdom embalming processes as well as the extensive use of amulets and spells.

The discovery of the complete funerary ensemble of Tutankhamun enabled scholars for the first time to examine the actual objects which previously had been seen only on tomb walls. According to Desroches-Noblecourt, the four rooms of Tutankhamun's tomb were filled with carefully arranged ritual objects, the purpose of which was to assist in the deceased king's transformation and rebirth. These ritual items revealed that, by the time of Tutankhamun's death, the Osirian burial rites, disregarded during the Amarna Period, had been restored.

Funerary ensemble of Tutankhamun

The decoration on coffins, sarcophagi, canopic jars and chests are a rich source of religious symbolism and add to the picture we have of the Osirian burial practices carried out in the New Kingdom.

Rolls of papyrus, written and illustrated with selected 'chapters' from the *Book of the Dead* and found on or near the body, reveal details of the funeral procession, the *Opening of the Mouth* ceremony, the judgment of the deceased, the presentation of the deceased to Osiris and life in the Osirian hereafter. The best examples of illustrated papyri come from

Funerary texts

the tombs of the Nineteenth Dynasty officials, Nakht (*Royal Scribe and Military Commander*), Hunefer (*Royal Scribe and Steward*) and Ani (*King's Scribe*).

Beliefs about life after death

A remarkable feature of the Egyptian funerary religion is its complexity, which developed as new beliefs were incorporated without older ones being discarded.[1]

The myth of Osiris

Osiris was a good and popular King of Egypt but his brother Seth was jealous of his reputation and planned to kill him.

Seth invited Osiris to a banquet and at the end of the feast Seth produced a beautiful chest. He promised to give it to the person who fitted it most exactly when lying in it. Of course Seth had it made to the exact measurements of his brother's body. After Seth's accomplices had all tried unsuccessfully to fit in the chest, Osiris lay down in it. Seth's accomplices then rushed forward, slammed down the lid, nailed it up and threw it into the Nile. The chest was carried down the river to the Mediterranean Sea where it was later washed up on the coast of Lebanon.

Osiris' wife, Isis, cut off part of her hair, put on mourning clothes and went in search of her husband's body which she eventually found at Byblos in Lebanon. She accompanied her husband's body back to Egypt and hid it in the papyrus thickets of the delta. According to one version of the story, Isis became pregnant to the dead Osiris by magical means during the voyage from Lebanon. Another version says that she was pregnant before her husband was killed and that she had given birth to Horus before she left for Lebanon.

For some reason, Isis left the body of Osiris unattended and Seth, who was hunting in the marshes, found it. The evil brother cut the body into 14 pieces and scattered the parts all over Egypt. Isis and her sister Nephthys (who was Seth's wife) wandered from one end of Egypt to the other looking for the pieces of Osiris' body. When they found a piece they preserved it carefully and held a funeral. They also made a wax model of the particular part and left it with the local priests who placed it in the temple where it was worshipped.

The two sisters collected all the pieces and then wept for Osiris. The great god Re heard them and sent Anubis, the jackal-headed god of embalming, and the ibis-headed god, Thoth, to help them. They put all the pieces together and wrapped the body in bandages. Thoth gave Isis the words to say over her husband's body. Then Isis and Nephthys changed themselves into birds and, using their wings, fanned life back into Osiris.

After his resurrection, Osiris did not take his place on the throne of Egypt again. He preferred to maintain his kingdom in the Underworld where he ruled as king of the dead. His son Horus eventually took revenge on Seth and was given the throne of Egypt by the gods.

Rebirth or resurrection

From earliest times, the Egyptians believed in the cycle of life, death and rebirth. This cycle was apparent in the patterns of nature — the constant movement of the sun across the sky, the germinating seed sprouting from the parched soil and the annual rise of the Nile after drought.

Cycle of life, death and rebirth seen in nature

The solar cult of the sun god, Re, associated with royalty throughout Egyptian history, promised survival after death. The Egyptians believed that just as the sun god *died* every evening in the west and was *reborn* every morning in the east, so too could humans survive death. However, the god Osiris, in his many aspects, offered more hope for resurrection and life after death.

It is believed that long before Osiris became associated with the Underworld, he was worshipped as a god of vegetation and grain. Throughout Egyptian history he continued to be held responsible for the forces that produced the sprouting grain and the rising Nile. The Egyptians believed that his power was manifested in anything that 'came forth from apparent death'.[2]

However, Osiris' importance to the Egyptians of the New Kingdom was as king of the Underworld. The people believed that Osiris had been a popular king who was killed and dismembered by his jealous brother Seth. Osiris' wife, Isis, his sister, Nephthys, and the gods Anubis and Thoth reunited the pieces of Osiris' body and he was resurrected to rule as the king of the Underworld. The Egyptians believed that they too could share Osiris' experience of resurrection.

Osiris and resurrection

The early writers of the Egyptian funerary texts did not bother to record a connected story of Osiris' experiences, possibly because they were so well known. The only connected narrative was written by the first century Greek writer, Plutarch, in his *De Iside et Osiride*. There appear to have been many variants of this myth.

It is possible to see from the following summarised version of the myth why the cult of Osiris became the dominant element in burial practices during the New Kingdom.

As well as illustrating the Egyptians' belief in resurrection and an afterlife with Osiris in the Underworld, the story explains some of the Osirian burial practices. For example:

Explanation of Osirian burial rites

- The body of Osiris was placed in a chest (coffin).
- The body parts were preserved and wrapped in linen bandages (mummification).
- Special words were spoken over the body (spells and prayers).
- Isis and Nephthys mourned the dead Osiris (the two *dryt* mourners in the funeral procession).
- Isis and Nephthys were transformed into birds and fanned life back into Osiris' body. These two winged goddesses were featured on canopic chests, coffins and sarcophagi spreading their wings around the body and its internal organs.

Osiris in a mummified form

In wall paintings Osiris was depicted as a mummified king usually with green or black-coloured flesh. Green was associated with new growth which emerged from the fertile black Nile mud. Black was the colour which the Egyptians associated with resurrection and eternal life.

The spiritual aspects of the individual

The Egyptians believed that the individual was composed of:

- a physical body
- a *double* or life-force — the *ka*
- a soul — the *ba*
- a spiritual intelligence — the *akh*
- a shadow
- a name.

At death the *ka*, *ba* and *akh* were believed to be released from the body and, if the correct burial practices were carried out, the deceased would enjoy eternal life.

The *ka* or life-force was symbolised by a pair of upstretched arms. The Egyptians believed that the *ka* was born with the individual and after death remained in the tomb with the body. In order to survive, the *ka* needed either the body in a recognisable form or a life-like statue.

The human-headed ba (soul) of Nefertari

At least one *ka* statue of the deceased, made of stone or wood, was placed in the tomb (see Chapter 7). The *ka* was believed to be able to eat, drink and enjoy the smell of incense and so it was important that the tomb was provisioned with these essentials and that regular offerings were made by the deceased's family.

The Egyptians had some difficulty reconciling their ideas about the *ba* or soul. It passed into the afterlife where it enjoyed eternal existence but it could also revisit the tomb at any time. There are many scenes showing the *ba* hovering over the mummy or entering the tomb shaft. It was believed to have the power to change itself into any form it desired, although it was generally depicted as a human-headed bird. The individual's shadow was frequently mentioned in connection with the soul and possibly remained with it.

The spiritual intelligence or *akh* was described as a shining, luminous form which, at death, severed all ties with the body and earthly existence.

Although a person's name was not a spiritual element, it was a vital part of the individual. The Egyptians believed that even if their mummy was destroyed and the substitute life-like statue smashed, they could still exist as long as their name was written or spoken. However, if their name was obliterated, they would cease to exist forever.

Nakht with his human-headed soul flying before him as he walks toward his tomb chapel

Judgment before Osiris

The idea of a judgment of the dead may have been accepted during the Old Kingdom but it was not until the New Kingdom that the concept was shown in pictorial form. The judgment of the individual before Osiris was depicted on the illustrated papyri placed somewhere near the mummy or on the tomb walls. It formed an important part (chapter) of the funerary texts called the *Chapter of Coming Forth by Day*, more commonly known as the *Book of the Dead*.

Illustrated papyri and the judgment

Two of the best sources illustrating belief in a judgment are the papyri of the Nineteenth Dynasty scribes, Ani and Hunefer. Although pictorial representations of the judgment varied in detail, the basic elements were always the same.

Some of the texts describe, as part of a hymn to Osiris, the deceased's entrance into the god's domain.

> I have come into the City of the God, the region which existed in primeval time, with (my) double and with (my) translucent form, to dwell in this land.[3]

Before the deceased could be brought before Osiris, he or she had to face 42 gods, each of whom had jurisdiction over a particular sin. According to the funerary text, the deceased said:

The 42 judges

> I know the names of the two and forty gods who live ... as watchers of sinners and who feed upon their blood on that day when the lives of men are reckoned up in the presence of the god Un-nefer (Osiris).[4]

The deceased then passed by the 42 gods, addressing each by name and declaring that he or she had not committed a particular sin. For example:

Negative confessions

> Hail, Eater of Shades, who cometh forth from the cavern where the Nile rises, I have not committed theft.
>
> Hail, Vigorous of Flame, who cometh forth from Memphis, I have not uttered evil words.[5]

These denials are referred to as the negative confessions and are evidence of the moral standards expected of the ancient Egyptians. The acts which the deceased denied committing covered the following categories:

- blasphemous behaviour such as cursing the gods or the king
- criminal acts such as murder and theft
- poor behaviour such as greed, anger and deceit
- destruction of the agricultural resources such as fouling running water and laying waste ploughed land.

The deceased concluded his denials by repeating several times, 'I am pure'.

Into the Hall of Maat

Once this trial was over, Anubis, the jackal-headed god of embalming and the necropolis, led the deceased into the *Hall of Maat* or the *Hall of the Two Truths*. At the far end, the enthroned Osiris sat under a shrine with the two goddesses, Isis and Nephthys, standing or sitting close to him. Nearby was the god Horus and sometimes the Sons of Horus.

The weighing of the heart

A set of scales, topped with either a feather representing truth or a symbol of the god Thoth, dominated the hall. These scales were for the *Weighing of the Heart* ceremony in which the heart of the deceased was balanced against the *Feather of Truth*. The heart had to balance the feather in order for the deceased to pass the test and proceed to the throne of Osiris.

It was during this ceremony that the Egyptians feared that their heart might fail them either physically or morally. So that the heart would not invent lies before the god, a heart-scarab, inscribed with Chapter 30 of the *Book of the Dead*, was placed among the mummy wrappings. The

The weighing of the heart and judgment before Osiris, from the papyrus of Hunefer

spell to prevent the heart from opposing the deceased included the following lines:

> Do not rise up against me as a witness,
> Do not oppose me in the tribunal
> Do not rebel against me before the guardian of the scales![6]

The ibis-headed god, Thoth, stood beside the scales to record the judgment. Standing ready to devour the heart, if the judgment went against the deceased, was Ammut, a composite monster, part crocodile, lion and hippopotamus. However, when the correct spells were written on the papyri and on the walls of the tombs, the deceased would make it safely through the judgment into the next life.

Recording the judgment

Horus then escorted the deceased before the throne of Osiris. In the papyrus of Ani, Horus informed his father Osiris that Ani's heart was found to be 'very true and right' and that he had 'not sinned against any god or goddess'.[7] Ani knelt before Osiris and asked that he might be favoured and 'beloved of the Lord of the World'.[8]

The nature of the afterlife

> The Egyptians did not necessarily hold a single view of the next world at any one time, but owing to their reluctance to abandon old ideas were quite capable of maintaining conflicting opinions at once.[9]

No single view of the afterlife

An afterlife spent travelling with the sun god

During the New Kingdom a convenient link was developed between the Osirian and solar views of the afterlife, particularly in relation to royalty. According to this view, the fate of the king was linked with that of Re and Osiris.

The ram-headed sun god travelling in his boat through the Underworld, from the tomb of Ramesses I

**The sun god's nightly
journey through the
Underworld**

The dead king joined the crew of the sun god's boat. In many scenes, the king is shown with a ram-headed Re and is often shown with Horus, Seth, Thoth and Maat. At sunset, the sun god's boat began its 12-hour journey through the Underworld, the kingdom of Osiris, bringing light and life to the blessed spirits who lived there. During these hours, Re became Osiris.

However, on their nightly journey, the crew faced many obstacles as there were enemies who wished to impede the boat's passage. The Underworld was believed to be divided into 12 regions, separated by 12 massive gates which were guarded by serpents. These gates represented the 12 hours of night. The sun god's enemies, who could deprive the dead king of food and drink, make him breathe fire or take away his name, had to be overcome. Re's chief enemy was the serpent Apopis. With the help of friendly spirits (four knife-carrying goddesses) who punished Apopis, and knowledge of the correct password, Re and the dead king passed safely from one region to another. They reached the Hall of Osiris in the middle of the night.

**The sun god's daily
journey through
the heavens**

The successful journey of the solar boat was a foregone conclusion and at dawn each day, the sun god and the deceased were reborn. When the sun god emerged from the eastern horizon, he was identified as Khepri, the scarab beetle or *he who comes into existence*. The deceased king spent the next 12 hours traversing the heavens with Re and his celestial crew.

*Khepri, the beetle-
headed god of the
morning sun,
from the tomb of
Nefertari*

A number of funerary texts followed the theme of the sun god's journey through the Underworld. These included the *Amduat*, or the *Book of What is in the Underworld*, the *Book of Gates* and the *Book of Caverns*. The pictorial representation of this journey was the main feature which distinguished the *decoration* of royal and non-royal tombs.

During the short Amarna period, when only the Aten (sun-disk) was worshipped, all the dramatic acts and supporting cast of gods in the hereafter were eliminated from the sun god's journey. No longer did he sail nightly through the domain of Osiris.

The Osirian afterlife in the Fields of Reeds

Most Egyptians preferred the idea of an eternity spent in the blissful and familiar environment of the *Fields of Reeds*, ruled over by Osiris. To enter the House of Osiris in the Fields of Reeds, the deceased had to know the spells for passing through the 21 portals, each of which was guarded by a doorkeeper.

The funerary texts state that after the deceased was given bread, wine and cakes at the altar of Osiris he would 'emerge into the Fields of Reeds in any form whatever he likes and he shall appear there regularly and continually'.[10]

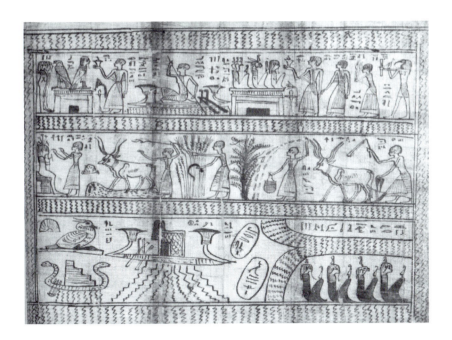

Kerquny carrying out various activities in the Fields of Reeds

It is possible that the delta region around Busiris (Buto), with its lush meadows and numerous watercourses, served as the prototype of the Fields of Reeds. It was in this area that the reconstitution of Osiris' body was supposed to have occurred.

Delta landscape in the *Fields of Reeds*

Life in the blessed fields was believed to be one of ease and plenty. The crops of wheat and barley grew very high, the harvests never failed and there were no pests. Although the papyri and tomb paintings show the deceased ploughing and reaping in the *Fields of Reeds*, the more oner-ous tasks were carried out by others. Ushabti figurines were placed in the tomb to answer all the deceased's demands in the next life. A prayer in Chapter 60 of the *Book of the Dead* included a request that the deceased would 'never be in a state of servitude and always be in authority'.[11]

Afterlife of ease and prosperity

As well as continuing their rural existence, the deceased expected to sail among the lakes, visit the cities and be reunited with their families — 'I have seen my father and gazed upon my mother, and I have made love'.[12]

The inhabitants of the Fields of Reeds were expected to help the sun god's boat pass safely through the Underworld on its nightly journey. These souls pushed the god's boat free from sandbanks and reeds.

Burial practices

The Egyptians believed that only if the correct burial practices were car-ried out would they enjoy eternal life. The dominant element in those burial practices was the cult of Osiris. The Egyptian people saw the experiences of Osiris as closely aligned to their own and they believed that they could share his experience of resurrection.

Practices aimed at reconstitution and reanimation of the body

The Osirian burial practices were intended to aid the reconstitution and reanimation of the body and to protect the deceased against the dangers lying in wait on its journey to the next life.

Like Osiris, the deceased's body had to be preserved by embalming and then reanimated by the use of prayers, magic spells and amulets (charms). This procedure was carried out according to the *Book of the Dead* (*The Book of Coming Forth by Day*).

Natural preservation in Predynastic times

Preservation of the body — mummification

Old Kingdom developments

Some form of artificial preservation of the body had been carried out in Egypt since the earliest dynasties. In primitive graves the body came into direct contact with the dry sand which absorbed its moisture and prevented it from decaying. However, as soon as the body was insulated from the preserving effects of the sand, by the use of wooden coffins and enclosed graves, it decomposed very quickly.

The earliest attempts at mummification simply involved wrapping the body in many layers of resin-soaked linen bandages. These were moulded to retain the body's shape and features.

Although very few mummies have survived from the Old Kingdom, the evidence suggests that the internal organs were being removed, preserved and stored separately as early as the Fourth Dynasty. A canopic chest found in the tomb of Queen Hetepheres (Fourth Dynasty), contained her linen-wrapped organs covered in a dilute solution of natron.

Middle Kingdom developments

During the Middle Kingdom, mummification became more common among the ordinary people. Most had their internal organs removed (eviscerated) through an incision in the side of the abdomen. Their bodies were packed with linen and their nostrils plugged with resin.

> A diffusion of ideas from the rich to the poorer is a regular feature of the development of Egyptian funerary practices.[13]

New Kingdom developments

It was not until the New Kingdom, however, that there were any significant advances made in the process. The minor variations in treatment from one body to another indicate that New Kingdom embalmers were experimenting with more effective forms of preservation.

Some of these New Kingdom developments included:

- removal of the brain, either through the nose or an incision in the neck

- a lower incision point in the abdomen, occasionally resealed with stitching but usually covered with a metal incision plate

- preservation and protection of toenails and fingernails by binding and the addition of tubular metal stalls

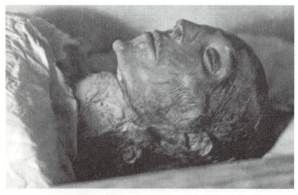

The mummified head of Seti I

- changes in the position of the arms — in a crossed position on the chest (for royalty)
- application of resin to the skin as insulation against moisture
- more elaborate methods of packing the body, including the limbs, to retain a life-like appearance.

The state of many of the royal mummies indicates that the Egyptians had reached a high standard of embalming by the middle of the New Kingdom. Two of the most remarkable mummies to have survived from the Eighteenth Dynasty were Yuya and Thuya, the parents of Queen Tiye. The head of the Nineteenth Dynasty pharaoh Seti I, is also an excellent example of the embalmer's skill. Unfortunately the rest of his body was damaged.

Embalming priests

Mummification was carried out by necropolis priests in an embalming booth (*the divine booth*) which was set up within a special enclosure on the west bank of the Nile. Like all priests, those responsible for mummifying the dead were organised in a strict hierarchy.

Priests of the *per-nefer*

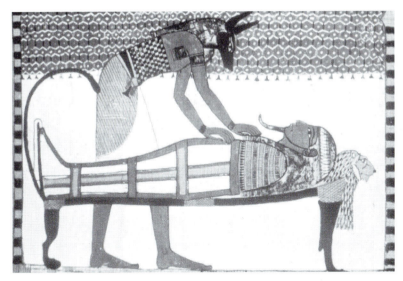

Anubis tending the mummy of Sennedjem in the embalming booth

The head priest in the *per-nefer* or *House of Vitality*, was called the *controller of the mysteries*. As he represented Anubis, the god of embalming, he often wore a jackal-headed mask during certain stages of the mummification process. His assistant was referred to as *god's sealbearer*. The lector priest was responsible for uttering the magical spells and reading the instructions from the funerary texts at each stage of the treatment.

At a lower level were numerous skilled technicians called *bandagers* who mixed and applied unguents, washed the internal organs and carried out the important task of bandaging the corpse. Other less skilled workers were probably responsible for more menial tasks such as carrying water and natron and heating up the resin.

The embalming process

The following description of the phases in the mummification process applies to the procedure at its most developed stage. It is believed to have taken approximately 70 days.

Purification

Initial washing

Immediately after death, the corpse was taken to a special site for purification. Because of Egypt's hot climate, it was necessary to carry out an initial treatment in case there was any delay in the embalming process. This involved washing the body in an antiseptic solution of water and dissolved natron. The only evidence for this stage comes from paintings in Late Period tombs where the deceased are shown either kneeling, as if still alive, or lying down while purifying liquid is poured over them.

Removal of the brain and evisceration

During mummification, the corpse was laid on large embalming tables, three elaborate examples of which were found in the tomb of Tutankhamun.

Removal of the brain

The brain, which was never preserved, was generally removed with a sharp instrument through the nose. There are some examples where it was removed through an eye socket or an incision in the skull.

> As much as possible of the brain is extracted through the nostrils with an iron hook and what the hook cannot reach is rinsed out with drugs.[14]

Evisceration

The removal of the stomach and intestines was done through an incision in the lower left side, while the lungs and liver were removed by puncturing a hole in the diaphragm. The body cavities were then washed out and the abdomen filled with crushed myrrh, cassia and various aromatic herbs.

> Next the flank is laid open with a flat knife and the whole contents of the abdomen removed; the cavity is then thoroughly cleansed and washed out, first with palm wine and again with an infusion of pounded spices.[15]

The importance of the heart

It was absolutely vital that the heart, regarded as the centre of intelligence and emotions, was never removed. In fact Chapters 27, 28 and 29 of the *Book of the Dead* contain a number of spells specifically aimed at preventing 'the heart being taken away from a man in the necropolis'. The heart had to remain in the corpse since it was weighed against the *feather of truth* during judgment of the deceased.

Dehydration

Before the body was covered with dried natron to remove all the moisture, it was temporarily packed with sawdust or even sand. This prevented distortion of the features and speeded up the drying process. During this vital part of the treatment, which is believed to have taken about 40 days, the body was placed on a special sloping table to allow the body fluids to drain away. At the same time as the body was drying out, so too were the internal organs.

Evidence from the tomb of Tutankhamun

Precious unguents were meant to restore vitality to the body. Unfortunately, despite the 12 layers of bandages, 13 around the chest, Tutankhamun's mummy was badly preserved. The priests had been too liberal with the use of unguents which had burnt away the tissues. However, those parts of the body which were covered directly with gold were well preserved.

Restoration of life-like appearance

Once the body was thoroughly dried out and cleansed, all the embalmer's skill was employed in restoring the mummy to as life-like an appearance as possible. A lotion of oil, beeswax, spices and wine was rubbed into the body to maintain the suppleness of the skin. The body cavities, and sometimes the cheeks and limbs, were packed with resin-soaked linen, bags of natron or sawdust.

Treatment of the skin

Cavities packed

The ears, nostrils and mouth were plugged and the abdominal incision was usually covered with an inscribed plate held in position with resin. During the New Kingdom, the eyes were covered with linen on which the eyelids were painted. At a later period, obsidian eyes were inserted into the sockets. Other cosmetic touches were added in individual cases.

Bandaging

Bandages, amulets, spells and unguents

This stage took about 15 days. The individual parts of the body were wrapped in numerous layers of fine linen strips coated in resin. Throughout the process, funerary jewellery, amulets and spells written on papyrus fragments were inserted between the bandages as the lector priest read from the *Book of the Dead*. Liberal amounts of unguents, which were believed to restore vitality, were poured over the bandaged mummy.

In the case of royal mummies, the arms were placed across the chest before bandaging. The bodies of ordinary citizens were generally wrapped with the arms stretched beside the thighs or, in the case of men, over the genital area.

After wrapping, the mummy was covered in one or more shrouds, held in place by longer bandages. A face mask, representing the deceased as eternally young, may then have been placed over the mummy. Face masks made from cartonnage (linen stiffened with plaster and then painted) were first used during the Middle Kingdom. The internal organs were anointed and also wrapped.

Protection of the body

The Egyptians attempted to protect the body from destruction so that it could be reanimated. They did this by the use of:

- amulets
- spells and prayers
- coffins and canopic chests
- sarcophagi.

Amulets and spells associated with mummification

Enormous numbers of amulets, many inscribed with prayers and spells, were inserted between the layers of bandages. The Egyptians believed that:

> amulets worked on the principle of sympathetic magic: that is the belief that an image of an object or creature could act for or against the item represented depending on the spells associated with its use.[16]

Amulets, placed on the body according to special instructions in the *Book of the Dead*, were of three kinds — those associated with protection, regeneration and rebirth.

The funerary texts were explicit about:

- the type of amulet to be used
- the exact position on the body of each amulet
- the material and colour of the amulets
- the spell associated with each one.

Since Osiris was believed to be the first person to have been embalmed, many of the amulets were connected with the Osiris myth.

Protective amulets

The texts specified that many amulets should be made from gold because it was believed to be non-corruptible. Those parts of the body protected by gold did not decompose.

In the case of royalty, the sacred cobra was placed on the head and around the face. Images of the vulture and falcon also played an important part in protecting the body. Two chapters in the *Book of the Dead* instructed the priests to place a gold vulture at the throat of the deceased. The outstretched wings were thought to protect the deceased, just as Isis had protected her son Horus. The falcon gave protection from the great gods of Heliopolis.

Another protective amulet associated with the myth of Osiris was the *tyet* or *knot of Isis*. The tyet was the symbol of the knotted girdle which Isis tied around her baby son, Horus, while they were hiding from Seth in the swamps of the delta. The texts dictated that this be made from a red stone such as carnelian or red jasper and hung around the neck or placed on the throat. The red colour represented the blood of Isis.

Sometimes a Y-shaped symbol, the hieroglyph for woven material, was placed on the body to make the bandages indestructible. Small images of gods and goddesses, such as the popular but ugly dwarf god Bes, gave added protection.

Regenerative amulets

One of the most important of the regenerative symbols was the *djed* pillar which was also connected to Osiris. It was originally the cult symbol of the town of Djedu (Busiris) in the delta, the earliest known centre of Osiris worship. The djed pillar represented the backbone of Osiris and so imparted stability and endurance. The *Book of the Dead* stipulated that 'a djed pillar of gold, strung upon a fibre of sycamore' should be 'placed at the throat of the deceased on the day of burial'.[17] The spell associated with it said:

> Raise yourself up, Osiris! You have your backbone once more O weary-hearted one; you have your vertebrae![18]

Djed pillar

Several chapters in the *Book of the Dead* refer to the importance of the udjet eye (wedjat eye). This represented the eye of Horus, which was torn out by Seth when Horus attempted to avenge his father's murder. Horus is supposed to have offered the eye to his dead father and the charm was so powerful that Osiris was restored to life.

Udjet eye

The Egyptians were particularly concerned about the possibility of losing their head. Because they believed that during reanimation, the neck helped the head to rise, particular attention was paid to the neck area. Amulets in the shape of head-rests (*weres*) were placed under the neck. They were often made of haematite (iron ore) so that the heat it was thought to give off would help the deceased to raise his or her head eternally, like the rising sun on the horizon.

In order to guarantee the deceased eternal youth and sexual vigour, the texts instructed the embalming priests to place a green feldspar image of a papyrus column (*wadj*) on the mummy. Just as the papyrus plant was filled with sap and promise of new life, so too would the mummy be imbued with new life.

In case a part of the body was damaged or destroyed, amulets of hands, legs, faces and arms were added to the wrappings. It was believed that these amulets restored movement and senses to the mummy. Images of animals, such as cats, cows, bull and rams were believed to give the deceased the qualities of the particular animal. For example, a bull would impart virility.

Amulets associated with rebirth

Perhaps the most important funerary amulet of the New Kingdom was the scarab, a symbol of rebirth and new life. The newly hatched scarab beetle, emerging from a ball of dung, was associated with the morning sun which was *reborn* every day. Numerous scarabs were placed on the mummy as part of the funerary jewellery or scattered loosely though the wrappings. The *Book of the Dead* devoted five chapters to scarabs, particularly the heart scarab (*ib*). Chapter 30 stated that the ib should be made 'of nephrite (green stone) mounted in fine gold with a silver suspension ring'.[19] Because it was important that the heart did not fail the test when it was judged against the *feather of truth*, the heart scarab was usually inscribed with a text similar to the one below.

> Do not stand against me as a witness! Do not oppose me in the tribunal! Do not tilt (the scales) to my disadvantage in the presence of the Guardian of the Balance.[20]

Front and back view of a green schist heart scarab, with gold mounting

Vignettes from the Book of the Dead showing the djed, tyet, ib and weres

The bennu bird

Small images of gods and goddesses were also thought to help in the rebirth of the deceased. These included the Osirian deities, and Taweret, the hippopotamus goddess of childbirth. Also, the bennu bird was sometimes found associated with the mummy. According to Egyptian legend it rose shining from the waters at daybreak, radiant with light, recreating itself like the sun.

The untouched mummy of Tutankhamun has provided the best evidence so far of the importance of magical protection.

Evidence from the tomb of Tutankhamun

During the bandaging process, 143 separate precious and magical objects were inserted between the layers of bandages. These treasures of gold and precious and semi-precious stones included pieces of the king's personal jewellery as well as special funerary items.

Four gold and beaded cobras were placed on Tutankhamun's shaved skull while two more, curling from a diadem, protected his face. Always associated with the cobra was the sacred vulture, and this adorned the front of his skull. These creatures represented the two goddesses of Lower and Upper Egypt.

Tutankhamun's neck was protected by two sets of necklaces and 20 amulets, some of incised gold, plus a prayer welcoming him to the kingdom of Osiris. Found around his neck were a carnelian *tyet* or *knot of Isis*; two Osirian *djed* pillars, one in solid gold; and a papyrus column in feldspar. Under the dead king's neck was a small amulet in the form of an iron head-rest.

The embalmers placed 35 objects within the 13 layers of bandages around Tutankhamun's chest. Among these were some of the most beautiful objects found in the tomb — magnificent necklaces and pectorals which incorporated other protective and regenerative symbols such as udjets, scarabs and the bennu bird.

Around the dead king's waist, the embalmers had placed a belt of gold and glazed terracotta beads, a ritual tail (reminiscent of primitive chieftains) and a ceremonial dagger. The sheath of this weapon was inscribed with a hunting scene in which animals, friendly to humans, attacked savage and dangerous animals such as bulls and ibexes. Another dagger, with a blade of iron, was placed alongside his body. With these weapons the dead man would be able to overcome all the demons lying in wait for him.

Covering the abdominal incision through which Tutankhamun's organs had been removed was a gold plate with a Y-shaped symbol to make the bandages indestructible.

Tutankhamun's arms and legs were covered with gold bracelets featuring udjet eyes and scarabs and each finger and toe was sheathed in gold. On his feet had been placed decorated gold sandals for trampling his enemies. Alongside his thighs were the sacred cobra and vulture taken from the king's headdress. They were placed in such a way that when Tutankhamun's reanimated body arose, facing the east, the cobra, representing Lower Egypt, would be on the north and the vulture, representing Upper Egypt, would be on the south.

After the individual parts of the body were bandaged, the whole mummy was wrapped in a large linen sheet. This was kept in place with bands inscribed with texts related to the rebirth of the king. For example, 'O, Osiris, King Nebkheprure, your soul lives and your veins are firm. You breathe the air and emerge like a god'.[21]

A solid gold death mask was placed over the face and chest. This represented the king as eternally young and returning to life. An inscription on the back of the breastplate proclaimed that this renewed being was like the bennu bird which recreated itself as does the sun — 'hail to thee, alive is thy face ... thy right eye is the boat of day, thy left eye the boat of night'.[22]

Coffins, sarcophagi, and canopic jars and chests

It was hoped that the coffins, canopic chests and sarcophagi would protect the mummy and its internal organs from damage and destruction. The Egyptians believed that spells, prayers and religious symbols painted or inscribed on these containers would magically increase the efficacy of the physical protection.

Jewellery from the tomb of Tutankhamun, which incorporates the udjet eye, vulture and cobra

The size, shape, material and decoration of these containers varied from period to period. The variations reflected religious and social changes.

Mummiform coffins became the standard during the New Kingdom. At first, the coffin was decorated in a simple fashion,

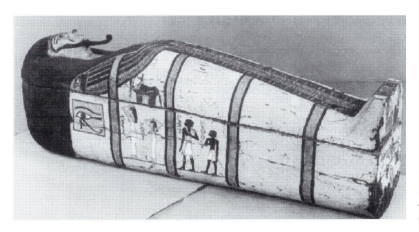

The early Eighteenth Dynasty coffin of the son of an official of medium rank

Mummiform coffins

The painted anthropoid coffin lid of a Nineteenth Dynasty woman, Iyneferty, the wife of Sennedjem

Guardians of the internal organs

representing the bandaged mummy. The arms were not represented on the early Eighteenth Dynasty coffins but were added later. The decoration became more detailed during the Ramesside period when every part of the exterior and interior surfaces of the coffins were covered.

Non-royals generally had anthropoid sarcophagi while royalty retained the massive stone type.

The sarcophagus of Amenhotep II

Common decorative themes for coffins and sarcophagi included wings. The four protective deities, Isis, Nephthys, Selket and Neith, were often shown on each corner, extending their wings around the precious contents. Images of falcons, vultures, winged scarabs and winged cobras were also used to protect the deceased. Other themes included funerary gods (Osiris, Sons of Horus, Anubis and Thoth), the djed pillar, Horus presenting the deceased to Osiris and Anubis tending the mummy, the funeral procession and rites performed at the tomb, the *weighing of the heart* and the sun god's boat being drawn through the Underworld.

Canopic jars were made from limestone, alabaster, wood, pottery and faience. During the Eighteenth Dynasty, the jar stoppers were in the shape of a human head, usually wearing a striped headdress. In the Nineteenth Dynasty canopic lids represented the *Four Sons of Horus* who were the spirits of the internal organs. Each of these guardians was identified with a particular organ and protected by a goddess, as shown in the table below.

Sons of Horus	Internal organ	Protective deity
Human-headed Imsety	liver	Isis
Baboon-headed Hapy	lungs	Nephthys
Jackal-headed Duametef	stomach	Neith
Falcon-headed Qebhsenuef	intestines	Selket

*Painted pottery canopic jars of the
Eighteenth Dynasty*

*Glazed figures of the canopic deities, the
four sons of Horus*

The jars were usually engraved or painted with
canopic formulae which identified the deceased, the
organ, its guardian spirit and the protective goddess.
For example:

> Isis your arms embrace that which is in you and
> your protection is over Imsety, who is in you, the
> one in honour with Osiris, the House Mistress
> Ruyu, the justified.[23]

Canopic chests were made either of painted wood
or stone. These became more and more elaborate
during the New Kingdom.

*The wooden, stuccoed and painted
canopic chest of Khonsu*

Evidence from the tomb of Tutankhamun

**Tutankhamun was interred in three nested coffins, two of gilded wood and one of
solid gold. They were Osirid in form. Osiris was always shown as a mummified
king, holding the insignia of royalty and wearing a long, curved beard.**

**These mummiform coffins were designed so that the facial features of the king
would show the stages through which he would pass. While the king's face on the
two outer coffins appeared to be a little weary of the world, the one depicted on the
solid gold coffin was more youthful. Under the third coffin, the face mask showed
the king as renewed and eternally young.**

**On the solid gold coffin the two protective winged goddesses, Isis and her sister
Nephthys enfolded the boy king in their interlaced wings. They shielded him just
as they had shielded the dead Osiris.**

**Representations of Isis and Nephthys appear again and again in the burial chamber.
They are found with Neith, a creator goddess from the delta and Selket, a scorpion
goddess, on either corner of the sarcophagus. At the end of the sarcophagus stood
a large, brightly coloured djed pillar.**

**Four nested, golden shrines surrounded the sarcophagus. The small inner shrine
immediately enclosing the sarcophagus was built in the shape of the pavilion used**

in the Sed festival. During this festival, the king underwent a ritual death and rejuvenation of his powers and vitality. Under this pavilion he was granted a new lease of life. Decorations on this first shrine show the two symbols of protection and transformation — the djed pillar and the tyet.

Tutankhamun's embalmed liver, stomach, intestines and lungs were protected separately. The whole canopic assemblage was guarded by a statue of Anubis, the god of mummification and *master of chests*. According to legend, it was he who buried Osiris. Desroches-Noblecourt believes that this black and gold figure of Anubis, represented the young Tutankhamun in the process of transformation. Many objects in the tomb were black (the colour of resurrection and eternal life).

The sarcophagus of Tutankhamun, in situ

One of Tutankhamun's three gilded coffins

The solid gold funerary mask of Tutankhamun

Funeral rites

> A funeral procession is made for you on the day of burial; the mummy case is of gold, its head of lapis lazuli. The sky is above you as you lie in the hearse, oxen drawing you, musicians going before you. The dance of the muu-dancers is done at the door of your tomb; the offering list is read to you; sacrifice is made before your offering stone.[(24)]

Of all the traditional scenes depicted in New Kingdom tombs, the one which was never omitted was the funeral procession. However, there were considerable variations from tomb to tomb.

Difficulties associated with interpretation

It is not easy to build up a complete picture of a New Kingdom funeral procession because some of the funeral rites are difficult to interpret.

Not all rituals shown on the tomb walls were actually carried out during the New Kingdom. When ordinary Egyptians adopted the Old Kingdom burial rites associated with royalty, they replaced the actual performance of some of them with symbolic representations. For example, the ancient boat journeys to Abydos and the sacred centres of the delta (Buto, Sais and Heliopolis).

Archaic and symbolic rites make interpretation difficult

In the case of New Kingdom royal burials, these journeys may have been carried out as the procession travelled across the Nile to the funerary temple in western Thebes. In the case of non-royals, a painting of the journey on their tomb wall, might have been sufficient.

Many of the titles given to participants in the procession were archaic reminders of much earlier burial rites. Although the original significance of these titles was often no longer understood, Egyptians of the New Kingdom continued to use them on tomb walls and funerary papyri.

Some of the scenes appear to be an amalgamation of stages in the funeral procession — the initial transportation of the body to the embalming place, the journey of the mummified body and the symbolic boat journeys.

Despite these problems of interpretation and the variations from tomb to tomb, the basic funeral rites remained much the same as those practised during the Old and Middle kingdoms.

The funeral procession

It appears that once the embalming was completed, the mummy was collected by the relatives and the funeral procession began.

According to artistic convention, which required that the mummy be seen, the corpse was shown lying inside an open booth. This was mounted on a boat-shaped bier covered with floral bouquets. In reality, a panelled shrine, decorated with amuletic designs, hid the mummy from view.

Funeral bier and shrine

As the corpse was ferried across or along the river to the necropolis, a symbolic pilgrimage may have been played out. The procession of boats

Symbolic boat journey to Abydos and delta centres

A funeral procession, from the tomb of Nakhtamun

stopped at various points along the river, which represented the ancient cult centres associated with Osiris — Buto and Sais in the delta and Abydos in Upper Egypt. At these stops the priests mimed parts of the old ceremonies, unveiled sacred statues and objects and left offerings on the river bank.

For the journey to the tomb, the bier was placed on a sled drawn by oxen. The canopic chest, on another sled, came behind, although in some scenes it is shown being carried on the shoulders of the mourners.

A mysterious symbolic addition to the funeral procession was the *tekenu* or *magic skin.* In earlier representations it took the form of a crouching man, enveloped in a skin and drawn along on a sled. Later, it appeared as a pear-shaped bundle, possibly the skin of a bull or a priest in a folded position, dragged along on a sled. The *tekenu* might have been associated with an archaic practice of human sacrifice but was more probably a symbol of rebirth. It has also been suggested that the skin represented an embryonic sac.

Mourners, from the tomb of Ramose

The panelled shrine and boat-shaped bier of Sennefer, from the tomb of Sennefer

In some scenes, the grieving widow is shown kneeling beside the bier while in others, two women, probably the widow and a relative, accompany the sled. These two *dryt* mourners represented the grieving wife (Isis) and sister (Nephthys) of Osiris. Among the other women in the funeral cortege were professional mourners, hired for the purpose. They were dressed in the traditional pale blue linen mourning dresses. As they wailed and screamed, they tore at their hair, beat their breasts and threw earth over themselves. A group of mourners referred to as the *nine friends* were probably officials.

***Dryt* mourners**

Offering bearers carried equipment such as trays piled with food and flowers, portable tables, jars of wine and beer, unguent cones, cuts of meat, clothing and ornaments. These were used during the rituals and the banquet held at the tomb. Sacrificial oxen were led by a priest called *mouth of god*. The number of animals depended on the wealth of the deceased. Other members of the funeral group carried the large assortment of funerary equipment for the *house of eternity*.

Of the priests associated with the funeral rites, it was the *sem* priest, wearing a panther or leopard skin, who was in charge of the whole proceedings. He was assisted in the rites by the lector priest who chanted prayers and uttered magical spells from an unrolled papyrus. Other priests burnt incense and sprinkled libations of milk over the ground during the procession to the tomb.

Funeral priests

The possessions of the vizier, Rekhmire, being carried to his tomb

Rituals at the tomb — the Opening of the Mouth ceremony

Muu — their origin and meaning

Once at the tomb, the bier might be greeted by the *muu*, with their tall, conical headdresses made from papyrus stalks. They appeared, apparently from the beyond, when the lead priest halted the procession and called out 'Come O Muu'. They are depicted with raised feet 'in the act of stepping across the threshold between this world and the next'.[25]

There is a great deal of argument in scholarly circles about the *muu*. Who were they? One view is that they represented the ancestral spirits of the delta while another suggests that they were divine ferrymen come to take the deceased to the next world. Real-life participants, wearing only kilts and white headdresses, may have played the part of the *muu*.

The most important ceremony was now carried out. It was the *Opening of the Mouth* ritual, the purpose of which was to magically restore the deceased's powers of speech, sight and hearing for his or her existence in the next life.

Three high-stepping muu dancers, wearing conical wicker headdresses, from the tomb of Tetiki

Ritual tools

Prior to the Eighteenth Dynasty, this ritual was performed on the *ka* statue but during the New Kingdom it was carried out on the mummy in its anthropoid case. The mummy case was supported by a priest wearing a jackal-headed mask, representing Anubis. A number of ritual implements — a chisel, an adze and a rod incorporating a snake's head — were used to touch the face of the mummy. This enabled the mouth to speak and receive food, the eyes to see, the ears to hear and the nostrils once again to breathe.

The Opening of the Mouth ceremony from the papyrus of Hunefer

Ay, Tutankhamun's vizier, performing the Opening of the Mouth ceremony on the mummy of the deceased king

This ritual was usually carried out by the dead person's eldest son, dressed in the leopard skin of the *sem* priest. The Egyptians believed that whoever performed this ceremony would inherit the deceased's position and property. The rite was particularly significant in the case of royalty. Like Horus, in the Osirian myth, whoever carried it out had a strong claim to inherit the throne. Sometimes a delegate, such as a priest, was chosen by the family to restore the senses to the deceased. This did not affect the right of inheritance.

Evidence from the tomb of Tutankhamun

Stored in the treasury in Tutankhamun's tomb were all the items that had played a part in the symbolic journey to Abydos and the delta. Many of them were enclosed in 22 black wooden shrines. In fact all the wooden objects were gilded and painted in black, the colour of rebirth. Also numerous models of boats of all kinds were found in the treasury.

Tutankhamun's funeral procession and Opening of the Mouth ceremony were depicted in part on the walls of his tomb. Because the boy-king had no son, the old vizier, Ay, carried out the ritual opening of the mouth and inherited the throne.

When Howard Carter opened the sarcophagus of Tutankhamun, *the crown of justification* (olive leaves, blue lotus flowers and cornflowers) was still in place and garlands of flowers still decorated some of the coffins. There were also remains of bouquets in a number of the rooms.

The remains of the banquet held on behalf of Tutankhamun, as well as some of the embalming bandages, were found buried outside his tomb.

The mummy was then anointed and the priests poured further libations, accompanied by the recitation of appropriate spells and gestures. Offerings of natron, incense, unguents, clothing, food and drink, as well as the all-important bull's foreleg and heart were then made.

Magical aids and equipment placed in tomb

While the burial furniture was being put into its appropriate place in the tomb, the priests placed a garland of flowers, referred to as the *crown of justification* around the mummy's neck. This declared that the deceased was triumphant over death. Bouquets were laid on the coffin which was then lifted into the sarcophagus.

After the priests placed appropriate magical and protective aids into position, they scattered a fresh layer of sand over the chapel floor, removing any footprints, and then sealed the tomb. A funeral banquet was held outside the tomb but there is some difference of opinion as to whether this was before or after the body was interred. The remains of the banquet and all the materials used in the embalming process were buried outside the tomb.

Providing for the dead

Food and drink

The Egyptians believed that the *ka* of the deceased continued to eat, drink and enjoy the smell of incense. These items were sometimes placed in the tomb at the time of burial. However, it did not matter to the Egyptians whether food and drink were actually stored in the tomb as long as they were depicted in some form. It was just as effective for the deceased to be shown on the wall of his or her tomb eating at a table laden with food or for workers to be shown engaged in various stages of food production. Sometimes models of food were placed in the tomb. As long as these representations of food and drink existed, they had the power to provide for the needs of the dead in the next life.

Equipment used in daily life

It was also believed that certain items of equipment used in daily life continued to be used in the hereafter. Although many tomb paintings depicted such objects as furniture, cosmetics, toys, musical instruments and tools, it was not until the discovery of the tomb of Tutankhamun,

Evidence from the tomb of Tutankhamun

There were very few *decorations* on the walls of Tutankhamun's tomb due to the haste necessary after his sudden death. However, in the annex of the tomb, were 34 vases for holding unguents (these were empty, probably robbed), 36 huge amphorae for holding wine and 116 baskets containing dried food and seeds (dried raisins, mandragora, melon, grape and nut seeds). Evidence from the antechamber indicates that there were originally more provisions than these. Wine strainers and even a miniature granary were included amongst the grave goods.

A large proportion of the objects were items of furniture — beds, chairs, stools, chests and lamps — but there were also mirrors, fans, jewellery, musical instruments, clothes, sandals, cosmetics, games, weapons and chariots.

that some of the actual objects were seen for the first time. Another valuable find of untouched grave goods was made in Deir el-Medina in the tomb of Sennedjem, *servant in the Place of Truth* (workman on the royal tombs). The number and quality of the grave goods of Sennedjem and his relatives are in stark contrast with those found in the tomb of a relatively insignificant boy-king. The gap between ordinary Egyptians and royalty and nobility was enormous.

Funerary equipment of a ritual nature

According to James, the term *funerary equipment* should be applied only to 'those objects, the purpose of which was more closely connected with the fate of the deceased in the afterlife and which had no part in daily life'.[26]

These included such objects as:

- papyrus rolls of funerary texts
- ushabtis (shabtis or shawabtis)
- Osiris and Ptah/Sokar/Osiris figurines
- 'corn' Osirises
- magical bricks
- model boats
- magic oars
- boomerangs and arrows.

Papyrus rolls containing funerary texts

The religious texts, prayers and magical spells written and beautifully illustrated in the funerary papyri are collectively called *The Chapters of Coming Forth by Day* or the *Book of the Dead*.

The purpose of placing these funerary papyri either between the legs of the mummy or inside hollow Osiris figures was to ensure the well-being of the deceased in the next world.

For those who could afford it, individually prepared papyri were written and illustrated with the tomb owner's choice of chapters. Poorer Egyptians tended to buy *off the shelf* versions which were already written and only needed the insertion of the deceased's name.

No surviving papyrus contains the entire work. Certain chapters, such as the Opening of the Mouth ceremony, the *negative confessions* and *Weighing of the Heart* ceremony, the *Heart* chapter, the deceased before Osiris and life in the Fields of Reeds, were considered more essential than others. Other chapters from the *Book of the Dead* were inscribed on amulets, ushabtis, coffins, canopic chests and the walls of tombs.

Ushabtis (shabtis or shawabtis)

The Egyptians believed that in the Osirian afterlife, agricultural tasks, such as sowing and watering the fields, harvesting the crops, rebuilding dykes and clearing out canals, would still need to be done. In real life, these labour-intensive jobs were done by peasants and conscripted workers. Many people avoided these tasks by paying someone else to do their share of the work for them. This concept was carried over into the next life. All the onerous jobs in the Fields of Reeds were to be

Mummiform 'answerers'

performed by *ushabtis* — little servant figurines who, when called upon to perform, would magically come to life and answer 'Here I am. I will do it'. They became known as *answerers*.

All ushabtis were mummiform. The earliest ones were made from wood and simply inscribed with the deceased's name, while later ones were made from a variety of materials such as stone, pottery and a glazed composition. Some of these little figures were provided with hoes, picks, seed bags, baskets and water pots.

Right: A painted shabti box and ushabtis from the tomb of a priestess, Henutmehyt

Far right: A 'corn' Osiris, from the tomb of Tutankhamun

Ushabti formula

The best examples were inscribed with the deceased's name and the ushabti formula:

> O thou shabti! If Osiris ... (the deceased) is counted off to do any work in the god's domain, as a man to his duties, thou art charged with all these tasks that need to be done yonder, to cultivate the fields, to irrigate the shore, to transport sand of the west and of the east. 'I will do them; here I am', thou will say.[27]

By the end of the New Kingdom, those who could afford it, had 401 ushabtis, stored in decorated boxes, buried in their tomb. There was one ushabti worker for each day of the year, plus 36 overseer ushabtis with whips to make sure the work was carried out satisfactorily. In the tomb of Seti I, there were supposedly over 700 ushabtis.

Osiris and Ptah/Sokar/Osiris figures

Osiris figures standing on pedestals were common in the earlier New Kingdom tombs. Some of these were hollow and held a copy of the *Book of the Dead* inscribed for the deceased.

Sokar, the god of the Memphite necropolis at Sakkara, was linked with Ptah, the Memphite god of creation. At some stage during the Old Kingdom, Sokar became associated with Osiris. In the Nineteenth

Dynasty, figures of a triune deity (a god representing the characteristics of three gods) appeared in some tombs. Like the Osiris figures, many of these were hollow and held funerary texts.

'Corn' mummies (the corn Osiris)

In one of his aspects, Osiris was regarded as a corn god and so the sprouting of the corn seed symbolised Osiris coming back to life. The Egyptians made little clay moulds in the image of the mummiform Osiris, filled them with Nile mud and pressed grain into them. These small 'corn' mummies were placed in the tomb and when the seeds germinated a miniature field, in the shape of Osiris, appeared. These were symbols of regeneration and magically aided in the rebirth of the deceased.

Grain moulds — symbols of regeneration

Magical bricks

The funerary texts instructed that four unbaked mud-bricks be placed in niches in each of the four walls of the burial chamber. Each brick was inscribed with a short text from Chapter 151 of the *Book of the Dead* and carried a prescribed amulet. The brick set in the north wall featured a wooden mummiform figure, the one in the south wall had a reed with a wick (a torch), the eastern brick carried an unbaked clay jackal and the brick placed in the western wall niche featured a blue djed pillar. The purpose of the bricks was to safeguard the deceased from intruders who might approach the tomb from any of the four cardinal points.

Protection from intruders from all directions

Evidence from the tomb of Tutankhamun

In Tutankhamun's tomb there were 113 ushabtis, some of which were lifelike portraits of the king. There were also 1816 tools which the ushabtis would use when called upon to work for the king in the next life.

The following list includes some of the objects that were placed in the tomb to protect the king from demons during his journey through the Underworld:

- **11 magic oars** — perhaps to use in the crossing of the waters of the Underworld
- **light-weight hunting chariots and bows and arrows** — to permanently destroy demons
- **statuettes of Tutankhamun in his papyrus boat, harpooning an unseen demon in the swamps and being borne on the back of a protective cheetah**
- **an ostrich-feather fan, decorated with a scene of an ostrich hunt** — in Egyptian symbolism, the ostrich was one of the evil animals of the desert
- **scenes showing the king showering arrows at wild ducks** — these were also symbols of evil.

There were also two walking sticks, one in gold and one in silver. According to the funerary texts, silver symbolised the permanence of the bones and gold symbolised the incorruptibility of the flesh.

A life size 'corn' Osiris, wrapped in linen, was found at the bottom of a long narrow box which contained Nile mud sown with grain. The grains, which had germinated in the darkness of the tomb, appeared to be sprouting from the figure of Osiris.

Two ritual head-rests reflected the Egyptian hope for rebirth. One was decorated with two heads of Bes (the god of births) and a lotus flower (symbol of the birth of the sun). The second head-rest was of a type normally found in what the Egyptians called *birth houses*. The one hundred and sixty-sixth chapter in the *Book of the Dead* refers to this item. A silver trumpet was placed in the tomb, possibly to announce the rebirth of the king.

A model of the head of Tutankhamun as a child, emerging from a lotus, recalls one of the creation myths and the birth of the sun.

Two small coffins, containing eight-month old foetuses, had been placed in the same room as the objects associated with the archaic delta rituals. Some scholars believe that these foetuses were related to the ritual of the placenta or were symbolic of the child Horus in the marshes.

The cult of the dead

Offerings to the deceased

Even after death and burial, the family of the deceased had to ensure that regular prayers and offerings of food and drink were made in the tomb chapel.

> Whether inspired by fear or piety, the Egyptians paid frequent visits to the *houses of eternity*. Parents, children and the widowed alike would scale the hill, bringing with them a few provisions and a little water to be laid on an offering table which stood in front of the stele or between the palm trees which overshadowed the entrance court, while to satisfy the wishes of the dead they would repeat the following rubric: 'Thousands of loaves of bread and jugs of beer, oxen and birds, oil and incense, linen and ropes, all things pure and good which the Nile brings, which the earth creates and on which the god lives, for the *ka* of (so and so), justified'.[28]

Warnings, that those who neglected their duties to the deceased would suffer the direst punishment, were often carved into the facades of tombs. Despite these threats, the practice of providing for the dead often became a great burden on the families of private individuals. After several generations, many of the offering tables were 'as bare as the tables of them that die in misery in the open field with none to survive them'.[29]

In the case of royalty, a special group of priests carried out a daily ritual in the elaborate mortuary temples built in western Thebes. To ensure an adequate and constant supply of offerings for the dead king or queen, special estates were placed under the control of the mortuary priests.

Mortuary temples

The mortuary temples had vast storehouses and granaries to hold the supply of goods from these estates. The granaries attached to the Ramesseum, the mortuary temple of Ramesses II, could hold enough grain to feed approximately 20 000 people for one year.

Houses of eternity

For all Egyptians it was of prime importance to be adequately prepared for death. The following description, from the papyrus of Ani, illustrates this:

> Furnish your place in the valley, the grave that shall hide your corpse. Make it a worthy target for you, as it was for the great departed, who now rest within their tombs.[30]

During the New Kingdom, most pharaohs, queens, nobles, minor officials and royal workmen were buried in the Theban necropolis. Their tombs were spread over a number of sites — the Valley of the Kings, the Valley of the Queens, Sheikh Abd el-Qurna, Dra Abu el-Naga and Deir el-Medina.

Location of New Kingdom tombs

However, for a brief time during the reign of Akhenaten, the royal family and many of the king's officials were buried in the eastern cliffs that encircled the site of Akhenaten's capital, Akhetaten (Amarna).

Some New Kingdom officials chose to build their tombs in the northern necropolis of Sakkara. One of these was General Horemheb. When he later became the first non-royal pharaoh, he built another tomb in the Valley of the Kings at Thebes. There were also officials like Paheri, Mayor of el-Kab, who chose provincial burial sites for themselves.

The poorer classes, who were unable to afford a tomb, were buried as in the past, in undecorated pits.

Tombs of the Theban necropolis

Royal tombs

During the Middle Kingdom and the Second Intermediate Period, pharaohs continued to be buried in pyramid-shaped tombs. Although many of these were very modest in size and made of mud-brick, they were still obvious targets for tomb robbers.

The Valley of the Kings

Changes in tomb location and construction

The rulers of the New Kingdom were more concerned with hiding their tombs. Thutmose I is believed to have instructed his architect, Ineni, to locate a well-hidden site for his tomb in the limestone cliffs beyond Deir el-Bahri. Ineni claimed that he supervised the excavation of the king's tomb in total secrecy. By building a rock-cut tomb, Thutmose broke a 1200-year-old tradition in royal tomb construction. Since his example was followed by 62 pharaohs from the Eighteenth to the Twentieth dynasties, the site today is referred to as the Valley of the Kings. Some of the New Kingdom queens and royal children of the Nineteenth Dynasty were buried in an adjacent valley.*

Attempts to guard royal burials

Each pharaoh went to a great deal of trouble to make sure his *house of eternity* was protected from tomb robbers. For example:

Protection for royal *Houses of Eternity*

- The burial sites were in an arid, desolate gorge, lost among rocky ravines.
- The tomb entrances, built at odd angles in clefts high in the cliffs, were small and inconspicuous and covered with rock and rubble after the tombs were sealed.
- The tombs were cut deep into the rocky hillsides, sloping down from one corridor to another.
- A variety of devices were used to fool tomb robbers who may have located the entrance — blind chambers, pits or wells, false walls and passages under the floor of what appeared to be the last chamber.
- The mortuary temples were separated from the tombs. They were built on the edge of the cultivated land between the river and the valley. Thutmose I hoped that this would allow his funerary cult to be continued, while his *house of eternity* remained safely hidden.

Tomb robberies

Despite the elaborate precautions, determined tomb robbers, driven by greed, plundered all the tombs in the Valley of the Kings except for that of Tutankhamun. Many of the tombs were robbed during the New Kingdom and involved necropolis workers (staff of mortuary temples and craftsmen who had worked on the tombs).

Fortunately for modern scholars, the priests of Amun during the Twenty-first Dynasty removed some of the royal mummies from their plundered tombs and hid them away. Some were placed in a side chamber in the tomb of Amenhotep II and the rest in an Eleventh Dynasty shaft at Deir el-Bahri.

A group of documents called the *Tomb Robbery Papyri* record an investigation carried out into a number of tomb robberies in the Twentieth Dynasty. The records contain the robbers' confessions which include details about the methods they used to gain entry to the tombs and what they did with the stolen goods. The form of punishment inflicted on them is also mentioned.

---

* Queens of the Eighteenth Dynasty were usually buried with their husbands. It was not until the Nineteenth Dynasty that the Valley of the Queens was used.

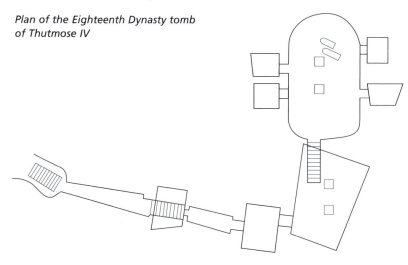

Plan of the Eighteenth Dynasty tomb of Thutmose IV

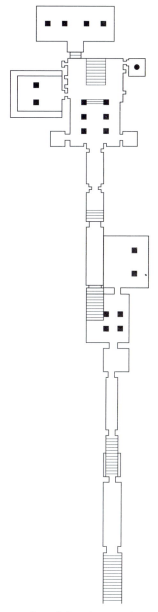

Architectural features of royal tombs

Most royal tombs incorporated the following features:

- A series of sloping corridors (often three) that led deep into the cliffs. These corridors varied in length. For example, the entrance corridor of the tomb of Thutmose I was 15 metres long while the two corridors comprising the entrance of Horemheb's tomb were 105 metres in length. In the case of most Eighteenth Dynasty tombs, these corridors took an obvious left-hand bend before the burial chamber. Later tombs were axial (they had a long central corridor) penetrating the cliff without any noticeable bends.

- A pit or well, some over six metres deep, was often constructed part-way along the main corridor. Since the room containing this well was referred to as the *hall of hindering*, its main purpose may have been to deter tomb robbers. However, some scholars believe that the pit symbolised the tomb of Osiris. A more practical purpose for it may have been to act as a collection point for drainage of water from flash floods.

- A number of intermediate chambers that were used for storing equipment or, as in the case of the tomb of Seti I, to deceive robbers.

- An antechamber at the end of the last corridor.

- The burial chamber, its roof supported by pillars, was usually the room farthest from the entrance.

Plan of the Nineteenth Dynasty tomb of Seti I

Decoration of the royal tombs

It is not really accurate to use the term *decoration* when speaking of the paintings and reliefs on the walls of tombs. The purpose was not to make the tomb attractive, but to help the deceased on his or her journey to the afterlife. The scenes were never intended to be seen once the tomb was sealed.

In most royal tombs, the walls of the corridors and chambers were covered with texts and illustrations from *The Book of What is in the*

*Scenes from
the Eighteenth
Dynasty tomb
of Amenhotep II*

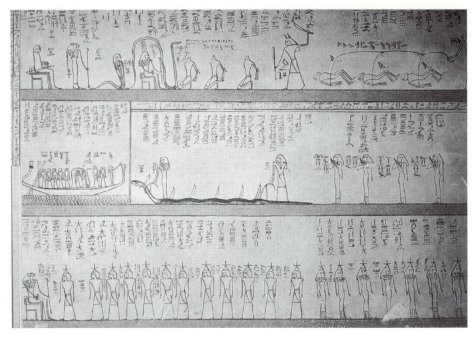

Underworld, The Book of Gates and *The Book of Caverns*. These funerary books followed the theme of the nightly progress of the sun god's boat through the Underworld and its re-emergence at dawn. The corridors of the tomb represented the various stages of the journey through the Underworld and the obstacles to be overcome.

Other scenes showed the deceased king or queen making offerings to a number of gods and standing before an enthroned Osiris.

*The ceiling of
the tomb of
Ramesses IV*

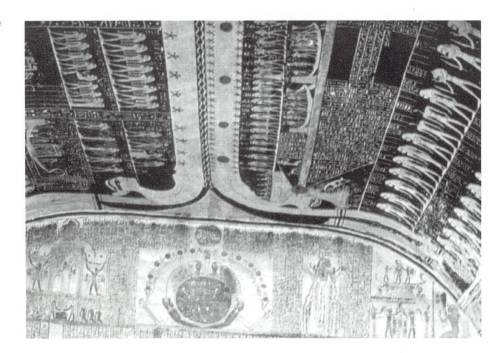

Most ceilings in the tombs, like the lids of coffins and sarcophagi, represented the sky. They were covered with gold stars on a dark blue background and some included astrological maps, figures of Nut, the sky goddess, and the passage of the sun across the sky.

Ceiling *decoration*

The tombs of high-ranking officials (nobles)

The preparation of a tomb was the biggest investment made during an official's lifetime. Even though the site in the necropolis would be granted to him by the king, the type of building materials and quality of the decoration usually depended on the person's individual wealth. The construction, cutting of reliefs, and painting may have extended over a long period of time, depending on the lavishness of the tomb.

Expense involved in tomb construction

From the evidence provided by the biographical inscriptions on the walls, it appears that most of the tombs were either started, or at least *decorated* when the official was at the height of his career. This might explain why so many of the tombs in the necropolis were unfinished. These unfinished tombs have provided valuable evidence on the methods and stages in construction. The beautifully decorated tombs at Thebes represent only a fraction of the burials in the necropolis.

Many unfinished tombs

Architectural features

Most tombs followed a basic pattern. The standard type was a T-shaped tomb. Variations occurred depending on the wealth of the tomb builder, the space available, the type of rock into which the tomb was cut and individual preferences for more rooms, pillars, niches and so on. However, they all shared the following architectural characteristics:

A conventional T-shaped tomb of the official class

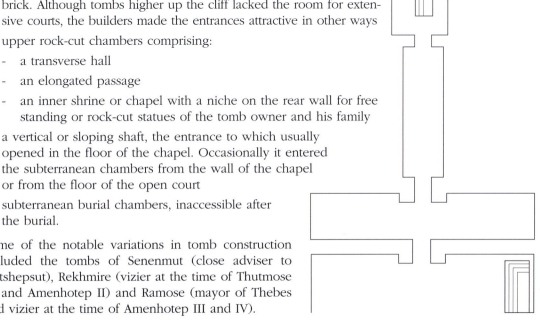

- an impressive entrance. Where space was available this took the form of a forecourt, partly cut into the rock and partly built of mudbrick. Although tombs higher up the cliff lacked the room for extensive courts, the builders made the entrances attractive in other ways

- upper rock-cut chambers comprising:
  - a transverse hall
  - an elongated passage
  - an inner shrine or chapel with a niche on the rear wall for free standing or rock-cut statues of the tomb owner and his family

- a vertical or sloping shaft, the entrance to which usually opened in the floor of the chapel. Occasionally it entered the subterranean chambers from the wall of the chapel or from the floor of the open court

- subterranean burial chambers, inaccessible after the burial.

Some of the notable variations in tomb construction included the tombs of Senenmut (close adviser to Hatshepsut), Rekhmire (vizier at the time of Thutmose III and Amenhotep II) and Ramose (mayor of Thebes and vizier at the time of Amenhotep III and IV).

*Part of the Theban
necropolis*

In the tomb of Senenmut, the outer and inner parts of the upper structure were built at different levels, connected by a ramp. He appears to
have been influenced by the design of Hatshepsut's mortuary temple at
Deir el-Bahri.

The elongated hall in Rekhmire's tomb, instead of getting lower and
narrower towards the chapel, opened out with the roof of the passage
reaching a great height. In the tomb of Ramose, the transverse hall was
made into a huge spacious room with papyriform columns.

Tomb *decoration*

The paintings and reliefs in the tombs of New Kingdom
nobles and officials are chiefly concerned with the concept
of rebirth. However, the tomb walls were also used to
commemorate, for posterity, the dec-eased's achievements
in life.

The decision to use reliefs cut into the rock or paintings
done on an overlay of plaster, was dictated by the quality
of the rock in the area. Those tombs located in the lower
cliffs at Thebes tended to have fine reliefs because the rock
was of good quality. The higher tombs were cut into rock
which tended to crumble easily. The walls of these tombs
needed an overlay of plaster and gypsum as a base for the
painted decoration.

There were fairly strict conventions with regard to the
themes depicted on the walls of non-royal tombs. It seems
that draughtsmen used *pattern books* from which the various scenes were copied. Prospective customers may have
been able to choose from a certain number of set themes
just as they were able to buy *off the shelf* papyrus rolls containing funerary texts.

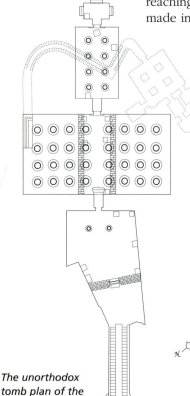

*The unorthodox
tomb plan of the
official, Ramose*

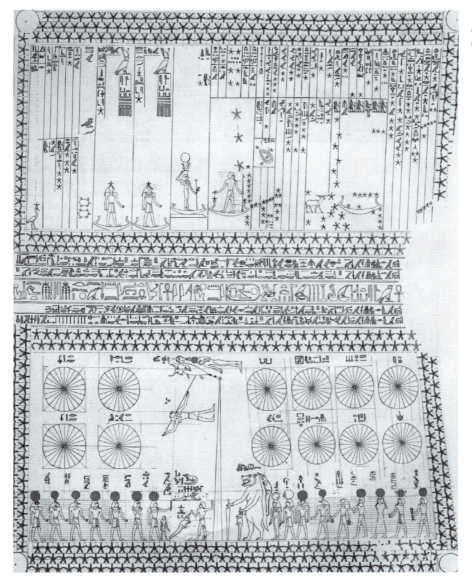

The astronomical ceiling in the tomb of Senenmut

However, there were major differences in the themes of Eighteenth and Nineteenth dynasty tombs.

In most New Kingdom tombs belonging to non-royals, the ceilings were decorated with geometrical patterns. Two unusual, but beautiful, variations occurred in the tomb of Senenmut, the adviser of Hatshepsut and Sennefer, an Eighteenth Dynasty mayor of Thebes. Senenmut's tomb featured an astronomical ceiling. Because the ceiling in Sennefer's tomb could not be smoothed off satisfactorily, he had it painted so that the bulges represented grapevines and bunches of grapes.

The table on page 669 lists a number of Eighteenth Dynasty officials whose tomb paintings and texts reflected their particular careers in the civil and military bureaucracies. The last column provides chapter cross references for this book, where you will find more information.

Eighteenth Dynasty tombs	Nineteenth Dynasty tombs
During the Eighteenth Dynasty, the burial chamber was painted or carved with funerary scenes while the chapel illustrated the life of the tomb owner, both private and public. The most common themes in these tombs were: • the deceased, with or without his wife, in front of an offering table laden with a variety of food. • some aspects of the funeral procession — the symbolic journey to Abydos and the *Opening of the Mouth* ceremony • agricultural scenes • fishing and fowling in the marshes • hunting in the desert • elaborate banquets • scenes associated with the official's particular role within the civil, military or religious bureaucracy.	During the Nineteenth Dynasty the scenes of daily life tend to become less frequent and in some cases disappear altogether. The chapel and burial chamber were both covered with more and more scenes from *The Book of What is in the Underworld* and *The Book of Gates*. The most common themes in these tombs were: • the weighing of the heart and the entrance to the kingdom of Osiris • the appearance and organisation of the hereafter and the creatures likely to be met on the way • the Hathor cow emerging from the hillside at the gate of the unknown • the tree goddess dispensing her gifts. The scenes showing the office of the tomb owner are reduced to a minimum IN Nineteenth Dynasty tombs.

Agricultural scenes

There is general agreement about the scenes showing the tomb owner in front of a table of offerings and scenes depicting agricultural activities. The food piled high on tables was to provide eternal nourishment for the deceased. Agricultural scenes were intended to guarantee the tomb owner a constant supply of food and drink in the hereafter. Some rural scenes were recorded in more detail because they illustrated aspects of an official's career.

However, there is a difference of opinion among historians about the meaning of some of the scenes of fishing, hunting and banqueting. Some scholars suggest that these themes represent activities enjoyed by the tomb owners during their lifetime and which they hoped would be transformed into reality in the next life. Kanawati, in his book *The Tomb and its Significance in Ancient Egypt*, thinks that they were 'a commemoration of the environment, pleasures and achievements of the tomb owner'.[31] He says that they were inscribed or painted on the walls of the chapel in order to provide a familiar environment for the *ka* throughout eternity.

Symbols associated with rebirth

To some scholars, the scenes have a deeper significance. For instance, Manniche, in *City of the Dead*, believes that the so-called *scenes of daily life* are far too idealised to be representations of the tomb owner's activities during his life. She believes that they are symbolic and refer to rebirth and the overcoming of evil. For example:

• In some of the fishing and fowling scenes, the presence of the tilapia fish is a symbol of rebirth. 'These fish have the habit of swallowing their young when in danger but expectorating them

Name	Title and reigning pharaoh	Scenes and text associated with their positions	Cross references
Rekhmire	Vizier of the South — Thutmose III	Installation of a vizier	Chapter 15
		Court of law, making judgments	
		Accepting taxes from local officials	
		Supervision of the delivery of jars of wine, oil and papyrus to the Temple of Amun	Chapter 15
		Supervision of the making of offering loaves for the Temple of Amun	
		Supervision of all the crafts in Amun's workshop	Chapter 16
		Procession of 'tribute' bearers from Nubia, Syria, Punt and Crete	Chapter 15
Menna	Scribe of Pharaoh's Fields — Thutmose IV	Ploughing, harvesting and tax assessment	Chapter 16
Userhet	Royal Scribe (of recruits) — Amenhotep II	Soldiers lined up for a meal	Chapter 15
		Engine bearers	
		Barbers shaving soldiers	
Nebamun and Ipuy	Royal sculptors — Amenhotep III	Supervision of crafts in the royal workshops	Chapter 16
Huy	Viceroy of Kush — Tutankhamun	Installation as a viceroy	Chapter 15
		Procession of tribute-bearers from Wawat and Kush (Nubia)	
		Voyage to Nubia in official ship	
		Freight boats	

unharmed when the crisis is over.'[32] The duck, which is always shown in the fowling scenes, was an erotic symbol and its purpose was to 'assist the tomb owner on the path to eternal life'.[33]

- The banqueting scenes are full of symbols of rebirth, such as the lotus flower. In one of the creation myths, the sun god was born from a lotus flower. Also featured in these scenes is the mandrake, a plant associated with love. To these symbols are added the transparent dresses of the women and the emphasis on wigs and perfume cones. Hair and perfume were closely associated with sexuality, and in ancient Egypt wigs were worn in bed.

The entire banquet scene had one definite purpose: to hint again and again at the proper atmosphere for creating new life.[34]

- The desert hunting scene may have represented the victory of good over evil since the desert was associated with Seth, the god of confusion.

Evidence of everyday life

Whatever the significance of these scenes, they do provide a wealth of detail on various aspects of Egyptian life and funerary practices.

Tombs of the workmen at Deir el-Medina

These tombs are in a category of their own. They were built around the village of Deir el-Medina for the workmen who constructed the royal tombs in the Valley of the Kings.

Architectural features

Variations according to site

The tombs were of two types, depending on the site.

- Where there was plenty of flat land, the tomb:
    - was constructed of mud-bricks with a small pylon marking the entrance to the forecourt
    - had a chapel with a vaulted roof
    - had a shaft or stairway leading from the outside court to the vaulted underground burial apartment.

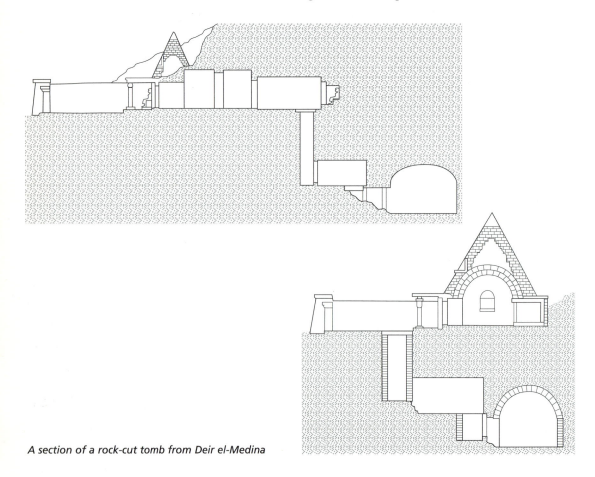

A section of a rock-cut tomb from Deir el-Medina

- Where no flat land was available, the tomb:
    - was cut into the rocky cliff with the front portico supported on pillars
    - had rock-cut stelae and statues on either side of the entrance
    - featured a two-roomed chapel with a flat roof and statue niches at the far end
    - had the entrance to the shaft inside the second room of the chapel
    - had a vaulted underground burial chamber.

One of the unusual features of both types of tomb was the small pyramid of brick or stone which crowned the chapel. The pyramidion (pyramid-shaped cap) was of limestone with sculpted decoration relating to the cult of the sun god.

Tomb *decoration*

Every part of the walls and ceiling was painted in brilliant colours. Many of these have survived to this day. Two outstanding tombs in the necropolis of Deir el-Medina belonged to Sennedjem and his son Khabekhenet. The paintings in these tombs were less stereotyped than in those of the Nineteenth Dynasty nobles. Although the usual funerary themes were still predominant, the

A pyramid-topped tomb from Deir el-Medina

Scenes less stereotyped than in tombs of nobles

Inside the chapel of Sennedjem

deceased's family played a prominent role in many scenes. Another variation was the inclusion of the village's patrons, the deified Amenhotep I and his mother, Queen Ahmose-Nefertari.

Kanawati says that these tombs at Deir el-Medina appear:

> to represent the deceased's world, both on earth and in the nether world, without a clear distinction between them which existed earlier.[35]

Royal and non-royal tombs at Amarna

Osirian features missing

Amarna tombs, both royal and noble, reflected the dramatic religious change that was implemented during the reign of Akhenaten. Gods, other than Aten, were not featured in the tombs and the usual scenes, associated with the cult of Osiris, were also missing from the walls.

The royal tomb

Changes in design and decoration

The royal tomb was excavated into the hillside of a barren wadi six kilometres from the city of Akhetaten (Amarna). It was unlike other royal tombs of the Eighteenth Dynasty in both design and *decoration*. It is believed to have been constructed with the intention of burying the entire royal family within its rock-cut chambers. Although it was unfinished at the time of Akhenaten's death, there are signs that it was to have been much more extensive.

Architectural features

The following plan shows at a glance how it differed from other Eighteenth Dynasty tombs.

Tomb *decoration*

Only fragmentary evidence

Most of the wall reliefs and paintings were obliterated when the tomb and its contents were viciously destroyed soon after the Amarna period. Fortunately, a number of fragments have survived and some of the reliefs can still be seen as marks in the rock beneath the original plaster walls. These scenes featured:

- the Aten (sun disk with its rays ending in human hands)
- the sunrise and the awakening of the temple personnel and worshippers
- the king and his family making offerings of food, drink and flowers in a temple court
- groups of officials and soldiers with chariots, waiting for the worshipping family
- the distraught king, queen and four daughters mourning the death of a woman who is generally believed to have been Akhenaten's second daughter, Meritaten
- the mourning of another royal woman, perhaps a minor queen
- nursemaids holding babies, indicating that the woman may have died in childbirth.

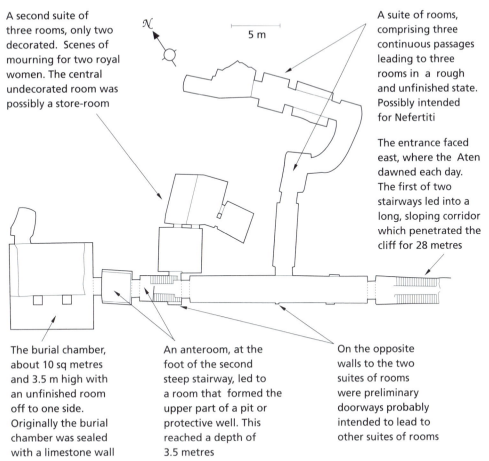

A second suite of three rooms, only two decorated. Scenes of mourning for two royal women. The central undecorated room was possibly a store-room

A suite of rooms, comprising three continuous passages leading to three rooms in a rough and unfinished state. Possibly intended for Nefertiti

The entrance faced east, where the Aten dawned each day. The first of two stairways led into a long, sloping corridor which penetrated the cliff for 28 metres

The burial chamber, about 10 sq metres and 3.5 m high with an unfinished room off to one side. Originally the burial chamber was sealed with a limestone wall

An anteroom, at the foot of the second steep stairway, led to a room that formed the upper part of a pit or protective well. This reached a depth of 3.5 metres

On the opposite walls to the two suites of rooms were preliminary doorways probably intended to lead to other suites of rooms

The plan of the royal tomb at Amarna

Tombs of the Amarna nobles

Many of Akhenaten's courtiers prepared tombs for themselves in the northern and southern hills to the east of the city of Akhetaten. The Amarna tombs, like other non-royal tombs, were T-shaped. While those at Thebes had their entrances in the transverse hall, those at Amarna had their entrance in the elongated hall. The burial chamber in the Amarna tombs was reached by a vertical shaft leading from the inner hall.

The *decorative* themes focused on the life of the royal family:

Scenes focused on royal family

- the royal family dining, riding in their chariots and inspecting buildings such as police quarters and storehouses
- the king at the window of the palace dispensing gifts and rewards — gold chains and decorations
- the royal family performing religious duties
- the personnel of the palace — chariot drivers, soldiers, scribes, fan-bearers, sentries and dancers.

The *Hymn to the Sun*, or portions of it, was inscribed on the walls of several tombs. Refer to Chapter 13.

Conventional versus controversial tomb *decoration*

**Old and new
styles combined**

Ramose, a vizier at the time of Akhenaten's father, Amenhotep III, built his tomb in the necropolis at Thebes and began to *decorate* it in the conventional way. When Akhenaten came to the throne, Ramose ordered the draughtsmen and painters to adopt the Amarna style of *decoration*.

His tomb is an excellent example of the radical changes that occurred in theme and style during the brief Amarna period.

> Thus we find the two styles side by side in one and the same tomb, the new decorations being exceedingly similar to that soon to be found in the tombs of el-Amarna, where the king moved with his entourage and officials. Ramose may have been invited to go, for even before the decoration in the hall had been completed, work was abandoned for good ... His tomb remains as a monument of conventional versus controversial concepts of art, a typical example of how nothing old was entirely discarded at the expense of the new in Egypt.[36]

Conclusion

For all Egyptians, it was of great importance that they should be adequately prepared for death. For those who could afford it, this meant building an elaborate tomb with walls carved or painted with the traditional funerary themes and preparing an anthropoid coffin or stone sarcophagus and a canopic chest. Other preparations included obtaining a papyrus copy of the *Book of the Dead*, and commissioning the manufacture of funerary and ritual objects such as shabtis to be placed in the tomb.

All Egyptians hoped that their families would arrange for their bodies to be adequately embalmed, for the correct rituals to be carried out during the funeral procession, particularly the Opening of the Mouth ceremony, and continue to make regular offerings in their tomb chapel after their death.

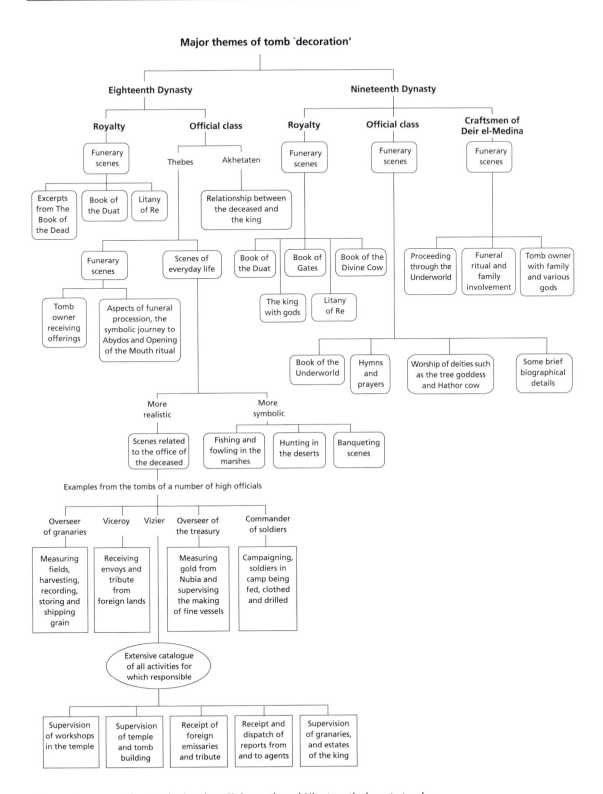

The most common themes depicted on Eighteenth and Nineteenth dynasty tombs

Chapter review

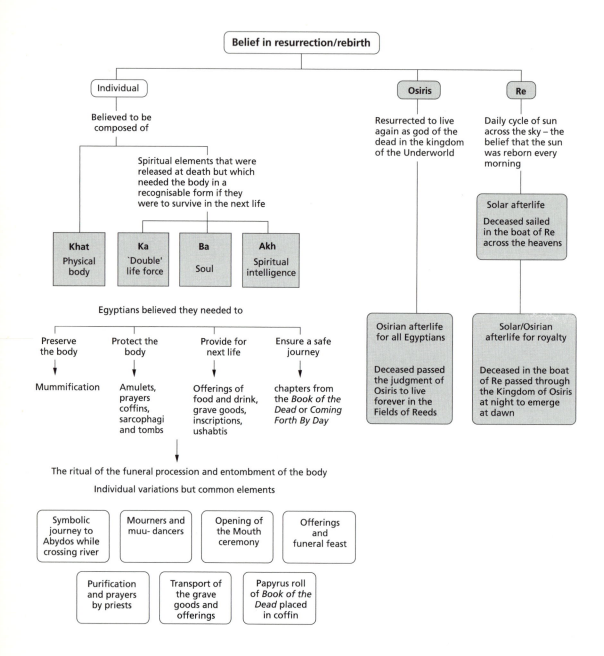

Belief in resurrection/rebirth

Individual

Believed to be composed of

Spiritual elements that were released at death but which needed the body in a recognisable form if they were to survive in the next life

| **Khat** Physical body | **Ka** `Double' life force | **Ba** Soul | **Akh** Spiritual intelligence |

Egyptians believed they needed to

Preserve the body → Mummification

Protect the body → Amulets, prayers coffins, sarcophagi and tombs

Provide for next life → Offerings of food and drink, grave goods, inscriptions, ushabtis

Ensure a safe journey → chapters from the *Book of the Dead* or *Coming Forth By Day*

The ritual of the funeral procession and entombment of the body

Individual variations but common elements

Symbolic journey to Abydos while crossing river

Mourners and muu- dancers

Opening of the Mouth ceremony

Offerings and funeral feast

Purification and prayers by priests

Transport of the grave goods and offerings

Papyrus roll of *Book of the Dead* placed in coffin

Osiris

Resurrected to live again as god of the dead in the kingdom of the Underworld

Osirian afterlife for all Egyptians

Deceased passed the judgment of Osiris to live forever in the Fields of Reeds

Re

Daily cycle of sun across the sky – the belief that the sun was reborn every morning

Solar afterlife

Deceased sailed in the boat of Re across the heavens

Solar/Osirian afterlife for royalty

Deceased in the boat of Re passed through the Kingdom of Osiris at night to emerge at dawn

REVISION QUESTIONS AND ESSAY TOPICS

1 **The following extract comes from a New Kingdom hymn. Read it carefully and answer the questions that follow.**

Geb's heir (in) the kingship of the Two Lands,
Seeing his worth he gave (it) to him,
To lead the lands to good fortune.
He placed this land into his hand,
Its water, its wind,
Its plants, all its cattle.
All that flies, all that alights,
Its reptiles and its desert game,
Were given to the son of Nut,
And the Two Lands are content with it ...

His sister was his guard,
She who drives off the foes,
Who stops the deed of the disturber
By the power of her utterance.
The clever-tongued whose speech fails not,
Effective is the word of command,
Mighty Isis who protected her brother,
Who sought him without wearying.
Who roamed the land lamenting,
Not resting till she found him,
Who made a shade with her plumage,
Created breath with her wings.
Who jubilated, joined her brother,
Raised the weary ones' inertness,
Received the seed, bore the heir,
Raised the child in solitude,
His abode unknown.
Who brought him when his arm was strong
Into the broad hall of Geb.

The Ennead was jubilant:
... His father's rank was given him.
He came out crowned by Geb's command,
Received the rule of the two shores.

They gave to Isis' son his foe,
His attack collapsed
The disturber suffered hurt,
His fate overtook the offender.

...The son of Isis who championed his father,
Holy and splendid is his name,
Majesty has taken its seat
Abundance is established by his laws ...[37]

a   Who was the son of Geb and Nut referred to in the first stanza and what was he given by the gods?

b   Who was Isis?

c   To what do the following lines refer?

Who sought him without wearying,
Who roamed the land lamenting,
Not resting till she found him,
Who made a shade with her plumage,
Created breath with her wings.

d   Explain how these lines are associated with several funerary practices carried out by the Egyptians.

e   Who was the child conceived by Isis and why did she bring him up alone, keeping his whereabouts a secret?

f   What is meant by 'he was given the rule of the two shores'?

g   How is the line 'His father's rank was given to him' related to the rites carried out for the deceased at the entrance to the tomb?

2   Write a short description to accompany the illustration below.

3 Identify the following collection of statements.

I have not caused pain
I have not ordered to kill
I have not depleted the cakes of the dead
I have not increased or decreased the measure
I have not cheated in the fields
I have not falsified the plummet of the scales
I have not killed
I have not done what the god abhors
I have not maligned a servant to his master
I have not stopped a god in his procession
I have not made anyone suffer
I have not caused tears
I have not robbed the poor.[38]

a What is the name given to this collection of statements?

b To whom were these statements made?

c What was their purpose?

4 The scene on the right is the second part of a larger papyrus.

a Identify each of the major components of this picture.

b Describe what part of the Egyptian's funerary beliefs it illustrates.

c List the features of the scene which would have formed the first part of this papyrus.

5 Identify the god represented in the figure on the right. Describe his funerary significance and the part he supposedly played in the burial practices of New Kingdom Egyptians.

6 **Answer the following questions and complete the tasks:**

a What part did natron, resin and precious unguents play in the embalming process?

b Identify the object pictured on the right and read the accompanying extract from the confession of a tomb robber.

The noble mummy of the king was completely bedecked with gold, and his coffins were adorned with gold and silver inside and out and inlaid with all sorts of precious stones. We collected the gold we found on the noble mummy of this god, together with his amulets and jewels which were on his neck and the coffins in which he was resting and we found the queen in exactly the same state. We collected all that we found on her likewise and set fire to their coffins. We took their furniture which we found with them consisting of articles of gold, silver and bronze, and divided them among ourselves. And we made into eight parts of gold which we found on these two gods coming from their mummies, amulets, jewels and coffins, and 20 *deben* of gold fell to each of the eight of us, making 160 *deben* of gold*, the fragments of furniture not being included.[39]

c Why was gold used, by those who could afford it, in such abundance around the body?

d What was an amulet?

e Draw up a table, and list information under the following three column headings:
  * Name of amulet
  * Category of amulet
  * Special features, such as colour, material and associated parts of the body.

7 **To which body of texts do the following belong?**

My head shall not be taken from me!
I am risen, renewed, refreshed,
I am Osiris.[40]

My mouth is given to me,
My mouth is opened by Ptah
With that chisel of metal
With which he opened the mouth of the gods.[41]

a Where are these texts likely to have been found?

b What is the purpose of the first one?

c To what funerary rite is the second referring?

---

* The total amount of gold is the equivalent of 14.5 kilograms.

8 **The text below comes from a papyrus recording the sale of a collection of shabtis:**

Pedikhons, son of Espenankh, son of Hor, the chief modeller of amulets of the temple of Amun, has declared to the beloved of the god, the priest Espernub, son of Inhafy, son of Iufenkhons: as Amun the great god endures, I have received from you the silver (the price) of these 365 shabtis and their 36 overseers, 401 in all, to my satisfaction. Male and female slaves are they, and I have received from you their value in refined silver of the 401 shabtis. O shabtis go quickly to work on behalf of Osiris, for the beloved of the gods, the priest Inhafy. Say, 'we are ready' whenever he shall summon you for service of the day.[(42)]

a   What was a shabti and what was its purpose?

b   What positions were held by Pedikhons and Espernub?

c   For whom was Espernub purchasing the shabtis?

d   Why was the deceased referred to as Osiris?

e   What was the significance of the number of shabtis purchased?

9 **Essay topics**

a   Write an account of the funeral procession of a New Kingdom noble. Explain the parts played by each of the participants and the rites carried out when the procession reached the tomb. Use the following extract and illustration as a guide.

Fair burial comes in peace when your seventy days are completed in the house of embalming. You are placed on a bier and drawn by young cattle. May the ways be opened by sprinkling of milk, until you reach the entrance of your tomb chapel. May the children of your children be collected in an unbroken circle and weep in affectionate mood. May your mouth be opened by the lector priest and your purification be performed by the *sem* priest. May Horus adjust your mouth. May he open for you your eyes, your ears, your members, your bones, so that your natural functions are complete. May the spells be read for you and a ritual offering, your heart being with you, the heart of your earthly existence, and you come in your former person as on the day on which you were born. May your beloved son and the friends be marshalled for you, performing the benediction of the ground and the burial of that which the king has proffered in the vault of the west. May there be a delivery of gifts for you as for the ancestors. May the forefathers come to you with chants and may the favours of the god to one he loves not come to an end for ever and ever.[(43)]

b   Compare the New Kingdom tombs of royalty and the official class with regard to:

   •   location

   •   architectural features

   •   'decoration'.

c   To what extent did the funerary assemblage of Tutankhamun provide evidence of the Osirian burial rites?

APPENDICES

Appendix A

The inscription 'discovered' by Colonel Howard Vyse in one of the 'relieving' chambers above the 'king's chamber' in the 1830s is quite possibly a forgery. Experts in various fields, quoted in Bauval and Hancock, *Keeper of Genesis*, suggest the following reasons for such a claim:

1 The hieroglyphics are a strange mixture of forms that have not been found in other Fourth Dynasty inscriptions. Several of the titles and cursive strokes were not used until the Eleventh and Twelfth dynasties, over 1000 years later, while others were not known until the Twenty-sixth Dynasty. There are also some strange expressions used in the inscription which have never been identified anywhere else in Egypt. There is a mistake in the spelling of the name Khufu and the only known sources containing this mistake were two books on hieroglyphics available to Vyse at the time. One of these was Sir John Gardner Wilkinson's *Materia Hieroglyphica*.

2 The angles and perspective of the inscription indicate that it was painted by someone working in a cramped space such as the 'relieving' chamber, and not by quarry workers before the stone was put into place.

3 The entry in Vyse's diary for the day he first opened the chamber did not mention the discovery of any inscription and yet, on the following day, when he was accompanied by witnesses, the inscription was there.

Appendix B

Modern Egyptologists claim that the Egyptians of the Pyramid Age had no iron tools and yet the ancient texts frequently refer to iron ritual objects. Also, an iron plate was found in one of the masonry joints in the southern shaft of the 'king's chamber' in 1837. When Sir William Flinders Petrie examined the plate in 1881 he was convinced it was very ancient. Modern metallurgists, after extensive investigation in 1989, came to the same conclusion and believe it was placed in the pyramid at the same time it was built. Despite these findings, spokespeople for the British Museum, where the iron plate is kept, have ignored the possible implications of its ancient origin for Egyptian history. If it were placed in the pyramid at the time of construction, the whole question of the dating of the Iron Age would have to be reconsidered.

Appendix C

The four narrow shafts in the Great Pyramid, two leading from the 'king's chamber' and two from the 'queen's chamber', were, for a long time, believed to be ventilation shafts. Modern astronomers are now able, with the help of computer technology, to recreate the skies as they were in 2500 BC and have found a remarkable correlation between the four shafts and four stars that were of great ritual significance to the ancient Egyptians (see the table on page 684).

Shaft	Angle	Star	Association with Egyptian funerary beliefs
North shaft of 'queen's chamber'	39 degrees	Beta Ursa Minor in the constellation of the Little Bear	Cosmic regeneration and immortality of the soul
South shaft of 'queen's chamber'	39 degrees 30 minutes	Sirius in the constellation of the Great Dog	The goddess Isis, cosmic mother of the kings of Egypt
North shaft of 'king's chamber'	32 degrees 28 minutes	Alpha Draconis in the constellation of the Dragon	Cosmic 'pregnancy' and gestation
South shaft of 'king's chamber'	45 degrees 14 minutes	Al Nitak or Zeta Orionis, the brightest star in the Belt of Orion	Osiris, god of resurrection and rebirth

Appendix D

An ancient body of writing called the *Hermetic Texts* described Egypt as an image of heaven. Considering the ancient Egyptians' belief in duality, it would not be surprising to find the ancient skies reflected on the ground ('as above, so below'). Many modern scholars now believe that the ancient astronomer priests of Egypt were more aware of the heavens than we once believed them to be and that ancient objects on the Giza plateau in particular, reflect the skies of the far distant past. Modern astronomers, using computerised images of the skies in various epochs, have provided valuable information which has enabled some scholars to reconsider their theories about the symbolism and age of the Sphinx and other monuments.

One of the astronomical features that fascinated the ancient astronomer priests was the constellation of the zodiac that rose just ahead of the sun in the eastern sky on the spring or vernal equinox. For example, from c. 2320 BC-160 BC it was the constellation of Taurus the bull, and from 10 500 BC-8800 BC it was the constellation of Leo the lion that was seen in the eastern sky. It is now worth considering whether the leonine Sphinx, which faces due east, was an equinoctal marker (the lion on the ground a pointer to the lion in the sky). This would mean reassessing the age of the Sphinx and putting its construction around 10 500 BC. This much earlier date than that usually suggested fits with the evidence provided so far by geologists and seismologists. It is also possible that the original figure of the lion had a lion, rather than a human head, which may have been added later.

NOTES

Part 1: Introduction

1 Gardiner, *Egypt of the Pharaohs*, p. 53

Chapter 1: The physical environment of ancient Egypt

1 Herodotus, *The Histories*, 2, p. 33
2 Ibid., 2, p. 8
3 Strabo, *The Geography of Strabo*, XVII
4 Wallis Budge, *Egyptian Religion*, p. 133
5 Herodotus, *The Histories*, 2, pp. 8–29
6 Lichtheim, *Ancient Egyptian Literature*, vol. I, pp. 205–9
7 Herodotus, *The Histories*, 2, p. 8

Chapter 2: Sources for Egyptian history

1 Herodotus, *The Histories*, 2, p. 33
2 James, *Pharaoh's People*, p. 17
3 Gardiner, *Egypt of the Pharaohs*, p. 53
4 James, *Pharaoh's People*, p. 18
5 Gardiner, *Egypt of the Pharaohs*, p. 55
6 Ibid., p. 57
7 Robins, *Women in Ancient Egypt*, p. 126
8 Steindorff and Seele, *When Egypt Ruled the East*, p. 6
9 Ibid., p. 6
10 James, *Pharaoh's People*, p. 17
11 Lichtheim, *Ancient Egyptian Literature*, vol. I, p. 18
12 Ibid., vol II, p. 121
13 Ibid., vol. I, p. 70
14 Kitchin, *Pharaoh Triumphant*, p. 199
15 Ibid., p. 132
16 Lichtheim, *Ancient Egyptian Literature*, vol. 2. p. 62
17 Kitchin, *Pharaoh Triumphant*, p. 125
18 Robins, *Women in Ancient Egypt*, p. 16

Chapter 3: The formative years of Egyptian greatness

1 Wilson, *The Culture of Ancient Egypt*, p. 51
2 Herodotus, *The Histories*, 2, p. 99
3 Ibid., 2, pp. 99–100
4 Emery, *Archaic Egypt*
5 Wilson, *The Culture of Ancient Egypt*, p. 50
6 Frankfort, *Kingship and the Gods*, p. 39
7 Wilson, *The Culture of Ancient Egypt*, pp. 64–5
8 Spencer, *Death in Ancient Egypt*, p. 39
9 Ibid.

Part 2: The Old Kingdom: the Pyramid Age

Chapter 4: The experimental phase of pyramid building

1 Fakhry, *The Pyramids*, p. 24
2 Edwards, *The Pyramids of Egypt*, p. 275
3 Ibid., p. 40
4 Ibid., pp. 51–2
5 Ibid., p. 67
6 Ibid., pp. 51–2
7 Fakhry, *The Pyramids*, p. 68
8 Edwards, *The Pyramids of Egypt*, p. 93
9 Gardiner, *Egypt of the Pharaohs*, p. 78
10 Edwards, *The Pyramids of Egypt*, p. 95
11 Fakhry, *The Pyramids*, p. 97
12 Edwards, *The Pyramids of Egypt*, p. 86
13 Ibid., p. 117
14 Fakhry, *The Pyramids*, p. 99
15 Herodotus, *The Histories*, 2, pp. 124–5
16 Fakhry, *The Pyramids*, p. 103
17 Lehner, *The Complete Pyramids*, p. 223
18 Ibid., p. 21
19 Ibid., p. 209
20 Fakhry, *The Pyramids*, p. 135
21 Lehner, *The Complete Pyramids*, p. 119
22 Scoch, 'Redating the Great Sphinx of Giza', p. 59

23   Ibid., p. 55
24   Ibid., p. 56
25   Ibid.
26   Fakhry, *The Pyramids*, p. 155
27   Edwards, *The Pyramids of Egypt*, pp. 51–2

Chapter 5: Religious and political changes

1   Kamil, *The Ancient Egyptians*, p. 55
2   Ibid., p. 63
3   Edwards, *The Pyramids of Egypt*, p. 158
4   Lichtheim, *Ancient Egyptian literature*, vol I, p. 41
5   Ibid., p. 46
6   Aldred, *The Egyptians*, p. 108
7   Edwards, *The Pyramids of Egypt*, p. 154
8   Lichtheim, *Ancient Egyptian Literature*, vol. I, p. 28
9   Wilson, *The Culture of Ancient Egypt*, p. 99
10   Ibid., p. 89
11   Manchip White, *Ancient Egypt, its Culture and History*, p. 58
12   Lichtheim, *Ancient Egyptian Literature*, vol. I, p. 18
13   Ibid., p. 19
14   Ibid.
15   Ibid.
16   Ibid., p. 20
17   Ibid.
18   Ibid., p. 21
19   Ibid.
20   Ibid.
21   Ibid., p. 23
22   Ibid., p. 25
23   Ibid.
24   Ibid., p. 26
25   Ibid.
26   Ibid.
27   Ibid., p. 27
28   Wilson, *The Culture of Ancient Egypt*, p. 95
29   Gardiner, *Egypt of the Pharaohs*, p. 84
30   Lichtheim, *Ancient Egyptian Literature*, vol. I, pp. 30–2
31   Ibid., p. 33
32   Ibid., p. 34
33   Ibid., p. 36
34   Ibid., p. 19
35   Manchip White, *Ancient Egypt, its Culture and History*, p. 58
36   Wilson, *The Culture of Ancient Egypt*, p. 69

Chapter 6: The life of the king and his people

1   Frankfort, *Kingship and the Gods*, p. 84
2   Redford, *Akhenaten, the Heretic King*, p. 136
3   Ibid.
4   Lichtheim, *Ancient Egyptian Literature*, vol. I, p. 64
5   Ibid., p. 65
6   Ibid., p. 69
7   Mertz, *Red Land, Black Land*, pp. 57–8
8   Lichtheim, *Ancient Egyptian Literature*, vol. I, p. 69
9   Ibid., p. 68
10   Ibid., p. 63
11   Ibid., p. 65
12   Ibid.
13   Mertz, *Red Land, Black Land*, p. 48
14   Kamil, *The Ancient Egyptians*, p. 130
15   Lichtheim, *Ancient Egyptian Literature*, vol. I, p. 64

Chapter 7: Preparing for eternity

1   Frankfurt, *Kingship and the Gods*, p. 185
2   Spencer, *Death in Ancient Egypt*, pp. 82–3
3   Lichtheim, *Ancient Egyptian Literature*, vol. I, p. 45
4   Ibid., p. 30
5   Spencer, *Death in Ancient Egypt*, p. 140
6   Ibid.
7   Lichtheim, *Ancient Egyptian Literature*, vol. I, p. 46
8   Spencer, *Death in Ancient Egypt*, p. 70
9   Ibid., p. 139
10   Kanawati, *The Tomb and its Significance in Ancient Egypt*, p. 22
11   Spencer, *Death in Ancient Egypt*, pp. 35–6
12   Ibid., p. 72
13   Kanawati, *The Tomb and its Significance in Ancient Egypt*, p. 22
14   Ibid., p. 130
15   Ibid.
16   Lichtheim, *Ancient Egyptian Literature*, vol. I, p. 58
17   Kanawati, *The Tomb and its Significance in Ancient Egypt*, p. 73
18   Ibid., p. 23
19   Lichtheim, *Ancient Egyptian Literature*, vol. I, p. 19
20   Kanawati, *The Tomb and its Significance in Ancient Egypt*, p. 70

21 David, *The Ancient Egyptians, Religious Beliefs and Practices*, p. 2

22 Kanawati, *The Tomb and its Significance in Ancient Egypt*, p. 100

23 Ibid., p. 29

24 Spencer, *Death in Ancient Egypt*, p. 140

25 Lichtheim, *Ancient Egyptian Literature*, vol. I, p. 41

26 Sethe, *Die Altaegyptischen Pyramiden Texte*, p. 722

27 Spencer, *Death in Ancient Egypt*, p. 72

28 Lichtheim, *Ancient Egyptian Literature*, vol. I, p. 44

29 Sethe, *Die Altaegyptischen Pyramiden Texte*, pp. 735–6

Part 3: The Middle Kingdom

Chapter 8: The achievements of the Eleventh and Twelfth dynasties

1 Manchip White, *Ancient Egypt, its Culture and History*, p. 152

2 Lichtheim, *Ancient Egyptian Literature*, vol. I, p. 85

3 Manchip White, *Ancient Egypt, its Culture and History*, p. 153

4 Wilson, *The Culture of Ancient Egypt*, p. 115

5 Ibid., p. 116

6 Lichtheim, *Ancient Egyptian Literature*, vol. I, p. 136

7 Wilson, *The Culture of Ancient Egypt*, p. 133

8 Lichtheim, *Ancient Egyptian Literature*, vol. I, p. 116

9 Wilson, *The Culture of Ancient Egypt*, p. 144

10 Breasted, *Ancient Records of Egypt*, vol. I, p. 309

11 Lichtheim, *Ancient Egyptian Literature*, vol. I, p. 143

12 David, *The Ancient Egyptians*, p. 95

13 Hayes, *Journal of Egyptian Archaeology*, 35, pp. 43–9

14 Ibid.

15 Ibid.

16 Breasted, *Ancient Records of Egypt*, vol. I, p. 251

17 Ibid., p. 213

18 Ibid., p. 215

19 Ibid.

20 Grimal, *A History of Ancient Egypt*, p. 164–5

21 Breasted, *Ancient Records of Egypt*, vol. I, p. 313

22 Adams, *Nubia, Corridor to Africa*, p. 185, in Kemp, *Ancient Egypt, An Anatomy of a Civilisation*, p. 176

23 Anthers, *Zeitschrift für Ägyptische Sprache und Altertum Kunde*, LXV, p. 108

24 Kemp, *Ancient Egypt, An Anatomy of a Civilisation*, pp. 170–1

25 Grimal, *A History of Ancient Egypt*, p. 177

26 Lehner, *The Complete Pyramids*, p. 167

27 Ibid., p. 182

28 Spencer, *Death in Ancient Egypt*, p. 86

29 Grimal, *A History of Ancient Egypt*, p. 179

30 Herodotus, *The Histories*, 2, pp. 147–50, 188–9

31 Grimal, *A History of Ancient Egypt*, p. 173

32 David, *The Pyramid Builders of Ancient Egypt*, p. 38

33 Lichtheim, *Ancient Egyptian Literature*, vol. I, p. 136

34 Ibid., p. 185

35 Ibid., pp. 140–1

36 Ibid., p. 169

37 Ibid., p. 172

38 Lichtheim, *Ancient Egyptian Literature*, vol. 1, p. 233

39 Ibid.

40 David, *The Pyramid Builders of Ancient Egypt*, p. 36

41 Robins, *The Art of Ancient Egypt*, p. 109

42 Wilson, *The Culture of Ancient Egypt*, p. 131

43 Breasted, *Ancient Records of Egypt*, vol. I, p. 233

44 David, *The Pyramid Builders of Ancient Egypt*, p. 33

Part 4: The New Kingdom

Chapter 9: A vigorous new beginning

1 Manchip White, *Ancient Egypt, its Culture and History*, p. 152

2 Lichtheim, *Ancient Egyptian Literature*, vol. I, p. 85

3   Manchip White, *Ancient Egypt, its Culture and History*, p. 153
4   Wilson, *The Culture of Ancient Egypt*, p. 115
5   Ibid., p. 116
6   Lichtheim, *Ancient Egyptian Literature*, vol. I, p. 136
7   Wilson, *The Culture of Ancient Egypt*, p. 133
8   Lichtheim, *Ancient Egyptian Literature*, vol. I, p. 116
9   Wilson, *The Culture of Ancient Egypt*, p. 144
10   Breasted, *Ancient Records of Egypt*, vol. I, p. 309
11   Lichtheim, *Ancient Egyptian Literature*, vol. I, p. 143
12   David, *The Ancient Egyptians*, p. 95
13   Hayes, *Journal of Egyptian Archaeology*, 35, pp. 43–9
14   Ibid.
15   Ibid.
16   Breasted, *Ancient Records of Egypt*, vol. I, p. 251
17   Ibid., p. 213
18   Ibid., p. 215
19   Ibid.
20   Grimal, *A History of Ancient Egypt*, p. 164–5
21   Breasted, *Ancient Records of Egypt*, vol. I, p. 313
22   Adams, *Nubia, Corridor to Africa*, p. 185, in Kemp, *Ancient Egypt, An Anatomy of a Civilisation*, p. 176
23   Anthers, *Zeitschrift für Ägyptische Sprache und Altertum Kunde*, LXV, p. 108
24   Kemp, *Ancient Egypt, An Anatomy of a Civilisation*, pp. 170–1
25   Grimal, *A History of Ancient Egypt*, p. 177
26   Lehner, *The Complete Pyramids*, p. 167
27   Ibid., p. 182
28   Spencer, *Death in Ancient Egypt*, p. 86
29   Grimal, *A History of Ancient Egypt*, p. 179
30   Herodotus, *The Histories*, 2, pp. 147–50, 188–9
31   Grimal, *A History of Ancient Egypt*, p. 173
32   David, *The Pyramid Builders of Ancient Egypt*, p. 38
33   Lichtheim, *Ancient Egyptian Literature*, vol. I, p. 136
34   Ibid., p. 185
35   Ibid., pp. 140–1
36   Ibid., p. 169
37   Ibid., p. 172

38   Lichtheim, *Ancient Egyptian Literature*, vol. 1, p. 233
39   Ibid.
40   David, *The Pyramid Builders of Ancient Egypt*, p. 36
41   Robins, *The Art of Ancient Egypt*, p. 109
42   Wilson, *The Culture of Ancient Egypt*, p. 131
43   Breasted, *Ancient Records of Egypt*, vol. I, p. 233
44   David, *The Pyramid Builders of Ancient Egypt*, p. 33
45   Breasted, *Ancient Records of Egypt*, vol. III, p. 186
46   Wallis Budge, *Egyptian Religion*, pp. 55–6
47   Lichtheim, *Ancient Egyptian Literature*, vol. I, p. 133
48   Ibid., p. 132
49   Robins, *Egyptian Art*, p. 105
50   Ibid., p. 118
51   Lehner, *The Complete Pyramids*, p. 171
52   Ibid., p. 176
53   Hayes, *Journal of Egyptian Archaeology*, 35, pp. 43–9
54   Erman, *Literature of the Ancient Egyptians*, pp. 75–84
55   Lichtheim, *Ancient Egyptian Literature*, vol. 1, p. 116

Chapter 10: 'The Female Horus' — Hatshepsut

1   Tyldesley, *Hatshepsut, Female Pharaoh*, p. 83
2   Breasted, *Ancient Records of Egypt*, vol. II, pp. 48, 142
3   Tyldesley, *Hatshepsut*, p. 97
4   Adapted from Breasted, *Ancient Records of Egypt*, vol. II, pp. 142–3
5   Dorman, *The Monuments of Senenmut*, p. 22
6   Lacau and Chevrier, *Une Chapelle d'Hatshepsout a Karnak*, pp. 97ff.
7   Robins, 'God's Wife of Amun', from *Images of Women in Antiquity*, Cameron and Kuhrt (eds), p. 74
8   Ibid.
9   Tyldesley, *Hatshepsut*, p. 100
10   Breasted, *Ancient Records of Egypt*, vol. II, p. 97
11   Adapted from Habachi, *Journal of Near Eastern Studies*, 16, p. 101

12 Tyldesley, *Hatshepsut*, pp. 135–6
13 Hayes, *Scepter of Egypt*, vol. II, p. 97
14 Tyldesley, *Hatshepsut, Female Pharaoh*, p. 137
15 Breasted, *Ancient Records of Egypt*, vol. II, p. 144
16 Ibid., p. 152
17 Ibid., p. 77
18 Ibid., p. 80
19 Ibid.
20 Ibid., p. 81
21 Ibid., p. 89
22 Ibid., p. 91
23 Ibid.
24 Ibid., p. 96
25 Ibid., p. 97
26 Ibid., p. 95
27 Ibid., p. 161
28 Hayes, *Scepter of Egypt*, vol. II, p. 106
29 Breasted, *Ancient Records of Egypt*, vol. II, p. 147
30 Ibid.
31 Ibid., p. 151
32 Ibid., p. 148
33 Ibid.
34 Hayes, *Mitteilungen des Deutchen Archaologischen Instituts Abteilung Kairo*, 15, p. 84
35 Dorman, *The Monuments of Senenmut*, p. 164
36 Breasted, *Ancient Records of Egypt*, vol. II, p. 131
37 Ibid., p. 125
38 Ibid., p. 124
39 Ibid., p. 132
40 Ibid., p. 142
41 Naville, *The Temple of Deir el-Bahri*, p. 1
42 Ibid.
43 Hayes, *Scepter of Egypt*, vol. II, p. 85
44 Breasted, *Ancient Records of Egypt*, vol. II, p. 131
45 Ibid.
46 Ibid., p. 133
47 Ibid., p. 137
48 Ibid., p. 133
49 Ibid., p. 134
50 Ibid., p. 131
51 Ibid., p. 273
52 Ibid., p. 129
53 Tyldesley, *Hatshepsut, Female Pharaoh*, p. 155
54 Gardiner, *Journal of Egyptian Archaeology*, 32, p. 46
55 Breasted, *Ancient Records of Egypt*, vol. II, p. 117
56 Ibid., p. 116
57 Ibid., pp. 121–2
58 Hayes, *Journal of Egyptian Archaeology*, 35, pp. 43–9
59 Breasted, *Ancient Records of Egypt*, vol. II, p. 107
60 Naville, *The Temple of Deir el-Bahri*, p. 1
61 Breasted, *Ancient Records of Egypt*, vol. II, p. 109
62 Naville, *The Temple of Deir el-Bahri*, book II, p. 15
63 Breasted, *Ancient records of Egypt*, vol. II, p. 109
64 Ibid., p. 109
65 From the Harris Papyrus, quoted in Kitchin, *Orientalia*, 40, p. 190
66 Breasted, *Ancient Records of Egypt*, vol. II, p. 113
67 Ibid., p. 121
68 Gardiner, *Egypt of the Pharaohs*, p. 189
69 Wilson, *The Culture of Ancient Egypt*, p. 174
70 Tyldesley, *Hatshepsut, Female Pharaoh*, p. 140
71 Redford, *History and Chronology of the Eighteenth Dynasty*, p. 58
72 Adapted from Habachi, *Journal of Near Eastern Studies*, 16, p. 101
73 Sethe, K. *Urkunden des Aegyptischen Altertums*, IV, 438, p. 10
74 Redford, *History and Chronology of the Eighteenth Dynasty*, pp. 58–9
75 Breasted, *Ancient Records of Egypt*, vol. II, p. 91
76 Säve-Soderburgh, 'Agypten und Nubien', p. 209
77 Mond and Meyers, *The Temples of Armant*, pl. 88, lines 8 ff
78 Breasted, *Ancient Records of Egypt*, vol. II, p. 124
79 Ibid., p. 116
80 Ibid., p. 115
81 Ibid., p. 139
82 Steindorff and Seele, *When Egypt Ruled the East*, p. 46
83 Mertz, *Temples, Tombs and Hieroglyphs*, pp. 179–80

84   Nims, *The Date of the Dishonouring of Hatshespsut*, pp. 97–100

85   Steindorff and Seele, *When Egypt Ruled the East*, p. 46

86   Mertz, *Temples, Tombs and Hieroglyphs*, pp. 179–80

87   Redford, *History and Chronology of the Eighteenth Dynasty*, p. 87

88   Gardiner, *Egypt of the Pharaohs*, p. 187

89   Steindorff and Seele, *When Egypt Ruled the East*, p. 46

90   Wilson, *The Culture of Ancient Egypt*, p. 177

91   Steindorff and Seele, *When Egypt Ruled the East*, p. 46

92   Mertz, *Temples, Tombs and Hieroglyphs*, p. 179

93   Nims, *The Date of the Dishonouring of Hatshespsut*, pp. 97–100

94   Robins, *Women in Ancient Egypt*, p. 52

95   Redford, *History and Chronology of the Eighteenth Dynasty*, p. 87

96   Ibid.

97   Ibid.

98   Breasted, *Ancient Records of Egypt*, vol. II, p. 124

99   Lichtheim, *Ancient Egyptian Literature*, p. 28

100 Breasted, *Ancient Records of Egypt*, vol. II, p. 156

101 Ibid., p. 162

102 Ibid., pp. 148–9

103 Ibid., pp. 107, 108, 111

104 Gardiner, *Egypt of the Pharaohs*, p. 189

105 Robins, 'God's Wife of Amun', in Cameron and Kuhrt (eds), *Images of Women in Antiquity*, p. 74

Chapter 11: 'Valiant like Montu' — Thutmose III

1   Breasted, *Ancient Records of Egypt*, vol. II, p. 166

2   Hayes, *Scepter of Egypt*, vol. II, p. 116

3   Tyldesley, *Hatshepsut, Female Pharaoh*, p. 143

4   Gardiner, *Egypt of the Pharaohs*, p. 188

5   Breasted, *Ancient Records of Egypt*, vol. II, p. 163

6   Ibid., p. 164

7   Gardiner, *Egypt of the Pharaohs*, p. 190

8   Hayes, *Scepter of Egypt*, vol. II, p. 116

9   Breasted, *Ancient Records of Egypt*, vol. II, pp. 67–8

10 Ibid., p. 68

11 Ibid., p. 301

12 Grimal, *A History of Ancient Egypt*, p. 213

13 Aldred, *The Egyptians*, p. 147

14 Breasted, *Ancient Records of Egypt*, vol. II, p. 179

15 Ibid.

16 Ibid., p. 184

17 Ibid., p. 179

18 Gardiner, *Egypt of the Pharaohs*, p. 189

19 Ibid.

20 Yeivin, *Journal of the Palestine Oriental Society*, pp. 194 ff

21 Wilson, *The Culture of Ancient Egypt*, pp. 177–8

22 Breasted, *Ancient Records of Egypt*, vol. II, p. 180

23 Ibid.

24 Ibid., p. 181

25 Ibid., p. 183

26 Ibid.

27 Ibid., p. 184

28 Ibid.

29 Ibid., p. 185

30 Ibid.

31 Ibid., p. 184

32 Ibid., p. 186

33 Yeivin, *Journal of the Palestine Oriental Society*, 14: 3, pp. 194 ff

34 Ibid.

35 Wilson, *The Culture of Ancient Egypt*, p. 181

36 Breasted, *Ancient Records of Egypt*, vol. II, p. 189

37 Ibid., p. 220

38 Ibid., p. 188

39 Ibid., p. 221

40 Steindorff and Seele, *When Egypt Ruled the East*, p. 56

41 Ibid., p. 170

42 Breasted, *Ancient Records of Egypt*, vol. II, p. 198

43 Ibid., pp. 196–7

44 Ibid., p. 198

45 Ibid., p. 232

46 Ibid., p. 200

47 Yeivin, *Journal of the Palestine Oriental Society*, 14: 3, pp. 194 ff

48 Breasted, *Ancient Records of Egypt*, vol. II, p. 202

49 Yeivin, *Journal of the Palestine Oriental Society*, pp. 194 ff
50 Ibid.
51 Breasted, *Ancient Records of Egypt*, vol. II, p. 233
52 Ibid.
53 Ibid., p. 215
54 Ibid., p. 233
55 Yeivin, *Journal of the Palestine Oriental Society*, 14: 3, pp. 194 ff
56 Breasted, *Ancient Records of Egypt*, vol. II, p. 181
57 Ibid., p. 166
58 Ibid., p. 260
59 Ibid., p. 261
60 Ibid., p. 195
61 Wilson, *The Culture of Ancient Egypt*, p. 186
62 Lichtheim, *Ancient Egyptian Literature*, vol. II, p. 36
63 Breasted, *Ancient Records of Egypt*, vol. II, p. 226
64 Ibid., p. 220
65 Grimal, *A History of Ancient Egypt*, p. 217
66 Breasted, *Ancient Records of Egypt*, vol. II, p. 239
67 Ibid., p. 242
68 Ibid., p. 241
69 Ibid., p. 245
70 Ibid., p. 252
71 Steindorff and Seele, *When Egypt Ruled the East*, p. 64
72 Breasted, *Ancient Records of Egypt*, vol. II, p. 267
73 Steindorff and Seele, *When Egypt Ruled the East*, p. 66
74 Aldred, *Akhenaten, King of Egypt*, p. 122
75 Gardiner, *Egypt of the Pharaohs*, p. 198
76 Daressy, *Fouilles de la Vallée des Rois*, p. 68, pl. XIX
77 Hassan, *Annales du Service des Antiquites de l'Egypte*, pp. 129 ff
78 Ibid.
79 Ibid.
80 Breasted, *Ancient Records of Egypt*, vol. II, p. 319
81 Adapted from Breasted by Forbes and Garner, The Australian Institute of Archaeology, *Documents of the Egyptian Empire*, doc. 13
82 Gardiner, *Egypt of the Pharaohs*, p. 202

83 Breasted, *Ancient Records of Egypt*, vol. II, p. 313
84 Ibid.
85 Ibid., p. 311
86 Gardiner, *Egypt of the Pharaohs*, p. 199
87 Breasted, *Ancient Records of Egypt*, vol. II, pp. 323–4
88 Ibid.
89 Ibid.
90 Yeivin, *Journal of the Palestine Oriental Society*, 14: 3, pp. 194 ff
91 Breasted, *Ancient Records of Egypt*, vol. II, p. 233
92 Lichtheim, *Ancient Egyptian Literature*, vol. II, pp. 36–7
93 Steindorff and Seele, *When Egypt Ruled the East*, pp. 67–8

Chapter 12: 'The Dazzling Sun-disk' — Amenhotep III

1 Gardiner, *Egypt of the Pharaohs*, p. 205
2 Redford, *Akhenaten, The Heretic King*, p. 45
3 Gardiner, *Egypt of the Pharaohs*, p. 206
4 Breasted, *Ancient Records of Egypt*, vol. II, p. 345
5 Ibid., p. 349
6 Adapted from Breasted, *Ancient Records of Egypt*, vol. II, pp. 346, 164
7 Breasted, *Ancient Records of Egypt*, vol. II, p. 346
8 Aldred, *Akhenaten, King of Egypt*, pp. 142–3
9 Breasted, *Ancient Records of Egypt*, vol. II, p. 343
10 Ibid., p. 336
11 Ibid.
12 Ibid., p. 339
13 Ibid., p. 341
14 Pritchard, *The Ancient Near East*, vol. I, p. 262
15 Ibid., p. 266
16 Knudtzon, *Die el-Amarna Tafeln*, (1907–15), 19, 21, translated in Redford, *Akhenaten, Heretic King*, p. 41
17 Steindorff and Seele, *When Egypt Ruled the East*, p. 110
18 Ibid., p. 111
19 Hayes, *Scepter of Egypt*, vol. II, p. 232
20 Breasted, *Ancient Records of Egypt*, vol. II, p. 345

21 Knudtzon, *Die el-Amarna Tafeln*, (1907–15), 4, 36–50, translated in Redford, *Akhenaten, Heretic King*, p. 41
22 Ibid.
23 Ibid.
24 Pritchard, *The Ancient Near East*, vol. I, p. 268
25 Breasted, *Ancient Records of Egypt*, vol. II, p. 343
26 Ibid., p. 375
27 Ibid., p. 376
28 Ibid., p. 378
29 Lichtheim, *Ancient Egyptian Literature*, vol. II, p. 45
30 Ibid., pp. 44–5
31 Hayes, *Scepter of Egypt*, vol. II, p. 234
32 Lichtheim, *Ancient Egyptian Literature*, vol. II, pp. 44–5
33 Hayes, *Scepter of Egypt*, vol. II, p. 234
34 Lichtheim, *Ancient Egyptian Literature*, vol. II, p. 46
35 Breasted, *Ancient Records of Egypt*, vol. II, p. 356
36 James, *Egyptian Painting*, p. 41
37 Redford, *Akhenaten, the Heretic King*, p. 162
38 Thomas, *Akhenaten's Egypt*, p. 9
39 Ibid.
40 Knudtzon, *Die el-Amarna Tafeln*, (1907–15), 19, 21 translated in Redford, *Akhenaten, Heretic King*, p. 54
41 Steindorff and Seele, *When Egypt Ruled the East*, p. 110
42 Redford, *Akhenaten, the Heretic King*, p. 35
43 Aldred, *Akhenaten, King of Egypt*, pp. 166
44 Grimal, *A History of Ancient Egypt*, p. 225
45 Breasted, *Ancient Records of Egypt*, vol. II, p. 348
46 Knudtzon, *Die el-Amarna Tafeln*, (1907–15), 14, 36–50, translated in Redford, *Akhenaten, Heretic King*, p. 41
47 Breasted, *Ancient Records of Egypt*, vol. II, p. 374
48 Ibid., pp. 350–1

Chapter 13: Akhenaten and the Amarna interlude

1 Kemp, *Ancient Egypt, An Anatomy of a Civilisation*, p. 264
2 Samson, *Nefertiti and Cleopatra, Monarch Queens of Ancient Egypt*, p. xiii
3 Kemp, *Ancient Egypt, An Anatomy of a Civilisation*, p. 262
4 Redford, *Akhenaten, the Heretic King*, p. 57
5 Aldred, *Akhenaten, King of Egypt*, p. 180
6 Hayes, *Scepter of Egypt*, vol. II, p. 280
7 Redford, *Akhenaten, the Heretic King*, p. 158
8 Gardiner, *Egypt of the Pharaohs*, p. 217
9 Ibid., p. 218
10 Lichtheim, *Ancient Egyptian Literature*, vol. II, pp. 98–9
11 Ibid., p. 98
12 Ibid., pp. 97–9
13 Ibid., p. 96
14 Ibid., p. 97
15 Redford, *Akhenaten, the Heretic King*, p. 178
16 Lichtheim, *Ancient Egyptian Literature*, vol. II, p. 93
17 Ibid., p. 99
18 Ibid., p. 93
19 Breasted, *Ancient Records of Egypt*, vol. II, p. 405
20 Ibid., p. 410
21 Redford, *Akhenaten, the Heretic King*, p. 178
22 Ibid., p. 170
23 Breasted, *Ancient Records of Egypt*, vol. II, 385
24 Aldred, *Akhenaten, King of Egypt*, p. 262
25 Breasted, *Ancient Records of Egypt*, vol. II, p. 406
26 Sethe, *Urkunden des Aegyptischen Altertums*, IV, 1966
27 Robins, *The Art of Ancient Egypt*, p. 165
28 Lichtheim, *Ancient Egyptian Literature*, vol. II, p. 91
29 Ibid., p. 94
30 Ibid.
31 Breasted, *Ancient Records of Egypt*, vol. II, p. 409
32 Robins, *The Art of Ancient Egypt*, p. 150
33 Ibid., p. 156
34 Ibid., p. 154
35 Kemp, *Ancient Egypt, An Anatomy of a Civilisation*, p. 265
36 Gardiner, *Egypt of the Pharaohs*, p. 227
37 Sethe, K. *Urkunden des Aegyptischen Altertums*, IV, 1975
38 Ibid., IV, 1969
39 Ibid.
40 Ibid.
41 Breasted, *Ancient Records of Egypt*, vol. II, p. 393

42 Ibid., p. 398

43 Ibid., p. 393

44 Ibid., p. 397

45 Ibid., p. 396

46 Kemp, *Ancient Egypt, An Anatomy of a Civilisation*, p. 276

47 Grimal, *A History of Ancient Egypt*, p. 232

48 Redford, *Akhenaten, the Heretic King*, p. 153

49 Grimal, *A History of Ancient Egypt*, p. 232

50 Lichtheim, *Ancient Egyptian Literature*, vol. II, p. 97

51 Ibid., pp. 94–6

52 Kemp, *Ancient Egypt, An Anatomy of a Civilisation*, p. 286

53 Thomas, *Akhenaten's Egypt*, p. 25

54 Breasted, *Ancient Records of Egypt*, vol. II, p. 403

55 Lichtheim, *Ancient Egyptian Literature*, vol. II, p. 92

56 Breasted, *Ancient Records of Egypt*, vol. II, p. 418

57 Redford, *Akhenaten, the Heretic King*, p. 235

58 Steindorff and Seele, *When Egypt Ruled the East*, pp. 220–1

59 Redford, *Akhenaten, the Heretic King*, p. 195

60 Aldred, *Akhenaten, King of Egypt*, p. 183

61 Ibid., p. 186

62 Redford, *Akhenaten, the Heretic King*, p. 194

63 *Egyptian Archaeology* 53 (Knudtzon, *Die el-Amarna Tafeln*, 1907–15) translated in Redford, *Akhenaten, Heretic King*, p. 198

64 *Egyptian Archaeology* 51 (Knudtzon, *Die el-Amarna Tafeln*, 1907–15) translated in Redford, *Akhenaten, Heretic King*, p. 198

65 Metz, *Temples, Tombs and Hieroglyphs*, p. 229

66 *Egyptian Archaeology* 140 (Knudtzon, *Die el-Amarna Tafeln*, 1907–15) translated in Redford, *Akhenaten, Heretic King*, p. 202

67 Ibid., p. 286

68 Ibid.

69 Ibid., p. 288

70 Davies, *The Rock Tombs of El-Amarna*, VI, p. 119

71 Samson, *Nefertiti and Cleopatra, Monarch Queens of Ancient Egypt*, p. 85

72 Redford, *Akhenaten, the Heretic King*, p. 192

73 Aldred, *Akhenaten, King of Egypt*, p. 230

74 Ibid., p. 202

75 Ibid., p. 109

76 Gardiner, *Egypt of the Pharaohs*, p. 220

77 Kemp, *Ancient Egypt, An Anatomy of a Civilisation*, p. 264

78 Thomas, *Akhenaten's Egypt*, p. 16

79 Hayes, *Scepter of Egypt*, vol. II, p. 180

80 Aldred, *Akhenaten, King of Egypt*, p. 305

81 Redford, *Akhenaten, the Heretic King*, p. 235

82 Ibid., p. 210

83 Ibid., p. 206

84 Ibid., p. 208

85 Bennet, *Journal of Egyptian Archaeology*, 125, p. 15

86 Redford, *Akhenaten, the Heretic King*, p. 211

87 Desroches-Noblecourt, *Tutankhamun, The Life and Death of a Pharaoh*, p. 182

88 Ibid., p. 275

89 Ibid.

90 Ibid., p. 221

91 Redford, *Akhenaten, the Heretic King*, pp. 218–19

92 Gardiner, *Journal of Egyptian Archaeology*, vol. 39

93 Ibid., p. 14

94 Ibid., p. 3

95 Aldred, *Akhenaten, King of Egypt*, p. 302

96 Redford, *Akhenaten, the Heretic King*, p. 228

97 Breasted, *Ancient Records of Egypt*, vol. II, p. 384

98 Ibid., p. 417

99 Ibid., pp. 410–11

100 Carter, *The Tomb of Tutankhamen*, p. 10

101 Breasted, *Ancient Records of Egypt*, vol. III, pp. 25, 31–2

Chapter 14: A change of dynasty — Seti I and Ramesses II

1 Kitchin, *Pharaoh Triumphant*, p. 19

2 Breasted, *Ancient Records of Egypt*, vol. III, p. 52

3 Ibid., p. 52

4 Kitchin, *Pharaoh Triumphant*, p. 22

5 Ibid., p. 24

6 Breasted, *Ancient Records of Egypt*, vol. III, p. 88

7 Kitchin, *Pharaoh Triumphant*, p. 26

8 Ibid.

9 Lichtheim, *Ancient Egyptian Literature*, vol. II, p. 53

10 Breasted, *Ancient Records of Egypt*, vol. III, p. 52

11 Ibid.
12 Breasted, quoted in Hayes, *Sceptre of Egypt*,
    vol. II, p. 329
13 Breasted, *Ancient Records of Egypt*, vol. III,
    p. 96
14 Gardiner, *Egypt of the Pharaohs*, p. 250
15 Lichtheim, *Ancient Egyptian Literature*,
    vol. II, p. 53
16 Ibid.
17 Griffith, *Journal of Egyptian Archaeology*,
    p. 201
18 Breasted, *Ancient Records of Egypt*, vol. III,
    pp. 92–3
19 Ibid., p. 100
20 Kitchin, *Pharaoh Triumphant*, p. 237
21 Gardiner, *Egypt of the Pharaohs*, p. 256
22 Breasted, *Ancient Records of Egypt*,
    vol. III, p. 109
23 Ibid.
24 Ibid., p. 107
25 Ibid., p. 97
26 Ibid., p. 107
27 Ibid., p. 110
28 Kitchin, *Pharaoh Triumphant*, p. 49
29 Ibid., p. 50
30 Ibid.
31 Wilson, *The Culture of Ancient Egypt*, p. 243
32 Ibid., p. 240
33 Lichtheim, *Ancient Egyptian Literature*,
    vol. II, p. 58
34 Breasted, *Ancient records of Egypt*, vol. III,
    p. 138
35 Lichtheim, Ancient Egyptian Literature, vol.
    II, p. 61
36 Ibid., p. 60
37 Kitchin, *Pharaoh Triumphant*, p. 54
38 Lichtheim, *Ancient Egyptian Literature*,
    vol. II, p. 61
39 Ibid.
40 Ibid.
41 Breasted, *Ancient Records of Egypt*, vol. III,
    p. 153
42 Ibid., p. 153
43 Lichtheim, *Ancient Egyptian Literature*,
    vol. II, p. 69
44 Ibid., p. 71
45 Wilson, *The Culture of Ancient Egypt*, p. 147
46 Lichtheim, *Ancient Egyptian Literature*,
    vol. II, pp. 65–6, 69
47 Ibid., pp. 61–2
48 McDonald, *The Tomb of Nefertari*, p. 14

49 Breasted, *Ancient Records of Egypt*, vol. III,
    p. 166
50 Kitchin, *Pharaoh Triumphant*, p. 75
51 Ibid., p. 84
52 Breasted, *Ancient Records of Egypt*, vol. III,
    p. 184
53 Kitchin, *Pharaoh Triumphant*, p. 86
54 Breasted, *Ancient Records of Egypt*, vol. III,
    p. 184
55 Kitchin, *Pharaoh Triumphant*, p. 90
56 Breasted, *Ancient Records of Egypt*, vol. III,
    p. 186
57 Wilson, *The Culture of Ancient Egypt*, p. 252
58 Metz, *Tombs, Temples and Hieroglyphs*,
    p. 276
59 Grimal, *A History of Ancient Egypt*, p. 266
60 Kitchin, *Pharaoh Triumphant*, p. 120
61 ibid.
62 Laloute, *L'Empire des Ramses*, p. 111, based
    on Pritchard, *Ancient Near Eastern Texts
    Relating to the Bible*
63 Kitchin, *Pharaoh Triumphant*, p. 107
64 Ibid.
65 Edwards, *A Thousand Miles Up the Nile*,
    pp. 411–2
66 Kitchin, *Pharaoh Triumphant*, p. 234
67 Wilson, *The Culture of Ancient Egypt*, p. 247
68 Breasted, *Ancient Records of Egypt*, vol. III,
    p. 226
69 Hayes, *Sceptre of Egypt*, vol. II, p. 334
70 Kitchin, *Pharaoh Triumphant*, p. 237
71 Lichtheim, *Ancient Egyptian Literature*,
    vol. II, p. 53
72 Ibid.
73 Ibid., p. 54
74 Ibid., p. 56
75 Ibid., p. 60
76 Ibid., p. 64
77 Ibid., pp. 63–4
78 Ibid., p. 60
79 Ibid., p. 64
80 Ibid., p. 61
81 Ibid., p. 64
82 Breasted, *Ancient Records of Egypt*, vol. III,
    p. 153
83 Lichtheim, *Ancient Egyptian Literature*,
    vol. II, p. 62
84 Ibid., p. 71
85 McDonald, *The Tomb of Nefertari*, p. 16
86 Breasted, *Ancient Records of Egypt*, vol. III,
    p. 218

87 Ibid., p. 222
88 Ibid., p. 181

Chapter 15: Egyptian expansion and its effects on New Kingdom society

1   Wilson, *The Culture of Ancient Egypt*, p. 204
2   Ibid., p. 168
3   Aldred, *Akhenaten, King of Egypt*, pp. 121–2
4   Ibid., p. 121
5   The Australian Institute of Archaeology, *Documents of the Egyptian Empire*, p. 16
6   Ibid., p. 19
7   Ibid., p. 25
8   Ibid.
9   Ibid., p. 31
10 Ibid., p. 37
11 Breasted, *Ancient Records of Egypt*, vol. II, pp. 184–5
12 Lichtheim, *Ancient Egyptian Literature*, vol. II, p. 12
13 The Australian Institute of Archaeology, *Documents of the Egyptian Empire*, p. 31
14 Ibid., p. 35
15 Ibid., p. 40
16 Wilson, *The Culture of Ancient Egypt*, p. 202
17 Tyldesley, *Daughters of Isis*, p. 197
18 Sethe, *Urkunden des Altes Reichs*, IV, 21
19 Breasted, *Ancient records of Egypt*, vol. II, p. 142
20 Tyldesley, *Daughters of Isis*, p. 200
21 Desroches-Noblecourt, *Tutankhamun*, p. 275
22 Ibid.
23 Ions, *Egyptian Mythology*, p. 92
24 The Australian Institute of Archaeology, *Documents of the Egyptian Empire*, pp. 40–1
25 Ibid., p. 32
26 Kemp, *Ancient Egypt*, p. 217
27 Ibid.
28 Ibid., p 209
29 Ibid., p 206
30 Ibid., p 208
31 Kitchin, *Pharaoh Triumphant*, p. 175
32 The Australian Institute of Archaeology, *Documents of the Egyptian Empire*, p. 40
33 Ibid., p. 28
34 Ibid., p. 35
35 Reisner, *Zeitschrift für Äegyptische Sprache und Altertumskunde*, p. 34

36 Kitchin, *Pharaoh Triumphant*, p. 86
37 Snape, *Egyptian Temples*, p. 28
38 Breasted, *Documents of Ancient Egypt*, vol. II
39 Snape, *Egyptian Temples*, p. 29
40 Breasted, *Documents of Ancient Egypt*, vol. II, pp. 357–8
41 Ibid., p. 359
42 Ibid.
43 Snape, *Egyptian Temples*, p. 33
44 Lichtheim, *A Book of Readings*, vol I, p. 117
45 Steindorff and Seele, *When Egypt Ruled the East*, p. 114
46 Aldred, *Akhenaten, King of Egypt*, p. 127
47 Aldred, *The Egyptians*, p. 179
48 Steindorff and Seele, *When Egypt Ruled the East*, p. 83
49 Manchip White, *Ancient Egypt, its Culture and History*, pp. 18–19
50 Steindorff and Seele, *When Egypt Ruled the East*, p. 83
51 Lichtheim, *Ancient Egyptian Literature*, vol. II, p. 53
52 Kemp, *Ancient Egypt*, p. 238
53 Lichtheim, *Ancient Egyptian Literature*, vol. II, p. 22
54 Davies, *The Tomb of Rekh-mi-Re*, pls. XI, XII
55 Ibid., pls XIII, XIV
56 James, *Pharaoh's People*, p. 61 (abridged from Faulkner in *Journal of Egyptian Archaeology*)
57 Ibid.
58 Ibid.
59 Ibid.
60 Ibid.
61 Davies, *The Tomb of Rekh-mi-Re*, pls. XI, XII
62 Ibid., p. 63
63 Ibid., pls. XXVI–XXVIII
64 Ibid.
65 Ibid.
66 Ibid., pls. XXIII
67 David, *The Ancient Egyptians, Religious Beliefs and Practices*, p. 139
68 Ibid., p. 135
69 Lichtheim, *Ancient Egyptian Literature*, vol II, p. 171
70 James, *Pharaoh's People*, p. 143
71 Lichtheim, *Ancient Egyptian Literature*, vol. II, p. 171
72 James, *Pharaoh's People*, p. 129
73 Ibid., p. 130

74   Lichtheim, *Ancient Egyptian Literature*,
     vol. II, p. 63
75   Ibid., p. 172
76   Pritchard, *The Ancient Near East*, vol. I,
     p. 263
77   Ibid., p. 266
78   Ibid., p. 268
79   Manchip White, *Ancient Egypt, its Culture
     and History*, pp. 18–19
80   Davies, *The Tomb of Rekh-mi-Re*,
     pls. XXVI–XXVIII
81   Lichtheim, *Ancient Egyptian Literature*,
     vol. II, p. 36

Chapter 16: Everyday life in New Kingdom Egypt

1   Montet, *Everyday Life in Egypt*, pp. 192, 195
2   Manchip White, *Ancient Egypt, its Culture
     and History*, p. 17
3   Montet, *Everyday Life in Egypt*, p. 173
4   Kitchin, *Pharaoh Triumphant*, p. 122
5   Ibid., p. 120
6   Gardiner, *Bibliotheca Aegyptiaca*,
     vol. VII, 1937
7   Erman, *Life in Ancient Egypt*, p. 174
8   Tyldesley, *Daughters of Isis*, p. 180
9   Robins, *Women in Ancient Egypt*, p. 176
10   Lichtheim, *Ancient Egyptian Literature*,
     vol. II, p. 136
11   Tyldesley, *Daughters of Isis*, p. 82
12   Lichtheim, *Ancient Egyptian Literature*,
     vol. II, p. 143
13   Tyldesley, *Daughters of Isis*, p. 121
14   Manchip White, *Ancient Egypt, its Culture
     and History*, p. 169
15   Gardiner and Sethe, *Egyptian Letters to the
     Dead*, p. 327
16   Tyldesley, *Daughters of Isis*, pp. 60–1
17   Lichtheim, *Ancient Egyptian Literature*,
     vol. II, p. 141
18   Tyldesley, *Daughters of Isis*, p. 159
19   Ebers Medical Papyrus, translated in
     Tyldesley, *Daughters of Isis*, p. 152
20   Adapted from Lichtheim, *Journal of Near
     Eastern Studies*, 4, p. 195
21   From the tomb of Paheri, translated in
     Tyldesley, *Daughters of Isis*, p. 111
22   Adapted from Lichtheim, *Journal of Near
     Eastern Studies*, 4, pp. 192–3
23   Montet, *Everyday Life in Egypt*, p. 174
24   Taylor and Griffith, *The Tomb of Paheri*, pl. III
25   Davies, *The Tomb of Rekh-mi-Re*, pls. XI, XII
26   Montet, *Everyday Life in Egypt*, p. 159
27   James, *Pharaoh's People*, p. 188
28   Ibid., p. 204
29   Lichtheim, *Ancient Egyptian Literature*,
     vol. I, p. 186
30   Tyldesley, *Daughters of Isis*, p. 149
31   Kitchin, *Pharaoh Triumphant*, pp. 196–7
32   Ibid., p. 191
33   Berbier, *Tomb Builders of the Pharaohs*, p. 29
34   Kitchin, *Pharaoh Triumphant*, p. 194
35   David, *The Pyramid Builders of Egypt*, p. 74
36   Kitchin, *Pharaoh Triumphant*, p. 192
37   Ibid., p. 199
38   Aldred, *Akhenaten, King of Egypt*, p. 273
39   Kemp, *Ancient Egypt, an Anatomy of a
     Civilisation*, p. 305
40   Ibid., p. 273
41   Lichtheim, M. *Ancient Egyptian Literature*,
     vol. I, p. 207
42   Lichtheim, *Ancient Egyptian Literature*,
     vol. II, p. 170
43   Erman, *Literature of the Ancient Egyptians*,
     p. 152
44   Taylor and Griffith, *The Tomb of Paheri*,
     pl. III
45   Ibid.
46   Ibid.
47   Lichtheim, *Ancient Egyptian Literature*,
     vol. I, p. 170
48   Herodotus, *The Histories*, 2, p. 13
49   Montet, *Everyday Life in Egypt*, p. 113
50   Taylor and Griffith, *The Tomb of Paheri*,
     pl. III
51   Ibid.
52   Ibid.
53   Ibid.
54   Lichtheim, *Ancient Egyptian Literature*,
     vol. II, p. 204
55   Ibid.
56   Gardiner and Sethe, *Egyptian Letters to the
     Dead*, p. 327
57   Erman, *Life in Ancient Egypt*, p. 255
58   Mertz, *Red Land, Black Land*, p. 238
59   Tyldesley, *Daughters of Isis*, p. 33
60   David, *The Ancient Egyptians, Religious
     Beliefs and Practices*, p. 142
61   Montet, *Everyday Life in Egypt*, p. 282

62 Lichtheim, *Ancient Egyptian Literature*, vol. I, pp. 186–7
63 Lichtheim, *Ancient Egyptian literature*, vol. II, pp. 170–1

Chapter 17: New Kingdom funerary beliefs and burial practices

1 Spencer, *Death in Ancient Egypt*, p. 163
2 Frankfort, *Kingship and the Gods*, p. 185
3 Wallis Budge, *Egyptian Religion*, p. 125
4 Ibid., p. 126
5 Ibid.
6 Lichtheim, *Ancient Egyptian Literature*, vol II, p. 121
7 Wallis Budge, *Egyptian Religion*, p. 150
8 Ibid.
9 Spencer, *Death in Ancient Egypt*, p. 139
10 Ibid., p. 149
11 Wallis Budge, *Egyptian Religion*, p. 190
12 Ibid., p. 190
13 Spencer, *Death in Ancient Egypt*, p. 37
14 Herodotus, 2, p. 160
15 Ibid.
16 Spencer, *Death in Ancient Egypt*, p. 120
17 Andrews, *Egyptian Mummies*, p. 34
18 Ibid., p. 35
19 Ibid., p. 33
20 Ibid.
21 Desroches-Noblecourt, *Tutankhamun, Life and Death of a Pharaoh*, p. 236
22 Ibid.
23 Hayes, *Scepter of Egypt*, vol II, p. 227
24 Lichtheim, *Ancient Egyptian Literature*, p. 229
25 Reeder, *KMT*, 6, p. 3
26 James, *Introductory Guide to the Egyptian Collections*, p. 155
27 Lurker, *The Gods and Symbols of Ancient Egypt*, p. 126
28 Montet, *Everyday Life in Ancient Egypt*, p. 327
29 Faulkner, *Journal of Egyptian Archaeology*, XLII, p. 21
30 Kanawati, *The Tomb and its Significance in Ancient Egypt*, p. 22
31 Ibid., p. 142
32 Manniche, *The City of the Dead*, p. 36
33 Ibid., p. 37
34 Ibid., p. 45
35 Kanawati, *The Tomb and its Significance in Ancient Egypt*, p. 141
36 Manniche, *The City of the Dead*, p. 52
37 Lichtheim, *Ancient Egyptian Literature*, vol II, pp. 83–5
38 Ibid., p. 125
39 Spencer, *Death in Ancient Egypt*, pp. 95–6
40 Lichtheim, *Ancient Egyptian Literature*, vol II, p. 121
41 Ibid., p. 120
42 Edwards, *Journal of Egyptian Archaeology*, 57, pp. 120–4
43 Manniche, *The City of the Dead*, p. 10

GLOSSARY

adze a heavy, chisel-like tool used to work timber

alluvium deposits of silt left by running water

akh a shiny, luminous spirit released from the body on death

Akhet the season of flood, one of the three seasons in Egypt, which began sometime in July

alabaster a semi-transparent, soft marble-like mineral used by the Egyptians for vases, sarcophagi and walls and floors of sacred places

amulet a magical charm used by the Egyptians for protection and regeneration

Amun/Amun-Re the chief god of Egypt throughout the New Kingdom; usually depicted in human form with a head-dress of tall ostrich feathers. Sometimes shown with a ram's head

ankh the hieroglyphs for *life* — the key of life

annals year-by-year accounts

Anubis the jackal-headed god of embalming and lord of the necropolis

astral to do with the stars

atef **crown** an elaborate triple crown with horns and feathers

Aten the disk of the sun. This was elevated to a god in its own right during the time of Akhenaten

Atum a creator god, a form of the sun god

ba the soul, represented as a human-headed bird

bark (barque) a mythological ship or portable shrine shaped like a ship

basalt a hard, dark igneous stone

ben-ben a sacred stone in the shape of a pyramidion which was the symbol of the sun god at Heliopolis. It was believed to represent the primeval mound which emerged from the waters of chaos during creation. It formed the tip of an obelisk

bennu bird a type of heron which, according to Heliopolitan tradition, represented Re-Atum and alighted on the ben-ben at the time of creation to disperse the darkness

bier a moveable stand on which a body or coffin was carried to the tomb

Black Land (or Kemet) the long, narrow river valley enclosed by desert cliffs (Upper Egypt) and the delta (Lower Egypt), made up of fertile black silt or mud which the Nile, in flood, deposited over the valley every year

Book of the Dead a New Kingdom funerary text usually written on papyrus rolls and placed near the body of the deceased

booty objects (spoil) taken from an enemy in war

bureaucracy government by officials. In Egypt, there were numerous religious, civil and military departments, and officials

canopic jars small, sealed containers used for holding the liver, lungs, intestines and stomach of a deceased person, and buried with the mummy

caravan a group of people such as merchants travelling together through desert land for security

cartonnage linen stiffened with plaster and then painted. Used for death masks and coffins

cartouche the oval figure that surrounded two of the pharaoh's names (the birth name and the coronation name) when carved or written

catafalque a decorated wooden support for a coffin

cataract rocky interruptions to the flow of water in a river, causing rapids. There were six cataracts along the upper Nile in Nubia

causeway a long covered paved corridor linking the valley and mortuary temples of a pyramid complex

cenotaph a monument to a deceased person whose body is buried elsewhere

chapel a chamber or series of rooms in a tomb which featured a false door, statues of the owner and perhaps his wife, an offering table and 'decorated' walls. Relatives and friends could visit the chapel and offer prayers, food and drink to the ka of the deceased

chronology a sequence of events

Coffin Texts funerary texts painted on coffins during the Middle Kingdom

concubine a woman who lives with a man and has a sexual relationship with him but is not his wife. In Egypt, men could have several wives as well as concubines

co-regency a situation in which a king shared his throne with another, usually a son, in order to ensure a smooth succession

'corn' mummies miniature outlines of the mummified Osiris, filled with mud, planted with grain and placed in the tomb. They were a symbol of rejuvenation

corvee annual conscription (forced recruitment) of workers for community tasks such as repairing canals after the flood

crook a sceptre carried by kings and gods as a symbol of authority. It originated from the shepherds' staff

cubit an ancient measure of length of approximately 45 centimetres

cult centre place where a local god was worshipped by a special group of priests, in a temple precinct

cult temple a temple dedicated to a particular god

cynocephalus a dog-faced baboon

decentralisatio movement away from the centre of power or population

delta the area between the ancient capital of Memphis and the sea, where the Nile divides into many branches and as it flows towards the Mediterranean Sea and silt is deposited in a large triangular or fan-shaped formation

Deshret the Red Land, or desert

divine god-like

djed **pillars** amulets thought to represent the backbone of Osiris. They were believed to impart stability and endurance

Double Crown a crown representing the Two Lands of Upper and Lower Egypt. It combined the White Crown of Upper Egypt and the Red Crown of Lower Egypt

dryt **mourners** professional mourners who represented the divine mourners, Isis and her sister Nephthys, who mourned the death of Isis' husband Osiris

dynasty a line of rulers from the same family

ebony a hard black timber

electrum an alloy of gold and silver

embalming a process of treating a dead body with resins, spices and other items to prevent it from decomposing

ennead a grouping of nine, such as nine gods

epigraphy the study of inscriptions

exotic something introduced from abroad, or foreign to a country

faience a glaze made by heating quartz sand with soda until the quartz melted and solidified. The most popular colours were green and turquoise, created by adding copper filings before heating

Faiyum an area to the south-west of Memphis where a branch of the Nile flows into a depression 50 metres below sea level. Surplus floodwaters are caught here and the area acts as a reservoir when the Nile is low. The land which was periodically reclaimed from this huge lake was fertile and rich in wildlife

false door an architectural feature of a tomb chapel which looked like a door. Its purpose was to allow the ka of the deceased to pass through to receive offerings

Fields of Reeds the place where ordinary Egyptians hoped to spend the afterlife. It closely resembled the delta area with its lush meadows, watercourses and canals

First Time the term used by the Egyptians for the creation of the universe

flail a short rod with two or three leather strips or strings of beads attached to one end, considered to be the shepherd's whip; one of the pieces of equipment carried by a king

frankincense a fragrant gum resin from African and Asian trees of the genus *Boswellia*, used for burning as incense

Geb god of the earth

God's Wife of Amun an influential religious title given to certain princesses and queens during the early Eighteenth Dynasty

gold of valour necklaces of gold given to officials by the king for outstanding bravery or merit. Presented in public ceremonies

granite a hard igneous rock containing quartz and feldspar, used extensively in Egyptian buildings, particularly monuments

Hapi the spirit of the Nile. The Egyptians depicted him as a man with a pendulous belly and the breasts of a woman

harem secluded part of a residence where the women of the household (mothers, wives, daughters, concubines, entertainers and servants) lived. In New Kingdom Egypt they were also self-contained economic institutions producing goods such as cloth

Hathor the goddess of love, often represented with the head, horns or ears of a cow

hierarchy a system in which people or things are graded in a particular order

hieratic a form of writing that was a simplified version of the hieroglyphic script, in which the images were replaced with strokes. It made writing easier and faster

hieroglyphs sacred carvings. These were miniature images that stood for objects, sounds and letters, and were originally only inscribed on stone. Later they were painted on walls and papyrus

Horus originally a falcon sky god, and the earliest state god of Egypt. Each reigning king was regarded as the 'living Horus'. Horus was also the son of Osiris and Isis. Eventually these two Horus gods merged

house of life a special place in the temple where books were written and interpretations were made. the priests of the *house of life* chose the names and titles of the king

Hyksos foreigners from Palestine who invaded and ruled Egypt from c. 1640 BC

hypostyle a massive, columned hall or reception area in an Egyptian temple

ib the heart scarab. An amulet placed in the wrappings of a mummy over its heart, so that the heart would not fail the deceased during judgment

incense an aromatic gum which, when burnt, gives off a sweet smell. It was used extensively in religious and funerary rituals

Instructions brief teachings aimed at guiding members of the noble class in the correct behaviour

inundation a flood

Isis the goddess wife of Osiris and mother of Horus

ivory a hard white substance which forms the tusks of animals, especially elephants

ka the life force

ka **statue** a statue in which it was believed the *ka* or *life* essence of a dead person could reside in order to accept offerings of food, drink and incense

Keftiu the Egyptian word for the people of the Aegean, particularly those from Minoan Crete

Kemet the Black Land — the fertile narrow valley of the Nile and its fan-shaped delta

kenbet local court

Khatte the Egyptian word for the land of the Hittites

khepresh the blue war crown of the pharaoh

Khepri (Kheper) the sun god in the form of the scarab beetle, symbol of rebirth and therefore the morning sun

king's son of Kush the Egyptian viceroy or governor of Nubia

kohl a fine black powder made from antimony (a metal) and used to darken around and protect the eyes

Kush Upper or southern Nubia

lapis lazuli a deep blue stone used extensively in Egyptian jewellery and decoration. Obtained from what is now Afghanistan

lector-priest priest who recited prayers at funerals

lotus a white or blue flowering water plant (water lily) which grew along the Nile

lustration basin basin in a temple which caught the remains of offerings such as blood or water

lyre a stringed musical instrument

ma'at divine order (rightness, truth and justice) established at the time of creation

macehead the head of a club-like weapon

malachite a green copper ore used by the Egyptians to protect their eyes

mastaba tomb a flat-topped, rectangular, mud-brick or stone tomb built by royalty and nobles in the Archaic and Old Kingdom periods

Medjay Nubians used by the Egyptians as mercenary soldiers and as a police force in Egypt

Mitanni the people and kingdom to the north-east of Syria and between the upper reaches of the Euphrates and Tigris rivers

Montu a Theban god of war

mortuary temple a temple built against the eastern face of a pyramid during the Old Kingdom in which the cult of the dead king was carried out by a special group of mortuary priests, who made daily offerings of food, drink and incense

mummification the process of preserving a dead body by embalming

muu **dancers** these are believed to have been ancestral spirits or divine ferrymen, who met the deceased at the mouth of the tomb. They were represented by real dancers dressed in kilts and high conical hats

myrrh a perfumed resin from a tree of the genus *Commiphora*, and used for making incense

Naharin the geographic area occupied by the Mitanni

natron a salt-like substance used to dry out the body and internal organs prior to embalming

necropolis cemetery or 'city of the dead'

Nekhbet the vulture-headed goddess of Upper Egypt

nemes **headdress** a striped linen headdress with two lappets which fell forward over the pharaoh's shoulders

nomarch a provincial governor

nome a province or district. of which there were 22 in Upper Egypt and 20 in Lower Egypt

Nubia the land to the south of the First Cataract. Made up of two parts — Lower Nubia (or Wawat) and Upper Nubia (or Kush)

oasis a fertile spot in the desert

obelisk a pillar of stone tapered towards the top and surmounted with a pyramidion which was usually gilded — regarded as the dwelling places of the sun god

obverse the front of an inscribed or decorated object

Opet festival an annual festival dedicated to the god Amun, his divine wife Mut and their son Khonsu. It involved a procession from the Temple of Amun at Karnak to the Temple of Luxor (the southern Opet or harem) and return

oracle a sign or communication from a god

Osiris the king of the Underworld and of resurrection; husband of Isis

ostracon (pl. ostraca) piece of broken pottery or flake of limestone often used by the ordinary Egyptians for jotting down notes and drawing

palace-facade a type of decoration used on early mastabas and sarcophagi which looked like the front of a palace (probably introduced from Mesopotamia)

palette a shield-shaped slate object for mixing cosmetics

papyrus a plant which grew along the Nile and was used for making paper, sandals, skiffs, baskets and many other things

Perit *the season of coming forth*. One of the three seasons in Egypt, which began in November. It was the time of sowing the seeds

pharaoh the term meant *great house* and originally referred to the palace, not the person who lived in it. During the New Kingdom it came to be used as a respectful term for the king

Predynastic Period the long period before the Lands of Upper and Lower Egypt were unified (c. 3100 BC) into one kingdom and ruled by the members of the first family or dynasty of kings

propaganda information aimed at furthering one's cause or damaging an opposing cause. The monumental inscriptions in Egypt may be described as propaganda since they always presented a favourable but often distorted view of the pharaoh

Ptah the creator god of Memphis

Punt an exotic land visited by the Egyptians and believed to have been in the vicinity of modern day Somalia in east Africa

pyramid complex the buildings centred on a pyramid — subsidiary pyramid, mortuary temple, enclosure wall, causeway and valley temple

Pyramid Texts the most ancient funerary texts, written on the walls of the pyramids of royalty during the Fifth and Sixth dynasties

quartzite a granular rock composed essentially of quartz

Re (Ra, Re-Atum, Re-Horakhte) forms of the sun god, usually represented as a hawk or falcon with a sun disk on its head

Red Land the ancient Egyptian name for the desert

regent usually a member of the royal family who ruled in the place of a child king until he was old enough to take responsibility alone

registers bands of painted or inscribed scenes in Egyptian tombs

reliefs pictures cut or incised into stone or plaster and usually painted. Sunk relief — the figures were cut below the level of the background. Raised relief — the background was cut away to leave raised figures

Retjenu a term used by the Egyptians for Palestine and parts of Syria

reverse the back of an inscribed or decorated object

sand-dwellers probably referred to desert tribesmen such as the Bedouin

sarcophagus a large stone outer coffin

scarab one of the most important and popular amulets used by the Egyptians. Shaped like a scarab beetle, it was the symbol of rebirth

scarab beetle a type of dung beetle sacred to the Egyptians

scimitar a curved, single-edged sword

scribe a person who could read and write the hieroglyphic and hieratic scripts and make mathematical calculations. They were employed at all levels in the religious and civil bureaucracies

Sed festival (heb-sed) the king's jubilee festival usually held after he had been on the throne for 30 years, in order to symbolically rejuvenate his powers

Sekhmet a lioness-headed goddess whose name meant 'powerful one'. She was goddess of war and strife as well as healing

***sem* priest** the chief funerary priest, who conducted the rites at the entrance to the tomb

sennet a board game similar to draughts

serdab a small enclosed cellar-like room in a tomb which contained the *ka* statue

serekh a rectangular-shaped frame containing the Horus name of early kings

Seth one of the oldest gods of Egypt, represented by an imaginary beast called the 'Seth-animal'. Seth was also the brother of Osiris. He was the god of the deserts and so was associated with all frightening things that the Egyptians believed came from the deserts

shadouf a device for raising water from the

river and for irrigation. It comprised a long suspended pole with a bucket at one end and a weight at the other

Shemau Upper Egypt, the long river valley that extended approximately 800 kilometres from the First Cataract to just north of the ancient capital of Memphis

Shemu *the season of harvest.* One of the seasons of Egypt that began sometime in March

shemset **girdle** a girdle with an apron of pendant beads or leather worn by kings of the Archaic Period as a symbol of their power

shendyt **kilt** a kilt with a stiffened front or apron which was part of the regalia of a king

Sobek the crocodile-headed god of the Faiyum

solar to do with the sun

solar boats the name often given to the large boats buried in pits around the tombs of Old Kingdom kings and queens

sphinx a large stone figure with the body of a lion and head of a human or animal. Kings of Egypt often had themselves portrayed as sphinxes

stela (pl. stelae) an inscribed pillar or upright slab of stone

subsidiary pyramid a small pyramid adjacent to the king's pyramid tomb the exact ritual purpose of which is unknown

tekenu *magical skin.* This mysterious funerary object, carried on a sled in the funeral procession, is believed to have been a crouching man covered in a skin, a symbol of rebirth

temenos wall an enclosure wall

theogamy a process by which a god took on the guise of the king in order to impregnate the queen so that the resultant child and future king would be regarded as the living son of the god

titulary a list of titles and names

Thoth the ibis-headed god of scribes and writing. The baboon, as well as the ibis, was sacred to Thoth

To-mehu Lower Egypt, or the delta area

tribute a contribution made by one ruler or state to another as a sign of submission or as the price of protection and peace

Tura limestone the fine white limestone used in funerary buildings, quarried at Tura in Lower Egypt

tyet *knot of Isis.* A protective amulet, usually in red, which represented the girdle which Isis tied around Horus to protect him. Usually placed on the upper part of a mummy

udjet or wedjat one of the most familiar protective amulets used by the Egyptians and referred to as the *Eye of Horus*

ushabti or shabti small mummiform statuettes of servants placed in the tomb. Their task was to answer the call of the deceased in the next life and carry out any tasks asked of them

valley temple a temple built on the edge of the area of cultivation and linked to the Nile by a canal in which funerary rituals such as purification of the body were carried out prior to burial

vizier *first under the king.* The vizier was the chief official in the administration of the Egyptian state

wadi an Arabic word meaning dried-up river bed

wadj a rejuvenation amulet in the shape of a papyrus sceptre

Wadjet (Edjo) the cobra goddess of Lower Egypt

was **sceptre** a sceptre usually carried by the gods, consisting of a forked staff with a dog or fox-like animal on top. It was a symbol of well-being and happiness

Wawat Lower Nubia

weres an amulet in the shape of a head-rest, often made of iron. The purpose of the weres was to reanimate the neck and head in the next life

White Walls this term referred to the residence city of Memphis in Lower Egypt

BIBLIOGRAPHY

Adams, W. Y. *Nubia, Corridor to Africa*, Allen Lane, London, 1977.

Aldred, C. *Akhenaten, King of Egypt*, Thames and Hudson, London, 1991.

Aldred, C. *The Egyptians*, Thames and Hudson, London, 1987.

Aldred, C. *Egypt to the End of the Old Kingdom*, Thames and Hudson, London, 1965.

Andrews, C. *Egyptian Mummies*, British Museum Publications, London, 1986.

Anthes, R. *Zeitschrift für Ägyptische Sprache und Altertum Kunde*, LXV, 1930.

Arnold, D. *The Temple of Mentuhotep at Deir el-Bahri*, Metropolitan Museum of Art, New York, 1979.

Australian Institute of Archaeology *Documents of the Egyptian Empire*, The Australian Institute of Archaeology, Melbourne, 1982.

Baines, J. and Málek, J. *Atlas of Ancient Egypt*, Phaidon, Oxford, 1980.

Bauval, R. and Hancock, G. *Keeper of Genesis*, Heinemann, London, 1996.

Bennet 'The Restoration Inscription of Tutankhamun', *Journal of Egyptian Archaeology*, 125, 1939.

Berbier, M. *The Tomb Builders of the Pharaohs*, American University in Cairo Press, Cairo, 1982.

Bouriant, U., Legrain, G. and Jéquier, G. *Monuments Pour Servir L'etude du Culte D'Atonu en Egypte*, L'Institut Français d'Archéologie Orientale du Caire, Cairo, 1903.

Breasted, J. H. *Ancient Records of Egypt,* vols I, II and III, University of Chicago Press, Chicago, 1906.

Breasted, J. H. *The Edwin Smith Medical Papyrus*, University of Chicago Press, Chicago, 1930.

British Museum *Introductory Guide to the Egyptian Collections*, ed. S. Quirke and J. Spencer, British Museum Press, London, 1992.

British Museum *British Museum Guide to Ancient Egypt*, ed. S. Quirke and J. Spencer, British Museum Press, London, 1992.

Busath, D. Simpkin's *Splendour of Egypt — The Temple of Hatshepsut*, Simpkins Souvenirs, Salt Lake City, Utah, 1983.

Cairo Museum *Fifty Wonders of Tutankhamun*, Crown Publishers, New York, 1978.

Cameron, A. and Kuhrt, A. (eds) *Images of Women in Antiquity*, Croom Helm, London, 1983.

Carter, H. *The Tomb of Tutankhamen*, Sphere Books Ltd, London, 1954.

Clark, S and Engelbach, R. *Ancient Egyptian Masonry*, Oxford University Press, London, 1930.

Daressy, V. I. G. *Fouilles de la Vallée des Rois*, Catalogue Général des Antiquités Egyptiennes du Musée du Caire, Cairo, 1902.

David, A. R. *The Pyramid Builders of Ancient Egypt, A Modern Investigation of Pharaoh's Workforce*, Routledge and Kegan Paul, London, 1986.

David, A. R. *The Ancient Egyptians, Religious Beliefs and Practices*, Routledge and Kegan Paul, London, 1982.

Davies, N. de G. *The Tomb of Rekh-mi-Re*, Metropolitan Museum of Art, New York, 1943.

Davies, N. de G. *The Rock Tombs of El-Amarna*, vols 1–6, Egyptian Exploration Fund, London, 1903–1908.

Davies, N. de G. *The Tomb of the Vizier Ramose*, Egyptian Exploration Fund, London, 1941.

Davies, N. de G. *Five Theban Tombs*, Egyptian Exploration Society, London, 1913.

Desroches-Noblecourt, C. *Tutankhamun — The Life and Death of Pharaoh*, Penguin Books, London, 1989.

Dodson, A. *Monarchs of the Nile*, The Rubicon Press, London, 1995.

Dorman, P. F. *The Monuments of Senenmut: Problems in Historical Methodology*, Kegan Paul International, London, 1988.

Dunham, D. *Naga ed-Der Stelae of the First Intermediate Period*, Oxford University Press, Oxford, 1937.

Edwards, A. B. *A Thousand Miles Up the Nile*, H. M. Caldwell, New York, 1888.

Edwards, I. E. S. *The Pyramids of Egypt*, Penguin Books, London, 1991.

Edwards, I. E. S. 'Bill of sale for a set of ushabtis', *Journal of Egyptian Archaeology*, 57, 1971.

Egyptian Antiquities Organisation, *Guidebook to Luxor Museum of Ancient Egyptian Art*, Egyptian Antiquities Organisation, Cairo, 1978.

Emery, W. B. *Archaic Egypt*, Penguin, Baltimore, 1962.

Erman, *A. Life in Ancient Egypt*, original publisher Mc Millan and Co., London, 1894, republished by Constable and Co, London, 1971.

Erman, A. *Literature of the Ancient Egyptians*, trans. A. M. Blackman, Methuen, London, 1927. New edition published as *The Ancient Egyptians, A Source Book of their Writings*, New York, 1966.

Fakhry, A. *The Pyramids*, University of Chicago Press, Chicago, 1961.

Faulkner, R. O. *The Ancient Egyptian Book of the Dead*, British Museum Press, London, 1985.

Faulkner, R. O. 'The man who was tired of life', *Journal of Egyptian Archaeology*, 42, 1956.

Frankfort, H. *Kingship and the Gods*, University of Chicago Press, Chicago, 1948.

Gardiner, A. H. *Bibliotheca Aegyptiaca*, vol. VII, Edition de la Fondation Egyptologique Bruxelles, Brussels, 1937.

Gardiner, A. H. 'The great Speos Artemedios inscription', *Journal of Egyptian Archaeology*, 32, 1945.

Gardiner, A. H. 'The Memphite tomb of King Horemheb', *Journal of Egyptian Archaeology*, 39, 1953.

Gardiner, A. H. *Egypt of the Pharaohs*, Oxford University Press, Oxford, 1961.

Gardiner A. H. and Sethe K. 'Egyptian letters to the dead', *Pap Leiden*, 37, Egyptian Exploration Society, London, 1928.

Gilbert, A. S. 'The slaughterhouse of Meketre', *Journal of Egyptian Archaeology*, 74, 1988.

Griffith, F. L. 'The Abydos decree of Seti I at Nauri', *Journal of Egyptain Archaeology*, 13, 1937.

Grimal, N. *A History of Ancient Egypt*, Blackwell, Oxford, 1992.

Habachi, L. 'Two grafitti at Sehel from the reign of Hatshepsut', *Journal of Near Eastern Studies*, 16, 1957.

Hassan, S. *Annales du Service des Antiquities de l'Egypte*, 36, 1937.

Hayes, W. C. *Scepter of Egypt, vol II, The Hyksos Period and the New Kingdom*, Metropolitan Museum of Art, New York, 1959.

Hayes, W. C. 'Varia from the time of Hatshepsut', *Mitteilungen des Deutchen Archaologischen Instituts Abteilung Kairo*, 15, 1957.

Hayes, W. C. 'The career of the Great Steward Henenu under Nebheptre Mentuhotep', *Journal of Egyptain Archaeology*, 35, 1949.

Herodotus *Histories*, Penguin Books, London, 1954.

Hornung, E. *The Tomb of Pharaoh Seti I*, Timkin, New York, 1990.

Ions, V. *Egyptian Mythology*, Hamlyn, London, 1968.

James, T. G. H. *Egyptian Painting*, British Museum, London, 1986.

James, T. G. H. *Pharaoh's People — Scenes from Life in Imperial Egypt*, University of Chicago Press, Chicago, 1986.

James, T. G. H. *The Hekanakhte Papers and Other Middle Kingdom Documents*, Metropolitan Museum of Art, New York, 1962.

James, T. G. H. and Shore, A. F. *Introductory Guide to the Egyptian Collections*, British Museum.

Kamil, J. *The Ancient Egyptians*, The American University in Cairo Press, Cairo, 1984.

Kanawati, *The Tomb and its Significance in Ancient Egypt*, Prism Publications, Cairo, 1987.

Kemp, B. 'Amarna from the air', *Egyptian Archaeology — Bulletin of the EES*, 2, 1992.

Kemp, B. *Ancient Egypt, An Anatomy of a Civilisation*, Routledge, London and New York, 1991.

Kitchin, K. '"As arrows in ... his quiver": The sons of Ramesses II', *KMT, A Modern Journal of Ancient Egypt*, vol. 7, no. 1, Spring 1996.

Kitchin, K. *Pharaoh Triumphant, The Life and Times of Ramesses II*, Aris and Hill Ltd, London, 1982.

Kitchin, K. 'Punt and how to get there', *Orientalia*, 40.

Knudtzon, J. A. *Die el-Amarna Tafeln*, 1, 2 vols., O. Zeller, Aalen, 1964.

Lalouette, C. *L'Empire des Ramses,* Fayard, Paris, 1985.

Lamy, L. *New Light on Ancient Knowledge, Egyptian Mysteries*, Thames and Hudson, London, 1981.

Leeau and Chevrier, H. *Un Chapelle d'Hatshepsout à Karnak*, Service des Antiquites de l'Egypte: Institut Français Archaeologie Orientale, Cairo, 1979.

Lehner, M. *The Complete Pyramids*, Thames and Hudson, London, 1997.

Lepsius, C. R. *Denkmaleer aus Aegypten und Aethiopien*, Nicolaische Buchhandlung, Berlin, 1848(58.

Lichtheim, M. 'The songs of the harpers', *Journal of Near Eastern Studies*, 4, 1945.

Lichtheim, M. *Ancient Egyptian Literature: A Book of Readings*, University of California Press, Berkely, 1973.

Lurker, M. *The Gods and Symbols of Ancient Egypt*, Thames and Hudson, London, 1980.

Manniche, L. *The City of the Dead*, British Museum Publications, London, 1987.

Manchip White, J. E. *Ancient Egypt, Its Culture and History*, Dover Publications Inc., New York, 1970.

McDonald, J. K. *The House of Eternity, the Tomb of Nefertari*, Thames and Hudson, London, 1996.

Metropolitan Museum of Art, *Facsimiles, Egyptian Wall Paintings*, Metropolitan Museum of Art, New York, 1983.

Mertz, B. *Red Land, Black Land, Daily Life in Ancient Egypt*, Peter Bedrick Books, New York, 1990.

Mertz, B. *Temples, Tombs and Hieroglyphs, A Popular History of Ancient Egypt*, Peter Bedrick Books, New York 1990.

Meyer, C. *Senenmut: Eine Prosopographische Untersuchung*, Verlag Borg, Hamburg, 1982.

Mond, R. and Meyers, O. H. *The Temples of Armant*, London, 1940.

Montet, P. *Everyday Life in Egypt in the Days of Ramesses the Great*, University of Pennsylvania Press, Philadelphia, 1981.

Naville, E., *Ahnas el Medineh*, Egyptian Exploration Fund, London, 1894.

Naville, E. *The Temple of Deir el-Bahri — Its Plan, its Founders and its first Explorers*, 7 vols, Egyptian Exploration Society, London, 1894–1908.

Nims, C. F. *The Date of the Dishonouring of Hatshespsut*, Zeitschrift f(r (gyptische Sprache und Altertumskunde, Leipzig, 1966.

Organisation of Egyptian Antiquities, *Cairo Museum Catalogue*, Verlag Phillip von Zabern, Mainz, 1987.

Petrie, W. M. F. *Journals, October 1888–January 1889*, University College, London.

Posener, G. *Literature et Politique dans l'Egypte de la XII Dynastie*, H. Champion, Paris, 1956.

Pritchard, J. B. *The Ancient Near East, An Anthology of Texts and Pictures*, vol. I, Princeton University Press, Princeton, New Jersey, 1958.

Pritchard, J. B. *The Ancient Near East, An Anthology of Texts and Pictures*, vol. II, Princeton University Press, Princeton, New Jersey, 1975.

Pritchard, J. B. *Ancient Near Eastern Texts Relating to the Bible*, Princeton University Press, Princeton, New Jersey, 1955.

Redford, D. *Akhenaten, The Heretic King*, Princeton University Press, Princeton, New Jersey, 1984.

Redford, D. *History and Chronology of the Eighteenth Dynasty*, University of Toronto Press, Toronto, 1967.

Reeder, G. 'The mysterious muu and the dance they do', KMT, *A Modern Journal of Ancient Egypt*, 6, 1995.

Robins, G. *The Art of Ancient Egypt*, British Museum Press, London, 1997.

Robins, G. *Women in Ancient Egypt*, British Museum Press, London, 1993.

Robins, G. *Egyptian Painting and Relief*, Shire Publications Ltd, Aylesbury, UK, 1986.

Romer, J. *Ancient Lives, the Story of the Pharaohs' Tomb Makers*, Michael O'Mara Books Ltd, London, 1984.

Rosellini, I. *Monumenti dell Egitti e della Nubia*, Edition des Belleslettres, Geneva, 1977.

Samson, J. *Nefertiti and Cleopatra, Monarch Queens of Ancient Egypt*, The Rubicon Press, London, 1987.

Säve-Soderburgh, T. *Agypten und Nubien*, Lund, 1941.

Scoch, R. 'Redating the Great Sphinx of Giza', *KMT, A Modern Journal of Ancient Egypt*, 1992.

Sethe, K. *Die Altaegyptischen Pyramiden Texte*, J. C. Hinricks, Leipsig, 1908.

Sethe, K. *Urkunden des Aegyptischen Altertums*, J. C. Hinricks, Leipzig, 1906 et seq.

Smith, G. E. *The Royal Mummies*, Institut Français d'Archaeologie Orientale, Cairo, 1912.

Smither, P. 'The Semnah despatches', *Journal of Egyptian Archaeology*, 31, 1945.

Snape, S. *Egyptian Temples*, Shire Publications Ltd, London, 1996.

Spencer, A. J. *Death in Ancient Egypt*, Penguin Books, London, 1982.

Stead, M. *Egyptian Life*, British Museum Publications, London, 1986.

Steindorff, G. and Seele, K. *When Egypt Ruled the East*, University of Chicago Press, Chicago, 1957.

Thomas, A. *Akhenaten's Egypt*, Shire Publications Ltd, London, 1988.

Taylor, J. J. and Griffith, F. L. *The Tomb of Paheri, at el-Kab*, published in one volume with E. Naville's *Ahnas el Medineh*, Egyptian Exploration Fund, London, 1894.

Trigger, B. G., Kemp, B. J., O' Connor, D. and Lloyd, A. B. (eds) *Ancient Egypt, A Social History*, Cambridge University Press, Cambridge, 1983.

Tyldesley, J. *Hatshepsut, Female Pharaoh*, Penguin, Middlesex, UK, 1996.

Tyldesley, J. *Daughters of Isis — Women of Ancient Egypt*, Penguin, Middlesex, UK, 1994.

Verner, M. *Forgotten Pharaohs, Lost Pyramids: Abusir*, Academia Skodaexport, Prague, 1994.

Verner, M. 'Archaeological survey of Abusir', *Zeitschrift fur Agyptische Sprache*, 119, 1992.

Wallis Budge, E. A. *Egyptian Religion and Egyptian Ideas of the Future Life*, Arkana, imprint of Routledge and Kegan Paul, London, 1987.

Watterson, B. *The Gods of Ancient Egypt*, B. T. Batsford Ltd, London, 1984.

Wilkinson, J. G. *Manners and Customs of the Ancient Egyptians*, J. Murray, London, 1837.

Wilson, J. A. *The Culture of Ancient Egypt*, University of Chicago Press, Chicago, 1951.

Winlock, H. E. *Models of Daily Life in Ancient Egypt*, Metropolitan Museum of Art Egyptian Expeditions XVIII, Cambridge, Massachusetts, 1955.

Yeivin, S. *Journal of the Palestine Oriental Society*, 14, 3, 1934.

ACKNOWLEDGMENTS

Figs 1.09, 1.16, 6.08, 6.16, 6.21, 6.22, 6.23, 6.27, 6.28, 7.07, 7.13, 8.06, 14.02, 15.07, 15.09, 16.04, 16.08, 16.13, 16.15, 16.16, 16.18, 16.22, 16.51 Erman, A. *Life in Ancient Egypt*, 1971, Dover Publications Inc.; **Figs 1.11a, 1.11b, 15.26, 16.38, 16.40** James, T.G.H. *Pharaoh's People*, 1985, Oxford University Press; **Figs 1.12, 4.20, 4.32, 4.41, 6.11, 6.12, 6.13a, 6.13b, 6.17, 7.21, 8.16, 8.17, 8.18, 8.21, 8.22, 8.23, 8.24, 8.25, 8.34a, 8.34b, 8.35, 8.36, 8.37, 9.04, 9.08, 10.06, 11.01, 12.03, 12.04, 12.06, 12.12, 12.17, 13.12, 13.13, 15.40, 16.11, 17.20, 17.21** The Egyptian Museum, Cairo; **Figs 1.13, 13.09, 13.14, 13.24, 13.37, 15.11, 15.16, 15.24, 15.37, 15.38, 15.45, 16.02, 16.48, 16.49, 17.19, 17.30, 17.32, 17.33, 17.47** Desroches-Noblecourt, C. *Tutankhamun: The Life and Death of a Pharaoh*, 1989, Penguin Books; **Figs 6.14, 16.25, 16.34, 16.50, 16.55** Stead, M. *Egyptian Life*, 1986, British Museum Press; **Fig. 2.09** Fitzwilliam Museum; **Figs 3.07, 4.19, 4.30** Fakhry, A. *The Pyramids*, 1969, University of Chicago Press; **Figs 3.08, 5.08** Aldred, C. *The Egyptians*, 1987, Thames & Hudson; **Figs 4.07, 4.35, 5.12, 6.32** Edwards, I.E.S. *The Pyramids of Egypt*, 1991, Penguin Books; **Figs 4.14, 4.21, 4.22, 4.23, 4.28, 4.29, 4.36, 8.08, 8.09, 8.10, 8.11, 8.12, 8.13, 8.33** Lehener, M. *The Complete Pyramids*, 1997, Thames & Hudson; **Figs 6.02, 6.03, 6.04, 6.05** Frankfort, H. *Kingship and the Gods*, 1969, The University of Chicago Press; **Figs 6.09, 10.19** Tyldesley, J. *Daughters of Isis*, 1984, Penguin Books; **Figs 6.15, 7.19a, 7.19b, 7.19c, 7.20, 8.29, 8.30, 8.31, 17.37, 17.39** Kanawati, N. *The Tomb and it's Significance in Ancient Egypt*, 1986, Prism Publications; **Fig. 6.33** Davies, N.D.G. *The Mastaba of Ptahhotep and Akethete*, 1900-01, Egypt Exploration Society; **Fig. 7.01** Lurker, M. *The Gods and Symbols of Ancient Egypt*, 1988, Thames & Hudson; **Figs 14.03, 14.05, 17.09, 17.12, 17.34** Lamy, L. *Egyptian Mysteries: New Light on Ancient Knowledge*, 1986, Thames & Hudson; Fig. 7.15 Aldred, C. *Egypt to the end of the Old Kingdom*, 1988, Thames & Hudson; **Fig. 7.18** Spencer, A.J. *Death in Ancient Egypt*, 1984, Penguin Books; **Figs 2.01, 2.03, 2.10, 8.01, 16.20** British Museum; **Figs 8.02, 9.09, 10.01, 10.02, 10.04, 10.05, 10.11, 10.41, 12.02, 12.11, 12.20, 13.26, 15.27, 16.06, 16.12, 16.14, 16.17, 16.19, 16.24, 16.26, 16.27, 16.28, 16.29, 16.30, 16.31, 16.37, 16.39, 16.41, 16.42, 16.43, 16.44, 16.52, 16.53, 16.54, 16.56, 17.07, 17.22, 17.23, 17.38** The Metropolitan Museum of Art, New York; **Figs 8.03, 8.07, 9.02, 9.05** Baines & Malek, *An Atlas of Ancient Egypt*, 1984, Time Life Books; **Figs 8.05, 13.11, 13.15, 13.19, 15.14, 15.15, 15.47, 16.05** Kemp, B.J. *Ancient Egypt — An Anatomy of a Civilisation*, 1994, Routledge; **Figs 8.19, 8.20, 14.18, 14.19, 14.25, 16.36, 16.54, 17.13, 17.45** Robins, G. *The Art of Ancient Egypt*, 1997, British Museum Press; **Fig. 7.25** BT Batsford Ltd; **Figs 12.18, 14.28, 15.13, 17.10, 17.14, 17.17, 17.18** Hayes, W. *Sceptre of Egypt*, 1990, The Metropolitan Museum of Art, NY; **Figs 10.07, 10.08, 10.09, 10.10, 10.16, 10.17, 10.28, 10.30, 10.31, 10.32, 10.33, 10.34, 10.37, 10.42a, 10.42b, 10.44** Naville, E. *The Temple of Deir el-Bahri, it's plans, its founders and its first explorers*, Egypt Exploration Society; **Fig. 15.42** Thomas, A.P. *Egyptian Gods and Myths*, 1986, Aylesbury; **Fig. 11.12** Abbas Chalaby, Egypt; **Fig. 11.06** *Documents of the Egyptian Empire*, 1982, Australian Instituate of Archeology; **Fig. 12.14** Boston Museum of Fine Art; **Figs 17.11, 17.16, 17.27, 17.44, 17.48** Andrews, C. *Egyptian Mummies*, 1984, Cambridge University Press; **Fig. 10.25** Landstrom, B. *Ships of the Pharaohs*, 1970, Allen & Unwin; **Fig. 2.11** Gardiner, Alan H. *Egypt of the Pharaohs*, 1961, Clarendon Press; **Figs 12.10, 15.25** Manniche, L. *City of the Dead*, 1987, British Museum Publications; **Figs 12.13, 13.05** Thomas, A. *Akhenaten's Egypt*, 1988, Shire Publications; **Figs 12.01, 12.15, 13.01, 13.03, 13.04, 13.06, 13.20, 13.25, 13.31, 13.32, 13.33, 13.34, 13.36, 15.17, 15.46, 16.07, 17.08** Aldred, C. *Akhenaten, King of Egypt*, 1988, Thames & Hudson; **Figs. 6.18b, 6.18c, 6.19, 13.02, 13.23** Egypt Exploration Society; **Figs. 6.25, 7.11, 7.12** Blackman, A.M. *Rock Tombs of Meir*, 1977, Egypt Exploration Fund; **Figs 7.10, 7.22** Simpson, W.K. *Mastabas of Qar and Idu*, 1976, Museum of Fine Arts, Boston; **Figs 13.08, 13.10, 15.18** Redford, D.B. *Akhenaten — The Heretic King*, 1984, Princeton University Press; **Figs 13.29** Samson, J. *Nefertiti and Cleopatra, Queen Monarchs of Ancient Egypt*, 1987, The Rubicon Press; **Fig. 13.27** Steindorff and Seele, *When Egypt Ruled the East*, 1957, University of Chicago Press; **Figs 9.03, 13.30, 13.35** Dodson, A. Monarchs of the Nile, 1995, The Rubicon Press; **Figs 14.08, 14.09, 14.10, 14.12, 14.16, 14.21, 14.26,**

14.27 Kitchin, K. *Pharaoh Triumphant*, 1982, Aris & Phillips Ltd; **Fig. 14.14** Grimal, N. *A History of Ancient Egypt*, 1994, Blackwell Publishers; **Fig. 15.04** Trigger, B.G. et al; *Ancient Egypt: A Social History*, 1983, Cambridge University Press; **Figs 14.22, 14.23, 17.01, 17.02, 17.46** McDonald, J. K. *The Tomb of Nefertiti*, 1996, Thames & Hudson; **Figs 15.41, 16.33, 17.04** James, T.G.H. *Egyptian Painting*, 1985, British Museum Press; **Fig. 17.29** Quirke, S. and Spencer, J. *British Museum Book of Ancient Egypt*, 1992, British Museum Press; **Figs 15.28, 15.31, 15.47a** Snape, S. *Egyptian Temples*, 1996, Shire Publications; **Fig. 16.35** Bierbrier, M. *The Tomb Builders of the Pharaohs*, 1982, British Museum Publications.

Every effort has been made to trace and acknowledge copyright but there may be instances where this has not been possible. Cambridge University Press would welcome any information that would redress this situation.

INDEX